CONTENTS

List of Figures	*page* vii
List of Tables	viii
Preface	xi
Acknowledgments	xiv

PART I: ADDICTION AND ADDICTIVE EFFECTS — 1

1. A General Introduction to the Concept of Addiction and Addictive Effects — 3
2. Addictive Effects and Appetitive Needs — 32
3. Variables that Increase the Likelihood of Developing an Addiction — 46
4. Consequences of Addiction — 71

PART II: TYPES OF ADDICTIONS — 87

5. Types of Addictions: General Overview — 89
6. Substance Addictions: Their Prevalence and Co-Occurrence — 103
7. Behavioral Addictions: Their Prevalence and Co-Occurrence — 118
8. Patterns of Addiction Co-Occurrence, Replacement, and Lifestyle Demands — 134
9. Assessing the 11 Focal Addictions — 148

PART III: RESOLVING THE PROBLEMS OF ADDICTION AND FUTURE DIRECTIONS — 183

10. Resolving the Problems of Addiction – Prevention: General Principles — 185
11. Prevention: Intrapersonal-Level Approaches — 199
12. Prevention: Extrapersonal-Level Approaches — 210
13. Resolving the Problems of Addiction – Cessation: General Principles — 242
14. Cessation: Intrapersonal-Level Approaches — 259

Contents

15 Cessation: Extrapersonal-Level Approaches 282

16 Future Considerations for Substance and Behavioral Addictions 301

Glossary 316

Bibliography 342

Index 390

FIGURES

2.1 A possible appetitive needs model of addictive effects: associational memory-appetitive system relations (AMASR) model *page* 36
5.1 The Addiction Matrix Self-Report Measure 99
13.1 A substance abuse treatment process model 253
13.2 Models of motivation relevant to addictions treatment 255

TABLES

1.1	Examples of 12-step organizations for substance and behavioral addictions ordered by year of formation	*page* 7
1.2	Definitions of the addictions	14
1.3	Withdrawal symptoms for different types of drugs based on the Sussman/Ames (2001, 2008) health behavior scheme of drug categories	16
2.1	Other alternatives to the appetitive needs notion of addiction	37
2.2	The five-component definition of addiction	39
3.1	Etiologic variables representing multiple levels of analysis	49
3.2	The PACE model	52
4.1	Consequences of addiction	75
4.2	Negative consequences of addiction by type of addiction	80
4.3	The ratio of lethal dose to effective dose for different drugs	82
5.1	Sixteen addictive behavior categories	91
5.2	Combinations of appetitive motivation pairs	96
6.1	Prevalence of substance addictions	105
6.2	Prevalence estimates of alcoholism	109
7.1	Prevalence of behavioral addictions	119
7.2	Estimated prevalence and co-occurrence of 11 different addictive behaviors	130
7.3	Prevalence of addictions among Russian, American, and Spanish youth – ever and last 30 days	132
8.1	Three patterns of involvement with an addiction	137
8.2	Human development and multiple addictions	138
8.3	Relations among multiple addictions	144
9.1	Means of assessing addictions	176
9.2	Similar and unique features of different addictions measures	180
10.1	Definitions/classifications of prevention	189

List of Tables

10.2	Five types of substantive contents shared by prevention and cessation programming	190
10.3	Drug education models	194
11.1	Intrapersonal-level prevention strategies	200
12.1	Components of the comprehensive social influences/life skills approach	217
12.2	Family-based prevention programming	225
12.3	Media-based prevention programming	230
14.1	Intrapersonal treatment of addictions	278
15.1	Extrapersonal-level treatment approaches	284
16.1	Future directions	303

PREFACE

As will be presented in the text, about half of us suffer from some kind of an addiction right now that is causing pain in our lives. We are having problems "shaking off" that addiction. Many of us are even suffering from multiple addictions. Some people may wonder how this is possible but there are also many people I talk to who agree, with no surprise in their voice, that it's simply a fact that we face difficulties with addiction at one time or another in our lives. "Addiction" is not just about drugs anymore. The recovery community has experientially known and written about both substance and behavioral addictions for decades. Several 12-step organizations were started by persons who reported developing a new detrimental addiction after sobering up from alcohol abuse (e.g., Gamblers Anonymous, Sex Addicts Anonymous). The neuroscience community generally expresses agreement, with suggestions that common neurotransmitter pathways, often involving mesolimbic dopamine and other ligands, underlie any number of addictive behaviors. Certainly, it is devastating to watch our media heroes succumb to wasting, overdoses, public shame, and death pertaining to imbibing alcohol, methamphetamine, crack, heroin, or pain killers, among other drugs, but also succumbing to frequent and strong cravings for sexual behavior, gambling, spending, iterative cosmetic surgery, or other excesses. Each year that I teach my Issues in Drug Abuse course I end up reporting on yet another celebrity who died, or experienced a great deal of embarrassment, due to a host of repetitive, seemingly out-of-control, addictive behaviors. Celebrities are in the limelight but they also represent a microcosm of the rest of us.

Many of us are aware that when an addict attempts to quit an ***addiction of choice*** (i.e., a most preferred or immediately troublesome addictive behavior) with a commitment to normalizing behavior, his or her subjective experience is often characterized by a series of phases – of feeling worse and then better with little predictability in terms of duration of each phase. Just quitting the substance or behavior does not seem to make the root of the problem go away. Rather, the "bold distraction" vanishes temporarily. The recovery movement gurus often use metaphors and talk about "the hole in the gut where the wind can blow through," "feeling lonely in a crowd," "feeling like one doesn't fit," or "feeling uncomfortable in one's own skin." The immediate solution is to again drink or use, or engage in some other activity that will make one feel "normal" or "better" or "distracted" or "excited" or "comfortably numb." Such is the subjective reality of addiction. The sufferer engages in the behavior for a "release," achieves the release for a brief period, and ends up repeating addictive behavior–satiation cycles. Sooner or later preoccupation with that addiction, loss of control when engaging in the addiction, minor daily negative consequential hassles, and even devastating negative consequences from engaging in the addictive behavior may occur.

Preface

My hope in writing this text is to broaden and deepen the understanding of just what addictions are and what perpetuates them in various forms. Too often we view "addicts" as people who are "obviously" out of control, immoral, and a small minority of the population. I believe, as do others, that this is because we often focus on relatively extreme and dramatic instances of the addictions. However, as an example, only 3–5 percent of alcoholics live on skid row. Only about 20 percent of compulsive gamblers file for bankruptcy due to gambling losses. "Workaholics" may even be praised by colleagues, though rejected or barely tolerated by significant others. Once we permit application of addiction definitional criteria across a variety of types of behaviors, and explore varying types and degrees of consequences, which may be very problematic but not so dramatic (e.g., sedentary and isolated living due to workaholism), we can see that this phenomenon applies to many people. If we understand that addiction has a wide reach, we may start to understand it not only as a problem of individual vulnerability but also as a problem of lifestyle. With a heightened awareness that lifestyle factors may interface with our neurobiological systems associated with obtaining **appetitive effects** (i.e., affect, arousal, and information regulation, inherently associated with biological fitness), we may begin to really grasp what the addiction phenomenon is. Specificity of forms of addiction is due to the variables of **pragmatics** (access to different avenues of addiction), **attraction** (finding an appeal of differential subjective effects and contexts), **addiction-related communication** (learning and using the language associated with specific addictions; for example, "chasing losses" in gambling), and the reality that during the life course an addiction at least temporarily meets one's **expectations** (what one expects from the behavior subjectively is delivered). I refer to this development-of-addiction scheme as the "PACE model" (pragmatics, attraction, communication, expectations).

This text presents an in-depth discussion of the concepts of addiction, and attempts to clarify these concepts. I argue that in some large part, and not contradictory with the assertions of many researchers and clinicians, addiction involves misapplication of neurobiological processes related to appetitive effects. While a rather wide variety of addictive behaviors are mentioned, the majority of the text focuses on 11 specific addictions. These 11 addictions account for the vast majority of cases of self-reported addiction (approximately 90 percent) including: tobacco use, alcohol use, hard drug use, food eating, gambling, Internet and other electronic media, shopping, love, sex, exercise and work. Relationships among different addictions are explored (e.g., concurrent, substitute, alternating). I also discuss the developmental trajectory of different addictions (e.g., TV viewing among young children may precede addiction to caffeine and nicotine) and provide an analysis of various types of negative consequences across the 11 types of addictions.

Very recent evidence is suggesting that up to 50 percent of the US or European adult population suffers significantly from one or more addictive behaviors in a 12-month period; and that 23 percent also exhibit co-occurring addictions. Thus, prevention and treatment of addictions must have wide reach reflecting recognition that perhaps a large minority or even a majority of the population can suffer from an addiction in the course of a lifetime. It is a challenge to envision how to modify lifestyle factors to better match or enrich our variable neurobiology, so as to avoid negative consequences of engaging in addictive behaviors.

Preface

I present several prevention and treatment solutions to addiction-related consequences provided at intrapersonal and extrapersonal levels of application. My objective in doing so is to give the reader a feel for how the 11 focal addictions might be addressed by multi-level prevention and treatment strategies. In reviewing these various strategies, I located whatever controlled trials I could, but realize that the current state of prevention and cessation of most of these addictions is very raw and new territory.

To summarize, covering addiction as a broad-based phenomenon is a distinctive approach. I present this approach with a major conceptual emphasis on misapplied appetitive processes. These processes are impacted by multiple levels of influence (i.e., neurobiological, cognitive, microsocial, macrosocial/physical environmental). Part I of the text begins by presenting concepts of addiction (and different definitional "camps"), followed by its etiology and consequences. Part II of the text presents types of substance and behavioral addictions, their co-occurrence, and assessment. Finally, Part III of the text presents potential prevention and cessation solutions, and future directions. My discussion includes a multidisciplinary perspective that is informed by the fields of social and clinical psychology, psychiatry, philosophy of science, social work, sociology, preventive medicine, and neuroscience, among others.

This text is primarily designed for upper level undergraduate students, graduate students, researchers, and practitioners interested in the breadth and depth of addiction processes from a multidisciplinary perspective to better understand the etiology, prevention, and treatment of addiction. This work may serve as a core or supplemental text. This is not a "how to"-type text. But importantly, the text may be applied to chemical dependence facilitator training venues where it can provide to trainees a fundamental understanding of addiction phenomena. Other academic venues may find this useful as a supplemental text for courses that review issues in drug abuse. I have written this text with the hope that anyone who has completed college general education requirements might be able to appreciate its contents while also recognizing that those with an advanced education may be better able to grasp some concepts presented (e.g., aspects of neurotransmission, appetitive effects, and evolutionary notions of addiction).

Because the text encompasses multiple addictions, all but substance use and gambling currently not being officially recognized as such by the DSM-V (due to need for additional research support though acknowledged as potential addictions), there may be resistance to some of the material. I believe that I make a bold move by addressing multiple addictions, also considering contexts which may or may not vary globally. I attempt to provide a cutting-edge, innovative presentation of material. I believe that this book is on the crest of the wave going the direction the field of the addictions is heading. Focusing on an overarching addictive process as opposed to merely discussing specific objects of addictions is of key importance. This text could spur research and practice in new directions.

ACKNOWLEDGMENTS

I would like to thank the University of Southern California for providing the research environment that permitted me to write this text. I would also like to thank Matthew D. Bennett of Cambridge University Press for appreciating the potential scope of the text. Further, I would like to thank Dominic Stock and Jo North for help in editing. I thank Soren Holm for his review of the text and assistance on tables, and Brian Cook, Mimi M. Kim, and Alan N. Sussman for their detailed reading, editing, and commenting on previous versions of the text. I would also like to thank four anonymous reviewers for their input. Finally, I would like to thank my family, Rotchana, Evelyn, Evan, and Max for their support while I grappled with the work involved.

PART I

Addiction and Addictive Effects

1 A General Introduction to the Concept of Addiction and Addictive Effects

Learning Objectives

- To understand the definition of substance and behavioral addiction
- To understand the history of conceptualizations of the addictions
- To learn examples of intensional models of addiction
- To learn examples of extensional models of addiction
- To have a sense of how to differentiate "addiction" from other disorders such as obsessive-compulsive disorder

Introductory Case Study: Johnny

Johnny as a young child used to run amok around the house. He tended to pace back and forth, not sitting down. His mom thought her 8-year-old just couldn't sit still. When he turned on the TV, though, he seemed entranced and his mom, while preferring that Johnny read, appreciated the fact that he would sit very quietly while he was watching TV. She permitted him to watch a great deal of TV each day, so she could clean the house and read the news.

When Johnny was 14 years old, instead of taking the bus home from school, he liked to jog the three kilometers to his home. It felt good, adventurous, and he felt accomplished. In his teens he was on his high school distance running team, perhaps unsurprisingly. He did pretty well, and he would run long workouts. Johnny did well in high school classes, and was respected for his intellect as well as his athletic skills. He loved to run, sometimes as much as three times a day, and he loved the friendships he had with his fellow runners. He also found gratification in eating huge bowls of ice cream after finishing his long-distance runs in the evening. He chuckled about how he would consume four meals a day. However, over the years he developed several injuries and had to continually stop running in order to heal. As a result, he gained some weight. When he was 19 years of age, he began to enjoy drinking beer. Sometimes he would drink beer, feel drunk, and fantasize about long-distance running.

He really liked drinking beer while he was in college. He remembered being with friends on their campus at their dormitory one night. His friends were urinating over the second-floor stairway balcony while Johnny was sitting in a car downstairs wasted from drinking beer. He recalled feeling like he was in a warm cocoon, knowing that it doesn't get any better than this. He felt secure, comfortable, relaxed, warm, and like he fitted in. He tended to drink beer only on weekends. On rare occasions he would smoke marijuana, mainly during winter and summer vacations.

Johnny did fairly well in college and decided to go on to graduate school. By the time he reached graduate school at 23 years of age, he was drinking five beers a day on average and this continued for almost ten years. By Johnny's estimation, that was not alcoholism. Six beers a day would be alcoholism, so he jokingly thought. He also discovered how good it made him feel to combine beer drinking with other concoctions such as antihistamines. He noticed that such combinations would help him to drink fewer beers. Soon he added regular use of marijuana to his regular alcohol and other drug use regimen. He noticed that marijuana reduced his anxiety and helped him perform better in school. He would also sometimes go on long-distance runs drunk or stoned. Soon, he was stoned too often – daily – including during his classes. He developed a pattern of having arguments as he came down from being high on marijuana. One night on vacation, he had an argument with his girlfriend while coming down from a "pot high." He stormed out of the hotel room. He ended up drinking beer until 7:30am with a homeless person at a seedy bar that was open all night. He rationalized that his marijuana use was "trouble" and he took great pains to quit it.

By the end of graduate school, Johnny stopped running or working out. He still ate a great deal and gained a lot of weight. He began a job as a faculty member of a large community college, where he engaged in numerous teaching and administrative tasks. Over time he achieved a solid reputation as an administrator and instructor. However, he took to enjoying $20 to $40 worth of crack cocaine from time to time, along with drinking alcohol. When he did this, he would experience "intimate times" with strangers – feelings of love for people he hardly knew, alternating over the weeks with bouts of work. He started feeling regret and shame regarding his drinking, with a large pinch of paranoia thrown in regarding his drug using, and he felt hopeless about his continued periods of binge eating.

He felt that he could stop drinking or using for a couple of months but then he would be at it again. He also went on diets but they did not last more than a couple of days. Sometimes he would attend 12-step meetings but his participation in "the program" was short-lived. The Higher Power talk and constant cigarette smoking was just too much for him to stomach. Also, he worried that people would gossip about him. At other times, Johnny found the meetings boring, repetitive, and it all seemed so vague. Yet, in concordance with the recovery stories and slogans that he heard at Alcoholics Anonymous and Overeaters Anonymous meetings, he truly identified with statements of feeling "a hole in the gut where the wind can blow through." He sometimes felt "lonely in a crowd." He definitely felt "discomfort in his own skin" and experienced cravings to drink, use, or eat to eliminate the discomfort.

He believed that these uncomfortable feelings existed prior to his ever engaging in addictive behaviors; though he also thought they may have worsened by continuing to engage in these behaviors. He longed for quick adventure. Slowly, in middle adulthood, he experienced a narrowing of his lifestyle.

He did not become homeless or otherwise fit into a "low-bottom" stereotype of alcoholism or other addiction. Instead, he was able to maintain a steady income from a steady job. In fact, sometimes he would work very long hours. He would even go on many work binges, working around the clock for days at a time. Sometimes he would drink or use and work all at the same time. He began to believe he must have been addicted to maybe ten different behaviors! He felt shame at times – but at other times he still felt "hip, slick, and cool" as he grew older and more forgetful. He did quit drinking and smoking marijuana for several years and got married. He enjoyed the adventure of marriage. After three years of marriage, however, he went back to his old ways. At the age of 45 years, his wife "adjusted" to his ways, and found solace in friendships with other women. Johnny spent more and more time alone. Eventually, he realized that if he continued to drink alcohol, in particular, he was facing the potential threats of serious arrests, isolation, and brain dysfunction – and that these threats were right around the corner. His also believed that his eating binges and overweight would lead to a heart attack or stroke.

He quit marijuana and other drug use on his own, but he lived erratically, with occasional lapses into drinking. He still would go on work "binges." Sometimes, he went on binges of television viewing, like when he was a child. His eating behavior seemed intractable to him. One thing seemed clear about Johnny. He thought he was suffering from multiple addictions, sometimes expressed together in the course of a day. However, the American Psychiatric Association (APA) currently only formally recognizes substance use disorder and, very recently, gambling disorder, as addictions (APA, 2013). Well, Johnny never had a problem with gambling. He never lost much money, didn't chase losses, and he knew he didn't enjoy it that much. Also, he never became a regular cigarette smoker. But he had engaged in so many other behaviors about which he was preoccupied, subjectively felt a loss of control, and experienced insidiously accumulating undesired consequences. Now, at 48 years old, he "knew" he had multiple addictions regardless of what others might think.

How can one know for sure whether or not Johnny was experiencing difficulties with multiple addictions? To Johnny, it was clear. He "knew" he was embedded in a world filled with his addictions. At least Johnny was behaving *as if* he was addicted to many different behaviors. This case study is not all that uncommon. Many of us have seen similar instances. It is easy to interpret the above narrative as describing an evolving set of addictions to television, food, exercise, alcohol, various drugs, "love," and work. But, then, what is addiction, really? The subsequent sections of this chapter discuss variously used definitions or conceptions of addiction.

Substance and Behavioral Addictions

Both substance and behavioral (process) addictions describe behavior that results in clinically significant impairment. **Substance addiction** pertains to repetitive intake of a drug (such as alcohol) or of food, whereas **behavioral addiction** pertains to engaging in types of behaviors repetitively which are not directly taken into the body such as gambling or sex (APA, 2013; Demetrovics & Griffiths, 2012; Sussman & Ames, 2008; Sussman, Lisha, & Griffiths, 2011b). Until recently, the scientific community focused on, or considered seriously, as an "addiction" only misuse of drugs that led to *physiological withdrawal symptoms* (the appearance of both physical and psychological symptoms which are caused by physiological adaptations in the central nervous system and the brain due to chronic exposure to a substance). In general, researchers considered those objects on which one could become addicted as being drugs which cross the *blood–brain barrier* (a filtering mechanism of the capillaries that carry blood to the brain and spinal cord tissue, blocking the passage of certain substances) and, as *exogenous ligands*, block, facilitate, or mimic *endogenous ligand* (naturally occurring neurotransmitter) functions. Certainly drug misuse may lead to a variety of negative life consequences. Drug misuse can result in overdoses or seizures during withdrawal leading to visits to emergency rooms, sickness, decreased function (e.g., paralysis), or even death. In 2010, 177,000 admissions to emergency rooms in the United States were due to negative effects of alcohol or other drug use (constituting 0.0014 percent of all emergency room visits; www.cdc.gov/nchs/data/ahcd/nhamcs_emergency/2010_ed_web_tables.pdf). Twelve-step organizations began to grapple with addiction to alcohol and other drugs in 1939 with the pioneering example of Alcoholics Anonymous (AA) (www.aa.org/; Alcoholics Anonymous, 1976). Several other 12-step organizations for substance addictions (e.g., tobacco, other drugs such as marijuana or cocaine, food) branched out from the AA model, continuing to the present day, as is shown in Table 1.1.

Behavioral addictions alter endogenous ligand functions. For example, if one engages in a novel activity, or imagines doing so (such as riding on an elephant), or engages in intensive gambling activity, endogenous mesolimbic dopamine levels may rise. If one lies down or imagines a sunset, or engages in fond memories of another person, endogenous serotonin may rise. It is also feasible that neurotransmission release may become reliant, in part, on participation in a behavioral addiction (through repetitive engagement in the behavior), leading to withdrawal-like symptoms upon abrupt termination of the addictive behavior. However, there is no direct contact with brain synapses through introduction of an exogenous ligand (i.e., a drug effect). Behavioral addictions (e.g., gambling, Internet, love, sex, exercise, work, shopping) were discussed informally for a long time among AA and other 12-step group participants (Rosenberg & Feder, 2014a, 2014b), subsequently resulting in new 12-step organizations targeting these dysfunctional behaviors. The pioneer behavioral addictions 12-step program was Gamblers Anonymous (GA), which began in 1957 (www.gamblersanonymous.org/ga/content/history). Other behavioral addictions 12-step groups were formed subsequently (up to the present time), asserting the experiential reality of the existence of various process/behavioral addictions. Examples of behavioral addiction 12-step programs also are shown in Table 1.1.

The Reality of Multiple Types of Addictions: General Theoretical Considerations

A variety of behaviors very recently have come to be considered addictions by researchers and practitioners, delineated by common features (e.g., appetitive effects [impact on mood, arousal, or thinking], preoccupation, subjective sense of loss of

Table 1.1 Examples of 12-step organizations for substance and behavioral addictions ordered by year of formation

Examples of 12-step organizations	Website	Year organization formed
Substance addictions		
Alcoholics Anonymous (AA)	www.aa.org/	1939
Narcotics Anonymous (NA)	www.na.org/	1953
Overeaters Anonymous	www.oa.org/	1960
Pills Anonymous (PA)	www.pillsanonymous.org/	1972
Cocaine Anonymous (CA)	www.ca.org/	1982
Nicotine Anonymous (NicA)	https://nicotine-anonymous.org/	1982
Food Addicts Anonymous (FAA)	www.foodaddictsanonymous.org/	1987
Marijuana Anonymous (MA)	www.marijuana-anonymous.org/	1989
Crystal Meth Anonymous (CMA)	www.crystalmeth.org/	1994
Food Addicts in Recovery Anonymous (FA)	www.foodaddicts.org/	1998
Heroin Anonymous (HA)	www.heroinanonymous.org/	2004
Behavioral addictions		
Gamblers Anonymous (GA)	www.gamblersanonymous.org/ga/content/history	1957
Debtors Anonymous (DA)	www.debtorsanonymous.org/	1971
Sexual Compulsives Anonymous (SCA)	www.sca-recovery.org/	1973
Sex and Love Addicts Anonymous (SLAA)	www.slaafws.org/	1976
Sex Addicts Anonymous (SAA)	https://saa-recovery.org/	1977
Sexaholics Anonymous (SA)	www.sa.org/	1979
Workaholics Anonymous (WA)	www.workaholics-anonymous.org/page.php?page=home	1983
Sexual Recovery Anonymous (SRA)	www.sexualrecovery.org/	1993
Online Gamers Anonymous (OLGA)	www.olganon.org/	2002
Love Addicts Anonymous (LAA)	www.loveaddicts.org/	2004
Internet and Tech Addiction Anonymous (ITAA)	www.netaddictionanon.org/	2009
Exercise Addicts Anonymous (EAA)	www.exerciseaddictsanonymous.org/	2014

control, negative consequences). In fact, the First International Conference on Behavioral Addictions took place in Budapest, Hungary in March, 2013 which demonstrated research consensus on the existence of multiple types of addictions (see http://icba.mat.org.hu/). When presenting definitions of addiction, I intend them to encapsulate both substance and behavioral addictions. As do others (Rosenberg & Feder, 2014a),

I assert that *when examining a wide variety of addictions, there are common underlying determinants and observable constituents.*

Obtaining a measurable description of a scientific concept such as addiction is useful to be able to make inferences regarding how the concept is related to other concepts (e.g., its overlap and non-overlap with other concepts), and subsequently how the concept can guide the development of useful applications (e.g., policy, prevention, control). A description of addiction that maps very well onto measurable criteria could serve as a useful phenotype that might assist in the explanation of gene–environment interactions in this arena, and best serve prevention and control efforts. Unfortunately the "addiction" concept has been the subject of much debate and several definitions (Sussman & Sussman, 2011). The different, current definitions are not mutually exclusive though. In fact, their boundaries tend to be fuzzy. It may be possible to provide a consensual empirical description of addiction that is applicable to multiple behaviors (e.g., shopping, working, gambling, or Internet use).

However, there may be some concern that if people can be said to be addicted to a myriad of activities then the concept of addiction becomes somehow trivial or is used too loosely (Orford, 2001), or misdirects focus to the individual rather than societal issues (Sinclair, Lochner, & Stein, 2016). However, as I will present in this text, people may indeed become addicted to many different behaviors, all of which lead to negative consequences that may be due to both societal and individual factors. That is, I assert that there are many recurrent, addictive patterns of behavior that lead to clinically significant impairment. The concept of addiction may apply broadly but it is not trivial.

Evolution of Definitions of Addiction

The etymology of the word "addiction" has a rather long history, though the concept of addiction as a serious type of problem in living is relatively new. "Addicere" (also see "addico," "addixi," or "addictus"), the Latin verb from which "addiction" derives, means "to give or bind, or even to enslave, a person to one thing or another" (Kor, Fogel, Reid, & Potenza, 2013; Koob & Le Moal, 2006). At its origin, **addiction** generally referred to "giving over" or being "highly devoted" to a person or activity (Alexander & Schweighofer, 1988), or engaging in a behavior habitually (Levine, 1978), which could have positive or negative implications. Over the last 400 years, statements have been made about addiction that began to frame it as a phenomenon that involved strong, overpowering urges. Over the last 200 years, the word "addiction" has come to be considered more and more to have a disease-like connotation (Orford, 2001). Many conceptualizations of the addictions, which date as far back as the end of the eighteenth century, pertain to a malfunction of the central nervous system in some way (Meyer, 1996). This word more recently is used as a concept involving neurobiological underpinnings (Goodman, 2009; Koob & Le Moal, 2006; Sussman & Sussman, 2011), sometimes considered a "brain disease" (Leshner, 1997; Levy, 2013; Sussman & Ames, 2008).

History of Substance Addictions

A brief glimpse at different substances of abuse provides evidence of common features of addiction, including achieving an appetitive effect (e.g., mood improvement), preoccupation, loss of control, and a variety of negative social or situational consequences. This section examines the history of tobacco, alcohol, other drug use addictions (opium, cocaine, marijuana), and food addiction.

Tobacco Addiction

Suspicion that tobacco may cause various diseases dates back at least 400 years. However, addiction to tobacco appears to have a brief "public" history. In occasional writings there is the suggestion of addiction to tobacco, at some points in history. For example, apparently, George Washington wrote from the front during the US Revolutionary War, in the 1770s, to send tobacco to the warfront if people couldn't send money (US Department of Health and Human Services, 1988). Thus, there was an importance placed on tobacco consumption, which suggests compulsive use. Deep inhalation of tobacco did not occur until after *flue-curing* (four- to eight-week air-curing, which results in tobacco low in sugar, and which gives tobacco smoke a light, sweet flavor, and a high nicotine content) was invented in 1839, and this certainly would have increased the likelihood of compulsive use. Identification of nicotine as the chemical that induced compulsive use of tobacco occurred in the 1920s and 1930s (US Department of Health and Human Services, 1988). The public consensus that nicotine was addictive, and the driving force behind regular tobacco use, occurred with publication of the Surgeon General's report on nicotine addiction in 1988 (US Department of Health and Human Services, 1988).

Alcohol Addiction

Perhaps the best-known addiction – which has been subjected to considerable research, has its own institute in the National Institutes of Health (i.e., National Institute on Alcohol Abuse and Alcoholism [NIAAA]), the substance from which the 12-step movement arose, and which has influenced the general concept of addiction – is *alcoholism*. Alcohol misuse has been noted throughout written history: for example, in writings of Herodotus (450 BC); in records from Pompeii (70 AD); in the proclamations of Domitian (80 AD) against widespread drunkenness in Rome; in the works of Shakespeare, such as in his descriptions of Sir John Falstaff (1600); in the passage of the "Gin Act" in England in 1751 (to restrict the distribution of gin and possibly decrease crime); and in a description of the behavior of pirates in Robert Louis Stephenson's book *Treasure Island* (1882); among many other examples (Warner, 1992). On February 22, 1842, Abraham Lincoln gave a "Temperance Address" before the Springfield, Illinois, Washington Temperance Society (the "Washingtonians"), in which he discussed the negative effects of intemperance and becoming a "redeemed specimen of long lost humanity." He attributed much vice, misery, and crime to the abuse of alcohol but also supported kind treatment of those who had fallen victim to alcohol addiction. In fact, he recognized a relatively high percentage of victims of alcoholism as having shown signs of brilliance and capacity for generosity (see Sussman & Ames, 2008).

Opium-Related Addiction

Another well-known substance addiction is that of *opium*. In *Confessions of an English Opium Eater* (De Quincey, 1822), initial use of opium was described as "divine enjoyment," as happiness that might be bought for a penny and carried in the waistcoat pocket. Social embarrassment while using opium (e.g., talking nonsense about politics, necessitating friends to apologize for the person with the acknowledgment that the individual was using opium) and a tendency to walk among the poor in London at night (potentially dangerous behavior) were documented – with an overall favorable attitude toward opium. However, De Quincey did note that he would die if he continued using the substance (Jonnes, 1996). In 1840, the Chinese government outlawed trafficking in opium (which was imported at the time), recognizing the ascendancy of opium smoking in China. However, the British compelled the Chinese to allow the opium trade, and after the "Opium Wars" (1839–1860), the opium trade was legalized and production in China increased, maintaining relatively high prevalence of opium addiction and related social and economic problems in China.

In *An Opium-Eater in America* (Blair, 1842), Blair describes multiple negative experiences he attributed to opium intake, including getting into fights, using even while continuing to suffer negative life consequences, experiencing a great increase in tolerance, suffering bad withdrawal and other physical symptoms (e.g., headaches, sickness, parched throat, restlessness, sleep difficulties, and skin peeling), experiencing psychotic reactions, losing friends, and feeling a sense of depression and hopelessness.

Recognition of the consequential increasing prevalence of opium misuse and addiction led to development of patent medications used to treat it. However, often these formulas contained opium themselves. The German pharmaceutical company Bayer sold an over-the-counter morphine substitute under the trade name Heroin from 1898 to 1910, reflecting the increased popularity of opiate use as a medication.

Cocaine Addiction

Replacement medications that did not contain opiate derivatives to treat opiate addictions also led to new problematic drug use. In 1880, Dr. Edward C. Huse wrote about the use of *cocaine* for the cure of an opium habit (Jonnes, 1996). Cocaine grew in popularity during this period. In "The Nightmare of Cocaine" (Anonymous, 1929), a man from the United States wrote about the development of his addiction to cocaine while fighting in France in World War I. He reportedly substituted cocaine for alcohol use and believed that he fought much better. Subsequently, he used cocaine regularly and experienced a sustained period of his life that included rushing thoughts and haphazard traveling, lack of sleep, weight loss, tolerance and withdrawal symptoms and cravings, loss of spouse, and social isolation. Dr. William Halsted, who later became chair of the Johns Hopkins University Department of Surgery, began in 1884 a lifelong struggle with cocaine that left him remote and eccentric, with occasional absences from work, after being considered very outgoing earlier in his life (Jonnes, 1996).

Both opium and cocaine were contained in numerous products back in 1900 (e.g., Bayer Heroin and Coca-Cola; Levinthal, 2005). By 1900, approximately 250,000 Americans (of 75 million) were opiate addicts and 200,000 were cocaine addicts. Controlling for overlap in drug use, approximately 1 in 200 Americans (0.5 percent) was an opium or cocaine addict (Jonnes, 1996). (In present times, 0.3 percent of Americans abuse these drug types [which are now illegal], representing a relative decrease in percentage prevalence, though the population is much larger; Sussman & Ames, 2008.) In 1905, Samuel Hopkins Adams, a famous muckraker at the time, exposed the patent medication industry's use of great amounts of opium and cocaine in their medicines (Jonnes, 1996).

Marijuana Addiction

Marijuana also has a history of misuse. In "The Tale of Two Hashish-Eaters" (from *1001 Arabian Nights*; www.druglibrary.org/schaffer/hemp/arab1.htm) marijuana was referred to as a "hilarious herb" that was purchased frequently and without good sense (one person spent his daily wage, after a little food, to purchase marijuana). Engaging in socially embarrassing behaviors, such as dancing naked in public while under the influence of marijuana, was noted. In 1857, Ludlow described his experiences with marijuana use. According to Ludlow (1857), his experiences included battles with marijuana dependence, particularly a preoccupation with marijuana use. This preoccupation replaced the pursuit of all other types of excitement, with continuous intoxication, attempts to quit with only relapse to follow, craving, depression, abnormal dreaming (including dreaming that he was intoxicated), and seeking the care of a physician to try to quit marijuana use. A much more in-depth presentation of the history of alcohol, opium, cocaine, and marijuana addictions may be found in Chapter 3 of Sussman and Ames (2008). However, this overview provides a reasonable picture of the evolution of these different addictions.

Food Addiction

There is no ancient history regarding *food addiction*. Binging and purging eating behaviors were noted in ancient Rome, though this may not have reflected consistent patterns of dysfunctional behavior but rather popular behaviors during ritualized banquets (in order to continue to gorge on food). Thinking about food or eating as an "addiction" appears to be a recent notion.

History of Behavioral Addictions

The historical literature presents descriptions of *gambling* and *sex* addictions. One example is Emperor Commodus (180–192 AD), who turned the Roman imperial palace into a casino, and gambling came to be considered a vice in ancient Rome.

Also noted in the writings of ancient Rome, during his reign and others, sex was described as occurring in many forms and excessively (e.g., Orford, 2001; Rosenberg & Feder, 2014b). Other behavioral addictions have been less often discussed in historical writings, or more ambiguously depicted. For example, Andre Matthey (1816) wrote about **diseases of the spirit** ("manias"), which had a major impact on conceptualization of behavioral addictions (e.g., kleptomania).

At the end of the nineteenth century, there was some suggestion that certain behaviors were morally wrong or problematic (e.g., being slaves to fashion [*shopping*] and gambling; Roumane & Conwell, 1897). These descriptors apparently were directed at various addictive behaviors. Various other out-of-self-control behaviors also may have been considered forms of mania or morbid appetites (Orford, 2001) such as *kleptomania* (craving to steal objects; Cuzen & Stein, 2014).

Except for gambling addiction, 12-step organizations created for behavioral addictions were established only from the 1970s (see Table 1.1). At the same time, addictions professionals coined names to refer to various addictive behaviors in popular writings. For example, "*workaholism*" was coined by Wayne Oates in his published work *Confessions of a Workaholic* (Oates, 1971). He was a professor of the psychology of religion and pastoral care, but discussed that topic in the role of a practitioner.

Internet addiction disorder was coined as a hoax by Ivan Goldberg in 1995 (Beard & Wolf, 2001), though it began to be studied seriously shortly thereafter by Mark Griffiths and Kimberly Young in 1998 (Griffiths, 1998; Young, 1998). Behavioral addictions have been studied empirically since the 1980s (e.g., Cook, 1987), and are also referred to as "process" addictions (Schaef, 1987). There is a relatively brief research history.

For hundreds of years, many behaviors I now refer to as addictions were considered examples of *vice*, that is, behaviors which are pleasurable, popular, possibly voluntary, and wicked (Bernhard, 2007; Skolnick, 1988). Such behaviors include gambling, drug use, adultery, and prostitution (Skolnick, 1988). Also among the seven "deadly sins" mentioned in the Bible and by Alcoholics Anonymous are lust, gluttony, and greed (Alcoholics Anonymous, 1976; www.allaboutgod.com/what-are-the-seven-deadly-sins-faq.htm), which might hint at *sex*, *food*, gambling, and shopping addictions.

Such is what is widely known regarding the "ancient" history of the behavioral addictions. Some addictive behaviors have a relatively very short history (e.g., addictions to *electronic devices* could not predate their invention). Similar consequences tended to arise from a wide variety of behaviors that, in general, appear to share a common thread – of being repetitively unusual in manifestation, involving motivated behavior of some type, preoccupation, and loss of control, resulting in clinically significant impairment in one or more life domains (e.g., social, work, health).

Summary of the History of Substance and Behavioral Addictions

While there apparently is not that much written information on the history of the addictions *as being addictions*, this does not mean that they did not exist. Of course, it is possible that the prevalence of addiction was either much lower than it is now, or that the "extremeness" of behavior needed to be categorized as a problem was much greater. The historical records do depict (a) increasing engagement in certain behavior and reduction of alternative behavior, (b) difficulties stopping the behavior, (c) thinking or acting bizarrely, (d) sleep difficulties, (e) social withdrawal, (f) depression symptomatology, and (g) such consequences as placing oneself in danger for accidents or violence. It seems clear that problematic behaviors, now coined as "addictions," existed for a long time. Furthermore, there existed common underlying parameters of these problematic behaviors (e.g., repetitive bizarre behavior, preoccupation, loss of control, and consequences such as social withdrawal) which pertain both to intake of substances and to engagement in various activities.

"Intensional" and "Extensional" Conceptions of Addiction

In the remainder of this introductory chapter, I provide several definitions of the addictions that are organized under two, more general classifications, of "intensional" and "extensional" definitions. An **intensional definition of addiction** pertains to *causal or process model* type statements of addictions. That is, intensional models attempt to describe at minimum an addictive behavioral process (i.e., this happens, that leads to this, and then to that), and at maximum an *etiology* (a causal story). These types of models have relatively good explanatory power though they often are more distant from observables than descriptive (extensional) models.

Described later on in this chapter there are also several schemes that present what might be labeled as "extensional," constituent, descriptive, or *listing-type* definitions (Sussman & Ames, 2008). An **extensional definition of addiction**, or listing/classification of addiction features, provides a taxonomy of addiction elements, which subsequently might be organized into a (more) intensional theory-based perspective. Just as Mendeleev's periodic table provided a taxonomy of chemical elements that were utilized for subsequent theories of the movement of electrons, an extensional scheme of constituents of addiction might later be similarly harnessed into higher-order theories in the field of addictionology. Specific examples of intensional and extensional models of addiction are shown in Table 1.2.

Major Examples of "Intensional" Definitions of Addiction

Five intensional models of addiction include those of (a) physiological and psychological dependence (cellular or acquired tolerance and withdrawal), (b) impulsive-obsessive/compulsive behavior, (c) self-medication, (d) self-regulation, and (e) addiction entrenchment (i.e., overwhelming involvement with an addiction object). These conceptions are somewhat overlapping; not mutually exclusive. However, these five models do summarize the most popular intensional-type conceptions currently used.

Table 1.2 Definitions of the addictions

Intensional definitions	Causal or process model type statements of addictions
Physiological and psychological dependence	Prolonged engagement in addictive behavior that results in its continued performance being necessary for physiologic and psychological equilibrium
Impulsive-obsessive/compulsive behavior	Engaging in addictive behavior due to a "building up of tension" which is released, resulting in pleasure or reduction of anxiety, relief, and perhaps later leading to self-reproach
Self-medication	Relief from disordered emotions and sense of self-preservation through engaging in addictive behavior (e.g., reaction to trauma)
Self-regulation	Engaging in addictive behavior in order to achieve an immediate temporary sense of comfort (ideal-current state match; e.g., BAS-BIS systems)
	Incentive-sensitization theory focuses on the influence of neural adaptation to addictive behaviors as the underlying mechanism perpetuating the addictive behaviors
	According to "allostasis," addiction is due to the dysregulation of the neurotransmission-hormonal (modulator) system that is caused by the addictive behavior
Addiction entrenchment: Overwhelming involvement with an addiction object	Over-attachment to a drug, object, or activity. Intrinsic and extrinsic incentives, addiction-promoting cognitive beliefs and expectancies drive the addictive behavior forward (e.g., behavioral economics-related models)
Extensional definitions	**Listing-type definitions with components that might be placed into higher-order theorizing**
Six-component definition	The six components are: salience, mood modification, tolerance, withdrawal symptoms, conflict, and relapse
Five-component definition	The five components are: appetitive effects, satiation, preoccupation, loss of control, and negative consequences
DSM-V: The current diagnostic criteria for "substance use disorder"	In DSM-V substance use disorder is diagnosed if the individual reports two or more of 11 criteria. The 11 criteria are intended to reflect impaired control, social impairment, risky use, and pharmacologic effects. Also, in the DSM-V, for the first time, appears a behavioral addiction, "gambling disorder," with nine criteria; four or more need to be endorsed for a diagnosis

Physiological and Psychological Dependence

The *physiological/psychological dependence* definition of addiction pertains to prolonged engagement in a behavior that results in its continued performance being necessary for physiologic and psychological equilibrium. Tolerance, withdrawal, and craving are hallmark criteria of a dependence definition of addiction. The addict is "trapped" into a pattern of increasing involvement with the behavior, while feeling more and more negative when trying to cut down or stop the behavior.

Tolerance

Tolerance refers to the need to engage in the behavior at a relatively greater level than in the past to achieve previous levels of appetitive effects (or achieving diminished effects at previous levels of behavior). As tolerance increases, one likely spends more time locating and engaging in the addiction. Tolerance phenomena are observed for various substance or behavioral addictions (e.g., drug tolerance, Sussman & Ames, 2008; food addiction, Yau, Gottlieb, Krasna, & Potenza, 2014; gambling addiction, Grant & Odlaug, 2014; Internet addiction, Weinstein, Feder, Rosenberg, & Dannon, 2014; sex addiction, Rosenberg, O'Connor, & Carnes, 2014; exercise addiction, Berczik et al., 2014). For example, an exercise addict seeks a continual increase in exercise intensity, frequency, or duration to achieve desired effects or benefits (Berczik et al., 2014).

Withdrawal

Upon abrupt termination of the addictive behavior, an abstinence syndrome, also known as *withdrawal*, will occur. This abstinence syndrome involves intense physical disturbances in the case of some types of drug abuse. Withdrawal symptoms vary across drugs of abuse (Sussman & Ames, 2008). For example, withdrawal related to alcohol, sedative, hypnotic, or anxiolytic addiction may involve autonomic hyperactivity, increased hand tremors, insomnia, nausea or vomiting, transient illusions or hallucinations, psychomotor agitation, anxiety, or grand mal seizures. In particular, autonomic hyperactivity involves a **catecholamine storm** or flooding of the central nervous system with norepinephrine and epinephrine neurotransmitters upon abrupt withdrawal, resulting typically in high temperature, tachycardia, and tremor. A list of physiological and psychological withdrawal symptoms for alcohol and related drugs, amphetamines or cocaine, opioids, nicotine, PCP, caffeine, cannabis, and hallucinogens is given in Table 1.3.

Behavioral addictions likewise exert withdrawal-like symptoms. For example, the exercise addict may have to stop working out abruptly, either due to injury or to other events, and then feels withdrawal-like symptoms such as irritability, anxiety, or tension (Berczik et al., 2014). Similar subjective feelings of irritability, restlessness, agitation, anxiety, depressed mood, or craving are observed for food or other behavioral addictions upon abrupt termination (e.g., food addiction, Yau et al., 2014; gambling addiction, Grant & Odlaug, 2014; Internet addiction, Weinstein et al., 2014; sex addiction, Rosenberg et al., 2014).

Table 1.3 Withdrawal symptoms for different types of drugs based on the Sussman/Ames (2001, 2008) health behavior scheme of drug categories

Drug type	Typical withdrawal symptoms
Alcohol, sedative, hypnotic, or anxiolytic	Autonomic reactivity, hand tremor, insomnia, nausea/vomiting, brief illusions or hallucinations, psychomotor agitation, anxiety, and/or convulsive seizures
Amphetamine or cocaine	Fatigue or exhaustion, depression, unpleasant and vivid dreams or nightmares, insomnia or hypersomnia, increased appetite, and/or psychomotor retardation or agitation
Opioid	Depressed mood, anxiety, abdominal cramping, nausea/vomiting, diarrhea, muscle aches, tearing, runny nose (rhinorrhea), sweating, fever, yawning, and/or insomnia
Nicotine	Depressed, anxious, or irritable mood, insomnia, difficulty concentrating, restlessness, decreased heart rate, constipation, sweating, and/or increased appetite
PCP	Little or no withdrawal symptoms
Caffeine	Little or no withdrawal symptoms; some fatigue, headache, and/or difficulty concentrating
Cannabis	Fatigue, difficulty concentrating, abdominal pain, changes in eating habits, agitation, restlessness, irritability, sweating, shakiness, fever, chills, depressed mood, anger, sleep problems, and/or vivid dreams
Hallucinogens	None, except for occasional flashbacks (rare)

Craving

Craving is now one of the criteria of substance use disorder in the DSM-V (APA, 2013). Craving refers to an "intense desire" to engage in a specific act (Foddy & Savulescu, 2010b; Pelchat, 2002). The intense desire for engagement reoccurs, is compelling, and one often gives in to this desire (Pelchat, 2002). Craving might be considered part of the withdrawal syndrome in a dependence model of addiction. That is, repeated participation in the behavior may lead to a psychic drive that requires continuous engagement to avoid craving (Bickel, Mueller, & Jarmolowicz, 2013; Koob & Le Moal, 2006). On the other hand, craving is not necessarily the same thing as physiological withdrawal and may, in fact, be more central to a concept of addictions (Leshner, 1997; O'Brien, Volkow, & Li, 2006; Potenza, 2010). Many drugs of abuse involve relatively little physical withdrawal (e.g., cocaine) but involve alterations in perception and psychological dependence or craving during use and upon abstinence, whereas other drugs involve relatively great physical withdrawal (e.g., nicotine, for some people) but involve relatively fewer alterations in perception during use and upon abstinence.

Regardless of physical withdrawal and psychological alterations in perception, addictions are identified by addictive object-seeking behavior and subjective urges to engage in the addictive behavior (craving) while in the midst of accumulative negative consequences (Leshner, 1997; Potenza, 2010). Some addicts who are new in recovery may even maintain a subjective sense of fear that catastrophic events will occur if they continue to refrain from their addictions (Jacobs, 1986). Of course, there is some ambiguity regarding the definition of craving. For example, this concept may overlap with implicit expectancy cognitive processes (Heather, 1998).

Summary

In summary, while many drug and non-drug addictions do not appear to produce obvious physical dependence (i.e., physiological-based tolerance and withdrawal effects), they do create a subjective need for increased involvement in the behavior to achieve satiation, and abrupt termination of the behavior often leads to such symptoms as depression, intense anxiety, hopelessness, helplessness, and irritability (e.g., also see Allegre, Souville, Therme, & Griffiths, 2006, and Hausenblas & Downs, 2002, regarding exercise dependence). The addictive behavior may seem to the addict "as if" it is the best solution to resolve these negative abstinence symptoms (Sussman & Unger, 2004). Regardless of level of physical dependence, relapse rates across various addictions appear to be relatively high (e.g., over 70 percent for a one-year period; Brandon, Vidrine, & Litvin, 2007; Hodgins & el-Guebaly, 2004; Miller, Walters, & Bennett, 2001; Schneider & Irons, 2001).

Impulsive-Obsessive/Compulsive Behavior

This second intensional definition of addiction might overlap with a psychological dependence notion of addiction, although the emphasis is on a "release"; that is, engagement in the addictive behavior leading to pleasure or relief rather than on a notion focusing on "maintaining an equilibrium." There are two variants.

Positive Reinforcement

An impulsive-obsessive/compulsive definition of addiction (Koob & Le Moal, 2006) generally pertains to engaging in the behavior due to a "building up of tension" which is released, resulting in pleasure and perhaps later leading to self-reproach. Cyclically, what occurs is another building up of tension or craving for pleasure again (an impulsion, positive reinforcement mostly). This might be referred to as the ***positive reinforcement variant*** of the impulsive-obsessive/compulsive model of addiction.

Negative Reinforcement

Alternatively, this intensional model of addiction may involve a building up of tension, anxiety, and stress which is released, resulting in relief from the anxiety but no particular pleasure; then, cyclically, leading to obsessions which produce anxiety and stress leading to a craving for relief again (compulsion, negative reinforcement mostly). It is possible that anticipation of negative affect, or experience of negative affect due to stress, which possibly originally stemmed from withdrawal-like reactions, may lead to engagement in addictive behaviors as a negatively reinforcing safety signal (Baker, Piper, McCarthy, Majeskie, & Fiore, 2004). This might be referred to as the ***negative reinforcement variant*** of the impulsive-obsessive/compulsive model of addiction.

Both Positive and Negative Reinforcement Apply

Some theoreticians conceive of the positive and negative reinforcement processes as pertaining to different definitions of addiction (Koob & Le Moal, 2006). However, it is plausible that both processes operate in the same person. That is, one may experience craving for pleasure and craving to release anxiety (positive and negative reinforcement). Some researchers have speculated that positive reinforcement operates early on in the addiction, whereas negative reinforcement operates relatively more later on (Wise & Koob, 2014). Of course, one might speculate that it is possible or even likely that both processes do operate at the same time (e.g., Cuzen & Stein, 2014; Goodman, 1990), as humans seldom function on single contingencies. That is, people live in a world of "free operants" and multiple simultaneous contingencies of positive and negative reinforcement operate for the same behaviors (Bouton, 2014; Epstein, 1992).

Differentiating an Impulsive-Obsessive/Compulsive Definition of Addiction from Obsessive-Compulsive Disorders

One may argue that such a definition is more applicable to ***obsessive-compulsive disorder*** (OCD) than to addictions (Kor et al., 2013). For example, sexual obsessions and related ritualistic behavior may be considered supplementary to an underlying obsessive-compulsive disorder, related to attempts at reducing anxiety. "Compulsions" involve (a) spontaneous desires to act a particular way, (b) a subjective sense of feeling temporarily out of control, (c) psychological conflict pertaining to the imprudent behavior, (d) "settling for less" to achieve the same ends (e.g., sexual release for money rather than love), and (e) a disregard for negative consequences (Hirschman, 1992). Arguably, OCD and addictions may be overlapping constructs (see Gillan & Robbins, 2014). However, many researchers and practitioners use the term ***compulsion*** more narrowly. Some define this term as a simple but intense urge to do something; only one feature of addictions but centrally definitive of obsessive-compulsive disorders (Hartney, 2010).

Obsessive-compulsive disorder-related behavior may be defined even more precisely as an intense ***egodystonic*** (separate from self) urge to engage in a simple, repetitive activity, to remove anxiety (Brewer & Potenza, 2008). Such activities may include repeated washing of hands or bathing, tying of shoes, or restricting areas in which one will travel (e.g., not walking on cracks). A narrow definition of compulsion does not, primarily, consider the interplay of higher-order cognitive processes, such as the planning that may go into completion of a cycle of addictive behavior. (Arguably, however, someone may decide to wash their hands where there is plenty of soap available and the facility is considered very clean; this may involve planning.) Also, the act may accomplish a temporary removal of anxiety, but it tends not to be experienced as pleasurable at any point in the engagement of the behavior (Hartney, 2010). Conversely, an addiction, by definition, involves the attempt to achieve some desired appetitive effect and satiation through engagement in some behavior. In fact, a whole constellation of purposeful behavior may be involved in attempts to achieve satiation (Sussman & Sussman, 2011). In summary, an ***obsessive-compulsive disorder*** may involve repetitive simple behaviors to remove anxiety, whereas an addiction may involve more complex behaviors to achieve an appetitive effect of some type (affect, arousal, or thought regulation).

Major Examples of "Intensional" Definitions of Addiction

Self-Medication

A *self-medication perspective* of addiction pertains to relief from disordered emotions and sense of self-preservation through engaging in the addictive behavior. The emphasis here is one where a person engages in the behavior because he or she feels "sick" and wants to feel "well." Possibly, different behaviors will relieve different negative emotions (opiates for anger, stimulants for anhedonia, alcohol to be able to express feelings; Khantzian, 1985, 1997; Mariani, Khantzian, & Levin, 2014). Support for this perspective is mixed, at best. However, phenomenologically, there is ample content (or at least face) validity.

Trauma and Self-Medication

A recent variant of this perspective is the view that in childhood one has experienced significant *trauma* (a life-threatening or disturbing experience or experiences) which sensitizes function of the amygdala, ever signaling potential for harm, threat, rejection, or disapproval, often in the absence of environmental triggers. One attempts to remove subjective experience of anxiety, depression, or post-traumatic stress disorder-like symptoms through engagement in the addiction, at minimum permitting focus of attention elsewhere (Markert & Nikakhtar, 2000). Certainly, self-medication perspectives may overlap with the previous two perspectives of addiction.

Self-Regulation

In a *self-regulation model*, the "present state"-of-being cues attempts to reach a "standard" at which point satiation is achieved, until the present state is no longer at the desired standard state. This type of systems model metaphorically is like that of a thermostat turning on and off depending on whether or not room temperature has reached the set-point temperature. A self-regulation view of addiction involves difficulties establishing standards of behavior, attentional failures, and misdirected attempts at regulation, planning, reasoning, self-monitoring, and emotion (Dvorak & Day, 2014; Koob & Le Moal, 2006; Lewis, 2011), that may lead to dysregulation.

BAS–BIS Model

One major addiction self-regulation model is that of Jeffrey Gray. Gray (1982) outlined two general motivational brain systems – the ***behavioral approach system (BAS)*** and the ***behavioral inhibition system (BIS)*** – that affect individual differences in behavioral responses to cues for reward. These interdependent systems influence whether an individual is likely to withdraw from or avoid situations that involve novel or threatening cues or whether a person is likely to engage in novel or risky behavior (e.g., drug use) in response to cues for reward. According to Gray, the BAS is mediated by ***dopamine*** pathways (associated with novelty and reward), involving the ventral tegmental area, ventral striatum, and nucleus accumbens. An active BAS is linked to more impulsive-type behaviors. Alternatively, the BIS is mediated by the ***septo-hippocampal system*** (which detects competing goals and leads to approach or avoidance behavior). An active BIS is linked to inhibiting behavior. Persons with difficulty in emotional self-regulation may be particularly prone to engage in addictive behaviors in order to achieve an immediate temporary sense of comfort (Dvorak & Day, 2014). That is, they are more likely to utilize the BAS which is not working in sync with the BIS resulting in a relatively dysfunctional do-loop. This perspective also overlaps with the others.

Incentive-Sensitization Theory

Robinson and Berridge's (1993, 2000) *incentive-sensitization theory* focuses on the influence of neural adaptation (i.e., sensitization) to addictive behaviors and addictive behavior-conditioned stimuli as the underlying mechanism perpetuating the addictive behaviors. They differentiate neural processes involved in motivational mechanisms or incentive salience to addictive behavior cues (***wanting***) (i.e., mesocorticolimbic circuitry) and the neural substrates of pleasurable effects or ***liking*** (i.e., nucleus accumbens [NAcc] opioid receptor neurotransmission [signaling]) (Robinson & Berridge, 1993, 2000, 2008). They have proposed that a progressive dysregulation of neural substrates occurs through repeated engagement in the behavior. This dysregulation is associated with an increase in behavioral sensitization contributing to addicts' "wanting" (or craving) the behavior becoming disproportionate to the pleasure derived from the behavior. Through repeated engagement in the behavior, behavior-associated stimuli that acquire *incentive salience* through neural representation (motivational "wanting" attribute encoded by the brain to reward-predicting stimuli) become "motivational magnets," able to "grab" the addict's attention (see Berridge & Robinson, 2003; Robinson & Berridge, 2008). According to Robinson and Berridge, adaptations in the neural substrates of "wanting" are affected by the pharmacological effects of drugs (in the case of substance addiction), or alterations in endogenous ligand (naturally occurring brain neurotransmitter) transmission as a function of regular participation in a behavioral addiction, as well as by processes of associative learning (e.g., of associated cues and contexts; Robinson & Berridge, 1993, 2000, 2008). These processes influence behavior outside of conscious awareness or implicitly (see Robinson & Berridge, 2000). Thus, it is possible to crave an addictive behavior, independently of its propensity to achieve pleasure or avoid withdrawal. A person may risk all sorts of negative consequences as a function of "giving in" to the craving related to the sensitized incentive value of the addictive behavior.

Allostasis Theory

Allostasis is another explanation of addiction due to dysregulation, in this case of the neurotransmission-hormonal (modulator) system that results from repetitive engagement in the behavior (see Koob & Le Moal, 2001). According to the notion of allostasis, addictive behavior leads to ***dopamine opponent-process counteradaptation*** (e.g., dopamine transduction mechanisms: reduced dopamine output and activation of brain stress systems) that masks the effects of the addictive behavior. Pituitary–adrenal axis activation is triggered by the release of adrenocorticotropic hormone (ACTH) from the pituitary gland. ACTH release is in turn controlled by the release of hypothalamic corticotropin-releasing factor (CRF) into the pituitary portal system. ACTH release leads to release of glucocorticoids, which increases CRF availability and its expression in the amygdala. Glucocorticoid receptors are in various brain regions, particularly the ventral tegmental area (VTA), the location where mesolimbic dopamine is released to traverse over to the nucleus accumbens. Arguably, glucocorticoid transmission may inhibit dopamine release, and heightened dopamine release could fire up stress systems. To increase dopamine availability and initially control feelings of anxiety or stress, the addictive behavior may be repeated again and again. New set points of **homeostasis** (the tendency toward a relatively stable equilibrium between interdependent elements, especially as maintained by physiological processes) may then be established. This adaptive response of one's neurophysiology, or the ability to achieve stability through these change processes, is referred to as allostasis (see McEwen, 2002), and dysregulation may express itself through repeated engagement in the addictive behavior.

Addiction Entrenchment

In this model, one is said to have an over-attachment to a drug, object, or activity (Orford, 2001). That is, one has developed an **excessive appetite** (Loonis, 2002; Loonis, Apter, & Szulman, 2000; Orford, 2001). The development of an excessive appetite may be due to a variety of factors. One may act along one's own unconventional attitudinal preferences, initially leading one to try out an addictive behavior. The qualities that would tend to make the behavior defined as "addictive" are in part the conventionality of the behavior and one's initial preferences (e.g., alcohol versus heroin intake), the excessiveness of involvement in the behavior (constrained versus regular use or involvement), and one's place in society (e.g., one's socioeconomic status, high versus low). Specifically, one's conventional behavioral inclinations, regulatory executive cognitive system, and social world would tend to place deterrence and restraint on excessive appetitive desires, whereas intrinsic and extrinsic incentives resulting from participation in the addictive behavior, along with addiction-promoting cognitive beliefs and expectancies would tend to drive the behavior forward (Orford, 2001; Wiers et al., 2007). With repeated participation in the behavior, the salience of alternative behaviors may decrease (Loonis, 2002; Loonis et al., 2000; Orford, 2001). In addition, there may be a narrowing range of alternative actions available or at least in immediate working memory and there may be difficulty finding adequate substitutes for the addiction (**vicariance**; Loonis, 2002; Loonis et al., 2000). Also, an erosion of discrimination may occur between when the behavior should and should not be engaged, and implicit cognition may increasingly associate internal and external cues with engagement in the appetitive behavior (Orford, 2001; Sussman & Ames, 2008; Wiers et al., 2007). Of course, one may also reach a state in which the addiction at times appears alien to one's own wishes, one experiences internal deterrents (e.g., gastric distress), and yet one craves the behavior (perhaps one's self-identity is enmeshed with engagement in the behavior) and one becomes secretive about it.

Entrenchment and Behavioral Economics-Related Models

The entrenchment notion is, perhaps, consistent with **behavioral economics-type models** of addiction-related behavior as being a choice (a self-destructive operant behavior); based on the existence of (a) multiple schedules or reinforcement associated with different behaviors (addictive versus non-addictive behaviors), and (b) involving different reinforcement values and delays in delivery of reinforcement. The idea here is that an addictive behavior that may have lower ultimate reinforcement value but a shorter delay of delivery, may guide behavior over alternative behaviors with higher ultimate reinforcement values but a longer delay of delivery (e.g., stable relationships such as marriage, improved health, financial security). Viewed as a function of a moment of choice, the notion is one of "melioration." Viewed as a function of delay discounting, the notion is one of "self-control." Alternatively, viewed as a function of response benefits and costs of alternative potential behaviors, the notion is one of "behavioral economics" (see Bickel, Jarmolowicz, Mueller, & Gatchalian, 2011; Bickel et al., 2016; Kurti & Dallery, 2012).

Summary of Intensional Addiction Models

The previous five notions of addiction were labeled as "intensional," rule-based, or theory-based definitions (Sussman & Ames, 2008). This list of theories is not exhaustive. There are a variety of related classical conditioning and operant models of addiction that could be introduced or discussed in more detail (Bickel et al., 2013; Gillan & Robbins, 2014; Koob & Le Moal 2006; Orford, 2001), or those that pertain to coping with intolerable affective states (e.g., hopelessness related to narcissistic rage [Dodes, 1990] or with pre-addiction isolation/negative states [Alexander & Hadaway, 1982], or as a reaction to childhood trauma [Mate, 2012], which may or may not reflect a self-regulation perspective). Agent (addictive behavior), host (genetics), and environment (opportunity) models of addiction (O'Brien, 2008) also have been proposed, as have transcriptional and epigenetic models of addiction (e.g., Maze & Nestler, 2011; Robison & Nestler, 2011). Most of these theories have been applied only to drug addiction. With all of these theories, some type of appetitive effect (positive affect enhancement or negative affect reduction, arousal enhancement or reduction, cognitive ideation enhancement or reduction), preoccupation with the behavior, and subjective loss of control appear inherent. An appetitive effect model of addiction will be discussed in the next chapter of this book.

Major Examples of "Extensional" Definitions of Addiction

Extensional models of addiction include the (a) six-component perspective, (b) five-component model, and (c) Diagnostic and Statistical Manual of the American Psychiatric Association (DSM) criteria. These conceptions are somewhat overlapping, not mutually exclusive. There are additional extensional models (e.g., Tenth Revision of the International Classification of Diseases and Health Problems [ICD-10] mental and behavioral disorders due to psychoactive substance use; see Sussman & Ames, 2008). (Interestingly, the ICD-11 proposal asserts that pathological gambling will continue to be categorized as an impulse control disorder [Sinclair et al., 2016].) However, these three models do summarize several of the most popular extensional-type conceptions currently used.

Six-Component Perspective

Griffiths (2005a, 2008) presented a *six-component definition* of addiction which has been influential among researchers of multiple addictive behaviors. These components are: (a) salience, (b) mood modification, (c) tolerance, (d) withdrawal symptoms, (e) conflict, and (f) relapse. *Salience* refers to the tendency for the addiction to dominate one's thoughts, feelings, and behavior. Mood modification refers to the rush, escape, or satisfaction that the addictive behavior serves. Tolerance refers to the process in which, over time, more of the behavior is required to achieve a level of mood modification. Withdrawal symptoms are the unpleasant feeling states or physical effects of not engaging in the addictive behavior (e.g., moodiness, irritability). Conflict refers to the discord between engaging in the addictive behavior and relations with others, oneself, or engagement in other activities (e.g., hobbies, responsibilities). Finally, relapse refers to the tendency to return to out-of-control addictive behavior after periods of trying to stop or control it. Each of these components is treated as just that – components which might be placed into higher-order theorizing later on. It would be fair to say that the six-component model is the most influential of the extensional models of behavioral addictions (e.g., used as a diagnostic basis of numerous presentations at the 2nd International Conference on Behavioral Addictions; also see such examples as Grall-Bronnec, Bulteau, Victorri-Vigneau, Bouju, & Sauvaget, 2015).

Five-Component Model

Sussman & Sussman (2011) presented a *five-component definition* of addiction based on an attempt at synthesis of previous conceptualizations, keeping the number of criteria to a minimum, and considering tolerance and withdrawal as examples of preoccupation. These components are: (a) appetitive effects, (b) satiation, (c) preoccupation, (d) loss of control, and (e) negative consequences. These five components are discussed in more detail in the second chapter of this text.

However, some explanation should be provided here on why tolerance and withdrawal have been considered as aspects of a more general concept of preoccupation. Tolerance refers to the need to engage in the behavior at a relatively greater level than in the past to achieve previous levels of appetitive effects. As tolerance increases, one likely spends more time locating and engaging in an addiction. Thus, tolerance may indicate increasing preoccupation. Withdrawal refers to physiological or acquired discomfort experienced upon abrupt termination of an addictive behavior. If withdrawal symptoms exist, and worsen, one is likely to be spending more and more time recovering from the after-effects of the addiction, and be focused in thought and action on how to cope (e.g., by using again or engaging in some addictive behavior). In summary, one is more preoccupied with the addiction when one is spending more time locating, engaging, and recovering from that behavior, and this preoccupation may be reflected in the processes of tolerance and withdrawal (Sussman & Sussman, 2011).

Brief History and Current Status of DSM Addiction Disorders (DSM-I, II, III, IV, V)

The best-known extensional definition of addiction is a set of diagnostic criteria based on work conducted in the context of framing substance use disorder, in the Diagnostic and Statistical Manual of the American Psychiatric Association (DSM). These addiction criteria have been used solely pertaining to drugs of abuse (except in the DSM-V, as will be discussed). However, the same criteria have been adapted widely to describe behavioral addictions (Rosenberg & Feder, 2014a; Sussman & Ames, 2008). There was no agreed-on system for the diagnosis and classification of substance abuse in the United States until publication of the DSM series.

DSM-I

Definitions of substance abuse/dependence have varied dramatically since the initial publication of the DSM-I in 1952 (Freedman, Kaplan, & Sadock, 1976). For example, in the DSM-I, there was a category of drug addiction; however, it was vague in scope. Alcoholism was not defined separately if it was symptomatic of another disorder. In addition, both alcoholism and other drug addiction were subsumed within a ***sociopathic personality disturbance*** category (mental condition in which a person has a long-term pattern of manipulating, exploiting, or violating the rights of others), suggesting that they stemmed from certain personality features.

DSM-II

In the DSM-II, published in 1968, a category of drug dependence was included that was composed of physiologic (addiction) and psychic (state) components to make the definition less vague. In the DSM-II, drug addiction or dependence referred to opium, synthetic analgesics, barbiturates, other hypnotics and sedatives, cocaine and other psychostimulants, cannabis, hallucinogens, and other drugs (e.g., volatile solvents). Tobacco and caffeine use were not included explicitly in any category.

Alcoholism was placed in its own category; that is, it became defined as a category regardless of its relation to other disorders in the DSM-II. In addition, four categories of alcoholism were defined (episodic excessive, habitual excessive, addiction, and other or unspecified), and physiological and psychological tracks were delineated. Physiological dependency to alcohol included withdrawal symptoms of gross tremor, ***hallucinosis*** (alcohol-related hallucinations or psychosis), seizures, delirium tremens, and tolerance. Evidence of tolerance included a blood alcohol level of more than 150 mg/dL (> 0.15 percent) without evidence of intoxication, a fifth (757 ml) of whiskey for more than one day for a 180-pound person, and blackouts. Several alcohol-related diseases (e.g., alcoholic hepatitis) were considered clinical features. A behavioral, psychological, and attitudinal track included drinking in spite of medical and social contraindications or loss of control.

DSM-III

The DSM-III was first published in 1980 (with a DSM-III-R revision in 1987), and this volume distinguished between abuse and dependence. In the DSM-III-R, psychoactive **substance abuse** required a maladaptive pattern of use that is demonstrated by continued use despite persistent (a) social, (b) occupational, (c) psychological, or (d) physical problems that were caused or made worse by use, or by recurrent use in physically hazardous situations, for at least a one-month duration or at least one symptom two or more times over the past year. Further, at least three of nine of the following criteria were necessary for a classification of psychoactive substance use dependence (some of the symptoms of the disturbance must have persisted for at least one month or have occurred repeatedly over a longer period of time):

1 Substance often taken in larger amounts or over longer periods than intended.
2 Persistent desire or one or more unsuccessful efforts to cut down or control substance use.
3 A great deal of time spent in activities necessary to get the substance (e.g., theft), taking the substance (e.g., chain smoking), or recovering from its effects.
4 Important social, occupational, or recreational activities given up or reduced because of substance abuse.
5 Continued substance use despite knowledge of having a persistent or recurrent social, psychological, or physical problem that is caused or exacerbated by use of the substance.
6 Marked tolerance – need for markedly increased amounts of the substance to achieve intoxication or desired effect (e.g., doubling quantity from early use), or markedly diminished effect with continued use of the same amount.
7 Characteristic withdrawal symptoms.
8 Substance often taken to relieve or avoid withdrawal symptoms.
9 Frequent intoxication or withdrawal symptoms when expected to fulfill major role obligations or when use is physically hazardous.

The DSM-III attempted to provide more empirical and within-person-based symptomatology; provided a **multiaxis diagnosis** (considers multiple life dimensions such as occupational impairment and medical impairment); and influenced greatly the DSM-IV. With the publication of the DSM-III, drug dependence was no longer included under a more general category of personality disorders, reflecting its importance as a separate entity. Thirteen drug categories classified in the DSM-III were retained in the DSM-IV (i.e., alcohol, amphetamines, caffeine, cannabis, cocaine, hallucinogens, inhalants, nicotine, opioids, phencyclidine, sedatives/hypnotics/anxiolytics, **polysubstance** [three groups of substances of equal preference, not including caffeine or nicotine], and "other" or "unknown" [e.g., anabolic steroids, betel nut]).

DSM-IV

The DSM-IV was first published in 1994, with a text revision published in 2000. "Drug abuse" was defined as a maladaptive pattern of drug use leading to clinically significant impairment or distress, as manifested by one or more of four symptoms or criteria in a 12-month period.

1. Recurrent drug use may result in a *failure to fulfill major role obligations* at work, school, or home. Repeated absences, tardiness, poor performance, suspensions, or neglect of duties in major life domains suggest that use has crossed over into abuse.
2. Recurrent drug use in situations in which it is *physically hazardous* is a sign of abuse. Operating machinery, driving a car, swimming, or walking in a dangerous area while under the influence indicates drug abuse.
3. Recurrent drug-related *legal problems*, such as arrests for disorderly conduct or for driving under the influence, are indicative of abuse.
4. Recurrent use despite having persistent or recurrent *social or interpersonal problems*, caused or exacerbated by the effects of the drug, is indicative of abuse. For example, getting into arguments or fights with others, passing out at others' houses, or otherwise acting in a socially disapproved way is indicative of abuse.

In summary, drug use that leads to decrements in performance of major life roles, dangerous action, legal problems, or social problems indicated substance *abuse* disorder in the DSM-IV and DSM-IV-TR. There were seven other criteria that, if met, constitute "substance dependence." A diagnosis of substance *dependence*, a more severe disorder, was intended to subsume a diagnosis of substance abuse. The criteria for **substance dependence provided by the DSM-IV** and DSM-IV-TR (APA, 2000) included a maladaptive pattern of drug use leading to clinically significant impairment of distress, as manifested by three or more of the following seven symptoms occurring in the same 12-month period:

1. *Tolerance is experienced.* There is either a need for markedly increased amounts of the drug to achieve the desired drug effect or a markedly diminished effect with continued use of the same amount of the drug.
2. *Withdrawal is experienced.* Either a characteristic withdrawal syndrome occurs when one terminates using the drug or the same or a similar drug is taken to relieve or avoid the syndrome.
3. The drug often is taken in *larger amounts or over a longer period* than was intended. For example, an alcohol-dependent man may intend to drink only two drinks on a given evening but may end up having fifteen drinks.
4. There is a *persistent desire or unsuccessful effort to cut down or control drug use.* For example, an alcohol-dependent man may decide to become a controlled drinker. He may intend to drink only two drinks every evening; however, he ends up having fifteen drinks on some evenings, two drinks on some evenings, and twenty drinks on other evenings.
5. *A great deal of time is spent on activities necessary to obtain the drug, use the drug, or recover from its effects.* For example, a person may travel long distances or search all day to "score" a drug, may use the drug throughout the night, and then may miss work the next day to recover and rest. In this scenario, two days were spent for one "high."
6. *Important social, occupational, or recreational activities are given up or reduced because of drug use.* For example, the drug abuser may be very high, passed out, or

hungover much of the time and thus may not visit family and friends like he or she did before becoming a drug abuser.
7 *Drug use continues despite knowledge of having a persistent or recurrent physical or psychological problem* that is likely to have been caused or worsened by the drug. For example, someone who becomes very paranoid after continued methamphetamine use and is hospitalized but continues to use it after release from the hospital exhibits this last symptom.

DSM-V

As of May of 2013, the current diagnostic criteria (DSM-V; APA, 2013) for **substance use disorder** were established. The number of drug classes is reduced slightly. Phencyclidine is considered a hallucinogen. Amphetamines and cocaine are combined into one "stimulant" category. Finally, there is no separate polysubstance category. These criteria now apply to ten drug categories: (1) alcohol, (2) caffeine, (3) cannabis, (4) hallucinogens (which subsumes phencyclidine and "other hallucinogens"), (5) inhalants, (6) opioids, (7) sedative/hypnotic/anxiolytic, (8) stimulants (which includes amphetamine-type substances, cocaine, and other or unspecified stimulants), (9) tobacco, and (10) "other" or "unknown" (e.g., anabolic steroids, antihistamines, betel nut).

The criteria are mostly a recombination of the DSM-IV criteria. First, the abuse and dependence categories were combined into one *substance use disorder* diagnosis. Second, the legal consequences criterion was removed from consideration (due to considerations including relatively low prevalence of legal problems, or sensitivity of that criterion). Finally, a **craving** criterion was added to the diagnosis (strong desire or urge to use the drug). Substance use disorder is diagnosed if the individual reports two or more of the following, involving recurrent use over the last 12 months:

(a) Use more than intended (larger amounts or longer period).
(b) Desire, but inability, to quit or cut down.
(c) Consumes life (great deal of time to obtain, use, or recover from effects).
(d) Craving, an intense desire or urge to use (new criterion).
(e) Failure to fulfill major role obligations at work, school, or home.
(f) Continued use despite related social problems.
(g) Other social, job, or recreational activities are neglected or given up.
(h) Hazardous use (physical danger).
(i) Continued use despite related psychological or physical problems.
(j) Tolerance.
(k) Withdrawal.

Criteria (a) through (d) are intended to reflect impaired control. Criteria (e) through (g) are intended to reflect social impairment. Criteria (h) through (i) are intended to reflect risky use. Finally, criteria (j) through (k) are intended to reflect pharmacologic effects. One may speculate whether or not using these criteria will end up increasing the prevalence of diagnoses such as for alcoholism (Wakefield & Schmitz, 2014).

Food addiction. The DSM-V, as with previous DSM systems, does not recognize a food addiction category. The manual does mention that some individuals may report eating-related symptoms resembling those typically endorsed by persons with substance use disorders such as craving and patterns of compulsive use. The manual also mentions that this might reflect involvement of the same neural systems (e.g., regulatory self-control and reward). However, the authors mention that not enough is known about shared and distinct factors to address potential overlap (see APA, 2013, p. 329).

Gambling disorder. With the publication of the DSM-V, there is now a non-substance-related addiction disorder category, which includes currently only gambling disorder. Gambling disorder involves four or more of the following, also involving recurrent behavior over the last 12 months:

(a) More money gambled to get desired excitement (tolerance-like).
(b) Restless or irritable when one tries to quit or cut down (withdrawal-like).
(c) Repeated unsuccessful efforts to control, cut back, or stop gambling.
(d) Preoccupied with gambling (reliving past experiences, planning next venture, thinking how to get more money to gamble).
(e) Often gambles when feeling distressed (e.g., helpless, guilty, anxious, depressed).
(f) "Chases" losses (returning to gamble and get even).
(g) Lies to conceal extent of involvement.
(h) Jeopardized or lost relationship, job, or educational opportunity because of gambling.
(i) Relies on others to provide money to relieve related debt.

The DSM-V mentions that there are other "behavioral addictions" which are not included as formal disorders at this time (such as sex, exercise, or shopping addictions) because of a lack of peer-reviewed evidence to establish the diagnostic criteria and course. However, the authors encourage more research on other potential behavioral addictions.

Summary of Extensional Addiction Models

These are listing-type, common features definitions, which are descriptive rather than etiologic (Sussman & Ames, 2001). The elements are treated as of equal valence and are summed to reach a threshold, which then leads to a diagnosis of a substance or behavioral addiction. For example, in gambling addiction, the total number of criteria ("four or more") is what is important in determining a diagnosis. Some practitioners, however, may argue that "lying" is not as central to gambling addiction as is "repeated unsuccessful attempts to stop gambling." Such is the potential weakness of an extensional approach.

Necessary and sufficient conditions, and family resemblances. While there is the tendency to consider extensional elements as exchangeable, and multiple elements summed to some number are diagnostic (e.g., the DSM scheme), there are several possibilities regarding how such elements of an addictive behavior might be interrelated. First, each of the elements alone, or in any combination with one or more of the others – perhaps all – may be a necessary condition of addiction. Second, each of the elements alone, or in any combination with one or more of the others – perhaps all – may be a sufficient condition of addiction. The six-component and five-component definitions of addiction intend to include elements, each of which is necessary. Also, all elements taken together are considered sufficient to define addiction. In other words, all six or five components are intended to be considered necessary and sufficient.

An alternative conceptualization when considering elements/components of an addiction is that of **family resemblances** (i.e., things which could be thought to be connected by one essential common feature may in fact be connected by a series of overlapping similarities, where no one feature is common to all; Sussman & Sussman, 2011; Wittgenstein, 1953). Consider the physical features of a family, for example. We may say that all of the family members appear similar (e.g., on any number of elements contained within the family set, such as weight, eye color, hair, last name) even though no two are identical in descriptors (elements) examined and two of them within the group (set) may have no feature in common. (e.g., one family member may have that family's prototypical weight and hair, but not eye color and last name; another member may have that family's prototypical eye color and last name, but not weight and hair). Yet, both members of the family will be considered to be from the same family. Likewise, there may be two people who are labeled as "addicted" but share none of the same elements in common. For example, one "addict" may experience loss of control and negative consequences whereas another "addict" may experience appetitive effects and preoccupation. As a second example, one gambling "addict" may exhibit lying and preoccupation whereas another may exhibit mood-related gambling and withdrawal-like symptoms. If such a non-overlap of extrapersonal components/elements exists, we can expect to discover new phenomena of addiction that bear only a family resemblance to the ones we now recognize (Sussman & Sussman, 2011).

Summary

Heterogeneity of phenomena, vagueness in conceptual boundaries, or use of numerous definitional elements may make it difficult to come to consensus regarding a "correct" intensional or extensional definition of addiction. Some authors have argued that to consider a substance or behavior an addiction, one needs to consider data regarding (a) co-occurring disorders, (b) clinical characteristics, (c) genetic contributions, and (d) central/peripheral neurobiological factors (Kor et al., 2013). Of course, an exploration of these different sources of data may reveal somewhat different patterns of findings across "addicts" reported to suffer from the same addiction (albeit the effects on mesolimbic dopamine appear pretty consistent; Sussman & Ames, 2008). More generally, it is difficult to identify a unifying framework when there is so much heterogeneity in extensional diagnostic features.

Also, there are some problems in logic here when trying to set boundaries on the concept of addiction. One key conceptual "bog" is the difficulty in trying to differentiate "addiction" from other disorders such as "obsessive-compulsive disorder." It might be argued that the difference between an OCD and an addiction is that only negative reinforcement operates with OCD, whereas both positive and negative reinforcement operate with addictions (see Kor et al., 2013). Yet, while positive reinforcement may lead to addiction to such substances as cigarette smoking, the maintenance of that addiction may be primarily through negative reinforcement (Raines, Unruh, Zvolensky, & Schmidt, 2014; Wise & Koob, 2014). One *reductio ad absurdum* argument stemming from this positive/negative reinforcement issue would be that early on the behavior is an addiction but later on the behavior becomes an instance of OCD.

Finally, a global perspective may add more confusion conceptually in terms of defining when a behavior is or is not an "addiction problem." Internationally, there may be some variation on when a repetitive behavior is considered an addiction, or at least a problem. For example, there may be differential tolerance of being drunk in public, or drinking hard liquor such as vodka in shots in restaurants (Japan or Russia versus the United States). Physical hazards or legal enforcement may vary depending on the environment (rural versus urban settings). For example, one is more likely to experience a DUI (driving under the influence) charge in locations in which public transportation is not as widely available and in which police enforcement is relatively high. Also, norms vary on what is addictive sexual behavior, work, or eating, as examples. As a specific example, it is not uncommon for persons in Asian countries to work over 60 hours per week, whereas such behavior might be considered workaholic in Western Europe (www.topuniversities.com/blog/differences-average-working-hours-around-world; http://stats.oecd.org/index.aspx?DataSetCode=ANHRS). One possible common criterion is that to the degree one's ability to fulfill context-based roles or duties (e.g., spouse, parent, co-worker, or citizen) is compromised, one is considered to suffer from a detrimental addiction (e.g., see Quinero & Nichter, 1996).

We are often left to go back to subjective experience of dysfunction (e.g., Johnny's self-perceptions provided at the beginning of this chapter) and what appear to be consensus-based clinical criteria (e.g., appetitive motive, satiation, preoccupation, loss of control, negative consequences) to build a case for what is and is not an addiction. Then, other types of assessment permit a better understanding on what are the parameters of that "addiction," which may show some variation (e.g., severity of behavior, topography of behavior). Chapter 2 explains in detail what Sussman and Sussman (2011) mean by appetitive effects and addiction – suggesting a common underlying basis of addictions. (For a philosophical discussion of appetitive versus volitive desires, see Davis, 2005.) Then, Chapter 3 will consider commonalities and differences in etiology of various addictions.

Bulleted Summary
- Substance addictions produce a more or less direct effect on brain neurobiology in part through introduction of exogenous ligands, whereas behavioral addictions produce a more indirect effect through motoric behavior and ideation which act on endogenous ligands.

- Over the last 400 years, the word "addiction" has evolved from referring to binding a person to something to being more or less a "brain disease."
- Intensional models of addiction include those of (a) physiological and psychological dependence (cellular or acquired tolerance and withdrawal, and craving), (b) impulsive-obsessive/compulsive behavior (involving positive and/or negative reinforcement), (c) self-medication (which may or may not involve coping with trauma), (d) self-regulation (e.g., BAS–BIS, incentive-sensitization, allostasis-dysregulation models), and (e) addiction entrenchment (i.e., overwhelming involvement with an addiction object, involving one's identity, or emotional attachment behavioral economics models).
- Extensional models of addiction include the six-component model, the five-component model, and the DSM models.
- Obsessive-compulsive behavior may be defined as an intense egodystonic (separate from self) urge to engage in a simple, repetitive activity, to remove anxiety (e.g., washing hands, tying shoes), whereas addictions involve an appetitive motive-satiation effect, preoccupation, loss of control, and negative consequences.

Suggestions for Further Reading

Koob, G. F. & Le Moal, M. (2006). *Neurobiology of Addiction*. London: Academic Press, ch. 1.

Rosenberg, K. P. & Feder, L. C. (eds.) (2014a). *Behavioral Addictions: Criteria, Evidence, and Treatment*. London: Academic Press/Elsevier.

Sussman, S. & Ames, S. L. (2008). *Drug Abuse: Concepts, Prevention and Cessation*. Cambridge University Press.

Sussman, S. & Sussman, A. N. (2011). Considering the definition of addiction. *International Journal of Environmental Research and Public Health*, **8**: 4025–4038.

2 Addictive Effects and Appetitive Needs

Learning Objectives

- To learn more about the five-component definition of addiction
- To begin thinking about the relations between appetitive needs and addictive effects
- To understand how lifestyle may contribute to creating addictions stemming from appetitive needs
- To contrast an appetitive needs notion of addiction with others (differential socialization, immorality, disease state)
- To learn examples of behaviors that might not be potentially addictive

Introduction

Why would Johnny continue to go on alcohol, work, TV, and eating binges? He was growing older and it would seem that the quality of his life was suffering. He has suffered socially. His quality of work likely has been decreasing and others have permitted him more limited work roles. He could suffer physically, and die prematurely. It appears that he did not keep engaging in these activities to ward off physiological withdrawal. It does appear to be the case that he kept trying to obtain a sense of "feeling OK" through dysfunctional behavior. He felt like he was satiating some sort of motivated drive by achieving addictive effects.

This chapter will attempt to provide an answer to what is leading Johnny to continue pursuing a course of addictive behavior. Perhaps Johnny was, at least temporarily, subjectively satiating "appetitive needs" through dysfunctional behavior. Perhaps an appetitive effects notion underlies addiction.

Addictive Effects

There is consensus that ***addictive effects*** (i.e., immediate impacts of an addictive behavior) share a common response of shifting subjective experience of oneself (Larkin, Wood, & Griffiths, 2006; Loonis, 2002). Experience of obtaining an addictive effect is often considered relatively quick, sometimes rush-like or sudden, also *subjective adaptation-directed* (achieving a sense of being fulfilled or fit); completing a subjective adaptation goal quickly and efficiently (Loonis, 2002). Self-reports of such experiential shifts consist of specific types which include: (a) positive affect enhancement or negative affect reduction (overall affect elevation); (b) arousal enhancement or sedation (change in general level of arousal); or (c) cognitive ideation enhancement (e.g., fantasy) or reduction (e.g., calm, or even sense of oblivion; Bejerot, 1972; Schneider & Irons, 2001; Sussman, 2012a, 2012b; Sussman & Sussman, 2011). One may also experience preoccupation in obtaining the addictive effect again, loss of control over the parameters of achieving this effect, and undesired or negative consequences resulting from engaging in the addictive behavior. In summary, engaging in an addictive behavior leads to a noticeably quick change in one's mood state, arousal state, or thinking state that pertains to achieving an appetitive effect.

Addictions generally are considered motivated behavior. The subjective state achieved at least temporarily is desired, and is referred to as "satiation" (Sussman & Sussman, 2011). Addictive effects, I assert, are initially experienced as relatively quick, temporary subjective fulfillment of appetitive needs. However, addictive effects are misdirected or under-regulated attempts at appetitive need fulfillment.

Fulfillment of Appetitive Needs and Addictive Behaviors

An ***appetitive need*** refers to drives, urges, or cravings, often instinctual, that serves to help regulate human function (e.g., see Alcoholics Anonymous, 1976; Angell, 1906; Griffiths, Kuss, & Demetrovics, 2014; Loonis, 2002). Early psychological theorizing suggested that humans experienced ***innate and secondarily acquired instincts*** (inborn and tied to associational memory), subjectively experienced, in need of satiation, including: desire to reduce shyness or increase sociability (to be part of a human "herd"); desire for fear reduction and submission to a social order (to feel safety); anger, rivalry, jealousy, envy, or dominance (to procure an optimal position in the human "herd"); curiosity, secretiveness, acquisitiveness (desire to explore and discover, desire to possess, to survive); affection, sexual love, parental love (self and other nurturance); and play, imitation, and constructiveness (to learn how to creatively adapt to new situations).

More recent evolutionary theories of human behavior have asserted that adaptation attributes such as survival ability and reproductive fitness are reflected in the biological operations of the mesolimbic dopaminergic system (probably the endpoint of, or nested within a cascade of neurobiological systems), which are subject to "hijacking" by addictive behaviors over time which will induce subjective increases in experience of these attributes (Bejerot, 1972; Blum et al., 2012; Newlin, 2002). While the appetitive effect generally is equated with changes in firing in the mesolimbic dopaminergic system, there are numerous brain neurotransmission and hormonal systems involved, including mu opioid, serotonin, norepinephrine, anandamide, and the hypothalamic–pituitary–adrenal axis (HPA), among others (Brewer & Potenza, 2008; Gunduz-Cinar et al., 2013; Johansson, Grant, Kim, Odlaug, & Gotestam, 2009; Schneider & Irons, 2001;

Volkow & Wise, 2005). *Addictive behaviors may cause a misleading (false) subjective sense of neurobiological fitness though induction of more positive emotional feelings, modulation of arousal (new opportunities associated with increases in arousal, or security or serenity associated with decreases in arousal), or providing a sense of cognitive exploration or solution* (e.g., Loonis, 2002; Panksepp, Knutson, & Burgdorf, 2002). Preoccupation ("wanting," "craving"), loss of control, and negative consequences may eventually occur while engagement in the addictive behavior still temporarily provides a subjective and misleading sense of neurobiological fitness. I believe that it is through appetitive mechanisms that addictive phenomena operate and why there may be many types of behaviors that are repeated, to achieve a subjective sense of neurobiological fitness, which unfortunately eventually lead to undesired negative consequences.

Modernization of Society, Appetitive Needs, and Addictive Effects

Neurobiological sociocultural theories of ill-health note that as persons are able to situate in one location, and easily fulfill needs for food, shelter, and protection, sedentary habits may accumulate (Fave, Massimini, & Bassi, 2011, p. 25). Once sedentary habits develop, a competition between cultural and biological fitness may arise. It is possible that persons may exhibit behaviors in order to recreate the feeling of grappling to satiate biological appetitive needs (Newlin, 2002), in a context which does not provide the arena for application of physiologic or psychological work to satiate those needs (Blum et al., 2012). Numerous addictions may operate in this way and reflect a problem of lifestyle (Sussman et al., 2011b). From an evolutionary perspective, instead of engaging in extensive "work" to satisfy an appetitive motive (e.g., hunting for food, growing one's own food, carefully planning meals, or cooking one's own food), the motive may be satisfied too easily and quickly (buying a fast food meal), perhaps even involving "products" that facilitate "rush" effects (e.g., processed, fatty, or sugary foods), possibly leading, for some people, to repeated cycles of attempting to satiate the motive with diminishing success, resulting in dysregulation (Koob & Le Moal, 2001; Robinson & Berridge, 2000; Sussman, Reynaud, Aubin, & Leventhal, 2011c).

Additionally, some writers suggest that modern free-market societies, such as the United States, are characterized by an out-of-control state of expectations, stresses, and quick-paced accomplishment-oriented behavior, along with the breaking of social cooperative links, which may be conducive to experimentation with addictive behaviors as a compensatory function (e.g., Alexander, 2012; Brown, 2014). Certain individuals may adapt well to fast-paced technologically enhanced lifestyles while others do not (Blum et al., 2012). Possibly, up to 50 percent of society does not adapt that well – and some of the resulting patterns of dysregulated behavior that occur may become addictions (Bechara, 2005; Griffiths & Larkin, 2004; Hatterer, 1982; Holden, 2001; Kourosh, Harrington, & Adinoff, 2010; Marks, 1990; Orford, 2001; Sussman et al., 2011b). Many potentially addictive activities are widely promoted and encouraged, and easily accessible, in modern society (Brown, 2014), with directions to distribution points (e.g., casino locations, fast food restaurants, clubs; Sussman et al., 2011a) and informed by the mass media, that facilitate experimentation with potentially addictive actions. These actions come to supplant other activities, directed by "acquired drives" (Bejerot, 1972).

In summary, there may be two forces at work in modern societies that facilitate development of addictions to several different types of behaviors. First, there may be a "pull" to engage in easily addicting behaviors that are present in modern society, that "simulate" the attainment of appetitive effects within a sedentary lifestyle. Second, simultaneously, there may be a "push" to seek out behaviors to satisfy one's drives in a fast-paced, technological, stressed-out world.

Appetitive Functions versus Addictive Behavior

Among many researchers and clinicians, "addiction" has come to refer to a disorder where an individual becomes intensely preoccupied with a behavior that at first appears to provide a subjectively desired appetitive effect (e.g., increase in pleasure or reduction of fear). The addictive behavior occurs with several, repeated pattern variations (e.g., bingeing, or sustained preoccupation) that involve a great deal of time thinking about and engaging in the behavior, which in general operates beyond the desire to remove intense anxiety common in compulsive disorders (Brewer & Potenza, 2008; Marks, 1990). Addictive behaviors at first appear to satisfy appetitive needs; ironically later on often depriving the addict of fulfillment of appetitive functioning.

Many behaviors may be in service of an appetitive function (e.g., eating behavior) but do not necessarily qualify as an addictive behavior (e.g., eating an occasional large meal versus binge eating, or reporting an addiction to eating). In one sense, of course, any appetitive-related behavior might be viewed as being engaged along a quantitative dimension which, at some point, would be defined as an excessive or addictive level (Orford, 2001).

In addition, what differentiates an addictive behavior from a non-addictive behavior maybe a function of the way in which the behavior is experienced. That is, with an addictive behavior, there is a greater likelihood of experiencing an immediate change of sense of oneself (e.g., a rush effect), and temporary satiation, and, over time, persons may become preoccupied with the behavior, exhibit a loss of control over the behavior, and suffer negative life consequences as a result (Sussman, Lisha, & Griffiths, 2011b; Sussman & Sussman, 2011). Loonis et al. (2000) explored the parameters of preoccupation among drug addicts. They found evidence that, when comparing drug addicts (in reception centers for drug treatment) to control subjects (in general medical offices), there is a much stronger focus on the addictive behavior relative to other behaviors (high salience), a lessened perceived availability of alternative behaviors (low variety), and a low perceived degree of ease at replacing engagement in the addictive behavior with another behavior (low vicariance).

There are many behaviors that could be experienced as appetitive which evolve into addiction. Popularly discussed behaviors include: (1) tobacco; (2) alcohol; (3) other drug misuse; (4) food addiction (binge overeating as a proxy); (5) gambling; (6) Internet use or other electronic media (e.g., online gaming); (7) love; (8) sex; (9) exercise; (10) workaholism; and (11) shopping/spending (Sussman et al., 2011b). These 11 specific behaviors will become the focus of most of the remainder of this text. However, there are many additional behaviors that might become addictive. Tanning is one example of a seldom studied behavior which some authors have considered to be addictive (versus an obsessive-compulsive disorder; Kourosh et al., 2010). Tanning-related behaviors include mirror checking, grooming, picking skin, and UV-exposure periods which may be experienced as a rush. Tanning often involves use of salons and timers, and the experience may involve primarily sensory processing. Tanning may be a means to attempt to make oneself more socially dominant, one type of appetitive motive, through attempting to increase one's physical attractiveness. Further, UV-exposure may lead to release of beta-endorphin and serotonin, as well as being a source of vitamin D, which could be interpreted as fulfilling pleasure and self-nurturance motives (two appetitive needs). More discussion on categories of addiction will be introduced in Chapter 5 of this text (the 11 "focal" addictions).

Contrasting an Appetitive Needs Notion of Addiction with Others

The *associational memory-appetitive system relations (AMASR) model* refers to an appetitive needs notion, that one's "instincts/drives," which otherwise would serve important survival and growth functions, through associational memory become excessive, atypically evoked, or misdirected. These excessive, atypically evoked, or misdirected appetitive motive-seeking behaviors, characterized by preoccupation and loss of control, are the essence of addictive behavior. A potential, perhaps simplified appetitive needs model of addiction is depicted in Figure 2.1.

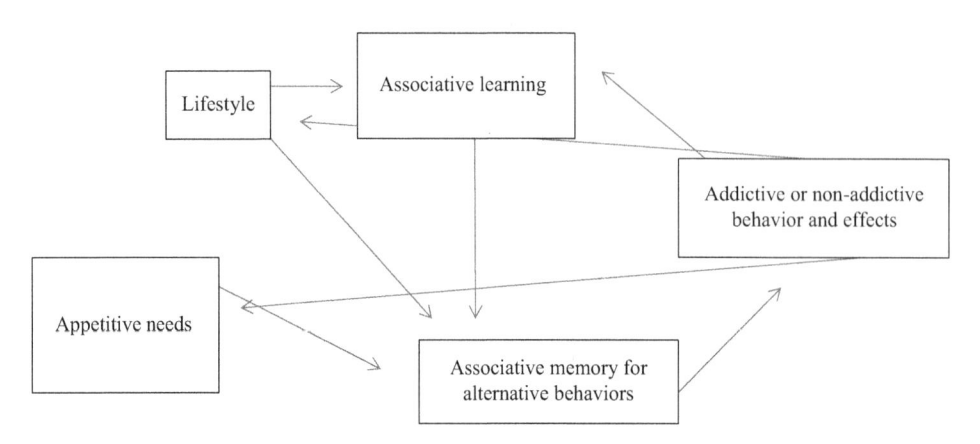

Figure 2.1 A possible appetitive needs model of addictive effects: associational memory-appetitive system relations (AMASR) model

Table 2.1 Other alternatives to the appetitive needs notion of addiction

Differential socialization	A person's values, expectations, and experiences are shaped and directed in counter-normative ways. Thus, addictive behavior can be considered a choice which terminates due to concerns of losing respect or money.
Immoral personality	The person doesn't care because he/she is "bad to the core." This notion is contradictory to the loss of control-related aspect of addiction. However, this theory is not taken seriously by most researchers and clinicians.
The disease notion	The notion of addiction as a disease is fraught with ambiguity but is likely consistent with the idea that one's appetitive needs are being met through faulty behavioral function.

There are apparently different perspectives of addiction, as were described in Chapter 1 (see Table 1.1). I would argue that most of these notions (e.g., allostasis, incentive-sensitization) are compatible with, or reflect specific mechanisms of, a more fundamental appetitive needs notion (the AMASR model). However, there are other theories, which may run further afield from such a notion, and might be more compatible with the general entrenchment conceptualization noted in the previous chapter. These alternatives are summarized in Table 2.1.

Differential Socialization

One may have become differentially socialized so as to act in what the observer would interpret as an addictive way (Akers, Krohn, Lanza-Kaduce, & Radosevich, 1979). That is, from a ***differential socialization*** perspective, an aspect of addiction entrenchment, one's values, expectations, and experiences are shaped and directed in counter-normative ways. This perspective seems inconsistent with the idea that one feels a loss of control; that the addiction is not giving the addict what he or she desires. That is, due to differential socialization, addiction would be considered a choice which terminates due to concerns of losing respect or money, or due to legal complications (Heyman, 2013a).

Immorality

Another conception is that the addict is immoral ("bad to the core"). However, this theory is not taken seriously by most researchers and clinicians since many drug addicts are not psychopathic (Lindesmith, 1940) and, while psychopathy shows notable comorbidity with substance abuse, for example, it appears to be a special case (is a moderator variable) of addiction experience, as opposed to serving as a main effects predictor (Cope et al., 2014), or being a constituent of addiction (contrary to the original DSM-I). Of course, this theory also seems contradictory to the loss of control-related aspect of addiction. Someone may be "good," and desire to stay out of trouble, but act "badly," and get into trouble, due to loss of control.

Disease State

Finally, one may try to contrast an appetitive needs notion with somehow having become "diseased." The disease model of addiction may help some persons seek out treatment to arrest its ***progression*** (movement to a more advanced state) and, for some people, may help reduce subjective stigma. Twelve-step programs support a disease model of addiction. However, the notion of addiction as a disease is fraught with ambiguity (see Sussman & Ames, 2001). One epidemiologic notion of a disease refers simply to impairment in daily functioning which may be acute or chronic, and infectious or non-infectious; alcoholism, for example, would be considered a chronic and non-infectious impairment in function (see Timmreck, 1998). Thus, it is possible that a disease notion could be consistent with the idea that one's appetitive needs have altered neurobiological function in such a way as to impair one's adaptation to the environment. It may not matter whether or not the AMASR perspective of addiction is or is not considered a disease-type notion.

More on Appetitive Needs and Constituents of Addiction

An appetitive needs (AMASR) conceptualization of addictions encapsulates five key addiction components. Desire for "appetitive effects" is the first component of the five-component, extensional model of Sussman and Sussman (2011) introduced briefly in Chapter 1, and which is summarized in Table 2.2.

Appetitive Effects

Appetitive needs are universal among human beings. However, the addiction process unfolds for some individuals but not others (perhaps up to 50 percent of a population in any 12-month period; Sussman et al., 2011b), and may also reflect individual differences in vulnerability prior to or while engaging in the addictive behavior (particularly among those who develop a wider breadth of addictive behaviors, or a greater extent of involvement with an addictive behavior). Anecdotally, some unknown percentage of self-described addicts have (retrospectively) reported feeling "different" from others long before developing readily identifiable addictions (e.g., feeling uncomfortable). Alternatively, other persons (retrospectively) report not feeling different prior to engaging in a problematic addictive behavior. In both cases, though, a behavior may be tried that is perceived as highly valued or enjoyable (alteration in affect, arousal, or cognition), generally with effects that occur rather rapidly, and that one desires to repeat (an appetitive state of some kind). Along with appetitive effects, examination of the other four components of the Sussman and Sussman (2011) model (satiation, preoccupation, loss of control, and negative consequences) is instructive and provides a more complete explication of an appetitive needs conceptualization.

Table 2.2 The five-component definition of addiction

Appetitive effects	Appetitive needs are universal among human beings. But for some a behavior may be tried that is perceived as highly valued or enjoyable, possibly with effects that occur rather rapidly, and that one desires to repeat (an appetitive state of some kind).
Satiation	Satiation is experienced when an individual feels as if appetitive needs are met by an episode of engagement in an addictive behavior. The immediate effect of the behavior may lead one to feel as if some bodily need has been satisfied. This experience may be identified as feelings of joy, alertness, safety, clarity, enlightenment, or sedation (calm).
Preoccupation	Preoccupation involves constantly (or very often) thinking about satiating the appetitive behavior. This can manifest as excessive thoughts about and desire to perform the behavior, excessive time spent to plan, engage in, or recover from the behavior, and less time spent on other activities, despite potentially diminishing appetitive effects.
Loss of control	The addictive behavior may have become increasingly automatic and a person may: become involved in the addictive behavior more often than intended; have problems regulating or stopping the behavior; and have difficulty in refraining from the behavior despite attempting to do so.
Negative consequences	An individual might continue engaging in the addictive behavior after suffering numerous negative consequences. Negative consequences include physical discomfort, social disapproval, financial loss, or decreased self-esteem, among others. The addiction may persist because it also provides motivation-related maintenance functions for the individual.

Satiation

One important aspect of an appetitive needs notion is that, at least for a brief period of time, the individual feels as if the appetitive needs are met by the addictive behavior. One is said to experience *satiation*. More precisely, the immediate effect of the behavior may lead one to feel *as if* some bodily or instinctual need has been satisfied. Also, as part of an addictive effect, some period of time may occur in which cravings/urges are not operative (Foddy & Savulescu, 2010a, 2010b; Marks, 1990; Orford, 2001); again, one may experience a subjective temporary sense of physiological fulfillment of the appetitive "need." During this generally brief period, one may feel self-sufficient or nurtured (Hirschman, 1992; Pearson & Little, 1969): subjective fulfillment of appetitive needs. One learns to associate in memory the appetitive need (internal cue) with the behavior that led to satiation (anticipatory satiation, with positive and/or negative reinforcing consequences), even though the result is not actually biologically adaptive. Repeated appetitive need–behavior–satiation cycles may become strongly associated in one's implicit memory (e.g., Stacy & Ames, 2001).

The ability to manipulate a subjective sense of satiating various bodily needs ("appetitive" effects) may underlie which behaviors may become addictive (Foddy & Savulescu, 2010a, 2010b; Goodman, 1990; Hatterer, 1982; Jacobs, 1986; Newlin, 2002). Later in this chapter, I discuss whether there are behaviors relatively likely or unlikely to elicit such need–behavior–satiation cycles. Fundamentally important, though, is that an addictive effect appears to involve repeated experiences that result eventually in a pathological relationship with a behavior that elicits an appetitive effect (Schneider & Irons, 2001; Sussman & Sussman, 2011). One may argue that some addicts are never satiated, or that an addict may seek an addiction object to once again try to achieve satiation that no longer exists. I assert that satiation effects continue to occur at least temporarily, if less potently, producing at least a brief period of satiation even for long-time addicts.

One point of clarification is needed regarding satiation. Just because a feeling of being satiated is elicited does not necessarily mean that the addict will then discontinue the behavior at that moment. The addict may want to continue to experience that sense of satiation and may continue the behavior to exhaustion. That is, it is possible that for many addictive behaviors, satiation is experienced while the behavior is being engaged in and may dissipate quickly upon termination of the behavior. In any case, preoccupation with and a "wanting" of the addictive behavior, a sense of loss of control, as well as experience of negative consequences are also definitive of that pathological relationship which develops. These components of addiction are discussed in the next subsections of this chapter.

Preoccupation

As just mentioned, repeated appetitive need–behavior–satiation cycles may occur. The more often and reliably these cycles occur, the more one may anticipate achievement of satiation though engagement in the addictive behavior. As one feels an appetitive need, one may then also relatively automatically consider the addictive behavior as a means to satiate the need (i.e., the thought about the behavior "pops into mind"; Stacy, Ames, & Knowlton, 2004). Appetitive needs for improvement in affect, regulation of arousal, or for an enriching or settling of one's cognitive environment, may become associated with repetitive thoughts about and behaviors directed toward participating in one or more addictive behaviors. One may experience excessive (a) thoughts about and desire to perform a behavior, (b) time spent to plan and engage in the behavior, and (c) time to recover from its effects (e.g., from **hangovers** [negative physical sensations at the end of an addictive behavior sequence], or due to remorse), and one may spend less time on other activities, despite potentially diminishing (though still existent) appetitive effects (Sussman & Sussman, 2011). When one considers negative consequences resulting from previous engagement in the addictive behavior, as one "thinks through" what one might end up doing, one may sense or recognize being preoccupied with that addictive behavior.

It is not known to what extent, or in what way, neurobiological processing of addictive desires is different from regular desires. However, addictive behavior-induced repetitive firing of certain brain systems (e.g., mesolimbic dopamine) does result in brain adaptations (e.g., activation of glutamatergic system; decrease in production of mesolimbic dopamine). This suggests a "hijacking" of the brain due to engagement in any of a variety of substance or process addictive behaviors (Goodman, 2008; Leshner, 1997; Potenza, 2010), which may contribute to the experience of preoccupation. One may become aware of a craving to engage in the behavior; the contextual demands to fulfill the appetitive need through engagement in the addictive behavior are taking up a great deal of time; and the addictive behavior may need to be engaged in incrementally more often to elicit a period of satiation.

Loss of Control

As one attempts to regulate involvement in the addictive behavior to fulfill that appetitive need, one may also realize that: (a) one is involved in the addictive behavior more often than one had intended, and (b) one is having problems regulating or stopping the behavior. Central to the loss of control aspect of addiction (see Heather, 1998 on **akrasia**) is difficulty in refraining from an addictive behavior despite attempting to do so. Many persons claim to be struggling with an addiction; feeling compelled, sensing incomplete control; and it is observed that they may disregard even basic self-care, suggestive of a loss of self-control. Attentional narrowing and impulsiveness, along with specific addictive behavior-directed short-term planning, and lack of attention to long-term planning, may all be related to the pattern of addiction-related loss of control (Sussman & Sussman, 2011).

Incomplete memory access, or biased memory of the initially pleasant effects of engaging in the addictive behavior (e.g., **automaticity/euphoric recall**), appear to be common aspects of addictions. According to Campbell (2003), the "cognitive impairment" associated with an addiction emerges only when a specific addiction associated with harmful consequences produces a simultaneous positive emotional response. This attentional narrowing minimizes or negates the memory (or access to aversive memory) of the negative effects or consequences of previous addictive behavior experiences. Due to these memory effects, recovering addicts with some "sober time" (and who no longer suffer from a cognitive narrowing) may look back at their active addiction days as being fraught with thinking that is disordered, illogical, fragmented, destructive, and nonsensical (Hirschman, 1992).

Negative Consequences

Lack of control over the appetitive need–addictive behavior relationship generally eventually leads to undesired consequences (e.g., physical discomfort, social disapproval, financial loss, or decreased self-esteem; Marlatt, 1985). Continuing to engage in the addictive behavior after suffering numerous negative consequences often has been a criterion of psychological or physiological dependence (APA, 2013). Stopping the behavior becomes difficult for several reasons, including incentive salience and comparatively immediate gratification resulting from the addictive behavior (i.e., satiation) relative to its delayed adverse effects (Bickel et al., 2011). The individual may also fear having to cope with day-to-day perceived stress and other life experiences upon cessation (possibly due to accumulation of addiction-related consequences), or having to endure "raw" emotional experiences without concurrent self-medication (Jacobs, 1986), as well as suffer withdrawal-related phenomena. Thus, the addiction persists and incurs cumulative negative effects.

Are There Behaviors that are Not Addictive?

Not every evolutionary-based motivated behavior is considered an addiction. An addictive effect is a subset of appetitive behavior. There are levels or styles of appetitive-related behavior that are not illustrative of addictive behavior. There also exists non-appetitive related behavior which, by definition, would not be addictive. What then is not addictive? People are known to say that they are addicted to one behavior but not to another. For example, Johnny, first mentioned at the beginning of Chapter 1, was not addicted to gambling though he was addicted to many other behaviors. Why might people become addicted to one potentially addictive behavior but not another? Are there any behaviors that generally are not addictive? I organize the examination of this issue by, again, using the five components of addiction (seeking an appetitive effect, achieving a period of satiation, preoccupation, loss of control, and experience of negative consequences; Sussman & Sussman, 2011; also see Table 2.2).

Appetitive Behavior and Satiation

There are two parameters of human activity that may not be addictive. First, there may be behaviors, or aspects of behavior, that are unlikely to elicit an appetitive state. Thinking out loud, deliberately focusing one's attention, or self-reflection (certain *executive cognitive functions*) are not likely to be intrinsically associated with seeking nurturance, joy, exploration (novelty-seeking), sedation, or arousal per se: that is, with addictive manifestations of appetitive behaviors (Sussman et al., 2011c). Second, the topography of a behavior that is addictive involves often a rapid change in subjective state (a "rush"), whereas behavior that is not addictive may involve a much slower tempo. Gardening, for example, is not addictive for most people because it often involves a slow tempo and patience (Griffiths, 2005a). Heading off to go to sleep certainly seems to serve important recuperative functions, but one is unlikely to become addicted to sleeping.

Furthermore, executive functions or slow-paced behavior may not be aspects of behavior that are likely to become satiated. Consideration of specific goals to be achieved, that necessitate engagement in attentional focus or step-by-step action, certainly may lead one to feel a sense of accomplishment. Such may be the case with planning activities such as completing a gardening sequence. However, this is likely not the same thing as satiating an appetitive motive. Upon ending a period of gardening, one may feel satisfied with the day's work, but with a realization that the job is not "done" – that more development of the garden can be completed, or that gardening is an ongoing process, and that what is improved needs to be maintained. There is not a quick rush to a sense of appetitive satiation. The pace is steady and is slow (Brown, 2014). On the other hand, going off to sleep is an example of an appetitive behavior that can satiate an appetitive need (for recuperation). The fact that it does not involve a rapid change in state may underlie its likely non-addictive status.

Certainly, if the duration of satiation were lengthened, arguably, one may speculate that the individual would have achieved a resolution of the subjective sense of discomfort that precedes engagement in the addictive behavior. Then, that behavior would be appetitive but not addictive. However, such periods are apparently short-lived, may not be fully experienced (e.g., may be slept through; or one may pass out), and are possibly met with counteradaptation processes (Koob & Le Moal, 2001). In addition, a person may want to maintain a sense of being satiated, continuing to engage in the behavior to exhaustion. If satiation of an addictive behavior operated in such a fashion, merely achieving that sense of satiation would not hint at potential solutions to the addiction. In general, though, satiation of appetitive processes is temporary. Hunger, or need for sleep, only subsides for a while, for example, as they should to keep one alive.

Preoccupation

Aspects of human function that minimize preoccupation (which is a type of **thought–do loop** – a repetitive thought sequence) and the likelihood of addiction, include: focusing on "not thinking"; breaking thoughts into "bits"; or focusing on the present moment. Certainly, some persons may engage in an addictive behavior such as drug use to try to pharmacologically stop thinking about some event that recurs in one's mind (e.g., post-traumatic stress disorder symptomatology; Mate, 2012; Yehuda, 2002). Still, drug-free thought modulation such as is the case with some **meditation practices** (e.g., focusing on one's breathing and letting thoughts pass by) does serve to reduce the potential for addiction preoccupation (Black, Milam, & Sussman, 2009; Sussman et al., 2011c, 2013b).

Also, flexibility in shifting one's thoughts to several activities would tend to be non-addictive. To the extent that (a) there is a relatively equal distribution of cognitive salience across any number of alternative behaviors/activities (one is able to think about participating in a number of different activities), (b) there is a wide range or variety of perceived alternative behaviors/activities, and (c) the subjective or actual ability to substitute one motivated behavior with another is high, then an addictive pattern of behavior is not likely to occur (Loonis et al., 2000). Consequently, one is relatively unlikely to be preoccupied with an addictive activity.

Loss of Control

One may report desiring to stop an addictive behavior but, even so, not having the ability to precisely predict when a bout of the behavior will be initiated, how it will be manifested, or when it will stop. Thinking out loud, focusing one's attention, or self-reflection are means of inhibiting loss of control (Sussman & Ames, 2008), as well as being likely not to elicit appetitive effects. Also, engaging in a behavior slowly and deliberately are ways to maintain a sense of control (e.g., as with walking meditation; Hanh, 2011). Certainly, merely sitting still is also a means of inhibiting loss of control (e.g., "Sit still and hurt").

Negative Consequences

Negative consequences of dysregulation of the appetitive-motivational system may lead to a variety of unwanted events (more details on consequences of addictions are presented in Chapter 4 of this text). To the extent that an individual finds (a) preoccupation with and (b) loss of control of the addictive behavior distressful these two constituents, themselves, may be both examples of and determinative of other negative consequences. Well-known consequences include financial, legal, social, role, or mental wellbeing (APA, 2013; Sussman & Ames, 2008). An addiction which does not cause obvious negative financial, legal, social, role, or mental wellbeing related consequences, or causes minor consequences, may still be considered addictive behavior by some (e.g., ***positive addiction***; Glasser, 1976). If so, the need for remediation would perhaps not need consideration. However, I might debate on whether or not fulfillment of an appetitive need that does not lead to negative consequences can be considered addictive; it may just be a motivated behavior that appropriately fulfills an appetitive need. However, if preoccupation and loss of control are associated with that "positive addiction," these components may be considered as negative or undesired consequences in need of remediation.

Summary

This chapter provides the appetitive effects conceptualization of the addictions (the associational memory-appetitive system relations [AMASR] model; see Figure 2.1). Too often we view "addicts" as a small minority of the population who are "obviously" out of control (no willpower) or immoral. I believe that this is because we focus on relatively extreme and dramatic instances of the addictions, though even in extreme cases it is questionable that addicts are, when sober, lacking in some sense of personal morality. A small percentage of all addicts die from overdoses, or end up homeless. However, many addicts do end up experiencing myriad negative life consequences as presented in Chapter 4.

Once we permit application of addiction criteria across behaviors (e.g., appetitive needs, satiation, preoccupation, loss of control, and negative consequences applied to eating, shopping, or gambling as examples), we can see that this phenomenon applies to many people and multiple behaviors. If we understand that addiction has a wide reach, we may start to understand it as a problem of lifestyle which interfaces with our neurobiological systems associated with obtaining appetitive effects. Also, we can see the interface of neurobiological dysfunction with lifestyle characteristics. Then, we may have some suggestion on what is not addictive and can provide a better fit of neurobiological function with lifestyle. Etiologic variables that determine which addictions one may pursue exist at different levels of analysis (macrosocial/physical environmental, microsocial, cognitive and neurobiological). Chapter 3 presents these different etiologic variables and suggests an integration of them within a model of addiction co-occurrence and specificity.

Bulleted Summary

- The appetitive needs notion of addiction involves an understanding of how appetitive needs may be satiated (appetitive effects) in maladaptive ways. Addictive effects occur when these effects lead to preoccupation with and loss of control over their occurrence, and undesired consequences.
- Civilization generally entails settling down in one location and time for sedentary living, but with demand for an accelerating pace of productive output. Such lifestyle factors may contribute to the translation of appetitive effects into addictive effects.
- An appetitive effects notion of addiction may be conceptualized as being very different from differential socialization-related notions, in which one engages in an addictive behavior voluntarily and, perhaps, immorally.
- Deliberate cognitive processing of information, self-reflection, slower processing of information, breaking thoughts into logical elements, grooming multiple types of activities, and experiencing no negative consequences are aspects of non-addictive experience.

Suggestions for Further Reading

Griffiths, M. D. (2005a). A "components" model of addiction within a biopsychosocial framework. *Journal of Substance Use*, 10: 191–197.

Loonis, E., Apter, M. J., & Sztulman, H. (2000). Addiction as a function of action system properties. *Addictive Behaviors*, 25: 477–481.

Newlin, D. B. (2002). The self-perceived survival ability and reproductive fitness (SPFit) theory of substance use disorders. *Addiction*, 97: 427–445.

Sussman, S. (2012b). Steve Sussman on Matilda Hellman's "Mind the Gap!" Failure in understanding key dimensions of an addicted drug user's life – addictive effects. *Substance Use & Misuse*, 47: 1661–1665

3 Variables that Increase the Likelihood of Developing an Addiction

Learning Objectives

- To learn key examples of large physical and social environment predictors of addiction
- To learn key examples of microsocial context predictors of addiction
- To learn key examples of cognitive-level predictors of addiction
- To learn key examples of neurobiological-level predictors of addiction
- To understand how the AMASR model of addiction might be impacted by multi-level predictors
- To learn the PACE model (pragmatics–attraction–communication–expectations) of addiction specificity (i.e., why someone might engage in one addiction but not another)

Introduction

While sitting in a casino somewhere in Nevada, a US state widely known through the mass media for its "adult entertainment," Johnny realized that there were numerous addictions, or cues to addictions, within "arm's reach," all legal through state or county policy (large physical environmental and large social environmental or "macrosocial" influences). These included: cigarette vending machines, several full bars and one with a number of televisions depicting a variety of sports events, an inexpensive food buffet (along with several other restaurants), a shopping mall nearby with a variety of impulse items for sale, legal houses of prostitution not far away, and of course, lots of slot machines and gambling tables. Johnny was with his wife, a religious Baptist. They each drank a cup of coffee and then did a little grocery shopping and walked around outside. This microsocial influence (being with his wife) narrowed the larger physical and social environmental options. He recalled "thinking" about how much he was enjoying the microsocial context (cognitive level) and walking around felt good (neurobiological level).

Each *etiologic level of analysis* here (large physical and social environment, microsocial context, cognitive-level, neurobiological level) all contributed to the direction of Johnny's behavior – which was laudatory at the time. This chapter is on the etiology of addictive behaviors, hence the introductory story.

Learning Objectives

There are several variables that appear to facilitate or prevent addictive behaviors. As just introduced, these variables operate at different levels of analysis (e.g., see Sussman & Ames, 2008), and appear to be at the etiological core of a variety of substance and behavioral addictions. First, one may consider a molar (macro-) level of etiology; how ***geographic/physical environmental and large social climate-level variables***, which traverse physical environments, facilitate the development of addictions. The examples of physical environmental predictors presented in this chapter are drug production and distribution routes; and environmental exposure/air pollution. The examples of macrosocial predictors presented in this chapter are culture-based (gender roles, and emerging adulthood) and mass media impact. The large-scale physical environment may provide ready access to locations or contexts of experimentation with addictive behaviors. The large social climate may instruct on a mass scale to participants that certain addictive behaviors are a means to satiate appetitive motives (e.g., being arousing, fun, or nurturing).

Second, one may consider a slightly more molecular group level of analysis. The ***microsocial (small group) level*** includes the impacts of different groups on one's behavioral options. These groups may include one's family, peers (friends, colleagues), or contact with community agents (e.g., teachers, elected officials, community groups). Through the microsocial environment, one is exposed to interpersonal-level pressures to engage or not engage in various addictive behaviors. One also learns and practices the "language" specific to an addiction. The examples of microsocial perspectives presented in this chapter are conceptualizations including social cognitive theory, differential socialization, deviant subculture, and prosocial bonding.

Third, one may consider an even more molecular level of analysis: what the individual thinks about the world, groups, and one's inner life (e.g., physical sensations). Executive, deliberate processes may inhibit engagement in deleterious addictive behaviors, whereas well-learned, implicit, automatic, or possibly "impulsive" cognitive processes may facilitate engagement in addictive behaviors. Sussman and Ames (2008) referred to this as a ***cognitive level of analysis***. The examples of cognitive-level predictors presented in this chapter include cognitive processes that may contribute to development of an addiction (cognition-information errors), and cognitive processes that lead to maintenance of a developing addiction (cognitive processing limits, belief–behavior congruence, and situational/contextual distortions).

Finally, one may consider individual differences in neurobiology which may make a person relatively more or less prone to experience different appetitive effects after engaging in various behaviors. One's genetics, brain structure, and neurotransmission are examples of constituents. The examples of predictors presented in this chapter are the ***neurobiological-level variables*** associated with the Reward Deficiency Syndrome (Blum et al., 2011b; Blum et al., 2012) and personality variables. Personality traits often are viewed as phenotypical of underlying neurobiological function.

Etiologic variables representing each level of analysis are presented in the next sections of this chapter, from molar to molecular. While the associational memory-appetitive system relations (AMASR) model discussed in Chapter 2 is mostly a cognitive and neurobiological perspective, certainly more molar variables "set the stage" for the operation of this model. For example, access to objects of addiction and learning about how to engage in an addictive behavior are examples of physical environmental/macrosocial or microsocial variables that may lead to experimentation with the addictive behavior, which when then found to elicit an appetitive effect may later result in addiction. The predictors presented in this chapter are summarized in Table 3.1.

The variables presented are illustrative of those that facilitate or deter development of an addiction. However, the list is not exhaustive (see Sussman & Ames, 2008 for a more exhaustive presentation on etiology as pertaining to substance abuse). Finally, I present an integrated stage model of the development of one addiction versus another (the PACE model). The PACE model is summarized in Table 3.2.

Environmental Level

Among environmental variables are: distribution routes, the impact of environmental exposure (e.g., air pollution), culture (e.g., gender roles, values associated with emerging adulthood), and the mass media. These variables, which also may reflect operation of other variables (e.g., distribution routes may operate maximally well in areas with *low defensible space* [low monitoring and visibility]), provide a molar-level approach regarding what might lead to engagement in any number of addictive behaviors.

Addictive Behavior Distribution Routes

Physical environmental factors may facilitate certain addictive behaviors (e.g., access to gambling venues; unpatrolled areas, safe houses, and drug use). As evidence on a very large scale, 95 percent of opium is currently grown in Myanmar (Burma) and Afghanistan (90 percent or more of the total is grown in Afghanistan). Much of the opium travels from Afghanistan into Iran, Tajikistan, and northern Pakistan. It then travels through Turkey, other Eastern European republics, and Russia, where it eventually travels into Western Europe or the United States. A great deal of opium also travels out from Myanmar (Burma) into China and into Canada and the United States. It also travels from Myanmar (Burma) through Malaysia and into Western Europe. Not surprisingly, the majority of treatment admissions in South Asia and East Asia are for heroin abuse. In most parts of Europe, the main problem drugs are opiates (mostly heroin). Approximately 70 percent of treatment demand in Europe is linked to opiates (Sussman & Ames, 2008). Rates of misuse tend to be higher around distribution routes. Rate of admissions for heroin abuse in the Americas is relatively much lower (though currently increasing; see: www.drugabuse.gov/publications/research-reports/heroin/scope-heroin-use-in-united-states), as heroin distribution tends to be more indirect. Likewise, rates of other addictions tend to be higher closer to distribution routes (e.g., sex trade locations and routes, and hubs of sex tourism; gambling casino locations and meccas such as Las Vegas and Nevada in the United States).

Environmental Level

Table 3.1 Etiologic variables representing multiple levels of analysis

Environmental level

Distribution routes	Physical environmental factors may facilitate certain addictive behaviors, and rates of addictions tend to be higher closer to distribution routes (e.g., opium production and heroin abuse in South Asia and East Asia; sex trade locations and hubs of sex tourism; gambling casino locations and meccas such as Las Vegas).
Impact of environmental exposure (air pollution)	Environmental exposures have been associated with a wide range of negative health outcomes and may also impair neurobiological functioning, leading to addictive disorders. Through "toxicant-induced loss of tolerance" (TILT) people exposed to pollutants may become more susceptible to the effects of lower quantities of drugs and face greater difficulties with withdrawal. However, the impact of air pollution on addictive behaviors has not been directly addressed.
Culture	Culturally defined roles have an important impact on the development of different addictions. Because of cultural permissiveness men are "permitted" trial of risky behaviors as part of adult development, whereas such behavior is consistently less tolerated in females. Thus, males are relatively more likely to use drugs, gamble, or become dependent on video games. Compulsive buying disorder (CBD) may be an exception. There is some debatable evidence that this disorder is more prevalent among females. Emerging adulthood, the period generally between 18 and 25 years of age in Western societies, is perhaps the only or main period of life in which risky behavior is most tolerated or promoted as a means to maximize "growing up," associated with such phrases as "you only live once" (YOLO) or "sowing one's wild oats," and is perhaps the peak risk period for addictions.
The mass media	The mass media are an important relay of information and, as such, influence behavioral options to achieve appetitive effects. The World Wide Web provides incredible access to information about drugs of abuse and means of producing these drugs, avenues for gaming, lots of free pornography, social networking sites, and information on locations of places to gamble. Also, television and movies may inadvertently promote drug use, gambling, sex addiction, or compulsive buying.

Microsocial level

Social cognitive theory	Addictive behaviors can develop through vicarious learning, modeling, and/or initially reinforcing consequences. Role models act as teachers of where and when, how much, and how an addictive behavior is "practiced."
Differential socialization	The process of socialization is a means of transmitting cultural or subcultural norms and obtaining a social identity. Differential socialization processes may lead one to hold beliefs and perceptions that drug use, gambling, high frequency of sexual behavior, compulsive buying, or excessive exercise are tolerated by others in one's social environment.

(cont.)

Table 3.1 *(cont.)*

Microsocial level

Deviant subcultures including neutralization theory	Differential socialization may lead to group norms that serve to rationalize problem behavior. In deviant subcultures the group norms exist in opposition to dominant social values. As individuals become more and more entrenched within a group of others who may share similar addictive behaviors, one may say that such persons have become part of a deviant subculture. There are several variants of the deviant subcultures perspective. Neutralization theory (Sykes & Matza, 1957) suggests that internalized dominant social norms are neutralized through techniques of neutralization. Techniques of neutralization include denial of responsibility for one's behavior, denial of injury, denial of the victim, condemnation of the condemners, and appealing to higher authorities.
Prosocial bonding or constraint	Prosocial bonding or constraint refers to ties to conventional society that might prevent deviant behavior. Without prosocial bonds available and actively restraining maladaptive behavior, it is relatively easy to form delinquent subcultures. Thus prosocial bonding or constraint may have a protective effect against addictive behaviors.

Cognitive level

Cognitive-information errors	Cognitive misperceptions are formed that might make an addictive behavior (e.g., drug use) appear to be a normal, prevalent, or attractive option to a perceiver. Cognition-information errors may facilitate interest in trying and experimenting with drug use behavior, engaging in online social network use, or buying numerous lottery tickets, as examples.
Limits in rational cognitive processing	Cognitive processing limits (e.g., of executive functions, or related to time pressure) may impair successful competition with previously learned and reinforced information that otherwise might inhibit participation in addictive behaviors.
Belief–behavior congruence maintenance	An individual may utilize cognitive processes that serve to distance the perceiver from incongruence between beliefs and behavior. Alternately, one may utilize logical-appearing processes that more directly attempt to maintain congruence between the behavior (e.g., drug misuse) and one's beliefs (e.g., relaxation is healthy).
Situational/contextual distortions	Through situational/contextual distortions an individual may distort the context of one's lifestyle to normalize one's behavior. One may perceive that it is normal to drink a half pint of vodka every night for example.

Table 3.1 *(cont.)*

Neurobiological level

Reward Deficiency Syndrome and related notions	Appetitive needs may be strong in some people and be subjectively experienced as negative affect. Subjectively experienced negative affect may lead one to search for a behavior to provide relief. Some individuals, because of their neurochemistry, have difficulty deriving feelings of reward or pleasure from ordinary activities and might seek alternative behaviors to compensate. Brain imaging studies indicate that gaming, gambling, substance misuse, and binge eating all activate brain regions associated with motivated behavior. Thus individuals with strong appetitive needs or difficulty deriving reward may engage in behaviors that produce physiological feelings of relief or reward, such as drug use, eating, gambling, love addiction, CBD, or other sensation-seeking behaviors.
Comorbidity and personality	Comorbid problems or personality issues may precede and facilitate engagement in addictive behaviors. Comorbid problems include attention deficit disorder, mood disorders (e.g., depression or anxiety), or OCD. Personality issues could reflect neurobiological events, and include low emotional stability, low self-esteem, loneliness, hostility, distractability, high sensation seeking, high impulsivity, low conscientiousness, and narcissism.

Environmental Exposure (Air Pollution)

Environmental exposures have been associated with a wide range of negative health outcomes and tissue, organ, and system effects, and may impair neurobiological functioning, leading to addictive disorders (Sussman, Ames, & Avol, 2015a). It is feasible given some empirical evidence that environmental exposures can contribute to dysregulation of mesolimbic dopamine (DA) turnover, resulting in an increased propensity for addictive behaviors. Recently, researchers have begun to investigate the effect of indoor and outdoor toxicants on **neurodegenerative disorders** (hereditary and sporadic conditions which are characterized by progressive nervous system dysfunction) and to examine the impact of toxicants on DA function. For example, Guxens and Sunyer (2012) reviewed epidemiological studies on child development and found some support for the impact of air pollution (e.g., car exhaust emissions) on increased inattention, prevalence of **attention deficit hyperactivity disorder** (ADHD; a chronic condition marked by persistent inattention, hyperactivity, and sometimes impulsivity), and lowered academic performance. However, the impact of air pollution on addictive behaviors has not been directly addressed. Miller (1999, 2000) presented a notion she termed **toxicant-induced loss of tolerance** (TILT) and argued (and provided anecdotal evidence) that people exposed to pollutants may become more susceptible to the effects of lower quantities of drugs and face greater difficulties with withdrawal. This physical environmental variable is interesting because it suggests that

Table 3.2 The PACE model

Pragmatics	Pragmatics variables operate to discern whether or not one can access a particular addictive behavior and then engage in this behavior regularly. Pragmatics involves four aspects: *Supply* of the object of the addiction must be available. *Awareness* must exist that there is a supply of the addiction object available. *Acquisition skills* are needed to know how to obtain the addiction object from the source. *Means of exchange* to offer in return for the addiction object also must exist.
Attraction	Attraction influences whether someone is likely to initiate and continue engaging in an addictive behavior. Individual differences in the acute effects of behaviors coupled with associative learning processes may be important driving factors that shape addiction specificity.
Communication	Earlier experienced environments may shape life experiences in part by repetition of learned patterns of communication. Differential communications associated with addictive behavior may prepare people for which types of addictions they pursue. Also a system of communication may develop in groups specific to different addictive behaviors. Communication about the addiction can be a way of forming or solidifying social relationships with other addicts or addictive object providers.
Expectations	Expectations are beliefs regarding the likelihood that or extent to which an addictive behavior is providing solutions to experiential requests. One may expect or anticipate that the addictive behavior will be rewarding or provide specific outcomes such as helping one live life more comfortably in the immediate present. Expectancies regarding the initiation of an addictive behavior (e.g., joy, pleasure) can differ from expectancies regarding the maintenance of the behavior (e.g., avoiding withdrawal symptoms).

through a polluted physical living space large numbers of people may become vulnerable to suffering from addictive behaviors.

Culture: Gender Roles and Emerging Adulthood

Culturally-defined roles provide an important macrosocial-level impact on the development of different addictions. **Gender roles** may reflect such a factor. In general, while norms are changing as times change, world-wide, men are "permitted" trial of risky behaviors as part of adult development, whereas such behavior is consistently less tolerated in females. (Females are relatively likely to be considered "bad" if they engaged in criminal or other risky behaviors; e.g., Ettorre, 2015; Rebellon, Wiesen-Martin, Piquero, Piquero, & Tibbetts, 2015; Sanguanprasit, Pacheun, & Termsirikulchai, 2006; Sussman & Ames, 2008). Thus, males are relatively likely to drink alcohol regularly and use other drugs, gamble, or become dependent on video games. However, as examples, females who do develop a difficulty with drug use or gambling tend to suffer more severe consequences more quickly than males (Grant & Odlaug, 2014; Kiraly, Nagygyorgy, Griffiths, & Demetrovics, 2014; Sussman & Ames, 2008). Since such behavior is more counter-normative for females, it is not surprising that some studies have provided evidence that genetic factors are predominant in adolescent females' substance use (and one may speculate regarding other addictions), whereas cultural permissiveness, family dysfunction, and deviant peers primarily mediate adolescent males' involvement (Silberg, Rutter, D'Onofrio, & Eaves, 2003). **Compulsive buying disorder** (CBD; obsession with shopping and buying) may be an exception. This disorder is prevalent in developed societies in which there is a great availability of a variety of goods and attainable credit, and plenty of advertising (Racine, Kahn, & Hollander, 2014). There is some suggestion that this disorder is more prevalent among females (Dittmar, 2005), although the data are equivocal (Racine et al., 2014), and may vary depending on location, self-report biases, and types of goods assessed (e.g., clothes versus tools).

Another important culturally defined role that may pertain to experimentation with a variety of addictions is the *emerging adulthood* stage of development (Sussman & Arnett, 2014). It is not surprising that prevalence of drug abuse and CBD tend to be relatively high among younger people (Racine et al., 2014). Emerging adulthood is the developmental period between adolescence and young adulthood (an extended transition period), is a distinct period demographically and subjectively, and reflects modern lifestyle (Arnett, 2000). In the course of this life transition, roughly from 18 to 25 years of age, individuals achieve relative autonomy from guardians and experience shifts in social roles and normative expectations for their behavior. Emerging adults typically are in a period of life in which they pursue higher education or vocational training over an extended period of time, and delay marriage or a permanent love relationship. Emerging adults are typically free from the dependency and monitoring that characterized childhood or adolescence (e.g., involving parents and junior high school teachers), yet are not burdened with the responsibilities of adulthood (e.g., caretaking for others). This freedom allows young people the opportunity to explore diverse potential life directions. During this period, more than any other stage of life, the near-future is uncertain, and individuals are making a variety of life decisions in terms of their education, work, leisure interests, romance, and worldviews. That is, emerging adults explore who they are or want to be, tend to no longer feel like adolescents but do not yet consider themselves as having reached adulthood, are extremely optimistic about their own life goals and opportunities, focus on their own needs and desires, and experiment with different life pathways. Emerging adults may feel particularly invulnerable to negative life consequences, be self-interested or even hedonistic, and may take an experimental stance toward living. Perceived invulnerability to negative consequences and hedonistic attitudes are associated with participation in risky behaviors and pursuit of appetitive effects among emerging adults (e.g., Stone, Becker, Huber, & Catalano, 2012; Sussman et al., 2011a). Emerging adulthood is perhaps the only or main period of life in which risky behavior is most tolerated or promoted as a means to maximize "growing up," associated with such phrases as "you only live once" (YOLO), "sowing one's wild oats," "live like you're dying," or "to live without risk is to risk not living" (Ravert, 2013; Sussman & Arnett, 2014). The lifestyle factors associated with emerging adulthood appear conducive to facilitating the development of addictions, and fit into the PACE model. (This model is discussed in detail toward the end of this chapter.) First, drugs and various other addictive objects are relatively readily accessible among emerging adults because many of their peers may take part in addictive behaviors (the *pragmatics* of addiction; Sussman et al., 2011a), particularly after the age of 21 years. Easy access permits participation in the addictive behavior for those who have the knowledge and skills to tap it. For example, venues such as raves, rock concerts, and clubs tend to cater to emerging adults.

Second, involvement in risky behavior is relatively well tolerated, and often celebrated, among emerging adults (Ravert, 2013). Therefore, the initial consequences of various addictive behaviors are relatively likely to be positive. Also, for many emerging adults, brain neurobiology still is rapidly changing, leading reinforcing events to be experienced as particularly positive (*attraction*) while connections with inhibitory structures are relatively weak (Agrawal et al., 2012; Sussman, 2013). Addictive disorders may be relatively likely to develop during emerging adulthood and young adulthood, particularly for those most genetically vulnerable to the rewarding effects of addiction-related objects or activities (Agrawal et al., 2102). Third, it is relatively likely that the emerging adulthood sociocultural milieu is one in which the language of addiction (e.g., shared slang terms) is well instructed and entrenchment into an addictive lifestyle is relatively well promoted (*communication*). Accordingly, slogans expressed from influential sources such as "live life like you're dying" would seem to promote any number of self-destructive addictive behaviors (e.g., Ravert, 2013). Finally, *expectations* regarding involvement in the addictive behavior are possibly relatively likely to be fulfilled. Arguably, addictive behaviors likely elicit new experiences of oneself, which appears to be a shared goal among addictions and emerging adulthood (Arnett, 2005; Larkin et al., 2006).

Mass Media

Another important macro-level sociocultural influence affecting involvement in various addictive behaviors is the increasing role of the media and world-wide access to information. For example, the World Wide Web provides incredible access to information about drugs of abuse and the means of producing these drugs, avenues for gaming, lots of free pornography, and social networking sites, information on locations of places to gamble, and information on shopping (e.g., eBay). Regarding drug abuse, different cultures may influence each other's beliefs regarding recreational drug use to the extent that they use a shared language on the Web (e.g., www.legalize.org/global/). Also, television and movies may inadvertently promote drug use, gambling, sex addiction, or compulsive buying by conveying images of role models or idols, such as rock stars romancing heroin addiction, rappers who sing about marijuana (Sussman, Stacy, Dent, Simon, & Johnson, 1996), advertisements for casinos (as being exciting), engaging viewers in purchases through info-commercials, or depicting celebrities involved in buying any number of items (e.g., http://en.wikipedia.org/wiki/AWE_[TV_network]). Movie images, in particular, are likely to be viewed internationally and influence the host culture within which they are viewed. Even if an individual does not attend to images portrayed by the media, the ***mere exposure*** to these images has been shown to affect preferences for objects (mere exposure is a psychological phenomenon by which people tend to develop a preference for things merely because they are familiar with them; for more about the mere exposure effect and preference literature, see Kunst-Wilson & Zajonc, 1980). Clearly the media are an important relay of information and, as such, influence behavioral options to achieve appetitive effects.

Microsocial Level

Social group factors may be very important as means to acquire and exchange information about addictive behaviors, and certainly such factors are relevant to participation in various addictive behaviors (e.g., tobacco hookah pipe smoking, drug misuse, social network addiction; Griffiths, Harmon, & Gilly, 2011; Griffiths et al., 2014; Sussman & Ames, 2008). As one hears about the potentially addictive behavior, is told how to engage in the behavior, and repeats engagement in the behavior, one also learns to participate in a social milieu in which the behavior is facilitated. As part of that milieu, context-specific language and customs are involved and mastered within groups. Relevant addiction-related concepts/theories that apply here include social cognitive theory (e.g., parental, sibling, or peer role modeling), differential socialization, deviant subcultures, and prosocial bonding (Sussman & Ames, 2008).

Social Cognitive Theory

According to *social cognitive/learning theory* (Bandura, 1986), involvement in an addictive behavior or behaviors can develop through vicarious learning, modeling, and/or initially reinforcing consequences. That is, role models act as teachers of where and when, and how an addictive behavior is "practiced." Initial reinforcing consequences observed in others, and experienced, can have a strong impact on subsequent trial behavior. For example, an individual might learn that it seems acceptable or of high prevalence to drink alcohol on weekends or during celebratory events, through watching parents, siblings, or peers drinking and talking about drinking. Watching significant others' enjoyment of drinking may lead one to want to try alcohol too. Processes of social/cognitive learning are intertwined with culture; that is, observing engagement in an addictive behavior within a different culture with different outcomes can influence one's perception of and attitudes toward the behavior. For instance, recreational marijuana use is tolerated in the Netherlands, whereas in the United States even the medical use of marijuana has been highly controversial until very recently. If one is raised in the Netherlands, one may not consider marijuana use as being a particularly deviant behavior (Sussman et al., 2011a). Given that recreational marijuana use is now legal in Alaska, Colorado, Oregon, Washington, and Washington, DC, it may cease to be considered deviant behavior in the United States. A large social climate change (legalization of marijuana) may impact microsocial processes (more opportunity for social learning), leading to increasing prevalence of use (see Cerda, Wall, Keyes, Galea, & Hasin, 2012).

Differential Socialization

The process of socialization is a means of transmitting cultural or subcultural norms. For example, people learn the appropriateness of: frequencies of different social behaviors, degree of personal space, amount of eye contact, voice volume, and various speech contents, and people obtain a social group identity. **Group socialization** is a form of learning appropriate behaviors of certain groups and differs across different groups of people. **Differential socialization** refers to the group-specific channeling of the development of beliefs, intentions, expectations, norms, perceptions, and modeling of social behaviors. Differential socialization processes may lead one to hold beliefs and perceptions that drug use, gambling, high frequency of sexual behavior, compulsive buying, or excessive exercise, as examples, are tolerated by others in one's social environment (Akers et al., 1979; Sussman et al., 2011a). For example, it is not surprising that exercise addiction is relatively high in prevalence and promoted among those involved in organized sports (Berczik et al., 2014), who may be differentially socialized to construct their lives around their sport. Poor parental supervision, inconsistent parenting or behavioral tolerance by parents, family modeling of addictive behavior, and deviant peer group association are processes associated with differential socialization that have been found to be quite influential in facilitating experimental drug use (for review, see Hawkins, Catalano, & Miller, 1992), Internet addiction disorder (Park, Kim, & Cho, 2008), and sex addiction (Rosenberg et al., 2014).

Deviant Subculture

As individuals become more and more entrenched within a group of others who may share similar addictive behaviors, one may say that such persons have become part of a **deviant subculture** (Akers et al., 1979; Sussman et al., 2011a); that is, reliably deviant from a mainstream, same-age peer group regarding means of achieving appetitive effects. The basic notion of delinquent subcultures is that differential socialization may lead to group norms that serve to rationalize and maintain problem behavior (Akers et al., 1979; Cohen, 1955). These rationalizations may reflect group norms that exist in opposition to dominant social values and occur in subcultural groups. Cohen, and some sociologists since (e.g., Bordua, 1962), argued that certain youth subcultures engage in problem behaviors due to a gross reaction against middle-class society, as an expression of a general negativism, and because they find such activities to be a great deal of fun in the short run.

There are several variants of the deviant subcultures notion. One such variant is **neutralization theory** (Sykes & Matza, 1957). Neutralization theory suggests that those who exhibit risky behaviors, including addictions, actually do internalize dominant social norms. Norms, however, are viewed as qualified guides for action, limited by situational variables (e.g., killing during war is OK; Agnew & Peters, 1986; Cutler, 2014; Dodder & Hughes, 1993; Shields & Whitehall, 1994; Sykes & Matza, 1957), or adherence to a "code of the streets" (Topalli, 2005). Techniques of neutralization include denial of responsibility for one's behavior (e.g., one's workaholism was way beyond his or her control; the individual's boss was encouraging working harder), denial of injury (e.g., believing one's gambling addiction is not harming anyone), denial of the victim (e.g., "ripping someone off" to obtain money for drugs and believing that the victim deserved it), condemnation of the condemners (e.g., being busted for involvement in illegal sexual behavior as part of one's sex addiction and feeling the police are hypocrites because some of them may also be customers of sex workers), and appealing to higher authorities (e.g., loyalty to one's drug-using network and their "causes").

Prosocial Bonding

Prosocial bonding or constraint refers to ties to conventional society that might prevent deviant behavior. Such ties result from learning and modeling of prosocial behavior exhibited among significant others, experiences of family harmony, and yielding to rules for good behavior instructed by family, grammar and high school personnel, and other public authorities. Without prosocial bonds available and actively restraining maladaptive behavior, it is relatively easy to form delinquent subcultures (Hirschi, 1969). There are, of course, some youth who strongly react against middle-class or mainstream norms and values but find alternative "acceptable" means of expressing their discontent (e.g., involvement in community activism).

Cognitive Level

Sussman (2005) inferred four general types of cognitive variables that are relevant to an understanding of the processes underlying the formation and maintenance of addictions: (1) cognition-information errors, (2) limits in rational cognitive processing, (3) belief–behavior congruence maintenance, and (4) situational/contextual distortions. While these variables have been mostly applied to drug use, they can operate with addictions in general. "Cognition-information" errors may facilitate interest in trying and experimenting with a potentially addictive behavior. Once the addiction begins to "take hold," continued subjective appetitive effects and peripheral experiences may reinforce continued involvement in the addictive behavior. Cognitive processing limits (e.g., of executive functions, or related to task demands or time pressure) may impair successful competition of other activities with previously learned and reinforced addictive behavior cues. There may also be cognitive processes that actively deter learning new information. First, an individual may be driven to maintain self-perceived belief–addictive behavior congruence. Second, one may distort the context of one's lifestyle to normalize one's behavior (situational/contextual distortions).

Cognitive Processing and Developing an Addiction

Cognitive misperceptions are formed that might make an addictive behavior appear to be an attractive option to a perceiver. ***Cognition-information errors*** may facilitate interest in trying and experimenting with drug use behavior, engaging in online social network groups (Griffiths et al., 2014; Sussman & Ames, 2008), or buying numerous lottery tickets, as examples.

Individuals' ascertainment of predictability and control in their lives is often based on previous experiences, which become their taken-for-granted world (Schutz & Luckman, 1973). This taken-for-granted world is one directed generally by implicit cognitive processes. What is "normal" may not even involve a deliberately processed moral dimension after a while. One concept that ties experience to judgments of probability of events is the *representativeness heuristic*. The representativeness heuristic involves making judgments about the probability of an event based on an individual's experiential schema of how representative an event appears to be and the ease with which mental content comes to mind (i.e., cognitive accessibility) rather than relying on further evidence. Thus, errors of frequency or importance occur for *rare* or *vivid* stimuli (Kahneman, 2003). These types of errors are those that serve to make an addictive behavior appear to be a statistically normative (popularly engaged in by peers), widely accepted, or subjectively desirable or safe behavior in which to satisfy appetitive needs. Specific types of cognitive-information errors include the *false consensus effect* (tendency to overestimate the extent to which one's opinions, beliefs, preferences, values, and habits are normal and typical of those of others), *illusory correlation* (tendency to overestimate the co-occurrence of two infrequent events, such as drug use and peak experience), *peer prevalence or acceptability overestimates* (tendency to overestimate involvement in an addictive behavior, or acceptability of such involvement, among one's peers), and *unrealistic optimism* (tendency to believe that one is less at risk of experiencing a negative event compared to others). Someone may falsely assume that others share one's beliefs and attitudes that are favorable toward gambling (false consensus), or that one is relatively invulnerable to negative consequences of drug use (unrealistic optimism), as examples of such cognition-information errors (Sussman, 2005; Sussman & Ames, 2008 for more details).

Once the behavior is initiated, subjective effects and experiences may reinforce continued participation in the addictive behavior. Both *explicit and implicit cognitive processes* (deliberate, conscious, and automatic processes) may lead the participant to develop associations of the addictive behavior to a variety of cues (e.g., internal cues such as anxiety, external cues such as the sight of a liquor store) and outcomes (e.g., relief, relaxation) that facilitate continued involvement (Stacy & Ames, 2001; Thush et al., 2008). Over time, internal and external cues may elicit automatically ("pop into mind") an addictive behavior of choice, which continues to be engaged in to achieve an appetitive effect, unless actively inhibited through deliberate higher-order processing.

Cognitive Processing and Maintenance of an Addiction

Over time, negative consequences of the behavior occur, discussed in Chapter 4 of this text. However, even while experiencing undesired consequences, corrective information may not become deeply processed in memory and the addictive behavior does not decrease in frequency. Perhaps, corrective information is simply overridden by an individual's earlier (and likely continued) positive response to the neurobiological consequences of involvement of the addictive behavior. Also, corrective information needs to compete with preexisting addictive behavior-relevant associations or learned information (Stacy & Ames, 2001; Sussman & Unger, 2004; Wiers, de Jong, Havermans, & Jelicic, 2004). ***Cognitive processing limits*** (e.g., of executive functions, related to task demand or time pressure) may impair successful competition of inhibitory executive processing with previously learned and reinforced information (e.g., Weinstein et al., 2014, regarding Internet addiction disorder). That is, when experiencing multiple task demands or time pressure to get tasks done, one may be relatively likely to fall "victim" to automatic processing and previously reinforcing activities such as an addiction.

There may also be cognitive processes that actively deter learning new (corrective) information. First, an individual may be driven to maintain **belief–behavior congruence**. To accomplish self-perceived congruence, one may utilize cognitive processes that serve to distance the perceiver from incongruence between beliefs and behavior, perhaps to keep incongruent information from consciousness. Alternately, one may utilize logical-appearing processes (experientially based but inadequate) that more directly attempt to maintain a sense of congruence between the behavior (e.g., drug misuse) and one's beliefs (e.g., relaxation is healthy). Second, one may distort the context of one's lifestyle to normalize one's behavior (**situational/contextual distortions**). One may perceive that it is normal and usual to drink a half pint of vodka every night for example. Certainly such logical-appearing processes may translate into deficits in reward-based decision-making which have been found to be associated with drug abuse and Internet addiction disorder (Holm, Sandberg, Kolind, & Hesse, 2014; Sun et al., 2009; Sussman & Ames, 2008), and likely apply to many other addictions.

Neurobiological Level

There are several theories of etiology relevant to neurobiological function, among which some of the intensional conceptualizations of addiction were presented in Chapter 1 (e.g., reward-sensitization, allostasis). Two general conceptions directly relevant to an appetitive needs and neurobiological perspective of addictions include the reward deficiency notion and considerations of comorbidity and personality.

Reward Deficiency Syndrome and Related Notions

Subjectively experienced negative affect or **anhedonia** (inability to experience pleasure) may reflect a "reward deficiency" and may lead relatively vulnerable persons to search for a behavior to provide relief. Specifically, negative affect or anhedonia may be subjectively experienced in various ways in such persons including not feeling self-contained, feeling uncomfortable in one's own skin, the odd person out, insecure, restless, bored, uncomfortable with ambiguity, inability to feel joy in positive situations (anhedonia), or fear (e.g., Leventhal, Chasson, Tapia, Miller, & Pettit, 2006). Brain imaging studies indicate that gaming, gambling, substance misuse, and binge eating all activate similar brain regions, associated with motivated behavior (e.g., dorsolateral prefrontal cortex, lateral and medial orbitofrontal cortex, parahippocampal gyrus, and caudate; Gearhardt et al., 2011; Han et al., 2011; Kiraly et al., 2014; Sussman & Ames, 2008; Volkow, Wang, Tomasi, & Baler, 2013). It is not surprising, perhaps, that the most popular hypothesis regarding neurobiological bases for the addictions is one asserting insufficient dopamine transmission in these structures. For example, Volkow et al. (2001) suggest that some individuals have relatively fewer D2 dopamine receptors, which might predispose them to fall victim to drug abuse and other addictive behaviors. This notion is consistent with physiological research on individual differences in neurotransmitter receptors.

Although the precise physiological mechanisms are still being debated, it has been hypothesized that low levels of D2 receptors may result in a generalized *reward deficiency syndrome* among some individuals (Blum et al., 1990). That is, some individuals, because of their neurochemistry, have difficulty deriving feelings of reward or pleasure from ordinary activities and this predisposes them to seek alternative behaviors to compensate for the lower level of activation of the brain reward circuitry (Noble, Blum, Ritchie, Montgomery, & Sheridan, 1991). In other words, these individuals may engage in behaviors that produce physiological feelings of reward, such as drug use, eating, gambling, love addiction, compulsive buying disorder, or other sensation-seeking behaviors, at least under conditions in which such activities are readily accessible and prosocial alternatives are not accessible (e.g., Fisher, 2014; Leventhal et al., 2006; Racine et al., 2014; Yau et al., 2014). Individuals exhibiting a reward deficiency syndrome appear more likely to have variations in genes that code for the production of dopamine receptors. One variant allele implicated in the reduction in the number of dopamine receptors is the DRD2 A1 allele (Blum et al., 1990).

As a reminder caveat, neurotransmission and the addictions is complex and involves several neurotransmitters and hormonal mechanisms, as was indicated in Chapters 1 and 2 (also see Sussman & Ames, 2008). As additional examples, relatively low levels of oxytocin and vasopressin are two hormonal neurobiological mechanisms associated with love addiction (Fisher, 2014; Sussman, 2010a), and involvement of the opioid system generally is discussed as being involved in exercise addiction (Berczik et al., 2014). Data are lacking regarding the neurobiological basis of some of the addictions (e.g., sex addiction, in particular; Rosenberg et al., 2014). One unique feature of the mesolimbic dopaminergic system, perhaps, is that most addictions are associated with increased turnover of dopamine, whereas increases or decreases in turnover of other neurotransmitters is associated with other addictions (e.g., an increase in gamma-aminobutyric acid or GABA is associated with alcohol use but a decrease in GABA is associated with opiate use; see Sussman & Ames, 2008).

Comorbidity and Personality

Comorbid problems or personality issues also may precede engagement in any of these addictions. Comorbid problems include such examples as attention deficit disorder, mood disorders or symptoms (e.g., depression or anxiety), or OCD (Kiraly et al., 2014;

Racine et al., 2014; Rosenberg et al., 2014; Sussman & Ames, 2008; Weinstein et al., 2014). Personality issues could reflect neurobiological events, and include low emotional stability, low self-esteem, lack of perceived interpersonal competence, loneliness, hostility, distractability, high sensation seeking, high impulsivity (e.g., regarding food addiction, when a variety of food is available), low conscientiousness, or narcissism (e.g., Berczik et al., 2014; Fisher, 2014; Griffiths et al., 2014; Racine et al., 2014; Rosenberg et al., 2014; Sussman & Ames, 2008; Yau et al., 2014). **Materialism** (a tendency to consider material possessions and physical comfort as more important than spiritual values) may be a personality issue relatively important in the genesis of compulsive buying disorder (Racine et al., 2014). Individuals who display some form of problematic exercise typically exhibit personality characteristics and/or psychological distress such as perfectionism, inhibition of anger, high self-expectations, tolerance of physical discomfort, depression, and anxiety (see Cook, Hausenblas, & Freimuth, 2014). Difficulty allocating tasks and perfectionism also are associated with workaholism (Sussman, 2012a).

Appetitive motives such as dominance, socializing, and exploration operate with many of these addictions (Sussman, 2012b). "Exploration" may reflect attempts to resolve a generalized sense of personal insecurity through engagement in behavior that "simulates" mastery of the unknown (e.g., one may speculate that this motive operates in some online or offline game addictions and some types of drug misuse). That is, persons relatively high in personal insecurity may attempt to "improve" themselves through an ***addictive exploration***. Different mental health or personality issues may be present with the same or different addictions (e.g., see Bancroft et al., 2003 regarding anxiety versus depression and differential functions of sexual addiction). As of yet there is no clear mapping of personality to different neurobiological functions and addictions.

Addiction Specificity and the PACE Model

A concept that pertains to why some addictions may *not* co-occur in individuals has been labeled as ***addiction specificity*** (Sussman et al., 2011a). Addiction specificity is a phenomenon complementary to addiction co-occurrence (Sussman et al., 2011b). Different people appear to show unique patterns of addiction (e.g., exercise is related to food addiction relatively closely; there may be a relatively strong association among alcohol, gambling, and sex addictions) and, while individuals struggle with some addictive behaviors, they may not have difficulty with other potentially addictive behaviors. There are people, for example, who develop problems with drugs and sexual behavior but who never experience difficulties with gambling (e.g., never lose much money when gambling, do not gamble long hours or lose control of their gambling behavior). The epidemiology of addiction specificity across substance and process addictions has not been well quantified, though some work on addiction clusters is now being examined and may pertain to addiction specificity as well as co-occurrence (e.g., see the pioneering work of Lesieur & Blume, 1993).

How different etiologic variables operate to facilitate different patterns of addiction is not clear. Theoretically, at least, Sussman and Ames (2008) and Sussman et al. (2011a) suggest a PACE model, in which *pragmatics* makes it more likely to try an addictive behavior through accessibility to the activity and acquisition skills, *attraction* leads to addictive behavior selection through relative enjoyment of effects, *communication* leads to an understanding and expertise regarding continuing to participate in the addictive behavior, and *expectations* that are met indicates continued functionality (meeting demands) of the addictive behavior. I originally proposed the PACE stage model to explain the development of intimacy in relationships between two people, summarized from within the interpersonal attraction literature in social psychology. Later, I applied the same model to drug misuse and even later to explanation of addiction specificity (see Sussman et al., 2011a). Each variable in this model is discussed next.

Pragmatics

Pragmatics variables determine whether or not one can engage in a particular addictive behavior, and then engage in this behavior regularly. Pragmatics involves four aspects. First, there must be a *supply* of the object of the addiction available in the environment (e.g., drug distribution point, gambling casino, brothel, potential love partner, workplace, gym). If not, no relationship with the addictive object can develop. For example, addiction to the Internet was not possible prior to the wide availability of the Internet. Objects of addiction tend to be available along distribution routes, which permit easiest passage from a manufacture/product/service origin point and where there tends to be higher consumer demand (Sussman & Ames, 2008). Changes in the availability of an addiction object or service can increase or decrease prevalence of addictive behavior. At a macro-geographical level, the explosion of crack cocaine use in the late 1980s in the United States or decline in heroin supply and use in Australia and the west coast of Canada are but two examples of this common phenomenon (Cornish & O'Brien, 1996; Jiggens, 2008; Wood, Stolz, Li, Montaner, & Kerr, 2006). At a micro-geographical level, distance from an addiction source or supply is associated with overall prevalence of the behavior as well as disordered forms of the behavior (e.g., regarding alcohol use and abuse; [Bluthenthal et al., 2008]; regarding gambling and problem gambling [LaBrie et al., 2007]). If the addiction object or service is readily available, then other pragmatics aspects must be considered.

Second, one needs to be *aware* that there is a supply of the addiction object available. In fact, perceived availability of the addiction object may be a more important predictor of behavior than actual availability (e.g., Bluthenthal et al., 2008). One may speculate that if the source of addiction is perceived to be available, the potential addict will be more active in trying to search out and obtain the object. Promotion of the addiction object reaches the potential consumer by way of any number of channels (e.g., word of mouth, observation of sales, public venues such as clubs or bars, television advertisements, provider or customer websites, or even early evening news stories). "Channels of introduction" to the addiction object likely contain specific cues and begin a process of differential exposure to and learning of information related to the context of the addiction (e.g., Akers et al., 1979), perhaps being the earliest aspect of addiction specificity. For example, beer advertisements and packaging may indicate the best types of stores to purchase the product and also suggest that when one drinks beer, one drinks multiple beers on a drinking occasion.

Third, an individual must have **acquisition skills**; that is, one needs to know how to obtain the addiction object or service from the source. An individual needs to be able to converse appropriately with people who possess the addiction object (e.g., drug, sex), how to bring up topics without being threatening (e.g., cost, location, type of service), and how to arrange an exchange (usually money for the object). Finally, an individual needs to have a *means of exchange*, that is, possess money or services to offer in return for the addiction object. For example, one can pay for a drug, provide a service as a drug transporter, or offer sexual favors, as means to procure one's drug of choice.

For some objects of addiction, such as food/binge eating, the pragmatics involved may render the behavior a relatively easy one in which to engage (e.g., fast food restaurants are everywhere and are reasonably affordable), whereas some objects of addiction, such as heroin use, may be relatively difficult ones in which to engage. However, many people have tried objects of addiction at least once. For example, by 12th grade 68 percent of youth in the United States have tried alcohol (52 percent have reported ever being drunk), 38 percent have tried cigarette smoking, 46 percent have tried marijuana, 50 percent of youth have tried an illicit drug, and 25 percent have tried an illicit drug other than marijuana (Johnston, O'Malley, Bachman, Schulenberg, & Miech, 2014a). A vast majority of the US adult population (over 86 percent) have tried gambling at some time in their lives (Potenza, Fiellin, Heninger, Rounsaville, & Mazure, 2002). Most people have purchased shopping items "on impulse," roamed the Internet for a substantial amount of time (Sussman et al., 2011b), and looked at an erotic photo (e.g., approximately 90 percent and 30 percent, of undergraduate student men and women, respectively, report using pornography; Carroll et al., 2008).

Situational opportunity and curiosity predict that a particular addictive behavior will be engaged in at least once. However, pragmatics per se is not the critical factor that leads to addiction specificity, particularly if multiple channels of addiction are readily available. Other processes are critical in channeling the transition from initiation of behavior to escalation, maintenance, and excessive or compulsive engagement in a specific addictive behavior or set of behaviors.

Attraction

Attraction plays an important role in addiction specificity by facilitating whether or not someone is likely to initiate and continue engaging in an addictive behavior. Numerous variables can shape what determines whether a behavior is attractive. These include *individual difference variables* that may influence selection of the addictive behavior. For example, some addictive behaviors (e.g., heroin, involving needle use) may be more normatively stigmatized and, hence, less attractive to many persons. However, those relatively vulnerable to engage in such behavior may prefer relatively stigmatizing addictive behaviors as a *prima facie* expression of defiance (Iacono,

Malone, & McGue, 2008). More specifically, persons attracted to relatively stigmatized behaviors such as heroin injection may initially intensely enjoy the reputation they obtain (e.g., deviant peer group credibility), or the reactions to their behavior that they observe from others, as being persons who are beyond the chains of social restraint, expressed in the addictive behavior (Freimuth, 2008). These individuals also may be less attracted to addictive behaviors that are more socially acceptable (e.g., shopping, Internet). Conversely, some of those who are attracted to relatively deviant addictive behaviors may be interested in engaging in relatively deviant manifestations of other addictions. As examples, they may favor shoplifting as a form of shopping addiction or may become a workaholic sex worker (i.e., work long hours at a relatively "extreme" job). In addition, those individuals who are relatively more enticed by deviance might be attracted to a greater variety of types of addictive behaviors (Brewer & Potenza, 2008; Freimuth, 2008; Goodman, 2008).

Attraction also involves the *experiential pleasantness ascribed to addictive behavior-related stimuli and context*. For example, researchers and practitioners have noted that drug addicts appear to become addicted to the routine of preparing and administering the drug, and contextual cues associated with the drug (Marks, 1990). One may feel attracted to the sight, smells, sounds, tactile stimulation, or social stimuli inherent in the context of the addiction (Pelchat, 2002). Over time, and through associative learning and memory processes, these contextual stimuli may come to represent or cue the behavior and appetitive effects (Stacy et al., 2004; Wiers & Stacy, 2006). It is important to note that external cues for an addictive behavior may be unique to that addictive behavior, and, hence, related behavior-specific urges would be elicited in response to those specific external cues (Carter & Tiffany, 1999; Marks, 1990).

Attraction may also impact addiction specificity via person-specific *differential reactions to the neurobiological effects* of addictive behaviors. Indeed, there is marked between-person variability in the acute effects of a variety of addictive behaviors (de Wit, 1998; Pepino & Mennella, 2005). That is, for some individuals a behavior can result in extremely pleasurable experiences (e.g., high, rush, relaxation, stimulation, social and performance enhancement). For others the same behavior can result in severe aversive effects (e.g., anxiety, undesired sedation, social and performance impairment, dysphoria, disappointment), or relatively few or weak acute effects (neither positive nor negative). Individual differences in the initial acute reinforcing effects of addictive behaviors can shape one's attraction to a behavior (e.g., Haertzen, Kocher, & Miyasato, 1983; Sussman & Ames, 2008).

Individual differences in the acute effects of behaviors coupled with *associative learning processes* (among stimuli, behaviors, and outcomes) may be important driving factors that shape addiction specificity. Attraction to an addictive behavior tends to be shaped by early experiences with it. In particular, accidental circumstances or initial physiological reactions may lead to avoidance of or preference for that addictive behavior (see Sussman et al., 2011a). For example, acting in a highly shameful way or experiencing pain following an accidental fall while using marijuana for the first time may cue one to avoid its use, though not the use of other drugs. As another example, some East Asians have a gene variant that produces an enzyme that inadequately breaks down alcohol's initial metabolite, aldehyde dehydrogenase, and hence, they tend to experience uncomfortable physiological reactions such as a *flushing response* (red flushing or blotches on the body such as the head, neck, or shoulders), nausea, and headaches when drinking alcohol. Thus, East Asians may be less attracted to using alcohol in comparison to other substances, such as marijuana or nicotine (Iacono et al., 2008).

Certain *intrapersonal traits* may impact initial sensitivity to specific addictive behaviors. Anhedonia – the incapacity to experience pleasure in response to natural rewards – is unlikely to increase propensity for behavioral/process addictions that produce relatively less positive reinforcing effects (e.g., shopping; Leventhal et al., 2006). By contrast, anhedonia is associated with increased sensitivity to the euphorogenic effects of stimulant drugs (e.g., amphetamine and cocaine; e.g., Tremblay, Naranjo, Cardenas, Herrmann, & Busto, 2002). The differential enjoyment of different drugs or of other addictive behaviors may or may not reflect development of a means of self-medication (Khantzian, 1985) or to satisfy a biologically based desire for stimulation as in sensation seeking (Zuckerman, 1994).

In some instances, the shaping of addiction specificity may involve extended access and involvement with a particular addictive behavior during a *critical point in childhood or adolescence*, which may facilitate an intense attraction toward the behavior. Neural adaptations may be especially likely when one is most neurobiologically vulnerable during adolescence and emerging adulthood. During adolescence some subcortical structures mature earlier and are more able to support the acquisition of appetitive-type behaviors (e.g., Giedd, 2008). As mentioned previously in this chapter, it is at this time of emerging adulthood that there exists relatively few higher-level inhibitory functions monitoring relatively greater motivational drive for novel experience, and this may affect the course of an addictive behavior.

Between-person differences in attraction also may be important for explaining the specificity in whether one maintains an addictive behavior after a habitual pattern is already established. There are reports of marked individual differences in the severity of *withdrawal* symptoms following discontinuation of an addictive behavior (e.g., Leventhal et al., 2007). It is possible that an individual has a greater propensity to experience severe withdrawal after abstaining from one addictive behavior compared to another behavior (Stewart & Brown, 1995). In this case, he or she is likely to continue one type of behavioral pattern to avoid severe withdrawal, and as a result, manifest addiction specificity.

Communication

People tend to select social and physical environments that are similar to earlier experienced environments, which may shape life experiences in part by repetition of learned patterns of communication (e.g., **Life Course Theory**; Elder, 1998). For example, youth who early on have learned to express anger-related words or cuss words are relatively likely to expose themselves to persons and situations that involve risky behaviors including addictive behaviors (Snyder et al., 2005; Sussman et al., 2011a). Further, it is possible that earlier life experiences, by perpetuating differential communications associated with addictive behavior, may prepare people for which types of addictions they pursue (Akers et al., 1979). That is, *early experiences with* *differential vocabularies* can direct behavior toward specific addictions. For example, observing older siblings engaging in marijuana use may teach younger ones the language associated with marijuana use (e.g., lighters, matches, bongs, rolling papers, pipes, or head highs versus body highs, inhaling), preparing them for how to use marijuana when they are older (e.g., Hyde, 1982). At the same time, if one does not learn the language associated with another addictive behavior and, hence, does not tend to think in terms of the language of the other addictive behavior (e.g., gambling addiction: bet, action, call, payout, all-in, ante, an arm, wad; www.ildado.com/casino_glossary.html), then communication becomes engrained specific to one addiction (marijuana use) but not another (gambling).

As one continues to engage in an addictive behavior, a pattern of behavior develops that involves craving, seeking, experiencing, and recovering from the effects of the addictive behavior. A system of *communication about these "preoccupation/entrenchment" aspects of the addiction* may develop, encompass important features of one's daily life, and call upon quite distinct personal and intergroup communication styles and techniques. For example, asking for a number of drinks in a bar requires different interpersonal communication skills than purchasing an ounce of cocaine from a dealer. The interactions among drinkers occur within the continuum of accepted social practices where both distributor and consumer often operate within the law (depending on other variables such as if the customer is "cut off" at some point in drinking, drugs are permitted at the bar, or whether drinking and driving are involved). In contrast, cocaine purchases may place users in jeopardy of physical aggression or theft from peers, and both users and dealers may incur legal consequences, possibly facilitating a different interactional style including "code words" to arrange a buy (e.g., someone may request to buy a "cup of soup" to indicate one "rock" of crack [Moreno, 2006]). In general, **insider speech** may develop to serve as a symbol of commonality and group identification pertaining to specific addictions within specific contexts (Tong, McIntyre, & Silmon, 1997).

As one becomes differentially socialized, one may become an *"expert" in the language of the addiction* and feel like a "regular" or someone who belongs in that context (as opposed to a "novice"). One may comprehend addictive behavior-specific words that associate the behavior with life experiences and show an understanding of the language of the behavior (e.g., "4:20" is jargon that refers to marijuana use in the United States by many experienced users: the time of day to use, marijuana appreciation day; **hand release** refers to a sex worker bringing a client to orgasm by using a hand, whereas **half and half** refers to engagement in a combination of oral and vaginal sex). Interaction with agents of an addiction (e.g., card dealers, sex workers) or other addicts becomes embedded with a commonality of terms that refer to the behaviors, associated objects or paraphernalia, or subjective experience. The person may self-identify with addiction-related groups or activities (e.g., running clubs, pertaining to exercise addicts). Communication about the addiction, therefore, can be a way of forming or solidifying social relationships with other addicts or addictive object providers (Dalzell & Victor, 2008).

There are several means by which communication processes may contribute to addiction specificity. Some people may originate from *cultural backgrounds* that cause them to feel comfortable or uncomfortable with taking part in the communication processes of a particular addiction, or lead them to be potentially unaware of words associated with the addiction. For example, Latter Day Saints or Baptist church members tend to avoid alcoholism or tobacco addiction (to be in good standing) and, in general, may avoid discussion of these drugs (e.g., Nace, 1984) (of course there are recovery programs provided by the Latter Day Saints; https://addictionrecovery.lds.org/?lang=eng). Conversely, members of the Latter Day Saints may be relatively likely to suffer from prescription pills abuse (www.cnn.com/2014/10/02/living/lisa-ling-mormon-drug-abuse-essay/), and possibly other addictions such as to sex (http://ldshopeandrecovery.com/).

Additionally, individuals with one addiction may communicate disparagingly about another addiction. For example, some methamphetamine users may operate within social contexts that ridicule people who drink alcohol or engage in other behaviors that are sedating or result in certain types of performance impairment (e.g., slurring words; Sussman et al., 2011a).

Expectations

In general, *expectancies* are subjective probabilities regarding the likelihood of achieving various outcomes by engaging in some behavior. Various conceptualizations of the expectancy construct have been applied to research on addictive behaviors since Rotter (1954) initially proposed expectancy theory. Expectancy as a construct relevant to addiction involves the anticipated consequences of behavior or beliefs held about the likelihood of appetitive effects (e.g., Goldman, 2002). In terms of the PACE model, addiction expectancies or expectations are beliefs regarding the likelihood that or extent to which an addictive behavior is providing solutions to experiential requests. One may expect or anticipate that the addictive behavior will be rewarding or provide specific outcomes such as helping one live life more comfortably in the immediate present (e.g., to lift self-esteem, provide a social lubricant effect, provide relaxation, satiate appetitive effects; Freimuth et al., 2008; Goldman & Darkes, 2004; Marlatt, Baer, Donovan, & Kivlahan, 1988).

There are several *individual difference factors* that contribute to development of a positive or negative expectation for particular addictive behaviors. These include one's genetically inherited sensitivity to the behavior (McCarthy, Brown, Carr, & Wall, 2001), emotional dispositions (e.g., some individuals with social anxiety tend to hold expectancies that alcohol facilitates social performance; Eggleston, Woolaway-Bickel, & Schmidt, 2004), or motivational state (e.g., those with weight concerns may hold positive expectations regarding the appetite suppressing effects of tobacco; Cavallo et al., 2010). Importantly, though, specific expectancies develop through the interplay of these individual difference variables with vicarious social learning, as well as with direct experience. For example, hearing comments relevant to expectancies for reinforcement from alcohol predate teens' first drinking experiences, and predict drinking onset (Smith, 1994).

Direct experience may refute, confirm, or enhance pre-use expectancies. The learned expectations and experiences of specific outcomes as they occur with a specific appetitive behavior likely play an important role in addiction specificity. For example, heavier drinkers differ from light drinkers on activation of expectancies of positive arousing effects versus sedating effects of alcohol (Kramer & Goldman, 2003; Simons, Dvorak, & Lau-Barraco, 2009). Additionally, research suggests that individuals with a single addictive behavior (e.g., alcohol only) differ from those who engage in multiple addictive behaviors (e.g., alcohol and marijuana) in the degree to which they hold positive expectations about the second behavior (often based on experienced realities), suggesting the possibility for an uncoupling of expectations across addictive behaviors (Simons et al., 2009). For example, some persons may prefer one drug over the other due to these different expectancies, with a preference for sedation or arousal. Others may use both drugs with the expectation that they can use them to fluctuate or balance out their level of arousal. Similar addiction interactions occur with behavioral addictions (e.g., see Carnes, Murray, & Charpentier, 2005, and Chapter 8 of this text). Experiences with addictive behaviors thus may create subjective physiological expectancies that are addictive behavior-specific.

Expectations associated with an addiction also may involve one's perceptions of the **social images** (general perceived or fanaticized lifestyle characteristics) associated with participation in the behavior. For example, gambling or shopping addictions may be associated with social images of living luxuriously, love or sex addictions may be associated with social images of intimacy or social power, and marijuana addiction may be associated with living a countercultural (or cognitively expanded) lifestyle (Herrnstein & Prelec, 1991). Perhaps socially learned through various modalities (e.g., mass media impact, family or peer social learning, experiences with an addictive behavior), it is likely that differential social image expectations impact addiction specificity.

In addition, perceptions of the **gradient of reinforcement value** functions portraying different addictive behaviors may vary in steepness, leading to selection of one addiction with a steeper gradient (more reinforcement value per unit time) over another (Herrnstein & Prelec, 1991). Such gradients may generalize across persons, or vary from person to person or within persons over time. For example, many people may expect a steeper gradient of reinforcement from drug effects versus exercise-related effects. An athlete, who previously expected that exercise would provide a steeper reinforcement gradient, may come to view a steeper gradient of reinforcement from drug effects while recovering from an exercise-related injury.

Expectancies regarding the initiation of an addictive behavior (e.g., joy, pleasure) can differ from expectancies regarding the *maintenance of the behavior* (e.g., avoiding withdrawal symptoms). However, as an individual's social activities begin to increasingly involve the addiction and other addicts or providers of the addiction, it may become possible to convince oneself that the addictive behavior does not interfere with and may even actually facilitate one's daily activities. One may come to rely on a specific addiction, avoiding all others, if this addiction is perceived to meet many of one's expectations for one's life (e.g., there are people who might say that their life is "all right" as long as they have their marijuana).

Summary

A large set of etiologic variables have been proposed as impacting on various addictions, though most such research has been conducted on drug misuse (e.g., Petraitis, Flay, & Miller, 1996). Level of analysis from the molar to the molecular was presented: the large physical and social environment, microsocial contexts, cognitive variables, and neurobiological variables (Sussman & Ames, 2008). An attempt was made to organize the specific examples of these variables (e.g., emerging adulthood as an example of a large social environment variable) in a way that might explain addiction co-occurrence or specificity (identifying reasons for overlap or non-overlap among different patterns of addictive behaviors).

There are several alternative models that might be envisioned to address relations among these multi-level variables. For example, a simple "additive model" suggests simply that variables at different levels of analysis add up to produce a "toxic combination" which produces an entrenched addiction of some type. A "multiplicative model" suggests that this toxic combination is elicited exponentially by the right set of predictors. A "nested model" suggests either that the large physical and social environment "draws" a net around which addictions may occur (an addiction can't exist if the product or service doesn't exist), or that specific neurobiological vulnerability determines which directions might be taken at more molar levels.

Finally, the PACE model delineates pragmatics, attraction, communication, and expectation as composing a useful framework for investigation on the determinants of addiction specificity. The PACE model was conceived of as a systems model with a stochastic base (Sussman et al., 2011a). That is, if one experiences numerous expectancies about an addiction, it is assumed that the other elements of the model already have been in operation (pragmatics, then attraction, and then communication); however, it is also assumed that feedback loops operate across all of the elements of the model. The PACE model serves as a theoretically plausible map of addiction specificity.

Bulleted Summary

- Large physical and social environment predictors of addiction include addiction object or service distribution routes (e.g., drugs, sex trade), the impact of environmental exposure (e.g., air pollution), culture (e.g., gender roles, values associated with emerging adulthood), and the mass media (which might glorify addiction, instruct how to engage in it).
- Microsocial context predictors of addiction include group influences (e.g., one's family, peers, or contact with community agents). Microsocial-level theories offered in this chapter included social cognitive theory, differential socialization, deviant subculture, and prosocial bonding.
- Cognitive-level predictors of addiction include cognitive processes that may contribute to development of an addiction (cognition-information errors), and cognitive processes that lead to maintenance of a developing addiction (cognitive processing limits, belief–behavior congruence, and situational/contextual distortions).

- Neurobiological-level predictors of addiction presented in this chapter include motivation-reward deficiency (Reward Deficiency Syndrome) and co-morbid problems (e.g., ADHD) and personality variables. Personality traits often are viewed as phenotypical of underlying neurobiological function.
- The AMASR model of addiction primarily operates at cognitive and neurobiological levels, though one's associational memory regarding one's appetitive operations likely is impacted by multi-level predictors. For example, one's status as an emerging adult likely results in differential exposure to pro-addictive behavior information that may bias associational ties to appetitive effects.
- The PACE model is composed of components including access to addiction objects or services (pragmatics), relative enjoyment of engagement in the addictive behavior (attraction), developing a language about the addictive behavior experience (communication), and fulfilling one's hopes for satiation through the addiction (expectation). This model might help explain why someone might engage in one addiction but not another.

Suggestions for Further Reading

Miller, C. S. (2000). Toxicant-induced loss of tolerance. *Addiction*, 96: 115–139.

Sussman, S. & Ames, S. L. (2008). *Drug Abuse: Concepts, Prevention and Cessation.* Cambridge University Press.

Sussman, S., Leventhal, A., Bluthenthal, R. N., Freimuth, M., Forster, M., & Ames, S. L. (2011a). A framework for the specificity of addictions. *International Journal of Environmental Research and Public Health*, 8: 3399–3415.

Wiers, R. W., Bartholow, B. D., Wildenberg, E. V. D., Thush, C., Engels, R. C. M. E., Sher, K. J., ... & Stacy, A. W. (2007). Automatic and controlled processes and the development of addictive behaviors in adolescents: A review and a model. *Pharmacology, Biochemistry and Behavior*, 86: 263–283.

4 Consequences of Addiction

Learning Objectives

- To learn more about how two of the components of addiction, preoccupation and loss of control, may in and of themselves be considered negative consequences
- To learn about more or less universal consequences of an addictive behavior
- To learn about variation in consequences across different addictions
- To learn about how consequences may vary as a function of context
- To learn about consequences of addiction as a function of cultural morality

Introduction

One may recall the case of Johnny, who was introduced in Chapter 1. After 30 years of "partying," he felt like he was at a crossroads of sorts. Continuing his story, he was spending a great deal of time socially isolated. He did not want his family to see him drunk so he wound up drinking late at night, combining the impact of the alcohol with long hours of working, binge eating, and "roaming" the Web when he was too tired or drunk to continue working. When he went to sleep he sweated profusely. In the morning his eyes were red, his skin felt hot and clammy, and he drank a very large cup of coffee as he began his workday. He only felt glimpses of tremors. But there was a clear narrowing pattern in Johnny's life. His community college administrative job roles, number of social contacts, and decision-making authority at work and in the family had all narrowed. Though he was not in legal trouble at the time, he believed that such trouble was around the corner. The dents on his car were minor, but reminded him of tattoos that represented remnants of addicted moments. He did not want to do this anymore and wanted to live a long life. He was not sure he would be able to stay stopped. He sometimes believed that he could and should punish himself in order to make amends for who he was, by engaging in an addiction just one more time. Afterwards, he felt that he "got even" with himself and might clean up his act for a week or two. In reality, however, even with all the messes he got into over the years, he also still subjectively, temporarily, satiated appetitive needs (exploration, pleasure, higher self-worth, and self-nurturance) with various addictions (notably, alcohol, work, TV, and eating). Obtaining consistent *sobriety* (a balanced life) was going to be difficult for Johnny.

Consequences of Addiction

Addictive behavior in this text is defined as engaging in behavior for an appetitive effect, achieving a period of satiation (a temporary lack of a feeling of "wanting"; e.g., Berridge & Robinson, 1995), then after repeated appetitive behavior–satiation cycles resulting in preoccupation over that behavior and a sense of loss of control regarding the when and where of engagement in the behavior, leading to *undesired or negative consequences* (Sussman & Sussman, 2011). People in recovery mention how drugs of abuse or a behavioral addiction did something *for* them at first (temporary subjective satiation of an appetitive need) and later did something *to* them (negative consequences accumulate). Substance and behavioral addictions at first may provide addiction-specific subjective positive consequences including feeling happier or less sad, more energetic or quieted temporarily, experiencing accomplishment and security, feeling a sense of dominance or self-nurturance, enjoying to some extent new adventures or exploration, or subjective experience of cognitive enrichment or decrease in obsessive thinking, as examples (Sussman, 2012b). The effects of substance and behavioral addictions would not be a problem if there were no *negative* consequences. There would simply be appetitive behavior–satiation cycles, with "harmless" preoccupation and loss of control (if that were possible) – and some temporary gains. Unfortunately, the reality is that participation in addictive behaviors will tend to lead to accumulation of various negative consequences (Sussman & Ames, 2008).

Fong, Reid, and Parhami (2012) suggested that common negative consequences definitive of addictive behaviors include (1) disruption of personal, family, social, or vocational pursuits (being a barrier in the flow of life); (2) causing distress to self or others (causing fear); and (3) leading to physical or social harm to self or others (causing direct harm). Even behaviors that some writers referred to as ***positive addictions*** (being addicted to an activity that is intrinsically healthy or self-fulfilling; Glasser, 1976; Griffiths, 1996) will have negative consequences for the addict (see Brown, 1993 on "mixed blessings"). For example, workaholism, while perhaps leading to praise from the boss and raises, may lead to performance burnout, distress to family due to not being available to them, and possibly self-harm from sleep deprivation. As a second example, exercise addiction, while possibly making one look younger and permitting greater mobility, may lead one to diminish the extent of one's work opportunities, may make one less available to family, and could lead to repeated injuries. This chapter addresses types of negative consequences that the addictions may elicit.

Preoccupation Could Be Considered a Consequence

While not stated as such in the five-component definition of addiction (Sussman & Sussman, 2011), *preoccupation* may be considered a negative consequence resulting from continued involvement in fulfilling an appetitive motive. Preoccupation with the addictive behavior might not be a bad problem if it did not interfere dramatically with other life demands. One difficulty with any addiction is that it may "take up space" in one's working memory, cloud one's thinking, and possibly diminish preferable alternative activity choices one may make. Other activities are given up or, if continued, are no longer experienced as being as enjoyable as they once were. To the extent that preoccupation interferes with enjoyment of other activities or successful fulfillment of life demands, it could be a negative consequence in and of itself. For example, thinking constantly about work during a family vacation may lessen enjoyment of that recreational time, and shortening the duration of a family vacation to get back to work may lessen the emotional recovery that could be experienced through involvement in the vacation, as well as potentially alienating co-vacationers (e.g., family).

If preoccupation with the addiction holds a prominent place in one's social interactions or activities, one's life may narrow, as with the example of Johnny, in terms of variety of activities engaged in. Significant others are placed in the position of either accommodating the addict's preoccupation (e.g., being a compliant listener to incessant explanation of an online game), possibly becoming a voluntary conspirer (e.g., feeding the addict with "drug talk"), or distancing from the addict and living an autonomous existence. Any of these options is less than optimal in terms of achieving intimacy, or resolving any ongoing group conflicts or issues.

Loss of Control Could Be Considered a Consequence

Also not stated as such in the five-component definition of addiction (Sussman & Sussman, 2011), *loss of control* may be considered a negative consequence resulting from continued maladaptive involvement in fulfilling an appetitive motive. For example, one may work non-stop to obtain a feeling of security. One goes on vacation, intending to spend time with family, and decides to complete a little work – maybe just one hour's worth (to renew that sense of security) – but then ends up working most of the time and not spending much time with family. The work binge may be socially isolating. Experiencing a loss of control over one's addictive behavior occurs when the person is no longer able to reliably predict when (a) the behavior or associated cravings will begin, (b) what the topography of the behavior will look like once initiated (e.g., where, when, how long), or (c) when it will end (e.g., Corwin & Hajnal, 2005). Thus, there may be an unexpected quantity of addictive behavior "output," such as number of alcoholic drinks or calories consumed, overload from working out, amount of money spent gambling, degree of safety when participating in any of these activities, or sheer number of hours spent engaging in the behavior. These behaviors, which signify loss of control, are undesired or negative consequences.

Second, there may be an unexpected frequency of episodes of engaging in the addictive behavior (e.g., regarding how many days in a month, or how many continuous days after at least a 24-hour break). The trade-offs one may make on daily activity due to loss of control over the addictive behavior may constitute a negative consequence (e.g., losing productive time).

Finally, fear of loss of control before and while engaged in the addictive behavior may be experienced as a negative consequence (i.e., "bad feelings"). That is, the "addict" may take a chance on trying to control the behavior, being afraid he or she will not be able to do so. Then, while engaging in the behavior, the addict may experience an abstinence violation effect (Marlatt, 1985), or realize that just a "taste" of the behavior does not satiate, and then feel disappointed and more fearful. The feelings associated with loss of control are likely to be negative (e.g., fear, worry, self-disgust, self-distrust, and hopelessness) even while experiencing subjective appetitive satiation effects.

Six Other More or Less "Universal" Types of Negative Consequences of Addictions

Examining the range of addictions, one might ask which negative consequences are common to most or all of them. There are at least six consequences that may apply to an addiction (in addition to preoccupation or loss of control). These consequences are depicted as the first six in Table 4.1.

First, unwanted *social consequences* are a hallmark of most or all addictions. Significant others will tend to complain if one is repetitively misusing tobacco, alcohol, or other drugs, eats addictively, gambles, shops, works, or engages in exercise or sex excessively, is on the Internet constantly, or demonstrates being addicted to love, as examples (e.g., Grant & Odlaug, 2014; Racine et al., 2014). These social complaints pertain to worry about the addict engaging in self-harm, acting strangely, harming them (e.g., catching an STD if the partner is a sex addict), or simply being inaccessible, as main examples.

Social complaints are likely to vary by **context** (the circumstances that provide the setting for an event) of the addiction. Griffiths (2005b) cites the example of a 23-year-old single male with no responsibilities who may work 16 hours a day seven days a week but suffer few obvious negative effects in his life as a result (and may be promoted, or receive huge financial rewards). However, another older male, married with three children also working 16 hours a day every day is likely to have many areas of conflict in his life (relationship problems, in particular). Although these two males may be engaged in identical work behaviors, only one of them may be deemed problematic and/or addicted. Of course, that young male may delay for a long time entering a committed relationship and thus may still suffer (delayed) social consequences of a different sort.

Second, the development of self-defeating, *unusual thinking* would seem to be a common negative consequence across different addictive behaviors. Addicts may, for many years of their addiction, tend to view the addiction as a saving grace in their lives rather than being self-destructive, for example; or that if they stop their addiction something terrible will happen (Jacobs, 1986). A gambler, by thinking that he or she can chase losses and get even with the house illustrates unusual and self-defeating thinking (APA, 2013). An exercise addict may believe that he or she is simply pushing the limits of what the human body is capable of doing (with objective evidence to the contrary, by overtraining), constantly focusing on the next race or exercise session. Likewise, a shopper who thinks that one can never have enough pairs of shoes, a marijuana addict who believes that he or she drives more safely due to driving more slowly while "stoned" (Sussman, 2010a), or a food binger who believes that he or she

"Universal" Types of Negative Consequences

Table 4.1 Consequences of addiction

Six "universal" types of negative consequences

Social consequences	Unwanted social consequences are a hallmark of most or all addictions. Significant others will tend to complain if one is repetitively misusing tobacco, alcohol, or other drugs, eats addictively, gambles, shops, works, or engages in exercise or sex excessively, is on the Internet constantly, or demonstrates being addicted to love. These complaints pertain to worry about the addict engaging in self-harm, acting strangely, harming them, or simply being inaccessible.
Unusual thinking	Addicts may tend to view the addiction as a saving grace in their lives, rather than being self-destructive. A shopper might think that one can never have enough pairs of shoes, a marijuana addict might believe that he or she drives more safely due to use, or a food binger might believe that he or she deserves to let go and have a "celebratory" meal.
Negative emotional consequences	If the person loses control over their behavior, suffers calamities due to the addiction, and becomes isolated socially, he or she is likely also to tend to feel a loss of self-esteem, suffer from sleep problems, and feel depressed and anxious as well.
Tolerance	Needing more of the behavior to achieve an appetitive effect may be perceived by some addicts as risky, more expensive, and uncomfortable.
Withdrawal-like symptoms	Experiencing irritability and difficulty concentrating are hallmark symptoms of withdrawal across addictions and could be considered negative consequences. One's performance and mood are likely to be impaired.
Relapse	Relapse implies failure to be able to maintain a course of action, and so tends to be perceived negatively by multiple parties (the addict, significant others, treatment institutions).

Five "addiction-specific" types of negative consequences

Financial problems	Financial problems may operate across several addictions, particularly regarding tobacco, alcohol, and illicit drug misuse; binge eating; shopping; sex; and gambling. However it is less likely that financial problems operate with Internet addiction, exercise addiction, love addiction, or workaholism. In fact, workaholics are likely to earn more than their peers, unless they "burn out."

(cont.)

Table 4.1 *(cont.)*

Five "addiction-specific" types of negative consequences	
Role consequences	Role consequences may not operate across all addictions. For example, a young workaholic or exercise addict may be perceived as excelling in their role as employee or athlete. However, to the extent that an addiction dominates one's life, it would encroach on one's other roles as spouse, parent, supportive friend, student, or possibly co-worker. Hence, role consequences may or may not be experienced across addictions depending on the extent to which the addiction dominates one's life.
Legal difficulties	Legal difficulties are relatively likely to occur for those addicted to alcohol and illicit drugs (public drunkenness in many countries, drunk and disorderly, DUI, illegal drug use). However, food addicts, exercise addicts, workaholics, and shopaholics are unlikely to experience problems in terms of legality.
Physical danger	One may become a physical danger (to self or others) regarding cigarette smoking (accidental fires caused by lit cigarettes), and alcohol and illicit drug use are well known to lead to dangerous circumstance (e.g., car accidents). Gambling and sex addictions could lead to physical danger if one interacts with criminal elements while engaging in these pursuits. However, it is probably not the case that food, Internet (unless texting while driving), love, exercise, work, or shopping addictions will immediately and directly result in physical danger.
Medical consequences	Medical consequences are particularly related to cigarette smoking, alcohol use, illicit drug use, food addiction, exercise addiction (injuries from overtraining), and possibly from sex addictions (STDs, HIV). Indirect medical consequences (e.g., obesity, or inadequate nutrition, chronic sleep deprivation) from gambling addiction, Internet or other electronic addictions, or work addictions could result from living a sedentary but addiction-focused lifestyle. Shopping and love addictions probably do not lead to negative medical consequences.
Addiction definition components as consequences	
Preoccupation	To the extent that preoccupation interferes with enjoyment or successful fulfillment of other events, it would be a negative consequence. An addiction may "take up space" in one's working memory, cloud one's thinking, inhibit one from making self-fulfilling decisions, and diminish alternative activity choices one may make.

"Universal" Types of Negative Consequences

Table 4.1 *(cont.)*

Addiction definition components as consequences	
Loss of control	Loss of control affects a person's ability to reliably predict when the behavior will begin, what its topography will look like, or when it will end. Thus, there may be an unexpected number of alcoholic drinks or calories consumed, overload from working out, unexpected amount of money spent gambling, and unreliable prediction of degree of safety and number of hours when participating in any of these activities.
Dramatic negative consequences	
Death or serious injury	These consequences appear with certain addictions (tobacco, alcohol, illicit drugs), and may tend to engulf the field, and pull attention away from other addictions which lead to serious but not so dramatic consequences.

deserves to let go and have a "celebratory" meal may all be said to be illustrating such unusual thoughts.

Third, eventual *negative emotional consequences* likely ensue across addictions (e.g., Grant & Odlaug, 2014). If the person loses control over their behavior, suffers calamities due to the addiction, or becomes isolated socially, he or she likely also is going to tend to feel a loss of self-esteem, suffer from sleep problems, and feel lonely, depressed, and anxious as well. Suicidal ideation is a related consequence of addiction (e.g., Kim et al., 2006 regarding Internet addiction; Petry & Kiluk, 2002 regarding pathological gambling).

Fourth and fifth, *tolerance* and *withdrawal-like symptoms* are defining features of all of these addictions (Griffiths, 2008), could be considered as constituents of preoccupation (Sussman & Sussman, 2011), and/or could be considered as two negative consequences prevalent across the addictions (Rosenberg & Feder, 2014a, 2014b). Needing more of the behavior to achieve an appetitive effect may be perceived by some addicts as more expensive and uncomfortable. Also, experiencing irritability and difficulty concentrating upon abrupt termination of the behavior, hallmark symptoms of (psychological or physiological) withdrawal across addictions, certainly could be considered undesired consequences.

Finally, *relapse* may be considered a universal negative consequence and definitive of addictive behaviors (Griffiths, 2008). Continuing to engage in the addictive behavior after suffering numerous negative consequences, and trying to quit but repeatedly failing to do so, often has been considered a criterion of psychological or physiological dependence (Marlatt, 1985). Stopping the behavior becomes difficult for several reasons, including influence of the cognitive salience of immediate gratification resulting from the addictive behavior (i.e., satiation, precluding thoughts about other activities) relative to its delayed adverse effects, and insufficient coping skills or practice. Relapse implies failure to be able to maintain a course of action, and so tends to be perceived negatively by multiple parties (the addict, significant others, treatment institutions).

Consequences of Addiction

Five Other "Addiction-Specific" Types of Negative Consequences

Consequences of addictions do vary by type of addiction and individual-contextual characteristics, and are also shown in Table 4.1. First, it is not likely that *financial problems* operate with Internet addiction (that is, if the person is not gambling, shopping, paying for a myriad of online games, buying the newest Internet equipment on which to play games, or paying for pornography online), possibly exercise addiction (although some exercise addicts do spend a lot of money on entry fees, equipment, treatments for injuries, travel to competitions, as well as losing missed opportunities at work due to exercise/competition commitments), love addiction (unless the person lavishes gifts on their love object), or workaholism. In fact, workaholics, in particular, are likely to earn more than their peers, unless they "burn out" (Sussman, 2012a).

Financial problems may operate across several other addictions, however, particularly regarding tobacco use (a pack a day smoker might spend $2,600 per year on cigarettes; e.g., see www.ibtimes.com/price-cigarettes-how-much-does-pack-cost-each-us-state-map-1553445), alcohol, and illicit drug misuse (and potential related legal fees); binge eating; shopping; sex; and gambling (e.g., Grant & Odlaug, 2014). Here, though, financial consequences may be considered to be excessive to society but not by the individual, if the individual earns a great deal of money. The consequences may be considered excessive to the individual and to the society at large if the individual earns very little. I speculate that the highest consensus on financial consequences pertains to alcohol use, illicit drug use, gambling, sex, and shopping addictions.

Role consequences (e.g., as co-worker, spouse, parent) may not operate across all addictions. It is not clear that there would be negative role consequences for cigarette smoking in many countries, though smoke-free office locations and campuses may be resulting in some disruption in role fulfillment (and higher quit rates; Sussman et al., 2013a). It also is not clear whether or not food addiction limits one's roles, except to the extent other aspects of one's behavior are involved (e.g., obesity, or "noticeable" purging or overeating). It is doubtful that there would be a negative role impact on exercise, work, or shopping addictions, though arguably there might be such consequences at the extremes of dependence. One would appear to be getting in good health, and be a good provider and consumer. Again, at the extremes, of course, any of these addictions might have an impact on the ability to carry out one's roles (e.g., Racine et al., 2014). For example, exercise addicts may lose relationships and jobs due to focusing their lives around their exercise (e.g., Lease & Bond, 2013).

Alcohol and illicit drug addictions, on the other hand, likely interfere dramatically with one's role as friend, co-worker, provider, spouse, or parent. Gambling may interfere with one's role as a provider, spouse, parent, or co-worker, depending on its impact on household finances, absences from home, or using company funds to pay for gambling debts (e.g., Grant & Odlaug, 2014). Likewise, involvement with the Internet could impact one's ability to hold on to responsibilities depending on how much time it takes away from engaging in other activities (e.g., Auer & Griffiths, 2015).

"Addiction-Specific" Types of Negative Consequences

Love or sex addictions may become disruptive to one's roles as a parent and spouse if they involve the need to search out third parties (e.g., "cheating"). Also, it may disrupt one's long-term relationships (i.e., once the "spark is gone"). In summary, role consequences may or may not be experienced across addictions depending on the extent to which it dominates one's life.

Legal difficulties are relatively likely to occur for those addicted to alcohol and illicit drugs (public drunkenness in many countries, drunk and disorderly, DUI, illegal drug use). Such consequences could also apply to those who violate cigarette no-smoking policies (if enforced). Those who gamble might wind up violating laws and get caught (e.g., embezzling office funds to pay off gambling debt). If one travels onto illicit Internet sites (e.g., child pornography), or pays for sex (or "love") in illegal ways, one may suffer such consequences. However, food addicts, exercise addicts, workaholics, and shopaholics are unlikely to experience problems in terms of legality (unless shopaholics become shoplifters; Racine et al., 2014).

One may be an immediate *physical danger* (to self or others) if one is addicted to cigarette smoking (half of all accidental fires are caused by lit cigarettes). Also, alcohol and illicit drug use are well known to lead to dangerous circumstances (and account for 20–50 percent of all fatal car accidents; Penning, Veldstra, Daamen, Olivier, & Verster, 2010; Sussman & Ames, 2008). Gambling and sex addictions could lead to physical danger if one interacts with dangerous criminal elements while engaging in these pursuits. However, it is probably not the case that food, Internet (unless texting while driving), love, exercise, work, or shopping addictions will *immediately* and *directly* result in physical consequences. It is unlikely that TV addiction is immediately physically hazardous, unless one has a TV in one's car.

Finally, one may suffer from serious negative *medical consequences* from substance and behavioral addictions, particularly related to cigarette smoking, alcohol use, illicit drug use, food addiction, exercise addiction (injuries from overtraining), and possibly from sex addictions (STDs, HIV). Indirect medical consequences (e.g., obesity or inadequate nutrition, chronic sleep deprivation) from gambling addiction, Internet or other electronic addictions, or work addictions could result from living a sedentary, addiction-focused lifestyle (e.g., Grant & Odlaug, 2014; Weinstein et al., 2014). However, such medical consequences may not occur directly and immediately for active persons who are addicted to gambling, Internet, or work, and it is not likely that medical consequences will occur for people suffering from shopping or love addictions. A matrix of 13 negative consequences of addiction by 11 addictions (tobacco, alcohol, illicit drugs, food, gambling, Internet, love, sex, exercise, work, and shopping) is shown in Table 4.2.

Consequences of TV Addiction

One example of an electronic addiction which may lead to many indirect negative medical consequences is television addiction (Kubey & Csikszentmihalyi, 2002; Sussman & Moran, 2013). Television viewing has remained for over 50 years the most

Table 4.2 Negative consequences of addiction by type of addiction

Negative consequence	\multicolumn{11}{c}{The "11 focal addictions"}
	Tobacco	Alcohol	Drugs	Food	Gambling	WWW	Love	Sex	Exer.	Work	Shop
Preoccupation	X	X	X	X	X	X	X	X	X	X	X
Loss of control	X	X	X	X	X	X	X	X	X	X	X
Social	?	X	X	?	X	X	X	X	X	X	X
Unusual thinking	X	X	X	X	X	X	X	X	X	X	X
Negative emotion	X	X	X	X	X	X	X	X	X	X	X
Tolerance	X	X	X	X	X	X	X	X	X	X	X
Withdrawal-like	X	X	X	X	X	X	X	X	X	X	X
Relapse	X	X	X	X	X	X	X	X	X	X	X
Financial	?	X	X	?	X	?	?	?	?	No	X
Role	?	X	X	?	X	?	X	X	No	No	No
Legal	X	X	X	No	?	?	?	X	No	No	No
Physical danger	X	X	X	No	?	No	No	?	No	No	No
Direct medical	X	X	X	X	No	No	No	X	X	No	No

Notes: X = consequence applies to this addiction; ? = consequence may apply to this addiction in some cases; No = consequence likely does not apply to this addiction; WWW = Internet addiction; Exer. = exercise addiction.

popular form of leisure activity in the United States (an average of 2.8 hours per day is spent viewing TV in the general population; US Bureau of Labor Statistics, 2012), as well as in Australia and Western Europe (e.g., www.hsph.harvard.edu/obesity-prevention-source/obesity-causes/television-and-sedentary-behavior-and-obesity/). Wide variation exists regarding what is considered heavy viewing, and the addictive aspect is more a function of interference with completion of life tasks rather than number of hours of viewing per se (Horvath, 2004). Furthermore, television has several positive features. TV viewing may facilitate relationship bonding (e.g., family gathering around the television). That is, television viewing can be a communal experience, as many television viewers come together to view and discuss programs. Also, a considerable body of evidence indicates that television operates as a form of entertainment-education and is a source of health information for many viewers (see Sussman & Moran, 2013, for a review).

However, just as alcohol use may serve a social lubrication function but is a source of drug dependence for some people, so might TV operate differentially. Although TV addiction may occur in some people but not others, TV addiction is perceived as a reality among a majority of research study participants (though research subjects generally have only been university students; McIlwraith, 1998). Negative consequences of heavy TV viewing and addiction mentioned in a cursory search of the literature include: (a) creating political or social biases (e.g., regarding presidential candidates, racial stereotyping) and shaping or increasing purchasing behavior, (b) increasing aggression or fear of being victimized, (c) leading to attention and cognitive deficits (e.g., may contribute to ADHD), (d) possibly having a negative impact on academic achievement at least at extreme levels of viewing, (e) predicting later cigarette smoking, (f) sleep difficulties, (g) avoidance of relationship maintenance, (h) lower life satisfaction, (i) poorer body image (among women), and (j) sedentary lifestyle leading to lower cardiorespiratory fitness, elevated serum cholesterol and obesity (Sussman & Moran, 2013). Regarding the last consequence, for example, children aged 8–16 who watched four or more hours of TV per day were found to have greater body fat and body mass index than those who watched less than two hours per day; Hancox, Milne, & Poulton, 2004; McIlwraith, Jacobvitz, Kubey, & Alexander, 1991). In fact, persons who watch six hours of television per day have been found to live an average of 4.8 fewer years than lighter or non-viewers (Veerman et al., 2012).

Dramatic Negative Consequences of Substance and Behavioral Addictions

The most dramatic consequence of the addictions is death. For example, alcohol can become lethal when the ***blood alcohol content*** (BAC, grams of alcohol per deciliter of blood) reaches about 0.35–0.40 percent. The ratio of lethal dose to effective (to experience a "high") dose for alcohol is 10.0 (where the effective dose is the equivalent of two 12-ounce beers). The lethal-to-effective dose is shown for 11 drugs in Table 4.3.

Table 4.3 The ratio of lethal dose to effective dose for different drugs

Drug	Lethal dose : effective dose
Heroin	5.0
GHB	8.0
Alcohol	10.0
Cocaine	15.0
XTC	16.0
Codeine	20.0
Mescaline	24.0
Rohypnol	30.0
Nitrous oxide	150.0
Nicotine	250.0
LSD	1000.0
Marijuana	1000.0

Several drugs exert lethal levels of intake alone or in combination with other drugs (particularly common is a mixture of alcohol with pills such as barbiturates or benzodiazepines; Sussman & Ames, 2008). Of course, accidental drug overdoses can occur among non-addicts.

Non-drug addictions are not likely to result in overdoses. Deaths occur only as indirect effects of behavioral addictions (e.g., not paying off a gambling debt to a loan shark, continual binge eating over a period of years, watching lots of TV and not being active over many years). Thus, it is easier to see why non-drug addictions have tended to become relatively ignored in the addictions literature.

Another related but somewhat less dramatic consequence is psychological or bodily damage (Orford, 2001; Sussman & Ames, 2001). Most drugs of abuse can cause injury and lead to psychosis, many have cardiovascular and digestive system complications (e.g., depressants, stimulants, steroids; alcohol can lead to alcoholic liver disease, or other liver problems), some cause lung damage (e.g., inhalants, nicotine embedded in tobacco smoke, THC embedded in cannabis smoke), and some are carcinogenic (e.g., nicotine in tobacco, THC embedded in cannabis smoke; alcohol use may be associated with cancers of the digestive and excretory systems). One of the most preferred inhalants is toluene, which is a solvent used in adhesives such as airplane glue, aerosols such as spray paint, and commercial solvents such as paint thinner. Its long-term use can greatly injure functioning of the cerebellum. Chronic use of amphetamines and cocaine may result in the at least temporary (four months to three years) loss of approximately 20 percent of dopamine receptors in the **nucleus accumbens** (consists of the caudate and putamen and is a region in the basal forebrain rostral to the preoptic area of the hypothalamus; it is an initial "station" for mesolimbic dopamine that runs up the medial forebrain bundle from where it is manufactured in the ventral tegmental area), or alter dopamine transporter density (e.g., McCann et al., 1998; Volkow et al., 2001).

These consequences also are unlikely to occur outside of drug addiction. One exception is that overuse of exercise could result in **rhabdomyolysis** (death of muscle tissue, myoglobin released into the bloodstream, which can cause kidney damage). Excessive exercise also can elicit cardiac events, deep vein thrombosis, or compartment syndrome (excessive pressure build-up in localized area of body, often due to injury; e.g., see Landau, Kenney, Deuster, & Campbell, 2012; Waterman et al., 2013).

Physical (bodily) consequences may result due *secondarily* to the addiction (e.g., sedentary lifestyle of TV addiction, as noted in the previous section). Again, since tobacco, alcohol, and other drug use may exert direct and often obvious physiological withdrawal symptoms, and directly lead to death and injury, these addictions tend to "engulf the field" when we consider the scope of addictive behaviors.

More on Variations in Consequences as a Function of Context

As alluded to previously in this chapter (e.g., workaholism in a young versus older person), negative consequences may vary across contexts (see Sussman & Sussman, 2011). For example, arrests for drinking and driving may not be well enforced in some countries (e.g., some rural areas in Southeast Asia), or may be enforced very strictly in other countries (e.g., Sweden). Thus, the legal consequences related to drinking alcohol may vary across contexts. As a second example, marijuana use is now legal in several states in the United States, though it was not legal in any state a couple of years ago. One will not be arrested now in these states for possession of small amounts of marijuana in one's home. However, a person may be arrested if they use marijuana in adjacent states. Physical consequences may vary likewise (e.g., there may be fewer injuries and deaths related to drinking and driving in locations where drinking-driving laws are well enforced).

Also, the social consequences of alcohol use and other addictions vary across history and cultures. Thus, when considering at least some of these consequences (role or social, in particular), one should note that they are not invariant (i.e., may not represent a **natural kind**; Williams, 2011; may reflect folk psychology conceptions, learned through experience; Churchland, 1981). To the extent that negative consequences of different addictive behaviors are considered inherent in the addictions themselves, as opposed to being a function of lifestyle factors within time and place, is to suggest that they do represent a sort of natural kind, apart from human interpretation. Certainly, drug overdoses will occur if enough of a certain type of drug is imbibed; this occurs regardless of time and place, and interpretation, and reflects a natural kind of sorts. Arguably, preoccupation, loss of control, tolerance, withdrawal, and relapse type constituents or consequences of addictions appear to occur regardless of time and place – though the "cut-off" values for "real" loss of control, for example, may be a function of culture; at the extremes there is much less question (Sussman & Ames, 2008).

How Should Morality Be Appraised Pertaining to the Addictions?

Behavior that may be considered immoral may or may not be addictive (e.g., paying for sex). Some behavior that may generally not be considered immoral may be considered as such when engaged in addictively (e.g., excessive alcohol consumption). Other behavior, even in the throes of addiction, may not be automatically considered immoral (e.g., workaholism, TV addiction). Still, even though there are addictive behaviors that generally are not considered immoral, as soon as the behavior is explicitly considered to be an extreme, an "addiction," it is possible that it might then be considered somehow immoral (i.e., wrongful, wicked, unprincipled).

Recently, *reintegrative shaming* has been considered a means of recovery or restorative justice. The notion is to shame the behavior (e.g., addiction, or other "deviant" act), but not the "offender" him- or herself. Indeed, persons in drug recovery tend to focus more on shame over their behavior and redeemed relationships, and those still using tend to focus more on others who are shaming them (Woodward, Misis, & Griffin, 2014). Also, morality of drug use has been found to be a mediator of the relations between spirituality and drug use (Sussman et al., 2013b); that is, spirituality is positively associated with immorality of drug use, which then may lead to lower drug use. Thus, there may be (equivocal) support for the utility of reintegrative shaming as a device of restorative justice. Still, there is a danger of stigma as a consequence of utilizing an approach like reintegrative shaming; many persons suffering from addictions avoid treatment to avoid humiliation (Woodward et al., 2014).

There is an enormous stigma associated with being an addict (Leshner, 1997); people commonly believe that drug addicts are bad people, weak-willed, immoral, or selfish (Sussman & Ames, 2008). If a stigma perspective was accurate (i.e., "addicts are bad people"), and the prevalence estimates calculated in the present text are also accurate (47 percent of the adult US population suffers from at least one addiction in a 12-month period), one might conclude that almost half of US adults are "bad people" (Sussman et al., 2011b). It is not clear that researchers, practitioners, or lay persons are willing to believe that generalization. Possibly, imparting a general awareness of the potentially high prevalence of the addictions could lower stigma associated with the condition (assuming that stigma is prefaced based in part on the assumption of low prevalence). Alternatively, social condemnation may not be of "addiction" per se, but only of certain extremes of addiction that may reasonably lead to negative social reactions (e.g., working long hours without bathing).

Larkin et al. (2006) argue that health professionals must be careful not to attach the pejorative label of "addiction" to people who, while they are heavily involved in, or strongly identified with, a particular activity, are not suffering unpleasant consequences. Additionally, as Larkin et al. (2006) note, unless people are at obvious risk for experiencing physical, emotional, relational, and financial difficulties as a result of their activity, it is both pointless and unfair to describe them as suffering from a disease-like condition.

Summary

In summary, negative consequences common to addictions likely include preoccupation, loss of control, social consequences, unusual thinking, emotional consequences, tolerance, withdrawal, and relapse. Negative consequences that are likely to vary as a function of addiction include financial, role, legal, physical, and medical. All of the consequences presented in this chapter are summarized in Tables 4.1 or 4.2. While I may have argued persuasively in favor of grouping these consequences into common versus addictive behavior type-specific sets, at the extremes of an addictive behavior, we might argue that most or all of the above consequences apply to some extent (e.g., financial and role consequences, being secondary to work burnout; regarding substance addictions, heavy use may result in consequences in many life domains; Rehm et al., 2013). However, it is still reasonable to believe – at least away from the extremes of behavior – that some consequences occur across addictions, but many of them may vary over time and place, or may be addictive behavior type-specific.

It is curious that addiction may be so highly prevalent. At present, most professionals consider addiction to be a chronic, relapsing disease (e.g., Leshner, 1997; Sussman & Ames, 2008), similar to other chronic disorders such as hypertension or asthma (O'Brien & McLellan, 1996). Therefore, it becomes imperative to distinguish whether or not addiction is a very common disease-like phenomenon (perhaps as common as some types of flu), or whether, with such apparently high prevalence, addiction reflects some other or additional (multiple) phenomena. For example, perhaps addiction also is a condition of lifestyle modeled by social-environmental conditions (Alexander, 2012; Brown, 2014; Sussman & Ames, 2008), possibly with critical periods of development making individuals most vulnerable to imprint an addictive lifestyle (Sussman & Arnett, 2014; Volkow & Wise, 2005). If addiction is popularly learned by victims, differing in objects of addiction by accessibility to the objects, social circumstances, time demands, and other social-environmental or developmental forces (recall the PACE model in Chapter 3), then arguably social policy changes are needed that could inhibit or redirect such excessive behavior away from self-destructive outcomes throughout the lifespan, and channel behavior in more constructive directions (see Griffiths, 2009a; Orford, 2001; Marks, 1990; Schaef, 1987).

One may now understand potential convergence of different notions of addictions by taking an appetitive effects perspective (Chapters 1 and 2). Also, one may now consider multiple levels of etiology of the addictions (Chapter 3) that might be integrated by such means as the PACE model. One may also begin to consider patterns of consequences across different addictions (Chapter 4). Now, one is prepared for Part II of this text. Part II will focus more on the empirical overlap and non-overlap of participation in substance and behavioral addictions, and their assessment.

Bulleted Summary

- While also definitive of addiction, preoccupation and loss of control may interfere with other life demands, and may be a source of worry. They, too, may be negative consequences of all addictions.
- There are at least six other universal consequences of an addictive behavior: negative social reactions from others, unusual thinking, negative emotional outcomes, tolerance and withdrawal-like symptoms (which might be viewed as aspects of preoccupation), and relapse (which might be viewed as an aspect of loss of control).
- Five consequences that tend to vary in prevalence across different addictions are: financial debt, role consequences, legal consequences, physical damage, and medical consequences.
- Negative consequences may vary as a function of various contextual factors including region (e.g., enforcement may vary, availability of public transportation may vary, attitudes toward addictions may vary) and time (e.g., legality of some drugs changes over time).
- Persons in recovery from an addiction may focus on shame over their behavior and redeemed relationships, whereas those still using may focus more on others who are shaming them. Stigma is a consequence that operates on socially disapproved addictions, or perhaps of socially tolerated addictions at their extremes (e.g., the extremes of shopaholism).

Suggestions for Further Reading

Jacobs, D. F. (1986). A general theory of addictions: A new theoretical model. *Journal of Gambling Behavior*, 2: 15–31.

Veerman, J. L., Healy, G. N., Cobiac, L. J., Vos, T., Winkler, E. A. H., Owen, N., & Dunstan, D. W. (2012). Television viewing time and reduced life expectancy: A life table analysis. *British Journal of Sports Medicine*, 46: 927–930.

Volkow, N. D., Chang, L., Wang, G.-J., Fowler, J. S., Ding, Y.-S., Sedler, M., ... & Pappas, N. (2001). Low level of brain dopamine D2 receptors in methamphetamine abusers: Association with metabolism in the orbitofrontal cortex. *American Journal of Psychiatry*, 158: 2015–2021.

Woodward, V. H., Misis, M. L., & Griffin, O. H. (2014). Examining the effects of social bonds and shame on drug recovery within an on-line support community. *Deviant Behavior*, 35: 938–958.

PART II

Types of Addictions

5 Types of Addictions: General Overview

Learning Objectives

- To learn a 16-category, exhaustive set of types of addictive behaviors
- To learn how types of addictive behaviors may fit into different sets of appetitive motives
- To learn how multiple addictions might be measured through use of an addiction matrix-type measure
- To learn why the remainder of the text presents primarily 11 "focal" addictions

Introduction

Johnny felt like he had been addicted to several different substances (alcohol, marijuana, other drugs, food) and behaviors (love, television, exercise, and work) in the course of his teenage or adult life. All of these addictive behaviors felt to Johnny like they accomplished satiation effects, relief from a state of "wanting," complemented each other, but involved preoccupation with them, loss of control, and consequences he worried about.

The only American Psychiatric Association (2013) officially recognized addictions are to substances (e.g., tobacco, alcohol, and other drugs) and gambling, though there are several other addictions that are recognized and on which research is being encouraged and conducted. In particular, the current Diagnostic and Statistical Manual of Mental Disorders (DSM-V; APA, 2013, pp. 795–798) discusses Internet gaming disorder as a condition for future study. In addition, other behavioral addictions, using the examples of sex addiction, exercise addiction, and shopping addiction, are mentioned but are not included at the present time due to insufficient peer-reviewed evidence to establish the diagnostic criteria and course descriptions needed to identify those behaviors as mental disorders (APA, 2013, p. 481). In Chapter 5, I wish to present material which goes beyond the current established system that identifies addictions. I present many types of addictions that have been self-reported and which should be at least mentioned here. Each type, by definition, would produce a "rush," temporary induction of satiation of some type of appetitive need, leading eventually to preoccupation with the addiction, loss of control, and negative consequences

(Sussman & Sussman, 2011). There is no consensus on how many specific types of addictive behaviors there are or how to classify addictions into more general categories.

However, in this chapter I will make an attempt at establishing all types or categories of addictions. In the next section I attempt to provide an exhaustive catalogue of addictions based on a Google search (Sussman, 2012b), which resulted in 16 categories. I discuss each category and whether or not the category was mentioned in any section of the DSM Manual. I also attempt to group these classes of addiction into types of appetitive motives.

General types or categories of addictions also have been attempted from empirical examination of the self-reported occurrence or co-occurrence of different addictions. Next, I discuss the empirical work examining multiple addictions, which has tended to use a matrix measure (i.e., single items to tap each addiction). Finally, I present the 11 specific addictions which are the focus of the remainder of this text and may reflect the majority of addictions in which people engage (the 11 "focal" addictions; Sussman et al., 2011b, 2014).

Speculation: A Catalogue of Addictions

To attempt to generate a (reasonably) exhaustive list of addictions, I engaged in an electronic search focusing on different types of addictions indicated on different websites (Sussman, 2012b). I used the key words "types of addictions," "types of addiction," "addictions list," and "addiction list" (June 5, 2012) examining Google, Google Scholar, OVID Medline, and PSYCInfo electronic search engines. Most websites or articles focused on one or two types of addictions. However, there were some websites and articles that addressed three or more types of addictions (e.g., www.addictionz.com/addictions.htm, suggesting 131 types of addictions). I merged specific addictive behaviors together (e.g., there were many types of hard drug use categories) into 16 general categories (e.g., similarly to what was found by Cook, 1987). The intention of engaging in this grouping was to examine what the websites indicated as being the breadth of addictive behaviors, as follows (I did the grouping, so certainly this was a flawed albeit heuristic exercise). These 16 addiction categories are summarized in Table 5.1.

1. Drug misuse. The first category is drug misuse, involving caffeine, tobacco, alcohol, marijuana, and various other illicit/hard drugs (e.g., prescription drugs, amphetamines, opioids, cocaine, XTC) (5 subcategories). Drugs are the mainstay of "addiction" conceptualizations, research, and practice (Orford, 2001).

2. Food-related. The second category is food-related. This category includes binge eating, use of diuretics, eating carbohydrates, hot peppers, fat, chocolate, ice, and "inedible objects" imbibed like food (e.g., dirt, toilet paper, chalk, household cleanser, gasoline, tape) (8 subcategories). Food-related objects may provide a direct neurobiological impact, or possibly an indirect one, e.g., an anticipatory response in brain regions such as the caudate – achieved via the novelty of the object that is ingested (see Yau et al., 2014; Gearhardt et al., 2011). More than 60 percent of higher frequency

Speculation: A Catalogue of Addictions

Table 5.1 Sixteen addictive behavior categories

Drug misuse	5 subcategories: Caffeine, tobacco, alcohol, marijuana, and various other illicit/hard drugs.
Food-related addiction	8 subcategories: Binge eating, use of diuretics, carbohydrates, hot peppers, fat, chocolate, ice, and "inedible objects."
Compulsive antisocial behavior	3 subcategories: Compulsive aggression, compulsive stealing, and compulsive fire setting.
Technology/communications related addiction	6 subcategories: Internet browsing, SNS, texting, telephone or smartphone, online and offline video games, and television.
Gambling addiction	The first behavioral addiction officially recognized as such by the American Psychiatric Association.
Working addiction	"Workaholism" involves negative social, emotional, and health consequences.
Relationships (sex/love)	8 subcategories: Sex, love, platonic relationships, codependence, being "cool," attention/applause, compulsive helping, and maintaining authority/control.
Physical attractiveness	4 subcategories: Tanning (tanorexia), teeth whitening, make-up, and cosmetic surgery.
Fantasizing	3 subcategories: Imagination, isolation, and laziness (i.e., under-achieving, being sedentary).
Exercise-related	2 subcategories: Aerobics and body building.
Spiritual obsession	4 subcategories: Occult, religion, self-help programs, and treatment seeking.
Pain seeking	5 subcategories: Cutting, self-mutilation, skin picking, trichotillomania (hair pulling), and scab picking.
Shopping	Compulsive buying disorder (CBD) has been categorized as an impulse control disorder, an example of OCD, a mood disorder, and a behavioral addiction.
Thrill/adventure seeking	4 subcategories: Auto-racing, cruising around in a car, dangerous sports, and thrills (compulsive sky diving, riding roller coasters).
Hoarding	8 subcategories: Anime/comics/cards, small collectables, rocks, puppets, coins, junk, trivia, and technology objects.
Voyeurism (i.e., "drama")	3 subcategories: Celebrity or other idolization, gossiping, and attending funerals

binge-eating disordered persons are likely food addicts (Gearhardt et al., 2012). It should be mentioned that eating of non-nutritive, non-food substances is referred to as ***pica*** in the DSM-V (APA, 2013, p. 329), a feeding and eating disorder rather than an addiction. Likewise binge eating disorder, and such behaviors as use of diuretics (part of anorexia nervosa) also are in the DSM-V as being feeding and eating disorders (APA, 2013, p. 350 and p. 341). Also, it should be noted that only 25 percent of persons identified as suffering from "obesity" show signs of having an eating addiction

(Davis et al., 2011). Thus, it is not surprising that obesity does not load on a common factor with nicotine, alcohol, drug, and gambling addictions (see Blanco et al., 2015).

3. Antisocial behavior. The third category refers to involvement in compulsive antisocial behavior: compulsive aggression (violence), compulsive stealing (also see Cuzen & Stein, 2014), and compulsive fire setting (3 subcategories). For example, kleptomania is characterized by an urge and preoccupation with stealing objects (often the same object which is not needed, and may not even be used) to achieve reduction in tension and pleasure during or following the action (Cuzen & Stein, 2014). Frequently, **kleptomania** is experienced as excessive and unwanted, but occurs over and over again, leading eventually to negative consequences (e.g., frustration, legal problems). Currently, kleptomania is considered as part of the DSM-V category of disruptive, impulse-control, and conduct disorders (APA, 2013, p. 478). For a second example, Bergen-Cico, Haygood-El, Jennings-Bey, and Lane (2013) provided a qualitative analysis of 12 men with histories of street crime and gang affiliation, who described themselves as being addicted to the action of the streets (***street addiction***; including preoccupation, loss of control, used to escape problems, and negative consequences).

4. Technology. The fourth category refers to addictions that are technology/communications related: Internet browsing, social networking sites (SNS), texting, telephone or smartphone, online and offline video games, and television (6 subcategories). For example, one may feel a subjective craving to view television a great deal to achieve a sense of satiation, become preoccupied with the idea of viewing television, not be able to predict how long one will watch TV (loss of control), and suffer negative life consequences as a result (Lee, Lee, & Kim, 2015; Sussman & Moran, 2013; Sussman & Sussman, 2011). Griffiths (2000a) argued that there is a need to distinguish between addictions *to* the Internet and addictions *on* the Internet (e.g., gambling, computer gaming, love, or sex). Of course, some behaviors engaged on the Internet (e.g., cybersex, cyberstalking, romance chat on the Internet) may be behaviors that the person would only carry out on the Internet because the medium may be perceived as anonymous, non-face-to-face, and disinhibiting (Griffiths, 2000a, 2000b; Young, 1996).

5. Gambling. The fifth category pertains to gambling. As previously mentioned, gambling disorder is the first behavioral addiction officially recognized as such by the American Psychiatric Association (APA, 2013). A unique aspect of gambling addiction is the cognitive misperception that one can "get even with the house" by continuing to gamble. It does not seem to be the case that such thinking operates in the other categories.

6. Workaholism. The sixth category is working ("workaholism"). While there is some debate regarding the parameters of the concept, and the extent to which it is an addiction with negative consequences, workaholism as a negative consequential addiction involves excessive time spent working, preoccupation with work to the exclusion of other life domains, loss of control over the parameters of one's work, and disenchantment with work (with "compulsive" workaholism), and negative social, emotional, and health consequences (Sussman, 2012a). A related, recently suggested addiction is "study addiction," which is viewed as an "offshoot" of workaholism and which satisfies the six component model criteria (Atroszko, Andreassen, Griffiths, & Pallesen, 2015).

7. Social group-related. The seventh category is social group-related: sex, love, platonic relationships, codependence (people-pleasing, hiding behind others), being "cool," garnishing attention/applause, compulsive helping, and maintaining authority/control (8 subcategories). For example, **love addiction** indicates a constricted pattern of repetitive behavior directed toward a love object that leads to negative role, social, safety, or legal consequences (Sussman, 2010a). It appears to involve brain neurotransmission processes similar to the effects of drug misuse, and may be a substitute addiction for drug misuse for some persons (Yoder, 1990). It appears to reflect most closely an anxious-ambivalent attachment style (Feeney & Noller, 1990), as opposed to a confident or avoidant style. It is likely depicted and promoted in the popular media as "ideal love" or "true love."

8. Physical appearance. The eighth category is physical attractiveness: tanning (tanorexia), teeth whitening, make-up, and cosmetic surgery (4 subcategories) (e.g., Kourosh et al., 2010). Tanorexia was described in Chapter 2 as a seldom-studied addictive disorder. If tanning or other such behaviors are intended as attempted solutions to **body dysmorphic disorder** (self-perceived defects in physical appearance not readily obvious to others), then it might be placed within the obsessive-compulsive related disorders category rather than in an addictions category, according to the DSM-V (APA, 2013, p. 242). Foster, Shorter, and Griffiths (2015) suggest that muscle dysmorphia, and attempts to make the body look stronger or more attractive could represent an addiction to body image (ABI), meeting all the six criteria put forward by Griffiths (2005a, 2008) and mentioned in Chapter 1 (six component model), namely salience, mood modification, tolerance, withdrawal symptoms, conflict, and relapse.

9. Fantasy. The ninth category is fantasizing: imagination (may also involve isolating, under-achieving, being sedentary) (3 subcategories, assuming that isolating, under-achieving, and being sedentary are addictions that also reflect involvement in fantasizing). There is almost no research about this category, though there are several websites and chat rooms that pertain to it (e.g., www.selfgrowth.com/articles/how-to-recover-from-fantasy-addiction; http://answers.psychcentral.com/General_Other/addiction-to-fantasy-1/). Fantasy-prone individuals tend to turn their attention inward, focusing on a rich internal world of imaginary people or stories, vivid memories or dreams, and emotions cued by internal stimuli (Cuper & Lynch, 2009). While fantasy is often considered a symptom of other addictions (e.g., gambling, love, or sex), this addiction can exist separately, and interfere with getting work done, limit one's social and family life, and cause great distress over time. Possibly a case example of addiction to fortune-telling reflects this category (if not spiritual obsession, the eleventh category below). One may fantasize about being able to foresee the future, and crave means to do that, and then seek out fortune-tellers. One may achieve a "buzz" seeking out the next experience, become preoccupied with fortune-tellers and fantasy, lose control over this behavior, and suffer financial, social, emotional, or other consequences (see Grall-Bronnec et al., 2015).

10. Exercise. The tenth category is exercise-related: aerobics (endurance) and body building (2 subcategories). Exercise addiction, at one time considered a "positive addiction" by some clinicians (e.g., Glasser, 1976), may lead to repeated injuries and neglect of work and family life. Amongst the scattering of research that has been completed, exercise addiction is said to include the presence of mood modification/regulation, tolerance, withdrawal symptoms, lack of control, detrimental social consequences, personal conflict, and several other negative effects such as disturbed psychological functioning, exercising despite medical contraindications, or interference with relationships or work, and relapse (Freimuth, Moniz, & Kim, 2011; Hausenblas & Downs, 2002; Sussman & Lisha, 2014; Weinstein & Weinstein, 2014). Types of exercise have unique features (e.g., one may consider reliance on endurance, strength, agility, or even ties to the arts such as dance as different types). It is possible that each type might best be identified to better understand unique addictive features (e.g., dance addiction; Maraz, Urban, & Demetrovics, 2015). Yet another approach to conceptualizing types of exercise addiction has been referred to as "primary exercise dependence" and "secondary exercise dependence" (Cook et al., 2013). **Primary exercise dependence** is defined as meeting criteria for exercise dependence and continually exercising solely for the psychological gratification resulting from the exercise behavior itself. On the other hand, **secondary exercise dependence** is defined as meeting criteria for exercise dependence, but using excessive exercise to accomplish some other end (e.g., weight loss or body composition changes) that is related to another disorder such as an eating disorder or addiction to physical appearance.

11. Spiritual obsession. The eleventh category is spiritual obsession: occult, religion, self-help programs, and treatment seeking (4 subcategories). Prayer, meditation, early romantic love, and drug abuse may have in common activation of mesolimbic dopaminergic pathways of the brain and the generation of intense emotional states. Intense emotional reliance on a Higher Power may operate as a substitute addiction, which replaces the psychobiological functions formerly served by drug use (Sussman & Black, 2008; Sussman et al., 2011c; Taylor, 2002). Preoccupation with religion or spirituality, loss of control over meditation or repetitive chant involvement, and interference with other life goals (e.g., working, social interaction), which can lead to worsened affect, may demonstrate the existence of this category of addiction (Sussman et al., 2011c; Taylor, 2002).

12. Pain seeking. The twelfth category is pain seeking: cutting, self-mutilation, skin picking, **trichotillomania** (hair pulling), and scab picking (5 subcategories). Non-suicidal self-injury (NSSI) has been conceptualized as an addiction (e.g., Najavits, Lung, Froias, Paull, & Bailey, 2014) and appears as such in popular culture (e.g., http://en.wikipedia.org/wiki/My_Strange_Addiction). It was identified as such in the literature search conducted by Sussman (2012b), and does appear to involve craving and loss of control with negative consequences (Victor, Glenn, & Klonsky, 2012), with some studies suggesting that pleasure (a type of satiation of an appetitive motive) is derived from such behavior (e.g., Chamberlain, Odlaug, Boulougouris, Fineberg, & Grant, 2009, regarding trichotillomania). However, there is some evidence that NSSI is mostly maintained by negative reinforcement (relief of anxiety), and may be better conceptualized as an OCD or one of emotional regulation (Victor et al., 2012). Clinically, the behavior generally involves simple, repetitive movements to reduce negative affect, consistent with OCD. It is possible that some behaviors such as hair pulling may reflect different mechanisms from a behavior such as cutting, which is more self-injurious. In the DSM-V, trichotillomania has been placed within the obsessive-compulsive related disorders category rather than an addictions category, along with skin picking with which it is sometimes associated (APA, 2013, p. 251). Clearly, conceptual clarification and empirical research are needed.

13. Shopping. The thirteenth category is shopping. CBD has been categorized as an impulse control disorder, an example of OCD, a mood disorder, and a behavioral addiction (Racine et al., 2014). In the DSM-V, CBD is considered, at least tentatively, as a behavioral addiction. Those suffering from CBD may tend to be more materialistic and do experience pleasure as well as remorse after a buying spree, and exhibit preoccupation, loss of control, and negative consequences consistent with an addictive process (Black, Shaw, McCormick, Bayless, & Allen, 2012; Racine et al., 2014).

14. Thrill seeking. The fourteenth category is thrill/adventure seeking: auto-racing, cruising around in a car, dangerous sports, and thrills (compulsive sky diving, riding roller coasters) (4 subcategories). Most authors appear to consider compulsive risk-taking as a temperament aspect of other addictions (e.g., drug use, gambling, or sex addiction; e.g., Petraitis et al., 1995). However, some authors have argued that there exist **adrenalin junkies** who engage in all sorts of activities for a rush, and some may do so repetitively. For example, rock climbing for some people may reflect a type of addiction to dangerous situations (see Heywood, 2006). Anecdotally, some people have told me that they are "addicted" to driving (cruising) to and from certain locations (e.g., a night scene, club area). I could locate no research pertaining to compulsive participation in such activities.

15. Hoarding. The fifteenth category is hoarding: anime/comics/cards, small collectables or trivia, rocks, puppets, coins, books or magazines, junk, and technology objects (8 subcategories). **Hoarding** refers to a persistent difficulty discarding objects, an experience of distress with discarding them, leading to accumulation of possessions that congest living space, and leads to social, safety, or other impairments. Hoarding has been placed within the obsessive-compulsive related disorders category rather than an addictions category (APA, 2013, p. 247). Indeed, case studies of hoarding reveal "eccentric" personality histories, various other ritualistic behaviors such as constantly washing hands, mood disorders, or memory difficulties consistent with OCD, mood disorders, or Alzheimer's disease (Thomas, 1997). Still, in nomothetic empirical research, hoarding is associated with compulsive buying and is strongly associated with cigarette smoking, and is sensitive to positive and negative reinforcements, which likely places it more within an addiction domain (Lawrence, Ciociari, & Kyrios, 2014; Raines et al., 2014).

16. Voyeurism. Finally, the sixteenth category is voyeurism (i.e., "drama"): celebrity or other idolization, gossiping, and attending funerals (3 subcategories). The idea is that one may become addicted to the drama in various everyday situations (e.g., www.wisdom-ink.com/3-ways-people-are-addicted-to-drama-and-how-to-stop-attracting-it; www.psychologytoday.com/blog/obesely-speaking/201411/excessive-attention-seeking-and-drama-addiction). It is possible that drama to capture others' attention may calm the amygdala, increase turnover of mu opioid-related function, and fire up mesolimbic dopamine (www.psychologytoday.com/blog/obesely-speaking/201411/excessive-attention-seeking-and-drama-addiction). I could not locate any empirical research studies on this phenomenon.

Grouping These Categories into Appetitive Motives

One may speculate that different categories of addictions are associated with different neurobiological motivations (e.g., Greenberg, Lewis, & Dodd, 1999; Rozin & Stoess, 1993; Sussman et al., 2011b). I considered how these 16 addictive behavior categories might operate from an appetitive motives perspective. I examined four types of motives in the addictions research literature that might apply. Work with the PROMIS questionnaire (www.s-p-q.com; Haylett, Stephenson, & Lefever, 2004; MacLaren & Best, 2010) has revealed at least two general factors associated with different addictive behaviors: "hedonist" types (illegal drugs, tobacco, prescription drugs, gambling, compulsive sex, alcohol, and caffeine) and "nurturant" types (compulsive helping, work, relationships, shopping, eating behaviors, and exercise). **Hedonist-type addictions** appear to focus on immediate pleasure, whereas **nurturant-type addictions** appear to focus on personal fulfillment.

Haylett et al. (2004), though not MacLaren and Best (2010), also found some support for **dominance and submissive-related factors**, possibly nested within hedonist and nurturant factors. Other literature also has focused on addictions as reflecting fight (e.g., dominance, power) or flight (e.g., retreat into fantasy, submission) motives (Blum et al., 2012; Goeders, 2004; Haylett et al., 2004; Newlin, 2002; Rawson & Condon, 2007; Sunderworth & Milkman, 1991), related to limbic system-based reward, or stimulation of the HPA axis.

As a heuristic exercise, I crossed the 16 addictive behavior categories with four motives as depicted in Table 5.2 (also see Sussman, 2012b).

I placed each of the 16 behavior categories into pairs of motives, with the assumption that multiple motives operate for any given addictive behavior (e.g., Haylett et al., 2004). There are six possible pairs of the four motives within which the behaviors could be placed. However, "dominance" and "submissive" would not be a plausible combination as they describe polar opposite motivations. Thus, I attempted to place each addictive behavior into the five remaining combinations of appetitive motivation pairs (see Table 5.2).

Avoidance/submissive-pleasure/hedonist behaviors included drug use and pain seeking. *Dominance-hedonist* behaviors included compulsive violence and adventure

Table 5.2 Combinations of appetitive motivation pairs

Avoidance/submissive-pleasure/hedonist behaviors	Dominance-hedonist behaviors	Hedonist-nurturance behaviors	Dominance-nurturance behaviors	Submissive-nurturance behaviors
Drug use and pain seeking	Compulsive violence and adventure thrills	Food intake, compulsive use of technology, gambling, social-related, exercise, shopping, and hoarding	Workaholism, physical attractiveness seeking, and compulsive voyerism	Spiritual obsession and fantasizing

thrills. *Hedonist-nurturance* behaviors included food intake, compulsive use of technology, gambling, social-related (e.g., love, sex), exercise, shopping, and hoarding. *Dominance-nurturance* behaviors included workaholism, physical attractiveness seeking, and compulsive voyeurism. Finally, *submissive-nurturance* behaviors included spiritual obsession and fantasizing. Again, this exercise is a heuristic suggestion that one could develop a Mendeleev-like classification of categories of addiction by appetitive effect type (www.rsc.org/education/teachers/resources/periodictable/pre16/develop/mendeleev.htm). It is not clear how accurate the above classification is. There may be fewer types of addictions, or more types of motives, and empirical work is needed to do the classification. However, this is a potential future research direction that could be fruitful.

Summary of the 16 Classes of Addictions and Appetitive Motives

The goal in this classification was to provide an exhaustive typology of addictions, which might spur new thought and research on the nosology of addictions. Certainly, though, it is premature to identify all different types of addictions and be able to group them into mutually exclusive and exhaustive categories. Possibly, considering the 16 categories of addictions created by Sussman (2012b), and trying to reduce them to five appetitive motive combinations, is way too much of a speculative leap. Again, these categories were: (a) Drugs, (b) Food-related, (c) Compulsive antisocial behavior (e.g., aggression), (d) Technology/communications related (e.g., video games, television), (e) Gambling, (f) Working, (g) Social group-related (e.g., sex, love, platonic relationships), (h) Physical attractiveness-focused (e.g., tanning, cosmetic surgery), (i) Fantasizing (e.g., isolation, laziness), (j) Exercise-related, (k) Spiritual obsession, (l) Pain seeking (e.g., self-mutilation, skin picking), (m) Shopping, (n) Thrill/adventure seeking, (o) Hoarding (e.g., small collectables), and (p) Voyeurism (e.g., celebrity or other idolization, gossiping). While speculative, I believe that these addictive behavior categories likely represent the vast majority of types of addictions located in the literature, as they were derived from an attempt at an extensive electronic literature review. Of course, it is debatable whether or not all of these behaviors qualify as addictions. In theory, each of these behaviors by definition may exhibit dysregulation features including repetitive, erratically experienced, phenomenological changes in appetitive motivation that bypass deliberate processing of information (Sussman et al., 2011c). The appetitive motives for which these behaviors may subjectively satiate include achieving a satisfying or pleasurable state (or novelty), nurturance (of self or others), dominance (feeling powerful), or submission (conformity, fitting in to a "pecking" order; e.g., Haylett et al., 2004).

To summarize, with a consideration of subjective effects, I perceived that all 16 behavior categories might be described by one of five appetitive motive combinations. One could withdraw (submission, flight) and feel satisfied/pleasure. *Arousal reduction/sedation* might be among subjective effects reported. One could dominate and feel pleasure. Subjective effects might include experience of peak moments, or *arousal enhancement*. One could achieve both pleasure and nurturance, subjectively feeling very *deeply satisfied* perhaps. One could dominate and feel nurturance (maybe feeling *self-contained*). Finally, one could withdraw and feel nurturance (engaged in *cognitive fantasy* or feeling *cognitive calm, reduction in thoughts*). Much empirical research is needed to truly make inroads and integrate addictive behavior experiences with neurobiologically plausible appetitive processes (Stacy et al., 2004). That is, much more work on co-occurrence of addictions may help identify the distinctive motivational systems that become excessive or misdirected. One may even speculate that work on addictions may enhance understanding of motivated behavior in general.

Use of Addiction Matrix Items

For two main reasons, few studies have examined multiple addictions utilizing extensive measures of each addiction. First, assessment through use of multiple inventories takes a great deal of time, which may not be practical particularly in large survey samples administered to general populations. Therefore, often only a few addictions can be measured at the same time. Second, there is a great deal of redundancy in the measurement of various addictions which share many common features (e.g., appetitive motives, preoccupation). Such redundancy is burdensome to measure. Thus, several previous studies have examined multiple addictions as a matrix measure. With this type of self-report measure, several addictions are tapped, generally with one item per type of addiction, arranged in a matrix format. While an addiction matrix measure does not extensively measure any addiction, and only one partial convergent validation study of such measures has been conducted (Sussman et al., 2014), this approach is practical, economical, and may actually tap different addictive behaviors. Prevalence and co-occurrence of different addictions can then be assessed. An example of the matrix measure format is described in Chapter 9 (see also Figure 5.1).

Cook (1987) was the first researcher to investigate use of a matrix measure to identify prevalence and co-occurrence of addictive behaviors. In a sample of 604 US college students, he examined ten among what will be referred to as "the 11 focal addictive behaviors" for the rest of this text, i.e., he measured use of cigarettes, alcohol, illicit drugs, a food addiction proxy (eating disorders [obesity, anorexia, and bulimia]), relationships/love, sex, gambling, exercise (running), work, and shopping, along with additional addictions (e.g., caffeine), and also partner violence and emotional disturbance constructs. He did not examine Internet addiction, due to the year the study was completed (the Internet as we know it today did not exist at the time). The highest prevalence addictions reported were: relationships/love (25.9%), caffeine (20.1%), work (17.5%), sex (16.8%), shopping (10.7%), alcohol (10.5%), and cigarettes (9.6%). He found that approximately a quarter of the sample (23.8%) responded "no" to all addictive behaviors, violence, or emotional disturbances, suggesting that a high prevalence of addictive behaviors exists. However, it must be noted that he did not separate between addictive behaviors, partner violence, and emotional disturbances when reporting that statistic. In addition, he found that all of the addictions were significantly associated with each other except for running/work/shopping with alcohol/illicit drugs.

Use of Addiction Matrix Items

Sometimes people have an "addiction" to a certain drug or other object or activity. An addiction occurs when people experience the following:
- They do something over and over again to try to feel good, for excitement, or to stop feeling bad
- They can't stop doing this thing, even if they wanted to
- Bad things happen to them or to people they care about because of what they are doing

Have you ever been addicted to the following things? Do you feel you are addicted to them now (in the last 30 days)?

Object or activity	Ever addicted to it? YES	Ever addicted to it? NO	Addicted to it in the last 30 days? YES	Addicted to it in the last 30 days? NO
1. Cigarette smoking	1	0	1	0
2. Alcohol drinking	1	0	1	0
3. Marijuana use	1	0	1	0
4. Other drugs (such as cocaine, stimulants, hallucinogens, inhalants, XTC, opiates, valium or others)	1	0	1	0
5. Caffeine (coffee, or energy drinks such as Red Bull)	1	0	1	0
6. Eating (way too much food each day, binge eating)	1	0	1	0
7. Gambling	1	0	1	0
8. Internet browsing (surfing the Web)	1	0	1	0
9. Facebook, Myspace, Twitter, MSN, YM or other online social networking	1	0	1	0
10. Texting (cell phone use)	1	0	1	0
11. Online or offline videogames (PS3, Xbox, Wii)	1	0	1	0
12. Online shopping	1	0	1	0
13. Shopping at stores	1	0	1	0
14. Love	1	0	1	0
15. Sex	1	0	1	0
16. Exercise	1	0	1	0
17. Work	1	0	1	0
18. Stealing	1	0	1	0
19. Religion	1	0	1	0
20. Self-mutilation (cutting, skin picking, hair pulling)	1	0	1	0
21. Driving a car	1	0	1	0
22. Gossip	1	0	1	0
23. Any other addiction? please specify:_____	1	0	1	0

Figure 5.1 The Addiction Matrix Self-Report Measure

One might conjecture whether or not a contrast was being demonstrated between prosocial daily activity-type addictions versus risky drug use-related addictions.

Alexander and Schweighofer (1989), in a partial replication study of 136 Canadian college students, found similar prevalence findings as Cook (1987) on two of the addictions (relationships and work), but prevalence was much lower on other categories (based on how use was described [as addiction, negative addiction, dependence, or regular use]). Defined only as regular use, prevalence was actually higher than the Cook sample on all types of addictive behaviors. Greenberg et al. (1999), in a sample of 129 college students, found significant inter-correlations among nine addictions (alcohol, caffeine, chocolate, cigarettes, exercise, gambling, Internet use, television, and video games) except for exercise with alcohol and cigarette smoking, cigarette smoking with chocolate, and video games with chocolate and exercise. Highest prevalence addictions were exercise (30%), caffeine (29%), television (26%), alcohol (26%), cigarettes (23%), and chocolate (23%), which were higher than the reported prevalence in Cook (1987) among the same addictions measured.

MacLaren and Best (2010), with a sample of 948 college students, examined the factor structure of a set of 16 addictions. Three factors were identified: (a) nurturant (e.g., compulsive helping [dominant and submissive], work, shopping, food [binging and starving], exercise, and relationships [dominant and submissive]); (b) hedonistic (illegal drugs, alcohol, tobacco, and sex); and (c) another hedonistic-like factor (prescription drugs, gambling, and caffeine). Highest prevalence addictions were exercise (25.6%), shopping (21.8%), relationships dominant and submissive (17% and 11.9%), caffeine (16.5%), food starving and binging (16.4% and 14.9%), compulsive helping dominant and submissive (12.5% and 12.1%), work (12.4%), prescription drugs (12.2%), sex (10.3%), and alcohol (10.2%). Though not replicated by MacLaren and Best (2010), earlier work by this same research group also had delineated dominant and submissive factors nested within nurturant and hedonistic factors (Christo et al., 2003; Haylett et al., 2004). Two of these three studies were conducted with college undergraduate students, but Haylett et al. (2004) studied 543 consecutive admissions to the PROMIS Recovery Center (mean age = 35 years). Perhaps additional factors emerge as a function of addiction severity or age of the sample studied.

Most recently, Sussman et al. (2014) investigated use of a matrix measure approach among former alternative high school youth (average age = 19.8 years) at risk for addictions. Lifetime and last 30-day prevalence of one or more of the 11 addictions reviewed in other work (Sussman et al., 2011b) was the primary focus (i.e., cigarettes, alcohol, hard drugs, eating, gambling, Internet, love, sex, exercise, work, and shopping; the **11 focal addictions**). Also, the co-occurrence of two or more of these 11 addictive behaviors was investigated. Finally, the latent class structure of these addictions, and their associations with other measures, was examined. Sussman and colleagues found that lifetime and last 30-day prevalence of one or more of these addictions was 79.2% and 61.5%, respectively. Lifetime and last 30-day co-occurrence of two or more of these addictions was 61.5% and 37.7%, respectively. **Latent class analysis** (LCA, a subset of structural equation modeling, used to find groups or subtypes of cases in multivariate categorical data, called "latent classes") suggested two groups: a generally Non-addicted group (67.2% of the sample) and a "Work Hard, Play Hard" addicted group that was particularly invested in addiction to love, sex, exercise, the Internet, and work (32.8% of the sample). Supplementary analyses that compared the matrix items assessment to other more detailed measures (for use of cigarettes, use of alcohol, use of illicit drugs, risky sexual behavior, compulsive Internet use, and strenuous exercise) suggested that the single-response type self-reports may be measuring the addictions they intend to measure (i.e., they demonstrated convergent validity). The one-year stability of the addiction class was very high as well (approximately 90%), as was indicated in a follow-up study (Sussman, Pokhrel, Sun, Rohrbach, & Spruijt-Metz, 2015b; also see Chapter 16).

Thus far, empirical work has not revealed replicable general types or classes of addiction. There is some support for the idea of relatively prosocial addictions versus risky behavior addictions; or addictions grouped by nurturance or hedonistic motives. However, there is other evidence suggesting that addictions tend to be associated with each other regardless of type. The Addiction Matrix Self-Report Measure used by Sussman and colleagues is shown in Figure 5.1.

Summary: The 11 "Focal" Addictions for the Remainder of this Text

The remainder of this text will present much more information on different addictions, but focusing on the 11 addictions on which there exists the most research, discussion, and highest prevalence, albeit not certified as such through an official system (e.g., Rosenberg & Feder, 2014b; Sussman et al., 2011b). These 11 addictions were the result of a recent exhaustive, systematic review of addiction prevalence and co-occurrence (Sussman et al., 2011b). To repeat, these 11 addictions are: cigarette smoking, alcohol use, illicit drug use (including marijuana), eating/food, gambling, Internet, love, sex, exercise, work, and shopping. Data from 83 studies (each study n = at least 500 subjects) were presented in Sussman et al. (2011b) and supplemented with smaller-scale data. Depending on which assumptions are made, overall 12-month prevalence of an addiction among US adults varies from 15% to 61%. We asserted that it is most plausible that 47% of the US adult population suffers from maladaptive signs of at least one of these 11 addictive disorders over a 12-month period, with a 23% co-occurrence of two or more addictions. We used this empirical review and these 11 addictions as background for examining previous work that involved use of an "addictions matrix item" to tap types of addictions.

Sussman et al. (2014) please recall, found that lifetime and last 30-day prevalence of one or more of these 11 addictions among former alternative high school youth was 79.2% and 61.5%, respectively. Expanding the number of categories to 22 addictions (23 with an open-ended option) in that study (also contained in the matrix measure; i.e., the measure also tapped caffeine use, offline video games, stealing, religion, self-mutilation, driving a car, gossip, or any other addiction as an open-ended category) increased ever and last 30-day prevalence to 84.8% and 68.2%, respectively, only slightly higher (about 5% and 7%, for lifetime and last 30-day prevalence, respectively). These 11 addictive categories accounted for 90.2% of self-reported last 30-day addictions (61.5%/68.2%). Thus, this text will focus on cigarettes, alcohol, hard drugs, eating, gambling, Internet, love, sex, exercise, work, and shopping, which not only reflect the addictions on which there is most consensus – but (albeit still somewhat speculative) also may reflect a majority of addictive behaviors.

Bulleted Summary

- The 16-category, exhaustive set of types of addictive behaviors included (a) Drugs, (b) Food-related, (c) Compulsive antisocial behavior (e.g., aggression), (d) Technology/communications related (e.g., video games, television), (e) Gambling,

(f) Working, (g) Social group-related (e.g., sex, love, platonic relationships), (h) Physical attractiveness-focused (e.g., tanning, cosmetic surgery), (i) Fantasizing (e.g., isolation, laziness), (j) Exercise-related, (k) Spiritual obsession, (l) Pain seeking (e.g., self-mutilation, skin picking), (m) Shopping, (n) Thrill/adventure seeking, (o) Hoarding (e.g., small collectables), and (p) Voyeurism (e.g., celebrity or other idolization, gossiping).

- The 16 types of addictions might be described by one of five appetitive motive combinations. One could withdraw (submission, flight) and feel satisfied/pleasure. Arousal reduction/sedation might be among subjective effects reported. Second, one could dominate and feel pleasure. Subjective effects might include experience of peak moments, or arousal enhancement. One could achieve both pleasure and nurturance, subjectively feeling very deeply satisfied. Fourth, one could dominate and feel nurturance (feeling self-contained). Finally, one could withdraw and feel nurturance (fantasy).

- With an addiction matrix-type item, several addictions are tapped, generally with one item per type of addiction, arranged in a matrix format. While an addiction matrix measure does not extensively measure any addiction, this approach is practical, economical, and appears to tap different addictive behaviors.

- The remainder of the text focuses on 11 addictions. These are cigarette smoking, alcohol use, illicit drug use (including marijuana), eating/food, gambling, Internet, love, sex, exercise, work, and shopping. The most research is available on these 11 addictions and they appear, in at least one sample, to account for 90 percent of addictions experienced.

Suggestions for Further Reading

MacLaren, V. V. & Best, L. A. (2010). Multiple addictive behaviors in young adults: Student norms for the shorter PROMIS scale. *Addictive Behaviors*, 35: 252–255.

Rosenberg, K. P. & Feder, L. C. (eds.) (2014a). *Behavioral Addictions: Criteria, Evidence, and Treatment.* London: Academic Press/Elsevier.

Sussman, S., Arpawong, T. E., Sun, P., Tsai, J., Rohrbach, L. A., & Spruijt-Metz, D. (2014). Prevalence and co-occurrence of addictive behaviors among former alternative high school youth. *Journal of Behavioral Addictions*, 3: 33–40.

Sussman, S., Lisha, N., & Griffiths, M. (2011b). Prevalence of the addictions: A problem of the majority or the minority? *Evaluation & the Health Professions*, 34: 3–56.

6 Substance Addictions: Their Prevalence and Co-Occurrence

Learning Objectives

- To learn about the prevalence and co-occurrence of tobacco use addiction
- To learn about the prevalence and co-occurrence of alcoholism
- To learn about the prevalence and co-occurrence of other drug use addiction
- To learn about the prevalence and co-occurrence of food addiction
- To understand the issue of considering food-related addiction "food addiction" (a substance addiction) versus "eating addiction" (a behavioral addiction)

Introduction

As first mentioned in Chapter 1, by the time he was 45 years old Johnny felt that he had become addicted to alcohol, marijuana – and food. He viewed them as substances that he would imbibe and then feel different and better than at "baseline." He dabbled with some other drugs but he viewed them as easier to quit. For example, he reported that one drug (crack cocaine) made him hear the sound of a railroad train or sometimes a police siren, when he was using it. He could not function much at all for several minutes (he would call this "the drug" most of the time and not identify its name). It was difficult to get him to talk much about his other drug use, which he quit simply when his "sources" disappeared and he had some time away from using the other drugs. It became difficult for him to talk even about his marijuana use. He did mention that he had been addicted to marijuana use, though he finally quit it on his own. He did not mind talking about his alcohol and food intake as they were both legal. He sometimes spoke about getting an alcohol or food "buzz." He viewed his substance addictions as being different from other addictions that involved movement of the whole body (exercise) or intense engagement in an activity (work). Alcohol and food intake was easier to do, with a greater immediate impact, but also with worse after-effects (feeling hung-over, foggy, sweaty, and with a bloated belly).

Substance addictions pertain to misuse of a variety of drugs or food (Schaef, 1987). The label "substance" refers to the fact that an object is imbibed as opposed to involving producing an effect through only motoric behavior. Drugs are consumed and produce a direct (exogenous) physiological effect on the brain. While drugs may have differential effects on some neurotransmitters (e.g., alcohol may decrease serotonin turnover whereas stimulants may increase serotonin turnover), all drugs appear to increase turnover of mesolimbic dopamine, relevant to the experience of reward or novelty (Sussman & Ames, 2008). Drugs that are fat-soluble, small-molecule, of light molecular weight, low hydrogen bond forming, and readily cross the blood–brain barrier are the types to produce an effect on neurotransmission (e.g., mimic endogenous neurotransmission, block neurotransmission reuptake, or stimulate neurotransmitter release; see Pardridge, 2012).

Food may also induce a direct (and indirect) effect on brain function (e.g., through stimulating the **vagus nerve** [each of the tenth pair of cranial nerves, supplying the heart, lungs, upper digestive tract, and other organs of the chest and abdomen]). In particular, intake of energy-dense foods may impact dopaminergic and opioid systems (Volkow, Wang, & Baler, 2011; Yau et al., 2014). It is possible that impairments in dopaminergic pathways associated with reward sensitivity, conditioning, and control may be involved in obesity as well as in food addiction (Volkow et al., 2011).

Importantly, though, regarding drug and food addictions, anticipatory responses in brain regions such as the caudate nucleus may precede intake of either type of substance (see Sussman & Ames, 2008; Yau et al., 2014; Gearhardt et al., 2011). Thus, there may be both a direct impact and an indirect impact of substances on neurobiological function. Again, what sets substance addiction apart from behavioral addiction is that a more or less direct impact may occur on brain function via ingestion of a substance of some type. Therefore, this chapter will focus on tobacco, alcohol, illicit drug, and food addictions; their prevalence and co-occurrence with each other and with behavioral addictions. Their prevalence is summarized in Table 6.1.

Studies Included in Chapters 6 and 7

In Chapter 6, I consider the prevalence of tobacco, alcohol, illicit drugs, and food addiction among adults, as well as their co-occurrence with other addictions. In Chapter 7, I consider prevalence and co-occurrence of the seven remaining behavioral focal addictions (gambling, various types of Internet use, love, sex, exercise, work, and compulsive spending). In almost all cases, the assessment of prevalence was determined through scores on self-report scales, though in less than 10 percent of the cases a DSM-like interview was conducted (see Sussman et al., 2011b, for details). The studies included were among those that had $n \geq 500$ participants, supplemented with smaller studies to discern prevalence and co-occurrence, with updated sources (since 2011). The studies vary by age of subject, region, country, and year. Certainly it is a challenge to consider the studies as a set. However, I believe the "grand" mean estimates are reasonably accurate (with an illustrative wide range). For example, in Chapter 7, I provided an estimate of 6 percent for last-year shopping addiction among US adults based on Sussman et al. (2011b). An updated, exhaustive meta-analysis of compulsive buying (non-clinical samples, $n > 144$ for studies included) provided a pooled world-wide single time-point prevalence estimate of 5 percent

Drug Addiction Categories

Table 6.1 Prevalence of substance addictions

Tobacco	Daily cigarette smoking varies considerably by country. Last 12-month tobacco dependence prevalence in the general adult population of the United States is approximately 15%. Daily use of cigarette smoking is shrinking a great deal among Western countries. However e-cigarette use appears to be on the rise.
Alcohol	One-year prevalence of alcohol use disorder, abuse or dependence generally is calculated as being around 10% for older teenagers and adults in the United States. Lifetime prevalence of alcohol use disorder is approximately 20%. These estimations are based on DSM criteria.
Marijuana and other illicit drug abuse	Daily marijuana smoking in the United States varies from 7% among 18-year-olds to 2% among 50-year-olds. Last 30-day use of marijuana is increasing, perhaps given recent emphasis on medical and legal marijuana use. Data on marijuana abuse/dependence among population samples indicated prevalence among older teenagers and emerging adults of approximately 7%. Prevalence of last 30-day illicit drug use, excluding marijuana use, is 8% among 18-year-olds and 5% among 50-year-olds. Other drugs of abuse are prescription drugs, amphetamines, sedatives, tranquilizers, ecstasy, and hallucinogens. Overall, prevalence of illicit substance abuse is estimated to be 5%.
Food addictions	Last-year prevalence rates of eating disorders varied between 1% and 2%. Eating disorders include anorexia nervosa, bulimia, overeating, and binge eating. Binge eating disorder (BED) arguably is most like other addictions in its behavioral topography. A study indicated that 57% of BED patients met the criteria for food addiction, and approximately 25% of obese persons meet the criteria for food addiction. If food addicts were a subset of BED patients then the prevalence of food addiction would be less than 1%. If food addicts were a subset of persons with obesity then the prevalence of food addiction would be 8.7%. Based on relevant literature the prevalence of food addiction is estimated to be 2%.

(Maraz, Griffiths, & Demetrovics, 2016). I believe that the means calculated provide a "ballpark" figure of how prevalent each addiction is, particularly useful when considered relative to the other ten addictions.

Drug Addiction Categories

The DSM-V includes ten categories of drugs of abuse: alcohol, caffeine, cannabis, hallucinogens (which include phencyclidine [PCP] and others), inhalants, opioids, sedatives (or hypnotics, or anxiolytics), stimulants (amphetamine-type substances, cocaine, and others), tobacco, and other (or unknown). A similar organization was developed by Sussman and Ames (2001, 2008) and will be discussed in more detail. The Sussman and Ames (2001, 2008) scheme contains eight categories. They divide drugs of abuse by subjective and behavioral effects into eight classes: (1) depressants (which include alcohol, sedatives for relaxation, hypnotics to induce sleep, anxiolytic to reduce anxiety, and anticonvulsants such as barbiturates), (2) PCP, (3) inhalants, (4) stimulants, (5) opiates, (6) hallucinogens, (7) cannabis, and (8) others (e.g., steroids, GHB, ketamine). All depressants are classified together because they slow down, relax, or "knock out" an individual. PCP is placed in a separate category because its effects are both depressant and hallucinogen-like and may precipitate violence. Inhalants generally exert sedative effects, but their administration (huffed, sniffed/fluted, or bagging [through mouth, nose, nose and mouth]) is quite different from other depressants. All stimulants tend to "speed up" the individual and make one nervous or more aware. All opiates relieve pain, and may relax or amotivate the user, whether or not they are derived from opium or are synthetic. All hallucinogens expand cognitive perceptions and may lead to perceptual distortions and easily agitated behavior. Marijuana may cause one to "mellow out" and/or "be paranoid" or alter one's perceptions (e.g., time may appear to slow down). Finally, there are "other" drugs of abuse (e.g., steroids, GHB, ketamine), which may or may not fit into one of the previous seven health behavior-related categories. These types of drugs are placed in the eighth category (other) because they have relatively short abuse histories or otherwise provide a unique label that does not appear to fit elsewhere. At present, steroids have had an abuse history spanning at least 50 years, and GHB and ketamine have a 30-year abuse history (see www.cesar.umd.edu/cesar/drug_info.asp). Thus, some of the "other" drugs are not new.

Sussman et al. (2011b) considered three general drug categories: cigarette smoking (15 percent previous year adult prevalence), alcohol use (10 percent previous year adult prevalence), and illicit substance use (5 percent previous year adult prevalence). Cigarette smoking, and other nicotine-containing tobacco products, while legal, is highly addictive and a leading behavioral cause of various diseases and premature death, but generally does not cause gross impairment in function while being used. Alcohol, also legal in most countries, is highly addictive, a leading cause of premature death, and a cause of obvious impairment in function if used excessively. Drugs of misuse, which singly are of relatively low use prevalence, often are grouped into categories such as "illicit" or "hard" substances (Sussman et al., 2011b). Most illegal/hard drugs (which can include prescription drugs that are used for recreation [used in illegal ways]) tend to lead to noticeable impairment in normal functioning, and users or distributors can be prosecuted.

Tobacco Addiction

Tobacco/Cigarette Daily Use

Among American teens and adults, a good source of data for examining prevalence of tobacco, alcohol, and other drug use is the Monitoring the Future research group in the United States (http://monitoringthefuture.org; Johnston et al., 2014a; Johnston,

O'Malley, Miech, Bachman, & Schulenberg, 2014b). Daily (20 or more days in last 30 days) cigarette smoking varies from 8.5 percent among 18-year-olds to 13 percent among 50-year-olds (Johnston et al., 2014a, 2014b).

Daily cigarette smoking prevalence among adults varies considerably by country. For example, Farrell et al. (2003) found that 24 percent of a large sample of adults in Great Britain smoked 10 or more cigarettes daily (which would likely reflect nicotine dependence). Ulrich et al. (Ulrich, Hill, Rumpf, Hapke, & Meyer, 2003) found a daily smoking prevalence of 38.6 percent in Germany. These prevalence rates are much higher than the US rates reported by the Monitoring the Future group, and vary considerably across these two countries.

Prevalence of Tobacco Addiction among Teens and Adults

One may infer that daily cigarette smoking is addictive use, though several studies do measure tobacco (nicotine) addiction specifically. Tobacco addiction (dependence) among older teenagers has been found to vary between 6% and 8% (Chen, Sheth, Elliott, & Yeager, 2004; Young et al., 2002). Cook (1987) found a prevalence of 9.6% for tobacco addiction among college students, while Dierker et al. (2007) found a tobacco addiction prevalence among incoming college students of 4.4% (4.9% of the full sample being daily smokers). MacLaren and Best (2010) found an even lower prevalence of tobacco dependence among a similar sample of 948 Canadian 19-year-old college students of 1.7%.

Grant, Hasin, Chou, Stinson, and Dawson (2004a) found a prevalence of 12.8% for tobacco addiction among a US national sample of adults (also see Falk, Yi, & Hiller-Sturmhöfel, 2006). Goodwin, Keyes, and Hasin (2009), on the other hand, found a prevalence of 21.6% and 17.8% for tobacco addiction among a US national sample of male and female adults, respectively. It appears that a measure of daily smoking demonstrates about the same level of prevalence as direct measures of dependence, particularly among adults (i.e., around 15%). I estimate last 12-month tobacco dependence prevalence in the general adult population of the United States as being approximately 15% (also see Hughes, Helzer, & Lindberg, 2006).

Prevalence of Tobacco Products Other Than Combustible Cigarettes

Daily use of combustible (conventional, traditional) cigarettes among US 18-year-olds decreased from 18.5% back in 1991, and 15.8% back in 2003, to 8.5% in 2013 (Johnston et al., 2014a, 2014b). Increase in prevalence of use of electronic or **e-cigarettes** may account, to some extent, for the decrease in combustible cigarette use (*e-cigarettes* are battery-powered vaporizers that simulate the feeling of smoking, but without tobacco); overall, nicotine dependence may not be decreasing among teens in the United States or elsewhere (Grana, Benowitz, & Glantz, 2014).

Corey et al. (2013) reported that from 2011 to 2012, e-cigarette prevalence doubled among teens in the United States. Among high school youth, ever and last 30-day e-cigarette use increased from 4.7% to 10%, and from 1.5% to 2.8%, respectively. When examined along with conventional cigarette smoking, an overall increase in 30-day nicotine product use was observed from 1.2% to 2.2%. Since e-cigarettes have only been on the market since 2007, this is of concern – given that there are negative consequences from nicotine itself including toxicity, inflammation of biological pathways, and effects on fetal and adolescent development (US DHHS, 2014); and the physical consequences of the vaporization of propylene glycol, vegetable glycerin, and flavorings (e.g., diacetyl) is likely negative (Grana et al., 2014). It is known that there are at least ten carcinogenic chemicals in e-cigarette vapor (Chapman, 2015).

In fact, in 2014, as measured by the National Youth Tobacco Survey (www.fda.gov/downloads/TobaccoProducts/PublicHealthEducation/ProtectingKidsfromTobacco/UCM443044.pdf), the tobacco products most commonly used (last 30-day use) by US high school students were e-cigarettes (13.4%), hookah (9.4%), cigarettes (9.2%), cigars (8.2%), smokeless tobacco (5.5%), snus (1.9%), and pipes (1.5%). Use of multiple tobacco products was common; nearly half of all middle and high school students who were current tobacco users used two or more types of tobacco products.

Adults also increased their use of e-cigarettes. From 2010 to 2013, current use of e-cigarettes ("every day" or "some days") among adults increased from 0.3% to 6.8% (McMillen, Gottlieb, Shaefer, Winickoff, & Klein, 2015), according to a random digit dialing US national probability sample survey conducted by Mississippi State University.

Summarizing Prevalence of Tobacco Use

To summarize, the topography of tobacco use is rapidly changing. While current use of cigarette smoking may decrease, and there is great variation across age cohorts and countries, it appears that overall tobacco use is staying constant (if not increasing slightly; about 15 percent reporting regular tobacco use/dependence in the last year among the US adult population). Still popular, with the longest consistent history of use, and about which the most research exists, I focus mostly on studies of cigarette smoking in this text. Unfortunately, measures of addiction to other tobacco products such as e-cigarette use are only now in development (e.g., Foulds et al., 2015).

Alcohol Abuse/Dependence

Estimates of current daily alcohol use rates in the United States varies from 2% to 11% among 18- to 50-year-olds, respectively, but may not reflect problem drinking (Johnston et al., 2014a, 2014b). Occasional heavy drinking (five or more drinks at least once in the last two weeks) varies from 22% among 18-year-olds to 40% among 21- to 22-year-olds, to 20% among 50-year-olds. Again, this may not indicate problem drinking. "Alcoholism" generally is estimated as being around 10% for older teenagers and adults (Essau & Hutchinson, 2008; Sussman & Ames, 2008). This is shown in Table 6.2 and in Sussman et al. (2011b), which includes measurement among sample sizes equal to or greater than 500. Certainly there is a great deal of variation as a function of age, location, and year of measurement. However, the average last 12-month estimate among adults does appear to hover around 10%.

However, a unique perspective on alcohol drinking which would reduce its prevalence estimate is the ***harmful dysfunction analysis*** (Wakefield & Schmitz, 2014).

Alcohol Abuse/Dependence

Table 6.2 Prevalence estimates of alcoholism

Age group	Prevalence estimate	Reference
Canadian college undergraduates (older teenagers and adults)	10%	Alexander & Schweighofer, 1989
14- to 21-year-old US teenagers and emerging adults	15%	Barnes et al., 2009
13- to 19-year-old US teenagers, abuse or dependent	16.4%	Chen et al., 2004
17- to 20-year-olds in the US	14.6%	Cohen et al., 1993
18- to 65-year-old (average age = 22) US college undergraduates	10%	Cook, 1987
18 years and older US adults	8.4%	Falk et al., 2006
16- to 64-year-old Great Britain adults, heavy or very heavy; dependent	10%; 5%	Farrell et al., 2003
18- to 98-year-old US adults (average age = 45 years), last year alcohol abuse or dependence	8.5%	French et al., 2008
18- to 98-year-old US adults	8.5%	Grant et al., 2004b
18- to 98-year-old US adults, alcohol abuse or dependence	8.5%	Hasin et al., 2007
US 12- to 50-year olds; 18- to 29-year-olds	5.8%; 10% to 15%	Harford et al., 2005
14- to 75-year-old German teens and adults, alcohol abuse or dependence	10.5%	Hill et al., 1998
12-year-old or older US general population; of last year baseline drinkers	3.4%; 5.3%	Kandel et al., 1997
12- to 17-year-old US teens, looking at 16- to 17-year-olds	9.5%	Kilpatrick et al., 2000
Canadian college student 19-year-olds	10.2%	MacLaren & Best, 2010
14- to 24-year-olds in Germany	9.9%	Nelson & Wittchen, 1998
Lifetime problem assessed with CAGE screener in the Netherlands, among 26- to 30-year-olds in 2000: males; females	14.6%; 4.8%	Poelen et al., 2005
General US adult population, 18 years and older during only the last 6 months	4.8%	Regier et al., 1990
US 17- to 18-year-olds	15.7%	Young et al., 2002

Note: Articles are simply presented in alphabetical order of authors; alcoholism prevalence tends to be estimated at 10%, although more physiological-based definitions hover at 5%.

"Harm" is defined as any type of social, physical, personal, legal, or role negative consequence, and "dysfunction" is defined as presence of a dependence syndrome or inability to function normally without use of alcohol. In work by Wakefield and Schmitz (2014), both harm and dysfunction were needed to diagnose an alcohol use disorder using large-scale survey data (Epidemiologic Catchment Area Study and the National Comorbidity Survey). This analysis revealed lifetime prevalence of alcohol use disorder of approximately 6 percent, as opposed to using DSM-based definitions that would yield a prevalence of about 20 percent. Of course, while not reported, 12-month prevalence would be even lower. In Sussman et al. (2011b), we estimated last 12-month alcohol abuse or dependence prevalence in the general adult population of the United States as being approximately 10 percent (alcohol dependence is approximately 4 percent world-wide; e.g., Pirkola, Poikolainen, & Lonnqvist, 2006; Regier et al., 1990; Teesson, Baillie, Lynskey, Manor, & Degenhardt, 2006). The harmful dysfunction analysis provides a figure similar to our estimate of alcohol use dependence world-wide, which makes sense since that analysis demands dependence as part of the definition of alcoholism.

Marijuana and Other Illicit Drug Abuse/Dependence

Marijuana Addiction

Daily (20 or more days in last 30 days) marijuana smoking varies from 7% among 18-year-olds to 2% among 50-year-olds (Johnston et al., 2014a, 2014b). Cohen et al. (1993) found a prevalence of marijuana abuse among 17- to 20-year-olds of 2.9%. Other data on marijuana abuse/dependence among population samples indicate a prevalence among older teenagers and adults of approximately 7% (Agrawal, Neale, Prescott, & Kendler, 2004; Barnes, Welte, Hoffman, & Tidwell, 2009; Coffey et al., 2002; Hall, Degenhardt, & Patton, 2008; Kandel, Chen, Warner, Kessler, & Grant, 1997; Kilpatrick, Acierno, Saunders, Resnick, & Best, 2000; MacLaren & Best, 2010; Young et al., 2002), though Chen et al. (2004) found a prevalence of 13.4% among teenagers, and Agrawal et al. (2004) found that the marijuana abuse/dependence rate among US college males and females was 18% and 7.5%, respectively. Alternatively, Compton et al. (Compton, Grant, Colliver, Glantz, & Stinson, 2004), Grant et al. (2004b), and Stinson et al. (Stinson, Ruan, Pickering, & Grant, 2006) assessed a very large sample and found a 1.5% prevalence of marijuana abuse/dependence among the US general adult population (between 4% and 5% prevalence among those 18 to 29 years of age), and Farrell et al. (2003) found a prevalence of 1.8% in Great Britain. Kandel et al. (1997) found 0.1% prevalence among US adults (9% prevalence among those who used in the last year).

Certainly, last 30-day use of marijuana is increasing, perhaps given recent emphasis on medical marijuana use (and use being legal in Alaska, Colorado, Oregon, Washington, DC, and Washington, in the United States). Back in 1991 last 30-day prevalence among 18-year-olds was approximately 14% but as of 2013 it was almost 23% (21% in 2014). Also, daily use among 18-year-olds increased from 2% to 6.5% over this same time period (Johnston et al., 2014a, 2014b). In 2011, 36% of all emergency department visits involving seeking detox services were due to marijuana use, which represented an increase by 62% from that in 2004 (www.samhsa.gov/data/2k13/DAWN2k11ED/DAWN2k11ED.htm#tab26; Drug Abuse Warning Network data).

This may represent the increase in potency of marijuana use, increased prevalence, greater willingness to go to emergency rooms due to marijuana use (suggesting increased acceptability of marijuana), or all three reasons (in 1983 marijuana potency or percentage THC was under 4% whereas currently it averages about 10% or higher; see www.cnn.com/2009/HEALTH/05/14/marijuana.potency/index.html?_s=PM:HEALTH).

Other "Illicit Drug" Addiction

"Hard" or "illicit" drugs is a sort of "catch-all" category for drugs that are either not legal (e.g., heroin), or are relatively dangerous (e.g., PCP, heroin, prescription opiate), or tend to be too low in prevalence to place in their own category (at least in drug studies which require a reasonable sample size; e.g., PCP). Marijuana is sometimes included in this category and sometimes is not, since it is sometimes legal, is relatively safe, and is of relatively high prevalence.

After marijuana, the most prevalent other "hard" drug of abuse (last 30-day use) among 18-year-olds in the United States is "prescription drugs" (7%), amphetamines (4.1%), narcotics other than heroin such as vicodin or oxycontin (2.8%), sedatives such as barbiturates (2.2%), tranquilizers such as xanax (2%), ecstasy (1.5%), and hallucinogens (1.4%), with all other illicit drug prevalence (i.e., inhalants, heroin, PCP, cocaine, methamphetamine) being at or under 1% (Johnston et al., 2014a, 2014b). The term **prescription drugs** is a more general label that subsumes several of the other categories of drugs used non-medically (amphetamines, other narcotics, sedatives, and tranquilizers). Older age groups report lower prevalence on all these drugs except amphetamines among college youth (5.3% last 30-day use; 3.2% among young adults), and other narcotic use is somewhat high among young adults and college youth (2.6% and 1.5%, respectively, last 30-day prevalence), as is use of tranquilizers (1.9% and 1.2%, respectively, last 30-day prevalence). Certainly, prescription drugs are not "illicit" although they may be used illicitly.

Prevalence of last 30-day illicit/hard drug use, including and excluding marijuana use, is 25% and 8%, respectively, among 18-year-olds and is 11% and 5% among 50-year-olds (Johnston et al., 2014a, 2014b) Prevalence of other illicit drug abuse disorders, which includes marijuana use in the calculation in some studies, varies between 2% and 5% among teenagers, college-age youth, and adults (Alexander & Schweighofer, 1989; Chen et al., 2004; Cohen et al., 1993 [1.1% among 17- to 20-year-olds, excluding marijuana use in the calculation]; Cook, 1987; Grant et al., 2004b; Kandel et al., 1997 [lower, at 0.3%; 11.6% among last year baseline users]; Kilpatrick et al., 2000; Regier et al., 1990; Sussman & Ames, 2008; Young et al., 2002). However, Agrawal et al. (2004) found a rate of 9% and 19.2% other illicit drug dependence (excluding marijuana) among 2,125 adult female and male twin pairs from the Virginia twin registry, respectively. On the other hand, Compton et al. (2004), and Warner et al. (Warner, Kessler, Hughes, Anthony, & Nelson, 1995), reported a US general adult 12-month prevalence of illicit drug abuse/dependence (marijuana and other illicit drugs) of 2.0% and 1.8%, respectively. In Great Britain, this prevalence within a general adult population was found to be 2.1% (Farrell et al., 2003). The adult last 12-month illicit drug dependence in Canada was found to be about 1%

(Gadalla & Piran, 2007). Based on this pool of studies (each with a sample size equal to or larger than 500), Sussman et al. (2011b) estimated last 12-month illicit drug abuse/dependence (marijuana and/or other drugs) prevalence in the general adult population of the United States as approximately 5% (any drug dependence is 1% to 3%; e.g., Regier et al., 1990; Teesson et al., 2006).

Co-Occurrence of Tobacco, Alcohol, and Illicit Drugs with Each Other and with Other Addictive Behaviors

Alcohol, Tobacco, and Other Drug (ATOD) Addictions with Each Other

Several studies (only four of which involved samples of 500 or more subjects) have found 30% to 60% co-occurrence of cigarette, alcohol, and other drug use disorders with each other among youth and adults in the United States or elsewhere (Essau & Hutchinson, 2008; Falk et al., 2006; Ford et al., 2009; Kaufman, 1982; Miller, Gold, & Klahr, 1990; Palmer et al., 2009 [lifetime use-based]; Regier et al., 1990 [lifetime use-based]; Stinson et al., 2006; Sussman & Ames, 2008). However, one exception is that in a large German adult sample, a last 12-month prevalence of only 18.4% alcohol hazardous use/abuse/dependence was found among general population daily smokers (Ulrich et al., 2003).

ATOD Addiction with Eating Addiction-Related Behavior

In a review by Holderness, Brooks-Gunn, and Warren (1994) there were three small US studies (ns =20, 27, and 138) that indicated that approximately 20% of drug abusers also exhibited an *eating disorder* (bulimia or bulimic behaviors), though Freimuth et al. (2008) suggested this co-occurrence is higher at 35%, and Lesieur and Blume (1993) suggested that the co-occurrence varies by age and is higher among older adults. Lesieur and Blume (1993) reported one US study of female alcoholics (n = 31) that showed 36% with symptoms of binge eating and 21% with a clinical eating disorder. Recently, one small sample of US substance abuse patients (86% were outpatients), with mostly alcohol, opiate, or cocaine, and marijuana use disorders (n = 51), revealed a 14% prevalence (endorsement of "yes") of being addicted to eating (31% endorsing either "yes" or "maybe"; Najavits et al., 2014). Among a small sample of Swedish chemical dependence inpatients and outpatients (n = 69), 48% reported some type of loss of control over eating (Punzi & Fahlke, 2015).

ATOD Addiction with Gambling Addiction

Sussman et al. (2011b) located only five studies with a sample size of at least 500 that examined co-occurrence of the eight other addictive behaviors among those suffering from tobacco, alcohol, or illicit drug use disorders, and all of these pertained to *gambling addiction* (Cunningham-Williams, Cottler, Compton, Spitznagel, & Ben-Abdallah,

2000 [lifetime use]; French, Maclean & Ettner, 2008; Griffiths, Wardle, Orford, Sproston, & Erens, 2010; Toneatto & Brennan, 2002; Welte, Barnes, Wieczorek, Tidwell, & Parker, 2001). Among a large sample of adults in Great Britain who reported having been "smokers" in the past year, 1.1% reported problem gambling (Griffiths et al., 2010). This was the only large study located pertaining to tobacco use and gambling. Among mostly large samples of weekly or greater drinkers, and among adult alcoholic inpatients, 3% to 5% reported a gambling problem (French et al., 2008; Griffiths et al., 2010; Lesieur, Blume, & Zoppa, 1986; Toneatto & Brennan, 2002), although in a representative sample of US adults, 24% of alcohol dependent persons also reported a gambling problem (Welte et al., 2001). In a convenience sample of 97 13- to 18-year-old US outpatient substance abusers (alcohol or marijuana abuse/dependence), only 1% (n = 1) met criteria for gambling addiction (Kaminer, Burleson, & Jadamec, 2002). Among a sample of 990 US adult drug abusers (ranging from 28% being sedative dependent, to 77% being stimulant dependent), 11% reported also being pathological gamblers (Cunningham-Williams et al., 2000 [lifetime use]), and other mostly small-scale research in various countries also indicated that 5–25% of illicit adult substance abusers were also gambling addicts (Freimuth et al., 2008; Lesieur & Blume, 1993; Lesieur et al., 1986; Petry, 2007; Najavits et al., 2014; Punzi & Fahlke, 2015; Spunt, Dupont, Lesieur, Liberty, & Hunt, 1998; Steinberg, Kosten, & Rounsaville, 1992; Toneatto & Brennan, 2002). Other adult data from various countries report co-occurrence of 15–19% problem gambling among cocaine addicts, and 20% among heroin addicts (see review by Ferentzy, Skinner, & Matheson, 2013).

ATOD Addiction with Sex or Love Addictions

Freimuth et al. (2008) estimated that about a third of substance abusers also exhibit *sex addiction*; however, that one report is speculative. Griffin-Shelley (1995) speculated that only 10% of those with drug dependence also suffer from *love addiction* or sex addiction. Najavits et al. (2014) found that 9.8% of a small sample of US substance abuse patients also reported sex addiction (13% endorsed "yes" or "maybe"). Punzi & Fahlke (2015) found that 48% of a small sample of Swedish chemical dependence inpatients and outpatients also reported problematic sexual activities.

ATOD with Other Behavioral Addictions

Najavits et al. (2014) also found a high co-occurrence of other addictions with that of substance abuse, including 9.8% with *Internet/computer* (28% "yes" or "maybe"), 5.9% with *exercise* (16% "yes" or "maybe"), 12% with *work* (20% "yes" or "maybe"), and 17.7% with *shopping/spending* (42% either "yes" or "maybe"). Punzi & Fahlke (2015) also found that 26% of their small sample (n = 69) of Swedish chemical dependence inpatients and outpatients also reported problematic exercise activities. We found no other studies indicating co-occurrence of other addictions among cigarette smokers, alcohol abusers, or illicit substance abusers.

Lisha and Sussman (2010) reviewed the literature, which indicated that exercise, or at least team sports participation, tends not to be related to tobacco, marijuana, and other illicit drug use. However, they found a positive relationship of sports participation with alcohol use and abuse (also see Lisha, Sussman, & Leventhal, 2013). Sussman and Lisha (2014) reviewed the literature on how exercise addiction might be related to alcohol abuse. The results of that paper are described in Chapter 7. However, in general, the relations between the two addictions are not strong. There is scant data indicating co-occurrence of about 20% (e.g., Freimuth et al., 2011; Najavits et al., 2014; Punzi & Fahlke, 2015), and one may speculate this percentage may be much smaller.

Summary of ATOD Addiction with Each Other and Other Addictions

Much more research is needed; there is a wide variation in how strongly cigarettes/nicotine, alcohol, and illicit drugs are associated with other addictions. Pedrelli et al. (2010) found gender differences among 904 undergraduate college youth; for males, "compulsive" drinking was associated with increased risk for compulsive illicit drug use, sex, and gambling, whereas for females, compulsive drinking was associated with compulsive illicit drug use and sex only. Of course, classification was vague in this study; again, more research is needed, also to examine moderator variables such as gender.

As Sussman et al. (2011b) reported, estimating the prevalence of cigarette, alcohol, and illicit drug use (marijuana or other drugs) addictions in US adults at 15%, 10%, and 5%, respectively, if one infers a 50% overlap among any two of the three drug use disorders, then one might sum half of each of these addictive behaviors and find that 15% of the adult population in the United States is addicted to either cigarettes, alcohol, or other drugs, controlling for overlap (30% total if there was no overlap). Tentatively, I estimate a 50% overlap among tobacco, alcohol, or illicit drug addictions. In addition, I tentatively estimate, based on the few gambling and binge eating reports (also see review by Lacey & Evans, 1986), and the studies just reviewed, that 20% of cigarette smokers, alcohol abusers, or illicit substance abusers may also experience any of the other eight addictions.

Food Addiction

Food addiction is a disorder characterized by a preoccupation with food, the availability of food, and, for many, the anticipation of pleasure from the ingestion of food. Food addiction can involve the repetitive consumption of food contrary to an individual's wishes, resulting in loss of control and/or preoccupation with restriction of food, body weight, and body image. Like drug addiction, food addiction may, over time, lead to neuroadaptive changes in the brain and an acquired so-called "brain disease."

Food addiction is different from other eating disorders. These other eating disorders include anorexia nervosa, bulimia, overeating, and binge eating. ***Anorexia nervosa*** (an emotional disorder characterized by an obsessive desire to lose weight by refusing to eat) is associated with (extreme) over-control, whereas addictions are associated with loss of control; it probably is not reflective of an addictive process (Kaye et al., 2013). For some people, the conditions of overeating-related ***obesity*** (e.g., Body Mass Index of 30 or higher) or ***bulimia nervosa*** (an emotional disorder involving distortion of body image and an obsessive desire to lose weight or not gain weight, in which bouts of extreme overeating are followed by depression and self-induced vomiting, purging, or fasting) may be a result of food addiction, but may not be examples of food addiction. Still, for some people, overeating-related obesity or bulimia nervosa might be considered to show an addictive pattern of behavior (Kaye et al., 2013). Binge eating disorder (BED) arguably is most like other addictions in its behavioral topography (Davis & Carter, 2009; Faber, Christenson, De Zwaan, & Mitchell, 1995; Goossens, Soenens, & Braet, 2009; Lewinsohn, Seeley, Moerk, & Striegel-Moore, 2002; Yau et al., 2014). Binge eating (eating large amounts of food in short periods of time, at least twice weekly) is the most prevalent food disorder in the United States. James, Guo, and Liu (2001) identified converging neuroimaging, cognitive, and behavioral indicators that suggested binge eating and other misuse of food intake reasonably fits within a theoretical model of substance addiction. Volkow and Wise (2005) reported similar results.

A recent study indicated that 57% of BED patients met the criteria for food addiction (Gearhardt et al., 2012) using the Yale Food Addiction Scale (see Chapter 9) and approximately 25% of obese persons met the criteria for food addiction (Davis et al., 2011). NIMH reports a prevalence of adult BED of 1.2% (www.nimh.nih.gov/statistics/1EAT_ADULT_RB.shtml). CDC estimates a prevalence of adult obesity of 34.9% (www.cdc.gov/nchs/data/databriefs/db131.htm). If food addicts were a subset of BED patients then the prevalence of food addiction would be less than 1%. If food addicts were a subset of persons with obesity then the prevalence of food addiction would be 8.7%. This is a fairly wide variation. Also, there likely are food addicts who are not obese or do not suffer from BED (Yau et al., 2014).

Last-year prevalence rates of BED among older teens and adults across several countries varies between 1 and 2% (Allison, Grilo, Masheb, & Stunkard, 2005; Gadalla & Piran, 2007; Gleaves & Carter, 2008; Hay, 1998; Hoek & Hoeken, 2003 [four large studies were cited in their review, but three examined only females]; Smith, Marcus, Lewis, Fitzgibbon, & Schreiner, 1998; Spitzer et al., 1992; Timmerman, Wells, & Chen, 1990 [examined bulimia nervosa]), though Goossens et al. (2009) found a prevalence of 7.4% among a sample of Belgian teenagers, Cook (1987) found a prevalence of 6.4% for overeating among US college youth (single item used), and MacLaren and Best (2010) found a prevalence of 14.9% food binging among 19-year-old Canadian college youth. Lewinsohn et al. (2002) found a prevalence of 3–4% for 24-year-olds. Spitzer et al. (1992) found a 30.1% prevalence among participants of hospital affiliated weight control programs (who were moderately obese). Based on these studies (9 of 12 including samples of at least 500 subjects), Sussman et al. (2011b) estimated a last 12-month prevalence of 2% for food addiction among general population US adults. Tentatively, I will stay with the 2% food addiction prevalence estimate of Sussman et al., (2011b), since their study examined the relevant literature most exhaustively. However, it is possible that prevalence of food addiction is much higher.

Food Addiction or Eating Addiction?

A recent review paper suggested that craving for types of food (e.g., carbohydrates, fats, sugars, salt) may not be the best way to frame the concept of food addiction, as consideration of how food might activate the brain is complex, and eating addiction may occur outside of food binges (Hebebrand et al., 2014). In addition, in a recent laboratory negative mood induction study, provision of comfort foods (e.g., chocolate, ice cream, cookies, or brownies) provided no mood benefit beyond non-comfort food, or no food (sitting quietly); that is, all conditions led to short-term mood improvement (Wagner, Ahlstrom, Redden, Vickers, & Mann, 2014). A wide variety of foods may be consumed addictively, and may be consumed in different ways that may be addictive. Hebebrand and colleagues prefer consideration of the term *eating addiction* as opposed to "food addiction." For the time being, given available work, I will continue to consider binge eating disorder as a proxy for food or eating addiction. However, its use should be considered with caution. (The implication, perhaps, is that food addiction is a substance addiction, but eating addiction is a behavioral addiction.)

Co-Occurrence

Found in primarily small samples (each composed mostly of women), between 20% and 46% of teens and adults in various countries with an eating disorder (of some type) reported *alcohol or other drug problems* (Freimuth et al., 2008; Gleaves & Carter, 2008; Holderness et al., 1994; Lacy & Evans, 1986; Lewinsohn et al., 2002; Timmerman et al., 1990 [alcohol abuse, about 6% of males and 23% of females with bulimia]), though only 1% of a small sample of 90 female and five male teenagers with an eating disorder reported alcohol or other drug use disorder (Castro-Fornieles et al., 2010).

Lewinsohn et al. (2002) found excessive *exercise* activity among males with BED, but not females; however, percentage overlap was not reported. Freimuth et al. (2008) summarized in their review of primarily small samples that of those with eating disorders, 39–48% also experienced an exercise addiction and 15% also experienced *buying addiction*. Faber et al. (1995), among a sample of 84 obese female subjects with BED, found that 15% could be classified as compulsive buyers (compared to 4.4% of obese female non-BED subjects). Faber and colleagues also mentioned that, in their earlier work, 23.8% of binge eaters reported also being compulsive buyers. There were no other studies reported that examined the relations of eating disorders with other addictions. Tentatively, Sussman et al. (2011b) estimated that 25% of those with an eating disorder, particularly binge eating disorder, experience one of the other ten addictive disorders. This estimate, while gross, does appear to reflect the available literature.

Summary

The five leading preventable causes of premature death include heart disease, cancers, chronic lower respiratory diseases, strokes, and unintentional injuries (www.cdc.gov/media/releases/2014/p0501-preventable-deaths.html). The four substance addictions presented in this chapter are major killers, accountable in large part for these leading preventable causes of death. Again, their prevalence is summarized in Table 6.1. The co-occurrence among tobacco, alcohol, and other drug addiction is fairly high, and among drug abusers, it appears that food addiction may be of relatively high prevalence (though not as high a co-occurrence as among the drugs with each other). These estimates do not consider lifetime co-occurrence or substitute addiction (e.g., food addiction or tobacco use starting after the individual stops drinking alcohol or using other drugs) which could elevate the co-occurrence among the substance addictions (i.e., viewed longitudinally). Chapter 7 will go on to discuss the prevalence of the other seven focal, behavioral addictions (gambling, Internet, love, sex, exercise, work, and shopping), and their co-occurrence with the other 11 focal addictions.

Bulleted Summary

- I estimate that the world-wide prevalence of tobacco addiction is 15%, that the co-occurrence of tobacco use addiction with addiction to alcohol and other drugs is 50%, and that the co-occurrence of tobacco use addiction with food and behavioral addictions is 20%.
- I estimate that the world-wide prevalence of alcoholism is 10%, that the co-occurrence of alcoholism with tobacco and other drug use addiction is 50%, and that the co-occurrence of alcoholism with food and behavioral addictions is 20%.
- I estimate that the world-wide prevalence of other drug use addiction is 5%, that the co-occurrence of other drug use addiction with tobacco addiction and alcoholism is 50%, and that the co-occurrence of other drug use addiction with food and behavioral addictions is 20%.
- I estimate that the world-wide prevalence of food addiction is 2% and that its co-occurrence with other addictions is 25%.
- Researchers currently debate whether or not food-related addiction directly alters neurobiological function through food intake (fatty and sugary food addiction) or whether it is the act of eating that one becomes addicted to (a behavioral addiction).

Suggestions for Further Reading

Hebebrand, J., Albayrak, O., Adan, R., Antel, J., Dieguez, C., de Jong, J., ... & Dickson, S. L. (2014). "Eating addiction," rather than "food addiction," better captures addictive-like eating behavior. *Neuroscience and Biobehavioral Reviews*, 47: 295–308.

Najavits, L., Lung, J., Froias, A., Paull, N., & Bailey, G. (2014). A study of multiple behavioral addictions in a substance abuse sample. *Substance Use & Misuse*, 49: 479–484.

Rosenberg, K. P. & Feder, L. C. (eds.) (2014a). *Behavioral Addictions: Criteria, Evidence, and Treatment*. London: Academic Press/Elsevier.

Sussman, S., Lisha, N., & Griffiths, M. (2011b). Prevalence of the addictions: A problem of the majority or the minority? *Evaluation & the Health Professions*, 34: 3–56.

7 Behavioral Addictions: Their Prevalence and Co-Occurrence

Learning Objectives

- To learn about the prevalence of gambling, Internet use, love, sex, exercise, work, and compulsive spending addictions
- To learn about the co-occurrence of gambling, Internet use, love, sex, exercise, work, and compulsive spending addictions with each other and with substance addictions
- To learn about the special case of team sports participation and alcohol use co-occurrence
- To get a sense of highest to lowest prevalence among the 11 focal addictions

Introduction

Johnny sometimes had dreams that he was fired from work or that he never completed his graduate program. The next day, to relieve this worry, he would get on one of his "work binges." He would work for many hours, days at a time. He might achieve a "buzz" at some point after he felt he really made headway, solving work issues. People at work might comment that he appeared to get more work done than two people generally do. At other times, he would work harder and harder but still felt that he might be fired at any moment and that less and less was accomplished. He suffered stomach aches and had trouble falling asleep, worrying about his job. He appeared to be suffering from workaholism.

Behavioral addictions comprise a series of pathological behaviors that lead individuals to experience "mood-altering events" (e.g., experiential changes, appetitive effects), in which they achieve such outcomes as pleasure, become preoccupied and experience loss of control, and become dependent (Robinson & Berridge, 2000; Schaef, 1987). The eventual impact is similar to that of drug misuse or food addiction (e.g., increase in mesolimbic dopaminergic turnover, dependence on the behavior to alter neurotransmitter function, decreasing effectiveness of the behavior, and negative consequences). Sussman et al. (2011b) completed a review of 11 addictions, seven of which are behavioral addictions. In this chapter, I will focus on these seven behavioral addictions: gambling, various types of Internet use, love, sex, exercise, work, and compulsive spending (Orford, 2001; Griffiths, 2005a, 2005b; Rosenberg & Feder, 2014a; Sussman et al., 2011b), and their prevalence and co-occurrence. A summary of the prevalence of the behavioral addictions is shown in Table 7.1. As in Chapter 6, in almost all cases, the assessment of prevalence was determined through scores on self-report scales, though in less than 10 percent of the cases a DSM-like interview was conducted (see Sussman et al., 2011b, for details).

Table 7.1 Prevalence of behavioral addictions

Gambling	Prevalence of gambling addiction is between 1% and 3% of the US adult population as well as in other countries such as Australia, Canada, China, Norway, Switzerland, and Spain (Sussman et al., 2011b estimated 2%). However, prevalence rates of pathological gambling may be as high as 15% in some unique populations of teens and adults.
Internet addiction	Sussman et al. (2011b) estimated a last 12-month prevalence of US general adult Internet addiction of 2%. This figure is consistent with studies on the prevalence of problematic online gaming and Internet addiction. While it is possible that prevalence of social networking addiction may become higher than other types of Internet addictions, it is premature to make an estimate.
Love and sex addiction	Most researchers place prevalence of love addiction or compulsive sexual behavior at 3–6% of the general adult population. Sussman et al. (2011b) speculated that 3% of US adults are love addicts and that 3% are sex addicts. Prevalence of love and sex addiction may be much higher among emerging adults; however, this may reflect developmental processes.
Exercise addiction	Exercise addiction has been estimated at being from 3% to 5% of the US population, although studies were completed primarily with college youth. A few studies of college youth report prevalence as high as 21.8–25.6%. Sussman et al. (2011b) speculated that the prevalence of last 12-month exercise dependence among US adults is 3%, though it may be lower because adults tend to become more sedentary as they age.
Workaholism	Current prevalence of workaholism in large samples has been found to be approximately 8.0–17.5%. However, others have estimated that only 5% of the US population are workaholics. Tentatively, Sussman et al. (2011b) estimated a prevalence of workaholism among 10% of the US adult population. Inconsistency in the measurement of workaholism may lead to variability in estimates.
Shopping addiction	Most estimates place prevalence of adult addiction to shopping ranging from 1% to 6%. Sussman et al. (2011b) estimated a prevalence of 6% of US adults suffering from shopping addiction based on the Koran et al. (2006) study.

Gambling

As introduced in Chapter 2, gambling involves risking something of value to obtain something of greater value (hence can involve chasing losses), but also involves achieving a sense of adventure or excitement, and is a means to relieve distress (APA, 2013), leading to preoccupation, loss of control, and negative consequences (e.g., sometimes lying to others about extent of involvement, losing the trust of other people, going into debt). Opportunities to gamble exist at casinos, at the racetrack, on the Internet, in governmental lotteries, and informally with peers or others (e.g., playing cards at homes, betting against friends on outcomes of sports games). Thus, there are a variety of venues for gambling to take place.

Problem Gambling Prevalence

North American research studies involving large samples, and meta-analyses, indicate that between 2.1% and 10% of older teenagers experience gambling problems (Barnes et al., 2009; Gupta & Derevensky, 2008; Ladouceur, Boudreault, Jacques, & Vitaro, 1999a; MacLaren & Best, 2010; Shaffer & Hall, 2001 [meta-analysis]; Shaffer, Hall, & Vander Bilt, 1999 [meta-analysis]; Welte, Barnes, Tidwell, & Hoffman, 2008; Westphal, Rush, Steven, & Johnson, 2000; Winters, Stinchfield, & Fulkerson, 1993). Problem gambling rates among older teenagers have shown variations world-wide. A review of large-scale studies by Volberg, Gupta, Griffiths, Olason, and Delfabbro (2010) examined studies on adolescent gambling in North America, Europe, and Oceania. The rates of problem/pathological gambling reported in non-North American countries were as follows: Australia, 1–13%; Denmark, 0.8%; Estonia, 3.4%; Finland, 2.3%; Germany, 3%; Great Britain, 2–5.6%; Iceland, 1.9–3%; Italy, 6% (7% among Italian 13- to 20-year-olds, see Villella et al., 2011); Lithuania, 4–5%; New Zealand, 3.8–13%; Norway, 1.8–3.2%; Romania, 7%; Spain, 0.8–4.6%; and Sweden, 0.9%. This variation may have resulted from the stringency of the instrument used to measure problem gambling, each country's gambling laws, or subject sampling methods used. On the other hand, using an addiction matrix item, Sussman et al. (2014) found that only 1.8% of (at-risk) former alternative high school youth from southern California in the United States (mean age = 19.8 years; n = 717) reported last 30-day addiction to gambling. Prevalence of gambling addiction appears generally low among adolescents. Cook (1987) found a prevalence of 2.4% among US college youth, and Lesieur et al. (1991) found a prevalence of 4–8% among a large sample of college youth in five US states.

Among adults, prevalence of gambling addiction is between 1% and 3% of the US population as well as other countries such as Australia, Canada, China, Norway, Switzerland, and Spain (Becona, 1993; Bondolfi, Osiek, & Ferrero, 2000; Cook, 1987; Desai, Desai, & Potenza, 2007; French et al., 2008; Griffiths, 2009b; Ladouceur, Jacques, Ferland, & Giroux, 1999b; Petry, 2005, 2007; Phillippe & Vallerand, 2007; Schofield, Mummery, Wang, & Dickson, 2004 [lifetime]; Shaffer & Hall, 2001; Shaffer et al., 1999; Stucki & Rihs-Middel, 2007; Sommers, 1988; Volberg, 1994 [lifetime];

Volberg & Steadman, 1988 [lifetime]; Wong & So, 2003), although two large-sample studies found a prevalence of 0.15% in Norwegian adults (Gotestam & Johansson, 2003) and 4.2% among US adults in Texas (Feigelman, Wallisch, & Lesieur, 1998 [lifetime measure]). Current prevalence rates of pathological gambling may be as high as 15% in some unique populations of teens and adults (e.g., the Aboriginal population in North America; Wardman, el-Guebaly, & Hodgins, 2001). Sussman et al. (2011b) estimated a last 12-month prevalence of gambling addiction of 2% in the general US adult population. I think that estimate is reasonable, and falls within the range of 0.4% to 5.3% estimated world-wide (Grant & Odlaug, 2014).

Co-Occurrence

Among large samples of adult gambling addicts across various countries, 41–75% reported being current *cigarette smokers* (Becona, 1993; Desai et al., 2007; Petry, 2007 [review]; Potenza, Steinberg, Wu, Rounsaville, & O'Malley, 2006). In several small samples, 4–11.4% of adult gambling addicts reported *alcoholism* (Black & Moyer, 1998; Lesieur & Rosenthal, 1991; Netemeyer et al., 1998). In one large sample of gambling addicted adults who called a gambling helpline in Connecticut, 18% reported problems with alcohol use (Potenza et al., 2006), and in large samples of Spanish and Swiss adults, 14% and 36%, respectively, of probable gambling addicted adults reported alcohol abuse (Bondolfi et al., 2000). Assessed from large representative samples of US adults, 25% and 33% of gambling addicts reported alcohol dependence (Desai et al., 2007; Welte et al., 2001).

Among large samples of US older teen heavy gamblers, co-occurrence with heavy use of alcohol or marijuana/other *illicit drugs* has been found to be 35% (Hammond et al., 2014 [lifetime use of marijuana]), 36% (Barnes et al., 2009), and 59% (Westphal et al., 2000). Among mostly small samples of US adult gambling addicts, co-occurrence with past year illicit drug problems has been found to vary from 2% to 13% (Black & Moyer, 1998; Lesieur & Rosenthal, 1991; Netemeyer et al., 1998; Petry, 2007; Potenza et al., 2006); however, in one large-sample study of US adults in Texas, 26% of gambling addicts reported a substance abuse problem (Feigelman et al., 1998).

In a large sample of US adult gambling addicts (using the National Epidemiologic Survey on Alcohol and Related Conditions [NESARC]), 33% were obese, though an *eating disorder* was not diagnosed (Desai et al., 2007). In a sample of 30 US adult gambling addicts, 6% reported an eating disorder (i.e., bulimia nervosa; Black & Moyer, 1998). Among 225 US adult gambling addicts, 19.6% also met the criteria for *sexual addiction* (Grant & Steinberg, 2005). Lesieur and Rosenthal (1991) reported two conference papers of small samples of US adult gambling addicts (Adkins, Rugle, & Taber, 1985, and their own), in which 20% were binge eaters (all females), 12% and 14% were sexually addicted, and 24% were *shopping addicts* (all females). Kausch (2003) reported on 94 US adult gambling addicts in Ohio, in which 30.9% suffered from sexual addiction and 24.5% suffered from buying/shopping addiction. In Netemeyers et al.'s study (1998) of 44 US adult gambling addicts, 29.3% reported buying addiction. I could locate no other data on co-occurrence of other addictions among gambling addicts.

Summary of Gambling Co-Occurrence with Other Addictions

Based on the studies reviewed, Sussman et al. (2011b) estimated that 50%, 30%, and 20% of gambling addicts also are cigarette, alcohol, and illicit drug use addicts, respectively. These estimates are similar to those suggested by Lesieur and Blume (1993). The alcohol and drug use co-occurrence estimates are a little lower than those suggested by Freimuth et al. (2008) and Kausch (2003), but are based on a larger pool of studies. In addition, we speculated that 20 percent of adult gambling addicts suffer from any of the other seven addictions. Gambling often involves sedentary behavior and probably would reveal a low relation with exercise addiction, but there are no data to support this speculation.

Internet Addiction

Young (1999) argued that individuals suffering from Internet addiction are likely to use the Internet to alter their mood state (i.e., attempt to "escape" when feeling lonely, down, or anxious), are preoccupied with Internet use (whether it involves gaming, social networking, or roaming), report symptoms of tolerance and withdrawal, have tried unsuccessfully to cut back on use, and have disturbances in their lives because of their Internet use. While there is an ongoing debate on to what extent Internet addiction is an addiction in and of itself, versus representing a medium for other addictions (i.e., shopping, gambling, gaming, sex, and love), studies still investigate prevalence of addiction to the medium – which may reflect a type of electronic device addiction (Sussman et al., 2011b). That is, one may obsess or daydream about the Internet as a medium, neglect responsibilities or sleep to be on the Internet, and conceal from others the amount of time spent on the Internet or feel a sense of loss of control over one's time on the Internet (Demetrovics, Szeredi, & Rozsa, 2008).

Internet Addiction Prevalence

In a nationally representative sample of 12-, 14-, 16-, and 18-year olds in Finland, only 1.7% and 1.4% of boys and girls, respectively, reported Internet addiction (Kaltiala-Heino, Lintonen, & Rimpela, 2004). A similar percentage was found for Italian teens of 1.2% (Villella et al., 2011). In Korea, 1.6% of a large school-based convenience sample of 15- to 16-year-olds reported Internet addiction (Kim et al., 2006). However, in a later study, in Korea, using similar inclusion criteria and scoring, 10.7% of a random school sample of 903 14- to 18-year-olds reported Internet addiction (Park et al., 2008). In China, 2.4% of a large sample of 12- to 18-year-old youth (mean = 15 years old) reported Internet addiction (Cao & Su, 2006). However, among 1,761 Chinese and 1,182 US female and male alternative (at-risk) high school youth, 5.8% (Chinese female), 15.7% (Chinese male), 9.7% (US female), and 7.3% (US male) reported compulsive Internet use (Sun et al., 2012).

Studies of mostly large samples of university students provided estimates of addictive Internet use of 5.9–9.3%, mostly for social contact and to reduce loneliness (Anderson, 2001; Chou & Hsiao, 2000 [in Taiwan]; Kubey, Lavin, & Barrows, 2001 [in United States]; Morahan-Martin & Schumacher, 2000 [277 US Internet-users]). However, Grusser, Thalemann, and Griffiths (2007) found that 11.9% of a large sample of over 7,000 online gamers (mean age = 21 years; various countries) were addicted to online games. Also, Niemz, Griffiths, and Banyard (2005) found a prevalence of 18.3% among 371 British college students (28.7% of males, 9.5% of females), and Leung (2004) found a 37.9% current prevalence among a large sample of Hong Kong 16- to 24-year-olds. Fortson et al. (Fortson, Scotti, Chen, Malone, & Del Ben, 2007) found that while 21.9% of a large sample of US college youth met criteria for Internet abuse, only 1.2% met criteria for Internet dependence.

Among large samples of adults contacted through online surveys, 3.5–9.6% were found to be Internet addicts (Cooper, Morahan-Martin, Mathy, & Maheu, 2002; Greenfield, 1999; Whang, Lee, & Chang, 2003). For instance, Greenfield (1999) conducted an online survey with 17,251 adult respondents from various countries. Internet addiction was assessed using ten modified items from DSM-IV criteria for pathological gambling. Greenfield reported that 6% of respondents met the criteria for addicted Internet use. A much lower prevalence of 0.7% was found by Aboujaoude et al. (Aboujaoude, Koran, Gamel, Large, & Serpe, 2006), through a random-digit-dialing telephone survey of general population US adults, and a 1.0% prevalence was found in a large, stratified probability sample of Norwegian adults (Bakken, Wenzel, Gotestam, Johansson, & Oren, 2009). Thus, as research criteria become more restrictive, involve a general population (i.e., include non-baseline Internet users as well as baseline users), and involve an assessment of adults, prevalence drops dramatically. Sussman et al. (2011b) estimated a last 12-month prevalence of US general adult Internet addiction of 2%. This figure appears fairly consistent with studies on the prevalence of problematic online gaming and Internet addiction (Kiraly et al., 2014 [young males being perhaps eight times more likely than young females to be online gamers]; Weinstein et al., 2014 [rates may be two to three times higher among teens than adults]).

While it is possible that prevalence of social networking addiction may be or become much higher than other types of Internet addictions as more and more people join such sites (e.g., Facebook, Twitter), it is premature to make an estimate (Griffiths et al., 2014). However, one can speculate. There are now 1.28 billion active (last 30-day log in) Facebook accounts world-wide (www.statista.com/statistics/264810/number-of-monthly-active-facebook-users-worldwide/). Assuming that there are 4.5 billion adults world-wide (62% of the total population), that 25% of them have Facebook accounts, and that 10% of those having Facebook accounts use them over two hours per day (as a rough proxy for addictive use), then the prevalence of social networking addiction would be estimated at approximately 2.5%. This could raise the overall estimate of Internet addiction, given the different types of usage of the Internet. For the time being, I will stick with the 2% overall estimate but acknowledge it could be twice as high overall.

Co-Occurrence

Among a large sample of teenagers and adults in Norway, 13.6% of Internet addicts self-reported also experiencing past year *alcohol and substance abuse* (Bakken et al., 2009). Shapira et al. (2003) reviewed two small-sample studies (ns = 21 and 20) by

Black and colleagues and Shapira and colleagues. Averaging across these studies, 12% of US adult Internet addicts reported alcohol abuse/dependence, 5% reported other drug abuse/dependence, 10% reported *binge eating*, 5% reported *gambling* addiction (Shapira study only), and 10% reported *sex addiction*/psychosexual disorders. In a study of 15 23-year-old Italian Internet addicts, one person (7.5% of sample) reported binge eating disorder (Bernardi & Pallanti, 2009). Sussman et al. (2011b) could locate no other studies that examined other addictions among Internet addicts. Based on these data we speculated that 10% of general adult Internet addicts are addicted to any one of the other ten addictive behaviors.

Love and Sex Addiction

Love addiction involves pleasurable feelings and obsessive thoughts that may be subjectively described as craving for continued union with a love object. A key element of love addiction is the belief that, somehow, romantic relations are magically potent; that they are relationships that can surmount all emotional obstacles (Peele & Brodsky, 1992, esp. pp. 144–157). Love addicts may also be sex addicts, but not necessarily, and the restrictive pattern of love addiction may be more like a substance abuse type addiction than sex addiction (Sussman, 2010a). Also, love addicts may engage in a pattern of love seeking (a) as a reaction toanxiety or depression, (b) to reduce fear of loneliness, and (c) as a function of idealization of the objects of romantic interest, and then blame these persons for not fulfilling one's fantasies and expectations (e.g., Feeney & Noller, 1990; Sussman, 2010a). Sex addiction involves sexual urges and fantasies, and engagement in sexual behavior to relieve distress, but also for adventure/excitement and to feel pleasure, which involves a loss of control and disregard of the physical or emotional harm to self or others (Fong et al., 2012; Rosenberg et al., 2014; Sussman, 2007).

Love and Sex Addiction Prevalence

Sussman et al. (2014) reported prevalence estimates of 23.2% and 16.5% for love and sex addiction, respectively, among US former alternative high school youth. Cook (1987) reported prevalence estimates of 25.9% and 16.8% for love and sex addiction, respectively, among US college youth. MacLaren and Best (2010) provided estimates of 11.9% for relationship submissive/love addiction and 10.3% for sex addiction among 948 19-year-old Canadian college youth. Likewise, among a sample of 240 US college students, Seegers (2003) found that 13.5% were at risk for, or were sexually addicted. Cooper et al. (2002) found a 9.6% online sexual addiction prevalence among a large sample of adult Internet users from various countries (80% from US). However, most researchers place prevalence of love addiction or compulsive sexual behavior at 3–6% of the general adult population (Fong et al., 2012; Freimuth et al., 2008; Krueger & Kaplan, 2001; Kuzma & Black, 2008; Rosenberg et al., 2014; Sussman, 2010a). Sussman et al. (2011b) speculated that 3% of US adults are love addicts and that 3% are sex addicts. Prevalence of love and sex addiction may be much higher among emerging adults; however, this may reflect developmental processes.

Co-Occurrence

Griffin-Shelley (1995) speculated that 50% of adult sex addicts also are drug dependent. Carnes (1991) found that in his sample of 932 US adult sex addicts, 42% also suffered from *alcohol or drug addiction*, 38% suffered from an *eating disorder* (compulsive eating, some suffered from anorexia or bulimia nervosa), 28% were *workaholics*, and 26% were *compulsive spenders*. Likewise, in a larger sample of 1,604 adult residential treatment sex addicts, Carnes et al. (2005) found that approximately 37% reported addiction to *nicotine*, 46% reported addiction to alcohol, 40% reported addiction to other substances, 24% reported addiction to eating, 6% reported addiction to *gambling*, 12% reported addiction to *exercise*, 34% reported workaholism, and 31% reported addiction to shopping/buying. Kuzma and Black (2008) reviewed three small-sample studies of US adult sex addiction (ns = 36, 26, and 25, respectively, by Black, Kehrberg, Flumerfelt, & Schlosser, 1997; Kafka & Prentky, 1992; Raymond, Coleman, & Miner, 2003). Averaging across these three small-sample studies, 60% of sex addicts also reported a substance use disorder of some type, 6% reported an eating disorder, 5% reported gambling addiction, and 5% reported buying/shopping addiction. Based on their review of five small-scale studies, Freimuth et al. (2008) calculated that 39–42% of adult sex addicts suffered from substance-related disorders, 22–38% suffered from an eating disorder, 4–11% suffered from gambling addiction, 8% suffered from exercise addiction, and 13–26% suffered from buying addiction. Based on these few studies completed, Sussman et al. (2011b) speculated that 50% of love addicts are also sex addicts, and the converse. In addition, they speculated that co-occurrence of love and sex addiction with the three substance use disorders is 40%, whereas co-occurrence with the remaining six addictions is 20%.

Exercise Addiction

Some addictions may be self-injurious but still receive social approval, at least initially. One such behavioral addiction is exercise. Both mere commitment to exercise and exercise addiction may involve experiences of satisfaction and achievement. However, exercise addiction may be distinguished from commitment to exercise in at least three ways: the degree of entrenchment/preoccupation in exercise, experience of and reliance on an appetitive effect (e.g., the runner's high, and/or to reduce distress), and strong deprivation sensations when unable to exercise (see Szabo, Frenkl, & Caputo, 1997). Exercise addiction, initially considered a "positive addiction" by some clinicians (e.g., Glasser, 1976), may lead to repeated injuries and neglect of work and family life (Adams, 2009; Allegre et al., 2006; Berczik et al., 2014; Freimuth et al., 2011; Griffiths,

1997; Thaxton, 1982). Amongst the scattering of research that has been completed, exercise addiction is said to include the presence of mood modification/regulation, tolerance, withdrawal symptoms (e.g., irritability or depression when the person is unable to work out), lack of control, detrimental social consequences, personal conflict, and several other negative effects such as disturbed psychological functioning, exercising despite medical contraindications, or interference with relationships or work (salience), and relapse (Freimuth et al., 2011; Hausenblas & Downs, 2002; Weinstein & Weinstein, 2014).

Exercise Addiction Prevalence

Exercise addiction prevalence has been estimated as affecting 3–5% of the US population, although large and small sample studies were completed primarily with college youth (Allegre et al., 2006; Cook, 1987; Downs, Hausenblas, & Nigg, 2004; Terry, Szabo, & Griffiths, 2004). A few studies of college youth report prevalence as high as 21.8–25.6% (Garman, Hayduk, Crider, & Hodel, 2004; MacLaren & Best, 2010), and Sussman et al. (2014) reported a 17.7% prevalence among US former alternative high school youth. On the other hand Griffiths, Szabo, and Terry (2005) reported only a 3% prevalence among British sport science and psychology students. Villella et al. (2011) reported a 7.6% prevalence among Italian 12- to 20-year-olds. Unfortunately, a vast majority of studies completed to date were not designed to examine prevalence of exercise addiction (Hausenblas & Downs, 2002), and could be subject to selection confounders (e.g., examining prevalence among athletes or sport science students will produce an inflated estimate). Based on the few studies completed, Sussman et al. (2011b) speculated that the prevalence of last 12-month exercise dependence among US adults is 3%, though it may be lower because adults tend to become more sedentary as they age.

Co-Occurrence

Sussman et al. (2011b) located no studies on the co-occurrence of exercise addiction with other disorders with a sample size of at least 500. There is some suggestion that there exist persons only dependent on exercise (primary exercise addiction) who are similar in other ways to non-addicts whereas there are others who also have eating disorder (secondary exercise addiction) and report the myriad features associated with addictiveness (Bamber, Cockerill, & Carroll, 2000). Among 125 Parisian male and female current exercise addicts (defined at 3 or more criteria of 7; mean age = 28.6 years), 20% reported *nicotine dependence*, 8% reported *alcohol dependence*, 70% reported being *bulimic*, and 63% reported being *shopping addicts* (Lejoyeux, Avril, Richoux, Embouazza, & Nivoli, 2008). They were about twice as likely as non-addicted exercisers to be bulimics and shopping addicts, but they were very similar in prevalence to non-addicted exercisers on cigarette and alcohol dependence. Among 265 US young adult women runners and non-runners, 25% of those who ran more than

30 miles per week showed a high risk for anorexia nervosa (Estok & Rudy, 1996). Sussman et al. (2011b) speculated that 15% of exercise addicts are also addicted to smoking, alcohol, or illicit drugs and that 25% exhibit the remaining addictions. One notable exception: a pooled estimate of anabolic-androgenic steroid (AAS) dependence among teenage or emerging adult athletes (e.g., weightlifters) is 32.5% (Pope et al., 2014). However, much more research is needed here.

The Special Case of Team Sports and Alcohol Misuse

As mentioned in the previous chapter, Lisha and Sussman (2010), and Lisha et al. (2013) found a positive relationship between team sports participation or physical activity and alcohol use and abuse (but not dependence). This relationship may not, however, reflect co-occurrence between exercise addiction and alcoholism. At least one study failed to find a difference in alcohol consumption between exercise dependent and non-dependent participants of a fitness club (Lejoyeux et al., 2008), and two other studies found only weak correlations of Pearson r = 0.06 and 0.09 that are not statistically significant (ps > 0.1), respectively, between alcohol and exercise addictions among males and females in a UK chemical dependence recovery facility (Haylett et al., 2004) and US college men and women (Greenberg et al., 1999).

Sussman and Lisha (2014) reviewed the possible relations among exercise and alcohol addictions. For some persons, it is possible that both addictions coexist. Both exercise and alcohol use increase release of mesolimbic dopamine, endorphins, and anandamide neurotransmitters (appetitive effects), and likely are met with counter-adaptation processes (Weinstein & Weinstein, 2014). Thus, they could "work off of each other," producing similar short-term impacts (satiation) and similar counter-adaptations. Exercise/alcohol co-addicts may be preoccupied with engaging in both activities. For most such persons it is doubtful that they would engage in drinking and sports participation *at the same time*. Rather, they may overtrain (loss of control), leading to tiredness or injury, which may then lead to drinking alcohol as a substitute addiction (Sussman & Black, 2008). Conversely, they may drink too much alcohol (loss of control), leading to being hungover, and then they may exercise extensively to decrease the duration of feeling hungover, or feel a contrast effect while getting into shape. Certainly, engagement in both addictions may lead to a variety of negative consequences such as impaired performance and injury.

Workaholism

Workaholism may at first induce pleasure, then later limit one's social life, induce subjective emotional pain (e.g., of feeling "burned out"), and may even lead to dangerous action (e.g., driving while preoccupied with work matters, driving and mobile telephone use, driving while being sleep-deprived). However, "workaholics" may also continue to receive ongoing social and financial rewards such as job promotions, salary increases, and/or praise from employers and work colleagues at least up to the point of burnout and reduction in productivity (Griffiths, 2005b; Sussman, 2012a).

Workaholism Prevalence

Current prevalence of workaholism in large samples has been found to be approximately 8% among Italian high school youth (Villella et al., 2011), 8–17.5% (Burke, 1999, 2000; Cook, 1987; MacLaren & Best, 2010) among college educated persons from various countries, and estimates as high as 23–25% have been provided in smaller samples (Doerfler & Kammer, 1986 [female attorneys, physicians, and psychologists/therapists]; Freimuth et al., 2008). Tentatively, Sussman et al. (2011b) estimated a prevalence of workaholism as 10% of the US adult population.

In the Sussman (2012a) review, I ascertained that self-identified workaholism may be as high as a third of a working population, if defined as excessive hours' working. Rates, of course, depend on the population being (a) between the ages of approximately 18 and 64 ("the working years"), which is 62% of the US population and (b) employed (which is approximately 90% in the United States). If a third of the working population self-identifies as workaholic, this could translate to 18% of the total population being workaholic (33% workaholic times 62% of working age times 90% employed). Interestingly, the estimate obtained from self-reports of US former alternative high school youth was 15.6% (Sussman et al., 2014). On the other hand, other researchers have estimated that only 5% of the US population was workaholic (Machlowitz, 1980). Along with a relative paucity in the number of prevalence studies, inconsistency in the measurement of workaholism certainly leads to variability in prevalence estimates. Also, excessive working may be a necessary but not sufficient criterion of workaholism (one should be "compulsively" into work, perhaps working harder and harder and subjectively feeling diminishing returns). Thus, a conservative estimate such as 10% may be more realistic also taking into account such characteristics as being hard driven and losing enjoyment of work.

Co-Occurrence

There are only a few, mostly anecdotal reports of the co-occurrence of workaholism with other addictions (e.g., Carnes, 1991; Carnes, Murray, & Charpentier, 2004; Carnes et al., 2005; Najavits et al., 2014), and these reports tend to link other addictions to workaholism rather than the converse. Tentatively, based on the few sources available, Sussman et al. (2011b) speculated that 20% of workaholics are addicted to other behaviors. It is possible that co-occurrence of workaholism may be higher with other "self-nurturing" addictions such as food, shopping, and exercise, as opposed to hedonistic addictions (i.e., drugs, sex, and gambling; see Sussman, 2012a, 2012b). However, given the few studies available to examine co-occurrence, the 20% co-occurrence estimate remains reasonable for the time being.

Shopping Addiction

Compulsive spenders repeatedly incur debt despite negative emotional, social, and financial consequences (Hodgson, Budd, & Griffiths, 2001). They may engage in a pattern of planning and purchasing behavior that at first glance appears normative, but on closer analysis may involve a pattern of repeated buying of one type of item, without using the item, to achieve a sense of pleasure (Black, 2007). They also tend to greatly value money as a solution to emotional problems (Hanley & Wilhelm, 1992).

Shopping Addiction Prevalence

Prevalence of addiction to shopping was 11.3% in the Villella et al. (2011) Italian high school sample, 10.7% in Cook's (1987) US college sample, 9.9% (last 30 days; 17.9% lifetime) in Sussman et al.'s (2014) former alternative high school sample, and a few reports place it between 12% and 21.8% among younger people (e.g., see Dittmar, 2005; MacLaren & Best, 2010), though most estimates place it as ranging from 1% to 6% among adults (Faber & O'Guinn, 1992; Freimuth et al., 2008; Racine et al., 2014). Koran et al. (2006) found a randomly sampled, telephone data collected, current prevalence estimate of shopping addiction for the US adult population (n = 2,513) of 5.8%. Neuner, Raab, and Reich (2005) provided a representative prevalence estimate of German adults (n = 974 in 2001) of 7.6%. Sussman et al. (2011b) estimated a prevalence of 6% of US adults suffering from shopping addiction based on the Koran et al. (2006) study.

Co-Occurrence

Among shopping addicts, in primarily small samples, prevalence of *substance use disorders* ranges from 21% to 46% (Black, 2007), and prevalence of bulimia nervosa and *binge eating* ranges from 8% to 35% (Black, 2007; Freimuth et al., 2008). Two surveys of small US samples (ns = 24 and 19) indicated that 46–47% of compulsive buyers also were *alcoholics* (which was found to subsume other drug abuse), 17% and 5%, respectively, suffered from binge eating disorder (the latter study failing to show elevated prevalence compared to non-shopping addicts), and 8% were also *gambling addicts* (Faber et al., 1995; Mitchell et al., 2002 [did not examine gambling]). Sussman et al. (2011b) speculated that the co-occurrence of shopping addiction with all other ten types of addiction is 20%, which is quite consistent with data provided by Racine et al. (2014; see p. 301); that is, with lifetime comorbidity involving relatively severe CBD. Regarding current comorbidity, co-occurrence may be higher with an eating disorder (17.2%) than with drug abuse/dependence (3.1%) regarding severe CBD. However, the sample sizes referenced were small, and it is reasonable to maintain a 20% co-occurrence with all other types of addictions for the time being.

Table 7.2 Estimated prevalence and co-occurrence of 11 different addictive behaviors (%)

IF, THEN	Prev	Cigs	Alc	Drugs	Eat	Gamble	Net	Love	Sex	Exercise	Work	Shop
Cigs	15		50	50	20	20	20	20	20	20	20	20
Alc	10	50		50	20	20	20	20	20	20	20	20
Drugs	5	50	50		20	20	20	20	20	20	20	20
Eat	2	25	25	25		25	25	25	25	25	25	25
Gamble	2	50	30	20	20		20	20	20	20	20	20
Net	2	10	10	10	10	10		10	10	10	10	10
Love	3	40	40	40	20	20	20		50	20	20	20
Sex	3	40	40	40	20	20	20	50		20	20	20
Exercise	3	15	15	15	25	25	25	25	25		25	25
Work	10	20	20	20	20	20	20	20	20	20		20
Shop	6	20	20	20	20	20	20	20	20	20	20	

Notes: Overall prevalence of these 11 addictions; prev = prevalence of abuse/dependence; cigs = cigarette (nicotine) dependence; alc = alcohol abuse/dependence; drugs = drug abuse/dependence; eat = binge eating disorder; gamble = gambling addiction; net = Internet addiction; love = love addiction; sex = sex addiction; exercise = exercise addiction; work = workaholism; shop = shopping/buying addiction; if do not remove co-addictions (assume non-overlap) = 61% overall prevalence; if remove highest prevalence addiction (15%) = 61% − 15% = 46% overall prevalence; if remove average of co-addictions (average over 110 pairs is 23.42%) = 61% − (61% × 23.42%) = 46.71% overall prevalence. [This table also appears in Sussman et al. 2011b.]

Summary

Again, a summary of the prevalence of the behavioral addictions is shown in Table 7.1. In addition, the prevalence of all 11 focal addictions and their estimated co-occurrence is shown in Table 7.2.

There appear to be some behavioral addictions that pertain to normative daily activity, and might be thought of as prosocial addictions. Work, Internet, exercise, and shopping addictions are often not likely to be thought of as addictions. They may be sometimes thought of rather as passions. However, the closer one is interpersonally to the addict, the more negative and serious such behavior may appear. Other addictions involve behavior that might be considered prosocial depending on the context: sex and love. These addictions may be considered pathological to the outsider if they involve infidelity, prostitution, or tales of stalking or revenge. Finally, gambling might be considered fun and tolerable but intrinsically risky, and gambling addiction might be relatively frowned on outside of certain venues (e.g., it would be considered normative in the contexts of raising money for the government, or in casino environments). It would not be surprising to find that estimates of the prevalence of the "prosocial" addictions tend to be highest, and gambling as lowest, among these behavioral addictions (e.g., Sussman et al., 2014).

My prevalence estimates in this text align with those of Sussman et al. (2011b), who provided the overall last 12-month prevalence of the 11 addictive behaviors among US adults as follows from highest to lowest: cigarettes 15%; alcohol 10%; work 10%; shopping 6%; illicit drug use 5%; love 3%; sex 3%; exercise 3%; eating 2%; gambling 2%; and Internet 2%. Addictions to eating, gambling, the Internet, love, sex, and exercise appear to have a prevalence rate around 2–3%, involving a minority of the adult population. Addictions to alcohol, cigarette smoking, illicit drugs (such as marijuana), work, and shopping appear to have a prevalence rate of around 5–15% of the adult population. It is not clear why these different behaviors differ in pattern of prevalence. One may speculate, as a more general "law of effect," that addictions directly involving relatively immediate aversive consequences (very quick financial loss, social rejection, injury from overtraining) would tend to be the lowest in prevalence. Behaviors that demonstrate the least immediately aversive consequences would tend to be of highest prevalence. This perspective appears to fit the data to some extent (e.g., cigarette smoking in some locations, alcohol use [if not too much is imbibed], work, and shopping are relatively less likely to lead to immediate aversive consequences).

On the other hand, Sussman and colleagues (2014), who studied US former alternative high school youth (average age = 19.7), found that ever (lifetime) addicted on the 11 addictions in order from highest prevalence to lowest prevalence was: love (34.3%), Internet (29.3%), other (illicit) drugs (29.2%), exercise (27.2%), cigarettes (24.3%), sex (24.1%), binge eating (23.4%), work (20.6%), shopping (17.9%), alcohol (14.8%), and gambling (3.2%). Last 30-day addiction in order from highest prevalence to lowest prevalence was: love (23.2%), Internet (18.4%), exercise (17.7%), sex (16.5%), cigarettes (13.4%), binge eating (12.7%), other drugs (12.7%), work (15.6%), shopping (9.9%), alcohol (5.7%), and gambling (1.8%). The prevalence of ever addicted and last 30-day addiction showed a nearly identical pattern across addictions, except that other drug

Behavioral Addictions: Their Prevalence and Co-Occurrence

Table 7.3 Prevalence of addictions among Russian, American, and Spanish youth – ever and last 30 days

	Ever (%) Russia	Ever (%) US	Ever (%) Spain	30 Days (%) Russia	30 Days (%) US	30 Days (%) Spain
Cigarette	6	1	–	3	1	–
Alcohol	1	4	–	1	3	–
Other drug	1	5	–	1	4	–
Internet	51	54	57	43	48	42
Shopping	12	27	19	8	23	14
Eating	15	21	21	11	18	10
Gambling	8	4	18	6	3	10
Love	18	23	28	14	22	21
Sex	9	9	17	7	8	13
Exercise	28	28	38	23	27	27
Work	12	7	6	9	7	4
Gaming	20	33	29	15	26	16

Notes: All youth were approximately 16 years old. Substance addictions were not measured in Spain using the addiction matrix measure. Numbers for these studies were: 715, Russia; 3,300, United States; and 811, Spain. A manuscript is under review regarding the Russia and Spain data (Tsai et al., under review).

addiction was relatively less prevalent among the behaviors for last 30-day addiction versus ever addicted. The representation of relatively prosocial addictions, at least regarding the last 30-day reports, perhaps followed a higher prevalence of prosocial addictions compared to the Sussman et al. (2011b) analysis. Still, the pattern was equivocal regarding prevalence of prosocial versus more antisocial addictions. Certainly, it is not clear that an immediate consequences explanation fits this sample as well. Also, since this was an emerging adult, former alternative high school sample, it is not clear how these results would generalize to a lower risk, general adult population.

A very recent unpublished analysis indicates the same ranking of the 11 last 30-day addictions among samples of regular US, Spanish, and Russian high school youth, using the same addiction matrix items. Internet, exercise, gaming, love, and food were the highest prevalence addictions, in that order, in all three countries (Table 7.3). Clearly, more research is needed.

Considering all 11 addictions (four substance addictions – tobacco, alcohol, illicit drugs, and food; along with the seven behavioral addictions), Sussman et al. (2011b) estimated a 47 percent prevalence of at least one of these addictions and a 23 percent co-occurrence of two or more of these addictions, in a 12-month period. However, such estimates do not consider lifetime co-occurrence, substitute addiction, or the existence of other addictions not presented in this chapter, which could elevate the prevalence and co-occurrence of addictions and lead me to further assert that addictions are a part of modern lifestyle. The next chapter will address such issues. In addition, Chapter 8 will revisit a discussion of addiction as a disease versus a problem in living.

Bulleted Summary

- The overall last 12-month prevalence among US adults (and perhaps world-wide) of gambling, Internet use, love, sex, exercise, work, and compulsive spending use addictions, is 2%, 2%, 3%, 3%, 3%, 10%, and 6%, respectively.
- Sussman et al. (2011b) estimated that 50%, 30%, and 20% of gambling addicts also are cigarette, alcohol, and illicit drug use addicts, respectively. In addition, they speculated that 20% of adult gambling addicts suffer from any of the other seven addictions. They speculated that 10% of general adult Internet addicts are addicted to any one of the other ten addictive behaviors. Further, they speculated that 50% of love addicts are also sex addicts, and the converse. In addition, they speculated that co-occurrences of love and sex addiction with the three substance use disorders are 40%, whereas co-occurrences with the remaining six addictions are 20%. They speculated that 15% of exercise addicts are also addicted to smoking, alcohol, or illicit drugs and that 25% exhibit the remaining addictions. They speculated that 20% of workaholics are addicted to other behaviors. Finally, Sussman et al. (2011b) speculated that the co-occurrence of shopping addiction with all other ten types of addiction is 20%. (See Tables 7.1. and 7.2.)
- While there is a negative relationship of participation in team sports with most recreational drug use, there is a positive relationship between team sports participation or physical activity and alcohol use and abuse (but not physical dependence).
- The overall last 12-month prevalence of the 11 focal addictive behaviors among US adults (and perhaps world-wide) from highest to lowest is cigarettes 15%; alcohol 10%; work 10%; shopping 6%; illicit drug use 5%; love 3%; sex 3%; exercise 3%; eating 2%; gambling 2%; and Internet 2%. Love, Internet, exercise, and sex addictions are relatively prevalent among teens and emerging adults. (See Table 7.3.)

Suggestions for Further Reading

Freimuth, M., Waddell, M., Stannard, J., Kelley, S., Kipper, A., Richardson, A., & Szuromi, I. (2008). Expanding the scope of dual diagnosis and co-addictions: Behavioral addictions. *Journal of Groups in Addiction & Recovery*, 3: 137–160.

Rosenberg, K. P. & Feder, L. C. (eds.) (2014a). *Behavioral Addictions: Criteria, Evidence, and Treatment.* London: Academic Press/Elsevier.

Sussman, S., Arpawong, T. E., Sun, P., Tsai, J., Rohrbach, L. A., & Spruijt-Metz, D. (2014). Prevalence and co-occurrence of addictive behaviors among former alternative high school youth. *Journal of Behavioral Addictions*, 3: 33–40.

Sussman, S., Lisha, N., & Griffiths, M. (2011b). Prevalence of the addictions: A problem of the majority or the minority? *Evaluation & the Health Professions*, 34: 3–56.

8 Patterns of Addiction Co-Occurrence, Replacement, and Lifestyle Demands

Learning Objectives

- To learn about patterns of single and multiple addictions
- To learn about changes in addictions over the course of human development
- To learn about "fusion addictions," concurrent addictions, and replacement addictions
- To consider addictions as a disease versus a problem in living

Introduction: Addiction or Addictions "of Choice"?

Johnny, we recall from Chapter 1, had all sorts of problematic addictions. At first, as a young child, maybe there was just one addiction (i.e., to TV viewing). Later, though, two or more addictive behaviors seemed to go together, being engaged in either at the same time or in some type of ritualized sequence (e.g., drinking alcohol and exercise addiction). His TV addiction remained, off and on throughout his life. However, Johnny never became addicted to cigarettes. Johnny would go to AA meetings sometimes, though, and be bombarded with cigarette smoke at the meetings. When no-smoking policy became the norm, he would be bombarded with cigarette smoke as he exited from the meeting rooms. He did not like the cigarette smoke at all. He sometimes felt that the AA "old timers" who claimed so many years of recovery were not really in full recovery because they were smoking. Still, Johnny realized that he shared in common with other "addicts" co-occurrence of multiple addictions and/or replacement (substitute) addictions.

Johnny's situation is not unlike many others. Among many persons who have struggled with substance addictions (not Johnny though), cigarette smoking in particular is known to co-occur with alcohol and other drug addictions (Sussman, 2002; Grigsby, Forster, & Sussman, 2015a, 2015b). The two people who began AA both died due to smoking-related diseases (Sussman & Ames, 2008). That is, Bill Wilson died of emphysema and Dr. Bob Smith died of pharyngeal cancer (Sussman, Patten, & Order-Connors, 2005). Many people in AA acknowledge that smoking is an addiction and an issue, but not as dramatic in immediate consequences as alcoholism. In addition, the thinking often has been to take "first things first." That is, the belief was that one should recover from alcoholism and then think about other things such as tobacco use (Sussman et al., 2005).

Learning Objectives

In this chapter I will attempt to examine relationships that may occur among different addictions, particularly the 11 addictions of focus in this text. I will examine the concept of the *"single addiction"* and patterns of **addiction co-occurrence**; i.e., two or more addictions that occur at the same time. Carnes et al. (2005) discuss different ways in which two or more addictions may co-occur in their study which included over 1,000 males who had sought treatment for a sexual disorder (46 percent also reported a history of alcoholism and 11 percent reported a history of exercise addiction). This work will be liberally referenced.

Addiction Co-Occurrence

Sussman et al. (2011b), in their examination of relations among the 11 focal addictions, mentioned that one might logically assume (a) total non-overlap (each person is addicted to one substance or behavior, the ***single addiction***), (b) total overlap (all persons are addicted to all substances or behaviors), or (c) partial overlap among the addictive behaviors (partial addiction co-occurrence). They surmised that partial overlap appears to fit the data the best. Given varying assumptions, they argued for a 23% (partial) overlap of two or more addictions among adults in a 12-month period. Subsequently, using a matrix item approach among former alternative high school youth (average age = 19.8 years old) who are at risk for addictions, Sussman et al. (2014) found that ever and last 30-day prevalence of one or more of these 11 addictions was 79.2% and 61.5%, respectively. Co-occurrence of two or more addictions, ever and last 30-day, was 61.5% and 37.7%, respectively. The average number of lifetime addictions was 2.48 (SD = 2.13) and the average number of addictions in the past 30 days was 1.48 (SD = 1.68). So, is there such a thing as a person who experiences a single addiction? Or are most addicts addicted to more than one behavior at the same time? One other possibility is that a person may quit (terminate) one addiction but then begin another addiction. That is, one may experience multiple addictions serially, as ***substitute addictions***.

How are Addictions "Terminated"?

Addictions may be terminated in one of two ways. First there may exist periods of deprivation, in which the addict misses his or her relationship with the addiction, may have stopped engaging in the addiction due to contextual factors, and may begin again if the opportunity exists. For example, Dr. Bob Smith (one of the two co-founders of AA) was mandated to quit alcohol use for two years in order to graduate from Rush Medical School (https://en.wikipedia.org/wiki/Bob_Smith_(doctor)), which he was able to do. It is not clear if he used another addiction as a substitute (maybe a greater reliance on cigarette smoking).

Second, there may be a real effort to stay stopped and/or there may be a "closure" to an addiction. The person is "sick and tired of being sick and tired" and wants to move on. Of course, he or she may begin a substitute addiction even when there is an earnest effort to stay stopped regarding that addiction of choice (Sussman & Black, 2008).

Summary

In this chapter, I will not only examine the single addiction, and patterns of addiction co-occurrence; I will also examine types of replacement or substitute addictions; i.e., addictions that replace an addiction or addictions that are terminated. Finally, in this chapter, I will again address social contextual demands (appetitive effects misdirected due to context). Human development-related (age), macrosocial contextual demands (e.g., the "speed" of life), and microsocial contextual demands (specific situational demands) are examined. Developmental and social contextual demands may have implications for how addictions might continue or become naturally terminated.

The Single Addiction

A fundamental query in this text pertains to an apparent assumption or cognitive set which practitioners or researchers have: that persons deal with single addictions. That is, the assumption is that most people suffer from a single addiction, or at least there is only one **addiction of choice** (the primary, most preferred, or most troublesome addiction) to be concerned about. We may discuss a "primary" drug use disorder – though recently we permit gambling to be considered a member of the set of "official" addictions as defined by the DSM-V. So, we may discuss an official "primary" gambling disorder. One might surmise that a sizable percentage of the general adult population is involved in one addiction at a time; perhaps only one type in one's lifetime. There exists at least one study which supports the idea of there being a single addiction phenomenon among adults, considered over a five-year period (Konkolÿ Thege, Woodin, Hodgins, & Williams, 2015, discussed in Chapter 16 of this text). Certainly, there is a great deal to grapple with in research studies and clinical treatment pertaining to even one addictive behavior.

An important consideration in studying any single addiction is that the pattern of involvement with the addiction may vary across persons. A person whom a researcher, treatment agent, or lay person might label an "addict" may demonstrate apparently controlled involvement in the behavior, and then demonstrate periods of being clearly out of control. This has been referred to as *"periodic" addictive behavior*. The periodic addict is involved in a behavior normatively for a while, then uses wildly; then goes back to normative behavior (e.g., Rotgers & Davis, 2006). Practitioners are not sure whether or not a "periodic" could attempt to become a **controlled drinker** (consistent, sustained regaining of control over behavior) or exhibit more consistently stable exercise regimens, as substance and behavior addiction examples.

There also exist persons who experience periods of abstinence followed only by periods of being out of control. There is no controlled engagement in the addictive behavior. This type of person might be referred to as the **binger**. (Sometimes the terms "periodic" and "binger" are used interchangeably.) Many treatment agents tend to feel that a "binger" probably should not engage in the addictive behavior at all, or would need to be closely monitored to prevent calamity. Indeed, regarding who might become a controlled drinker, as an example, the literature suggests the following

(Sussman & Ames, 2008). This person tends: (a) to drink relatively less (e.g., six beers [or the equivalent] a day rather than 12 or 24 beers); (b) not to experience legal consequences; and (c) not to demonstrate personality changes when under the influence of the addiction (e.g., Dr. Jekyll and Mr. Hyde). Perhaps few or no bingers could learn to demonstrate controlled involvement in the addictive behavior.

Decision-making is easiest regarding the person who demonstrates continual, uncontrollable involvement in the addictive behavior (constant, regular addict). This person should quit engaging in the addiction. Of course, things get more complicated if one were to consider certain addictions – one has to eat food regularly or die; one has to buy things such as clothes and places to live; one needs to work to have enough money to live; to engage in sex with another is to keep the species going; and we are now living in an Internet-dependent social and vocational world. Whether or not one is a food addict, shopaholic, workaholic, love addict, or Internet addict, these behaviors have to become normalized to achieve a state of balance (i.e., *sobriety*); other addictions could more or less be abstained from. The periodic, binger, and regular patterns of addiction are reviewed in Table 8.1.

Single addictions are complex to study because they vary in topography (e.g., periodic, binger, regular pattern of involvement), and focusing on alleviating negative consequences of even one addiction may take a great deal of effort. Not surprisingly, in research and practice, the existence of multiple addictions across one's lifetime often has been ignored. This quandary exists even given many testimonials such as the introductory example to this text. Often people in recovery are asked about their "drug of choice" (i.e., preferred or most problematic drug that is abused), on which treatment becomes focused. As noted earlier in this section, we could generalize that phrase to apply to any of the addictions by asking what is the person's "addiction of choice." However, there may be different addictions of choice at different time points; that is, there may be an addiction which causes the most difficulty at present but there might have been a different addiction of choice in one's past. Alternatively, or additionally, there really may be several patterns of co-addiction among persons entering treatment. Such alternative patterns of behavior ("addictions of choice" or "addiction set") are grossly understudied.

Table 8.1 Three patterns of involvement with an addiction

The periodic addict	The periodic addict is involved in a behavior normatively for a while, then uses wildly; then goes back to normative behavior. Treatment agents are not sure whether or not a "periodic" addict should attempt to become a "controlled drinker" or participant in another potentially addictive behavior.
The "binger"	A "binger" is a person who experience periods of abstinence followed by periods of being out of control. There is no controlled engagement in the addictive behavior. Many treatment agents tend to feel that a "binger" probably should not use at all.
The regular addict	A regular addict is a person who demonstrates continual involvement in the addictive behavior. This person should quit engaging in the addiction.

Human Development and Multiple Addictions

Involvement in different addictions may vary over the course of human development. That is, it is feasible that development of different types of addictions within the same person may occur over the lifespan. In other words, it is possible that the same person may suffer from multiple addictions, considered longitudinally. Persons as young as three years of age may suffer from television addiction (Sussman & Moran, 2013). There is little research on this point. However, anecdotally, parents have observed the consequences of turning off the television on their young children. Persons as young as eight years of age may become addicted to caffeine (Collins, Graham, Rousculp, & Hansen, 1997; Sussman & Ames, 2008). That is, they may use caffeine to regulate their affect and they may suffer withdrawal symptoms when they are not using caffeine. There is only one study on this topic. However, this study found that relatively high and frequent intake of caffeine is predictive of other addictions later on (tobacco, alcohol). Persons as young as 11 or 12 years of age may become addicted to cigarette smoking and then go on to use other drugs when they are maybe 14 or 15 years old (e.g., Kandel, 1990). Beginning in the older teen years, people may become addicted to other behaviors (e.g., sex addiction; Sussman, 2007). A person may give up a previous addiction and acquire a new one – or a person may simply add new addictions to their repertoire (i.e., the **addiction spectrum** may "*fan out*"). If a person experiences one addiction at a time then there is only one addiction to treat at that time. A changing of one addiction to another over time, due to changes in human development or other events (e.g., bariatric surgery) has been coined "addiction transfer" (Blum et al., 2011a). A summary of different patterns of addiction as one grows older is shown in Table 8.2.

"Fusion Addictions"

There are persons who appear to suffer from two or more (almost) **"fused" addictions** (e.g., conjoined smoking and drinking, eating and drinking, love and sex, gambling and drinking; see Carnes et al., 2005). Addiction involvement may increase and involve both (multiple) behaviors and be exchangeable to some extent. There are at least four types or aspects of fused addictions. **Cross-tolerance** from one addiction to another occurs when tolerance for one addiction transfers to another. In fact, part of

Table 8.2 Human development and multiple addictions

Different types of addictions may occur over the lifespan:

Persons as young as three years of age may suffer from television addiction.
Persons as young as eight years of age may become addicted to caffeine.
Persons as young as 11 or 12 years of age may become addicted to cigarette smoking.
Persons 14 to 15 years old may go on to using other drugs.
Emerging adults may be relatively likely to suffer from sex addiction.

current chemical dependence treatment may implicitly involve disassociating two addictions in particular: smoking from alcohol abuse (Sussman, 2002). (There may be some argument as to whether nicotine and alcohol can be said to demonstrate cross-tolerance since they exhibit somewhat different neurobiological effects. Possibly, there are psychosocial parameters of cross-tolerance that operate there; if this is even a truly reasonable example of cross-tolerance.) There is some evidence that treatment targeting both addictions may not lower cessation rates for either one (e.g., Sussman, 2002, regarding smoking cessation and alcoholism), and in fact may increase likelihood of cessation of both (Tsoh, Chi, Mertens, & Weisner, 2011), contrary to speculation in 12-step programs (Sussman, 2002).

A second type of addiction fusion is **combining**. Combining involves any number of addictions involved to maintain a certain high. For example, one may combine heroin with cocaine (a "speed ball") in order to obtain the right "edge" to the "high." A third type of fusion, **intensification**, involves combining addictions for a total experience. For example, some people have suggested that they use cocaine just prior to having sex to intensify the sexual experience, the latter of which may also be addictive. A fourth type, **numbing**, involves following a stimulating addictive behavior with one that is calming or medicating. One may follow a sex addiction experience with getting drunk, for example, to distance oneself from the first experience.

In summary, the first type of fusion addiction discussed (cross-tolerance) suggests that tolerance for levels of involvement in one addiction may operate for another; that the addictions may be in part exchangeable, or reflect similar underlying motives. The three other fusion addiction types (combining, intensification, and numbing) involve a cocktail of addictions to achieve certain meshed subjective effects. Fusion addictions may be somewhat different in goal from the other concurrent addiction processes (which are used to justify one behavior with another, for example). Certainly, there may be more than two "fused" addictions at a time, and the same two addictions may demonstrate multiple types of fusion addiction; research is needed to better understand these phenomena, and to consider implications for new treatments.

Multiple, Concurrent Addictions

One may become involved in multiple, concurrent addictions that are not conjoined (i.e., not "fused") but appear together nevertheless. There are persons – like Johnny – who report suffering from multiple addictions, some of which appear in ritualistic sequences in the course of a day. Carnes et al. (2005) suggested several models pertaining to the relations among multiple addictions, in addition to their discussion of fusion addictions.

Withdrawal mediation occurs when one addiction permits one to avoid withdrawal from another. The two addictions are not subjectively experienced as being the same "type" but one may be used to control the other. For example, someone in early recovery may drink a lot of coffee (caffeine), eat a lot of sweets, smoke a lot of cigarettes (nicotine), or engage in impulsive sexual activity as a means of helping to moderate, cope with, or relieve withdrawal from alcohol or another drug (Baker et al., 2004).

A second type of concurrent addiction, *masking*, is the hiding of a more normatively unacceptable addiction by first participating in a less shameful one. For example, one may engage in sex addiction only when one is drunk or high. Then, one may attribute participation in the sex addiction to the fact that one was drunk or high. A third type, *disinhibiting*, is roughly the same thing; one gathers up courage to be involved in one addiction due to inhibitions that have been lowered while participating in another. For example, one may engage in sex addiction when one is "loosened up" through drinking.

A fourth type, *ritualizing*, involves a chain of behavior that includes a series of preparation steps and pattern of engaging in a chain of addictive behaviors, all which invest one into altered states. For example, one may begin a night on the town through drinking a fixed number of drinks at a strip club and then proceed to engage in sex addiction at the massage parlor down the street. Masking, disinhibiting, and ritualizing are overlapping processes conceptually, engaged in for somewhat different reasons. Masking refers to a justification reason. Disinhibiting refers to a gathering courage reason. Ritualizing refers to a fixed set of behaviors ordered and completed that involve two or more addictions to invest one in a more variable experience.

Multiple Addictions Viewed at a Dyadic Level

Multiple addictions may be examined within an individual or in a social context (e.g., a dyad, with each member of the dyad having one or more addictions). For example, Schneider (2005) discusses "bartering" which involves two or more people trading addictions (e.g., one person may trade sex to a sex addict for their own use of drugs). Members of couples may create *implicit contracts* with each other – that indicates tolerance of each other's addiction. For example, one person in the relationship may eat addictively and gain a tremendous amount of weight. The other person in the relationship is "permitted" to drink alcohol excessively. Anecdotally, such relationships exist and likely operate in families, with close friends, or in love relationships. Perhaps, co-dependency is a popular sort of dyadic-level addiction. One person may be addicted to a drug or to a behavior such as gambling, while the other person may be addicted to the relationship (be a love addict; e.g., Lee, 2014). There is scant empirical research on dyadic-level multiple addictions.

Replacement (Substitute) Addictions

One addiction may begin after another addiction terminates. That is, one may engage in a replacement or *substitute addiction* – likely serving the same appetitive functions (Schneider, 2005; Sussman & Black, 2008). Carnes et al. (2005) mention two types of substitute addictions. *Replacement* occurs when one addiction replaces another with a passing of some duration of time (substitute addiction). For example, some people in recovery from alcoholism, after they have quit alcohol use, begin cigarette smoking at 12-step meetings and become addicted to nicotine (Friend & Pagano, 2004).

Alternating addiction cycles pertains to replacement addictions that cycle back and forth, in a systematic way, over stretches of time. For example, an exercise addict may get injured and then become a heavy drinker. After developing a drinking problem such as experiencing a DUI or complaints from significant others (and healing from the physical injury), the individual "goes on the wagon" (quits drinking) and again becomes an exercise addict, becomes injured again, and repeats the cycle (Sussman & Lisha, 2014).

In the recovery movement, substitute addictions have been addressed as an issue about which persons in recovery should be vigilant (e.g., www.wikihow.com/Get-Sober-with-a-12-Step-Program). For example, the popular recovery movement catch-phrase of *13th Stepping* may reflect the tendency to replace one's drug of choice with a sexual compulsion. Some authors have even argued that 12-step programs function as a substitute addiction (Buddy, 2003; Galaif & Sussman, 1995; Sussman & Black, 2008; Sussman et al., 2011c), albeit more safe than involvement in many harmful alternatives.

Horvath (2006) discusses several parameters of substitute addictions. On the one hand, some replacement behaviors may be relatively adaptive to the addict (e.g., eating celery or carrots for dessert instead of chocolate cake, smoking marijuana instead of using cocaine, exercising excessively rather than drinking alcohol). As a recent example, recovering alcoholics and other substance abusers often report the belief that the Internet is a safe substitute to subdue their cravings and avoid relapse (Young, 1999). Moreover, some cocaine-addicted people may attempt natural recovery with potentially healthy substitutions such as religion, volunteer work, formal education, and interpersonal relationships (Chiauzzi & Liljegren, 1993; Shaffer & Jones, 1989). Some substitutes that may cause dependence, such as methadone maintenance treatment and AA membership, may be associated with lower relapse rates among heroin addicts and alcoholics (Vaillant, 1988).

Even though engaging in a substitute addiction allows the addictive pathway to remain functional, this substitute may, over time, permit a "weakening" of the original (hopefully worse) addiction. The substitute addiction also may then be eliminated or channeled into a healthy and moderate level of behavior (Horvath, 1999, 2006) that could not be reached with the more intense/harmful addiction. This redirection, perhaps described by the phrase "All things in moderation," or self-regulation of lifestyle maintenance functioning (Brisman & Siegel, 1984), entails in itself much-needed conceptual understanding and research. In fact, in one study, the authors found patient reports indicating a notable functional replacement of alcohol abuse by overeating (Kleiner et al., 2004). Thirty years ago, researchers thought that some people substitute drugs to reach an intoxicated state to achieve the sense of release and abandonment of control previously experienced with bulimia (Zweben, 1987), or that bulimia nervosa may be a means of symptom substitution for substance abuse (Brisman & Siegel, 1984). While recent research has failed to support bulimia nervosa and drug abuse as being substitute addictions for each other, some support for this possibility remains (Kaye et al., 2013).

Murphy and Hoffman (1993) found that up to 25 percent of their sample of alcoholics who had maintained at least one year of sobriety substituted new addictions such as eating desserts, smoking cigarettes, and working extended hours, to replace their previous alcohol use behaviors for up to 36 months post-abstinence. These researchers mentioned that these new behaviors appeared to be common, or even tolerated, aspects of early recovery until life processes were normalized. Likewise, Vaillant (1983) found that alcoholics remitted to treatment utilized chain smoking, compulsive work, or benzodiazepines as their major replacement methods. Friend and Pagano (2004) examined the substitute addiction process in patients being treated for alcohol dependence, and found that 15 percent of patients initiated smoking during treatment for the first time, and 54 percent of that group continued to smoke 12 months after treatment, during which time their tobacco use increased. Moreover, former smokers were particularly susceptible to return to heavy tobacco use during their alcohol treatment. Similarly, Mansky (1999) found that in a New York State recovery program for physicians, gambling, eating disorders, sex, excessive exercise, workaholism, and overspending were observed to be substitute addictions for alcohol and drug abuse.

Substitute addictions specific to narcotic abuse have been identified. These include marijuana, **chloriazepoxide** (i.e., a benzodiazepine which increases sleepiness and muscle relaxation, and reduces anxiety), religion, food, participation in AA, obsession with possessions, and alcohol (Vaillant, 1966). The prescribed use of anti-anxiety agents such as benzodiazepines, which are effective for anxiety, has been noted as being problematic in addiction treatment due to a high potential for abuse and conversion into a substitute addiction (Zweben, 1987). These studies suggest the operation of both replacement and alternating addiction cycles.

Of course, substitute chemical addictions often do not occur. Blanco et al. (Blanco, Okuda, Wang, Liu, & Olfson, 2014), using a large US nationally representative sample (NESARC), investigated the occurrence of one substance use disorder (SUD) taking the place of another SUD that remitted (stopped, at least when queried again after a three-year duration), versus a new SUD occurring on top of one that had not remitted, in a two-group analysis. Approximately 13 percent of those who remitted developed a new SUD, whereas 27 percent of those who did not remit developed a new SUD. This paper did not address the issue of substitute addiction as described by Sussman and Black (2008), which pertains to many different types of addictions (e.g., food, gambling, and sex). Blanco and colleagues did find that people who have a problem with one substance (drug) may develop a concurrent problem with a second substance; and that they are more likely to do so than persons who have been able to quit using a substance. This makes sense in that personal application of principles of substance use cessation may generalize to other substances. There is little other empirical work on substitute addiction though this term has been a topic of concern in the recovery movement for a long time (Sussman & Black, 2008).

Potential Interplay of Cigarette Smoking and Alcohol Addictions

Curiously, 15% of smokers have a current and 40% have a past alcohol problem (Sussman, 2002); also, approximately 75% of alcoholics and 79% of opiate addicts also self-report being addicted to nicotine through cigarette smoking (Guydish et al., 2011).

(Recall, that Sussman et al., 2011b provided a 50% co-occurrence, overall, a little lower.) Drug users who smoke differ in up to at least six ways from non-users who smoke. First, drug users who smoke often began smoking at a younger age. Second, drug users who smoke are relatively more addicted to nicotine. In fact, they smoke an average of ten cigarettes more per day, among adults. Also, the prevalence of "heavy smoking" (e.g., two packs a day or more) is 72 percent among drug users versus 9 percent among non-users. Users with a severe drug problem smoke more (2.5 to up to 4 packs/day) than those with a moderate (around a pack and a half), or a mild (around a quarter pack) problem. Third, these smokers generally have relatively more cognitive deficits, perhaps due to the effects of using drugs. Fourth, they have relatively more psychological problems, including depression, anxiety disorders, and personality disorders. Fifth, they have more medical problems, including upper digestive and respiratory cancers, heart disease, pancreatitis, and cirrhosis. Finally, they report relatively low levels of smoking cessation self-efficacy (see Sussman, 2002).

Potential Interplay of Exercise and Alcohol Addictions

Since exercise addiction would seem to imply a drive for good health (albeit too much of one), one would envision it not being associated with alcohol addiction. In fact, the relations between exercise addiction and alcohol addiction are not strong, as mentioned earlier in this text. However, they may be positively associated for some people. (They were associated in Johnny's case.) It is feasible that exercise and alcohol addictions may alternate among some individuals (Sussman & Lisha, 2014). Recall that "alternating addiction cycles" refers to engaging in a fixed pattern of alternating addictions, in part contingent on life event changes. Suffering a sports injury may lead an exercise addict to engage in heavy drinking. Negative consequences of sustained drinking may lead to "going on the wagon" and beginning to train again if the injury has healed. The addict may alternate between these two addictions over long spans of time. Longitudinal research studies are needed to explore the potential interplay of these two types of addiction. Examples of patterns of interplaying among the addictions are summarized in Table 8.3.

Addiction as a Problem that Varies with Lifestyle Demands

The relative likelihood of participating in multiple addictive behaviors concurrently may be impacted by lifestyle demands (context). One type of context is *human development-related*. Very young children often are exposed to television. There are TV shows developed for very young children (e.g., Teletubbies; https://en.wikipedia.org/wiki/Teletubbies). They may become addicted to television if: (a) they have the opportunity (e.g., their parents are busy and want their children to sit still), (b) they initially do enjoy the medium, and (c) they are relatively vulnerable (e.g., perhaps relatively anxious, irritable, anhedonic, or restless children may find the TV more pleasurable). If a person maintains this addiction and takes a new one on later (e.g., to caffeine) then multiple addictions result. Drug abuse is not an issue with most young

Table 8.3 Relations among multiple addictions

Fused addictions (cross-tolerance, combining, intensification, numbing)	There are persons who appear to suffer from two or more (almost) "fused" addictions (e.g., smoking and drinking, eating and drinking, love and sex, gambling and drinking). Addiction involvement may increase and involve both (multiple) behaviors and be exchangeable to some from one addiction to another occurs when tolerance for one addiction transfers to another. "Combining" involves any number of addictions involved to maintain a certain high. For example, one may combine heroin with cocaine (a "speed ball") in order to obtain the right "edge" to the "high." "Intensification" involves combining addictions for a total experience. For example, some people have suggested that they use cocaine just prior to having sex to intensify the sexual experience, the latter of which may also be addictive. "Numbing" involves following a stimulating addictive behavior with one that is calming or medicating. One may follow a sex addiction experience with getting drunk, for example, to distance from the first experience.
Multiple, concurrent addictions (withdrawal mediation, masking, disinhibiting, ritualizing)	"Withdrawal mediation" occurs when one addiction permits one to avoid withdrawal from another. Someone in early recovery may drink a lot of coffee (caffeine) or smoke a lot of cigarettes (nicotine) to cope with or relieve withdrawal from alcohol or another drug. "Masking" is the hiding of a more shameful addiction by first participating in a less shameful one. For example, one may engage in sex addiction only when one is drunk or high. "Disinhibiting" involves gathering up courage to be involved in one addiction due to inhibitions that had been lowered while participating in another. "Ritualizing" involves a chain of behavior that includes a series of preparation steps and pattern of engaging in a chain of addictive behaviors, all of which invest one into an altered state.
Replacement	One addiction may begin after another addiction terminates. That is, one may engage in a replacement or "substitute addiction" – likely serving the same appetitive functions. Alcoholics remitted to treatment can utilize chain smoking, compulsive work, or benzodiazepine as their major replacement methods.

children (exceptions being young children [e.g., five years old] who engage in smoking or inhalant use to decrease hunger; Sussman & Ames, 2008), nor are other addictions that result only after developing secondary sexual characteristics (sex addiction), or possibly until the access to a channel of addiction is introduced at school (e.g., exercise addiction related to team sports), or until they have a need to support themselves or others (workaholism).

Social contextual demands certainly are important. From a *macrosocial* perspective, if one indeed lives in a modern, high technology, alienating society that pushes one to do more and more, the "speed" or quick pace of life may facilitate all sorts of addictions (Alexander, 2012; Brown, 2014). These addictions serve to demonstrate conformity to the structure of this demanding, fast-pace world (e.g., workaholism, Internet addiction), to demonstrate mastery of this world (e.g., workaholism, Internet addiction, shopaholism, love addiction, sex addiction, gambling disorder, exercise addiction), or to cope emotionally with existence in this world (e.g., tobacco, alcohol, illicit drugs, food addictions). That is, modern lifestyle may dictate that one conforms efficaciously to difficult overarching demands which, inevitably, for a large percentage of the population, leads to addictive engagement.

Also, developing any particular addiction is a partial function of microsocial financial cost and activity demands (*microsocial contextual demands*). As an example, for an addicted gambler who spends much time in a casino, possibly most financial resources will go into the maintenance of the gambling behavior leaving very few financial resources left to participate in other costly activities (e.g., taking care of a family). Also, the addicted gambler may not have much additional time to leave the casino and engage concurrently in shopping, sex, work, or exercise addictions.

On the other hand, the casino social context may promote tobacco and alcohol addictions, and may tolerate other drug addictions, permitting concurrent addiction to gambling and alcohol or other drug use. This may partly explain why drug addictions tend to have a higher prevalence and co-occurrence than some process/behavioral addictions – drug addictions can be adapted into most behavioral repertoires including day-to-day work and leisure time (if they do not grossly or obviously impair behavior). That is, drug misuse, while potentially costly, is readily transportable.

On Becoming Considered a Disease-Like Phenomenon

Future research is needed to better understand why some people quit easily and others don't, and whether differences in ease of quitting might be a function of the relative influence of physiology versus social context, or some interaction (vulnerability-related behavior may shape one's environment and the converse). Certainly, to the extent that a disease label facilitates compassion in treatment, it may continue to serve a heuristic function as at least a metaphor for entrenched neurobiological adaptations (Sussman & Ames, 2008). If the disease label is used to describe a non-infectious, chronic alteration and impairment of functioning, then viewing addictions as a disease would seem appropriate (Sussman & Ames, 2001; Timmreck, 1998). To the extent that etiology, course, and prognosis information is required, it may be premature to utilize a disease label.

Summary

Regardless of one's perception of "addiction," consistent engagement in any of the 11 focal behaviors presented in this text may cause significant deleterious changes in the brain pathways, in particular the mesolimbic dopaminergic (reward) system (Leshner, 1997; Sussman & Ames, 2008). These changes, in turn, may be involved in difficulty with cessation of addictive behavior. What is perhaps most important to target by health professionals is the compulsion to engage in certain behaviors repeatedly even with knowledge of potentially dire health or social consequences. This compulsion may be a function of neurobiological changes, associated psychological states (e.g., subjective sense of restlessness, irritability, or discontent; Alcoholics Anonymous, 1976), and social contextual facilitation of the behavior.

Simply identifying co-occurrence of addictions does not identify causation of their "unique" and "shared" components. Future research needs to assess possible reasons why some people might suffer from one addictive behavior but not another, or why some people tend to suffer particular multiple addictions (e.g., such as may be the case among sufferers of borderline personality disorder; Bagby, Vachon, Bulmash, & Quilty, 2008). Furthermore, one must still account for the fact that, for example, a significant minority of people become addicted to heroin or gambling, but very few are thought to become addicted to, say, gardening.

Vulnerable individuals may attempt to manipulate continuously their neurobiological circuitry in order to obtain a more comfortable subjective state. Also, it is likely that society promotes some addictive behavioral processes, such as drinking alcohol, overeating, or working to excess. It is quite reasonable to assert that at least a large minority of the world's population suffers from an addictive process at any point in time. While controversial, a high prevalence of some type of addiction among a significant minority of the population might suggest that addiction is a natural state of affairs as a human being. As Marks (1990) provocatively suggested, "life is a series of addictions and without them we die" (p. 1389). Clearly, much more research is needed in this arena. The next chapter concludes Part II of this text by examining assessment of substance and behavioral addictions.

Bulleted Summary

- It is complex to even understand varying patterns of single addictions, or "addiction of choice." This may account for the tendency to focus study on single addictions and then act as if there is only one addiction of relevance for treatment. However, many people are addicted to more than one behavior either concurrently or serially.
- Very young children may become addicted to television viewing. Somewhat older children may become addicted to caffeinated sodas. Tweens may become addicted to nicotine or food. Teens may begin a course of drug use or exercise addiction. Emerging adults are at highest risk for a slew of addictions.
- Addiction to two or more behaviors that become more or less part of the same ritual generally to modulate the addiction "high" is known as "fusion addiction." Engaging

in two separable addictions in the course of a day is known as "concurrent addiction." Concurrent addictions may interplay in various ways. For example, "masking" refers to hiding a more normatively disapproved of addiction by first participating in a less shameful one. Stopping completely one addiction and replacing it later with a substitute is known as "replacement addiction."
- To the extent that one demonstrates neurobiological vulnerability to the addictions, one may consider addictions as a disease-like phenomenon. However, human development-related, and macro- and microsocial contextual demands play an important role in determining which type of addiction one may suffer from or, perhaps, even if one will experience an addiction at all.

Suggestions for Further Reading

Brown, S. (2014). *Speed: Facing Our Addiction to Fast and Faster – and Overcoming Our Fear of Slowing Down.* New York: Berkley Books.

Carnes, P. J., Murray, R. E., & Charpentier, L. (2005). Bargains with chaos: Sex addicts and addiction interaction disorder. *Sexual Addiction & Compulsivity*, 12: 79–120.

Marks, I. (1990). Behaviour (non-chemical) addictions. *British Journal of Addiction*, 85: 1389–1394.

Schneider, J. P. (2005). Coexisting disorders. In R. H. Coombs (ed.), *Addiction Counseling Review*. Mahwah, NJ: Lawrence Erlbaum Associates, pp. 293–316.

Sussman, S. & Black, D. S. (2008). Substitute addiction: A concern for researchers and practitioners. *Journal of Drug Education*, 38: 167–180.

9 Assessing the 11 Focal Addictions

Learning Objectives

- To learn about the different types of assessments that could be applied to multiple addictions
- Interview assessments of the 11 focal addictions will be described
- Self-report assessments of the 11 focal addictions will be described
- Potential use of the matrix measure of multiple addictions will be described
- Similarities and differences in features assessed across the 11 focal addictions will be described

Introduction

Johnny saw a psychologist through his health maintenance organization. He wanted assistance with "social anxiety." After an hour of unstructured interviewing, followed by completion of a few brief self-report measures (for depression, for lifestyle difficulties), his psychologist asked him if he might be suffering from alcoholism. Johnny said that he did but that he did not want that diagnosis to be placed on paper. He did not want people to know or for him to possibly be unable to obtain life insurance. The psychologist wanted to make an alcohol dependence diagnosis for Johnny's records and insurance payments. Johnny left treatment. Thus, this chapter on assessment begins.

Recent work suggests shared symptomatology across substance and process/behavioral addictions with, at least preliminarily, comparable diagnostic criteria (Rosenberg & Feder, 2014b; Sussman et al., 2011b). In particular, the DSM diagnostic criteria for alcohol and substance use disorders (introduced in Chapter 1) have been generalized to capture the behavioral addictions. Key criteria include:

(a) engaging in the behavior to enhance affective, arousal, or cognitive state (shift subjective sense of self; achieve an *appetitive effect*);
(b) engaging in the behavior over a *period of time* (e.g., for more than 12 months);
(c) continued engagement in the behavior despite neglecting other life tasks (all of which indicate **entrenchment** in the behavior [its "salience"; see Loonis et al., 2000]);

(d) ***preoccupation*** with the behavior (which may be the same thing as entrenchment, the difference – if any – being that preoccupation is generally noticed when the person is engaged in other incompatible behavior [e.g., on vacation but thinking about working]);
(e) *tolerance*, needing more of the behavior to experience desired effects (which also indicates entrenchment/preoccupation; see Sussman & Sussman, 2011);
(f) *withdrawal*, experiencing undesirable symptoms or signs upon cessation (i.e., if not physiological withdrawal, then craving to do the behavior again [which also indicates preoccupation with the behavior; see Sussman & Sussman, 2011]);
(g) apparent *loss of control* regarding involvement in the behavior; and
(h) experiencing *negative consequences* such as complaints from family and friends, legal problems, or role-related problems.

While there are many similarities among the addictive behaviors, which result in similarities in diagnostic criteria and assessment items, there are unique aspects of each addiction that require specification. This chapter will review the ways the 11 addictions of focus in this text (tobacco, alcohol, other/hard drugs, food/eating, gambling, Internet, shopping, love, sex, exercise, and work) have been assessed. Specifically, interview data, self-report assessments, and "other" assessments (i.e., corroborative reports, neurobiological, and biochemical) will be described. The organization of the chapter is by type of assessment with discussion of each of the 11 addictive behaviors nested within assessment-type.

At the end of this chapter I review the overlap and non-overlap of the general domains of behavior (e.g., appetitive effect, preoccupation, loss of control, negative consequences) tapped by these measures, considered across the 11 different focal addictions. While the research contexts within which the assessment data were collected were quite variable (e.g., college undergraduates, adults, or treatment patients), the reader may see that there is a great deal of substantive overlap regarding the types of items across the different addictions, with some differences primarily reflecting the behavioral topography of the specific addiction.

Clinical Interviews: Overview

Clinical interviews serve several functions. As examples, they may be used proactively to check for presence of (consequences of) addictions (e.g., to drugs, sex, gambling, exercise) among employment candidates for jobs in which public safety is paramount (e.g., lifeguards, delivery personnel, vehicle drivers, babysitters, or airplane pilots), or those participating in athletics (e.g., to detect presence of performance-enhancing drugs; tendency to overtrain; ***proactive assessment***). Second, interview data may be used as a tool to clarify a presenting medical or social-psychological problem (***reactive assessment***). As examples, professionals may be asked to assess those who suffer from certain physical or medical problems which may be related to an addiction (e.g., liver problems, sleep difficulties) or those who have been garnering complaints or concern from significant others or public authorities (e.g., because the person being assessed has been showing behavioral signs of drug misuse such as slurring words, shaking, showing uncontrolled anger; or performance-related signs of any number of addictions such as demonstrating lackluster performance at work or home due to Internet addiction). Both proactive and reactive assessments of addiction are important to differentiate addictions from other problems, and to facilitate appropriate treatment planning, to begin the process of helping an individual arrest negative consequences and permit recovery of functioning, as well as to minimize consequences to significant others and protect the public (Grigsby, Sussman, Chou, & Ames, in press).

Mental Status Examination

The mental status of the person being interviewed is of relevance to help suggest other means of assessment which might determine whether a formal psychiatric diagnosis of an addiction-related disorder and/or of a comorbid condition should be made. The *mental status examination* includes the assessment of appearance, attitude and behavior, speech, affect, thought and language, and perceptions and cognitive functioning, such as insight and judgment (Schottenfeld & Pantalon, 1994). When performing a mental status examination (MSE), the following questions are examples of those that might help to provide a guideline to determine whether an individual is suspected of suffering from an addiction or comorbid psychopathology. Relevant questions to consider during the mental status examination include:

- Does the individual appear to be withdrawn, socially isolated, undernourished, agitated or depressed, tired, unable to concentrate, indifferent to pleasurable activities, or unkempt in physical appearance?
- Is the individual hostile or uncooperative, evasive, or defensive and are there any discrepancies in reports of autobiographical events (i.e., lies, missing information about consequences stemming from addictive behavior)?
- Did the individual report any delusions, visual or auditory hallucinations? If so, what were the circumstances?
- Did the individual appear to be disoriented to time and place?
- Was the individual under the influence of mood-altering drugs at the time?
- Does the individual give any indication of having lost control or of being preoccupied with an addictive behavior?

After answering these questions (which are not only specific to the addictions) the individual might be assessed through a more specific (i.e., unstructured or structured) interview assessment, which can provide much more information on the parameters of the suspected addictive behavior.

Unstructured Interview Format

The *unstructured interview* format, which contains a number of open-ended questions, can produce detailed information that is specific to the individual being questioned. Types of unstructured interview questions that are likely to be asked pertain to the person's understanding of why they are being interviewed, current living situation, significant life events, history of any psychosocial problems, any medical or psychological treatment, what the person does during their work, educational, and recreational time, and family and personal history of addiction (what type, how long, behavioral topography, who with, where, what functions the addiction serves). This can assist clinicians in recommending more thorough assessments, and if conducted properly can be efficacious in determining a diagnosis and subsequent treatment plan (Jones, 2010) although some researchers and clinicians are in disagreement as to whether or not unstructured interview formats have any notable advantages (Samet, Waxman, Hatzenbuehler, & Hasin, 2007; Sussman, 2001). That is, as these techniques typically do not have a psychometric structure, it is difficult to determine the reliability and validity of unstructured interview formats used to collect addiction information. The general lack of consistency between assessments in the frequency, type, and content of the questions asked makes it possible to overlook important information across cases. To the extent that different professionals and treatment facilities consider as part of their territory multiple types of addictions, unstructured interviews certainly are being employed to tap them. The research evidence for accuracy of assessment of the different addictions through unstructured interviews is nonexistent as of present.

Structured Interviews

There are several advantages to using a *structured interview* process, which is constructed in a fixed format often with quantitative as well as qualitative data being collected, as opposed to an unstructured one. First, structured interviews are more effective in collecting quality information, as there are fewer digressions into areas of little substantive concern. This improves the efficiency of the interview process by saving time and effort for the interviewer and interviewee. Second, structured interviews produce consistent results across individuals allowing researchers and clinicians to identify similarities across different addictive behavior experiences. Finally, by using this method of assessment, the researcher or clinician can produce consistent results across cases that produce an objective and information-based result.

While this approach may appear advantageous to unstructured interview methods, there are several limitations that should be considered. First, the effectiveness of the structured interview process, though greater than that of the unstructured interview, is a direct reflection of the interviewer's skills. Experience, intuition, and rapport with clientele can greatly influence the interpretations made. Second, structured interviews are often time consuming and expensive to develop and administer. Third, the constraints on the questions asked and method of evaluation leave little room to explore other pertinent areas or diagnoses. This could lead to oversight of important facts that contribute to a greater understanding of a person's addiction or addictions (Grigsby et al., in press; Sussman, 2001).

Most of the structured interviews that have been developed pertain to tobacco, alcohol, or other drug misuse. There are very few such assessments of food addiction, or behavioral addiction-type interviews. Thus, examples are drawn primarily from the drug assessment arena. Still, one can envision how such interviews can be extended to tap many other types of addictions.

Structured Interviews of Substance Addictions

Examples of Structured Interviews of Tobacco, Alcohol, and Other Drug Use

Tobacco use and dependence may be addressed in interviews that focus on other drugs; almost no well-established formal interviews on tobacco use per se exist. Perhaps the main ones include use of the Structured Clinical Interview for the Diagnostic Statistical Manual (SCID), which is described below, and items from the *National Health Interview Survey* (NHIS; see www.cdc.gov/nchs/nhis/tobacco/tobacco_overview.htm and www.cdc.gov/nchs/nhis/tobacco/tobacco_questions.htm). NHIS items include: lifetime smoking, age at time of first cigarette, recent smoking, number of cigarettes per day, number of cigarettes in last 30 days, smoking during pregnancy, use of various tobacco products such as snuff and chewing tobacco, and attempts at quitting.

The *Comprehensive Drinker Profile* (CDP; Miller & Marlatt, 1984) is a structured interview that was originally designed in 1971 to assess alcoholism in male inpatients, but it was revised for broader alcohol and other drug misuse clinical applications. The 88-item CDP collects detailed information on an individual's alcohol consumption history, motivation, behavior, and self-efficacy to control or quit drinking, and has shown acceptable reliability for regular (consistent) drinking patterns, but may not be optimal for assessing episodic or infrequent, but heavy, drinking sessions (Miller, Leckman, Delaney, & Tinkcom, 1992; Miller & Del Boca, 1994). The CDP includes a section related to alcohol-related problems (that can also be used to assess other drug misuse). The measure produces two scores: a score for alcohol abuse symptomatology (problems) derived from the Michigan Alcohol Screening Test (described below, a self-report instrument) and an indicator of physical dependence. This interview was developed to suggest optimal treatment directions. The CDP has been used more extensively in clinical settings, and while reliability and predictive validity have been established, exact estimates are not commonly reported in the literature for this measure. Three additional instruments were designed to complement the CDP including a brief interview, the Brief Drinker Profile (Miller & Marlatt, 1984); a parallel outcome measure for use in treatment settings, the Follow-Up Drinker Profile (Miller & Marlatt, 1987); and a corroborative measure given to "significant" others that can be compared to responses on the CDP, the Collateral Interview Form (Miller & Marlatt, 1987).

The *Substance Dependence Severity Scale* (SDSS; Miele et al., 2000a) is a 13-item clinician-administered semi-structured interview that was developed to assess severity and frequency of dependence across a range of drugs, based on the DSM-IV diagnostic criteria for substance use disorders. The left column contains behavior probes, the middle column contains anchor points for severity ratings (absent, subthreshold, mild, moderate, severe, extreme), and the right column is used for the content ratings (e.g., spending time drinking/using instead of: working or doing school work; spending time with family or old friends; spending time doing things one used to enjoy, like sports, or some kind of regular activity or hobby). The test/retest, joint rating, and internal consistency reliabilities across alcohol, cocaine, heroin, marijuana, and sedative users range from fair to good (intraclass correlation coefficients [ICCs] = 0.41 to 0.87) with estimates ranging by drug and subscale. In a sample of 172 alcohol, cocaine, and heroin users entering substance abuse treatment, the SDSS demonstrated better convergent and discriminant validity when compared to other measures of substance abuse (e.g., the Addiction Severity Index) and survival analyses demonstrated predictive validity (one to six months later) when time to first post-treatment use of alcohol, cocaine, or heroin was used as an outcome (Miele et al., 2000b).

The *Addiction Severity Index* (ASI) is a structured clinical research interview designed to provide information about various areas of an individual's life in which there often exists dysfunction associated with drug abuse. The 200-item ASI assesses problem areas including medical, legal, drug abuse, alcohol abuse, employment, family, and psychiatric problems. Reliability and predictive and discriminant validity data for the ASI have been extensively reported (McLellan et al., 1980; McLellan, Luborsky, Woody, & O'Brien, 1985; Rounsaville, Kosten, Weissman, & Kleber, 1986; Leonhard, Mulvey, Gastenfield, & Schwartz, 2000; Mäkelä, 2004). Early work by McLellan et al. (1985) has resulted in a strategy for obtaining a composite score based on the sum of several individual questions within specific problem areas. However, use of the composite score as a primary measure of drug use and related problems should be completed with caution. As outlined by Mäkelä (2004), composite scores are not always independent of one another, and could be an indicator of poor reliability instead of discriminant validity. Previous work has demonstrated that self-administered formats of the ASI produce similar results to the interview format (Rosen, Henson, Finney, & Moos, 2000).

The *Structured Clinical Interview for the Diagnostic Statistical Manual* (SCID) is a broad-spectrum instrument that adheres to the DSM decision trees for psychiatric diagnosis and encourages multiple paths of exploration, clarification, and clinical decision-making, with specific clarification regarding efforts to decrease or control use, continued use despite problems, specific withdrawal symptoms of a drug, and assessment of comorbidity. This interview is a primary measure of substance use disorders in the field of clinical psychology, but requires extensive training to use efficiently. The Structured Clinical Interview for the DSM-IV was a primary measure of substance abuse and substance dependence disorders. The research version of the SCID-5 (SCID-5-RV) and User's Guide was released on November 24, 2014, and other versions are in development (see www.scid4.org/). This general DSM interview structure is being used to assess both substance and behavioral addictions (Rosenberg & Feder, 2014a, 2014b). However, little research has been completed on use of this format with addictions other than substance use. It has been used widely with tobacco, alcohol, and other drug use.

Structured Interviews of Food Addiction

While *food addiction* has not been assessed through a validated structured interview, binge eating disorder is assessed in an interview format in the DSM-V as a feeding and eating disorder involving recurrent episodes, for at least three months, of binge eating (lots of food in a discrete period, a sense of lack of control over intake), associated with eating more rapidly than normal, until feeling uncomfortably full, when not physically hungry, eating alone due to embarrassment over intake, and feeling disgusted with oneself afterward, with no compensatory behavior such as with bulimia nervosa (APA, 2013). It is strongly associated with food addiction and has been used as a proxy measure (Sussman et al., 2011b). Food addiction is related to more frequent binge eating episodes (Yau et al., 2014), may involve addiction to eating behavior as opposed to the intake of specific foods as in a substance addiction (Hebebrand et al., 2014), and perhaps is associated more with preoccupation about food to achieve a "rush" effect.

Structured Interviews of Behavioral Addictions

Gambling

Zimmerman, Chelminski, & Young (2006) adapted the January 1995 DSM-IV patient version of the SCID for *problem gambling* (PG). Using the same format as the SCID they wrote a diagnostic module for the DSM-IV PG criteria. At the beginning of this module, PG is screened for by the following questions: "Did you ever gamble? IF YES: When in your life did you gamble the most? (How long did that last?) During that time, how often did you gamble? How much were you betting? Did you ever think that you had a problem with gambling? Has anyone else ever thought that you have a gambling problem? How often do you gamble now? How much money are you gambling?" If there is no evidence of a potential gambling problem then the rest of the module is skipped. The presence of a manic episode, a potential exclusion for the diagnosis of PG if the gambling behavior is limited to periods of mania or hypomania, is assessed as well in the SCID interview. For patients with current PG, they are asked whether the gambling behavior was a reason for currently seeking treatment. The SCID-5-RV assesses problem gambling similarly, adhering closely to the DSM-V criteria for gambling disorder (see Chapter 1 of this text).

Other interviews to assess PG include the *Structured Clinical Interview for Pathological Gambling* (SCI-PG; Grant, Steinberg, Kim, Rounsaville, & Potenza, 2004) and the *Diagnostic Interview for Gambling Severity* (DIGS; Winters, Specker, & Stinchfield, 2002). The SCI-PG asks how often one gambles now, how much money is typically gambled, the last time one gambled, and gambling history items. Next, if one suspects a problem, items assess "absent," "subthreshold," or "threshold" levels of criteria including five items that tap preoccupation (e.g., "How often do you think about gambling?"), three items that tap gambling to cope (e.g., "Did you ever gamble to escape problems in your life?"), two items that tap tolerance (e.g., "Have you needed to increase the amount of money you gambled in order to get what you sought from gambling?"), one item on chasing losses ("When you have lost money gambling, have you ever chased after your losses?"), three items on lying about one's gambling ("Have you ever lied to anyone about gambling such as how long you gambled, or the amount of money gambled, or that you were gambling at all?"), two items about negative consequences of gambling

("Has your gambling caused problems for you in your family, work, school, or social life to the extent that you lost or risked losing something or someone important?"), three items on loss of control (e.g., "How successful have you been in trying to cut down or stop?"), two items on withdrawal-like symptoms (e.g., "Did you experience restlessness or irritability when you tried to cut back or stop gambling?"), and one item on getting bailed out of trouble by borrowing money ("Have you ever asked for money or been given money from a family member or close friend to relieve a desperate financial situation caused by gambling?"). The DIGS is very structured and consists of 19 questions, which are scored as "very true," "somewhat true," or "false." These questions are very similar to the SCI-PG and the SOGS (described later in this chapter).

Internet Addiction

A little research has involved interview studies of *Internet addiction*. Interview items tap: experiences using the Internet, symptoms and possible sources of Internet addiction (e.g., preoccupation with Facebook), and friends' or significant others' views about one's Internet use or addiction (e.g., Tsai & Lin, 2003 [among Taiwanese youth]). In at least one instance, interviews were conducted – but only to develop a self-report questionnaire for game addiction – on one type of Internet addiction (Wong & Hodgins, 2013). One study attempted to carefully establish SCID-like diagnostic criteria for Internet addiction, but did not utilize an interview as the method for establishing the criteria (seven, which were preoccupation, withdrawal, tolerance, loss of control, and three entrenchment/preoccupation criteria [use even though problem, loss of other interests, using Internet to escape]; Tao et al., 2010). There are many sources of addiction from the Internet, including gambling, shopping, working, sex, love, gaming, as well as the overall medium. Certainly, future interview studies will need to consider the type of activity engaged in.

For example, Internet gaming disorder (IGD) is a "Condition for Further Study" in the DSM-V (APA 2013); that is, IGD is acknowledged as a potential addiction contingent on the need for more research. Eight tentative criteria that could be tapped through a SCID-type interview include: (1) preoccupation or obsession with Internet games, (2) withdrawal-like symptoms when not playing, (3) a build-up of tolerance – more time needs to be spent playing the games, (4) tried to stop or curb playing Internet games, but failed to do so, (5) loss of interest in other life activities, (6) continued overuse of Internet games even with the knowledge of how much they impact a person's life, (7) lied to others about his or her Internet game usage, and (8) use of Internet games to relieve anxiety or guilt.

Shopaholism/Buying Addiction

The one research-based interview which taps *compulsive buying disorder* is the *Minnesota Impulsive Disorder Interview* (MIDI; Christenson et al., 1994). The MIDI is a 36-item semi-structured interview that includes separate screening modules diagnosing pathological gambling, hair pulling, fire starting, intermittent explosive disorder, compulsive buying, and compulsive sexual behavior. A screening item then leads to assessment of such criteria as increasing tension before shopping followed by relief afterwards. Certainly, as with some of the other addictions, interviewing for shopping addiction has been used to develop self-report scales (e.g., Faber & O'Guinn, 1992; the Compulsive Buying Scale).

Love Addiction

There are no research-based interviews of *love addiction* (Sussman, 2010). Development of love addiction interviews is needed. Such an interview would tap: always needing a love object to feel complete, preoccupation with a love object, dissatisfaction with a love object after a period of time (tolerance), feeling irritable or having difficulty focusing when not with the love object (withdrawal), and experiencing negative consequences such as relationship breakups and negative affect.

Sex Addiction

There has been interview work completed on *sex addiction*. A recent DSM-V-type field trial utilized a structured diagnostic interview and self-report scales to examine hypersexual disorder (Hypersexual Disorder-Diagnostic Criteria Interview, HD-DCI; Reid et al., 2012). An interview format similar to the SCID was used, yoked to proposed diagnostic criteria. The interview permitted follow-up questions for clarification. The criteria applied to persons over 18 years of age covering a period of at least six months, involving recurrent and intense sexual fantasies, urges, and behavior. This status was examined in association with five additional criteria: excessive time involved in procuring and engaging in sex, in response to negative mood states, in response to stressful life events, unsuccessful efforts to control one's sexual behavior, and disregarding safety of others. The interview demonstrated reasonable validity and two-week test–retest reliability.

Exercise Addiction

Exercise addiction assessment has involved in-depth interviews (Bamber, Cockerill, Rodgers, & Carroll, 2003; Muller et al., 2014; Sachs & Pargman, 1979), though not often. Bamber and colleagues engaged in a semi-structured clinical interview of 56 adult female exercisers to formulate diagnostic criteria for exercise addiction. The interviewer requested a discussion of events over the last three months. Participants made notes on a calendar. Detailed probing took place regarding significant events for evidence of preoccupation/entrenchment, withdrawal, tolerance, urges, and loss of control. Qualitative analysis of responses was engaged in to search for emergent themes. Uncovered themes included psychological (intrusive thoughts), social and occupational (e.g., social isolation), physical (injury and exercise), behavioral impairment (inflexible), and withdrawal/loss of control. The authors asserted that these themes should be core in consideration of exercise addiction.

Muller et al. (2014) examined the concordance of a questionnaire-based categorization as at-risk for exercise dependence (German version of the Exercise Dependence

Scale-21; EDS-G) with an interview-based diagnosis of exercise dependence among 134 subjects. The interview targeted the same aspects of exercise dependence as the EDS-G. First, all participants were asked to describe their sport activities within the last three months. The interview also examined if exercise was used to avoid negative feelings, how much exercise interfered with social or role functioning, and if there was a need to permanently increase the amount of time exercising or an inability to reduce exercise despite negative consequences. The agreement between questionnaire-based and interview-based diagnoses was fair to moderate, though over-diagnosing appeared to occur with the EDS-G.

Workaholism

Workaholism has seldom been measured by use of interviews. I could locate only one widely cited qualitative interview study of 100 workaholics (Machlowitz, 1980). Ten characteristics were examined (e.g., whether or not the person wakes up early no matter how late the person goes to sleep). That study revealed the existence of enthusiastic workaholism. All other studies have involved self-report inventories. One other paper mentioned engaging in interviews but the workaholism data reported were based on self-report scales (Harpaz & Snir, 2003).

Self-Report Assessment Instruments: Brief Introduction

There are many *self-report assessment instruments* available to tap any one of the 11 addictions of emphasis in this text. These assessments often have ***cut-off scores*** (minimum scores to indicate "true" presence of the addiction). They permit the treatment agents and perhaps the suffering person to gauge the degree of difficulty with a particular addiction. Summaries of many of the substance (tobacco, alcohol, other drug or food addiction) and behavioral addiction self-rating scales that are presented in this chapter may be located online (see www.knowmo.ca/Capacity/AddictionMeasures.aspx). This large collection of psychometric summaries of addiction-related measures was organized by David Hodgins and Cayla Martin at the University of Calgary, Department of Psychology Addictive Behavior Laboratory in Alberta, Canada. Many of these measures are also described in Rosenberg and Feder (2014a). In this section of the chapter, I will attempt to describe some of the more popular measures used. In doing so, one may notice that there is a great deal of overlap in terms of contents covered.

Self-Report Assessment Instruments of Substance Addictions

Tobacco Dependence

Many self-report measures of tobacco dependence have been developed. Prominent examples include the *Fagerstrom Scale for Nicotine Dependence* (FTND; Heatherton,

Kozlowski, Frecker, & Fagerstrom, 1991). This six-item measure taps number of cigarettes smoked, whether smoking begins within 30 minutes of waking, two items related to smoking in the morning, difficulty refraining from smoking where it is forbidden, and smoking even while ill in bed. This type of measure taps physiological dependence and, perhaps, does not tap directly some aspects of addiction as defined in this text (i.e., appetitive effects, negative consequences).

The *Cigarette Dependence Scale* (CDS; e.g., Courvoisier & Etter, 2010) is a 12-item measure which taps a self-rating of level of addiction to cigarettes, quantity of cigarettes smoked, whether smoking begins within 30 minutes of waking up, whether quitting would be difficult, urges to smoke, feeling stressed without cigarettes, feeling a prisoner of cigarettes, dropping other activities to smoke, and smoking even though knowing of health dangers. The CDS is more closely related to an appetitive drive–satiation notion as well as DSM criteria, and is a very good predictor of abstinence in the short term (Couvosier & Etter, 2010).

Other tobacco dependence measures may also tap subjective tolerance, craving, and relative salience of tobacco (e.g., *Hooked on Nicotine Checklist* [HONC]; DiFranza et al., 2002). The ten-item HONC, which was developed for adolescents, taps failed quit attempts, smoking because it is hard to quit, feeling addicted, strong cravings to smoke, needing a cigarette, hard to keep from smoking where forbidden, when quitting feeling irritable, having difficulty concentrating, having urges to smoke, and feeling anxious because not smoking. Clearly there is a lot of overlap among the cigarette smoking dependence measures as well as variants such as the 10-item *Penn State Electronic Cigarette Dependence Index* (PSECI; Foulds et al., 2015), which also taps waking up at night to have an e-cigarette. All of these measures show good internal consistency (Cronbach's αs $>$ 0.68), discriminate heavier from lighter smokers, and predict relapse (e.g., Couvosier & Etter, 2010; DiFranza et al., 2002; Foulds et al., 2015; Heatherton et al., 1991).

Alcohol Misuse

The *Michigan Alcohol Screening Test* (MAST) is a 25-item questionnaire used to screen for consequences of problematic alcohol use and perceptions of alcohol-related problems. This questionnaire was originally developed to place drinkers into early (mild impairment), middle (moderate impairment), and late (severe impairment) stages (or levels of impairment) of alcoholism (Selzer, 1971). This measure can be self-administered and used to identify abnormal drinking by addressing social and behavioral consequences (Selzer, Vinokur, & van Rooijin, 1975). More than a decade after its introduction, a review of studies using the MAST concluded that the scale had acceptable inter-item consistency (Cronbach's α = 0.83–0.93), but tended to over-diagnose alcoholism (Gibbs, 1983). The SMAST is a shorter ten-item version that is relatively effective in discriminating alcoholics from non-alcoholics. The items are designed to describe extreme drinking behaviors and to establish the presence of negative consequences of excessive alcohol consumption. Examples of discriminating items are as follows: Have you ever attended a meeting of Alcoholics Anonymous? Have you ever gone to anyone for help about your drinking? Have you ever been in a hospital because of drinking? Arguably, since one item that has a higher scoring weight refers to attendance at meetings of AA, over-diagnosis still could result, for example, due to a DUI being committed by a non-alcoholic who is then mandated by the court to attend meetings.

The *Alcohol Use Disorders Identification Test* (AUDIT), developed by the World Health Organization, is an index of consequences experienced from drinking over the past year (Saunders, Aasland, Babor, de la Fuente, & Grant, 1993). The AUDIT is often used as a self-report measure, but it can also be administered by a clinician orally (e.g., at initial screening). Three questions assess quantity and frequency of use, and seven questions assess alcohol-related problems (loss of control, not completing tasks, drinking in morning, remorse, blackouts, injuries, social consequences; alpha range, 0.75 to 0.94; Saunders et al., 1993). After summing responses for the ten items, the practitioner can determine a risk level and employ suggested intervention strategies. The AUDIT has shown convergent validity across a wide range of populations (Reinert & Allen, 2007).

The *Alcohol Use Inventory* (AUI; Horn, Wanberg, & Foster, 1986; Littrell, 1991; Rychtarik, Koutsky, & Miller, 1998) is a 228-item, multiple-choice, self-report inventory. It was systematically developed to measure alcohol problems and has demonstrated strong content, construct, and criterion validity. There are 24 subscales with 17 primary scales characterizing individuals along various dimensions with internal consistency ranging between subscales ($\alpha = 0.57$–0.88). The dimensions are grouped according to benefits from drinking, drinking styles, drinking consequences, and concerns about and recognition of a drinking problem. The primary scale factors include the following: (1) drinking to improve sociability; (2) drinking to improve mental functioning; (3) drinking to manage or change mood; (4) drinking to cope with marital problems; (5) gregarious versus solitary drinking; (6) obsessive-compulsive drinking or constantly thinking about drinking; (7) continuous, sustained drinking; (8) loss of behavioral control when drinking; (9) social-role maladaptation; (10) perceptual withdrawal symptoms such as alcohol hallucinosis (hallucinations without impairment of consciousness), **delirium tremens** (agitation, general confusion, visual and auditory hallucinations), and *formication* (a sensation like insects crawling on or under the skin, which can be fatal); (11) somatic or physical withdrawal (e.g., shakes, hangovers, convulsions); (12) drinking provokes marital problems; (13) quantity of alcohol used; (14) post-drinking worry, fear, and guilt; (15) external support to stop drinking; (16) ready to quit; and (17) recognition of drinking problems.

The AUI primary scales may identify three general profiles of problem drinkers: low impairment problem drinkers, medium impairment problem drinkers, and high impairment problem drinkers (Rychtarik et al., 1998; Rychtarik, Koutsky, & Miller, 1999). Low impairment problem drinkers are likely to show a later onset of problem drinking, drink relatively less, and seek treatment as outpatients. They also are likely to be relatively successful in their social and vocational lives. The medium impairment problem drinkers are similar to the first type of drinker in that they show relatively good social adjustment. However, they are more likely to report a history of physical, emotional, or sexual abuse, and depression, and they drink a greater quantity of alcohol. Finally, the high impairment drinkers show the greatest social and vocational impairments, high levels of previous physical, emotional, or sexual abuse, highest levels of sustained drinking, and highest levels of psychopathology (i.e., depression, anger, or sociopathy).

Other Drug Misuse

The *CRAFFT* (car, relax, alone, forget, family or friends complain, trouble) is a brief six-item screener. The CRAFFT has demonstrated good convergent validity and nearly acceptable internal consistency ($\alpha = 0.68$). The items on this assessment represent neurobiologically based (drinking or using to relax), cognitively based (poor decision-making, as in riding in a car driven by someone under the influence; forgetting things while drinking or using [blackouts]), and non-socially based (drinking or using alone) drug use motivations, as well as interpersonal-based consequences of use (family or friends telling one to cut down; getting into trouble while under the influence). Moreover, the CRAFFT is capable of detecting problems related to alcohol and other drug use whereas most similar measures capture alcohol use only (Knight, Sherritt, Shrier, Harris, & Chang, 2002).

The original *Chemical Dependency Assessment Profile* (CDAP) is a 232-item multiple-choice, true/false, and open-ended self-report questionnaire used to assess substance use, dependence problems, and treatment needs among adolescents and adults (Davis, Harrell, & Honaker, 1989). Further analysis of a modified version of the instrument – including only the multiple-choice and true/false items – revealed dimensions of dysfunction addressing quantity/frequency of use, physiological symptoms, situational stressors, antisocial behaviors, interpersonal problems, affective dysfunction, treatment attitudes, impact of use on life functioning, and expectancies (Harrell, Honaker, & Davis, 1991). Original findings indicate good internal consistency ($\alpha = 0.78$–0.88), but normative data were only based on a sample of 86 individuals. This assessment is unique in that it taps into neurobiologically based, cognitively based, and socially based use motivations and consequences for alcohol users, non-alcohol drug users, and polydrug users.

The *Drug Use Screening Inventory* (DUSI) is a self-report inventory which consists of 149 items (the revised version, the DUSI-R, consists of 159 items) and is used to quantify problems in ten areas, including alcohol or other drug use, behavior problems, health status, psychiatric disorders, social competence, family adjustment, school adjustment, work adjustment, peer relations, and leisure/recreational time. The scale demonstrated good internal consistency for males ($KR20 = 0.76$) and females ($KR20 = 0.72$) and has been shown to be a valid measure of drug misuse in normal and clinical populations (Tarter & Hegedus, 1991). An adolescent version is also available (Tarter, Laird, Bukstein, & Kaminer, 1992) that is adequate at discriminating between normal and clinical drug users based on the DSM-III criteria for a psychoactive substance use disorder (Kirisci, Mezzich, & Tarter, 1995).

Food Addiction

There are a variety of self-report measures that tap binge eating disorder (e.g., EDE-Q, EAT-26, CIDI, QEWP-R; see Sussman et al., 2011b), anorexia nervosa, bulimia, or emotional eating (also as are found on the University of Calgary website provided at the beginning of this chapter). However, these measures are not of food addiction per se. There are few measures of food addiction. A 25-item measure of food addiction has been developed and is the one most widely used (*Yale Food Addiction Scale* [YFAS]; Gearhardt, Corbin, & Brownell, 2009), and an updated 35-item version (YFAS 2.0) reflecting DSM-V diagnostic criteria, which demonstrates reasonable internal consistency, and convergent, discriminant, and incremental validity, has been developed (Gearhardt, Corbin, & Brownell, 2016). The YFAS refers to "certain foods" (focused on high-fat, high-sugar types). It consists of items tapping *loss of control* (eating more than planned, continuing to eat certain foods though no longer hungry, worry about cutting down on certain types of food, avoiding situations because one is afraid of overeating), *negative consequences* (eating to the point of feeling physically ill, feeling sluggish from overeating, dealing with feelings from overeating instead of dealing with job or social demands, causes distress, difficulties functioning effectively because of food and eating, causes self-loathing or guilt, causes physical problems or makes a physical problem worse), *entrenchment/preoccupation* (constantly eating certain foods throughout the day, going out of the way to purchase certain types of food, start eating food rather than job or social activities, avoiding certain situations because not able to consume certain foods there, keep consuming even though having emotional/physical problem), *tolerance* (eating more and more to get the feeling desired, eating same amount does not reduce negative feelings like it used to), *withdrawal* (symptoms such as agitation or anxiety when cutting down or stopping eating certain foods, consuming certain foods to avoid feelings of agitation or anxiety, feeling urges to consume certain foods when cutting down or stopping eating them), and *trying to stop/relapse* (desire to cut down or stop eating certain types of food, tried to cut down or stop, success at cutting down or stopping, number of times tried to cut down or stop).

The YFAS 2.0 (Gearhardt et al., 2016) reflects role, social and physically hazardous consequences, and craving, as well as dependence-related symptoms (e.g., also includes items such as problems with family and friends because of overeating; avoiding school, work, or social activities because of fear of overeating; feeling so bad about overeating that the person doesn't want to do other things such as work or social activities; overeating getting in the way of taking care of family and doing household chores; cutting down on certain foods resulting in craving for them; such strong urges for certain foods that the person can't think of anything else; keep eating certain foods even though the person knows it is dangerous [sweets/diabetes]; distracted by eating or thinking about eating to the extent that the person could have got hurt [driving a car]; family and friends worry about the overeating). All items now are on eight-point scales from "never" to "every day"; see http://supp.apa.org/psycarticles/supplemental/adb0000136/adb0000136_supp.html.

There exists a 15-item measure developed for Overeaters Anonymous (OA; www.oa.org/newcomers/is-oa-for-you/) which includes: *affect enhancement* (eat when emotions are intense), *loss of control* (eat when not hungry, eating binges, use laxatives/excessive exercise/diet pills/etc. to control weight, fast to control weight, need to have something in mouth all the time, ever eaten food that is spoiled, certain foods can't stop eating after the first bite, lost weight with a diet followed by bouts of uncontrolled eating), *entrenchment/ preoccupation* (eat a lot when alone, fantasize about how much better life would be if a different size or weight, spend too much time thinking about food, etc.), and *negative consequences* (eating affecting health, eating making self or others unhappy, feelings of guilt or shame about weight or way of eating). Likewise, there are 12 Food Addicts Anonymous (FAA) items (www.foodaddictsanonymous.org/are-you-food-addict), which include: *loss of control* (especially junk food or high sugar foods, failed at diets, efforts to avoid weight gain), *affect enhancement* (eating when upset or to reward self), *entrenchment/ preoccupation* (hiding eating, avoid social interactions because don't look good enough, steal others' food, look forward more to food served at gatherings rather than being with other people there), and *spiritual/negative consequences* (ashamed about eating or weight, becoming more irritable after eating sugar or flour or wheat, life would be fine if persons or things would change, ask for divine help and feel let down). OA and FAA items involve a "yes" or "no" type of response. Neither OA nor FAA items have been subjected to rigorous psychometrics research.

Another food addiction measure is the *ACORN Assessment* tool which attempts to assess food addiction by stages (Werdell, 2009). These stages are: *early stage* (seven items; e.g., enjoy eating almost more than anything else, occasionally eat more than want but can control it), *middle stage* (12 items; e.g., there are special foods or treats which one eats quite frequently, dieted more than once in the last five years, experience of not remembering that one ate something), *late stage* (13 items; e.g., have foods that one eats every day [such as foods containing sugar, flour, caffeine], suffer from consequences that one doesn't want from overeating and can't stop), and *final stage* (five items; e.g., do not enjoy eating as much as one once did, would sometimes rather die than stop eating binge foods). While this measure is a promising direction to contemplate, because it could in theory anchor treatment type to stage of addiction, I could locate no research on it.

Self-Report Assessment Instruments of Behavioral Addictions

Gambling

Gambling is now in the DSM-V, and the diagnostic criteria were introduced in Chapter 1. Screening and diagnostic instruments are described in several sources, including Albrecht, Kirschner, and Grusser (2007) and Grant & Odlaug (2014). Instruments described by Grant and Odlaug (2014) include the *South Oaks Gambling Screen* (SOGS, 20 items; Lesieur & Blume, 1987), *Gamblers Anonymous 20 Questions* (Toneatto, 2008), the *Massachusetts Gambling Screen* (MAGS, 28 substantive items; Shaffer, LaBrie, Scanlan, & Cummings, 1994), the *Lie/Bet Questionnaire* (two items; Johnson et al., 1988), *Early Intervention Gambling Health Test* (EIGHT, eight items; Sullivan, 1999, 2007), and *National Opinion Research Center* (NORC) *DSM-IV Screen for Gambling Problems* (34 items; National Opinion Research Center, 1999).

Albrecht et al. (2007) also mention the *Canadian Problem Gambling Index* (CPGI; nine core severity items among a total of 33 items; also includes items on frequency and duration of involvement in gambling, cognitive expectancies, and family history of problem gambling), adaptation of the *Yale-Brown Obsessive Compulsive Scale* to gambling (PG-Y-BOCS; 10 items) as a simpler measure of problem gambling (PG), and the *Gambler's Belief Questionnaire* (GBQ; 21 items), which assesses cognitive distortions related to gambling.

I will provide details on a couple of these. Perhaps the most widely used and researched of these self-report measures are the Lie/Bet Questionnaire and the SOGS. The Lie/Bet Questionnaire is a two-item screen: "Have you ever had to lie to people important to you about how much you gamble?" and "Have you ever felt the need to bet more and more money?" The SOGS was developed by Lesieur and Blume (1987), and is the longest among the PG self-report measures at 20 items scored (mostly "yes/no" type). The SOGS scale was derived from DSM-III criteria for pathological gambling (PG). Respondents scoring "3" and "4" are classified as "potential pathological gamblers" and those scoring "5" or more are classified as "probable pathological gamblers." This classification has been used widely in epidemiological studies. Items assess *type of gambling* (cards, bet on horses or other animals, sports, dice, casinos, lotteries, bingo, stocks [the market], slot or other machines, game of skill [pool, bowling, golf], paper games such as **pull tabs** [lotto, tickets that may have winning combinations]), *entrenchment/preoccupation* (the largest amount of money ever gambled, going back another day to win money lost, hiding signs of gambling from others, where borrowed money for gambling from [e.g., household, relatives, loan sharks, credit line]), *loss of control* (gamble more than intended, felt one would like to stop gambling but didn't think one could), and *negative consequences* (family members with gambling problems, claiming to be winning money gambling but weren't really, felt had a problem with gambling, people criticized one's gambling, felt guilty about the way one gambles or what happens, argued over how one handles money [arguments centered on gambling, borrowed money but not paid back due to gambling], lost time from work or school due to gambling). The SOGS has also been promoted as an interview, administered as such in its initial research (Lesier & Blume, 1987). The SOGS can be used to fit the DSM-V criteria, though research studies are needed.

An example of one other type of self-report scale examined *gambling-related problems* (French et al., 2008). The items were included in the National Epidemiological Survey on Alcohol and Related Conditions (NESARC) Wave 1, a large and nationally representative survey (originally administered as an interview). Respondents were asked 15 questions on problems associated with gambling. These problems included using gambling as a means to improve one's mood (*affect enhancement*), and raising gambling money by writing a bad check, signing someone else's name to a check, stealing, and cashing someone else's check, as examples; generally reflecting likely loss of control and impending *negative consequences*. The authors found that alcohol consumption and gambling were complementary activities. The measure has not been used clinically; however, it could be.

Internet and Communications Addictions

Internet Addiction Disorder

The most popularly used general assessment of Internet addiction disorder (IAD) is Young's *Internet Addiction Test* (IAT; Young, 1998), which consists of 20 items on six-point-type scales ranging from "does not apply" to "always." The IAT items involve *loss of control* (stayed online longer than intended, lose sleep due to late night log-ins, try to cut down and fail), *entrenchment/preoccupation* (anticipating going online again, fear life without Internet would be empty, annoyed if interrupted while online, preoccupied with Internet when offline, saying "just a few more minutes" when online, neglect household chores to stay online, prefer excitement of Internet to intimacy with partner, check e-mail before doing something else one needs to do, new relationships with fellow online users, secretive when others ask what one does online, hide how long on Internet, choosing to spend time online rather than going out with others, block out disturbing thoughts about life with soothing thoughts of Internet), *withdrawal* (feel depressed or nervous when offline which goes away when online), and *negative consequences* (others complaining about one's Internet use, grades or school work suffers, job performance suffers).

Using factor analysis among 410 Hong Kong university undergraduates, three underlying dimensions of the IAT were found: withdrawal and social problems (moodiness or difficulties being away from the Internet), time management and performance (entrenchment [preoccupation] and loss of control), and reality substitute (dependence on Internet to relieve real-world problems; Chang & Law, 2008). These authors also found that the degree of Internet addiction was more severe among those in cyber-relationships and those who gambled online, compared to those in chat rooms, shopping, or looking for information online. Discussed in detail in Weinstein et al. (2014), other Internet addiction measures include the *Internet Addiction Scale* (IAS; 31 items), *Chen Internet Addiction Scale* (CIAS; 26 items), *Questionnaire of Experiences Related to the Internet* (QERI; 10 items), *Compulsive Internet Use Scale* (CUI; 14 items), *Problematic Internet Use Questionnaire* (PIUQ; 18 items), *Generalized Problematic Internet Use Scale* (GPIUS; 29 items), and the *Internet-Related Problem Scale* (IRPS; 20 items).

Sun and colleagues (2012) used a four-item index to assess *Compulsive Internet Use* (CIU; Davis, Flett, & Besser, 2002). These items were "I use the Internet more than I ought to," "I usually stay on the Internet longer than I had planned," "Even though there are times when I would like to, I can't cut down on my use of the Internet," and "My use of the Internet sometimes seems beyond my control." The Likert-type response options were (1) Never, (2) Rarely, (3) Sometimes, (4) Most of the time, and (5) Always. The CIU construct showed a good internal consistency (Cronbach's $\alpha = 0.81$). The mean of all four items was used as a continuous measure of CIU. In Sun et al's (2012) study, baseline CIU predicted one-year changes in tobacco and alcohol use among female but not male high school students in the United States and China.

Online and Video Gaming

Measures pertaining to online gaming include the *Problematic Online Game Use Scale* (POGU, 20 items), *Online Game Addiction Diagnostic Scale* (OGADS; 30 items), and *Problematic Online Gaming Questionnaire* (POGQ, 18 items). Factors underlying these questionnaires include the same types mentioned in the IAD (see Kiraly et al., 2014, pp. 71–73). For a relatively new example, one recent such assessment is the online *Gaming Addiction Inventory for Adults* (GAIA; Wong & Hodgins, 2013). This measure consists of 31 items (26 of which are used in an overall score; five items load on an unimportance of video game factor). The items load on six factors (one being the "not addicted" factor) and show convergent validity with other gaming addiction measures. Items on the six factors (as labeled by the authors) tap: *loss of control and consequences* (10 items; e.g., sometimes late for engagements because playing video games, fail to get enough sleep because of playing video games, unsuccessful attempts to reduce the time spent playing video games, social life has sometimes suffered because playing video games, spend more money than can afford on video games), *agitated withdrawal* (four items; e.g., angry when unable to play, irritable when unable to play, anxious when unable to play), *engagement* (five-item unimportance factor; e.g., video games are unimportant in my life, I rarely think about playing video games when I am not using a computer or gaming console), *coping* (four items; e.g., play to feel better, to release stress, to change mood), *mournful withdrawal* (five items; e.g., miss game character [avatar] when unable to play, have nothing else to do, feel sad when unable to play), and *shame* (three items; i.e., hide negative effects of video game play, shame about negative effects in life resulting from game play, regret neglecting other task due to game play).

There are other problem gaming measures including the *Problem Video Game Playing Scale* (PVP, nine items) for adolescents, and the *Game Addiction Scale* for primary school age children (GAS; 21 items), for games that are not necessarily online-based (see Albrecht et al., 2007; Salguero & Moran, 2002). These measures also get at entrenchment/preoccupation, tolerance, withdrawal, loss of control, and negative consequences. For example, the PVP negative consequences item is: "Because of the video game playing I have reduced my homework, or schoolwork, or I have not eaten, or I have gone to bed late, or I spent less time with my friends and family." As with other measures, these show adequate internal consistency and convergent validity.

Social Network Addiction

Social network addiction generally is tapped through use of the IAD but there is a *Facebook* (FB) *Addiction Scale* (FAS) (Cam & Isbulan, 2012: Griffiths et al., 2014; Koc & Gulyagci, 2013). This eight-item measure includes: *preoccupation* (difficulty focusing on academic work due to FB use, first thing on mind when get up is to log into FB), *affect enhancement* (log into FB to feel better when down), *withdrawal* (anxious if can't access FB), *loss of control* (attempted to spend less time on FB but not succeeded), and *negative consequences* (family or friends think spend too much time on FB, lose sleep over spending more time on FB, interferes with social activities). This measure demonstrates good internal consistency (reflecting a single factor). Another measure, six items retained from the *Bergen Facebook Addiction Scale* (BFAS; Andreassen, Torsheim, Brunborg, & Pallesen, 2012), include: *entrenchment/preoccupation* (spent a lot of time thinking about FB or planned use of FB), *affect enhancement* (used FB in order to forget about personal problems), *tolerance* (felt an urge to use FB more and more), *loss of control* (tried to cut down on the use of FB without success), *withdrawal* (become restless or troubled if have been prohibited from using FB), and *negative consequences* (used FB so much that it has had a negative impact on job/studies). This measure demonstrates good internal consistency, test–retest reliability, and convergent validity. There are other social network websites (e.g., Twitter, Pinterest, LinkedIn, Tumbir, Xing, Renren). However, SNS measures do tend to focus on FB. New measures of social media addiction continue to be developed (e.g., notably, a 48-item *Smartphone Addiction Scale* tested among approximately 200 South Korean adults, derived in part from the IAT; Kwon et al., 2013).

Shopaholism/Compulsive Buying

The two most-used self-report measures are the *Compulsive Buying Measurement Scale* (CBMS; Valence, d'Astous, & Fortier, 1988) and the *Compulsive Buying Scale* (CBS; Faber & O'Guinn, 1992). The CBMS consists of 16 items, with reasonable reliability (though estimates vary from study to study) and concurrent validity. Items tap: *affect enhancement* (buying to cope with stress in daily life and relaxing), *entrenchment/preoccupation* (some things bought are not shown to anybody, respond to direct mail offers, if financial problems know could rely on somebody to help out), *loss of control* (have money/cannot help but spend part or the whole of it, often impulsive in buying behavior, something inside oneself pushed one to go shopping, strong urge to buy, irresistible urge to buy, bought a product one did not need with very little money left, spendthrift), *history* (during adolescence had enough money to buy things enjoyed, teen years told what to buy), and *negative consequences* (felt somewhat guilty after buying a product, feel sorry for something done or said).

The CBS, initially 29 items, retained seven core items in a revised version, on five-point scales (strongly disagree to strongly agree) and includes: *affect enhancement* (buying something to feel better), *entrenchment* (felt others would be horrified to find out one's spending habits, making only minimum payments on credit card), *loss of control* (having to spend money left at the end of a pay period, buying things one couldn't afford, writing a check that one knew would bounce), and *withdrawal* (feeling anxious or nervous if one didn't go shopping). Another measure is the *Yale-Brown Obsessive Compulsive Scale – Shopping Version*, which focuses relatively more on shopping preoccupation/entrenchment (10 items; see Racine et al., 2014, for more detail). While the CBMS and CBS were developed some time ago, the internal consistencies of these scales are moderately high and they appear to have reasonable discriminant validity between clinical and normal groups of buyers (Albrecht et al., 2007).

Love Addiction

There are some assessments of love addiction available (e.g., see www.loveaddictionhelp.com/love_addiction_assessment). There have been three evidence-based assessments that are love addiction-related. Feeney and Noller (1990) constructed 12 love addiction-related Likert scale type items that were scored from "strongly agree" (1) to "strongly disagree" (5) and formed two factors, reliance on partner (e.g., "want us to be together all the time," "happiest, most alive with partner," and "self-worth most positive with partner") and unfulfilled hopes (e.g., "never satisfied with partners," "daydreaming, planning about partners," and "pursuit more exciting than love"). Use of this self-report measure, or of interview items that indicate developing dependence on a search for ideal love for self-fulfillment, which appears consistently thwarted, could be used to screen persons with love addiction.

Likewise, Hunter, Nitschke, and Hogan (1981) developed a 20-item four-point "strongly agree" to "strongly disagree" closed-ended self-report *Love Scale* (e.g., "Soon after I met my partner, I knew this person was my 'other half' and made my life complete") which they administered to 58 undergraduates (mean age 28 years) twice during a two-week period, and found high test–retest reliability. Some of these types of items also are reflected in the *Passionate Love Scale* (PLS; Hatfield & Sprecher, 1986). Feeney and Noller's measure, the Love Scale, and the Passionate Love Scale (14 items; see: www.elainehatfield.com/Passionate%20Love%20Scale.pdf) failed to provide replication work, and only college undergraduate students were assessed. All three measures tap dependence on an ideal love.

Examples of popular "yes/no" items that may be used to identify persons at risk for love addiction include (from the *Sex Love Addicts Anonymous* [SLAA] 40 questions): "Have you ever tried to control how often you would see someone?," "Do you get high from romance?," "Do you believe that a relationship will make your life bearable?," "Do you believe that someone can 'fix' you?," "Do you feel desperation or uneasiness when you are away from your lover?," and "Do you feel that you're not 'really alive' unless you are with your romantic partner?" (www.slaafws.org/download/core-files/The_40_Questions_of_SLAA.pdf). Examples of popular love addiction type "yes/no" items that indicate experience of *loss of control*, *preoccupation*, or *negative consequences* include: "Do you find yourself unable to stop seeing a specific person even though you know that seeing this person is destructive to you?," "Do you make promises to yourself concerning your romantic behavior that you find you cannot follow?," "Do you find that you have a pattern of repeating bad relationships?," "Do you find yourself in a relationship that you cannot leave?," "Does your romantic behavior affect your reputation?," "Do you have relationships to try to deal with, or escape from life's problems?," "Are you unable to concentrate on other areas of your life because of thoughts or feelings you are having about another person?," "Do you believe that your life would have no meaning without a love relationship?," and "Do you find yourself obsessing about a specific person even though these thoughts bring pain, craving, or discomfort?" (www.slaafws.org/download/core-files/The_40_Questions_of_SLAA.pdf). Certainly, much assessment research remains to be completed.

Sex Addiction

Some researchers have addressed sex addiction as the self-reported number of orgasms per week (e.g., at least seven days a week), as opposed to consequences criteria. However, the relation between sexual frequency and adverse consequences is not clear (Kaplan & Krueger, 2010). The most popular assessment of sex addiction is the 25-item *Sex Addiction Screening Test* (SAST), which contains some items that do not tap sex addiction per se. SAST items include: *abused* (sexually abused as a child, stayed in romantic relationships after became abusive), *entrenchment/preoccupation* (purchase romance novels or sexually explicit magazines, multiple romantic relationships at the same time, fantasies to escape problems, sadomasochistic behavior, sex with minors, preoccupied with sexual thoughts or romantic daydreams, feel sexual behavior is normal, worried about people finding out, hide some sexual behavior from others), *loss of control* (have trouble stopping sexual behavior when know it is inappropriate, sex for gifts, periods of sexually acting out followed by periods of celibacy, efforts to quit type of sexual behavior have failed, feel controlled by sexual desires or fantasies of romance, think sexual desire stronger than self), and *negative consequences* (significant others worry or complain, feel bad about sexual behavior, created problems for self and family, sought help, others hurt emotionally, felt degraded, depressed afterwards, interferes with family life). Various modifications of the SAST (made longer, made shorter) have been developed including a six-item brief version, *PATHOS* (Preoccupied with sexual thoughts, hide behavior/Ashamed, sought help/Treatment, someone hurt emotionally/Hurt, feel controlled/Out of control, and feel depressed afterwards/Sad; Rosenberg et al., 2014). This measure has achieved reasonable reliability and convergent validity support.

The 19-item *Hypersexual Behavior Inventory* (HBI; Reid, Garos, & Carpenter, 2011) has demonstrated adequate internal consistency and concurrent validity. The HBI includes three factors: *affect enhancement* (use sex to forget about the worries of daily life, helps one feel less lonely, turn to sexual activities when experiencing unpleasant feelings, turn to sex in order to soothe self, helps one cope with stress, way for one to deal with emotional pain, way to try and help deal with problems), *loss of control* (promised oneself not to repeat a sexual behavior, find oneself returning to it over and over, engage in sexual activities knowing one will later regret, attempts to change sexual behavior fail, do things sexually that are against personal values and beliefs, even though sexual behavior is irresponsible or reckless find it difficult to stop, feel like sexual behavior is taking one in a direction one doesn't want to go, sexual cravings and desires seem stronger than one's self-discipline, behave in ways one thinks are wrong), and *negative consequences* (sacrifice things really want in life in order to be sexual, fantasies distract one from accomplishing important tasks, sexual behavior controls life, interferes with aspects of one's life such as work or school).

Non-researched clinical measures include what appears to be a very useful 20-item (yes/no) measure utilized as part of a self-help program ("sex addiction workbook" items; Sbraga & O'Donohue, 2003). Items include: *entrenchment/preoccupation* (wake up and fall asleep planning new sexual encounters, free time consumed by sexual fantasizing/planning, can't get rid of sexual thoughts, use Internet to keep sexually stimulated, secret [pornography] collection, sexually available even if in serious relationship, spend money on sex, spend time cruising for sex partners, use sex to feel better, sex partners who one can't remember, find self in places would feel ashamed to be caught in, lie to people one cares about in regard to what one is doing sexually, keep people at a distance so that they don't know about other life, look for weak people for sexual encounters), *tolerance* (sexual experiences frequently disappointing), *loss of control* (feel controlled by sexual drive), and *negative consequences* (almost been caught and vowed to stop only to start again, isolated and lonely due to sexual activities, lost a job/relationship/home due to sexual activities). Other measures mentioned by Reid et al. (2011) include the *Sexual Compulsivity Scale* (SCS, 10 items; Kalichman et al., 1994; Kalichman & Rompa, 2001) and the *Compulsive Sexual Behavior Inventory* (CSBI, 28 items; Miner, Coleman, Center, Ross, & Rosser, 2007), assessed primarily among gay males or to also tap sexual violence, respectively.

Sex Addicts Anonymous provides a series of 13 questions the member can ask to complete their first step (sex as out of control and unmanageable), including: activities that are part of one's sexual behavior, ways one has been preoccupied with sex, ways one has not been able to control or stop the behavior, ways one has been lured into sexual activities, ways one tried to deny sexual behavior to self, lies told to conceal sexual activity, ways disrespectful of others while engaging in sex, examples of euphoric recall of sex, ever risked arrest, ways put self in danger of disease, how compulsive sexual activity has affected various areas of life (education, job, awareness of feelings, relationships, financial, spirituality, physical health, mental health, morals, and personal goals), description of one's most recent episode, and sexual history (https://saa-recovery.org/SAALiterature/English/FirstStepGuide/).

Exercise Addiction

There is a fair amount of overlap among the exercise addiction self-report scales, though there are some which are specific to forms of exercise (e.g., bodybuilding, running). Also, some measures tap whether one exercises to meet more people (e.g., the *Exercise Dependence Questionnaire*), whereas others tap whether one is becoming socially isolated due to exercise (e.g., *Exercise Dependence Scale*). Scales described by Berczik et al. (2014) or Cook and Hausenblas (2014) include the *Obligatory Exercise Questionnaire* (OEQ; 20 four-point scale items), *Exercise Dependence Scale* (EDS; 21 six-point scale items), *Exercise Dependence Questionnaire* (EDQ; 29 seven-point scale items), *Exercise Addiction Inventory* (EAI; six five-point scale items), *Bodybuilding Dependence Scale* (BDS; nine seven-point scale items), *Running Addiction Scale* (RAS; 11 seven-point scale items; also see Chapman & de Castro, 1990), and *Commitment to Exercise Scale* (CES; eight four-point scale items, or use of a continuum line with bipolar adjectives). The most studied measures include the OEQ, EDS, EDQ, and the EAI, all of which have some evidence of reliability and convergent validity. The *OEQ* (also see Ackard, Brehm, & Steffen, 2002) taps: *frequency of training* (e.g., engaging in exercise on a daily basis), *entrenchment/preoccupation* (e.g., feeling guilty if one does not exercise, exercise when advised against such activity by a doctor or friend, finding mind wanders to thoughts about exercising), *loss of control* (e.g., sometimes feeling like don't want to exercise but go ahead and push oneself anyway), *social exercise* (e.g., best friend likes to exercise), *withdrawal* (e.g., when miss a scheduled exercise session may feel tense, irritable, or depressed, exercise to avoid feeling anxious), and *appetitive effects/affect enhancement* (experience feeling euphoria or a "high" during or after an exercise session).

The *EDS* (also see Hausenblas & Downs, 2002) taps: *withdrawal* (exercise to avoid feeling irritable), *entrenchment/preoccupation* (exercise despite recurring physical problems, rather exercise than spend time with family/friends, spend a lot of time exercising, exercise when injured, spend most of free time exercising, exercise despite persistent physical problems, choose exercise to get out of spending time with family/friends, great deal of time spent exercising, think about exercise when one should be concentrating on school/work), *tolerance* (increase intensity to achieve desired effects/benefits, continually increase exercise frequency to achieve the desired effects/benefits), *loss of control* (exercise longer than intended, unable to reduce how long exercise, exercise longer than intend, unable to reduce how often, longer than expected, longer than planned), and *withdrawal* (exercise to avoid feeling anxious, exercise to avoid feeling tense).

The *EDQ* (also see Ogden, Veale, & Summers, 1997) taps: *affect enhancement* (after exercise session feel happier about life, after exercise feel less anxious, after exercise feel more positive about self, exercise to look more attractive), *entrenchment/preoccupation* (level of exercise makes one tired at work, rest of life has to fit in around exercise, after exercise feel one is a better person, exercise to meet more people, exercise to keep one occupied, if can't exercise can't cope with life, exercise to control weight, being thin is most important thing in life, exercise to be healthy, after exercise feel thinner, exercise to feel fit, exercise to prevent heart disease and other illnesses, if can't exercise miss the social life), *withdrawal* (if can't exercise feel irritable, if can't exercise feel agitated, hate not being able to exercise), *loss of control* (miss time at work due to exercise, little energy for partner/family/friends due to exercise, make decision to exercise less but can't stick to it), *tolerance* (exercise same amount of time each week or not, weekly pattern of exercise is repetitive), and *negative consequences* (feel guilty about amount one exercises, exercise has become a problem, exercise interferes with social life). The EDQ loads on six to eight factors depending on the study completed (Ogden et al., 1997).

The *EAI* (also see Terry et al., 2004) taps: *affect enhancement* (use exercise as a way to change mood [buzz, escape]), *entrenchment/preoccupation* (exercise most important thing in life), *tolerance* (increase amount of exercise in a day), *withdrawal* (if have to miss exercise session feel moody and irritable), *loss of control* (if cut down the amount, and then start again, one ends up doing as much as before), and *negative consequences* (conflicts with family or partner about amount of exercise).

Workaholism

Besides records of number of hours worked per week (e.g., 50 or more; Snir & Zohar, 2008), which may reflect need for money as opposed to addiction to work, and collaborative reports, currently there are no alternative, commonly used measures of workaholism other than that assessed through self-report. As summarized by Sussman (2012a), a couple of studies have examined simple self-reported identification as a workaholic as being a single-item measure. However, such subjective measures are of questionable content validity. There exist three main tested self-report questionnaire measures of workaholism that provide multiple studies of reliability and validity: the *Work Addiction Risk Test* (WART; Robinson, 1998; Taris, Schaufeli, & Verhoeven, 2005), the *Workaholism Battery* (WorkBAT; Andreassen, Hetland, Molde, & Pallesen, 2011; Spence & Robbins, 1992), and the *Dutch Work Addiction Scale* (DUWAS; Shimazu & Schaufeli, 2009; Shimazu, Schaufeli, & Taris, 2010). (One other questionnaire, the *Work Attitude Questionnaire* [WAQ] attempts to differentiate enthusiastic versus compulsive workaholism, though little research on it is available; see Albrecht et al., 2007.)

The *WART* is composed of 25 items and consists of five dimensions: *compulsive tendencies* (e.g., "I seem to be in a hurry and racing against the clock"), *control* (e.g., "I get impatient when I have to wait for someone else or when something takes too long"), *self-absorption/impaired communication* (e.g., "I forget, ignore, or minimize birthdays, reunions, anniversaries, or holidays"), *inability to delegate* (e.g., "I prefer to do most things myself rather than ask for help"), and *self-worth* (e.g., "It is important that I see the concrete results of what I do"). Collapsed across the five dimensions, the internal consistency of the measure is reasonable ($\alpha = 0.88$), as is its two-week test–retest reliability ($r = 0.83$). However, the first three factors demonstrate the greatest number of item-factor loadings and discriminant validity for separating workaholics from non-workaholics. I think "compulsive tendencies" may tap loss of control, whereas the other four dimensions tap aspects of preoccupation.

The *WorkBAT* is composed of 25 items (there also exists a 14-item short scale and a 20-item short scale) and consists of three dimensions: *high work involvement* (e.g., "I spend my free time on projects and other activities"), *high work drive* (e.g., "I seem to have an inner compulsion to work hard"), and *work enjoyment* (e.g., "Sometimes I enjoy my work so much I have a hard time stopping"), though in several studies only two dimensions (i.e., work drive and enjoyment) have been identified, and in a recent Chinese assessment five dimensions have been identified (n = 1,235; 24-item scale after factor analysis; enjoyment, work involvement-enjoyment, drive-work involvement, drive-3, work involvement-3; Huang, Hu, & Wu, 2010). Internal consistency for the drive and enjoyment subscales is reasonable ($\alpha = 0.75$ or 0.85 and 0.85 or 0.88, respectively [McMillan, Brady, O'Driscoll, & Marsh, 2002; Sussman, 2012a]), and less consistently internally consistent for the involvement subscale ($\alpha = 0.65$ or 0.80). There is also some evidence of convergent validity, with moderate correlations of (a) the drive subscale with an intrinsic job motivation measure ($r = 0.39$), (b) the enjoyment subscale with a job satisfaction measure ($r = 0.48$), and (c) both subscales with the Schedule for Nonadaptive and Adaptive Personality – Workaholism scale (SNAP-W; rs = 0.61 and 0.27, respectively). However, criterion validity of these subscales with number of hours worked (rs = 0.22 and 0.16, with drive and enjoyment subscales, respectively) is weak.

Schaufeli and colleagues (e.g., Schaufeli, Shimazu, & Taris, 2009) developed a newer measure, the *Dutch Work Addiction Scale* (DUWAS), derived from WART and WorkBAT items, which consists of two dimensions: *working excessively* (e.g., "I seem to be in a hurry and racing against the clock") and *working compulsively* (e.g., "It's important for me to work hard even when I don't enjoy what I am doing"). The working excessively subscale shows marginal internal consistency ($\alpha = 0.67$), whereas the working compulsively subscale shows adequate internal consistency ($\alpha = 0.77$). There are 17-item and 10-item versions of this measure, and both dimensions have shown some evidence of concurrent validity, with negative relations with perceived health and happiness among large, heterogeneous samples of Dutch and Spanish employees (collapsed across version and sample, mean rs between working excessively with perceived health and happiness are –0.21 and –0.20, respectively, and between working compulsively with perceived health and happiness are –0.28 and –0.28, respectively). One may speculate that maybe working excessively taps loss of control, whereas working compulsively taps preoccupation and negative consequences.

Using the DUWAS, Schaufeli, Bakker, Heijden, & Prins (2009) found that the combination of working excessively and working compulsively (16 percent of the sample) was related to the most unfavorable conditions in terms of medical residents' (n = 2,111) self-reported job demands (i.e., work overload, work–home conflict, overwork, role conflict, mental demands, emotional demands, and organizational demands), job resources (i.e., in terms of: perceived lack of social support from colleagues, participation in decision-making, feedback, supervisory coaching, and opportunities to learn), wellbeing (i.e., burnout, happiness, recovery after the workday), and organizational behavior (i.e., **presenteeism** [going to work despite feeling sick] and medical performance [making errors that impact patients]). Thus, the DUWAS demonstrates reasonable concurrent validity, at least among medical residents.

Two other self-report measures of workaholism were located in the literature, though relatively less research has been completed using these measures. The *SNAP-Work* is an 18-item, forced-choice (true/false) instrument containing 13 work items and a further five items shared with an Obsessive-Compulsive subscale (McMillan et al., 2002; Sussman, 2012a). (The full SNAP measure, which taps various personality constructs, is much longer, consisting of 375 total items.) Second, a *workaholism behavior measure* was developed and examined by Mudrack and Naughton (2001). This measure consists of two scales, each containing four items: the Non-Required Work Scale asks respondents how much time and energy they spend on thinking about ways to improve their work and Control of Others reflects the interpersonal and intrusive nature of workaholism (Sussman, 2012a).

These measures overlap in substantive contents of workaholism though there are a few differences, such as in wording of items. The main substantive difference is that the "workaholism behavior measure" emphasizes responsibility more than do the other measures. However, all measures appear to tap some aspect of lack of conscientiousness such as forgetting birthdays of significant others due to work. Also, lack of work enjoyment and a sense of compulsive involvement with work are tapped by all measures. In general, the currently examined workaholism measures appear to measure loss of control and preoccupation/entrenchment, and sometimes measure negative consequences. These measures don't tap much the process of seeking an appetitive effect (obtaining a high or rush by working). A sense of trying to control others appears unique to measurement of this addiction.

Use of a Multi-Response Self-Report Addiction Matrix Measure

The justification and history of use of this type of measure were introduced in Chapter 5, begun with categories developed by Cook (1987). As further mentioned in Chapter 5, others followed, adapting this measure to their subject populations. This type of item is perhaps the only means to tap multiple addictions in large-scale survey, avoiding item redundancy. The final matrix measure developed by Sussman et al. (2014) used a template adapted from Cook. Subjects endorsed ever and past 30-day addiction categories that applied to them, and could write in additional addictions that they felt they experienced. The final version of the matrix measure included responses reported by at least ten subjects in a pilot study of one class of alternative high school youth and two classes of college undergraduate students. After completing the measure, they were asked for feedback regarding wording of the measure's items to assist in enhancing its clarity. The measure included a detailed header. Then, 22 response categories of addictions were provided along with a 23rd which permitted participants to indicate an open-ended response to "Any other addiction? Please identify: ____"

The full measure is included as Figure 5.1. For the purposes of the Sussman et al. (2014) study, only 11 categories were emphasized for most analyses, to approximate the categories examined in Sussman et al.'s (2011b) study. Marijuana was combined with the other drugs response category to reflect hard (or illicit) drug addiction. Internet browsing and Facebook categories were combined to create an Internet addiction category. The online or offline video games category was not included in the Internet addiction category because gaming might have been offline. Shopping at stores and online shopping were included to assess shopping addiction.

This measure demonstrated a plausible prevalence among former alternative high school youth, and very high (90%) one-year stability of addiction (36% of sample) versus non-addiction (64% of sample) class membership (recall that two LCA classes were identified; Sussman et al., 2015b). In addition, this measure demonstrated convergent validity with other measures including compulsive Internet use, rigorous exercise, frequency of cigarette, alcohol, and other drug use, and risky sexual behavior (Sussman et al., 2014).

Other Types of Assessment

Some "addicts" may not identify as having a problem, be unwilling to disclose to others consequences of their behavior, or may exhibit gaps in memory as a function of "motivated forgetting" or perhaps due to being inebriated in the case of alcohol or other drugs. **Corroborative reports** of other persons, which might confirm self-reports, might be used in assessment of any of these addictions to provide another means of examining the addictive behavior. However, valid and reliable measures are almost nonexistent throughout the addictions. For example, a Google Scholar search using the words "validity," "corroborative reports," and "addictions" yields only 57 web pages. Still, the little work that has been done suggests that client–collateral agreement is reasonable (e.g., 75% regarding substance abuse since treatment; 79% regarding participation in AA/NA; see Kedia & Perry, 2005). In the Kedia and Perry (2005) study, not surprisingly, those collaterals who saw the clients more frequently and recently (spouses, parents, children) had relatively higher agreement rates. Much work might be accomplished in this direction, as one of the main consequences of behavioral addictions is difficulties in relationships with significant others.

Neurobiological assessments also are promising for establishing the existence of multiple addictions, and include use of fMRI or neurotransmitter metabolites (e.g., activity in the nucleus accumbens, related to firing of mesolimbic dopamine, is associated with activity among perhaps all of the addictions). Such work is reported in various sources (e.g., Rosenberg & Feder, 2014a). However, neurobiological work is in its preliminary stages, is quite expensive, and is not practical to use as a clinical assessment device for different addictions.

Biochemical assessment has been a useful tool to provide accurate and objective information regarding the type and amount of a particular drug that is present in the body at the time of measurement. Urine **immunoassays** (a procedure for detecting or measuring specific proteins or other substances through their properties as antigens or antibodies) have been a popular biochemical method of assessing level of drug use as a cheap and effective method of corroborating self-report information (Grigsby et al., in press). However, this method is not without its limitations. Detection of drug metabolites is dependent on the sensitivity of the assay used. Drug concentrations are highest several hours after drug use and decrease to undetectable levels over time. The length of time a drug or its metabolites can be detected in urine is referred to as the *retention time*. Retention times differ according to (1) the type and amount of drug consumed, (2) whether use is occasional or chronic, (3) the method of drug use, (4) individual metabolic rates and excretion, (5) diet, (6) acidity of the urine (higher then quicker excretion of basic drugs; lower then quicker excretion of acidic drugs), (7) fluid intake, and (8) the time of day (Moeller, Lee, & Kissack, 2008).

Generally, the length of time drug metabolites stay in the body varies across drug types. For example, cocaine and some hallucinogens (e.g., LSD) are present in the body for 12 to 48 hours. Drug metabolites that are present in the body one to three days include methadone, opiates (heroin, morphine, codeine), proposyphene (Darvon), methaqualone (Quaalude), barbiturates (e.g., Phenobarbital), and amphetamines (crystal, ice, crank, methamphetamines; one to two days). Phencyclidine (PCP) used occasionally remains present in the body for one to eight days, whereas when chronic use is present, PCP remains in the body up to 30 days. Finally, cannabinoids (marijuana) used occasionally are present in the body for one to seven days, whereas daily chronic use causes cannabinoids to remain present in the body for one to six weeks (Moeller et al., 2008).

Evidence has also suggested that ***false positive rates*** (false alarm rates, incorrectly detecting presence of drug use for example [specific example, of opium by eating poppy seeds]) are more common with certain drugs, particularly benzodiazepine, than others – such as marijuana and crack cocaine use (Vincent, Zebelman, & Goodwin, 2006). Prescription and non-prescription drug use may also contribute to false positive rates and should be considered during the screening process (Brahm, Yeager, Fox, Farmer, & Palmer, 2010). It is generally recommended that additional "confirmatory" testing be performed in lieu of drawing definitive conclusions from urine-based assessments (e.g., immunoassays confirmed by use of ***chromatography*** techniques [the separation of a mixture by passing it in solution or suspension or as a vapor, as in gas chromatography, through a medium in which the components move at different rates]; Sussman & Ames, 2008). In addition to these limitations of popular biological drug screening methods, there has been little to no work that has attempted to determine how these measures are associated with the criteria of drug addiction provided in this text. For example, while the biochemical assessment may indicate that the experienced user has more drugs in their system, they may be experiencing fewer intrapersonal or interpersonal difficulties relative to a new user. Despite these limitations, the continued research of drug concentration levels is not without merit as it can be useful in predicting outcomes and improving treatment decisions for drug-using patients in clinical and natural settings beyond self-report measures of drug use (Isbister, 2010). For example, the installation of breathalyzer-enabled ignition interlock devices can assess the level of alcohol in a driver's system before allowing the car to operate. If judged to be beyond the legal limit, it can prevent the individual from driving under the influence of alcohol – a common and dangerous form of alcohol misuse (also see Grigsby et al., in press).

It is difficult to envision how biochemical assessments would play a role in the assessment of behavioral addictions. It is possible that evidence of the metabolites of fatty foods might be measured to indicate non-compliance with treatment for *food addiction*. The consequences of *sex addiction* (e.g., such as potential STDs) or *workaholism* (e.g., levels of stress-related hormones, such as cortisol levels or DHEA [dehydroepiandrosterone]; www.directlabs.com/Resources/Hormones/StressHormones.aspx) might be assessed through biochemical assessments. However, the sensitivity and specificity of STDs for sex addiction, or stress hormones for work addiction, are not high. As behaviors are not external agents which are imbibed, biochemical assessment would have no relevance to many addictions. Brief descriptions of the various assessments discussed above (screening, mental status, interviews, self-reports, other assessments) are summarized in Table 9.1.

Assessing the 11 Focal Addictions

Table 9.1 Means of assessing addictions

Screening interview data	Clinical screening interviews may be used proactively or reactively to check for addictions or to clarify a presenting problem. Both proactive and reactive assessments of addiction are important to differentiate addictions from other problems, and to facilitate appropriate treatment planning.
Mental status examination	The mental status examination includes the assessment of appearance, attitude and behavior, speech, affect, thought and language, and perceptions and cognitive functioning, such as insight and judgment. It helps suggest other means of assessment to determine whether a formal psychiatric diagnosis of a comorbid condition should be made.
Unstructured interview format	The unstructured interview format can produce incredibly detailed information that is specific to the individual being questioned. This can assist clinicians in recommending more thorough assessments, and if conducted properly can be efficacious in determining a diagnosis and subsequent treatment plan.
Structured interviews	Structured interviews are more effective in collecting quality information, as there are fewer digressions into areas of little substantive concern. Furthermore this format produces consistent results across individuals allowing researchers and clinicians to identify similarities across different addictive behavior experiences. There are very few assessments of food addiction, or behavioral addiction-type interviews. Thus, examples are drawn primarily from the drug assessment arena. (e.g., the SCID).
Self-report assessment instruments	There are many self-report assessment instruments available to tap any one of the 11 addictions of emphasis in this text. Some examples are:
Tobacco, alcohol, or other drug misuse	**Tobacco**: Fagerstrom Scale for Nicotine Dependence (FTND); Cigarette Dependence Scale (CDS); Hooked on Nicotine Checklist (HONC). **Alcohol**: Michigan Alcohol Screening Test (MAST); Alcohol Use Disorders Identification Test (AUDIT); Alcohol Use Inventory (AUI). **Drugs**: CRAFFT; Chemical Dependency Assessment Profile (CDAP); Drug Use Screening Inventory (DUSI).
Food addiction	Yale Food Addiction Scale; 15-item scale developed in Overeaters Anonymous; ACORN Assessment tool.
Gambling	DSM-V diagnostic criteria; South Oaks Gambling Screen (SOGS); Gamblers Anonymous 20 Questions.
Internet and communications addictions	**Internet**: Young's Internet Addiction Test (IAT); Internet Addiction Scale (IAS); Chen Internet Addiction Scale (CIAS); Questionnaire of Experiences Related to the Internet (QERI); Compulsive Internet Use Scale (CUI); Problematic Internet Use Questionnaire (PIUQ); Generalized Problematic Internet Use Scale (GPIUS); Internet-Related Problem Scale (IRPS).

Summary

Table 9.1 *(cont.)*

	Online and video gaming: *Problematic Online Game Use Scale (POGU); Online Game Addiction Diagnostic Scale (OGADS); Problematic Online Gaming Questionnaire (POGQ); Gaming Addiction Inventory for Adults (GAIA); Problem Video Game Playing Scale (PVP); Game Addiction Scale (GAS).* ***Social network addiction***: *Facebook (FB) Addiction Scale (FAS); Bergen Facebook Addiction Scale (BFAS); Smartphone Addiction Scale.*
Love and sex addiction	***Love***: *Love Scale; Passionate Love Scale.* ***Sex***: *Sex Addiction Screening Test; Hypersexual Behavior Inventory.*
Exercise addiction	*Obligatory Exercise Questionnaire; Exercise Addiction Inventory; Bodybuilding Dependence Scale.*
Workaholism	*Work Addiction Risk Test; Workaholism Battery; Dutch Work Addiction Scale (DUWAS); SNAP – Work/Workaholism Behavior Measure.*
Shopaholism/compulsive buying	*Compulsive Buying Measurement Scale (CBMS); Compulsive Buying Scale (CBS); Yale-Brown Obsessive Compulsive Scale – Shopping Version.*
Multi-response Addiction Matrix Measure	There is a great deal of overlap regarding the types of items across the different addictions. Similarities among the addictive behaviors translate into similarities of assessment and can be measured using a multi-response addiction matrix. The Multi-response Addiction Matrix Measure developed by Sussman et al. (2014) demonstrated plausible prevalence of 11 addictions, very high one-year stability, and convergent validity with other measures.
Other types of assessment	Corroborative reports (of other persons). Neurobiological assessments. Biochemical assessment.

Summary

Similar features of different addictions measures. The criteria and items used across measures of substance and behavioral addictions overlap greatly. In general, these measures tap (a) an appetitive effect (e.g., affect enhancement), (b) extensive involvement, precluding other activities to achieve an appetitive effect, and relatedly preoccupation with the addiction when not engaged in the addictive behavior, (c) loss of control, and (d) suffering negative consequences. Most of the measures, but not all, consider tolerance and withdrawal as separate features (though Sussman & Sussman [2011] would tend to think of them as aspects of preoccupation). Several of the measures consider duration of engagement as an aspect, which, for some unclear reason, varies using DSM-type criteria from three months to one year (e.g., food addiction – three months, sex addiction – six months, substance addiction – 12 months).

Unique features of different addictions measures. Measurement of different addictions involves some unique features. First of all, and most obviously, *different behaviors are being measured*. Thus, the questions focused on the topography of these behaviors differ. For example, when addressing *tobacco, alcohol, or other drug addiction* the manner of imbibing the drug might be assessed (e.g., taken orally, absorbed through the skin, inhaled, sniffed, or smoked, or injected). Discussion of acute physiological withdrawal symptoms also appears unique to tobacco, alcohol, or other drug addiction. Type of *food* might be assessed (e.g., high fat, high sugar, perhaps). For some food addiction measures, but not others, means to control weight (e.g., use of laxatives, exercise, diet pills, fasting) might be considered. *Gambling* addiction may address type of gambling (e.g., slots, cards). Attempting to make up for lost money through more gambling appears unique to that addiction.

Several different types of activities might be assessed on the *Internet* (which has led to assessments specific to the online activity). The envelopment in text language which often is used online may be unique to Internet addiction, and some of this language has become mainstreamed, though current Internet addiction items do not tap this dimension (e.g., LOL = laughing out loud; BFF = best friends forever). *Shopaholism* might address the type of item most preferred as an object of purchase (e.g., shoes). One may respond to direct mail offers or other questionable avenues of buying products when addicted to shopping. Preferred objects of a *love* addiction might be assessed. The use of poetic-sounding language (e.g., "you complete me") may be unique to love addiction and be used in its assessment. Type of *sex* addiction might be assessed (e.g., type of sex act such as preoccupation with sadomasochism, sex for gifts, looking for vulnerable people to have sex with). A history of sexual abuse may be present. (Of course, a history of sexual abuse may occur regarding many types of psychopathology; e.g., see Molnar, Buka, & Kessler, 2001).

Preferred type of *exercise* might be assessed in exercise addiction and there exist some activity-specific measures (e.g., running, body building). Attempting to exercise to achieve good health yet also when injured or advised against it by a physician seems unique to exercise addiction. Finally, job tasks that are most addictive might be assessed in *workaholism* measures (e.g., one could assess constant travel, doing all-nighters). Also, such items as feeling one is racing against the clock, impatient when having to wait for someone else to complete a task, being controlling, or keeping going even when the returns appear to be diminishing appear unique to workaholism.

Relatedly, while speculative, it is possible that ease of engagement (lack of effort) may be definitive of some addictions (tobacco, alcohol, drugs, food, Internet gaming) but not others (exercise, work, gambling, shopping, love or sex; that may demand more focused engagement but also produce a "rush" effect). Also, impact on one's biological clock may vary across different addictions. For example, duration of sleep, controlling for difficulties with or quality of sleep and resulting sluggishness, may vary. With tobacco, alcohol, or several types of drugs, food, shopping, love, sex, or exercise, it is less clear that one's overall duration of sleep would be impacted, whereas with certain drugs such as stimulants (e.g., cocaine or methamphetamine), gambling,

Summary

Internet, or workaholism, one may experience diminished duration of sleep to continue to engage in the activity.

Second, there appear to exist *irrational perceptions specific to the behavior*. For example, one may believe that one is labeled a tobacco, alcohol, or drug misuser due to others' hypocrisy. One may believe at least half-heartedly that one will not gain as much weight if food makes one feel good (or that one has a "second stomach" for desserts). Regarding gambling addiction, one may believe that one can "chase" one's losses, or double down, to win in gambling. Also, one may exaggerate one's winnings to oneself and others. On the Internet, one may use it as a reality substitute, and, for example, miss one's game character (*avatar*) when unable to play online games. Regarding shopping, one may recall being told what to buy as a child and now purchase objects without restraint (even compulsively). Regarding love addiction, one may feel the most self-worth with a partner yet never stably feel satisfied with partners, looking to be fixed by someone. Regarding sex addiction, one may believe that one won't catch an STD if one's partner is attractive. Regarding exercise addiction, one may overtrain into injury perceiving that one is getting into superior health. Regarding workaholism, one may believe that it is possible to do a perfect job.

Third, *physiological dependence* on an addiction is at least most obvious, or most directly related in the case of drug addictions, in which there may be physical withdrawal reactions (e.g., sweating, shakes) that are relatively unlikely to occur with other addictions. Still, hallmark withdrawal-like symptoms, particularly difficulty concentrating and irritability, may occur with all addictions. Neurobiologically, one may speculate that if one consistently induces greater endogenous mesolimbic turnover through engaging in an addictive behavior, over time, counteradaptation processes may diminish available dopamine at the receptor sites when not engaging in that behavior.

Fourth, *medical consequences* are most obvious, or most relevant, in the case of tobacco, alcohol, or other drug addictions, in which there may be disease implications, overdoses and emergency room visits, hospital stays, or death. In addition, **blackouts** (loss or gaps of memory of certain events that occurred while drinking or using) are most likely to be experienced in the case of alcohol or other drug addictions, but not other addictions (in general, besides the experience of trauma-related gaps of memory). Certainly diminished quality of sleep may occur as a function of any of these 11 addictions, leading to medical complications eventually. Weight problems may also occur as a function of many of these addictions, though perhaps not with shopaholism. An STD may be experienced as the result of sex addiction.

Fifth, *immediate physical danger* is relatively likely pertaining to alcohol or other drug addictions (e.g., driving drunk or high, riding in a car with someone who is drunk or high), or exercising to injury, but is relatively unlikely with most other addictions (although meeting up with a stranger one initially has contact with on the Internet might be physically dangerous).

Sixth, there may be some variation in *financial implications*. One may try to get financially bailed out of trouble with gambling and shopping addictions, or may make minimum payments back on a credit card due to desire for liquid cash for spending on gambling or shopping, but probably not with the other addictions (although one may

Table 9.2 Similar and unique features of different addictions measures

Similar features	All of the measures consider entrenchment or preoccupation in the addiction, loss of control, and suffering negative consequences. Most of the measures consider affect enhancement (appetitive effects), tolerance, and withdrawal as separate features. Some of the measures consider duration of engagement as an aspect.
Unique features	Measurement of different addictions involves some unique features: Different behaviors are being measured. Different irrational perceptions are specific to different behaviors. Physiological dependence is most directly related to alcohol or other drug addictions. Medical consequences are most obvious in the case of alcohol or other drug addictions. Immediate physical danger is relatively likely pertaining to alcohol or other drug addictions. There is some variation in financial implications. Legal problems would seem most obvious regarding participation in illegal behaviors.

steal from others to keep some drug addictions going). Of course, one may spend too much money in many of the addictions, but probably not with exercise or workaholism, at least in and of themselves.

Finally, *legal problems* would seem most obvious regarding participation in illegal behaviors including use of certain drugs, use of many types of drugs while driving (except tobacco), underground gambling, illegal activity on the Internet, writing bad checks or falling into debt in shopping addiction, or participation in certain sex addiction venues (e.g., illicit prostitution, with a minor). However, food, love, exercise, or work addictions are relatively unlikely to involve illegal behavior, except in extreme cases (e.g., stalking in love addiction may lead to arrests). Similarities and differences regarding information tapped from measures of different addictions are summarized in Table 9.2.

Conclusions. There is much overlap in measurement of addictions across assessments, and across addictions, though some addiction-specific features are also evident and in need of assessment. There is much research to be done on the assessment of different addictions to be able to place them as an official category within the DSM. One may speculate that this will occur over the next ten years or so, perhaps the earliest new categories being Internet and sex addictions (Rosenberg & Feder, 2014a, 2014b). The debate about whether to call some addictions impulsive or compulsive disorders, or addictions, will take some time to resolve, depending on how broadly one is willing to define "addiction" and how narrowly one is willing to define the other disorders. Attempts to differentiate these disorders through neurobiological measurement may or may not lead to fruitful results. However, based on the five criteria suggested by Sussman and Sussman (2011) – trying to achieve an appetitive effect, brief periods of satiation (of an appetitive need), preoccupation/entrenchment, loss of control, and negative consequences – it does seem fairly clear that all 11 behaviors focused on in this chapter are measurable addictions, at least through self-report items.

Bulleted Summary

- Unstructured-to-structured interviews, self-report assessments, a multi-response matrix measure, and perhaps some neurobiological assessments could be applied to multiple addictions. Most such assessments have been applied to alcohol and other drug use addictions, although new instruments to tap the other focal addictions have been and are being developed and validated.
- Tobacco use generally is not assessed through use of validated structured interviews (other than the SCID and the NHIS). Structured interviews of alcohol and other drug use include such acronyms as the CDP, SDSS, ASI, and the SCID. Also, there is no formal interview assessment of food addiction yet, though there is a SCID assessment of binge eating disorder.
- There are at least three formal interview assessments of gambling (SCID-PG, SCI-PG, DIGS), one interview assessment for shopaholism (MIDI), one SCID-based sex addiction interview assessment (HD-DCI), and two pertaining to exercise interview assessment (Bamber and colleagues; Muller and colleagues). There currently are no formal interview assessments for Internet, love, or work addictions.
- Many self-report assessments of the 11 focal addictions exist.
  - Regarding tobacco dependence, assessments include the FTND, CDS, HONC, and PSECI.
  - Regarding alcohol, these include the MAST, AUDIT, and AUI.
  - Regarding other drug use, these include the CRAFFT, CDAP, and DUSI.
  - There are three measures of food addiction now namely the YFAS, OA measure, and ACORN.
  - Self-report assessments of gambling include the SOGS, GA questions, MAGS, Lie/Bet Questionnaire, EIGHT, NORC Screen, CPGI, PG-Y-BOCS, GBQ, and NESARC gambling problem items.
  - Internet addiction-related self-assessments include the IAT, IAS, CIAS, QERI, CIU, PIUQ, GPIUS, IRPS, POGU, IGADS, POGQ, GAIA, PVP, GAS, FAS, and BFAS.
  - Shopaholism self-assessments include the CBMS and CBS.
  - Love addiction self-assessments have included the Feeney and Noller items, the Love Scale, the PLS, and the SLAA questions.
  - Sex addiction self-assessments include the SAST (and PATHOS), HBI, sex addiction workbook items, and SAA questions.
  - Exercise addiction self-assessments include the OEQ, EDS, EDQ, EAI, BDA, RAS, and CES.
  - Workaholism self-assessments include number of hours worked per week, WART, WorkBAT, DUWAS, WAQ, SNAP-Work, and a workaholism behavior measure.
- The matrix measure of multiple addictions involves providing a definition of addiction in the heading of the item, and asking the subject if he or she suffers from a list of addictions. This measure is economical, shows some evidence of convergent validity, and may be the only way to assess multiple addictions in a practical way.

- All addictions involve an appetitive need and search for satiation of it, preoccupation, loss of subjective control, and negative consequences. Unique features of different addictions include that (a) they do pertain to different specific behaviors, (b) irrational perceptions exist specific to different behaviors, (c) physiological dependence exists for some addictions (e.g., alcohol) but perhaps not others (e.g., work), (d) medical consequences are direct and pronounced for some addictions (e.g., alcohol) but not others (e.g., shopping), (e) immediate physical danger is more prevalent for some addictions (e.g., alcohol) than others (e.g., shopping), (f) financial implications are more prevalent for some addictions (e.g., gambling) than others (e.g., work), and (g) legal implications are more prevalent for some addictions (e.g., cocaine) than others (e.g., work).

Suggestions for Further Reading

American Psychiatric Association (APA) (2013). *Diagnostic and Statistical Manual of Mental Disorders* (5th edn.). Washington, DC: APA.

Grigsby, T., Sussman, S., Chou, C.-P., & Ames, S. L. (in press). Assessment of substance misuse. In J. Van Geest, T. Johnson, & S. Alemagno (eds.), *Handbook of Research Methods in the Study of Substance Abuse*. New York: Springer.

Rosenberg, K. P. & Feder, L. C. (2014b). An introduction to behavioral addictions. In K. P. Rosenberg & L. C. Feder (eds.), *Behavioral Addictions: Criteria, Evidence, and Treatment*. London: Academic Press/Elsevier, pp. 1–18.

Sussman, S., Arpawong, T. E., Sun, P., Tsai, J., Rohrbach, L. A., & Spruijt-Metz, D. (2014). Prevalence and co-occurrence of addictive behaviors among former alternative high school youth. *Journal of Behavioral Addictions*, 3: 33–40.

PART III

Resolving the Problems of Addiction and Future Directions

10 Resolving the Problems of Addiction – Prevention: General Principles

Learning Objectives

- To learn about levels of prevention, and to differentiate prevention from cessation
- To learn about the history of prevention research and practice
- To learn about mediation of prevention effects
- To consider the different age ranges in which prevention programming might be applied

Introduction

If Johnny had only been provided with prevention strategies when he was young, maybe many of the negative consequences he experienced as an adult would have been minimized. His mother wondered if he was hyperactive but he was never prescribed medication. Would that have helped? As might be instructed by a prevention practitioner, his TV viewing as a young child should have been monitored and regulated more closely by his parents. Maybe he could have been provided with evidence-based drug misuse prevention information in middle school. Then, perhaps he would not have used TV viewing or alcohol as a means to regulate his appetitive functioning. His behavior was not way out of the ordinary as a child. Perhaps others thought he would simply grow out of any behavioral quirk. Johnny received almost no formal prevention programming other than viewing a couple of films in his high school driver's education class on the dangers of drinking and driving. Certainly, as an adult, with numerous consequences already having been experienced, many types of prevention programming were not appropriate courses of action. That is, prevention of regular use, or prevention of any social or role consequences was no longer relevant; prevention of alcohol-related diseases and death still was relevant.

The central focus of addiction prevention work is on **antecedents**, events, contexts, and behaviors that precede and facilitate or deter engagement in the addiction. Program participants are taught how to anticipate the impacts of *internal* (e.g., such as desiring to feel good, desire to block out negative thoughts) and *external* (e.g., drug paraphernalia, escort web pages, casinos, gyms, social influence, or cultural norms) addiction-related cues, and how to counteract them with instruction of protective cognitions, behaviors, or access to protective social units (e.g., drug-free community settings, mentors of moderate behavior). Prevention interventions are often designed for use in a particular setting or settings (e.g., schools, home) and tailored to address the needs of specific groups (e.g., children, teenagers). Moreover, different prevention programs target persons at different developmental periods across the lifespan. Programs have targeted young children, elementary school youth, teens, emerging adults, middle age adults, and older adults (Sussman, 2013).

The *level of application* of prevention programming can be either **intrapersonal** (within the person) or **extrapersonal** (beyond the individual) (see Sussman & Ames, 2008). That is, one general type of programming includes strategies that attempt to change the individual's neurobiology, thinking, affect, or behavior (intrapersonal). Another type of programming is targeted at a unit that involves at least two or more individuals (extrapersonal). This level of application may focus on small groups (microsocial level) or on the large social or physical environment.

There has been a fair amount of prevention research and practice as applied to tobacco, alcohol, and other drug use (Sussman, 2013; Sussman & Ames, 2008). However, there has been relatively little prevention work applied to other behaviors. This chapter, and the next two, borrow heavily from the tobacco and other drug abuse prevention literature – for potential translation to other addictive behaviors. Most of the writing on prevention of other addictive behaviors is theoretical, or based on current clinical practice, without the support of empirical research.

For example, in Rosenberg and Feder's (2014a) text, the recent forerunner to this book, prevention strategies are offered but only in three chapters. Specifically, in the Yau et al. (2014) chapter, there is brief discussion of the possibility that policy-based strategies may impact food addiction. The authors highlight that taxation of sweetened beverages (or other foods), and food labeling, could lower their intake, but the few evaluations completed provided equivocal results. In two other chapters, about problematic online gaming and about social networking addiction, prevention strategies were derived from clinical practice including suggestions that parents become familiar with their child's online games to show interest in their child and begin to set rules on their use, have parents use **content-control software** for their children (to restrict contents that a youth would be able to access; e.g., see https://en.wikipedia.org/wiki/Comparison_of_content-control_software_and_providers), or instruct youth in meditation (Griffiths et al., 2014; Kiraly et al., 2014).

Prevention of TV, love, sex, and work addictions has been discussed by Sussman and colleagues (Sussman, 2007, 2010a, 2012; Sussman & Black, 2008; Sussman & Moran, 2013), but primarily speculatively. Likewise, Dickson, Derevensky, and Gupta (2002) speculate how strategies for prevention of alcohol, tobacco, and other drug use (ATOD) might be applied to prevention of gambling. Additionally, they assert (consistent with Sussman & Ames, 2008) that prevention strategies should consider a multi-level approach that includes variables within the individual (e.g., neurobiology, personality/cognition), and outside the individual (e.g., the microsocial environment, and the larger sociophysical environment).

In this chapter, I will present general principles of prevention (i.e., as a function of modalities, levels, differences and similarities from cessation, history, mediators, and developmental age considerations). Then in Chapters 11 and 12 I will discuss potential application of two general levels of analysis, intrapersonal and extrapersonal, to the prevention of the 11 focal addictions, borrowing heavily from drug abuse prevention (Sussman & Ames, 2008). Presentation of examples of theoretical or empirical work on the prevention of specific addictions is nested within discussion of types of prevention strategies. In a subsequent parallel presentation, general principles of cessation, followed by intrapersonal and extrapersonal cessation strategies, will be discussed in Chapters 13 through 15.

Why has most prevention work been on alcohol, tobacco, and other drugs? To repeat, a fair amount of the discussion to follow is inferred from the drug abuse prevention literature (see Sussman & Ames, 2008). Of the 11 focal addictions addressed in this text, only three of them have been approached extensively through prevention programming (i.e., cigarettes, alcohol, and illicit drug use), though there has been a little prevention work completed on other addictions (in particular, on food addiction-related behavior, problem gambling, and Internet addiction prevention), as will be described in subsequent chapters. There are at least three reasons that the other addictions (shopping, love, sex, exercise, and work) have hardly been examined for relevance to prevention programming. First, among several researchers and practitioners, these behaviors may not even be perceived as problems. Many other professionals may view such behaviors often as prosocial excesses (e.g., it being good to engage in work marathons), or possibly as being secondary to or part of other types of disorders such as OCD (recall the discussion of addiction versus OCD in Chapter 1 of this text). Even food addiction-related behavior may be considered part of other eating disorders (e.g., obesity, binge eating disorder), as opposed to being a separate addiction entity.

Second, relatedly, differentiating negative consequential types or levels of involvement in these behaviors is a source of contention and perhaps more difficult to conceptualize for the purposes of prevention programming. People need to eat to live, shop to have necessity items, fall in love and engage in sex at least for procreation and the protection of others (nurturance), exercise to maintain good health, and work to provide for the family. Possibly more fine-tuning is needed for each of these behaviors to understand what it is that needs to be prevented. For example, prevention of "compulsive" workaholism (working harder and harder, but getting less and less out of it), not "enthusiastic" workaholism (working harder and harder, and getting more and more out of it), may be what needs to be targeted among those at risk (Sussman, 2012a). Also, the degree to which workaholism interferes notably with social time or sleep time may need to be considered.

Third, there are commercial industries that may not whole-heartedly support prevention of behaviors which might decrease their net incomes or curtail their freedom of operation (e.g., fast food industry, retail stores, pornography industry, or the workplace in general). Still, given that it is possible to provide careful assessment and convincing explanation to stakeholders, prevention of these behavioral addictions at extreme levels could and should be addressed, as they do cause distress to self and others.

Modalities of Prevention

The largest body of addictions prevention work has been applied to tobacco use. Many *modalities* (settings, means of delivery) of tobacco use prevention programming have been implemented including (a) policy regulations (tax increases, warning labels, limits on access, smoke-free policies, and restrictions on marketing), (b) mass media programming, (c) school-based classroom education, (d) family involvement, and (e) involvement of community agents (i.e., medical, social, political). In a majority of trials, community-wide programming, which includes multiple modalities (e.g., [a] through [e]), has not been found to achieve impacts greater than single modality programming (Sussman et al., 2013a). Possibly, the most effective means of prevention involves a careful selection of program type combinations. Also, it is likely that a mechanism for coordinating maximally across program types (e.g., staging of programming, integration of community units taking a systems approach) is needed to encourage a synergistic impact. Considerations of different and multiple types of modalities of prevention programming across different addictions are explored in the subsequent two chapters of this text.

Levels of Prevention

Historically, public health researchers and practitioners have divided the field of prevention programming into three levels. These levels are *primary prevention* (before the problem behavior starts), *secondary prevention* (before the disease starts), and *tertiary prevention* (before death is likely). This chronicity definition is consistent with "progression" notions of addiction (Sussman & Ames, 2008). Arguably, Johnny might benefit from secondary, but more likely, tertiary preventive care

However, there is another target population-type terminology used by most researchers nowadays regarding grouping of prevention programming. Prevention may be considered *universal* (designed to affect the general population), *selective* (designed to affect subgroups at elevated risk for developing a problem, based on social, psychological, or other factors; e.g., the child of someone suffering from an addiction), or *indicated* (designed to affect high-risk subgroups already identified as having some detectable signs or symptoms of a developing problem; Gordon, 1987; see Table 10.1). The two sets of terminology may overlap to some extent (i.e., secondary or tertiary prevention would be most strongly associated with indicated prevention), but they do have a rather different focus.

Differences and Similarities of Prevention and Cessation

Differences

Another, different set of terms used to describe levels of an intervention is *prevention* versus *cessation*. Both prevention (at all levels) and cessation approaches encourage

Differences and Similarities of Prevention and Cessation

Table 10.1 Definitions/classifications of prevention

Types of prevention	Definitions. Programming …
Chronology definition	
Primary prevention	Implemented on a population before the problem behavior starts
Secondary prevention	Targeting the population after the problem behavior starts but before the disease sets in
Tertiary prevention	Aimed to improve conditions for diseased individuals before death is likely
Target population definition	
Universal prevention	Designed to affect the general population
Selective prevention	Designed to affect subgroups at elevated risk for developing a problem, based on social, psychological, or other factors (e.g., children of alcoholics)
Indicated prevention	Designed to affect high-risk subgroups already identified as having some signs or symptoms of a developing problem (e.g., experimental drug users)

Note: All prevention programming focuses on preventing future behaviors or consequences from occurring, as opposed to recovering from consequences (cessation).

adoption of alternative, healthy behaviors and "prevention" of premature death. However, cessation efforts address healing the "wreckage" of one's addiction. **Cessation programs** instruct one how to cope with psychological dependence (emotional reliance) on an addictivebehavior, and with withdrawal-like symptoms (getting past irritability and difficulties concentrating without resorting to the addiction). Cessation work focuses on stopping a current behavior from continuing, to arrest ongoing consequences, and permit recovery of health. The goal also may involve teaching one how to live with permanent changes resulting from the addiction (e.g., drug-related injury, divorce due to gambling debt or sexual exploits).

One of the main justifications offered to pursue prevention considers that there are high relapse rates in adult cessation programs (approximately 75 percent at one-year post-treatment return to baseline use in the drug abuse cessation arena [e.g., for cigarettes, alcohol, heroin, and marijuana]; Sussman & Ames, 2008). Arguably, prevention programming among children, teens, or emerging adults might inhibit, delay, or halt the addiction process that makes cessation so difficult. Effects of drug abuse prevention programming have been replicated in a variety of settings, particularly among young teens (Skara & Sussman, 2003; Sussman, 2013; Sussman et al., 2013a), with small to moderate effect sizes. One might further speculate that exposure to early prevention programming could potentially provide a type of proactive interference against later addiction-facilitative-type information – that is, resulting in protection against addictive behavioral processes (Sussman, 2013). Thus, there exists the expression "an ounce of prevention is worth a pound of cure" (Hirsch, Kett, & Trefil, 2002).

Sometimes youth may already be strongly addicted to one behavior (e.g., cigarette smoking) but may not be dependent on another behavior (e.g., alcohol use, gambling, sex). Possibly, cessation programming would be needed to address the one behavior, whereas prevention programming would be needed to address the other. In other words, it is feasible that both prevention and cessation material could be used in the same program.

Similarities

Across ATOD prevention and cessation programs, some similar content themes have emerged (e.g., Hansen, 1992; Sussman & Ames, 2008). These themes are directly relevant to any of the substance or behavioral addictions. Five types of substantive contents that exist in both prevention and cessation programs include the following (also see Table 10.2):

1 The ***social influence**-oriented approach* focuses on counteracting social influences that serve to promote or maintain an addiction. Program information includes instruction in awareness and counteraction of media, peer, or other social influences, and correction of social informational inaccuracies. For example, in a media literacy activity, a television commercial that advertises a casino may be analyzed for the social images that it portrays (e.g., excitement, winning), and to correct inaccuracies in the advertisement (e.g., casinos may be fun, but most people do lose money), possibly involving development of "corrective" ads (e.g., showing people losing money, setting firm limits on losses).
2 Instruction in ***cognitive-behavioral techniques*** focuses on uncovering the topography of one's at-risk situations or escalating addictive behavior through self-monitoring, and learning how to cope effectively with stressful situations. For

Table 10.2 Five types of substantive contents shared by prevention and cessation programming

Social influence-oriented approach	Focuses on counteracting social influences that serve to promote or maintain an addiction. Includes instruction in awareness and counteraction of media, peer, or other social influences, and correction of social informational inaccuracies.
Cognitive-behavioral techniques	Focuses on uncovering the topography of one's at-risk situations or escalating addictive behavior through self-monitoring, and learning how to cope effectively with stressful situations and not resorting to the addictive behavior.
Motivation enhancement	This approach attempts to increase a person's motivation not to start, not escalate, or to quit an addictive behavior. Motivational enhancement approaches assist individuals in clarifying their direction of change and increase their willingness to change.
Response-contingent reinforcement	Focuses on reducing occurrence of problem addictive behaviors with extrinsic rewards such as money, prizes, or vouchers. This approach can also include differential reinforcement contingencies designed to strengthen more prosocial alternative behaviors.
Supply reduction approaches	Focuses on arranging the social environment so that objects of addiction are more difficult to obtain (e.g., access restriction).

example, monitoring what sexual addiction-related situations one comes across during the day may help one to avoid them. Monitoring one's at-risk situations may help one to anticipate and cope with sexual urges. Stress coping strategies include: how to seek out social support; utilize relaxation strategies; "sit with feelings" (e.g., wait out curiosity to try out a new illicit massage parlor); engage in role playing to enhance social competency or general assertiveness; self-management and behavioral regulation; and learn and utilize effective problem-solving strategies.

3 **Motivation enhancement** focuses on techniques to clarify desire for change and reduce ambivalence toward change. This may include, but is not restricted to, a specific strategy such as motivational interviewing. This approach dedicates a significant amount of programming to attempt to increase a person's motivation to not start, not escalate, or to quit an addictive behavior. Motivational enhancement approaches assist individuals in clarifying their direction of change and increase their willingness to change. Motivation enhancement may include such strategies as giving advice, removing cognitive impediments to change, providing choices, and reconciling discrepancies between current behavior and desired goals (Barnett, Sussman, Smith, Rohrbach, & Spruijt-Metz, 2012).

4 The **response-contingent reinforcement approach** focuses on reducing occurrence of problem addictive behaviors with extrinsic rewards such as money, prizes, or vouchers. Additionally, this approach can include differential reinforcement contingencies designed to strengthen more prosocial alternative behaviors (e.g., contingency-based management [CM] where an individual is rewarded for desired behavioral changes). This approach has been used with young children in targeted prevention programming to decrease negative behaviors and increase cooperative behaviors, as well as with older youth and adults in cessation programming (Kellam et al., 2014; Sussman, 2002a; Sussman & Ames, 2001; Sussman et al., 2004).

5 The **supply reduction approach** focuses on arranging the social environment so that objects of addiction are more difficult to obtain (e.g., access restriction). By making addiction objects harder to obtain, it is theorized that costs (financial, time, or social) will increase for potential addicts, giving the individuals reason to think about behaviors other than the potential addiction. In addition, supply reduction approaches diffuse larger social environmental disapproval of the addictive behavior (Pentz, Bonnie, & Shopland, 1996).

History of Prevention of the Addictions

Prior to 1900

This section pertains more to ATOD prevention simply because there is relatively little documented history on the prevention of behavioral addictions. Certainly, there also is a dearth of information prior to the late 1800s even on types of ATOD prevention education for youth. One could speculate, however, that for untold years such education was provided by religious authorities in sermons delivered at religious services and through one-to-one moral or spiritual instruction. Parents (and sometimes governments) have warned children about all sorts of behaviors including unsafe diets (e.g., see governmental attempts to ban coffee, http://mentalfloss.com/article/12662/5-historical-attempts-ban-coffee), gambling, uncontrolled sexual behavior, excess drinking, or drug intake. In the United States, there was sentiment against social "vices" and anti-gaming legislation pushed gambling onto boats in the Mississippi River and Western territories in the United States by the mid-1800s. By 1901, every state and territory in the United States had passed legislation mandating some form of **temperance instruction** (self-restraint or abstinence in drinking) to be taught in the public schools (Beck, 1998), in part because of the efforts of Mary H. Hunt and the Women's Christian Temperance Union (WCTU). At that time gambling also became illegal in most locations in the United States.

1900 to 1930

The WCTU believed that alcohol, tobacco, opium, and other drugs, gambling, and pornography were the primary cause of social ills in the United States. Temperance education focused on the moral evils of engaging in these behaviors. Scare tactics were developed, including the use of graphic descriptions of physical consequences and moral degradation associated with drug use or other vices. For example, it was asserted that tobacco use stunts one's growth, poisons the heart, and impairs mental powers. More prominently, the use of alcohol was publicized as dulling the moral centers of the brain, which, in turn, would lead to criminal behavior (Beck, 1998). In addition, small quantities of alcohol were thought to create an abnormal desire for more, which might become uncontrollable and destructive. **Prohibition** was a US nationwide constitutional ban on the sale, production, importation, and transportation of alcoholic beverages that remained in place from 1920 to 1933. Alcohol intake prevalence was cut in half but began climbing again in the late 1920s. Preventive impact among youth was not assessed to my knowledge.

In France, at this same time, drug prevention education emphasized avoiding the use of hard liquor while the moderate use of beer or wine was acceptable. More favorable attitudes also existed regarding gambling. This perspective was more in keeping with the views of the research community at the time. There was no formally recognized prevention of behavioral addictions at this time (except perhaps for the use of "supply reduction" strategies pertaining to "vices").

1930 to 1970

When Prohibition was repealed in 1933, temperance instruction began to lose its foothold in prevention education. At that time, some locations in the United States still continued to provide temperance instruction, some locations provided little such instruction, and in some locations the use of **responsible behavior programs** began. Responsible drug use programs emphasized no use of restricted drugs but responsible use of alcohol and waiting until one is grown up (18 years of age) so that one can make a responsible, mature choice. Responsible choice education likely created a forbidden fruit *contingency* in which youth envied what adults were allowed to do (e.g., drink and smoke), and wanted to engage in such behaviors to demonstrate adult-like behavior. It is unlikely that this type of education could have shown any effectiveness (Beck, 1998; Sussman, 2002c). Concurrently, scare tactics remained popular in mass media campaigns (e.g., the movie *Reefer Madness* [1936]), and additional laws went into effect restricting marijuana use (e.g., the Marijuana Tax Act of 1937).

Prevention of drug abuse programs in school education began to be addressed seriously again in the United States after the President's Advisory Commission on Narcotic and Drug Abuse report was published in 1963 (Beck, 1998). At that time, fear-arousal, information, and values or affect clarification programs began to be implemented in schools. Many drug education programs were developed and implemented haphazardly by private companies, individual educators, and through an influx of federal support (Beck, 1998). Most of these prevention programs were based on the premise that if children knew why drug use was bad for them, they would choose not to start using (Edmundson, McAlister, Murray, Perry, & Lichtenstein, 1991; Evans, 1998; Sussman, Dent, Stacy, Burton, & Flay, 1995). The *fear-based model* assumed that if youth were frightened about the potential negative effects of drugs, then they would not want to experiment with drugs. Unfortunately, the arousal of fear and its impact tend to "wear away" over time, or fear-based messages are poorly manipulated (i.e., persons do not become fearful when exposed to those messages) such that effects of physical consequences programming have been equivocal (Evans, 1998; Sussman et al., 1995).

The **information-based model** assumed that providing adolescents with factual information about drug use (or another addiction) would prevent them from engaging in the behavior (Evans, 1998). This approach, which is essentially a form of fear arousal according to Evans (1998), was found to be largely ineffective (Goodstadt 1978; Thompson, 1978). The **affective or values-based model** of drug abuse prevention addresses more global attitudinal changes directed at such factors as enhanced self-esteem, improved decision-making and goal setting, and clarification of one's life values. This model often does not include specific information about self-destructive behaviors, such as smoking or drug use (Durell & Bukoski, 1984; Evans, 1998). There is little evidence that this type of model is an effective means of drug use prevention (Hansen, Johnson, Flay, Graham, & Sobel, 1988; Tobler et al., 2000).

1970 to the Present

Many notable events occurred in the 1970s. The so-called **parent power movement** gained widespread support, which led to the use of testimonials by former drug addicts, drug-free school weeks, removal of drug paraphernalia shops ("head shops"), and eventually use of a simplified version of social influence programming (e.g., "Just Say No" campaign). The effects of these programs generally are not known and are questionable. (A renewed interest in a parent power movement was evidenced by the establishment of and research on Parent Corps [see www.parentcorps.org/].) In addition, in 1971 Wayne Oates coined the term "workaholic" (Oates, 1971), the term "junk food" apparently was coined in 1972 by Michael Jacobsen (Center for Science in the Public Interest; Jacobsen, 1993), and in 1976 William Glasser coined the term "exercise addiction" (Glasser, 1976). Most of these terms pertained to misdirected or over-canalized prosocial behaviors, though Glasser's use of the term recognized that, while someone might suffer withdrawal-like symptoms if they stopped, the positive addiction would tend to make them a stronger or more accomplished person (Glasser, 1976). Of course, at the extremes, one might also suffer injuries or perhaps reduce one's social life. Thus, there was recognition of social lifestyle influences that could facilitate addictive, possibly unhealthy extremes of behaviors of a variety of sorts unless prevented.

In 1976, Richard Evans and colleagues at the University of Houston developed the earliest *social influence-based programs*. The basic assumption was that "inoculation" to resist social pressures that serve as precipitants of ATOD use would prevent initial trial and experimentation. The idea was to expose young people to social pressures involving ATOD use in a safe environment and to teach them skills that could then be transferred to the real world. Subsequent generations of researchers were influenced to varying degrees by the work of the Houston group. Additional theoretical influences in these generations of research included McGuire's social inoculation and attitude change (e.g., persuasive communications) theories, Bandura's social learning theory, Jones and colleagues' attribution theory, Kiesler's commitment theory, Jessor's problem behavior theory, Levanthal's and Flay's tobacco use development models, wellness notions, and Meichenbaum's cognitive-behavavior therapy (see Flay, 1985; Skara & Sussman, 2003; Sussman et al., 1995). The four main drug education models are summarized in Table 10.3.

Table 10.3 Drug education models

Fear-based model	The fear-based model assumes that if youth are frightened about the potential negative effects of drugs or other addictive behaviors, then they will not want to engage in them. The effects of physical consequences programming have been equivocal.
Information-based model	The information-based model assumes that providing adolescents with factual information about drug use (or another addiction) will prevent them from engaging in the behavior. This approach has been found to be largely ineffective.
Affective or values-based model	The affective or values-based model of addiction prevention addresses more global attitudinal changes directed at such factors as enhanced self-esteem, improved decision-making, goal setting, and clarification of one's life values. There is little evidence that this type of model is an effective means of drug use prevention.
Social influence-based model	The basic assumption was that "inoculation" to resist social pressures that serve as precipitants of addiction would prevent initial trial and experimentation. The idea was to expose young people to social pressures in a safe environment and to teach them skills that could then be transferred to the real world. There is some support for this model with alcohol, tobacco and other drug use prevention, as a comprehensive life skills approach.

The Twelve Mediators of Preventive Effects

This history of prevention research and practice has led to the current understanding of what works in prevention programming. Hansen and colleagues (e.g., Hansen, 1992, 1996; Hansen & McNeal, 1997) summarized 12 variables that mediate change in substance use prevention programs (a mediation model is one that seeks to identify and explicate the mechanism or process that underlies an observed relationship between an independent variable and a dependent variable via the inclusion of a third hypothetical variable, known as a mediator variable). It is reasonable to speculate that these same *mediators* generalize to any of the 11 focal addictions, and that prevention strategies which manipulate these mediators of change may be considered at intra-personal and extrapersonal levels of application:

1 **Normative beliefs** or the perceptions about the prevalence or acceptability of an addiction among close friends and same-age peers (perceptions that an addictive behavior is more prevalent and more acceptable than it actually is will tend to lead to involvement with the addiction; correction of inflated prevalence or acceptability estimates tend to reduce involvement).
2 *Lifestyle/behavior incongruence* or the degree to which an individual views an addictive behavior as incongruent with personally held current lifestyle and future aspirations (e.g., adolescents who perceive that their desired lifestyle does not fit with drug use, gambling, or binge eating are somewhat protected).
3 *Commitment* regarding an addiction, such as public statements of intention (e.g., statements such as "I have signed my name to show that I have promised not to engage in this behavior"); also, items that assess a youth's private intentions (for example, placing a personal statement on a wallet-sized card such as: "I have made a personal commitment to never smoke cigarettes").
4 *Beliefs about social, psychological, and health consequences* (e.g., an individual's beliefs about what it means to engage in risky behaviors in a group, beliefs about having fun, dealing with personal problems, having bad breath or appearance, experiencing health problems, and the perceived probability and severity of getting into trouble); beliefs that an addiction leads to relatively fewer benefits in the long run, or decreased reward demand and delayed discounting, may lead to less interest in engagement in the addiction.
5 **Resistance skills** or the perceived ability to identify and resist social pressure to use tobacco, alcohol, other drugs, intake large quantities of food, or engage in sex, gambling, or other behavioral addictions (this refers to an individual's ability and self-efficacy to say no [refusal assertion] in a variety of contexts).
6 *Goal-setting skills* or the degree to which one is able to engage in goal-setting behaviors (this includes being able to frequently establish goals, develop strategies for achieving goals, and persistence in achieving goals).
7 *Decision-making skills* or the degree to which one understands and applies a rational strategy for making decisions.
8 *Alternatives* or awareness of and participation in enjoyable activities that do not involve engagement in an addictive behavior.

9 *Self-esteem* or the degree to which one feels personal worth or possession of characteristics that contribute to a positive self-evaluation.
10 *Stress management skills* or skills for coping with stress (this includes skills for relaxing as well as for confronting challenging situations).
11 *Social skills* or the ability to establish friendships, be generally assertive with friends, and get along with others.
12 *Assistance skills* or the degree to which an individual is able to seek out or provide assistance to oneself or others who have personal problems.

Interactive Techniques

Strategies that manipulate these mediators are taught through the use of **interactive techniques** (e.g., role play, interactive peer discussions, where participants generate the appropriate behavior and are relatively likely to "own" the behavior), which have been found to increase involvement in the learning process. Interactive approaches may be a *sine qua non* for prevention efficacy, at least regarding tobacco and other drug use prevention programs (see Botvin, Baker, Dusenbury, Botvin, & Diaz, 1995; Sussman et al., 1995; Sussman, Rohrbach, Patel, & Holiday, 2003; Tobler et al., 2000).

This is the status of knowledge regarding mediation of tobacco, alcohol, and other drug abuse prevention as of this current date. These same types of strategies may be translated to various behavioral addictions, and this should be examined in future research studies.

At What Age Should Prevention Programming Be Delivered? (Developmental Considerations)

Most thinking regarding ideal ages of implementation of prevention programming has, as with other areas of prevention, been focused mostly on drug abuse. Some researchers and practitioners argue that prevention should focus on the very young (e.g., three to six years of age), to try to recognize those at high risk for drug abuse (or other addictions) as soon as possible and provide needed assistance while they are rapidly developing (Tarter et al., 2003). At that age, programming tends not to pertain directly to substance use but to focus on learning how to recognize emotions in others and how to bond with others. Also, youth may learn rules of good behavior (Sussman, 2013). A focus on young children has been suggested by researchers as also an important likely avenue of problem gambling prevention and TV addiction prevention, though no empirical work exists to support the assertion (Sussman & Moran, 2013; Williams, West, & Simpson, 2012).

Findings from animal and human research indicate that those who initiate substance use at younger ages (e.g., 10 to 12 years of age) are more likely to become dependent on drugs, suggesting that substance exposure may disrupt normal processes of neurobiological development (De Bellis et al., 2000; Levin, Rezvani, Montoya, Rose, & Swartzwelder, 2003). These findings support the perspective that prevention programming should target young at-risk children, so that they may avoid such tampering with their neurobiology when they reach adolescence. Researchers have found early intervention beneficial in directing individuals away from problem behaviors and toward prosocial activities (see Ialongo, Poduska, Werthamer, & Kellam, 2001). Some of the strategies used with younger children (emotional learning), instruction in decision-making and planning, and perhaps brief instruction in the dangers of the addiction, may have a preventive impact (Sussman, 2013).

Many other drug abuse prevention researchers have argued that prevention programming should be applied during the critical period of young adolescence, in which tobacco and alcohol onset and experimentation increases dramatically (Flay, 1985; Sussman et al., 1995). In fact, most programming has focused on combating social influences, relatively strong antecedents of drug use during young adolescence.

Others suggest that drug abuse prevention programming would be more effective if it was implemented when drug use is truly beginning to become problematic, among older teens for most people (Sussman, 2013), focusing on motivation enhancement, life skills, and decision-making instruction. Still others suggest that programming should continue throughout childhood, adolescence, and emerging adulthood.

Sussman (2013) argues that prevention programming might be best offered throughout the lifespan, with different types of programming for different ages (even for the elderly). Also, possibly different addictions might be targeted during "critical periods" as individuals develop (e.g., television among young children, caffeine among elementary school children, tobacco and Internet among junior high school youth, sex among older teens and emerging adults).

Summary

This chapter introduced addictive behavior prevention terminology, similarities and differences from cessation programming, and the history of prevention programming primarily in tobacco and other drug abuse prevention. Also, key mediators of change were discussed that might apply across different addictions. Finally, age of maximal application of programming was discussed. The next chapter provides details of intrapersonal approaches to prevention of addiction, and then Chapter 12 provides details of extrapersonal approaches.

Bulleted Summary

- Prevention has been delineated as an issue of chronicity (primary, secondary, tertiary), population-based (universal, selective, indicated), and level of application (intrapersonal, extrapersonal). While prevention targets severing connections between antecedents and behavior, cessation is focused on arresting behavior and consequences resulting from it.
- The work of prevention likely fell to informal change agents (family, religion, enforcement authorities) prior to the 1900s. Next, legal, fear, information, and values

clarification approaches were attempted without apparent success. Drug abuse prevention advanced at least for young teens through an emphasis on comprehensive social influences programming.
- There are 12 key mediators of (drug abuse) prevention effects such as changing normative beliefs, decision-making skills, lifestyle alternatives, and assistance skills.
- Drug abuse prevention for very young children helps them recognize emotions in others and bond with significant others. Among elementary children, drug use consequences information can be instructed. Comprehensive social influences information might be applied to young teens, whereas motivation/skills/decision-making material might be applied to older teens and adults.

Suggestions for Further Reading

Botvin, G. J., Baker, E., Dusenbury, L., Botvin, E. M., & Diaz, T. (1995). Long-term follow-up results of a randomized drug abuse prevention trial in a white middle-class population. *Journal of the American Medical Association*, 273: 1106–1112.

Hansen, W. B. (1992). School-based substance abuse prevention: A review of the state of the art in curriculum, 1980–1990. *Health Education Research: Theory and Practice*, 7: 403–430.

Sussman, S. (2013). A lifespan developmental-stage approach to tobacco and other drug abuse prevention. *ISRN-Addiction*. doi: 10.1155/2013/745783.

Sussman, S. & Ames, S. L. (2008). *Drug Abuse: Concepts, Prevention and Cessation*. Cambridge University Press.

Sussman, S., Levy, D., Hassmiller, K., Cena, D. W., Kim, M., Rohrbach, L. A., & Chaloupka, F. (2013a). A speculation on modalities of tobacco use prevention. *Tobacco Induced Diseases*, 11.

11 Prevention: Intrapersonal-Level Approaches

Learning Objectives

- To learn about neurobiological-level addiction prevention strategies
- To learn about cognitive-level addiction prevention strategies
- To learn about any research on intrapersonal-level approaches that have been applied to gambling, an addiction which is now recognized as such in the DSM-V
- To learn about any research on intrapersonal-level approaches that have been applied to addictions other than drug use or gambling

Introduction

While this did not actually happen, possibly, as a child, Johnny could have seen a physician and been prescribed a drug for ADHD, been taught how to recognize emotions better in others, been assisted in feeling emotional bonds with others at a young age, or experienced strengthening of his executive inhibitory cognitive processes through early prevention education. Any of these intrapersonal-level strategies might have helped him not to begin a series of addictions. Johnny has thought, though, that his cognitive processes function at a pretty high level. He has argued that we all die so why not be hedonistic in some ways? Perhaps he was experiencing a cognitive misperception?

This chapter pertains to prevention strategies that might be applied at an intrapersonal level. That is, the focus is on strategies that attempt to alter something about the person, as opposed to the environment outside of the person. Neurobiological-level and cognitive-level strategies are the focus here. The strategies to be discussed are shown in Table 11.1.

Neurobiological-Related Strategies

Pharmacotherapy and Vigilance

Quick progress is being made in the characterization of mechanisms that underlie the generation and processing of inter- and intracellular signals in work completed by

Table 11.1 Intrapersonal-level prevention strategies

Neurobiological-related strategies	Though pharmacotherapy is used mostly in the context of cessation treatment with adults, drugs that alter unhealthy signaling mechanisms that are precursors to any number of addictions may exert preventive effects. Drugs related to key co-occurring disorders (e.g., ADHD, depression) might serve an addiction preventive function. It is possible that in the future a set of genetic markers could be identified and used to predict an individual's "risk" for developing an addiction. Vigilance programs could then be developed to target youth at high genetic risk for an addiction.
Enhancing social and emotional competence	The importance of social and emotional competence is becoming increasingly evident in being preventive of addictions. Education programs might focus on recognizing feelings in oneself and others, being respectful of others' feelings, understanding meanings of emotions, learning self-control, how to communicate effectively with others, how to seek support, how to build relationships with others, and how to negotiate.
Cognitive-information strategies	These strategies focus on beliefs and thoughts that affect feelings and behaviors. Education programs might target cognitive-information error-related myth formation and try to counteract that process through use of elaborative processing, as an example. Cognitive strategies elaborate on the difference between more immediate gratification and the impact of longer-term negative consequences of an addiction so that meaningful memories are constructed. Prevalence overestimates reduction also may be considered a cognitive-information corrective strategy.
Executive functioning capacity enhancement	Executive functions are relevant to inhibitory control over behavior. To counteract deficits in executive functioning capacity, prevention materials could be tied to risky situations so that this information is stored in long-term memory as new associates of addictive behavior-related experiences. In this way executive functioning may become less of an issue because program materials are more likely to be automatically activated in relevant situations.
Implementation intentions	Implementation intentions specify a plan of action. The person may practice the self-statement "When situation X occurs, I will perform behavior Y." When an individual is then confronted with a particular situation, the initiation of the specified goal-directed behavior has a greater chance of being automatically initiated, requiring little or no conscious intent.

Neurobiological-Related Strategies

Table 11.1 *(cont.)*

Belief–behavior discrepancies	Making youth aware of belief–behavior discrepancies can induce a preventive effect among those already engaged in risky behavior. For example, a person's general attitude about him- or herself as a moderate person may appear contradictory with some specific attitude (e.g., participation in an addictive behavior). If confronted with this discrepancy, an individual will tend to try to reduce it, which, in the present context, could lead to specific anti-addictive behavior statements and sections.
Coping skills	Coping skills involve behavioral or cognitive methods of handling precarious situations. Coping can be defined as stress-coping skills or as temptation-coping skills. Coping skills may involve: substitution behavior, lifestyle alternatives, distraction, avoidance, delay, social support seeking, self-enriching expectancies, cognitive distraction, problem-solving, cognitive restructuring, hardy cognitive style, and self-instructional training.

biochemists, molecular biologists, cell biologists, immunologists, pharmacologists, and clinical researchers. Drugs that alter unhealthy signaling mechanisms that are precursors to any number of addictions (e.g., drugs that decrease sensation-seeking tendencies) may exert preventive effects. In general, though, pharmacotherapy is used mostly in the context of cessation treatment with adults, which is presented in Chapter 14. Their use with youth for the purposes of prevention is mostly a matter of future-think and fraught with ethical dilemmas (Sussman & Ames, 2008). Arguably, drugs related to key co-occurring disorders (e.g., ADHD, depression) might serve an addiction preventive function.

Most complex human behaviors (including the addictions) appear to be multigenic. Indeed, to date, no single gene has been identified that can alone explain the complex traits that lead to drug misuse or other addictions, though some dopaminergic gene parameters (e.g., DRD2 and DAT1 polymorphisms) may be related to a variety of addictions within families (Blum et al., 2011b). It is likely that the genomic substrates of the addictions are much more complex than research has revealed to date. Given this caveat, it is possible that in the future a set of genetic markers could be identified and used to predict an individual's "risk" for developing an addiction. **Vigilance programs** could then be developed to target youth at high genetic risk for an addiction. Strategies that could be used include not only (1) screening and (2) assigning youth to receive tailored prevention programming but also (3) use of prophylactic medications to attempt gene function manipulation. For example, it is known that children of alcoholics/drug abusers are at increased risk for drug abuse (e.g., see www.nacoa.org). Current selective prevention programs for children of alcoholics/drug abusers may be the precursors of what eventually may be genetically based vigilance programs. Selective prevention programs for children of alcoholics/substance abusers show some promise especially when their duration is longer than ten weeks and when they involve family skills training components (e.g., teaching children and parents appropriate roles; Broning et al., 2012). Of course, the use of vigilance programs to target children at risk for specific addictions, such as sex addiction or workaholism, may seem a little far-fetched, fraught with ethical dilemmas and uncertainty regarding when such targeting would best be accomplished in the lifespan, although youth are likely impacted by their parents' addictions, may be at elevated risk themselves, and might benefit from prevention of any number of addictive tendencies.

As a general rule, *structuring* youths' lives such that they are limited from extensive involvement with addictions – at least until they are age 20 or older, when the brain is more mature – might help to reduce the neurobiological consequences of repetitive involvement in an addictive behavior (Casey, Tottenham, Liston, & Durston, 2005). This may include instruction in warning signs of addiction, monitoring by adults, making available palatable hobbies or jobs for youth, creation of extended communities, and other venues, while avoiding the perception that behavioral addictions are okay for adults but not youth (a "forbidden fruit"; e.g., Sussman, Grana, Pokhrel, Rohrbach, & Sun, 2010).

Social-Emotional Competence

The importance of *social and emotional competence development* is becoming increasingly more evident as a successful means of preventing addictive behaviors, as well as promoting prosocial behavior. Some researchers and practitioners feel that prevention programming ought to be applied to very young children to enhance social and emotional learning, while the brain is still rapidly developing (Fishbein, 2000). An example of a program for young children that focuses on social and emotional learning is the I Can Problem Solve (ICPS) program. This program was implemented with 4-year-olds to teach these children how to think in ways that would help them successfully resolve interpersonal problems with peers and adults. The program consisted of daily 20-minute small group activities in the classroom for a three-month period (using words, pictures, puppets, and role playing). Words that are precursors to understanding consequences and problem-solving are instructed. Some research indicates that through the ICPS, young children learn alternative ways to solve interpersonal problems (www.researchpress.com/books/590/icps-i-can-problem-solve). This program has been found to improve behavioral adjustment, impulsivity, and self-control up to 12 months post-program implementation in quasi-experimental work (M. B. Shure's work reviewed in Sussman, 2013). These results are suggestive of preventing later addictive behavior development (also see www.thinkingchild.com/).

Education programs might include instruction on emotional regulation as an adjunct to an early intervention. For example, an intervention could focus on helping youth to recognize feelings in themselves and others (e.g., facial expressions), being respectful of others' feelings, understanding meanings of emotions, and learning self-control (see Fishbein, 2000). In addition, instruction in how to communicate effectively with others, how to seek support, how to build relationships with others, and how to negotiate fairly might be reasonable prevention components (see Elias, 2006) even for younger children. Early instruction in these areas may improve social and emotional competence, which could, in turn, minimize a sense of relative imbalance for some youth, and possibly help in normalizing one's wiring if exposure to these lessons occurs during critical periods in neural development; hence preventing later development of addictive behavior.

Cognitive Strategies

Cognitive strategies have been used in some addictions prevention programming. These strategies attempt to alter the way in which a person thinks, and may be organized into (a) correction of cognitive-information errors, (b) maximizing executive processing, (c) focusing on belief–behavior discrepancies, and (d) decreasing situational distortions.

Cognitive-Information Errors Reduction

Cognitive-information error-related myth formation can be counteracted through use of *elaborative processing* (Stacy & Ames, 2001). For example, as operationalized in a curriculum by Sussman and colleagues (Project Towards No Drug Abuse [TND]; Sussman, Craig, & Moss, 2002), a program could initially provide a discussion about the "kernel of truth" in any given addictive behavior "myth" and then discuss why the myth is, in fact, a myth. To illustrate, a prevention lesson might discuss the myth that individuals use drugs as a means of being emotionally protected from life stresses. The *kernel of truth* in this myth is that a person might initially feel that their drug use is protective, at least temporarily, from negative life stressors; that is, they experience some temporary relief or pleasure from drug use that distracts them from real life events. It is a *myth*, however, because an individual thinks less clearly under the influence; that is, one's thinking may be distorted, and the individual may be more likely to become increasingly uninhibited and become victimized (e.g., get robbed or mugged) and, hence, incur greater stress over time (Sussman & Ames, 2008). In terms of prevention programming, it may be important to elaborate on the difference between more immediate gratification and the impact of longer-term negative consequences of an addiction so that meaningful memories are constructed. Very recently, use of narrative stories has been used to try to decrease reward demand and delayed discounting of addictions (William Bickel, personal communication, August 12, 2016).

Enhancing Executive Processing

Executive functions are relevant to inhibitory control over behavior and counteracting the influence of more spontaneous cognitions or implicit processes. There is evidence that **executive functions** (e.g., working memory capacity, planning) affect behavior by moderating the availability of resources an individual has access to during addictive behavior-related decision-making in complex social situations (e.g., Finn & Hall, 2004; Payne, 2005; Thush et al., 2008). Complex social situations are likely to tax aspects of executive functioning. *Executive functioning capacity enhancement* prevention efforts might assist individuals to make behavior more deliberate (step-by-step) in taxing situations. One purpose of the use of **meditation** is to enhance executive function capacity in this way (Black et al., 2009). That is, by focusing on thoughts as they "pass by" without acting on them immediately, one may increase the ability to engage in deliberate processing of information.

In addition, to make content or skills that are learned in programs more automatically accessible from memory in **high-risk situations** (i.e., situations in which objects of addiction are readily available or in which addictive behaviors are otherwise promoted), prevention materials could be tied to risky or other daily social situations so that this information is stored in long-term memory as new associates of addictive behavior-related experiences. Then executive functioning or cognitive control becomes less of an issue because program materials may be more likely to be *automatically activated* in situations along with other associates of addictive behavior when individuals are immersed in situations with strong cues (see Stacy et al., 2004).

Implementation intentions programming may be another means of linking specific intentions to perform a behavior with situational cues such that a behavior becomes relatively spontaneously initiated. Implementation intentions specify a plan of action. The person may practice the self-statement "When situation X occurs, I will perform behavior Y" (see Gollwitzer, 1999). This type of intervention requires the individual to identify aspects of an intention, such as specifying when, where, and how responses will be carried out (i.e., forming a mental representation of the situation), which delegates the initiation of goal-directed behavior to situational cues. When an individual is then confronted with a particular situation, the initiation of the specified goal-directed behavior has a greater chance of being automatically initiated by the situational cues (an established cue–response association), requiring little or no conscious intent. Implementation intentions focus on more spontaneous processes and have shown effects across a variety of health behaviors (see Hagger et al., 2012; for review, Prestwich, Conner, & Lawton, 2006; Varley, Webb, & Sheeren, 2011). For example, Hagger et al. (2012) examined the effectiveness of an implementation intention and/or mental simulation/motivation manipulation among undergraduate students from Estonia, Finland, and the United Kingdom to prevent heavy or binge drinking. One-month follow-up tests revealed significant reductions in the implementation intention group regarding amount of drinking in the United Kingdom and Estonia, and on binge-drinking occasions for the United Kingdom sample only. At least some support is suggested for use of implementation intentions in alcohol indicated prevention efforts.

Belief–Behavior Discrepancies Reduction

Making youth aware of *belief–behavior discrepancies* sometimes can induce a preventive effect among those already engaged in risky behavior. One example of making participants aware of a belief–behavior discrepancy is derived from **Attitudinal Perspective Theory** (Upshaw & Ostrom, 1984), a concept from cognitive social psychology. This theory posits that there are two different aspects of one's attitudes about behaviors or events. First, an individual has a general attitudinal perspective (e.g., as being a moderate). In fact, most youth and adults prefer to consider themselves as being "moderate" people (Sussman et al., 2002). Separately, the individual has specific attitudes about specific behaviors or events (e.g., beliefs about gun control laws, no-smoking policy, or appropriate patterns of drug use). It is possible that someone's general attitude about him- or herself as a moderate person may appear contradictory with some specific attitude (e.g., tolerance regarding addictive levels of a behavior). If confronted with this discrepancy, an individual will tend to try to reduce it, which, in the present context, could lead to specific anti-addictive behavior statements and actions. Another example of a belief–behavior discrepancy is that one may desire to attain certain goals (e.g., good grades), know that good health is important to help one achieve these goals, be instructed to recognize that an addictive behavior (e.g., online gaming) may interfere with goal attainment (lack of sleep, diminished health), and therefore need to change either goals or that addictive behavior. Possibly, most youth would tend to modify the addictive behavior (Sussman et al., 2002).

Coping Skills to Decrease Situational Distortions

Exhibiting maladaptive behavior may lead to reinterpreting situation-related reactions in a distorted fashion (normalization of deviant responses, or ***reinterpretation***). That is, one may search for ways to justify maladaptive responses such as addictive behavior (e.g., addiction-induced relaxation being equated with learning a skill to achieve relaxation; Lennard, Epstein, Bernstein, & Ransom, 1971). Instruction in *coping skills* was mentioned among the cognitive-behavioral strategies shared across prevention and cessation programming, and as serving as a mediator of prevention effects, introduced in Chapter 10. Coping may exert a proactive effect on one's life circumstances (e.g., applied to new situations), or may serve a reactive function (e.g., buffering stressful events). In the former sense, coping exerts a main effect on subsequent adjustment. That is, the better one copes with new, perhaps ambiguous situations, the less likely one is to resort to maladaptive behavior such as addictions, leading to situational distortions and repeated addictive behavior episodes. Learning to delay reactions to new situations, seeking social support, or problem-solving in the new situation may assist in successfully addressing many new situations.

As a reactive function, if coping enhances adaptation under stressful conditions, then a stress-times-coping interaction effect is expected (a "buffer" interaction). For example, one may attempt to escape a difficult situation that places one at "high risk" for engaging in an addictive behavior or seek social support, or use self-instructions so as to not react in a maladaptive way in a stressful situation.

Coping responses can be categorized in a variety of ways. One reasonable cognitive-behavioral typology is as follows, involving six behavioral coping strategies and six cognitive coping strategies (see Meichenbaum, 1977; Sussman & Ames, 2008; Wills, 1986).

Behavioral Coping
1 Substitution behavior (e.g., walking instead of smoking, if not also an addiction)
2 Lifestyle alternatives (e.g., increase relaxation, physical activity, meditation)
3 Distraction (e.g., keeping busy)

4 Avoidance, escape, assertion refusal (from high-risk situations)
5 Delay (wait out high-risk situation)
6 Social support seeking (e.g., to vent feelings, feel spiritual constancy)

Cognitive Coping
1 Expectancies (think of the benefits of engaging in positive activities and the costs of engaging in negative activities)
2 Cognitive distraction (think about other things to minimize cravings)
3 Problem-solving (think "through"the problem)
4 Cognitive restructuring (minimization, accentuate the positive, social comparison, humor)
5 Cognitive style (think of life as a challenge, to be controlled, to be involved)
6 Self-instructional training (add missing elements in stream of speech to gain self-control)

Behavioral coping may also have an indirect effect on addictive behavior, in part through alterations in cognitive coping. Conversely, behavioral coping may facilitate greater efforts at cognitive coping. Both types of coping are important means of counteracting the development of an addiction.

Application of Intrapersonal Strategies to Gambling Prevention

There is a small literature on intrapersonal-level prevention of gambling among youth (e.g., Gaboury & Ladouceur, 1993; Ladouceur, Goulet, & Vitaro, 2013). The basic strategies involved in gambling prevention at the individual level include instruction in correction of gambling misperceptions, coping skills and decision-making, providing personalized feedback, and risk reduction techniques (e.g., limiting length of gambling time, or type of gambling). Gambling misperceptions involve any type of attempt to think one's way around chance events. The ***hot hand fallacy*** involves the idea that one can elicit winning numbers or determine how one chance event will turn out based on a previous chance event. One type of hot hand fallacy is where a gambler believes he or she can "chase losses" by continuing to gamble after losing several times (as if luck will change). An "illusion of control" is when one believes that a particular day, gambling machine, or gambling location will be a lucky one. *Instruction in the true odds* of winning for specific games *and negative consequences* suffered from repeated trials of not winning are used to counteract such thinking.

Coping skills may involve helping one to sit still with negative affect, or with urges to alleviate uncomfortable feelings through gambling. *Decision-making skills* as applied to whether or not one should gamble may help one to resolve to engage in activities incompatible with gambling. ***Personalized feedback*** involves understanding where one is situated relative to past behavior and peer norms pertaining to a developing entrenchment in gambling (or any other addiction). This strategy provides a means of warning the gambler when he or she is entering a perilous degree of gambling behavior. Arguably, feedback may be considered an extrapersonal type of activity to the extent that peer behavioral norms are contrasted with one's own behavior. *Risk reduction* involves attempting to assist the gambler to gamble at more "responsible levels" (within one's economic means, and time-limited gambling).

Gaboury and Ladouceur (1993), in one of the earliest prevention studies (also see Ladouceur et al., 2013), provided instruction on the legality, commercial nature, and automaticity of gambling, pathological gambling, and coping in classrooms at five high schools in the Quebec City area (n = 289; classroom level of assignment to program and control conditions) and found increases in knowledge and coping skills related to prevention of pathological gambling at a six-month follow-up. Ferland, Ladouceur, and Vitaro (2002) found that a video was able to increase knowledge and correct misperceptions about gambling among 7th and 8th grade youth. It should be mentioned that while intrapersonal-directed changes are the focus of this programming, it is delivered in a classroom setting in general, which is an extrapersonal context. Certainly, group processes operate as a moderator of material instruction, though such effects are not discussed, in general. More information on classroom-based gambling prevention programming is presented in Chapter 12.

Speculation on Potential Application of Intrapersonal Strategies to Other Addictions

These same types of intrapersonal-based prevention strategies might be applied to other addictions, though almost no prevention research has been conducted. Sussman (2010) discussed potential techniques relevant to *love addiction* prevention. **Mood management** (self-regulation of negative mood states, use of positive techniques to enhance mood such as meditation) might be instructed, to counteract one motive for love-seeking. Cognitive restructuring techniques could help one separate inner speech pertaining to "love-with-love" versus "love with love-objects." For example, one may first be made aware that the thought that "only one specific person could ever satisfy one's needs" tends to lead to a love-addictive process. One may then practice repeating alternative self-statements such as that "there is never just one person in the world," or "there are many fish in the sea" to provide a restructuring. Participants also might be engaged in cognitive restructuring to remove fantasy-based thinking (e.g., being rescued or being a rescuer) that could reflect or lead to later love-addictive behavior. Also, prevention programming might include types of counseling that attempt to facilitate a secure attachment style. One may be instructed through use of role play or dramatizations, or direct instruction, that dependent romantic love does not contribute to a healthy relationship and, as such, is not really love.

Sussman (2007) discussed prevention strategies that might have some relevance to teen *sexual addiction*, mostly packaged as prevention of risky sexual behavior. Teens are now exposed to more conflicting information about sex than ever before. Some schools offer counseling on birth control and sexual disease prevention. Others preach absolute abstinence. An emphasis on abstinence-only education has shown some effects on creating conservative shifts in attitudes in some studies (Carter-Jessop, Franklin, Heath, Jimenez-Irizarry, & Peace, 2000). However, in general, this approach has had little impact on behavior (Rose, 2005). Sexual disease prevention programs generally include the delineation of specific objectives for specific populations, have multiple components delivered through multiple modalities, and involve guidance from behavioral theories (Eke, Mezoff, Duncan, & Sogolow, 2006). Most sex education programming, however, has produced only short-term effects (up to three months; Coyle, Kirby, Robin, Banspatch, & Glkassman, 2006; Malow, Rosenberg, & Devieux, 2006), although this programming hasn't been found to do any harm such as encourage sexual activity (Sabia, 2006). There is no consistent set of treatment strategies consensually agreed on.

Relatively recently, a study examined the effectiveness of a computer-delivered, individually tailored HIV/AIDS risk reduction intervention in a randomized trial with 157 college students (Kiene & Barta, 2006). Two brief computer-delivered sessions that used elements of motivational interviewing were implemented (HIV prevention intervention versus a nutrition education tutorial control group). Subjects in the HIV prevention intervention group reported a greater frequency of keeping condoms available, and greater condom use, at a four-week follow-up. Much research needs to be completed, and risky sexual behavior is only a proxy measure for sexual addiction (Sussman, 2007), but computer-based prevention does appear to be a promising intrapersonal-level prevention modality.

Sussman (2012a) examined prevention of *workaholism*. Attempts to counteract characteristics of individuals that promote workaholism, or promoting opportunities for recreation that restrict work–personal life overlap may be helpful. For example, cognitive approaches such as instruction and practice of self-statements to assist in helping individuals decrease their tendency to try to control other workers (e.g., focusing on "keeping one's own side of the street clean") may assist in decreasing workaholism tendencies. Discount tickets to recreational events provided through the workplace also may provide a preventive function for individuals. Prevention research is nonexistent in this addiction arena.

Summary

This chapter introduced examples of intrapersonal (neurobiological and cognitive function-related) prevention strategies, along with available research findings. Neurobiological-level strategies include use of pharmacotherapy and vigilance (monitoring), and instruction in social-emotional competence. Cognitive strategies include use of elaborative processing to better tie thinking to situational-behavioral events, strengthening executive processing capacity, and using implementation intentions as a means to control how one might act in high-risk situations. In addition, one might make use of cognitive exercises to make one's own equivocations explicit in working memory so as to create a means to reduce them and, thereby, reduce one's tendency to react by engaging in an addictive behavior. Six behavioral (e.g., seeking social support) and six cognitive (e.g., problem-solving) coping strategies were provided as examples on how one might, in part, prevent cognitive-situational distortions that reinforce participation in addictive behaviors. A little research on intrapersonal-level prevention of gambling problems (e.g., coping skills), and speculation on preventive strategies (e.g., mood management) that might be applied to other addictions, was presented.

Bulleted Summary

- Neurobiological-level addiction prevention strategies include vigilance programs (screening those at risk and providing tailored programming which might include use of medication), structuring youths' time, and social-emotional competence instruction (e.g., problem-solving, recognizing others' feelings).
- Cognitive-level addiction prevention strategies include use of elaborative processing, strengthening executive control, use of implementation intentions, equivocation awareness and reduction (e.g., attitudinal perspective activity), and cognitive/behavioral coping skills.
- Intrapersonal-level approaches that have been applied to gambling include correction of gambling misperceptions (true odds), coping skills and decision-making, providing personalized feedback, and risk reduction techniques (e.g., time-limited gambling).
- There is no research on intrapersonal-level approaches that have been applied to the prevention of addictions other than drug use or gambling, though several plausible strategies include such approaches as motivational interviewing.

Suggestions for Further Reading

Broning, S., Kumpfer, K., Kruse, K., Sack, P.-M., Schaunig-Busch, I., Ruths, S., ... & Thomasius, R. (2012). Selective prevention programs for children from substance-affected families: A comprehensive systematic review. *Substance Abuse Treatment, Prevention, and Policy*, 7. doi: 10.1186/1747-597X-7-23.

Fishbein, D. H. (2000). The importance of neurobiological research to the prevention of psychopathology. *Prevention Science*, 1: 89–106.

Ladouceur, R., Goulet, A., & Vitaro, F. (2013). Prevention programmes for youth gambling: A review of the empirical evidence. *International Gambling Studies*, 13: 141–159.

Sussman, S. (2013). A lifespan developmental-stage approach to tobacco and other drug abuse prevention. *ISRN-Addiction*. doi: 10.1155/2013/745783.

Sussman, S. & Ames, S. L. (2008). *Drug Abuse: Concepts, Prevention and Cessation*. Cambridge University Press.

12 Prevention: Extrapersonal-Level Approaches

Learning Objectives

- To learn about school and other community unit-based addiction prevention strategies that have been used for drug- and non-drug-related addictions, which generally utilize comprehensive social influences/life skills strategies
- To learn about family-based prevention strategies that have been or could be used across the 11 focal addictions
- To learn about extrapersonal-level electronic media-based prevention strategies that have been or could be used across the 11 focal addictions
- To learn about policy-based prevention strategies that have been or could be used across the 11 focal addictions
- To learn about resource acquisition or alternative approaches that have been or could be applied to prevention of the 11 focal addictions

Introduction

Johnny saw some films at school on driving while tired and on drinking and driving. He really felt little impact from seeing those films. His health education classes did teach him about the existence of drugs such as LSD and marijuana. The consequences of using these drugs led Johnny to wonder. He thought he might be interested in trying those drugs for himself. He was a little frightened when he learned in health education class about STDs and thought he should be careful if he began to have sexual relations. In any case, he was doing well at school. His addictive "tendencies" such as they reportedly were "went under the radar" at school and home. He studied hard, worked out very hard as a member of his high school cross-country and track teams, and was responsive at home when needed to help out around the house. He simply would not have been ear-marked for targeted prevention programming. However, extrapersonal universal prevention programming that could have reached his attention might have helped him to be vigilant lest he became too preoccupied, or experience loss of control, with some behavior (e.g., alcohol or marijuana use over the next couple of years). Learning about what is normative behavior regarding alcohol and other drug use for his age, within the classroom setting, may have assisted him. Unfortunately, no evidence-based programming was provided to Johnny at school.

Learning Objectives

A great deal more extrapersonal-level prevention programming has been conceptualized and evaluated than intrapersonal-level programming. Extrapersonal-level approaches refer to alterations made in small groups, or to the large social/cultural environment, or to associated physical environments. There are several advantages of extrapersonal approaches to prevention, to the extent that they can be realized and implemented. Among microsocial (group-level) approaches, making use of the group can help correct youths' cognitive misperceptions, as well as provide a venue for practicing newly learned behavioral skills in social settings, with corrective input from educators, and peer feedback that may mimic real-world social situations (Sussman, 2015). This form of programming often makes use of simulations of real-world settings. For example, learning how to avoid, escape, refuse, or even correct social pressures (***activism***) facilitative of any behavior one does not wish to engage in (e.g., drug use, eating fast food, buying items beyond one's financial resources), particularly among young teens, can be practiced in group settings. Practice facilitates performance if and when such pressures occur naturally in one's social environment.

As with the intrapersonal strategies, thinking about the prevention of behavioral addictions at the extrapersonal level requires making generalizations; translating work from what has been completed in drug abuse prevention to prevention of the other eight focal addictions such as gambling or sex addiction. That is, a fair quantity of tobacco, alcohol, and other drug prevention programming has been implemented in schools and other social settings. However, much less extrapersonal-level prevention programming has been applied to other addictions.

Certainly, there may be some resistance to actually trying to provide some types of prevention programming in institutional contexts, such as schools. Would schools permit instruction in the prevention of love and sex addiction in their classrooms? Some instruction in prevention of risky sexual behavior has been permitted, and possibly some material could be added if administrators could take these two addictions seriously. (They may not believe that teens could suffer from a developing love or sex addiction due to "raging hormones" being part of adolescence; Sussman, 2007, 2010.) Would schools want to teach prevention of workaholism? Workaholism is somewhat widespread among professional groups (Sussman, 2012a), and tends to be condoned by the workplace, especially for young employees.

Would many social settings even consider instruction in prevention of shopping or exercise addictions? Shopaholism may simply not even be recognized as a problem; at least not until it has become severe. I also would speculate that prevention of exercise addiction is unlikely at the current time because many schools, for example, have limited resources to even provide any instruction in physical education and it might be more of a problem to convince many youth to exercise at all, rather than addressing a minority who may continue to exercise despite clear physiological and psychological contraindications.

This chapter provides several examples of prevention programming that involve social interaction and the group, including the elements of comprehensive social influences/life skills programming in schools and other community units, and family-based involvement. Information from outside the person's immediate social environment can also help direct persons toward prosocial resources. Thus, this chapter also provides

School or Other Community Unit-Based Approach to Tobacco, Alcohol, or Other Drug Abuse Prevention: Comprehensive Social Influences

The most effective and widely used microsocial-based ATOD prevention approach for young teens involves *comprehensive social influences/life skills prevention programming*. This type of programming generally is implemented in schools and occasionally in other community units (e.g., youth clubs, after-school programs). This approach is most applicable to young teens; who are most responsive to such an approach (see Sussman, 2013). Examples of this type of programming include Life Skills Training, Project ALERT, All Stars, and Project TNT (see Sussman, 2013). For older teens, a motivation enhancement-skills instruction-decision-making (MSD) approach is more appropriate and, while often implemented in a classroom setting, is more intrapersonally oriented (see Sussman & Ames, 2008; Sussman et al., 2004; also material in Chapter 11).

The comprehensive social influences/life skills approach generally is divided into 11 substantive components (Sussman & Ames, 2008; Sussman et al., 1995; Tobler et al., 2000). These key components have been provided mostly in school-based programs but are adaptable to any number of modalities (e.g., family, mass media) and might be best used in a systems approach (Sussman et al., 2013a). While currently tested with tobacco, alcohol, and other drug abuse prevention, and while their presentation herein focuses on drug use, the reader may be able to envision how they might be applicable to other addictions (as is suggested in their description below). A twelfth component, the "talk show" (see Sussman, 2015), while generally not included as a social influences/life skills component, will be mentioned here as well because it involves similar, social-level mediators of change.

1. Listening and communication skills. The objective of *social skills training* is to teach different skills (e.g., listening and communication skills), using a well-researched sequential process, including (1) demonstration of appropriate behavior, (2) modeling of appropriate behavior, (3) behavioral rehearsal, and (4) feedback. One can improve both listening and speaking skills by learning how to ask *open-ended questions* (questions that require more than a one-word answer), establishing eye contact appropriately, nodding, and orienting one's body toward the other speaker. One can ask questions of the speaker or listener to check for mutual understanding of the communication. One can also make sure that one's non-verbal behavior matches one's verbal behavior to exchange a consistent message. These skills are useful in social group situations.

Nevertheless, social skills training can create problems for some high-risk teens. Among high-risk youth, enhancing communication or general assertiveness skills may increase the scope of social entertainment options and inadvertently improve a teen's ability to acquire drugs or other addictive objects from new sources (*conversation initiation skill*; Wills, Baker, & Botvin, 1989; e.g., the ability to be able to walk to a random adult and convincingly request that the adult buy alcohol or another addiction object for the youth). Utilizing methods to enhance motivation to live addiction-free prior to instructing specific skills may involve providing non-addiction directions and increasing flexibility of an individual's range of behavioral options (Sussman et al., 2004).

There are cultural variations on what constitutes good social skills. For example, different norms exist regarding degree of personal space, acceptability of establishing eye contact, degree of smiling considered appropriate, and appropriateness of stating opinions that may diverge from the group (see Unger, Hamilton, & Sussman, 2004; Wyer, Chiu, & Hong, 2013). Thus, one needs to make sure that the skills being instructed accurately reflect group norms of the participants. Overall, increasing social competence will have protective effects for teens.

2. Refusal assertion. **Refusal assertion skill** is one type of assertiveness skill, a social skill that involves how one might best refuse an offer or request of someone else. Generally, an assertive refusal is a simple, direct response that is not too passive (weak statement, such as "ask me tomorrow") or too aggressive (e.g., yelling at the requester). With an assertive refusal strategy one may acknowledge positive intent of the requester ("I know you are trying to be nice by offering me a cigarette"), state one's own position ("but I don't smoke"), and possibly offer an alternative ("I'll see you later in class"). Refusal assertion, although emphasized as being very important in earlier consensus statements, is not considered to be as central a feature of ATOD prevention programming as it was in the past. Rather, manipulation of *social normative perceptions* (beliefs regarding social norms) appears to mediate program effects among young teens, perhaps not refusal assertion skills training per se. For example, MacKinnon and colleagues found that perceived peer disapproval, negative outcome expectancies for drug effects, and relatively low prevalence estimates mediated effects obtained in the Midwestern Prevention Project. Refusal assertion skills instruction did not (Donaldson et al., 1996; MacKinnon, Johnson, Pentz, Dwyer, & Hansen, 1991). Similar findings have been uncovered in the arenas of alcohol use prevention (Project Alcohol Abuse Prevention Training) and tobacco use prevention (Project Towards No Tobacco Use [TNT]) (see Donaldson et al., 1996). Refusal assertion training can be useful to those who need such skill only if closely linked to normative perceptions material. Provided alone, one (a young teen) may come to believe that everyone "out there" uses tobacco or other drugs and that drug use offers are ubiquitous. As a consequence, one's refusal self-efficacy may decrease, and one may increase intention to conform to such perceived pressures by using tobacco and/or other drugs. One may conjecture that similar unexpected effects of naïve instruction of refusal assertion skills may be found for the prevention of other addictions. In addition, training in refusal assertion may create reactance in some older adolescents who, at their developmental level, do not want to engage in such an activity or already have taken a stance toward the addictive behavior. In particular, these older teens may feel that such an activity is demeaning or irrelevant (Sussman et al., 1995).

3. Short- and long-term physical consequences information. These prevention activities do not address social influences but are included in some form in most comprehensive social influences programming. Certainly, a discussion of physical consequences is necessary to justify why one should learn to resist different types of influences to use drugs. One activity used in Project TNT includes discussion of a chain of consequences that begin with smoking and smokeless tobacco use initiation, progresses to addiction, to disease, and through to death. By uncovering a chain of consequences that conforms to use development transitions (e.g., regarding cigarette smoking: coughing, enjoyment, addiction, disease, and death), youth can see how consequences accumulate as they continue to use drugs (Sussman et al., 1995). In addition, some myths about tobacco and other drug use can be corrected. For example, many youth believe that when coughing stops in early smoking experimentation, they are merely "getting used to" smoking. If youth are taught that what is really happening is that their bodily defense systems are giving up, and that they are beginning to become addicted to nicotine (increased tolerance), this information is likely to exert a preventive effect (Glynn, Leventhal, & Hirschman, 1985). Although this type of reasoning is a cognitive misperception type of correction, types of group activities might be used to instruct effectively the physical consequences of tobacco or other drug use. For example, as was completed in Project TNT, this material might be instructed by lining up students and having them take on different "roles" in the different phases of tobacco use-to-consequences. Also, this information might be instructed through a group "game" or group dramatizations (e.g., role playing a funeral of someone who died from a drug overdose; Sussman et al., 1995). A consequences progression-type activity could be developed for any of the other addictions, if the focus was more on development of the habit and progression of different types of consequences (e.g., tolerance and withdrawal-like symptoms, social consequences, financial consequences).

4. *Peer group unacceptability of the addictive behavior.* Group activities involve participation of a whole set of youth (e.g., a classroom or youth group) and can affect conservative shifts in attitudes of its members by taking *group polls*. For example, instructors might take a class poll regarding whether *peers approve* of getting drunk on alcohol, using tobacco, or getting high on marijuana. Young individuals tend to believe that they, but not their peers, are the only ones who view tobacco and other drug use as unacceptable behavior. By taking a group poll youth learn that most of their peers also disapprove of drug use (Sussman & Ames, 2008).

Effective programs have used 20-minute activities to decrease perceived approval of use. To illustrate, in a well-planned **normative restructuring activity** youth are instructed to stand under (or hold up) approve/disapprove signs regarding acceptability of tobacco and other drug use. A conservative shift in attitudes results as youth visibly understand that they and the majority (if not all) of their peers disapprove of use (see Sussman et al., 1995). Such an activity is readily applicable to other addictions.

5. *Correction of addictive behavior prevalence overestimates.* A similar type of activity is used to reduce *addiction prevalence overestimates* (Sussman et al., 1988). Instructors may attempt to modify overestimates of the prevalence of drug use, for example, by taking an anonymous poll of self-reported drug use in the class along with youths'

estimate of the number of their peers in the class who use drugs. The instructor then provides a comparison of the actual frequency of use to student estimates of that frequency among peers, the latter of which are generally markedly higher. The instructor explains, through group discussion, that youth may tend to overestimate the number of users among their peers, that relatively few youth use drugs, and that there is little actual pressure "out there" to use by peers. Possibly, this activity might be applied to other addictions.

6. *Awareness of adult influences.* *Adult influences* refer to modeling influences of adult role models among youth who may aspire to appear older to others. Youth are made aware of these influences through group discussions about adults, including celebrities in the news and significant others (Sussman, 2002c). In addition, one homework assignment that is sometimes used is to have young teens observe or interview an adult who has an addictive behavior problem. The interviewed adults may reveal that they no longer enjoy their addiction; that they continue to engage in an addiction because they feel trapped. They may plead with that youth not engage in the addictive behavior and suffer the same fate. Adolescents may appreciate that innocent curiosity as to why people begin an addictive behavior can lead to problematic levels of participation in it, which, in turn, makes some adults very unhappy.

7. *Media influences.* *Advertising influences* may socially model and glamorize such addictions as alcohol, other drug use, gambling casinos, or shopping sprees, as examples, and influence those individuals who aspire to express social images portrayed in advertising (e.g., "having fun," "risk taking," or "sophistication"). In prevention education, youth engage in a deliberate analysis of media programming and are made aware of advertising influences (referred to as instruction in **media literacy**) so that they are less likely to yield to these, often subtle, informational social influences. They may learn to correct false advertisements or act on various media influences through activism activities. For example, in Project TNT youth correct tobacco magazine advertisements by creating new ads that provide the opposite message (e.g., unattractive, boring) of that portrayed in the tobacco advertisement (e.g., beauty, fun). Tobacco counteradvertising activities also may include coloring smoker's teeth yellow in ads (Sussman et al., 1995). Corrective advertisements might work very well to correct images associated with problem gambling, and research in that arena might be considered, as well as some of the other addictions (e.g., food, shopping).

8. *Activism.* Activism activities also assist in the prevention of an addiction such as drug use. For example, youth may write letters to significant others, celebrities, the tobacco or alcohol industry, or the media requesting that these industries provide a correct portrayal of tobacco or to encourage others not to use tobacco or engage in heavy alcohol use. Engaging youth in such writing exercises may help them to personalize knowledge, become active learners, and encourage belief change through activism (Sussman & Ames, 2008).

9. *Self-confidence building.* Self-confidence building involves the use of cognitive techniques, such as making positive affirmations to self or others. The individual may engage in a series of steps that involve consideration of their assets and liabilities to

assist them in making decisions that could increase self-confidence. They may engage in a "pass the compliment" activity that involves making simple, realistic, positive personal statements passed from person to person (e.g., having a nice smile, being a good friend, dressing nicely). By engaging in such activities, a change in personal self-beliefs may occur (Sussman et al., 1995).

10. Decision-making. **Decision-making** involves learning how to rationally combine information to make self-fulfilling decisions in different problem areas. A range of possible options that include considering the benefits and costs of each option and then making a decision based on carefully considered information aid in leading to a wise decision. Self-confidence building and decision-making are distinguishable from ethical/moral decision-making (e.g., "maturity" and "responsible" adult behavior) and values clarification materials, which have not been shown to aid in the prevention of drug use (Sussman et al., 1995).

11. Making a commitment not to engage in a problematic addiction. Obtaining a *public commitment* is another activity that involves writing and group action. Here, the participant engages in a writing activity (i.e., stating the commitment) that is then stated publicly to the group. Often, a decision-making sequence about drug use, for example, is completed first (e.g., to not misuse, not abuse). Next, a contract *not to use* drugs or to discuss drug misuse with others, as examples, is provided. The signed contract is shared among the other youth in the group (Sussman et al., 1995). This activity is relevant to young teens but not older teens who may resent being requested to state a commitment in public. For older teens, instructing them on obtaining a personal and private commitment may be attempted (Sussman, 2015).

12. The talk show. While not employed as a comprehensive social influences/life skills strategy, the **talk show format** is an activity highly preferred by older teens and merits mention (see Sussman & Ames, 2008; Sussman, 2015). Use of psychodramas in the format of "talk shows" can assist in eliciting responsibility, consequences information, and achieving healthy changes. For example, in a "marijuana panel" talk show in Project Towards No Drug Abuse (Sussman et al., 2002), various panelists report their (scripted) experiences. Scripts are provided to all participants in the group who volunteer to take on various roles, and they can work off the scripts. Participants in this activity serve either as panelists or as audience members. An ex-marijuana abuser reports that he or she "used to smoke weed every day. It became a problem." This type of activity also could be applicable to any of the 11 focal addictions. These components are summarized in Table 12.1.

School or Other Community Unit Approaches for Non-Drug Addiction-Related Behavior

Most of the strategies indicated above would likely apply well to other addictive behaviors. However, describing how they might apply effectively mostly is a matter of conjecture. There is no literature on community unit-based prevention of shopping and exercise addiction in any clinical or research literature. Arguably, such work

School or Community Approaches to Non-Drug Addiction Behavior

Table 12.1 Components of the comprehensive social influences/life skills approach

Listening and communication skills	Listening and communication skills can be improved by learning how to ask open-ended questions, establishing eye contact appropriately, nodding, and orienting one's body toward the other speaker. Like other forms of social skills training the instructional process includes (1) demonstration of appropriate behavior, (2) modeling of appropriate behavior, (3) behavioral rehearsal, and (4) feedback components.
Refusal assertion skills	Refusal assertion skill is one type of assertiveness skill. It is a social skill that involves how one might best refuse an offer or request of someone else. An assertive refusal is a simple, direct response that is not too passive or too aggressive. With an assertive refusal strategy one may acknowledge positive intent of the requester, state one's own position, and possibly offer an alternative.
Short- and long-term physical consequences information	A discussion of physical consequences is necessary to justify why one should learn to resist different types of influences to use drugs. By uncovering a chain of consequences that conforms to use development transitions, youth can see how consequences accumulate as they continue to use drugs. In addition, some myths about tobacco and other drug use can be corrected. Consequences regarding other addictions also might be provided as a "chain" of consequences.
Peer group unacceptability	Young individuals tend to believe that they, but not their peers, are the only ones who view tobacco and other drug use, or some other addictions perhaps, as unacceptable behavior. By taking a group poll youth learn that most of their peers also disapprove of the behavior. A conservative shift in attitudes results as youth visibly understand that they and the majority of their peers disapprove of the behavior.
Correction of behavior prevalence overestimates	Behavior prevalence overestimates can be modified, for example by taking an anonymous poll of self-reported drug use, or other addictive behavior, in a class along with youths' estimate of the number of their peers in the class that engage in the behavior. The comparison will often show that youth tend to overestimate the number of their peers that engage in the behavior and that relatively few youth actually do.
Awareness of adult influences	Adult influences refer to modeling influences of significant others or other adult role models, particularly among youth that aspire to appear older to others. Youth are made aware of these influences through group discussions about adults, including celebrities in the news and significant others.

(cont.)

Table 12.1 (*cont.*)

Media influences	By working with media influence youth are made aware of adult advertising influences so that they are less likely to yield to these informational social influences. They may learn to correct false advertisements (media literacy) or act on various media influences through activism activities.
Activism	Youth may write letters to significant others, celebrities, the tobacco or alcohol industry, or the media requesting that these industries provide a correct portrayal of tobacco or to encourage others not to use tobacco or engage in heavy alcohol use. Engaging youth in writing exercises may help them to personalize knowledge, become active learners, and encourage belief change through activism. A similar activity might be aimed at other addictions (e.g., gambling).
Self-confidence building	Self-confidence building involves the use of cognitive techniques, such as making positive affirmations to self or others. The individual may engage in a series of steps that involve consideration of their assets and liabilities to assist them in making decisions that could increase self-confidence.
Decision-making	Decision-making involves steps of learning how to rationally combine information to make self-fulfilling decisions in different problem areas.
Making a commitment	The participant (young teen) engages in a writing activity that is then stated publicly to the group. Often, a decision-making sequence about drug use is completed first. Next, a contract not to use drugs or to discuss drug misuse with others, is provided. The signed contract is shared among the other youth in the group.
The talk show	Use of psychodramas or "talk shows" can assist in eliciting responsibility and consequences information and achieving healthy changes. Scripts are provided to all participants in the group who volunteer to take on various roles, and they can work off the scripts. Participants in this activity serve either serve as panelists or as audience members.

should be done. For example, possibly many shopaholics at first are not even aware that their behavior is way out of line with the norm. Instruction in peer normative prevalence estimates of shopping frequency contrasted with self-ratings of shopping frequency may be instructive, and instruction in building self-confidence might assist in the prevention of shopping addiction.

As another example, it might be important to intervene on faulty attitudes and perceptions that coaches and society in general have regarding pathological patterns of exercise. For example, clichés such as "No pain, no gain," "Don't hit the wall, run through it," and even the Nike slogan "Just do it" all encourage exercise but place no limit on when to stop and tacitly encourage exercising beyond physical and/or psychological limitations (Brian Cook, personal communication, July 25, 2015). Media literacy instruction might help here. Published empirical and theoretical work on potential prevention of non-drug use addictions in school or other community settings deserves some discussion. While currently there is no literature on the prevention of shopaholism and exercise addiction, there is some literature among the remaining focal addictions, or at least some related behaviors, as follows.

Food Addiction-Related Behavior

Some work has been completed on eating disorders prevention. In particular, a lot of work has been completed recently on the prevention of childhood obesity (e.g., Davis et al., 2007; Waters et al., 2011). However, prevention of "food addiction" is another matter. There remains some controversy regarding the existence of food addiction as an entity, and there is still debate about whether food disorders such as obesity or binge eating disorder might be considered a good proxy for food addiction. Assuming there is the beginning of establishing a consensus on the existence of food addiction (Yau et al., 2014), one may ponder whether or not the food industry would want us teaching prevention of food/eating addiction. This has been an issue with childhood obesity prevention and nutrition (e.g., regarding regulation of sugary foods such as sodas in schools; Yau et al., 2014, p. 166).

Childhood obesity is moderately (not highly) associated with food addiction. Waters et al. (2011) conducted a Cochrane review on *childhood obesity prevention* studies that used a controlled study design. The majority of studies targeted children aged 6–12 years. The meta-analysis included 37 studies and demonstrated that programs were effective at reducing adiposity, although not all individual interventions were effective, and there was a high level of observed heterogeneity. They found strong evidence to support the beneficial effects of child obesity prevention programs on body mass index (BMI). Promising strategies included school curricula with options for healthy eating (e.g., quality food at school), physical activity (e.g., daily movement skills), and body image components (e.g., desensitization to body image through relaxation and imagery). By changing one's knowledge and lifestyle, more temperate behavior and improved physical function may result.

There is one promising study on prevention of eating disorders and obesity with emerging adults. Stice, Rohde, Shaw, and Marti (2013) examined the effects of a prevention program targeting both eating disorders and obesity at one- and two-year follow-ups among female college students at risk for these outcomes because of body image concerns (n = 398). Participants were randomized to the "Healthy Weight 2" group-based four-hour prevention program, which promotes healthy dietary intake and physical activity, or an educational brochure control condition. Intervention participants showed significantly less body dissatisfaction and eating disorder symptoms and lower eating disorder onset through two-year follow-up versus controls. There were no main effects for BMI, depressive symptoms, dieting, caloric intake, physical activity, or obesity onset. A 60 percent relative reduction in eating disorder onset over the two-year follow-up was clinically significant.

It is not clear what lessons might be derived here for food addiction. However, tentatively, one may conjecture that instruction in healthy eating behavior and physical activity involvement may help prevent food addiction. One may also conjecture that intervening on affect regulation and decision-making skills, sometimes used as modalities in the prevention of eating disorders, may also be an effective strategy to consider for food addiction (Brian Cook, personal communication, July 26, 2015).

Gambling Addiction

Some work has been completed on prevention of gambling, though prevalence among youth is not high (e.g., Sussman et al., 2014). Elementary and high-school based prevention programs for *problem gambling* are relatively uncommon, but they do exist in some jurisdictions. Such programs typically have a broad scope of topics that include teaching statistical knowledge about gambling, providing information on the potentially addictive nature of gambling, explaining gambling fallacies, building self-esteem, and developing peer resistance skills (Williams et al., 2012). Examples of these types of programs are "Don't Bet On It" in South Australia for ages 6 to 9; "Gambling: Minimizing Health Risks" in Queensland for Grade 5 students; "Facing the Odds" in Louisiana for Grades 5 to 8; "All Bets are Off" in Michigan for Grades 7 and 8; "Kids Don't Gamble ... Wanna' Bet" in Minnesota and Illinois for Grades 3 to 8; "Youth Making Choices" for high school students in Ontario; "Count me Out" in Quebec for ages 8 to 17; the "Problem Gambling Prevention Program" in Florida for middle and high school students; and "Gambling: A Stacked Deck" in Alberta for Grades 9 to 12.

Stacked Deck is a set of five to six interactive lessons that teach about the history of gambling, the true odds and **house edge** (that gambling odds favor the gambling establishment and not the customer), gambling fallacies, signs of problem gambling, and skills for good decision-making. An overriding theme of the program is to approach life as a "smart gambler" by determining the odds and weighing the pros versus cons of one's actions. A total of 949 Grade 9 through 12 students in ten schools throughout southern Alberta received the program and completed baseline and follow-up measures. These students were compared to 291 students in four control schools, in a blocked randomized controlled trial. Four months after receiving the program, compared to the control group (which did not change), students in the intervention group reported significantly more negative attitudes toward gambling, improved knowledge about problem gambling, improved resistance to gambling fallacies, improved decision-making and problem-solving, decreased gambling frequency, and decreased rates of problem gambling. There was no change in involvement in high risk activities or money lost gambling (Williams, Wood, & Currie, 2010).

There appears not to be longer-term data on behavioral changes as a function of use of microsocial-level gambling prevention programming. Ladouceur et al. (2013) reviewed the literature on the effectiveness of youth gambling prevention programs. Two categories of preventive strategies, all universal and mostly school-based, were presented: gambling-specific prevention programs and gambling and related skills workshops. The first type of program, the prevention programs, provides information on gambling to encourage more realistic perceptions (e.g., accurate probability information, erroneous beliefs correction, signs of problems). The second type of program, the skills workshop, focuses more on problem-solving and coping skills instruction, and self-monitoring. These authors concluded that programs in both categories are generally effective in reducing misconceptions and increasing knowledge about gambling. However, only a total of 15 program evaluations were located, and a lack of long-term follow-ups and of behavioral measures made it difficult to draw any clear conclusions about prevention program effectiveness.

Love Addiction

Sussman (2010) suggested several microsocial strategies to address *love addiction* prevention. For example, since it is possible that development of love addiction may occur through social learning processes (e.g., exposure to the behavior of significant others, mass media influences), corrective information about healthy and unhealthy romantic relationships may be provided as part of school health curricula, or through other types of community health promotion programming. One may, for example, be presented with a set of age-appropriate love addiction relationship scenarios. One could be guided through a decision-making sequence about the benefits and costs to self and others for each scenario, and learn that costs outweigh benefits to both partners. These scenarios may be contrasted with realistic love types (e.g., feeling good about a love partner's abilities to function independently and achieve happiness outside of the relationship). One also may be instructed in myths of ideal romantic love (e.g., the myth that there is only one "right" person for each and every other person; or the myth that showing obsessive thinking toward another person is definitive of love). Persons may be asked if there is a "kernel of truth" regarding the myth and then explain why it is a myth (e.g., people do get married again; people would not be able to build lives together if all they thought about was each other).

Sex Addiction-Related Behavior

Sussman (2007) discussed prevention strategies that might have some relevance to teen *sex addiction*. There is no consistent set of strategies consensually agreed on. Among teens, modalities of prevention programming to decrease risky sexual behavior, which may have some overlap with sex addiction, have included (a) school group-based or other small-group, (b) one-on-one counseling, (c) case management, (d) family-based, and (e) community-level programming (e.g., media, health services, outreach, and group support), most research being addressed with small group (microsocial) programming (Malow et al., 2006). Key strategies that overlap across several different levels of programming but provide a significant preventive impact include instruction in STI (sexually transmitted infection) knowledge, goal setting, alteration of perceived peer group norms (acceptability and prevalence of risky behaviors), cognitive-behavioral skills instruction (e.g., refusal assertion, how to use condoms [as a harm reduction method], conversational skills), personalization of consequences information, motivational enhancement to engage in responsible sexual behavior and goal attainment, and, pertaining to other extrapersonal modalities presented below in this chapter, family education and counseling, media awareness and education, and use of community outreach services (Auerbach, Hayes, & Kandathil, 2006; Fisher, Fisher, Bryan, & Misovich, 2002; Malow et al., 2006).

Creating links to social, health, and instrumental support, which can then create "human capital" and increase social competence, is thought to be another "key" to successful HIV prevention among teens, particularly among at-risk groups (Malow et al., 2006). In addition, instruction that emphasizes ethnic and gender pride may be better able to impart risky sex prevention information among minority females (Wingood et al., 2006). Evidence-based HIV/STI prevention interventions have shown generalizability effects in developing countries (e.g., Karnell, Cupp, Zimmerman, Feist-Price, & Bennie, 2006; Kirby, Obasi, & Laris, 2006).

Life Skills Training, a 30-session school-based drug abuse prevention program, was examined for long-term generalization effects to HIV-risk behavior (Griffin, Botvin, & Nichols, 2006). The program instructed personal and social competence (e.g., developing personal relationships, conversation skills), and skills to resist drug use. Little information was provided regarding risky sexual behavior in the program contents; hence the exploration for a generalizability effect from drug use to sexual behavior. Data were collected in 1985 among 12-year-olds in Grade 7 and at a long-term follow-up in 1998 (average age of 24 years). HIV risk behavior was measured as an index score composed of items including number of sex partners, having sex while intoxicated, and extent of condom use. An approximate 5 percent absolute reduction on each of the HIV risk behaviors was found 13 years later comparing the program condition to the control condition in this randomized design, apparently mostly mediated by reduction in drug use. However, efforts to replicate such generalizability effects proved to be disappointing among older teens utilizing other school-based programming (e.g., Project Towards No Drug Abuse; Sussman, Sun, Rohrbach, & Spruijt-Metz, 2012).

An accumulation of evidence-based, primarily school-based prevention efforts for teen pregnancy or HIV/AIDS can be adapted for specific populations, including potential sex addicts (Eke et al., 2006; Solomon, Card, & Malow, 2006). This may be accomplished by knowing the core elements of the program and the population it is being adapted to, and then fitting the two together. Because sexual addictions are correlated with other addictive or problem behaviors among teens (e.g., substance misuse, violence), prevention programming might best target multiple behaviors. In so doing, this programming may provide a more time-efficient format for also including information relevant to prevention of sex addiction (Guilamo-Ramos, Litardo, & Jaccard, 2005). Of course, prevention of risky sexual behavior is not the same as prevention of sex addiction, in that the preoccupation and loss of control definitive of sex addiction may or may not occur among those who engage in risky sexual behaviors, and sex addicts may or may not engage in risky sexual behaviors. Still, these sets of behaviors are related and prevention of one set may apply to prevention of the other set (Sussman, 2007).

Electronic Media-Related Addiction

TV addiction (as an example of addiction to electronic media in general [e.g., Internet-based shows, YouTube]) may be impacted through school-based/community unit approaches. Sussman and Moran (2013) examined TV addiction prevention. Whether TV is harmful is a function of what programming is being viewed (e.g., violence on TV), who is viewing (e.g., addiction prone), how often TV is viewed (e.g., more than two hours per day may become a problem), and whether viewing involves other significant others (which may or may not be relationship enhancing; Kubey, 1990). Media literacy could be promoted through a variety of modalities (e.g., schools, public community settings, home), and involves a deliberate analysis of media programming. In such an analysis, depending on the age of the viewer, one may be asked to search contents for advertising ploys, stereotypes, major themes and purposes of a show, whether contents are attempting to be realistic or a fantasy, and how shows might impact one's feelings (Singer & Singer, 1998). Also, among young teens, corrective information about healthy (non-addictive) and unhealthy television viewing patterns may be instructed as part of school health curricula, or through other types of community units. One may, for example, be presented with a set of age-appropriate/ inappropriate television viewing scenarios. One could be guided through a decision-making sequence about the benefits and costs to self and others for each scenario, and learn when costs outweigh benefits (Sussman & Moran, 2013). Several impactful media literacy curricula have been implemented over the last 20 years (Singer & Singer, 1998), and these could focus more on limiting the amount of television viewed as well as interpretation of programming.

Workaholism

Prevention of *workaholism* might be considered (Sussman, 2012a). For example, children of workaholics (who may be at elevated risk for workaholism themselves) might be involved in group discussions, or might be taught how to monitor themselves for signs of developing workaholism (e.g., a tendency to work to achieve a "high," a tendency toward perfectionism, and favoring instrumental activity over relationships). Planning recreational time on a weekly calendar might be guided by a facilitator. Addressing issues pertaining to working to achieve a sense of normalcy might be discussed, possibly using an approach such as motivational interviewing (i.e., the person may need to realize a sense of normalcy regardless of work role). Providing peer norms on work patterns might help persons to decrease work hours (through realizing that their own behavior is non-normative). In addition, career selection methods might assist in matching cases of potential workaholism to jobs that might maximize enjoyment while permitting a healthy outlet for being hard-driving. Finally, education on the progressive nature of workaholism-related consequences might help curb a developing pattern of workaholism (e.g., through use of a "talk show" curriculum activity format). Possibly, such programming might be best offered in a community college or university context, or possibly as part of workplace education.

Family-Based Prevention Programming for Tobacco, Alcohol, and Other Drug Abuse

Family involvement is a relevant means of providing prevention material outside school or other public community units and can lead to a 10–15 percent incremental tobacco or other drug use prevention effect in families willing to participate in and comply with a program (Broning et al., 2012; Sussman et al., 2013a). Families differ from other groups because of the often close and historical patterns of interaction within the unit. Therefore, it is important to recognize the influence of the family unit while providing assistance to the target individual or individuals (e.g., the "addicts"). According to Kumpfer's (1999) *transactional framework of resilience* the "transactional processes involved in the relationship between parents and their children are extremely important in moderating posited biological risk characteristics and promoting resilience" or resistance against risky behaviors (Kumpfer & Bluth, 2004, p. 673). Therefore, it is necessary to strengthen and promote positive **transactional processes** within the family (i.e., mutual social interaction and impact). Strategies that have been utilized to strengthen family dynamics include family skills training, brief family therapy (including structural, functional, and behavioral therapy), cognitive/behavioral parent training, and family support and education (for review, see Kumpfer, Alvarado, & Whiteside, 2003). One caveat, however, is that persons at highest risk for various addictions likely are relatively unlikely to be part of families who will take on the responsibility of teaching the prevention material to them or serve as support persons. Some family-based prevention programs are summarized in Table 12.2.

Strengthening Families Program

Examples of evidence-based *family drug abuse prevention programming* include the Strengthening Families Program and Family Matters. Kumpfer and colleagues developed the original Strengthening Families Program in 1983 (http://www.strengtheningfamiliesprogram.org/). It is a family skills-training program designed to increase **resilience** (skills to buffer oneself from stressful conditions facilitative of addictions) and reduce risk factors for problem behaviors in high-risk children aged 6–12 years, defined as behavioral, emotional, academic, and/or social problems (see Kumpfer & DeMarsh, 1985). The program emphasizes improving family relationships, parenting skills, and youth social and life skills. The program generally includes three 14-week courses: Parent Training, Children's Skills Training, and Family Life Skills Training. Parents learn to increase desired behaviors in children by using attention and rewards, clear communication, effective discipline, substance use education, problem-solving, and limit-setting. Children learn effective communication, understanding feelings, social skills, problem-solving, resisting peer pressure, consequences of substance use, and compliance with parental rules. Families engage in structured family activities, practice therapeutic child play, conduct family meetings, learn communication skills as a family, practice effective discipline, reinforce positive behaviors in each other, and plan family activities together. Effects have been found on antisocial

Family-Based Prevention Programming for Drug Abuse

Table 12.2 Family-based prevention programming

Strengthening Families Program	A family skills-training program designed to increase resilience and reduce risk factors in high-risk children and older youth. The program emphasizes improving family relationships, parenting skills, and youth social and life skills. Effects have been found on antisocial behavior, such as tobacco and other substance use, conduct problems, and improvement in social and life skills.
Family Matters	Family Matters is a home-based program designed to prevent tobacco and alcohol use in children 12 to 14 years old. The program is delivered through four booklets mailed to the home and follow-up telephone calls to parents by health educators. This program showed effects on both tobacco and alcohol use at three- and 12-months' follow-up.
Functional Family Therapy (FFT)	FFT is an indicated intervention involving family treatment designed for delinquent teenagers. FFT focuses on family communication, and the establishment of rules and consequences. Several studies provide encouraging reports of the program's effectiveness on repeated felonies, violent crime, and misdemeanors.
Multisystemic Therapy (MST)	MST targets individual, family, peer, school, and community influences of youth offenders with serious problems that may include violence, substance abuse, and severe emotional problems. Consistent findings are decreased drug use, rearrest, self-reported criminal offense, and days in out-of-home placements.
Multidimensional Treatment Foster Care (MTFC)	MTFC includes placement of youth in a foster home with a foster parent trained in behavior management who receives support from intervention staff. After the adolescent has begun to respond to the intervention in the foster home, and after the parents have received the same training and support as the foster parents received, the adolescent returns home. MTFC has shown positive outcomes: fewer days in detention or lock-up, more time living with parents, fewer misdemeanor and felony arrests, and fewer self-reported index crimes and general delinquency. MTFC is a cost-effective alternative to incarceration.

behavior, such as tobacco and other substance use, conduct problems, and improvement in social and life skills.

The Strengthening Families Program for youth aged 10–14 years consists of seven sessions and four boosters. In two-hour sessions, parents and youth spend the first hour apart and the second hour together in supervised family activities. Emphasis on creating a positive future orientation, age-appropriate expectations and roles, mutual empathy, making house rules, and listening to each other are central to the program. Effects have been found on drug use in several trials (e.g., a 33 percent relative reduction in ever-tried alcohol use at a four-year follow-up, 10th-grade final wave of data collection; Kumpfer, Molgaard, & Spoth, 1996; Spoth, Reyes, Redmond, & Shin, 1999; Sussman, 2013). Such programming could, in theory, be effective on other addictions, though it has not been so applied.

Family Matters

Karl Bauman and colleagues developed Family Matters in the late 1980s (http://www.sph.unc.edu/familymatters/Program_materials.htm). Family Matters is a home-based program designed to prevent tobacco and alcohol use in children 12–14 years old. The program is delivered through four booklets mailed to the home and follow-up telephone calls to parents by health educators. The booklets contain readings and activities designed to get families to consider general family characteristics and tobacco and alcohol use attitudes. Topics discussed include adult supervision and support, rule setting and monitoring, family communication, attachment and time together, education encouragement, family/adult substance use, substance availability, and peer attitudes and media orientation toward substance use. This program was delivered to 1,300 treatment and control parent–child pairs in a randomized controlled trial and showed effects on both tobacco and alcohol use at three and 12 months follow-up (83 percent of the families in the program completed one or more of the units, and 62 percent completed all four units; achieving approximately 15 percent relative reductions in tobacco and alcohol use; Bauman et al., 2000, 2001, 2002).

At least three other family-based multiple-problem targeted prevention programs, discussed below, have had an important impact in the drug abuse prevention field (see Sussman et al., 2004). These programs have been designed to prevent even more severe problems in the future, although they are used with families of youth that already show problems in living.

Functional Family Therapy

Functional Family Therapy (FFT) is an indicated intervention involving family treatment designed for delinquent teenagers (http://www.fftinc.com/). Developed in the early 1970s by Alexander and colleagues, FFT focuses on family communication, and the establishment of rules and consequences. Several studies provide encouraging reports of the program's effectiveness. In a study by Waldron and colleagues (Waldron, Slesnick, Brody, Turner, & Peterson, 2001), researchers used FFT and a cognitive-behavior therapy intervention on teens referred for marijuana use. Each of the interventions alone produced significant results on marijuana use at four months, but only the two interventions combined maintained these results at seven months. In two earlier studies that utilized FFT, Alexander and colleagues (Alexander, Barton, Schiaro, & Parsons, 1976; Alexander & Parsons, 1973) found that improvement in family communication post-treatment led to a reduction in delinquency among the teens in the study. Note that all of the teens in these studies had histories of serious antisocial or delinquent behavior. Thus, achieving positive outcomes, even if only short-term, should encourage further research into the efficacy of FFT.

Multisystemic Therapy

Multisystemic Therapy (MST), as its name suggests, targets individual, family, peer, school, and community influences of youth offenders with serious problems that may include violence, substance abuse, and severe emotional problems (http://mstservices.com/index.php#). MST was developed in the 1970s and numerous researchers have since published the results of randomized trials of MST with the most consistent findings across studies being decreased (1) drug use, (2) rearrest, (3) self-reported criminal offense, and (4) days in out-of-home placements. Other consistent findings are improved family relations, school attendance, and psychiatric functioning. The effectiveness of this program, however, is considerably lower when not implemented with fidelity (Henggeler, Pickrel, & Brondino, 1999). In other words, all or key lessons need to be delivered as written by educators who are well trained in using the strategies employed, and youth need to be able to receive all material in an atmosphere conducive to learning it. The program developers have instituted training strategies that address these fidelity issues, thus shaping MST to be a very promising program for at-risk youth. For example, in one randomized control trial, in which 118 juvenile offenders received either MST or community services, alcohol, marijuana, and other drug use was significantly reduced (by 50 percent) immediately post-test (Henggeler et al., 1999). MST treatment can last three to five months. Effects on felony and misdemeanor arrest rates have been found to be two to five times lower among persons exposed to MST compared to individual therapy an average of 21.9 years later (Sawyer & Borduin, 2011).

Multidimensional Treatment Foster Care

Multidimensional Treatment Foster Care (MTFC) is an evidence-based program that targets community, family, and peer factors that influence adolescents with a pattern of repeat criminal offending and drug misuse (http://www.mtfc.com/). The program is based on social learning principles (e.g., vicarious learning, practice, and motivation) and emerged from ongoing research at the Oregon Social Learning Center. Chamberlain and colleagues developed the first program in 1983, which targeted juvenile offenders. It has since been adapted to target various age groups with a variety of problem behaviors, including substance use and misuse (with an impact on self-reported behavior lasting two years or more compared to usual care; e.g., Rhoades, Leve, Harold, Kim, & Chamberlain, 2014). This intervention includes placement of youth in a foster home with a foster parent trained in behavior management who receives support from intervention staff. After the adolescent has begun to respond to the intervention in the foster home, and after the parents have received the same training and support as the foster parents received, the adolescent returns home.

Chamberlain and Reid (1998) tested the intervention with 85 boys with felony and other criminal histories and found substantial benefits of the program. That is, following treatment the boys assigned to MTFC, when compared to those receiving community-based group care in a randomized controlled trial, served fewer days in detention or lock-up, had twice as much time living with parents, and had fewer misdemeanor and felony arrests and fewer self-reported index crimes and general delinquency. MTFC is a cost-effective alternative to incarceration; however, staff requirements are extensive, which may influence the ability of some groups to apply the program with fidelity. Nevertheless, as with each of the programs described above, results of the randomized trials are encouraging.

Application of Family-Based Prevention Programs to Non-Drug Use Addictions

There has been only a little application of family-based programming to non-drug-related addictions. Certainly, family planning of meals and foods kept in the home might help prevent *food addiction*. It is known that low and/or declining parental monitoring of children between the ages of 11 and 14 is associated significantly with *problem gambling* when those children reach young adulthood (Lee, Stuart, Ialongo, & Martins, 2013). Thus, it is feasible that **parental monitoring** (i.e., being around the youth, showing interest) may assist in lowering the probability of future problem gambling among children (and perhaps lead to better overall adjustment).

Regarding prevention of *love addiction*, programming that attempts to facilitate a **secure attachment style** (feeling connected to and nurtured by significant others) with teachers, parents, and peers, attempted in some programs with young children including the Strengthening Families Program (see Sussman, 2010a, 2013), may help limit reliance on love addiction-related social learning modalities for relationship development information (e.g., romantic television shows or movies). Certainly, such programming also would be protective against other addictions that may stem from inadequate attachments (e.g., drug abuse).

While speculative, there are some programs that may have relevance to prevention of *sex addiction*. Family-based sex education programs have been promoted by organizations such as the National Association of Social Workers (Malow et al., 2006) and the Sex Information and Education Council of the United States (SIECUS). Debra Haffner, president and CEO of SIECUS, advised: "Don't wait for your teens to ask you about sex – they may not. We don't wait to talk to our kids about other important matters of health and safety. Why should the subject of sex be any different?" (see Sussman, 2007). If parents monitor their children, and provide accurate information to them, they may help instill values for responsible sexual decision-making. Some parents feel that if they bring up the subject of birth control, they may be encouraging the child to have sexual intercourse. But offering information isn't the same as offering the tools themselves. According to SIECUS, "with open communication, young people are more likely to turn to their parents in times of trouble.

Without it, they will not" (also see Burgess, Dziegielewski, & Green, 2005). **Outcome and self-efficacy expectations** (expecting that completing an action will result in desired outcomes and that one is able to take that action, respectively) may mediate the likelihood that parents will communicate with their children about sex (e.g., father–son communication; DiLorio, McCarty, & Denzmore, 2006), and thus might need instruction.

Of course, parents can implement some health protection preventive measures, particularly regarding online exposure to porn (related to *Internet sex addiction*). The computer with Internet access can be placed in the house where it can be easily monitored, the web history of the child's Internet usage can be checked, home web pages (e.g., Facebook) can be monitored, and blocking software can be installed. In addition, the parent can talk with their teen about the importance of hiding their identity online (Weiss & Schneider, 2006). Parents can assist in making their children media literate and screen out certain types of programming, which has implications for prevention of online addiction and TV addiction (Jusoff & Sahimi, 2009; Singer & Singer, 1998).

Parental social modeling of appropriate purchasing patterns might assist in preventing *shopping addiction*. It is not clear whether store employees could be trained to spot shopping addicts and, at least, provide flyers on warning signs of compulsive buying behavior, and hand out these flyers to parents. Transmission from parent to teen of balanced views about work, relationships, and physical activity might help prevent *workaholism* or *exercise addiction*. Much more could be explored in terms of family-based prevention of various addictions. For the time being, such suggestions are speculative.

Electronic Media-Based Tobacco, Alcohol, and Other Drug Abuse Programming

Media-based programming may elicit preventive effects contingent on the adequacy of the reach of programming, the opportunity facilitated for interaction about the media program, and *supplementation* with other types of programming (Flay, 1981). The mass media can be a useful adjunct to a variety of interventions. Six stochastic steps that have been identified as needed for media-based programming to impart behavioral effects on individuals are as follows: (1) exposure to the communication, (2) awareness of the key messages, (3) knowledge change, (4) belief change, (5) behavior change, and (6) maintenance of belief and behavior change (see Flay, 1981). Operationally, utilizing multiple media channels at prime viewing times, repetition, arousing personal involvement, being entertaining, involving discussion, and providing opportunities to act are important for a media message to exert influence on people. The mass media can affect very large social regions because of their potentially unlimited reach.

DeJong (2002) and DeJong and Wallack (1999) propose several criteria that need to be met by mass media campaigns. First, a media campaign has to prompt reevaluation

Table 12.3 Media-based prevention programming

Six stochastic steps of media-based programming
Exposure to the communication
Awareness of the key messages
Knowledge change
Belief change
Behavior change
Maintenance of belief and behavior change
Criteria that need to be met in mass media campaigns
Prompt reevaluation of individual risk and consideration of action
Bring about a change in beliefs about the behavior being addressed
Model or instruct new behavioral skills
Facilitate the conviction that one can carry out the new behaviors, and that in so doing health will improve
Instruct the importance of monitoring changed behavior and continued self-management

of individual risk and consideration of action. Second, the campaign must bring about a change in beliefs about the behavior being addressed. Third, the campaign should model or instruct new behavioral skills. Fourth, the campaign needs to facilitate the conviction that one can carry out the new behaviors, and that in so doing health will improve. Finally, the mass media programming needs to instruct the importance of monitoring changed behavior and continued self-management. The contents of mass media campaigns that appear to have exerted the strongest effects on drug misuse have been those that depict a dramatic true consequence of drug use, take an activism stance, assert a greater autonomy experienced by non-drug use (addiction-prone) lifestyles, make appeals to sensation-seeking youth through fast-paced material with exciting activities being depicted, or attempt to correct misperceptions of drug use norms (Dejong, 2002; Emery et al., 2005; Hafstad et al., 1997; Palmgreen, Donohew, Lorch, Hoyle, & Stephenson, 2001; Slater et al., 2006). General principles of mass media-based prevention programming are summarized in Table 12.3.

Flynn and colleagues conducted perhaps the most rigorous assessments of the use of the mass media in studies of cigarette smoking prevention. They assessed the incremental effects of adding a mass media component to school-based programming. The media program involved airing about 15 television spots and eight different radio spots during each of the four years of the intervention. The media program consisted of themes of positive non-smoker images, negative smoker images, improved refusal assertion, and attempts to lower prevalence estimates. Classroom teachers delivered the school-based program four days per year in Grades 5 through 8, and three days per year in Grades 9 and 10. With the use of a matched pairs design of school versus school plus media conditions in two metropolitan areas in Vermont and New York, these researchers found that the media component provided an incremental effect after four years of programming (2.6 percent versus 4.4 percent [at least one cigarette per week smoking prevalence] for school plus media versus school only; Flynn et al., 1992) and two years after that, when students were in the 10th to 12th grades (about 17 percent versus 25 percent, respectively; Flynn et al., 1994). The findings from this study were also moderated by risk. Those at higher risk for continued smoking (they or their family member smoked at baseline) were impacted more strongly by the program (showed a relatively greater decrease in prevalence) than those at lower risk (Flynn et al., 1997).

Sensation-seeking is a risk factor for drug and possibly other addictions (Sussman & Ames, 2008; Zuckerman, 1994). Palmgreen et al. (2001) attempted to tailor materials for sensation-seekers in the development of a mass media marijuana use prevention campaign. In the sensation-seeking mass media campaign, program elements were integrated through use of advertisement storyboards and were evaluated by additional focus groups (Palmgreen et al., 2001). Revisions based on these evaluations were incorporated into five professionally produced 30-second television spots that involved material likely to appeal to youth high in sensation-seeking (e.g., fast-paced and novel). After the program development was completed, the campaign was implemented and evaluated using a controlled interrupted time-series design in two matched communities. The campaign reversed upward developmental trends in 30-day marijuana use among high sensation-seeking individuals (i.e., about a 10 percent decrease in use was observed the year following the campaign).

A review of the literature on Internet-based teen smoking prevention and cessation programming uncovered a total of 19 studies, four of which pertained to teen prevention (Walters, Wright, & Shegog, 2006). Of those studies, in the two that were completed regarding the same project that involved mailed computer-generated feedback reports, smoking incidence was cut by more than one-third among program recipients when compared to controls in randomized designs at six-month and one-year follow-ups. Effects of programming failed to be found in the other two studies. Another fairly recent study, which utilized group randomized trials to test the effectiveness of Internet-based programs to reduce smoking prevalence and positive smoking-related outcome expectancies, found a decrease in 30-day smoking prevalence (about a 4 percent difference between program and control subjects in Australia, but not the United States) and lower expectations for smoking in the future among its Australian and American adolescent subjects, respectively (Buller et al., 2008). This program ("Consider This") contained 73 online activities that instructed media literacy, relationships, mind and body (e.g., negative consequences of smoking), decision-making and refusal assertion components.

The Smoking Prevention Interactive Experience (ASPIRE) is a relatively recent computer-based smoking prevention and cessation curriculum for high school youth (Prokhorov et al., 2008). It consists of five weekly sessions in one semester and two booster sessions in the following semester (each 30 minutes long). Subjects engage in either the prevention program if they are non-smokers or the cessation program if they are current smokers. Module contents are further tailored based on the subject's decisional balance, smoking temptations, depression, and addiction. At an 18-month follow-up of a randomized controlled trial at inner city high schools, among baseline non-smokers, smoking initiation rates were lower in the ASPIRE condition than in a standard care control condition which used a self-help booklet (NCI's *Clearing the Air*; https://pubs.cancer.gov/ncipl/detail.aspx?prodid=P133), 1.9 percent versus 5.8 percent.

The results for cessation were not significant. The Internet remains a promising modality (Sun et al., 2005).

Electronic Media-Based Programming Applied to Non-Drug Use Addictions

There have been some *gambling* prevention efforts that involved use of the media. Walther, Hanewinkel, and Morgenstern (2013) investigated a media-based program that was delivered in schools. They engaged in a two-wave clustered randomized control trial among approximately 2,000 12-year olds (intervention versus control group) in Germany. The intervention group received a four-unit media education program, which contained one unit on gambling (gambling myths, actual odds, gambling industry profits, and symptoms of a problem, involving media viewing and classroom interaction). The program was implemented by trained teachers during class time. The control group attended regular classes without any specific intervention. The results seven weeks after exposure to the 90-minute segment on gambling indicated increased gambling knowledge, decreased problematic gambling attitudes, and decreased current gambling (though a very small effect size and no change in lifetime gambling) in the intervention group compared to the control group.

There also have been several media awareness campaigns directed toward teens or adults to attempt to prevent problem gambling (Williams et al., 2012). A majority of these have not involved comparison groups. Several months after being exposed to campaigns or other media (e.g., interactive CDs) participants show significantly improved knowledge about gambling, more awareness of the signs of problem gambling, and fewer gambling fallacies. However, in general, evidence for an impact on gambling behavior is lacking. One exception is a study by Doiron and Nicki (2007). These researchers delivered a two-session program to 20 **video lottery terminal** (**VLT**) gamblers (similar to a slot machine; one gambles on the outcome of a video game) who scored in the "at-risk" range on the Canadian Problem Gambling Index. The program focused on problem-solving and cognitive restructuring material. Session One consisted of a 20-minute video providing information on gambling and problem gambling and a homework manual with exercises to practice cognitive restructuring (replacing maladaptive with an adaptive stream of inner speech) and problem-solving. In Session Two, material covered the role of problem-solving and faulty thinking, and a plan for the future. Apparently, some group discussion was involved here. Still, most material was instructed through automated educational presentation, video and text vignettes, audio training tapes, and skill rehearsal. The program was evaluated after the second session and one month later compared to a wait-list control group of 20 people (100 percent retention of participants at one month). Large decreases in erroneous gambling beliefs and actual gambling behavior (number of VLT sessions [mean of about 7 to 2 sessions; non-VLT gambling sessions [about 17 to 9 sessions]; VLT expenditure [mean of about $132 to $21]) occurred in the experimental group at both post-training and one month follow-up, with no changes in the control group.

Regarding prevention of *sex addiction/risky sexual behavior*, there are many books, pamphlets, and videos available for parents and teens, including a comprehensive and very readable report from the National Commission on Adolescent Sexual Health entitled *Facing Facts* (see http://eric.ed.gov/?id=ED391779). Possibly, tailoring these mass media materials for sensation-seeking youth and adults may exert a stronger preventive effect on sexual attitudes and behavior (Noar, Zimmerman, Palmgreen, Lustria, & Horosewski, 2006). Again, there is no research support here.

One may speculate that prevention efforts can also take advantage of the fact that the source of addiction is also a prevention communication medium. For example, public service announcements (PSAs) could be run on television to alert individuals to the signs of *dysfunctional television viewing* and provide information on how to seek assistance prior to developing a deeply ingrained addiction. Prevention efforts could also take advantage of entertainment education strategies, whereby educational story-lines are embedded within a television program, that attempt to limit number of hours of viewing or unhealthy viewing motivations. Media-based prevention regarding other addictions needs conceptualization, development, and testing.

Policy-Based Prevention Programming and Tobacco, Alcohol, and Other Drug Abuse

Tobacco

In the tobacco, alcohol, or other drug abuse prevention arena, legal regulation of substances can be accomplished by use of a ***prohibitory scheme*** (of production or distribution; e.g., zoning, age restrictions), a ***regulatory scheme*** (setting conditions of use, information about use, sanctions; e.g., taxation, legal limits, ***interdiction*** [delaying or disrupting drug use or distribution; forbid use by actions of authorities]), and large social climate influence (policy facilitating an overarching norm that an addiction is good or bad behavior because it is legal or illegal; Pentz et al., 1996). The primary policy tactic used regarding illicit drug use generally is interdiction. Interdiction has been expensive and of equivocal success (other than some street-level tactics to reduce availability; Pentz et al., 1996; Sussman & Ames, 2008).

Tobacco prevention-related policy has become a rather strong force nowadays in guiding tobacco-related research and practice. The Framework Convention on Tobacco Control (FCTC; www.who.int/fctc/en/) provides both prevention and control guidance through primarily policy regulations. There are 179 countries party to the FCTC. Sussman et al. (2013a) discussed the importance of several modalities of tobacco use prevention, including policy-related types. Tax increases on cigarettes can curb youths' intention to begin smoking, and a 20% increase in price may lead to a reduction in use of 6–10% among youth. Large warning labels placed on tobacco products using clear language in ways that might cue behavior may also be helpful (e.g., 33–50% of the pack or more; maybe a 2% reduction). Also important are enforcement of access laws for tobacco and advertising regulations, and passive smoking laws among youth.

For example, a full ban on smoking (no-smoking policy) in all public locations may lead to up to a 10% reduction, full bans on ads for tobacco may lead to a 5% reduction, and strict enforcement of no youth access may lead to a 2% reduction in youth smoking prevalence. The two policy interventions that appear to have the greatest impact are tax increases, and enactment and enforcement of restrictions of smoking (e.g., no smoking policies) in public places (Sussman et al., 2013a).

A whole new field of *tobacco regulatory science* has at least indirect implications for potential prevention work (the emphasis is on minimizing harm, as opposed to tobacco prevention or cessation; Ashley, Backinger, van Bemmel, & Neveleff, 2014). In tobacco prevention and control or cessation work, generally the endgame is the eradication of nicotine addiction and tobacco-related disease. In the new field of tobacco regulatory science, the endgame is less clear, but focused more on minimizing harm from various nicotine delivery systems (cigarettes, e-cigarettes, cigars, pipes, smokeless tobacco, dissolvables, pharmacological adjuncts). In part, to better understand and inform the impact of tobacco-related policy actions, the passage of the Family Smoking Prevention and Tobacco Control Act of 2009 established the Food and Drug Administration's (FDA) Center for Tobacco Products (CTP) (FSPTC Act, 2009; see www.fda.gov/tobaccoproducts/guidancecomplianceregulatoryinformation/ucm246129.htm). A primary goal of the CTP is to assess scientific evidence and support new research that will inform regulatory decision-making and protect public health, also known as tobacco regulatory science. The FDA's public health framework for tobacco regulation includes eight elements: (1) understand regulated products, (2) restrict product changes to protect public health, (3) prohibit modified risk claims that state or imply reduced risk without an order (i.e., official FDA approval achieved as an outcome of a careful examination protocol), (4) restrict marketing and distribution to protect public health, (5) decrease harm of tobacco projects, (6) ensure industry compliance with FDA regulations through education, inspections, and enforcement, (7) educate the public about the FDA's regulatory actions, and (8) expand the science base for regulatory action and evaluation. The emergence of the field of tobacco regulatory science will be critical as new policies are developed that dictate access to and use and marketing of new tobacco and alternative nicotine delivery products, such as e-cigarettes, hookahs, and *snus* (a moist powder tobacco product originating from a variant of dry snuff in early eighteenth-century Sweden, that may show reduced risks). It is not clear whether or how tobacco regulatory science, which is in its infancy and subject to a rapid developmental process, will impact tobacco-related research and practice outside of the United States.

Alcohol

Policy-related *supply reduction programming* that focuses on changes in the *alcohol use* environment has shown promise. There are many types of specific strategies that have shown effects on when, where, and how much alcohol is used. Environmental prevention strategies include prohibitory policy mechanisms (e.g., raising the minimum drinking age, zoning [limiting use locations]) and regulatory policy mechanisms (e.g., alcohol taxation, setting blood alcohol level limits for driving, and enforcement). Additional environmental prevention strategies include traffic safety education, server training and monitoring, and community involvement (e.g., coalitions of businesses and government leaders, point-of-sales stings, and media and family involvement; Hansen, 1994; Komro & Toomey, 2002; Williams & Perry, 1998), which can alter demand for alcohol and provide a means of regulation. Interestingly, for example, a point-of-sales **sting event** (e.g., having someone pose as a minor and try to purchase alcohol while law enforcement is watching) can reduce sales drastically to minors for approximately three months (Wagenaar, 2006). Use of warning labels on alcohol beverages and provision of alternative youth activities outside of school also may serve to reduce demand for alcohol, though there is little current research support other than to stimulate discussion about alcohol use consequences (Wilkinson et al., 2009). Most of these strategies have not been examined much for their incremental effects. However, results of these types of programs in combination may effect decreased heavy drinking among youth and decreased the number of fatal car crashes (see reviews in Komro & Toomey, 2002; Wagenaar, Lenk, & Toomey, 2005). Taken together, these various policy-related environmental/community-based prevention strategies attempt to make alcohol less accessible and less socially desirable and to make the social environment more supportive to non-use (Hansen, 1994; Komro & Toomey, 2002; Williams & Perry, 1998). These strategies are likely to be of some importance in the prevention of youth alcohol use because currently alcohol is so widely available to youth, both outside and inside the home (Komro, Stigler, & Perry, 2005; Wagenaar et al., 2005).

Other Drugs

Regarding US drug policy expenditures, two-thirds of the allocated budget goes to disrupting the drug market (supply control; e.g., Caulkins, 2006; Strang et al., 2012). Disrupting the drug market can have both prevention and cessation effects. Policies include crop eradication (e.g., of marijuana, coca, or opium fields), controls on precursor chemicals, interdiction, criminal investigation, street-level enforcement, imprisonment, fines, diversion programs (for users), or legalization. Unfortunately, crop eradication measures often shift production to other growing regions, and costs to enforce controls on precursors are very high and substitute chemicals are used. Although costly, there is some evidence that interdiction efforts can raise prices of a drug which could lead to prevention or cessation effects. In theory, high-level criminal arrests could be quite disruptive but little empirical work exists to this effect. Street-level enforcement may deter only the more visible use of drugs (e.g., high use areas); imprisonment is of questionable service and is expensive; and there is little impact of fines other than to reduce the stigma of other approaches. **Diversion programs** are a form of sentencing and such programs are often run by a police department, court, a district attorney's office, or an outside agency designed to enable offenders to avoid criminal charges and a criminal record. They seem to have some effectiveness in some locations, including California, and research should continue in this regard.

Legalization/harm reduction may be of some use though there is little controlled research completed (Strang et al., 2012). The current legalization of marijuana in several states in the United States may provide natural laboratories to assess this option. One recent study suggests that enactment of medical marijuana policies may lower initiation of use of marijuana by 18 percent nine years post-enactment but then lead to relatively greater initiation after nine years (Shi, 2016). Possibly, linking drug supply policy measures to microsocial, group-level prevention or treatment options may provide a stronger impact (Pentz et al., 1996; Strang et al., 2012).

Application of Policy-Based Programming to Non-Drug Use Addictions

Food Addiction

Yau et al. (2014) discussed the possibility that policy-based strategies may impact *food addiction*. They asserted that taxation of sweetened beverages (or other foods), and food labeling, could lower their intake, but the few evaluations completed provide equivocal results. One may speculate that endorsement of healthy food policy (e.g., see http://publichealthlawcenter.org/topics/healthy-eating) could lower the prevalence of food addiction if food addiction is associated with intake of unhealthy food. Other policy research may be found on the website of the UConn Rudd Center for Food Policy & Obesity (www.uconnruddcenter.org/). However, little enforced food addiction-related policy is in operation.

Gambling Addiction

There have been several efforts pertaining to gambling prevention policy. Gambling prevention policy initiatives can be organized into three categories: (a) restrictions on the general availability of gambling; (b) restrictions on who can gamble; and (c) restrictions on how gambling is provided (Williams et al., 2012). Restrictions tend to elicit weak effects on decreases in gambling, though there are some suggestions that controls over the number of casinos constructed in an area, and times of operation, may have some impact. Restriction of continuous gambling (**automated electronic gambling machines** [**EGMs**]; e.g., slot machines), casino table games, and continuous lotteries (such as Keino) has been suggested as being associated with decreases in treatment seeking.

There is limited evidence that a raise in the minimum age of legal gambling may reduce slot machine use (perhaps related to use in casinos). Restriction on Internet gambling is legislated in several countries (e.g., through restricting financial transactions via banking institutions), though the relationship between Internet gambling and problem gambling is not clear at this point.

Modifying the parameters of EGMs generally has a weak relation with behavior, though pop-up messages (e.g., that might say "you have been gambling for 30 minutes") may impact behavior. A slower speed of play and reducing maximum wins may have a weak impact. A *pre-commitment* (limiting time or amount that will be played; perhaps involving electronic smart cards) may serve as a harm reduction device, though evidence of efficacy is lacking thus far (e.g., people can swap cards). There is no evidence as to whether casino employee training to recognize at-risk gamblers and alert supervisors is efficacious. Most casinos won't limit overall amounts gambled, so the effectiveness of capping strategies is not known. Also, although perhaps a good idea, it is not known if restricting alcohol or tobacco use at casinos will limit gambling.

Other Addictions

Regarding *media addiction* prevention (Internet, TV), warning statements might be placed on Internet or television consumer channel packages/plans to encourage limiting viewing time to no more than two hours per day (Sussman & Moran, 2013). Likewise, Sussman (2010a) suggested a potential *love addiction* policy-related effort. Warning statements might be placed on some media outlets. For example, in theory, a warning message placed at the beginning of a romance movie might say "This movie portrays fantasy material and does not reflect healthy real-life love relationships." Certainly, some persons might view such action as extreme. However, if there is evidence that the media promotes love addiction, and if love addiction prevalence is sizable (e.g., 5 percent or greater of the population), then such action would seem justified. Also, while seldom investigated, state governmental policies, such as taxes on beer, restrictions on location of cigarette vending machines, and placement of family planning clinics, seem to influence adolescents' behavior (i.e., they have been shown to exhibit significant deterrent effects; Bishai, Mercer, & Tapales, 2005). Possibly such policy-determined, large environmental manipulations may provide a preventive effect on risky *sexual behavior* among teens. There is much research needed regarding policy prevention programming.

Some policy-related *workaholism* prevention strategies have been considered (Sussman, 2012a). From the level of the organization, use of **employee assistance programs** (employer-sponsored services designed for personal or family problems, including mental health, substance abuse, various addictions, marital problems, parenting problems, emotional problems, or financial or legal concerns), enforced vacations, development opportunities for better engagement or flexible roles, and management training to facilitate enjoyment on the job may be of assistance to prevent as well as treat workaholism. Periodic assessments of work enjoyment at the workplace may assist in determining if the workload needs to be decreased. At a societal level, a shift in policy-facilitated cultural emphasis to the importance of work–personal life balance, making use of work closings during national holidays to promote the importance of recreational and family interests, and mass media campaigns that attempt to counteract workaholism could be undertaken (e.g., development of a "work smarter, not harder" campaign). Little work has been discussed in the academic literature in this regard, and no empirical studies are available.

Resource Acquisition and Alternatives Programming

This domain of programming redirects youth to more self-fulfilling behaviors. Youth who take on responsibility for the care of others, who adaptively emotionally distance themselves from problem others (e.g., create a palatable bedroom environment in their parents' house), and who take on more prosocial pursuits (where they can find them, such as seeking out school activities) appear to be more resilient against drug misuse (Sussman & Ames, 2008), and possibly other addictions. Thus, programming that facilitates such behavior (e.g., opportunities for involvement in community service) may provide a protective effect. Also, individuals who learn to maintain a more hopeful outlook, develop good communication skills, and seek out prosocial support when needed tend to be more resilient (reactively) against drug abuse and other risky behaviors (Hawkins et al., 1992). While plausible, there is little research on use of resources acquisition instruction or involvement in alternatives programming as means of prevention for any addiction.

There is some suggestion of effectiveness in *resource acquisition-type programming* on indicated drug use prevention in single-group studies of attendance of high-risk preteens and teens at community-based programs. These community programs involve bringing in an intensive and costly in-house network of social service resources to teens under one roof and appear to facilitate surmounting of hurdles in development these youth face (Sussman, Skara, & Pumpuang, 2008). Perception of availability of environmental resources, such as access to jobs, education, recreation, transportation, or drug and other counseling services in one's community could be enhanced among emerging adults by receiving such information through any number of modalities (e.g., as a telephone education program, through mass media communications).

If provided as booster programming (e.g., by telephone) following receipt of some type of addiction educational programming in school or elsewhere in the community, a resource acquisition strategy could enhance hope for lifestyle stability with satisfactory self-fulfillment in a time- and location-efficient way. Provision of such resources might assist in helping at-risk persons avoid involvement in negative addictions. The drawback would be if resource acquisition skills also enable youth to locate sources of addictions (e.g., new fast food restaurants, gambling outlets). Considering a common underlying appetitive effects notion of addictions may help in appropriate planning of a resources acquisition component.

Similarly, there have been but a few evaluations of **alternative resource programming** for teens. Alternative programs attempt to provide community resources to teens, enhance their perception of the availability of resources, or enhance their self-efficacy to find and utilize these resources (http://archives.drugabuse.gov/about/organization/despr/hsr/da-pre/KumpferLitReviewPartC.html; also see Swisher & Hu, 1983; Tobler, 1986). Generally, use of alternatives programming has been considered relatively important among at-risk teens who arguably may not have access to or know how to seek out alternative resources for living. Kumpfer (1997) noted that a meta-analysis of the Center for Substance Abuse Prevention's high-risk youth and family programs suggests that alternative programs are effective for drug abuse or delinquency prevention. However, some *iatrogenic effects* (undesired worsening of an addictive behavior, increase in drug use) have resulted from involvement in certain alternative recreational activities. These activities include such venues as rock band concerts (e.g., "Battle of the Bands"), drug-free parties, or sports that involve peer or adult drug user involvement. In addition, some iatrogenic effects have resulted from youth involvement in some vocational or community service involvement (e.g., housing construction and house painting, where adult drug users might be involved with youth). Conversely, academic achievement, religious activities, anti-drug activism-related involvement, and active personal hobbies are inversely related to drug use (Kumpfer, Williams, & Baxley, 1997). These latter activities tend to promote attachment to social institutions and adults in such a way that drug use is relatively less likely to be modeled. While these sorts of programs seem to be "politically correct," there is a rather small evidence base regarding their prevention of any addiction. It is not clear whether or not alternatives programming might discourage one addiction (e.g., drug misuse) while encouraging another (e.g., workaholism).

Summary

This chapter described extrapersonal-type prevention programming for various addictions. In particular, this chapter discussed strategies in different modalities: the school or other community unit, the family, media-related efforts, policy-based prevention programming, and resource acquisition/alternatives programming as a strategy. The strategies discussed were generic attempts; to be generalizable across a wide range of individuals.

Individual–environment matching is an approach that goes way beyond most of what is presented in this text. Still, a brief suggestion of approaches might stimulate further thinking on the topic in the future. The idea is to minimize harm of or engagement in addictive behaviors by considering specifically an approach intended to match individual appetitive function to environmental contexts. There are at least three specific approaches that might be considered. One attempt is that of ***containment***, reducing engagement in a potentially addictive behavior to a safe level. In other words, one may attempt to restrain situations of participation in the addictive behavior through social monitoring and influence, or location access. Second, one may attempt *lifestyle matching*, finding a better lifestyle fit to reduce likelihood of addictive behavior initiation or escalation (e.g., change in living arrangements, embedding oneself into non-using or other non-addictive behavior-participating contexts), Finally, one may consider ***environment enrichment***, that is, providing a more saturated reinforcing environment may decrease negative affect-situation reasons for initiating an addictive behavior; appetitive needs being satisfied in productive ways.

Individual–environment matching principles might be overlaid on generic programming in the future, though certainly any such attempts may at times be considered too personally intrusive. Handled with care, and derived from an evidence base, prevention programming will help many people. For others, an addiction may still develop and cessation programming may be needed. The next three chapters pertain to cessation.

Bulleted Summary

- School and other community unit-based addiction prevention strategies that have been used for drug and non-drug related addictions, generally utilize comprehensive social influences/life skills strategies. Program components include:
    - listening and effective communication skills (e.g., asking open-ended questions);
    - refusal assertion skill;
    - short- and long-term physical consequences information (or other sorts of factual correction, such as instruction of the "house edge" in gambling);
    - correction of misperceptions regarding peer group acceptability of engaging in the addictive behavior;
    - correction of misperceptions of peer group prevalence overestimates of engagement in the addiction;
    - awareness of sources of social influences and how they might bias one's own expectancies and behavior (adult influences, media influences);
    - activism efforts to counteract dysfunctional social influences (e.g., writing to the entertainment industry against glamorization of alcohol use among teens in the movies);
    - self-confidence building;
    - decision-making skills; and
    - making a public or private commitment not to engage in the addiction.
    - Another skill useful in teaching perspective taking, often used among older teens, is the talk show.
- Family-based prevention strategies that may be applicable to several addictions include:
    - teaching appropriate family roles;
    - communication skills; and
    - sometimes other remedial skills (e.g., education tutoring).
    - Programs introduced include the Strengthening Families Program, Family Matters, Functional Family Therapy, Multisystemic Therapy, and Multidimensional Treatment Foster Care.
- Electronic media-based prevention strategies that have been or could be used across the 11 focal addictions would need to reach the audience, arouse interest, impart relevant information (e.g., correct misperceptions), facilitate belief change (e.g., cognitive restructuring, problem-solving), and provide cues to action.
- Policy-based prevention strategies that have been or could be used across the 11 focal addictions include prohibitory schemes (e.g., illegal drugs, tobacco advertisements on billboards in the United States), regulatory schemes (e.g., minimum age and restricting youth access to tobacco or alcohol, restricting locations of casinos, restricting gambling time or type of gambling, taxation, use of warning labels), and large social climate influences (in support of prohibitory or regulatory limitations).
- Resource acquisition or alternatives approaches are plausible means to elicit addiction preventive effects by providing self-fulfilling behavioral pathways (e.g., healthy recreation, education). However, almost no research exists on any of the 11 focal addictions, and no controlled trials have been carried out.

Suggestions for Further Reading

Broning, S., Kumpfer, K., Kruse, K., Sack, P.-M., Schaunig-Busch, I., Ruths, S., . . . & Thomasius, R. (2012). Selective prevention programs for children from substance-affected families: A comprehensive systematic review. *Substance Abuse Treatment, Prevention, and Policy*, 7. doi: 10.1186/1747-597X-7-23.

Ladouceur, R., Goulet, A., & Vitaro, F. (2013). Prevention programmes for youth gambling: A review of the empirical evidence. *International Gambling Studies*, 13: 141–159.

Sussman, S. & Ames, S. L. (2008). *Drug Abuse: Concepts, Prevention and Cessation*. Cambridge University Press.

Sussman, S., Skara, S., & Pumpuang, P. (2008). Project Towards No Drug Abuse (TND): A needs assessment of a social service referral telephone program for high risk youth. *Substance Use & Misuse*, 43: 2066–2073.

Yau, Y. H. C., Gottlieb, C. D., Krasna, L. C., & Potenza, M. N. (2014). Food addiction: Evidence, evaluation, and treatment. In K. P. Rosenberg & L. C. Feder (eds.), *Behavioral Addictions: Criteria, Evidence, and Treatment*. London: Academic Press/Elsevier, pp. 143–184.

13 Resolving the Problems of Addiction – Cessation: General Principles

Learning Objectives

- To learn what leads to cessation attempts without formalized treatment, and about a stepped-care approach to cessation
- To learn about abstinence versus moderation as the goal of treatment, and about harm reduction
- To learn about the history of addictions treatment
- To learn about stages of recovery and models of treatment motivation

Introduction

As an adult, Johnny felt that he needed to get things under control. He needed some means of stopping his addictive behaviors. He was experiencing negative consequences of his drinking including a couple of altercations with the police. He was tired of being drunk and wandering out in public. He was tired of experiencing a swollen uvula, sore throat, heartburn, clammy skin, and sweating. He now also experienced high blood pressure. He also felt a slight dullness in his head, that he could not think all that crisply. Yet, he often thought about drinking and looked forward to sneaking away from family to drink. He could hardly talk about some of his other addictions with others though he knew he was experiencing financial consequences and embarrassment, and felt like he was placing a wedge between himself and his wife and children. Rumors began to surface at his workplace; he was provided with fewer and more specific administrative tasks. His history of workaholism was of little value considered alongside the other addictions he experienced. He knew he needed to change his behavior soon; but how? His experiences with 12-step programming had not been very positive. He thought that maybe he should head back to the recovery community he had left several times. However, he was worried that his agnosticism, dislike of tobacco use, and his personal secretiveness at meetings would lead to his perceived ostracism yet again. Still, he was not sure he could get things "under control" on his own.

Recall the associational memory-appetitive system relations [AMASR] model (Figure 2.1), discussed in Chapter 2. Over repeated engagement in the behavior, the individual becomes intensely preoccupied with it despite potentially diminishing subjective appetitive effects. That is, whether engaged in the behavior or not, the person often thinks about that addictive behavior – what it has done for and to the person. The addict may have difficulty imagining life without that addiction. The individual may fear loss of the adventure associated with the addiction. The individual also may experience either a loss of control over when the behavior is initiated, how it is manifested when engaged (e.g., risky or crazy actions taken such as becoming disorderly in public while intoxicated; some individuals may skip meals or sleep while gaming), or when it will stop. Stopping an addictive behavior becomes difficult for several reasons, including having a lack of awareness of the "stimuli" or triggers that influence the behavior and the cognitive salience (dominance in working memory) of immediate gratification relative to delayed adverse effects. That is, the behavior becomes increasingly more automatic. At this point, the individual also may fear having to cope with day-to-day perceived stress and other life experiences upon cessation, possibly due to accumulation of addiction-related consequences, or having to endure "raw" emotional experiences without concurrent self-medication provided by engagement in the addiction, as well as having to suffer withdrawal-related phenomena.

The Costs of Addiction Lead to Cessation Attempts

One may incur negative (undesired) consequences (e.g., social, role, physical, emotional) though still continuing to engage in the self-defeating addictive behavior. However, as the costs of the behavior are reliably greater than the benefits, the sufferer will tend to want to moderate or quit the addictive behavior (Prochaska, 2008). That is, attempts at cessation of any addiction are commonly linked to its *negative consequences*. For example, an individual may experience legal consequences, such as being arrested, resulting in court mandated treatment. An individual may experience social consequences, such as interpersonal conflict related to involvement in the addiction, and may be persuaded to enter a treatment program as a result. An individual may suffer an accident such as a car crash while engaged in the addiction (e.g., related to being distracted by a cell phone conversation while driving due to workaholism, or under the influence of a substance addiction). An individual may acknowledge the need for treatment after losing his/her job, home, car, friends, and family (job, personal role, and social consequences). There are many possible scenarios that bring individuals into treatment, but most are linked to negative consequences of participating in the addictive behavior.

Some researchers and practitioners have suggested that being arrested and court ordered to treatment may not be such a bad event for many individuals, because it may actually disrupt negative behaviors earlier than otherwise expected (minimizing more severe future problems such as social isolation and physiological deterioration) and keep individuals in treatment longer with potentially better outcomes (Fletcher, Tims, & Brown, 1997). Some studies investigating treatment outcomes have found no difference between those coerced into treatment and those who voluntarily enter treatment. Several other studies showed that those individuals coerced into treatment had better outcomes. However, still other studies have found that those coerced into treatment do not do as well as those volunteering (see Farabee, Prendergast, & Anglin, 1998). **Stigma** (a mark of disgrace associated with a particular circumstance, quality, or person) resulting from being forced into treatment, social expectations and pressure that one needs life-long treatment to keep the addiction in check, subjective feelings that one now has less to lose due to experiencing negative consequences, and side effects of treatment among persons involuntarily engaged (e.g., possibly learning a new addiction from another person in treatment), can lead to worse outcomes.

Natural Recovery: Quitting Without Formalized Treatment

There are several different ways that people are able to solve their difficulties with an addiction. There is evidence that individuals do recover from substance abuse problems spontaneously, without the help of formal treatment programs. In fact, most people self-initiate their own recovery (natural recovery, self-initiated cessation). In particular, many people "grow out of" the addiction as they reach adulthood (Wakefield & Schmitz, 2014). Some people are able to quit after experiencing a physical complication or, eventually, they become "tired" of the addiction and are able to stop. Others stop through support of friends or informal counselors.

However, there is a dearth of evaluation research on factors contributing to spontaneous recovery. According to a large-scale general population study of Canadians, only one in three people with alcohol abuse or dependence diagnoses ever seeks treatment (Cunningham & Breslin, 2004). Of the 1,000 respondents in the study that sought some type of treatment in the past, 30% reported talking with a doctor, 12% reported attending self-help groups, 8% reported seeing other professionals (e.g., psychologist, social worker), and 7% sought inpatient or outpatient services. In another study, Cunningham (1999) found that between 54% and 88% of problem drinkers quit without formalized treatment, depending on the number of reported consequences (one to six reported; also see Bischof, Rumpf, & Ulrich, 2012). One may conjecture that the numbers of teens or emerging adults exposed to formal drug treatment programs are much fewer than the numbers of adults exposed to treatment (also see Heyman, 2013b). Toneatto, Sobell, Rubel, and Sobell (1999) summarized data suggesting that up to a third of heroin or cocaine addicts exhibit natural recovery (also see Bischof et al., 2012). Heyman (2013b) provided data for cigarettes, alcohol, cocaine, and marijuana suggesting up to 80% *remission* rates (after 30 years of dependence; i.e., cessation, a diminution of the seriousness or intensity of disease), with 60% stability of remission – and no more than 30% of subjects ever seeking treatment. These data leads one to speculate that natural recovery occurs among a third of problem tobacco, alcohol, or other drug users ($0.8 \times 0.6 \times 0.7 = 0.33$). It does appear that more people recover on their own than with some type of formalized treatment.

Some data suggest high rates of natural recovery among the behavioral addictions (e.g., Konkolÿ Thege et al., 2015, regarding excessive exercise, sexual behavior, shopping, online chatting, video gaming, and eating; though a single item was used to identify each addiction). In a convincing example, using Gambling Impact and

Behavior Study data and National Epidemiologic Survey on Alcohol and Related Conditions (NESARC) data (total n = 45,000), Slutske (2006) found that approximately one-third of persons suffering from pathological gambling disorder were characterized by natural recovery. A great deal more research is needed to understand natural recovery across the 11 focal addictions. For the time being, it appears reasonable to suggest that a third of persons suffering from a serious addiction will recover without being involved in formal treatment of some type.

It is not clear how many people quit an addiction on their own as a function of duration of use, but I conjecture that the longer and heavier a person uses a drug, or is involved in another addiction, the less likely the person will be to quit the addiction without formalized treatment (Cunningham, 1999; Sussman & Ames, 2008), or perhaps the longer it will take prior to successful natural remission (Heyman, 2013b). Factors sustaining an addiction may include relative ease of access and early numerous pleasurable experiences associated with involvement in the addiction (a subsequent strongly encoded and automatic *euphoric recall*).

Quitting With Formalized Treatment: Considering a Stepped-Care Approach

One may consider thinking in terms of a stepped-care approach to treatment. First, the "addict" might attempt informal means to quit. If that fails, next the person may attempt an outpatient approach (e.g., attending individual and group support groups several days per week). Finally, if that does not work, the person may need to consider an inpatient approach; that is, treatment may need to become more structured or "addict-bounding," as more unstructured and self-initiated attempts fail. Inevitably, though, regardless of the "step," as mentioned above, cessation of any of the 11 focal addictions is commonly linked to *negative consequences* resulting from engagement in them.

Some persons suffering from an addiction may experience discrete events leading them to reach a treatment system and quit their addiction through seeing a counselor or attending support groups as an outpatient (Bischof et al., 2012). More severe cases (e.g., when the person becomes a "dramatically" financial, legal, or physical danger to self or others) may do better beginning as an inpatient. Approximately 15–30 percent of drug abusers manage to reach formal treatment settings (Heyman, 2013b; Nurses Research Publication, 1999; also see www.drugabuse.gov/publications/drugfacts/treatment-statistics). It is not clear what percentage of alcohol and other drug abusers reach treatment voluntarily versus involuntarily (e.g., through the courts or prison system; one may speculate that perhaps half reach treatment through the courts; https://report.nih.gov/nihfactsheets/ViewFactSheet.aspx?csid=22). The percentage of persons suffering from food or behavioral addictions that attempt some type of formalized treatment is unknown. Of course the history of treatment of food or the behavioral addictions is briefer than tobacco, alcohol, or other drug abuse addictions. One may speculate that 30–35 percent solve their addiction problems informally, and 20 percent solve their addiction problems through some type of treatment, generally involving an iterative process. Perhaps another

30–35 percent suffer life-long addiction problems, while the remaining approximately 20 percent suffer from addictions periodically. Some researchers assert that spontaneous recovery may be more common among the behavioral addictions than among chemical addictions (Sinclair et al., 2016). More research is needed.

Abstinence or Moderation as the Goal of Treatment?

Tobacco, Alcohol, and Other Drug Abuse: Tolerating Other Drug Use in Treatment, Abstinence, Moderation

Among alcohol or other drug use treatment programs that are based on 12-step models, abstinence has been considered necessary to recover from an addiction. ***Total abstinence*** is defined as no use of tobacco, alcohol, or any other mood-altering drugs. While abstinence from tobacco use sometimes is encouraged, considered as a problem that might be handled after the alcohol or other drug problem has been resolved, tobacco use (along with caffeine) tends to be tolerated or even sometimes promoted in many treatment programs (Grigsby et al., 2015a, 2015b; Sussman, 2002).

Alcohol use in general has not been viewed as a safe alternative among drug addicts. Many substance abusers misuse alcohol in addition to other drugs, but some do not have a history of alcohol abuse. In general, though, abusers of drugs other than alcohol ("drug addicts") believe that use of alcohol quickly disinhibits control processes and may trigger associative memories compatible with drug use, reducing the probability of effective coping in high-risk situations. A drug lapse may then be very likely if the individual values immediate gratification and loses perspective of long-term goals (Bickel et al., 2011, 2016; Zweben, 1993).

Sometimes marijuana use has been addressed as an alternative among drug addicts. Swartz (2010) found some data suggesting that medical marijuana users admitted to substance abuse (e.g., methamphetamine) treatment (n = 18, eight successful completers) fared equal to or better than non-medical marijuana users (n = 60) in some outcome categories (e.g., treatment completion, criminal justice involvement, medical concerns), though they were more likely than controls to either increase or decrease use of their drug of choice at the end of treatment (no overall effect). At this time, there are no data to strongly support what anecdotally has been coined "marijuana maintenance" for cessation of other drug use.

For many individuals total abstinence from alcohol or other drugs is necessary; any use at all results (eventually) in out-of-control use and negative consequences. The "disease model" produces a dichotomous restriction on the possible range of treatment outcomes; one is either "abstinent (exerting control) or in relapse (losing control)" (Marlatt, 1985, p. 7). Alternatively, for those who accept the concept that addictive behaviors are overlearned habits that are modifiable, controlled use is a feasible treatment outcome.

Strategies aimed at moderation of consumption (e.g., controlled drinking) may benefit some individuals. Of course, the ability to maintain controlled use of alcohol varies among individuals and may not be a viable or reliable option for most individuals abusing alcohol or other drugs. However, controlled drinking or use as a goal may at least bring individuals into treatment sooner. Those who fail at controlled use may then be willing to consider abstinence as a goal. In fact, the abstinence rate among those who choose controlled drinking as a treatment goal is about the same as those who choose abstinence as a goal (about a third of alcoholics who seek formalized treatment achieve multi-year abstinence; Galaif & Sussman, 1995).

Those few alcoholics (approximately 5 percent of alcoholics) who become controlled drinkers (e.g., **one drink** [e.g., 12 ounces of 5 percent alcohol] per day for females, two drinks per day for males) tend previously to have been lighter drinkers (e.g., they may have imbibed six drinks per day or less). In addition, they have suffered fewer legal and social consequences, may report having been less likely to experience gross behavioral changes when drinking (not experiencing the "Dr. Jekyll/Mr. Hyde" effect), and have been abstinent a few years before drinking again. They tend to drink one to four drinks on social occasions and/or only occasionally (see Sussman & Ames, 2001). Interestingly, it appears that problem drinkers who receive treatment are twice as likely to become abstinent, but are half as likely to become controlled drinkers, than those who do not receive treatment, followed one year after treatment (Peele, 1998). Possibly, this could reflect a social bias in which problem drinkers in recovery come to believe in an ***abstinence violation effect*** (Marlatt, 1985). In other words, if they ever drink alcohol, they may feel that they "lost the game" and that they might as well give up and drink regularly again. For information on current popular moderation-allowable programs, see Addiction Alternatives (www.addictionalternatives.com/), DrinkWise (www.drinkwise.org.au/), or Moderation Management (www.moderation.org/).

Food Addiction and the Other Behavioral Addictions

People have to eat (or be force-fed) or they will die. Perhaps eating is the only one of the 11 focal addictions which people can't live without. Gambling is not a necessary activity, rather a source of recreation. The Internet is part of modern living and is needed for work as well as being a source of recreation and keeping up with current events. However, some people still do live without the Internet. Love and sex are needed for procreation, though people can continue to live without having children. People can live without love though there may be some debate regarding their quality of life. Exercise is important to maintain physical health. However, while people need to walk (or otherwise exert themselves or achieve others' assistance) to get from one place to another, they don't have to exercise vigorously. One needs to work to be able to provide for self or others, unless one is provided for by others (e.g., welfare). People need to shop to buy goods, unless others buy necessity items for them (which can happen). Of course, to not engage in any of these activities is an impossible goal for most of us, who must rely on ourselves for resources and to maximize the quality of our lives. Arguably, people are better adapted to their social environment if they engage in most of these behaviors. While quitting tobacco, alcohol, other drug use, and gambling addictions would appear difficult but a logical goal, with the other seven focal addictions the focus of treatment tends to be quite different. The goal of treatment of food or the remaining behavioral addictions is moderation.

How to frame treatment so as to help persons engage in moderate activity is not easy. Among other things, "moderation" may be defined within social contexts. For example, many people may be seen using smartphones in shopping malls as they walk around. Moderate use may be frequent use in that case. (If a person can't stop thinking about smartphone use when not using it, can't refrain from using it, and suffers decreased productivity or accidents due to its use, then it is an addiction.) Of course, controlled moderate use may be difficult for someone with an addiction who is trying to achieve moderation. One means is to try to provide regulatory controls over the behavior (e.g., to facilitate moderate or controlled involvement). This would include setting time limits on a behavior, limiting venues in which to engage in the behavior, or involving monitoring of the behavior from others. For example, a parent may be able to limit their child's total Internet use time, or set specific times that the Internet can be used. Restrictions might involve use of filtering and blocking tools to limit access to certain sites, words, or images. It may also be possible to use software to block outgoing content that is questionable (e.g., a child's personal information) or that might be utilized in aberrant forms of sex addiction (see http://parental-time-control-software-review.toptenreviews.com/). Some of these regulatory controls might seem untenable for some people, who might view them as a violation of their human rights (particularly independent adults). Several alternative means of achieving moderation regarding these behaviors are discussed in Chapters 14 and 15.

Harm Reduction Strategies

Many individuals have a long history of being reinforced by their addictive behavior as well as suffering increasingly frequent and severe negative consequences. Relapse rates are disconcertingly high (around 70 percent for a single attempt). Abstinence (or moderation) may be very difficult to establish, and may take several attempts over an extended period of time. Thus, the concept of harm reduction as a treatment strategy is important. A principal feature of **harm reduction** is the acceptance that some addicts cannot be expected to cease their problematic behavior at the present time. Harm reduction is defined as attempts to (a) sever connections of the addictive behavior from its consequences to self or others (e.g., heroin use from heroin overdoses), (b) slowly or in small steps change the form of the addictive behavior to a less dangerous one (e.g., injectable to oral form, or heroin to methadone perhaps), and (c) eventually lead to cessation or minimal harm (Duncan, Nicholson, Clifford, Hawkins, & Petosa, 1994; Marlatt, Somers, & Tapert, 1993; Pentz, Sussman, & Newman, 1997). Harm reduction, as tertiary prevention or treatment strategy, is respectful of responsible decision-making, emphasizing the need to understand an individual's fluctuating ability to control his or her behavior (Erickson, 1995).

Harm reduction focuses on short-term goals that are accessible and achievable (Single, 1995). For example, a harm reduction approach goal might be to gradually guide an individual away from engaging in problem behaviors as well as to reduce the risks associated with involvement in target behaviors (Marlatt et al., 1993). Alternative behaviors may be seen as less immediately harmful and a step in the direction of decreased risk. In the example just mentioned, methadone use might be considered a relatively safe substitute behavior for another problem behavior, such as heroin addiction.

Much of the harm reduction work has been on *tobacco, alcohol,* or *other drug use* addictions, and *risky sexual behavior.* Harm reduction programs began in the United Kingdom with drug abusers being prescribed controlled dosages of heroin and cocaine for maintenance of their habits. The Netherlands subsequently adopted a policy in which drug addicts and users were viewed as normal citizens and not as criminals or dependent persons (Marlatt, Larimer, & Witkiewitz, 2012). Currently, many harm reduction strategies for tobacco, alcohol, and substance abuse have been implemented in various countries, including use of pharmacological adjuncts (e.g., nicotine gum, patch, or inhaler) in place of cigarette smoking, designated driver programs for drunk drivers, needle exchange programs (to decrease the risk of contracting HIV, hepatitis C, and other bloodborne diseases transmitted by shared needles), legal needle sales, methadone maintenance programs (see discussion of pharmacological treatments in Chapter 14), and gradual detoxification programs for drug addicts where they can legally obtain a daily dose under the care of a physician to help minimize physical withdrawals.

Other beneficial harm reduction tactics used in various private community settings such as clinics or "street settings" include the instruction in safe methods of inhalant huffing, instruction in methods of safer sex and the distribution of condoms, AIDS awareness, and the use of marijuana (and sometimes tobacco) as a maintenance drug for other drugs (see Marlatt et al., 2012; Pentz et al., 1997; Swartz, 2010). Some research suggests that harm reduction approaches may decrease disease prevalence (e.g., STDs) and arrest rates, and may lead to eventual abstinence though much more research is needed (Marlatt et al., 2012).

Non-Drug Addictions

Very little research on harm reduction and *food addiction* or the *behavioral addictions* exists. The only work I could locate was on setting *Internet* restrictions, which may or may not be considered an example of harm reduction. Also, instruction in *safer sexual behavior* may or may not serve as a harm reduction strategy for sex addiction, though there is some research on harm reduction and safer sex completed (Marlatt et al., 2012). Harm reduction is an approach to at least consider in future work as more knowledge accumulates on the treatment of behavioral addictions.

History of Cessation Treatment: Drug Abuse and Other Addictions

Very few references to treatment are mentioned in historical sources prior to the 1800s. Generally, early on, individuals with addiction problems, mostly alcohol-related, sought assistance from religious authorities, or they were detained and "dried out" by legal authorities or sometimes sought the assistance of physicians or faith healers (Sussman & Ames, 2008). According to some sources, addicts were, to the extent possible, tolerated within society and would continue to work or go to school if not disruptive to others (Levinthal, 2005; White, 2005). It is not clear how effective these strategies were in reducing addiction-related problems.

From 1820 to 1940, treatment approaches included beginning to perceive inebriates (alcoholics) as "sick" rather than as simply immoral, pairing off reformed drunkards with those still having problems (the use of a "pathfinder" which may have influenced the notion of sponsorship in 12-step programs), engaging reformed drunkards as lecturers on their former degradation and current redemption, use of lodging houses and inebriate asylums, providing rewards for improvement, emphasizing use of relaxation and rest, and developing fulfilling roles for reformed drunkards in a life of service and spirituality (see McCarthy, 1984, on the Emmanuel Movement). The *moral treatment* approach involved community support to help direct the individual away from alcohol or other drug use. Inebriate homes were established to provide for short-term stays, followed by affiliation with local recovery support groups (White, 2005). In addition, religion-oriented urban rescue missions and rural colonies formed (e.g., the Water Street Mission opened in 1872).

Starting in the mid-1900s, many communities adopted public detoxification facilities for alcoholics and drug addicts. These types of facilities were popular in Europe, but trends toward criminalization led to a relatively low number of these facilities in the United States. In the 1940s and 1950s, several developments led to the "modern alcoholism movement" (White, 2005). The "Big Book" of Alcoholics Anonymous was published in 1939, and was reviewed positively by leading popular and scientific journals of that year (e.g., *New York Times, Lancet*). The advent and growth of Alcoholics Anonymous (AA) led to renewed hope about the prospects of long-term recovery (it is discussed in Chapter 15 of this text). The Research Council on Problems of Alcohol and the Yale Center of Studies on Alcohol were created. The "Minnesota Model" of treatment of substance abuse was developed, evolving from the combined program ideas and philosophies of the Wilmar State Hospital treatment program, Hazelden (a private treatment facility), and the Minneapolis Veterans Administration Hospital Program (Nurses Research Publication, 1999; White, 2005). This model emphasized (1) inpatient or residential care for a few weeks or months; (2) a focus on psychoactive substance use disorder with little or no attention to associated psychiatric conditions or individual psychosocial factors; (3) use of AA concepts, resources, and precepts including the "12 steps" being central to recovery; (4) referral to self-help groups such as AA on discharge from residential or inpatient care, with limited or no ongoing professional treatment; (5) provision of limited family therapy, although the family may be oriented to AA principles and Al-Anon (a 12-step group for the family members of alcoholics who, in general, meet separately from the alcoholic family member); and (6) non-acceptance of psychotherapy and pharmacotherapy for either substance abuse or psychiatric disorders. In addition, in 1958, the Synanon drug treatment program was established, marking the beginning of the *therapeutic community*, in which the treatment agents include a community of staff and other patients. Twelve-step programs for the other behavioral addictions began subsequently, as was mentioned in Chapter 1.

Substance abuse treatment seems to have been heading toward specialization of treatment methods at least since the mid-1970s (e.g., dual diagnosis, family dynamics, high-profile clients, counseling disabled clients; see Nurses Research Publication, 1999) and ascertainment of addictions counseling competency and accountability (White, 2005). Treatment programs are now being tailored to a variety of populations (e.g., children, adults, individuals, and groups) and utilize a variety of treatment agents (e.g., medical doctors, psychologists, social workers, nurses, or recovering addicts). Programs are provided in a variety of settings (e.g., hospitals, outpatient clinics, prisons, and inpatient or residential programs) and utilize a variety of treatment models (e.g., AA, NA, milieu, cognitive-behavioral, behavioral, and pharmacologic).

Non-Drug Addictions

Consideration of treatment programming and professional organizations for multiple addictions has now begun (e.g., Orford, 2001; Rosenberg & Feder, 2014a; Sussman et al., 2011b). I have already mentioned several of the other 12-step programs that sprang up after AA (e.g., Gamblers Anonymous, in 1957; Exercise Addicts Anonymous which is just beginning; see Chapter 1 of this text and Table 1.1). An annual meeting now has just been initiated to share ideas on etiology and treatment of the behavioral addictions; the first and second meetings of the International Conference of Behavioral Addictions met in Budapest, Hungary in March 2013 and 2015 (http://icba.mat.org.hu/). The third meeting met in Geneva, Switzerland in March 2016 (www.icba2016.org/). Inpatient and outpatient treatment settings exist now for food disorders (generally though in community mental health settings, binge eating is secondary to anorexia nervosa/bulimia nervosa treatment), gambling, Internet addiction, sex and love addiction, and there are some inpatient treatment settings for shopping, exercise, and work addictions as co-occurring addictions (e.g., www.recovery.org/topics/gambling-addiction-recovery/; www.recovery.org/topics/Internet-addiction-recovery/; www.recovery.org/topics/sex-addiction-recovery/; www.recovery.org/topics/love-addiction-recovery/; www.recovery.org/topics/shopping-addiction-recovery/; www.recovery.org/topics/exercise-addiction-recovery/; www.recovery.org/topics/work-addiction-recovery/).

The treatment of multiple addictions currently is progressing toward a multidisciplinary approach to the problem. As new knowledge about drug dependence or a behavioral addiction is revealed, this new information is being translated into additional treatment methods. Treatment increasingly focuses on identifying the addictive behavior-dependent individual and on prevention of the progression of the dependence.

In general, there is a blending of therapeutic influences in these settings derived from various combinations of cognitive-behavioral therapy (see Chapter 14 of this text) and 12-step programming (Nurses Research Publication, 1999; Sussman & Ames, 2008; see Chapter 15 of this text). This chapter and the next two summarize the major treatments considered (and some novel entries), mainly tested for treatment of substance use disorders but also for other addictions as per availability of theoretical or empirical literature. While the present chapter provides an overview of cessation, Chapter 14 reviews specific intrapersonal approaches and Chapter 15 reviews extra-personal approaches.

While numerous changes are occurring in treatment nowadays, third-party payment options are limited for most of these addictions – unless they are diagnosable within the DSM-V or ICD schemes. Thus, treatment of substance use disorders, gambling disorder, and some other addictions (e.g., if considered as examples of obsessive-compulsive or impulse control disorders) might be subsidized through insurance.

"Stages" of Recovery Models

A generic treatment model which considers stages of recovery is depicted in Figure 13.1.

The general idea of a stages-of-recovery model is that the person suffering from addiction arrests immediate physical and lifestyle consequences first and then gradually learns how to live life without the addiction. There are several addiction cessation treatment stage models. In certain ways these models overlap. For example, all of the models concur that recovery is a developmental process that varies from individual to individual, progressing in stages, and that relapse is always a possibility. Unfortunately, there is little empirical support for any these approaches. They do guide clinical treatment, however.

Mueller and Ketcham Model

This model highlights that comprehensive addictions treatment programs include formalized phases to guide "addicts" through "healing" changes in their behavior, including (a) stabilization, (b) early recovery, and (c) middle-to-late recovery (e.g., Mueller & Ketcham, 1987). During stabilization, goals include initial detoxification or withdrawal from substances, or psychological withdrawal from another addiction, assessment of any comorbid psychological problems, medical care for health-related problems, and nutritional status assessment. While it is known that victims of various addictions report withdrawal-like symptoms (e.g., Grant, Potenza, Weinstein, & Gorelick, 2010), it is not known how long such symptoms last. Thus, it is not clear for how long one might consider providing a stabilization period in treatment of various behavioral addictions. Erring on the side of caution, it might be wise to have someone who is suffering from a behavioral addiction do very little for a day or two prior to having them enter "early recovery." There needs to be some time to experience psychological withdrawal in a safe environment, where informal social support is readily available. However, while cravings are likely to be experienced with some regularity, the addict should be prompted into early recovery very soon; prior to thinking too much about leaving the treatment setting.

Early recovery typically includes treatment planning for the change of behavior for the long term, involving use of cognitive-behavioral therapies, skills training,

"Stages" of Recovery Models

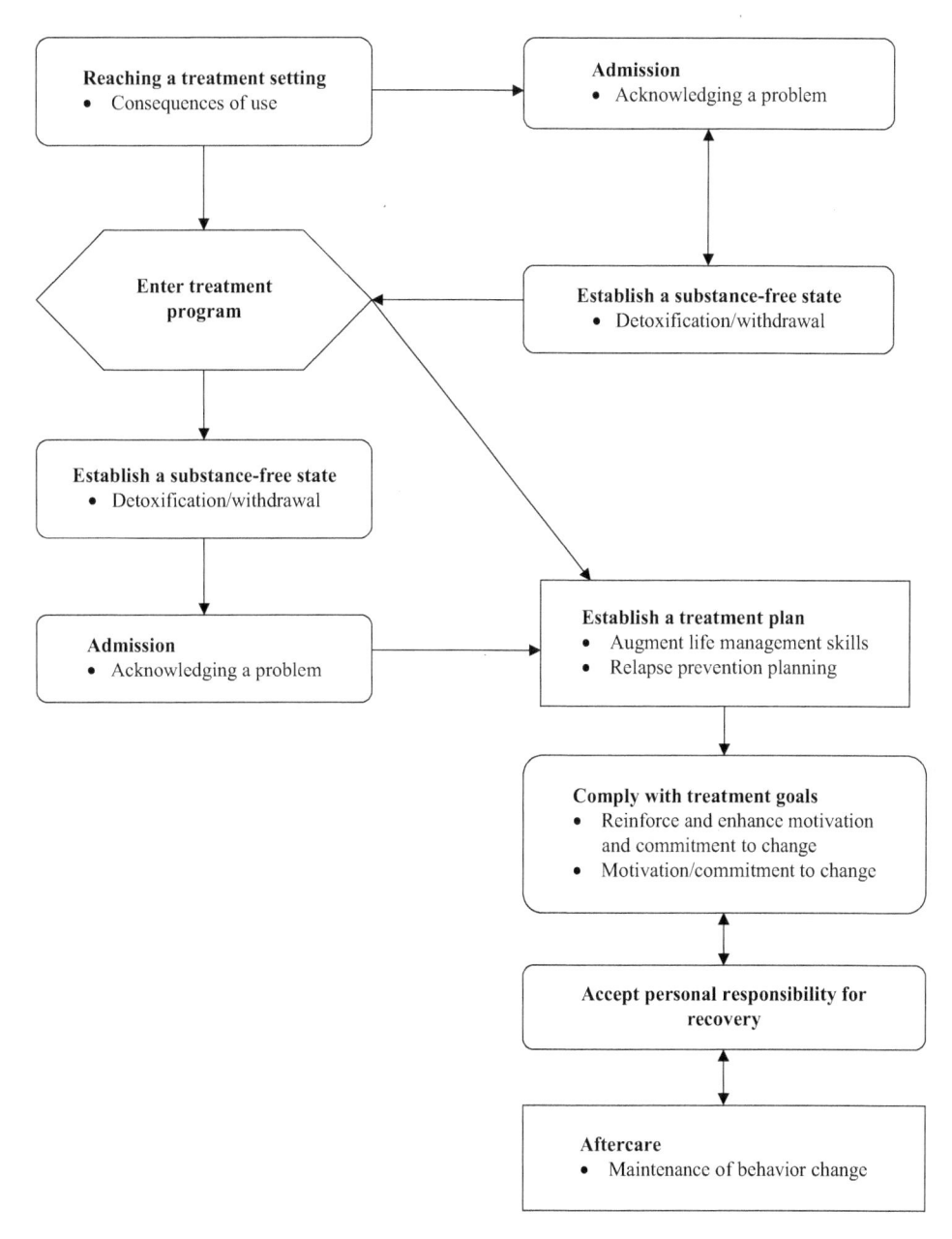

Figure 13.1 A substance abuse treatment process model (Sussman & Ames, 2001, 2008)

counseling, and rehabilitative therapies. Oftentimes, recovery reading material and workbooks are provided at that time. The treatment planned should fit the severity of the addiction, but also be manageable enough such that the addict will be retained in treatment.

Middle-to-late recovery typically includes instruction in relapse prevention and provision of aftercare programs. With most addictions for most persons, once arrested, attempt at controlled engagement is likely to lead to failure (though, as discussed earlier in this chapter, may be essential regarding eating, Internet, love, sex, work, shopping, or exercise). Learning alternative, moderate ways of living is essential at this point in recovery.

Johnson Model

Johnson (1980) proposed a widely used scheme of recovery that introduces four stages which indicate changes in treatment motivation. Individuals progress through the following stages of recovery: *admission, compliance, acceptance,* and *surrender*. The first stage of *admission* occurs when individuals enter treatment settings and accept or admit that they have a serious problem with an addiction. The second phase of recovery is *compliance*. Compliance involves a change in an individual's attitude from resisting to complying with treatment. **Resistance** is an individual's unwillingness to change or participate in his or her treatment and can be problematic. Without compliance, it is unlikely that cognitive and behavioral changes will occur. The third stage of recovery, *acceptance*, involves that point when one takes personal responsibility for one's own recovery. According to Johnson, this occurs when an individual gains some insight into the severity of his or her problem. Gratitude may replace feelings of alienation from others. During this stage, there exists an increase of self-awareness and self-acceptance, and congruency in an individual's verbalizations, affect, and body language. Individuals presenting for treatment come to recognize that they are responsible to engage themselves in a process of recovery to overcome the addiction (Marlatt, 1985; Zweben, 1993).

The fourth stage of recovery, *surrender*, is signaled by an "appropriate display of caution about the future" and the realization that aftercare is necessary for the continued maintenance of change. At this time, individuals may need the support of groups, such as AA and NA, or a program for a behavioral addiction (e.g., Gambler's Anonymous), to help cope with future difficulties. At this stage of recovery, individuals are ready for outpatient programs and sober-living homes. The beginning of a lifelong path of vigilance is set in motion, to not fall back into the "pit" of that addiction.

Gorski and Miller Model

Gorski and Miller (1984, 1986) developed another more detailed formal model of the stages of recovery involving a series of developmental periods that affect physiological changes, including neurobiological changes and various goals for each developmental period. These developmental periods are as follows: (1) the *transition period* or recognition of the addiction and need to pursue abstinence as a lifestyle goal; (2) the *stabilization period*, which involves crisis management or recovery from acute withdrawal and symptoms of post-acute withdrawal (see Chapter 14 for a discussion of post-acute withdrawal symptoms); (3) the *early recovery period*, or acceptance and healthy coping (e.g., how to replace addictive thoughts, feelings, and behaviors with sobriety-based thoughts feelings and behavior); (4) the *middle recovery period*, at which time balanced living becomes a goal and repairing lifestyle damage is engaged in;

(5) the *late recovery period*, which involves personality changes, and resolution of family of origin issues, to maximize quality of recovery; and (6) the *maintenance period*, which entails continuation of a significant period of growth and development, and sets in action an ongoing recovery maintenance program.

The Importance of Motivation

Motivation is an essential component of the cessation of any addiction and the maintenance of behavior change. Motivation varies between individuals and may fluctuate within an individual at any given time during an effort to stop engaging in a behavior addictively and during the maintenance of change (Sussman & Ames, 2008). Several definitions of the concept of motivation for change have been proposed. Motivation may be a function of goals (*direction*) or tendencies to act (*energy*) (Bindra & Stewart, 1966). That is, motivation may be defined by the goal objective and amount of work that one is willing to put in to achieve that goal. Additionally, the motivational source may be extrapersonal or intrapersonal (i.e., stem from social sources or from within the person). Conversely, others view motivation as an intrapersonal *state of readiness* to change (e.g., DiClemente et al., 1991; Miller & Rollnick, 2013; Prochaska & DiClemente, 1982). Conceptually, definitions of motivation all describe awareness of discrepancies between possible desired goals and current states (also see Nezami, Sussman, & Pentz, 2003). While negative consequences experienced due to the addiction may drive initial thoughts of change, there are various models of motivation that might actually "drive" behavior. I describe four models of motivation that, in principle, might be applied to cessation of any of the 11 focal addictions in future research. These models are depicted in Figure 13.2.

Motivation
In the field of health behavior, motivation refers to the willingness and ability to overcome unpleasant affect to achieve improved physical and emotional wellbeing

Direction–Energy model of motivation
Addresses the need to consider two components of motivation – a goal and the energy to reach that goal

Transtheoretical model of motivation
Consists of a series of stages of change with early stages involving commitment to a goal, and later stages involving skills to complete the goal

Intrinsic–Extrinsic model of motivation
Proposes that goals are more likely to be obtained if the individual identifies with the desirability of obtaining the goal as opposed to some external reward

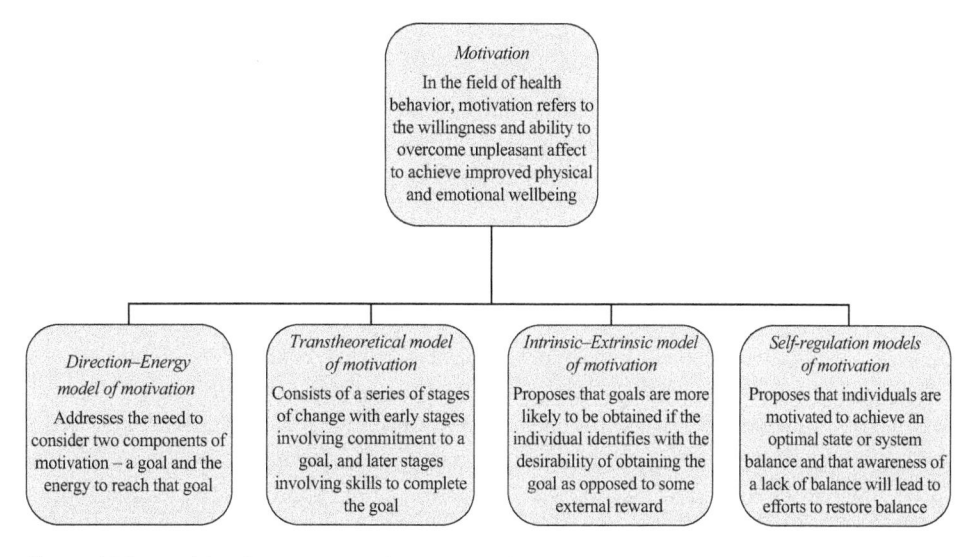

Self-regulation models of motivation
Proposes that individuals are motivated to achieve an optimal state or system balance and that awareness of a lack of balance will lead to efforts to restore balance

Figure 13.2 Models of motivation relevant to addictions treatment (also appears in Sussman & Ames, 2008)

Direction–Energy Model

The *direction-energy model* addresses the need to consider two components of motivation – a *goal* and the *energy* to reach that goal (Bindra & Stewart, 1966; Emmons, Glasgow, Marcus, Rakowski, & Curry, 1995; Miller & Rollnick, 2013; Sussman, 1996; Young, 1936). According to Sussman (1996), (a) a desire for self-image change, (b) curiosity, and (c) a desire for mood enhancement guide the goal component of motivation. The amount of energy invested in behavior change is guided by (a) perceiving a match between one's behavioral responses with the demands of reaching the goal. In addition, the amount of energy invested in change is guided by (b) one's embeddedness in a lifestyle about which a comfortable end state is perceived to be reachable and (c) social or intrapersonal pressure to change (e.g., fear; Sutton & Eiser, 1984).

Transtheoretical Model

The **Transtheoretical Model** (DiClemente et al., 1991; Prochaska, 2008; Prochaska & DiClemente, 1982; Prochaska, DiClemente, Velicer, Ginpil, S., & Norcross, 1985; Prochaska, Velicer, DiClemente, Guadagnoli, & Rossi, 1990) consists of a series of stages of change with early stages involving establishing a commitment to a goal and later stages providing the energy to complete the goal. According to this model, an individual's *state of readiness* for change is conceptualized as his or her motivation for change. I discuss it here as a model of motivation. However, some researchers and practitioners might also consider it a model of stages of recovery. This model includes five stages.

The first is *pre-contemplation*, which is marked by a lack of interest in change. The second is *contemplation*: the realization of a problem, the evaluation of the consequences of one's present behavior, and consideration of behavior change. The third stage is *preparation*, when individuals are motivated to make behavioral changes; individuals focus on actions that will bring about behavior change. The fourth stage is *action*, the actual change attempt and willingness to stay abstinent or controlled even though experiencing withdrawal symptoms. The final stage is *maintenance*, which reflects an individual's efforts to avoid relapse and solidify changes made.

Intrinsic–Extrinsic Motivation Model

The **Intrinsic-Extrinsic Motivation Model** proposes that goals are more likely to be obtained if the individual identifies with the desirability of obtaining that goal, as opposed to reaching the goal for some other, extrinsic reward (Curry, Wagner, & Grothaus, 1990). Different strategies, including motivational interviewing and proximal goal setting, have been shown to enhance intrinsic motivation (Manderlink & Harackiewicz, 1984). Several theories of behavior change emphasize intrinsic motivation (e.g., Health Behavior Model: Becker, 1974; Protection Motivation Theory: Rogers, 1975). Other theories focus on socioenvironmental elements (extrinsic rewards) that facilitate or motivate change (e.g., Social Learning Theory: Rotter,

1954), whereas others combine personal (intrinsic) and social (extrinsic) aspects as influencing motivation for behavior change (e.g., Theory of Reasoned Action: Fishbein & Ajzen, 1975). There is an indication that extrinsic motivation will work as well as intrinsic motivation as long as extrinsic reinforcement pertains to behavior that is performance dependent (see Nezami et al., 2003).

Self-Regulation (System) Models of Motivation

Self-regulation models of motivation propose that individuals are motivated to achieve an optimal appetitive state or system balance and that awareness of a lack of balance will lead to efforts to restore balance. Physiological mechanisms and self-initiated behavior are pursued to reach homeostasis of an ideal state (Sommers, 1972). In other words, individuals seek to reach a desirable subjective state (e.g., level of arousal: O'Connor, 1989), level of coping or store of psychosocial assets (Leventhal, Diefenbach, & Leventhal, 1992; Ockene, Nutall, Benfari, Hurwitz, & Ockene, 1981), or physiological homeostasis (tendency toward a relatively stable equilibrium between interdependent elements: Sommers, 1972). This model may be most consistent with an appetitive state–satiation model of addiction.

Summary

This chapter introduced general concepts of cessation, including what leads one to change behavior on one's own (natural recovery) or get into treatment, general treatment goals, the history of cessation programming pertaining mostly to substance misuse, and stages of recovery and the types and importance of motivation. Based on available research, at least a third of people who suffer an addictive problem appear to resolve that problem without formal treatment; possibly only 15 percent of persons suffering from an addiction will receive formalized treatment and many of them will relapse. Of those who do receive formal treatment (voluntarily or involuntarily), relapse for a single attempt may be as high as 50–75 percent of those who attempt to quit their addiction of choice (Heyman, 2013b; Sussman & Ames, 2008). Of those who do quit one addiction, some percentage may end up suffering from another addiction (e.g., quitting alcohol and becoming a sex addict, gambling addict, or workaholic; Sussman & Black, 2008). Very recently, there are inpatient recovery centers that will accept a wide variety of addiction problems, not just a substance use disorder. Whatever informal or formalized treatment is attempted, with whatever addiction, motivation to change appears vitally important. For example, in one study on teen tobacco use cessation, baseline motivation and program-induced motivation enhancement together mediated 50 percent of the smoking cessation effect (McCuller, Nutall, Benfari, Hurwitz, & Ockene, 2006). The next two chapters will present intrapersonal and extrapersonal treatment strategies that have been used or could be used with the 11 focal addictions. Guided by motivation to change, these strategies hold promise for cessation of the addictions, as will be discussed.

Bulleted Summary

- Undesired consequences of one's addictive behavior lead to cessation attempts. At least a third of persons suffering from addictions quit without formalized treatment. A ***stepped-care approach*** to cessation involves gradually structuring treatment based on severity and length of time the person has suffered from the addiction.
- Based on available research, only perhaps 15 percent of addicts receive formalized treatment. Consideration of abstinence versus moderation as the goal of treatment may lead to more people considering means to normalize their behavior. Harm reduction may assist one at the beginning of treatment to arrest consequences and gradually grapple with the addiction.
- Formalized addictions treatment has had a relatively brief history; throughout history the main treatment providers have ended up being family members, the clergy, or enforcement agents. Treatment facilities, pathfinders, and 12-step programs have been considered only over the last 100 years or so.
- Stages of recovery models include those of Mueller and Ketcham, Johnson, and Gorski and Miller, in general involving stabilization, and early, middle, and late recovery. Motivation is the driving force behind cessation and models include direction–energy, transtheoretical, intrinsic–extrinsic, and self-regulation aspects.

Suggestions for Further Reading

Grigsby, T., Forster, M., & Sussman, S. (2015a). A perspective on cigarette smoking during alcohol and substance use treatment. *Substance Use & Misuse*, 50: 1199–1204.

Heyman, G. M. (2013b). Quitting drugs: Quantitative and qualitative features. *Annual Review of Clinical Psychology*, 9: 29–59.

Johnson, V. E. (1980). *I'll Quit Tomorrow: A Practical Guide to Alcoholism Treatment*. San Francisco, CA: Harper & Row.

Nezami, E., Sussman, S., & Pentz, M. A. (2003). Motivation in tobacco use cessation research. *Substance Use & Misuse*, 38: 25–50.

Prochaska, J. O. (2008). Decision making in the transtheoretical model of behavior change. *Medical Decision Making*, 28: 845–849.

Sussman, S. & Ames, S. L. (2008). *Drug Abuse: Concepts, Prevention and Cessation*. Cambridge University Press.

14 Cessation: Intrapersonal-Level Approaches

Learning Objectives

- To learn about detoxification and pharmacotherapy approaches
- To learn about the application of cognitive-behavioral and motivational interviewing therapies to the 11 focal addictions
- To learn about cue exposure and implicit-cognition strategies in cessation of the addictions
- To learn about relapse and relapse prevention of the 11 focal addictions

Introduction

For a couple of years, Johnny did receive medication for generalized anxiety disorder. A psychiatrist thought it might also help reduce his alcohol intake. He took selective serotonergic and dopaminergic reuptake inhibitors as prescribed. He thought that they might have dampened his addictive tendencies a little. He was curious about that. However, he did not feel that much of a difference of an effect on his anxiety and eventually discontinued their use. He looked around for a cognitive-behavioral therapist. He thought that maybe irrational thinking or impulsive responses were part of his problem. However, he could not locate any reputable cognitive-behavioral therapists that were covered by his health insurance plan. He saw a couple a counselors for both his addictions and anxiety but they were 12-step oriented. The counselors seemed to think that the anxiety might be part of an addictive personality (being restless, irritable, and discontent), and that Johnny needed to reach out to a Higher Power, go to AA meetings, and work the steps. Johnny was not convinced that they were correct. He could not handle that sort of counseling for more than a couple of months. He did stay sober from alcohol with or without outside help for months at a time, and experienced improvements at work (sometimes experiencing workaholic binges). However, triggering events led him to relapse. For example, after being sober 100 days, a person who worked in a liquor store recognized him and motioned non-verbally to a friend that Johnny liked to drink. Johnny observed this behavior and took offense by the implication that he might be a drunk. Upset, he "went out" and drank. On another occasion, after having difficulty with a staff person at work, Johnny blamed himself for not exhibiting good self-control. To punish himself after 60 days of sobriety, he drank and then met strangers on the Internet who "really understood him." He felt he might have several intrapsychic issues, wanted some type of private therapy, but he often felt hopeless about obtaining such treatment.

Cessation: Intrapersonal-Level Approaches

Intrapersonal strategies of cessation target the individual directly, not the social environment. Pharmacotherapy, cognitive-behavior therapy, motivational interviewing, cue exposure therapy, implicit cognition-related strategies, and relapse prevention strategies are the techniques presented in this chapter.

Detoxification and Pharmacotherapy

Detoxification: General Information

Drug addiction recovery differs from other addictions in that the initial stage (i.e., stabilization, mentioned in Chapter 13) may demand a period of detoxification. **Detoxification** or managed withdrawal from drugs involves removing the toxic materials from an individual's body. Many people "detox" from a drug or drugs in private, without going into formalized treatment. They may suffer a range of symptoms (e.g., sweating, heart palpitations, difficulties sleeping, irritability, difficulty concentrating, or cravings). Sometimes a friend stands by to assist, perhaps providing less and less of a drug to gradually wean (taper) the drug abuser off of the drug or drugs. Many others go into formalized treatment to better reduce medical risks of withdrawal (e.g., seizures, sleep disturbances, perceptual distortions; see Trevisan, Boutros, Petrakis, & Krystal, 1998, regarding alcohol withdrawal), or to be monitored so as to successfully complete the withdrawal process instead of opting for continued use of a drug or drugs.

As an institutionalized process, detoxification generally involves a three- to five-day inpatient stay (e.g., a "72-hour hold") at a detoxification facility with 24-hour intensive medical management. For those persons physiologically dependent on a drug, the individual is likely to suffer relatively severe withdrawal symptoms that need to be managed to reduce potential for medical complications (e.g., with alcohol, opiates, or benzodiazepines, could include seizures, aspiration of vomitus, dehydration, or acute psychosis). Evaluation is very important because medical aspects of detoxification are contingent on the type of drug abused. Pharmacotherapy might help not only with withdrawal symptoms but also with associated features of drug addiction (e.g., such as anxiety or depression, or craving).

In behavioral addictions, the "withdrawal" is more psychological and mood related. Certainly there may be neurotransmission adjustments involved. For example, with frequent repetition of the addictive behavior, one may conjecture that there would be some reduction in manufacture of endogenous ligands (e.g., mesolimbic dopamine), or reliance on the behavior for release of available ligands from the pre-synapse. However, there are no dangerous abrupt withdrawal effects that demand immediate medical attention (Grant et al., 2010). The notion of "detoxification" for addictions that are not directly and obviously physiologically addicting may seem far-fetched, though there are at least two related reasons to take such a perspective. First, as introduced earlier in this text, all of the addictions involve withdrawal-like phenomena, in particular, difficulties concentrating, irritability/anxiety, and cravings to engage in the addiction of choice. Removing individuals from their usual social environments may assist them in obtaining a temporary reprieve from their addiction and give them some time to get motivated to abstain. Second, for severe cases of behavioral addiction, persons may not be able to stop engaging in the behavior for more than very brief periods, necessitating the need for a formalization of a period of time insulated away from opportunity to engage in the addiction. Various recovery centers do provide residential treatment for any number of addictions – at a price. Thus, there is recognition of a "detoxification" (or "withdrawal" or "stabilization") for any addiction, physiological, learned, or both. There is no research on the utility of such a treatment notion.

Pharmacotherapy: General Information

Pharmacotherapies for drug abuse may serve a variety of functions. As just presented, they may ease withdrawal symptoms. In addition, targets for pharmacotherapy include (a) reducing intoxication or overdoses, (b) assisting with abstinence initiation, (c) relapse prevention, or (d) assisting with associated symptomatology (e.g., agitation, depression). Types of drugs used include agonists (which mimic the effects of endogenous [naturally occurring] neurotransmitters), antagonists (which counteract the effects of endogenous neurotransmitters), and aversive-negative reinforcement type drugs. **Agonists** provide similar effects as the drug of choice but are relatively safe or produce fewer psychotropic (disabling) effects. **Antagonists** block the effect of the drug of choice, so that the person using them will not experience pleasant effects when using the drug of choice. Some drugs produce subjectively aversive effects if the drug of choice is used (the aversive-negative reinforcement drugs).

Similarly, pharmacotherapy might be considered for behavioral addictions to (a) reduce enjoyment of the addiction (e.g., serotonin reuptake inhibitors [SSRIs] may reduce sexual response and make sex addiction less enjoyable), (b) reduce cravings and perhaps aid in relapse prevention, and (c) assist with associated symptomatology (e.g., depressed affect or anxiety). Unfortunately, as will be described below, most pharmacotherapy for the behavioral addictions is speculative and has little empirical support.

Detoxification and Pharmacotherapy with Drug Addictions

I provide a very brief summary here for tobacco, alcohol, and opiate detoxification and pharmacotherapy. These are three prototypical examples of how drugs might be used as treatment adjuncts (more details are in Chapter 16 of Sussman & Ames, 2008; see also www.drugabuse.gov/publications/principles-drug-addiction-treatment/evidence-based-approaches-to-drug-addiction-treatment/pharmacotherapies). (Also see Blum et al., 2016. These authors assert a claim for the potential restorative use of pharmacotherapy, which is beyond the scope of the present discussion. In short, prolonged involvement in various addictions may lead to long-term changes in brain function, suggesting alterations in gene activity [epigenetic effects] and amino acid deficiency. Use of neuronutrient-amino-acid therapy [NAAT] may be a means to restore mesolimbic dopamine in the reward system and possibly reduce craving [Blum et al., 2016].)

Tobacco

There are seven primary recommended medications to assist in *tobacco cessation* among adults (Fiori et al., 2008). These include buprorion SR (which may block reuptake of dopamine, norepinephrine, or nicotinic acetylcholinergic receptors, serving an agonist substitution function perhaps), varenicline (which is a partial nicotine agonist and antagonist), and five nicotine-containing products (nicotine gum, nicotine inhaler, nicotine lozenge, nicotine nasal spray, and nicotine patch, which may serve an agonist function as well as ease withdrawal). Other possible pharmacotherapies either show promise but have less research support (e.g., use of clonidine [an antihypertensive medication] or nortriptyline [a triclyclic antidepressant]; Fiori et al., 2008), or may have little research support and might even be dangerous (e.g., use of e-cigarettes; Chapman, 2015).

Alcohol

Various drugs are used to help in the acute and post-acute withdrawal from *alcohol* abuse; the list of these drugs is provided by Julien (2005, p. 120; also see updated edition by Advokat, Comaty, & Julien, 2014). Librium and other benzodiazepines are used to ease withdrawal symptoms. Other medications used with alcohol include carbamazepine (mood stabilizer; may reduce withdrawal), γ-hydroxybutyrate (GHB; may reduce withdrawal symptoms), disulfiram and calcium carbimide (which allow aldehyde accumulation, resulting in noxious effects if any alcohol intake occurs; these drugs are also used for relapse prevention), naltrexone (reduces opioid receptor-related effects, reduces consumption), acamprosate (GABA modulator, reduces craving), SSRIs and buspirone (reduces depression or anxiety-related symptoms), ondansetron and ritanserin (serotonin antagonist; may reduce craving), and bromocriptine (dopamine agonist; may reduce craving).

Opioids

Treatment of *opioid* withdrawal may involve a variety of pharmacological approaches. One may use symptomatic medication (agonists such as methadone and/or L-α-acetylmethadol [LAAM]), clonidine (which is used to treat high blood pressure and may relieve craving), use of ultrarapid detoxification (heavy sedation with an anesthetic and use of an antagonist such as naltrexone or nalozone; e.g., Salimi et al., 2014), or use of buprenorphine (which has both agonist and antagonist properties; for a recent review, see Mattick, Breen, Kimber, & Davoli, 2014). Methadone may do better than buprenorphine in retaining people in treatment though both drugs are about equivalent in suppressing illicit opioid use (Mattick et al., 2014). In addition, for easing opiate withdrawal, darvon (propoxphene), methadone, or a combination of naloxone with clonidine, while the patient is under sedation, have been used.

Use of Pharmacotherapy with Non-Drug Addictions

Pharmacotherapy with *food addiction*-related behavior was discussed by Davis, Edge, and Gold (2014), including mention of Lorcaserin (may be satiety inducing, and an agonist targeting a specific serotonin receptor, 5-HT$_{2C}$; e.g., see http://en.wikipedia.org/wiki/Lorcaserin), Qsymia (combines an appetite suppressant [phentermine] with a migraine medication [topiramate]), Contrive (combines buprorion and naltrexone), tesofensine (combines norepinephrine, serotonin, and dopamine reuptake inhibitors), metformin (antihyperglycemic agent), Exenatide or Liraglutide (antidiabetic medications), pramlintide (adjunct for diabetes), and Empatic (combines antiepileptic [zonisamide SR] with bupropion SR). While Lorcaserin and Qsymia have been tested with promise for weight control among overweight and obese individuals, the overall discussion by Davis et al. (2014) was speculative and no applications to BED or food addictions have been tested as yet.

Pharmacotherapy has been utilized with *compulsive gamblers* (Grant & Odlaug, 2014), including use of opioid antagonists (e.g., naltrexone, nalmefene), and glutamatergic agents (e.g., N-acetylcysteine, NAC), with some success over periods as long as 18 weeks. Use of antidepressants (e.g., sertraline, paroxetine, fluvoxamine, escitalopram, or bupropion), lithium carbonate, anti-epileptics, and atypical antipsychotics has not revealed efficacious results for gambling or *Internet addiction disorder* (IAD). One research group has found weak evidence of the utility of buprorion (which may in part be a selective dopaminergic reuptake inhibitor) for problematic online gaming and IAD (Kiraly et al., 2014). One study indicated potential efficacy of use of methylphenidate (a dopamine reuptake inhibitor, used most often for treatment of ADHD) among 62 youth with IAD and ADHD after eight weeks of treatment (Han, Lee, Na, & Renshaw, 2009).

Pharmacotherapy for *sex addiction* was discussed by Rosenberg et al. (2014) and includes citalopram and other SSRIs, which have been found to decrease masturbation and pornography use, and selective norepinephrine reuptake inhibitors (SNRIs), anti-anxiety agents, anti-impulsive medications (e.g., lithium), ADHD medications (e.g., methylphenidate), naltrexone, and anti-androgens in extreme cases (to decrease sexual responsiveness). The only medication for which any research support was suggested was use of SSRIs.

Pharmacotherapy for *compulsive buying disorder* was discussed by Racine et al. (2014) and includes use of mood stabilizers (e.g., valproate, lithium), and antidepressants (e.g., buprorion, nortriptyline), which in combination have been found to reduce CBD. An SSRI, fluvoxamine, has been found to reduce preoccupation with shopping in both pilot and controlled trials (i.e., a two-group trial of drug versus placebo, subject n = 23, nine-week period; Black, Gabel, Hansen, & Schlosser, 2000).

It is interesting that there is an overlap among medications used for withdrawal or treatment of a variety of addictions. This either suggests that there are similar underlying mechanisms of action of different addictions, or perhaps reflects limitations in the advancement of pharmacotherapy for the addictions.

Cognitive-Behavior Therapies (CBT)

In early recovery and through later phases, different types of therapeutic regimens may be attempted. **Behavior modification interventions** historically address observable antecedents and consequences of a behavior without acknowledging cognitive mediation of behavior. Even so, behavior modification techniques consist of a variety of behavior-rewarding modeling, reinforcement, and guiding (shaping) experiences to change addictive behavior that may indirectly change cognitive processes. **Cognitive interventions** include strategies to directly modify thinking to enhance executive control or other cognitive processes (e.g., classically conditioned; implicit processes) to facilitate addictive behavior cessation. As a "cognitive behavior therapy" (CBT) approach, changing behavior patterns or frequency is instructed through use of any number of stimulus–organism–response–reinforcement techniques (SORR). These techniques alter effects of stimuli confronting the person (**stimulus control**), the way the person interprets these stimuli (**organism control**), responses the person emits (**response control**), or introduce new contingencies of reinforcement (**reinforcement control**; Goldfried & Davison, 1994; Gottman & Leiblum, 1974). CBT, in general, requires extensive training to deliver it adequately.

Certainly, CBT might be applied as both an extrapersonal-type treatment (e.g., Yau et al. [2014] mentioned use of CBT family therapy with binge eating disorder, but with no research evaluation having been conducted) and as an intrapersonal-type treatment (individual therapy or counseling). When CBT is viewed from an intrapersonal perspective, organism control techniques are particularly important. One major organism control technique is **problem-solving**. Problem-solving involves a series of steps in cessation programming, including generating as many behavioral options as possible to avoid engaging in the addictive behavior in different life circumstances, examining the benefits and costs of each behavioral option (e.g., switching behaviors, stopping the addictive behavior of choice, or beginning meditation to be more mindful), and then trying to make the best decision or set of decisions based on the available options with the most benefits and least costs. After this examination, one might make a commitment to that decision and act, knowing that one can always reevaluate the decision after trying things out (Sussman & Ames, 2008).

Directly modifying one's inner speech can be accomplished through use of such cognitive strategies as **cognitive restructuring** or **self-instructional training**. For example, when there is a self-defeating or irrational element to one's inner voice, cognitive restructuring helps in replacing or changing these cognitions. Cognitive restructuring involves recognizing and examining self-defeating cognitions and replacing them with self-fulfilling thoughts that may lead to a better, more rational direction of thought and behavior (Meichenbaum, 1977).

When elements of one's inner voice are missing (e.g., one is impulsive), self-instructional training may help in guiding the individual to regulate his or her behavior. Self-instructional training involves examining and recognizing missing cognitions and adding cognitions through practice (e.g., out loud, then subvocally, and then thinking about it) so that one is led to a better direction of thought and behavior (Meichenbaum, 1977).

CBT often includes other strategies that may enhance its purported strength. Motivational interviewing (MI) strategies (also discussed in this chapter), self-management of triggers or cravings to engage in the addiction, increasing consideration of alternative activities, interpersonal conflict skills, correcting cognitive biases involved in the addiction, relapse prevention, and sometimes imaginal desensitization are included along with what is generally considered CBT (Grant et al., 2009; Petry et al., 2006; Rash & Petry, 2014 [review included 25 studies]).

Tobacco, Alcohol, and Other Drug Addiction

Most CBT work has pertained to *substance use disorders* (e.g., Sussman & Ames, 2008). There have been numerous studies that have been completed regarding ATOD misuse and dependence. Effects tend to be maximized when combined with pharmacological treatments regarding tobacco cessation (Fiori et al., 2008), but a small, often non-significant effect of combined pharmacologic plus CBT treatment is found regarding alcohol or illicit substance use cessation (e.g., Magill & Ray, 2009). CBT appears to exert a significant though generally small main effect size in randomized controlled trials as applied to alcohol or other drug misuse (moderate effect for marijuana use; Magill & Ray, 2009). CBT is considered an evidence-based approach regarding tobacco, alcohol, and other drug misuse and dependence cessation (see Carroll et al., 1998; Fiori et al., 2008; Magill & Ray, 2009; Sussman & Ames, 2008).

CBT as Applied to Food Addiction

There is only one evaluated CBT trial of *food addiction*; that had considered food addiction as a moderator of outpatient obesity treatment (Lent, Eichen, Goldbacher, Wadden, & Foster, 2014), which failed to indicate a moderating effect on weight loss or attrition. However, there are some studies on BED (see Yau et al., 2014). Specific to BED, body image concerns and perfectionism may be addressed with CBT programming. Brownley et al. (Brownley, Berkman, Sedway, Lohr, & Bulik, 2007) systematically reviewed evidence on efficacy of treatment for BED. Twenty-six studies, including medication-only, medication plus behavioral intervention, and behavioral intervention only designs, met inclusion criteria. The strength of the evidence for medication and behavioral interventions was moderate, and for self-help and other interventions was weak. Individual or group CBT reduced binge eating and improved bingeing abstinence rates for up to four months after treatment but did not lead to weight loss.

Castelnuovo et al. (Castelnuovo, Manzoni, Villa, Cesa, & Molinari, 2011) described the results of the STRATOB (Systemic and STRATegic psychotherapy for OBesity) study, a two-group randomized controlled trial comparing Brief Strategic Therapy (BST; similar to extended MI, attempted solutions are discussed, use of reframing) with CBT (involving self-monitoring, goal setting, time management, problem-solving, cognitive restructuring, stress management, and relapse prevention) for the inpatient and telephone-based outpatient treatment of obese people with BED seeking treatment for weight reduction. Data were collected at baseline, at discharge from the hospital (one month after), and after six months from discharge. A significant association emerged between treatment groups and BED remission at six months in favor of BST (only 20 percent of patients in the BST group reported a number of weekly binge episodes >2 versus 63.3 percent in the CBT group).

Yau et al. (2014) reported outcomes of use of interpersonal psychotherapy (IPT) for BED (IPT is basically CBT with an interpersonal context emphasis; see http://interpersonalpsychotherapy.org/about-ipt/). IPT focuses on significant interpersonal events (e.g., death of a loved one, role disputes, role transitions), and management of impulsivity as a reaction to these events. That is, IPT is an intrapersonal self-control device used to elicit extrapersonal-level changes. IPT was noted as having an impact on number of binge episodes up to a four-year follow-up, in what appeared to be a single-subject design. In addition, another related treatment was mentioned (relational psychotherapy [stop relating to the world through food]; Yau et al., 2014), but no evaluations were provided for this other therapy. Yau et al. (2014) also described two other intrapersonal treatments, Dialectic Behavior Therapy (DBT: mindfulness, emotional regulation, and distress tolerance components), and nutritional counseling. Only one small DBT pilot study was completed, and no nutritional counseling impact studies were reported. The result of that work was only suggestive; research is needed.

Summary

In summary, the research on cessation of food addiction is lacking. The impact of CBT appears limited to short-term (four-month) impacts on episodes of binge eating (among persons suffering from BED) and related cognitive misperceptions, but has no impact on weight loss or control. IPT shows promise as well, though research is needed.

CBT as Applied to Behavioral Addictions

Cognitive restructuring is a CBT approach that has been demonstrated to be efficacious for *problem gambling*, often combined with other CBT components (Grant & Odlaug, 2014). In fact, Cowlishaw et al. (2012) examined 14 CBT randomized controlled trials of problem or pathological gambling cessation (n = 1,245). Eleven studies compared CBT with control comparison groups at 0- to 3-months post-treatment and showed medium to large beneficial effects of therapy. Only one study (n = 147), however, compared groups at 9- to 12-months follow-up and produced smaller effects that were not significant. In one rather unique study, eight-session CBT (in addition to referral to Gamblers Anonymous [GA]) had been found to provide significant improvements in pathological gambling behavior relative to those referred to GA only, and those in a workbook condition (plus GA) which, in turn, had been found to achieve marginal improvements over the GA-only referral condition at a 12-month follow-up (Petry et al., 2006). Basically, this means that in-person CBT programming with some extrinsic push for involvement may be relatively efficacious for the treatment of gambling addiction.

There is one review of *Internet addiction disorder* studies conducted in China (Liu, Liao, & Smith, 2012). The authors systematically reviewed the outcomes and methodological quality of 24 IAD treatment studies. The authors used 15 attributes from quality-of-evidence scores to evaluate the 24 outcome studies. Only sequence generation and intention-to-treat attributes were reported by more than 50 percent of the studies. CBT combined with family therapy or group therapy emerged as possibly efficacious treatments. CBT is being used for problematic online gaming, but there are no empirical studies completed (Kiraly et al., 2014). CBT plausibly might have participants engaged in cognitive restructuring to remove fantasy-based thinking (e.g., if there was over-identification with Internet online game avatars) that, if not intervened on, could lead to worsening of addictive behavior or relapse. Mood management techniques might be instructed to reduce the desire to search out external sources of relief such as online gaming or any electronic media. Research is needed.

Timmreck (1990) suggested that the sufferer of *love addiction* should learn how to construct a self-support system through the use of guided healthy self-talk. This self-talk might guide one toward getting used to less intense, more constructive feelings toward self and others (Timmreck, 1990). He also mentioned that self-management training should be considered to help one redirect one's behavior. These approaches are plausible CBT techniques. However, no research was completed.

Weiss and Schneider (2006) suggest that the *sex addict* be requested to engage in a variety of cognitive-behavioral-type tasks, including use of stimulus control strategies (e.g., throwing out all pornography, and actively planning and avoiding risky situations), organism strategies (self-affirmations to separate self from behavior, self-efficacy to resist temptation), response strategies (development of a "sexual boundary plan" such as not keeping secrets from significant others about sexual behavior, limiting sexual behavior to one significant other, going to support groups, and focusing on physical health), and reinforcement strategies (e.g., enjoyment of new activities, family involvement, work, and having one's emotional needs better taken care of). While very plausible and clinically useful, research is needed.

While there have been no controlled trials of CBT with *compulsive buying disorder* addiction, single-group work suggests fewer episodes after treatment (see Racine et al.'s 2014 discussion of Mitchell, Burgard, Faber, Crosby, and Zwaan, 2006). Certainly, more research is needed.

Also, only theoretical and clinical work has been applied thus far regarding use of CBT with *workaholism*. Relevant cognitive-behavioral strategies for workaholism might include instruction in **environmental advocacy** (how to get one's needs met within systems: for example, regarding workaholism, setting realistic goals, seeking enjoyment with work, decision-making for work–personal life balance), self-instructional training and cognitive restructuring (to help one better direct purposeful thinking), and problem-solving (considering the benefits and costs of alternatives to solving a problem, to assist in time management; Holland, 2008; Sussman, 2012a). These cognitive-behavioral techniques could be utilized to help (a) reduce or redirect tendencies to be hard-driven in a relatively healthy, balanced direction, (b) select or control the tempo of work tasks so as to maximize enjoyment, and (c) modify organizational inputs to assist with drive and enjoyment of work.

While CBT has been recommended for *exercise addiction* (e.g., Berczik et al., 2014), no conceptual or clinical work has been published. One can envision use of **behavioral contracting** (a simple positive-reinforcement intervention to change behavior). It spells out in detail the expectations of the participant in carrying out the intervention plan, with costs and benefits of non-compliance and compliance, time duration, and "out" clauses) to regulate limits on exercise or cognitive restructuring of misperceptions related to exercise as potential CBT strategies. However, this is a topic for future research and practice.

Residential CBT Programs

Possibly, residential CBT programs might be relatively effective for persons suffering from severe levels of addiction since persons are contained in safe environments and can be better monitored. For example, cognitive-behavioral community-based residential programs for substance abuse consist of 24-hour supervised treatment. These residential treatment programs are frequently also based on the principles of NA or AA (e.g., they may have residents complete the first five steps among 12 steps, prior to discharge, and attend meetings), but they use a variety of methods to eliminate chemical dependency or other addictions through continuous exposure to structured cognitive-behavioral programming. This programming includes both behavioral tasks to modify habits, as well as cognitive restructuring.

The objectives of residential CBT programs include (1) the elimination of dependency on all problematic addictions, (2) the development of self-awareness and self-worth, (3) the practice of self-discipline, (4) identification and clarification of problems that may threaten sobriety (i.e., life balance without addictions), (5) problem-solving or effective decision-making strategies, (6) the enhancement of physical and psychological wellbeing, (7) the enhancement of coping skills training (e.g., cognitive coping such as cognitive restructuring), and (8) alternative solutions to self-destructive behaviors (Sussman & Ames, 2008). These programs also assist in establishing or enhancing social support and healthy familial and interpersonal relationships through counseling, educational classes, and milieu group therapy (such extrapersonal approaches are discussed in more detail in the next chapter). In addition, many of these programs provide relapse-prevention programming (described later in the present chapter), assist in determining vocational aptitude and educational needs through skills development, assist in establishing realistic personal goals, and enhance access to and the utilization of community resources. They may also provide nutritional training and parenting skills training.

Empirical support for these CBT inpatient programs regarding drug abuse, food addiction, or behavioral addictions cessation is sorely lacking. One would think that these programs would be relatively effective. Research is needed (Sussman, 2010b; Sussman & Ames, 2008).

Motivational Interviewing

Motivational interviewing (Miller & Rollnick, 2013) is based on principles of cognitive therapy, Carl Rogers' client-centered approach, and the Transtheoretical Model. **Motivational interviewing** involves a series of procedures for therapists to help clients clarify goals and follow through with their efforts to change behavior. Motivation is conceptualized as the probability that a person will enter into, continue, and adhere to a specific change strategy (Council for Philosophical Studies, 1981). Motivation for change can fluctuate over time, especially for some highly ambivalent individuals unsure of change. Addressing this ambivalence is considered a key for facilitating behavioral change. MI is conducted in a spirit of respect and collaboration. Personalization of material is very important (Ray et al., 2014).

I placed MI in the intrapersonal cessation chapter because its focus is on client-directed change. MI pertains in part to making explicit and resolving discrepancies between one's behavior and attitudes (in common with other motivation enhancement strategies). However, it also might be an extrapersonal device because fundamental to its efficacy is the quality of the relationship and interaction between the client and the facilitator (Barnett et al., 2014). Recently, *group MI* has become popular, which is clearly an extrapersonal treatment (Sussman, 2015). Group MI is conducted rather similarly to individual-based MI, although there are several notable differences. In particular, in group MI the interpersonal dynamics of a group are critical concerns – including consideration of group structure (size, formalized leadership), roles (expressive and instrumental leaders), and individual experiences that filter into the group process. Group MI requires resolution of equivocation and production of commitment language among group members, at a group as well as individual level (Engle, Macgowan, Wagner, & Amrhein, 2010; Sussman, 2015).

MI, in general, involves eight strategies to motivate behavior change: (1) giving advice to elicit and reinforce change goals, (2) removing impediments to change through use of problem-solving and other techniques, (3) providing positive choice options as elicited by the client, (4) decreasing desirability of not changing, (5) showing empathy (warmth, caring, understanding), (6) providing accurate feedback on clients' behavior, (7) clarifying goals by confronting the client with discrepancies between future goals and the present situation, and (8) supporting the development of self-efficacy through active helping. Positive reflections of a facilitator (e.g., "It seems like you are saying you can do it") are more likely to lead to change talk regarding drug misuse than negative or neutral reflections (Barnett et al., 2014).

Motivational interviewing is a valuable brief treatment option for teens as well as adults; the most current data suggest its advantage over no treatment or other modalities in approximately 60 percent of the studies within which it has been examined (see Barnett et al., 2012). Adaptations of motivational interviewing also have been shown to be effective among some groups, especially among alcohol abusing adult populations (for review, Burke, Arkowitz, & Dunn, 2002; Burke, Arkowitz, & Menchola, 2003; Dunn, Deroo, & Rivara, 2001; Noonan & Moyers, 1997). Work with MI has been applied with promising results to a wide variety of problem behaviors, separately or in combination with CBT.

MI Use in Treatment of Tobacco, Alcohol, or Other Drug Abuse Addictions

Hettema, Steele, and Miller (2005) conducted a meta-analysis on the utility of MI in 72 studies that included a treatment and a comparison group (6 studies of cigarette smoking, 31 studies of alcohol use, and 14 studies of drug use, among other health behaviors). An average of 3.6 characteristics/aspects of MI were included in the program conditions, with an average of two sessions provided (2.2 hours total); 75 percent were manual-guided protocols. Subjects' mean age was 34 years. Effect sizes on tobacco, alcohol, or other drug misuse studies were an average of d = 0.3 from 6–12 months post-intervention (lower for cigarette smoking, d = 0.14) and dipped down to around 0.2 (small effect) at greater than 12 months, except when MI was used to supplement other programming (e.g., when MI was being used as an initial screening tool or as a means of follow-up). In the latter case, the effect size was stable at d = 0.6.

Barnett et al. (2012) provided an exhaustive empirical review that summarizes the most up-to-date MI interventions with adolescents on tobacco, alcohol, or other drug abuse. Of the 39 studies included in this review, 67 percent reported statistically significant improved substance use outcomes (seven or more studies showed changes in each drug category, though relative impacts on different drugs were not compared). Chi square results failed to show a significant difference between interventions using feedback or not, or interventions combined with other treatment versus MI alone.

Food Addiction

There are no studies of MI with food addiction per se. There is empirical support that MI may work for use with childhood or adolescent obesity (e.g., Pakpour, Gellert, Dombrowski, & Fridlund, 2015), and adult obesity, binge eating, and to maintain a healthy diet (Copeland, McNamara, Kelson, & Simpson, 2015). In a review of 37 studies, counselor empathy, counselor reflections, **MI spirit** (client sense of autonomy and collaboration with counselor), and client change talk appeared to mediate the relations between use of MI and increase in healthy behavior or weight loss. It is likely that MI may be a fruitful treatment modality for food addiction.

MI Use in Treatment of Behavioral Addictions

MI has also been used some in the treatment of behavioral addictions (e.g., Rash & Petry, 2014). For example, Larimer et al. (2012) utilized an important element of MI with a *problem gambling* college student population. They engaged in a randomized clinical trial with assignment to a ***personalized feedback intervention*** (PFI; a key component of MI, involves feedback about the participant's behavior in comparison to peers, and tips to change), cognitive behavioral intervention (CBI), or assessment-only control (AOC). PFI was delivered individually in a single session and included feedback regarding gambling behavior, norms, consequences, and risk-reduction tips, delivered in a motivational interviewing style. CBI was delivered in small groups over four to six sessions and included functional analysis and brief cognitive correction, as well as identification of and alternatives for responding to gambling triggers. Probable college student pathological gamblers (n = 147; 65.3 percent male) participated in the study. Relative to the control condition, results at six-month follow-up indicated medium effect size reductions in both interventions for gambling consequences and DSM-IV criteria, and reductions in frequency for the PFI condition (e.g., ds = 0.48 and 0.23, respectively, comparing PFI and CBI to the control condition on frequency reduction). The CBI was associated with reduced illusions of control, whereas the PFI was associated with reduced perceptions of gambling frequency norms.

In a recent review by Cowlishaw et al. (2012), four studies of MI therapy were identified for problem gambling. Data suggested reduced financial loss from gambling following MI therapy at 0 to 3 months post-treatment, although comparisons on other outcomes were not significant. The effect approached zero when defined by gambling symptom severity. Studies compared groups at 9 to 12 months follow-up and found a significant effect of MI therapy on frequency of gambling, with comparisons on other outcomes that were not significant. Two studies of integrative therapies (CBT+MI) found no significant effects of therapy at 0 to 3 months post-treatment. However, comparisons at 9 to 12 months follow-up suggested a medium effect from the combined therapy on gambling symptom severity, with no significant differences for other outcomes. Grant and Odlaug (2014) also reviewed ten trials of MI alone or in combination with other components (mainly CBT), in controlled trials, and did indicate some longer-term effects on reduction in gambling (not abstinence) for as long as a two-year follow-up (total ns ranged from 29 to 314 per study).

Use of MI-related telephone support along with use of self-help materials (e.g., via the Internet with personalized feedback) has been found to be efficacious in small-scale studies, at least on gambling frequency (not on amount gambled), and use of MI telephone support appears to elicit relatively strong program effects beyond baseline motivation to change (see Rash & Petry, 2014). The data on only use of self-help materials are equivocal, in part due to reliance on the participant to be motivated enough to complete the materials. Self-directed interventions appear to benefit some gamblers; however, the involvement of therapist support, either in person or by telephone, may bolster these effects and such support need not be extensive. Self-directed options reduce the barriers associated with treatment-seeking, and may reach a wider range of gamblers than professionally delivered treatments alone, though an extrapersonal support element does seem essential (Rash & Petry, 2014).

There appear to be no controlled MI trials on other behavioral addictions currently. However, it is plausible that it might work well with any of the behavioral addictions. For example, MI may help *love addicts* understand maladaptive functions of love objects. Individuals may learn through MI techniques that their romantic relationships involve an ongoing pattern of equivocation about issues of trust and intimacy (Sussman & Ames, 2008). One may then try to reduce the discrepant feelings by deciding to enter relationships more slowly (Sussman, 2010a). As another example, a key aspect of MI may involve providing accurate feedback on the *workaholic's* behavior and outcomes as an aid in altering self-and-other destructive work habits, which might also involve exploring the client's reinforcement history (see Sussman, 2012a).

Cue Exposure Approaches

The Cue Reactivity Paradigm

Less popularly used in clinical practice than CBT, cue exposure/reactivity approaches are based on conditioning/learning models that underlie associative learning processes (Yin & Knowlton, 2006). The general theory of cue exposure and engagement in addictive behavior is that repeated exposure to addiction-related cues (conditioned stimuli) automatically results in craving or arousal that is uncomfortable (conditioned responses), and may lead to addiction-seeking behavior to reduce the craving. In other words, cue reactivity often is interpreted as a conditioned response to addiction-related cues learned from repeated engagement in addictive behavior (Drummond, 2000; Monti, Rohsenow, & Hutchison, 2000; Niaura et al., 1988; Rohsenow et al., 1994). Thus, cue reactivity paradigms involve the monitoring of a variety of physiological responses (e.g., salivation, heart rate, sweat gland activity, and neuroimaging) and obtaining self-reports of craving (or urges, as in Monti et al., 2000) during exposure to addictive behavior-related cues (e.g., paraphernalia and drug use situations).

Significant increases in self-reports of craving have been found when tobacco, alcohol, or drug addicted individuals are exposed to drug-related versus drug-neutral stimuli (Carter & Tiffany, 1999). While cue-related reports of craving in response to alcohol-related cues is more pronounced and reliable (less error variance) than physiological measures of cue reactivity (Carter & Tiffany, 1999), the ability of urges (cravings) to predict drinking after treatment is inconsistent (Monti et al., 2000), and cue-elicited craving may be less predictive of relapse than physiological cue reactivity (e.g., salivation, skin conductance; Drummond & Glautier, 1994; Rohsenow et al., 1994). In any case, regarding tobacco, alcohol, or other drug addiction there is empirical support for the assertion that cue-related responses to condition cues predict subsequent addictive behavior.

Cue Exposure Response Prevention Treatment

Preventing responding to the conditioned stimuli may lead to extinction of the conditioned responses and, hence, reduction in addiction-seeking behavior. Thus, the goal of cue exposure and cue reactivity treatment paradigms is to minimize responses to addiction-related stimuli to minimize continued participation in the addiction. **Cue exposure treatment protocols** involve extinguishing conditioned responses through unreinforced exposure to conditioned stimuli. For example, someone who abuses cocaine might be exposed to cocaine-related stimuli (imaginal exposure [*in vitro*], or *in vivo* [actual handling of cocaine]) such as white powder while simultaneously working toward reducing craving or a desire to use. Cue exposure protocols can reduce the desire to use that may be attributed to particular cues and prepare individuals to manage these cues outside of treatment in real-life situations. In addition, cue exposure paradigms provide an opportunity to practice coping responses (e.g., relaxation) that may, in turn, increase one's self-efficacy when re-exposed to cues in the natural environment (Monti, Abrams, Kadden, & Cooney, 1989).

Although promising, there are several limitations to these approaches, including the possibility of **spontaneous recovery** over the passage of time (i.e., reintroduction of an addiction object may facilitate reoccurrence of conditioned responses), the unreliability of some conditioned responses as predictors of addictive behavior, the possibility that cue exposure treatment interacts with or is mediated by various cognitive processes (e.g., expectancies or implicit cognitive processes), the possibility that treatment does not generalize to the natural environment, and availability of the addiction object in one's natural environment (Conklin & Tiffany, 2001). In fact, it is possible that repeated exposures to cues could result in enhanced self-reporting of addiction-related cognitions through exposure (Sussman, Horn, & Gilewski, 1990). Then, differential exposure to non-addiction-related cues would be needed to reduce the associational retrieval strength of drug-related cues. One other potential limitation is that the effects of cue exposure approaches on brain function (use of fMRI) have not yet revealed consistent findings, though some treatment effects on reduction of cue-elicited activation of the dorsal prefrontal cortex and amygdala have been found (Courtney et al., 2016).

There is some evidence of the efficacy of cue exposure approaches for the treatment of *problem gambling* (see Grant & Odlaug, 2014), but only in the short term with small sample sizes. There is no other cue exposure treatment research on other addictions.

"Implicit Cognition"-Oriented Approaches

Implicit cognition refers to relatively automatic thinking (thoughts that "pop" into mind, that may tend to direct behavior), which may serve a deleterious function via its role in maintenance of addictions (Stacy et al., 2004). Newer intervention approaches to address and reduce the influence of implicit processes on addictive behaviors are now being evaluated in laboratory settings. One approach currently being evaluated uses varieties of **attentional retraining**. The general idea is that an attentional bias for addiction-related cues is an important determinant of cue approach behavior, addiction craving, and addiction-seeking behavior (see Cox, Fadardi, Intriligator, & Klinger, 2014; Franken, 2003) so, for example, retraining drug-dependent individuals to focus attention away from drug-related cues may, in turn, reduce craving and drug-seeking behavior. An attentional retraining approach may prevent dysfunctional attentional bias from increasing in strength and promoting continued addictive behavior, though the relation between attentional bias and craving varies by drug and generally is modest (Field, Munafo, & Franken, 2009). In the attentional retraining approach, measures used to assess an attentional bias are adapted to train attention away from addiction-related cues. For example, in a visual probe task (**dot probe paradigm**), a target replaces a drug-related picture in a number of cases (with quick presentations, e.g., 500 milliseconds), whereas, in retraining sessions, the target replaces a neutral picture in most cases. For example, alcohol stimuli might be contrasted with non-alcohol stimuli such as enjoyed non-alcoholic drinks (Cox et al., 2014). In this way, substance-dependent individuals implicitly learn to not attend to cues for their drug of choice. Initial findings from different labs have shown some promising findings using attentional retraining paradigms (e.g., Field & Eastwood, 2005).

In more recent work, McGeary, Meadows, Amir, and Gibb (2014) examined impact of a computer-delivered, home-based, alcohol-specific attention modification program (AMP) with 41 heavy *alcohol* drinking college students. The participants were randomly assigned to AMP or an attention control condition (ACC). Participants selected ten alcohol-related words most relevant to their own drinking experience as well as ten neutral words not related to alcohol. These personalized stimuli were used in an attention retraining program based upon the probe detection paradigm twice weekly for four weeks. Participants in the AMP condition reported decreased drinking, whereas those in the ACC condition reported no change in their drinking.

Most attentional bias modification (ABM) research has been completed with cigarettes, alcohol, or other drugs. However, Kemps, Tiggemann, Orr, and Grear (2014) found that, using a modified dot probe paradigm, undergraduate women could be redirected from consumption of chocolate and craving for chocolate during that experiment. Thus, *food addiction*-related cues might be modified through attentional retraining. Other addictions have not been examined yet.

A second approach includes implementation of memory enhancement components through elaborative processing of new associations. **Elaborative processing** (EP) may help minimize the influence of preexisting associations. The use of EP promotes more protective associative cognitive structures in long-term memory. The idea is that EP can connect in memory addictive behavior cessation materials with contexts associated with the related addiction. Then program materials may be more likely to be spontaneously activated in memory when an individual is confronted with strong addictive behavior-related cues in risky situations (for discussion, see Stacy et al., 2004). For example, an intervention could focus on tying non-drug use coping program information (e.g., seeking social support) and high-risk situations (e.g., finding beer on a kitchen counter) together in memory (Stacy & Ames, 2001). The individual then might seek social support when actually encountering that high-risk situation. With sufficient semantic relatedness to preexisting memories, through repetition, or simply through the novelty of the new memory created, program information may become accessible enough to spontaneously "pop into mind" when an individual is in a risky situation (e.g., the person may make a phone call to a support person rather than drink the beer). Research is needed on this approach.

Third, an approach that enhances *executive inhibitory or planning functions* might be used. For example, the therapist might help the client repeatedly role play some complex social situations that might tax working memory to make coping responses more spontaneous. Aspects of working memory involved in making use of treatment information in demanding situations (i.e., high-risk situations) may be important determinants of effective behavioral control. Reduced attentional resources, whether based on individual deficits in one's executive functions or on working memory load inherent in a given situation can reduce the chance of behavioral control. It may be helpful to tailor treatment components to train working memory (cf. Olesen, Westerberg, & Klingberg, 2004) for individuals with lower working memory capacity that may need improved attentional resources. Such an approach might be utilized with any of the 11 focal addictions.

Finally, another approach is to try to automatize action plans that lead to alternative behaviors instead of the addiction of choice. For example, implementation intentions or simple if–then action plans may lead to action without controlled cognitive processes. That is, establishing a cue–response association may give a specified goal-directed behavior a greater chance of being automatically initiated by situational cues.

For example, one implementation intention statement is: "If I go to a party, then I will drink only cola." Because drugs negatively affect controlled processes, this type of strategy may help individuals to automatically regulate or control their use of alcohol and drugs, or engagement in another addictive behavior (Prestwich et al., 2006). Implementation intentions have shown strong and positive effects with several health behaviors (Chatzisarantis & Hagger, 2010; Gollwitzer, 1999; Hagger et al., 2012; Henderson, Gollwitzer, & Oettingen, 2007; Orbell & Sheeran, 2002; Tam, Bagozzi, & Spanjol, 2010; for review, Prestwich et al., 2006). Tam et al. (2010) found evidence that use of an implementation intentions protocol can place consumption of *food* (i.e., healthy snacks) more under deliberate voluntary control (when matching regulatory motivations; see Adriaanse, Vinkers, DeRidder, Hox, & DeWit, 2011 for a food-related review). Certainly, entering a risky situation (a "slippery slope") may present competitive contingencies that could overwhelm preexisting implementation intentions (e.g., intending not to engage in sexual behavior when entering a questionable massage parlor). Research is needed to better understand the potential operation of all of these implicit cognitive treatment strategies for all 11 focal addictions.

Relapse and Relapse Prevention

Relapse

Relapse refers to the engagement in an addictive behavior after a period of abstinence. Recurrence of participation in the addiction can vary from a single event ("slip" or "lapse") to a time-limited episode or "binge" to a full-blown return to the frequency and pattern of behavior prior to abstinence (Marlatt, 1985). The concept of a relapse also can refer to a chain of events preceding the recurrence of the drug use behavior (the relapse situation). "Staying stopped" is the most difficult aspect of breaking an addiction. No one can monitor an addict 24 hours a day to make sure the person does not engage in addictive behavior. In this very important sense, relapse prevention is an intrapersonal treatment.

There are several notions from the work on substance abuse that can be generalized to any of the 11 focal addictions. The phenomenon of **post-acute** withdrawal (PAW; Gorski & Miller, 1984, 1986) refers to the period of up to approximately 18 months following acute withdrawal from drug use and perhaps other addictions (e.g., see Yung et al.'s case study [Yung, Eickhoff, Davis, Klam, & Doan, 2015] of PAW and Google Glass [glasses, Internet wearable technology]). PAW is a biopsychosocial syndrome involving the occurrence of a variety of symptoms indicating dysfunction occurring during abstinence, perhaps involving neurobiological readjustment and related to the psychosocial stresses of coping with life addiction-free. Also, PAW may be affected by personality factors (e.g., depression, sensation-seeking, and obsessive-compulsive disorders) and triggering events. Symptoms of PAW include the following: (1) the inability to think clearly; (2) emotional overreactivity, numbness, or artificial affect; (3) memory impairment or problems; (4) stress sensitivity; (5) sleep disturbances; and (6) physical coordination problems. PAW symptoms such as sleep disturbances may lead to early relapse. Two means to cope with PAW symptoms are (a) to become aware of and responsive to PAW-related relapse cues (e.g., perhaps coping with them through such means as meditation practices or seeking social support) and (b) mood management.

Gorski and Miller (1984, 1986) developed a list of relapse phases and warning signs based on analyses of histories of relapse-prone individuals committed to maintaining sobriety but who were unable to stay sober and returned to compulsive use. The process they outlined (for alcoholics or drug addicts) could potentially be applied to any of the 11 focal addictions. The relapse process entails several sequential phases. First, individuals may experience *internal changes* in thinking, feelings, and behavior. They may not feel as though they are balanced. Next, they may engage in *denial* – individuals may stop being honest with others about their thoughts and feelings. Next, these individuals may engage in *avoidance* and *defensiveness*. Individuals might begin avoiding others or any situation that might force them to be honest about changes in thoughts, feelings, and behaviors. Soon individuals may experience *crisis building* – problems in sobriety that they do not understand. Soon these individuals may feel a sense of *immobilization*, of being trapped while problems seem unmanageable. Soon individuals may begin to experience *confusion and overreaction*. That is, the individuals have difficulty thinking clearly and regulating their feelings and emotions. Next, they may experience *depression*. In other words, they may come to believe that life is not worth living and lack the desire to take action. At this point, *behavioral loss of control* begins. These individuals may feel that they can no longer control their thoughts, feelings, and behaviors and they may experience feelings of helplessness. Next, *recognition of loss of control* occurs. That is, individuals may realize that their life has become unmanageable. After that, these individuals may experience a sense of *option reduction*. They may feel trapped and unable to manage their lives; they may believe self-medication with drugs or alcohol, or another addictive behavior, is their only or best way out, or a relief. At this point comes the final phase of *engagement in the addiction of choice*. Individuals return to the addictive behavior; they try to control their behavior and they lose control. Certainly, research is needed here. However, this work suggests that if one is experiencing any of these warning signs, which may be aspects of PAW, seeking out therapeutic support immediately is essential. As mentioned above, engagement in meditation, mood management, and seeking social support may be important means to counteract the impact of PAW on the potential for subsequent relapse.

Relapse Prevention

Relapse appears to be linked to factors such as *failure to avoid addictive behavior-related settings* (e.g., inappropriate social support networks, social pressure, and opportunity); *failure to maintain effective coping mechanisms* in high-risk situations (i.e., a loss of perceived self-efficacy when exposed to addictive behavior-related objects or services); *interpersonal problems* (e.g., conflict); *negative affective states* such as anger, sadness, boredom, anxiety, depression, guilt, fear, apprehension, and loneliness; and addictive behavior *cravings or intrusive thoughts about engaging in the addiction* (Henderson, Witkiewitz, George, & Marlatt, 2011; Marlatt, 1985).

Marlatt (1985, p. 3) conceptualized relapse prevention as a "self-management program designed to enhance the maintenance stage of the habit-change process." Relapse prevention interventions assist in the acquisition and practice of effective coping strategies (i.e., cognitive and behavioral skills) for managing high-risk situations and to enhance self-efficacy when faced with those situations (Henderson et al., 2011; Larimer, Palmer, & Marlatt, 1999; Marlatt, 1985). Relapse prevention is a self-control program that combines *behavioral skills training*, *cognitive interventions*, and *lifestyle-change procedures*, and is based on the principles of Social Learning Theory. The goals of the program for relapse prevention are (1) to anticipate and prevent the occurrence of a relapse after the initiation of a habit change attempt and (2) to help someone recover from a "slip" or lapse before it escalates into a full-blown relapse. Relapse prevention methods were envisioned by Marlatt to apply to any number of addictions, following any number of means to achieve initial cessation. Individuals acquire new skills and learn new coping strategies through involvement in *self-management* of relapse prevention. Additionally, individuals are actively involved in the learning of mental processes including *awareness* of high-risk stimuli (vigilance) and *responsible decision-making*.

Individualized *assessment of high-risk situations* is an important element of Marlatt's relapse prevention model. In general, assessment of high-risk situations is carried out either through therapist–patient interviews and descriptions about past relapse experiences, through various self-report instruments that assess likely addictive behavior-related situations, or through self-monitoring of behavior (Larimer et al., 1999). Cognitive processes operate to recognize and monitor high-risk situations and relapse warning signs and to prepare an individual to avoid, escape, or cope with the situation when encountered (Henderson et al., 2011).

The ability of an individual to adequately cope when in high-risk situations is a key for maintaining abstinence and enhancing self-efficacy. Enhancing one's **self-efficacy** or the expectation that one is able to effectively cope with high-risk situations without reverting to prior addictive coping responses is central to relapse-prevention therapy (Larimer et al., 1999; Marlatt, 1985). Nevertheless, should a lapse occur, relapse-prevention therapy involves implementing strategies to address a type of cognitive distortion, referred to as an **abstinence violation effect** (AVE), or the feeling of loss of control over one's addictive behavior and the perceived inability to engage in healthy behaviors. *Cognitive restructuring* strategies may help in challenging this type of distortion (e.g., challenging one's belief that one is a failure and unable to live an abstinent lifestyle) and help one to recover from temporary setbacks.

In Marlatt's relapse prevention model, *urge management* is also an important treatment technique to help individuals avoid relapse. For example, self-monitoring techniques can be used to evaluate urges (Marlatt, 1985) and stimulus control techniques (e.g., removing drug use paraphernalia) can help in managing urges. Although there are several conceptualizations of urges in Marlatt's model, urges are considered to be mediated by (1) conditioning elicited by stimuli associated with past gratification, and (2) cognitive processes associated with anticipated gratification (i.e., the expectancies for the immediate pleasurable effects of the addictive behavior; Larimer et al., 1999, p. 155).

Table 14.1 Intrapersonal treatment of addictions

Detoxification and pharmacotherapy	Detoxification or managed withdrawal from drugs involves removing the toxic materials from an individual's body. Various drugs are used to reduce acute withdrawal symptoms. In behavioral addictions, the "withdrawal" is more psychological, mood-related. However there is recognition of a "detoxification" of sorts for any addiction and there is an overlap among medications used for withdrawal or treatment of a variety of addictions.
Cognitive-behavior therapies	"Cognitive" interventions include strategies to directly modify thinking to enhance executive control or other cognitive processes to facilitate addictive behavior cessation. Changing behavior patterns is instructed through stimulus–organism–response–reinforcement techniques (SORR). SORR alter stimuli confronting the person ("stimulus control"), the way the person interprets these stimuli ("organism control"), responses the person emits ("response control"), or contingencies of reinforcement ("reinforcement control"). Even though most CBT work has pertained to substance use disorders CBT is used with behavioral addictions as well. Cognitive restructuring has been demonstrated to be efficacious for problem gambling.
Motivational interviewing	Motivational interviewing is based on principles of cognitive therapy. MI involves a series of procedures for therapists to help clients clarify goals and follow through with their efforts to change behavior. Work with MI has been applied to a wide variety of problem behaviors and it is plausible that it might work well with any of the 11 focal addictions.
Cue exposure approaches	Cue reactivity involves the monitoring of a variety of physiological responses during exposure to addictive behavior-related cues. The goal of cue exposure and cue reactivity paradigms is to minimize responses to addiction-related stimuli to minimize continued participation in the addiction. Cue exposure treatment involves extinguishing conditioned responses through unreinforced exposure to conditioned stimuli. There is some evidence of the efficacy of cue exposure approaches for the treatment of problem gambling.
Implicit cognition	There are several newer approaches that address the influence of implicit processes on addictive behaviors. In *attentional retraining* individuals are retrained to focus attention away from addiction-related cues to reduce craving and addiction-seeking behavior. Initial studies have shown some promising findings using attentional-retraining paradigms. Another approach includes *memory enhancement* components that focus on the strengthening of new associations in memory. These approaches may help minimize the influence of preexisting associations and promote the influence of more protective associative cognitive structures.

Table 14.1 *(cont.)*

	Enhancing executive functions might assist working memory to make coping responses more spontaneous. Such an approach might be utilized with any of the 11 focal addictions. Another approach is to try to automatize *implementation intentions* that lead to alternative behaviors instead of the addiction of choice. Establishing a cue–response association ("if–then") may give a specified goal-directed behavior a greater chance of being automatically initiated by situational cues.
Relapse and relapse prevention	"Staying stopped" is the most difficult aspect of breaking an addiction. There are several notions from the work on substance abuse that can be generalized to any of the focal addictions. The relapse process entails several sequential phases, including: (1) internal changes, (2) denial, (3) avoidance and defensiveness, (4) crisis building, (5) immobilization, (6) confusion and overreaction, (7) depression, (8) behavioral loss of control, (9) recognition of loss of control, (10) option reduction, and (11) engagement in addiction. *Relapse prevention* is a self-control program that combines behavioral skills training, cognitive interventions, and lifestyle change procedures, and is based on the principles of Social Learning Theory. The goals of the program for relapse prevention are to anticipate and prevent the occurrence of a relapse after the initiation of a habit change attempt and to help someone recover from a "slip" or lapse before it escalates into a full-blown relapse. Relapse prevention interventions have been found to be beneficial in reducing the intensity of relapse episodes and improving psychosocial functioning.

Outcome expectancies also are important cognitive determinants of relapse emphasized in relapse prevention therapy – that is, when an individual encounters a high-risk situation, he or she may ignore or discount possible negative outcomes resulting from unhealthy behavior while anticipating only positive outcomes or the desire for immediate gratification. Relapse prevention therapy assists in identifying high-risk situations, challenging expectancies affecting decision-making in those situations, challenging denial and rationalizations in those situations, and encouraging the generation of available alternative behavioral choices, which relatively recently may include use of the practice of meditation (see Henderson et al., 2011; Larimer et al., 2012; Marlatt, 1985, 1999).

The efficacy of relapse prevention interventions relative to no-treatment controls has support in the literature (for reviews, see Henderson et al., 2011; Irvin, Bowers, Dunn, & Wang, 1999). Relapse prevention interventions have been found to be as effective as other treatment approaches and beneficial in reducing the intensity of relapse episodes and improving psychosocial functioning (Henderson et al., 2011; Irvin et al., 1999). As with the other intrapersonal approaches to cessation mentioned above, almost all work has been on tobacco, alcohol, or hard drug use, though application is suggested to food or behavioral addictions (Grant et al., 2010). Intrapersonal treatment of addiction approaches are summarized in Table 14.1.

Summary

This chapter introduced several intrapersonal approaches to cessation treatment. These approaches include: pharmacotherapy, CBT, MI, cue exposure approaches, implicit cognition approaches (attentional retraining, elaborative processing, strengthening executive functions, and implementation intentions), and information on relapse and relapse prevention. These approaches are perhaps a majority, but not all of the individual-level treatments being considered. For example, transcranial magnetic stimulation (TMS), which uses magnetic fields to directly stimulate brain nerve cells, may serve a restorative function and decrease addiction reward valuation (Bickel et al., 2016). A second approach not discussed in this chapter is use of narratives read by participants to elicit episodic future thinking and improve valuation of temporally distant reinforcers (i.e., decrease a delay discounting slope so as to increase motivation to avoid engaging in the addictive behavior; see Bickel et al., 2016). While any of these approaches may be important for all of the 11 focal addictions, outcome research studies are needed for most of them. The next chapter discusses cessation considered within an extrapersonal context.

Bulleted Summary
- Pharmacological adjuncts may assist in (a) decreasing withdrawal symptoms, (b) reducing craving (urges) to engage in the addictive behavior, (c) lifting associated negative affect, and (d) preventing relapse. Also (e) restoring neurobiological function is another possible goal of this treatment type.
- CBT includes stimulus control strategies (e.g., removing addiction-related objects from one's physical environment), organism control strategies (problem-solving, cognitive restructuring, self-instructional training and other self-control strategies, self-monitoring, goal setting, time management, and stress management), response control strategies (coping), and response-reinforcement control techniques (e.g., self-reward).
- MI involves a series of procedures for therapists to help clients clarify goals and follow through with their efforts to change behavior, and this approach may overlap to some extent with some of the CBT methods.
- Cue exposure treatment protocols involve extinguishing conditioned responses through unreinforced exposure to conditioned stimuli, and might be attempted regarding any of the 11 focal addictions though published work exists only on tobacco, alcohol, other drugs, and gambling.
- Implicit cognition strategies in cessation of the addictions include attentional retraining, elaborative processing of new healthy associations, inhibitory/planning operations training, and use of implementation intentions.
- Relapse may involve post-acute withdrawal symptoms (difficulty functioning cognitively, emotionally, and behaviorally due initially to losing a sense of balance in sobriety). Relapse prevention involves learning how to cope in high-risk situations without engaging in addictive behavior. Self-management skills, decision-making, and cognitive and behavioral coping skills (e.g., use of meditation) all are part of a relapse prevention package.

Suggestions for Further Reading

Cowlishaw, S., Merkouris, S., Dowling, N., Anderson, C., Jackson, A., & Thomas, S. (2012). Psychological therapies for pathological and problem gambling. *Cochrane Database of Systematic Reviews*, 11: Article CD008937.

Julien, R. M. (2005). *A Primer of Drug Action* (9th edn.). New York: W. H. Freeman (13th edn. C. D. Advokat, J. E. Comaty, & R. M. Julien, eds., 2014).

Marlatt, G. A. (1985). Relapse prevention: Theoretical rationale and overview of the model. In G. A. Marlatt & J. R. Gordon (eds.), *Relapse Prevention*. New York: Guilford Press, pp. 3–70.

Rosenberg, K. P. & Feder, L. C. (eds.) (2014a). *Behavioral Addictions: Criteria, Evidence, and Treatment*. London: Academic Press/Elsevier.

Sussman, S. & Ames, S. L. (2008). *Drug Abuse: Concepts, Prevention and Cessation*. Cambridge University Press.

Yin, H. H. & Knowlton, B. J. (2006). Addiction and learning in the brain. In R. W. Wiers & A. W. Stacy (eds.), *Handbook on Implicit Cognition and Addiction*. Thousand Oaks, CA: Sage, pp. 167–173.

15 Cessation: Extrapersonal-Level Approaches

Learning Objectives

- To learn about the "motivational intervention" and 12-step programs for the addictions
- To learn about the application of family and group therapies for the 11 focal addictions
- To learn about social skills training and behavioral contracting application to the addictions
- To learn mass media, physical environmental, and other large social environmental treatment strategies (e.g., policy) relevant to the 11 focal addictions

Introduction

Johnny went to AA meetings off and on for 20 years. His first six months of involvement in AA provided him with hope. He liked the idea of "cleaning house" and that he could be with people who understood what it was like to struggle with addictions. He even went out to eat with people from the group after meetings early in sobriety. However, he had difficulty with sponsors; he felt like they spoke at him but often did not really converse with him. He found the talk about a Higher Power untenable. He was trying to grapple with his addictions, not find religion. He found the tobacco use at meetings hypocritical. He thought they really could not be truly sober if they were highly addicted to tobacco. He did really appreciate the sacrifice others made when they talked openly about the things they did while under the influence. Johnny sometimes tried to share his embarrassing moments, at least in a general way. Afterwards, he often felt frightened that he would get in trouble for revealing his exploits. He worried that people would gossip about him. He would start to think that he was in the wrong organization. However, he was unable to locate alternatives to AA that were close to where he lived, such as Life Ring. He ended up going to a speaker's meeting where he did not have to say anything. However, he also felt like he was not really accepted as part of the group. After a while he felt quite expendable. Then, he slipped. When he slipped he felt too embarrassed to return to meetings. He was worried that awareness of his slips would get back to his workplace. He felt no anonymity after a while. He tried to become a controlled drinker but often failed. He kept going back to meetings with the hope that eventually he would fit somewhere in AA and that he would not feel embarrassed about being a member of a group of drunks. He went back to meetings in a different location. He went through a similar chain of events. How would Johnny ever get it together?

Extrapersonal-level treatments approach change in the individual through microsocial (group) and macrosocial (e.g., cultural, physical environmental) contexts. There are many cessation-related strategies that involve social processes. Mobilizing a person into treatment often involves social forces, including the "nudge from the judge," complaints from co-workers, discussions with family and friends, or suggestions made by physicians sometimes in the emergency room. Likewise, improving one's behavior often involves inputs from others. That is, others may provide direction on alternative activities. Maintenance of change may also involve social rewards, which could include simply spending time with people who are sober and content. The extrapersonal treatment strategies to be presented are depicted in Table 15.1.

Motivational Intervention

Sometimes a ***motivational intervention*** (not to be confused with motivational interviewing) is implemented to confront the addict with his or her detrimental effects on others, particularly family and close friends (Johnson, 1980). The Johnson Institute-style motivational intervention is a confrontational method used to encourage addicts to acknowledge the negative impact of his or her addiction on self and others and to be motivated to change through confrontation with family and significant others. This intervention involves the following five steps: (1) inquiry, (2) assessment, (3) preparation, (4) intervention, and (5) follow-up/case management (Storti, 2001). During an *inquiry*, individuals gather contact information and screen whether a particular individual requires an intervention. The *assessment* process generally involves interviewing and gathering family members or significant others who will participate in the intervention. *Preparation* involves rehearsal of what significant others will say when confronting the addict. During the actual confrontation (the *intervention*), significant others express their feelings, their specific current concerns, and their worries about the future. During the *follow-up/case management* phase, the addict enters treatment of some type. While there are difficulties recruiting families to use the intervention approach (only 30 percent will follow through with this approach), those who do use it are highly successful (i.e., 75 percent) in getting the targeted addict into treatment (Miller, Meyers, & Tonigan, 1999).

Once recognition of the problem behavior is understood or perhaps debated among the addict and significant others, informal or formal treatment providers (e.g., a therapist, 12-step group) may be selected either by the addict or by external agents. Next, therapeutic relationships are attempted. If a solid ***therapeutic alliance*** is created (i.e., a trusting and mutually respectful relationship is developed), progress toward solutions to problematic addictive behavior will be achieved. The person in recovery may attempt to learn alternative social behaviors. Social skills training, such as assertiveness training, and anger or other mood management, may be needed for some individuals to attempt reintegration into a relatively addiction-free social world. Additional social-level therapeutic modalities may need to be provided as well, including involvement in a recovery community.

Table 15.1 Extrapersonal-level treatment approaches

12-step programs	12-step programs such as AA and NA provide the basic philosophy of change for many inpatient and outpatient addictions treatment facilities. 12-step programs are abstinence-oriented, multidimensional, non-profit, humanistic, voluntary, socially supportive, self-help fellowships. There are several 12-step programs for other addictions such as Overeaters Anonymous (OA), Gamblers Anonymous (GA), and Workaholics Anonymous (WA). AA or NA programs appear to work as well as other well-established, research-based approaches (e.g. motivational interviewing or cognitive therapy).
Social skills training	Social skills training may include self-control skills, listening/conversational skills, assertiveness, and stimulus–response control. Training often involves modeling of assertive behavior, behavioral rehearsal, practice through role playing, performance, and immediate feedback. There is little research evidence on the efficacy of social skills training in the addictions arena, other than substance use disorder.
Family therapy	Family therapy tends to view the addictions as a family (systems) problem. In family therapy the family's strengths and resources are utilized to minimize the negative consequences of the addict's behavior. The goal is to help the system integrate and heal. Family therapy research has been conducted pertaining to alcohol/drug abuse, with rather promising results. Family therapy is also used with pathological gambling, eating disorders, and Internet addiction and may work for these and other addictions as well.
Group therapy	Group therapy provides peer support, feedback, and confrontation, guided by a trained therapist. The therapist helps group members resolve issues of trauma and learn intimacy with others, as well as learn how to express feelings appropriately. Regarding substance use disorder, group therapy appears to be as effective as individual-level treatment. There is also some promise that group therapy for gambling addiction and compulsive buying disorder may be efficacious.
Behavioral contracting	Contracting is a method of formalizing or reinforcing an individual's commitment to change. It usually involves a written agreement, signed and agreed on by involved parties. Contracting can include contingencies describing penalties and positive reinforcers for violating or conforming to the contract. While achieving mixed results in substance use disorders, there is little discussion of the use of behavioral contracting with the behavioral addictions.
Mass media-related cessation	Public health media cessation messages may be defined to include any media announcement, for which there is no charge, which educates and increases awareness about the consequences of an addiction. A mass media campaign tends to involve multiple public service announcements (PSAs) and other media channels (e.g., Internet, flyers, radio, TV). Although the effectiveness of PSAs is yet to be fully

Table 15.1 *(cont.)*

	determined, some anti-drug misuse public health messages have been found to be effective. There is almost no information on cessation of other addictions through use of the mass media.
Environmental and policy changes	Environmental and policy changes include modification of the larger environment through civil engineering modifications or policy. Environmental and policy changes may help individuals avoid the object of addiction and approach healthy alternatives. Geographic applications may effectively enhance cessation efforts and decrease relapse rates by manipulating the availability of supportive physical structures in addition to removing addiction-related locations. Such large-scale policy modifications have not been envisioned to pertain to most of the addictions.

12-Step Programs

While 12-step programming involves both intrapersonal and extrapersonal features, the involvement in a recovery group (extrapersonal) is arguably most fundamental to these organizations. 12-step programs such as AA and NA provide the basic philosophy of change for many inpatient and outpatient addictions treatment facilities in the United States (over two-thirds) in particular but also world-wide (Sussman, 2010b). More importantly, these programs are main sources of peer social support for the maintenance of habit change. 12-step programs are abstinence-oriented, multidimensional, non-profit, humanistic, voluntary, socially supportive, self-help fellowships for individuals for whom an addiction has become problematic (Galaif & Sussman, 1995; Sussman, 2010b; Sussman & Ames, 2008).

The *prima facie* only requirement for membership in 12-step programs is the desire to stop the problematic addiction. The 12-step program model is self-supporting, does not accept outside contributions, and has no opinion on outside issues. Bill Wilson and Dr. Robert Smith, both self-identified alcoholics, founded AA in 1935. Alcoholics Anonymous has become one of the most widely disseminated self-help treatment groups, where membership is estimated at more than two million (www.aa.org/assets/en_US/smf-132_en.pdf; accessed 2-18-2015). The organization begat more than 100 other 12-step programs based on the structure and principles of AA, as was mentioned in Chapter 1. All of the 12-step sobriety-based programs are based on a **disease model of addiction**. Addictions are thought to be "allergies" that are manifested by a baseline subjective sense of restlessness, irritability, and discontent ("r.i.d."; Alcoholics Anonymous, 1976; Marijuana Anonymous World Services, 1995; Narcotics Anonymous, 1988), in conjunction with (implicit) processes that perpetuate uncontrolled participation in the addiction in high-risk situations. The addict, when sober, may feel quite uncomfortable within his or her "skin" and can fall victim to his or her addict "voice." Self-statements such as "I won't go on a work binge as long as this terrible event doesn't happen, but it happened," "I could smoke marijuana safely under a certain condition; this is it," or automatic thoughts of "It would be nice to have a drink" may suddenly pop into mind as individuals pass by a club or experience emotional turmoil. When the addictive behavior is engaged in, often without much forethought, there may be a great calming effect, perhaps subjective alterations in sensory perceptions, and perhaps a greater subjective sense that one's role in the world is quite different than it was before engaging in the behavior. At the same time, there may be a loss of control over the extent and quality of the behavior, generally after involvement in the behavior for a brief period of hours or days.

The solution to addiction in 12-step programs is very much group-based (Kelly, Hoeppner, Stout, & Pagano, 2011). AA, as the template for other 12-step groups, is formalized through 12 concepts, traditions, and steps. The Twelve Concepts outline the general governmental structure and function of AA. The Twelve Traditions outline AA's basic premises about the organization, such as ensuring members' anonymity and protecting the privacy and integrity of the organization, its leadership, and the sobriety of its members (Yoder, 1990). The Twelve Steps of AA, which involve use of the first-person plural throughout ("we"), provide an internal process of change through which members break through the "denial" that may accompany the addiction, admit to being powerless over alcohol (or other drugs), and learn to make lifelong changes in daily living that include helping others (Spiegel & Mulder, 1986). By following the 12-steps program, members learn to trust a "Higher Power," which could be their "home group" as well as a deity or another form as a means to obtain a daily reprieve from urges or thoughts of drinking alcohol (e.g., Chappel, 1992; Sussman et al., 2013b). Individuals "work the steps" along with other members of the organization. A nearly identical protocol operates across 12-step programs for the different addictive behaviors.

Anonymity is an essential component of 12-step programs, affirming the concept of *principles before personalities*. The anonymity of membership creates an atmosphere of intimacy, trust, and support. Members maintain personal anonymity at the level of the press, radio, and films. The 12-step program is not connected with political, religious, or law enforcement groups (though many judges order persons who committed a DUI or were drunk and disorderly to AA meetings; www.rehabs.com/pro-talk-articles/you-cant-make-me-or-can-you-mandated-aa-attendance/). Individuals of all ages, races, sexual identity, and religion, or lack of religion, may join the program. However, an attitude of indifference or intolerance toward spiritual principles may defeat one's recovery. Honesty, open-mindedness, and willingness (H.O.W.) are essential components of the recovery process.

Another essential component of 12-step programs is that addicts help one another to stay clean and sober. These programs are built on the principle that a recovering person can altruistically and effectively help a fellow addict to gain or maintain sobriety. Members openly talk about their struggles and successes and learn problem solving skills (e.g., how to avoid drinking in high-risk situations), as well as form friendships with others, comforted in the knowledge that they are not alone in their plight.

An important aspect of the program is self-selecting a sponsor who provides support and helps to guide the individual in the program, such as going through the 12 steps (Sussman & Ames, 2001, 2008). 12-step programs provide a means of social support through meetings, fellowship, and sponsorship as well as through clubs (particularly the AA Alano Clubs) that provide a gathering place for fellowship. AA weddings, funerals, and other events often are held within specific groups, meeting many of 12-step program members' social needs in sobriety.

Sober-Living Homes

Community-based residential or *sober-living homes* are safe environments for those who have completed residential treatment or inpatient care or for those who need a structured living situation to maintain sobriety (Heslin, Singzon, Aimiuwu, Sheridan, & Hamilton, 2012; Mueller & Jason, 2014). While not officially part of 12-step organizations, often 12-step meetings are held in the group home, or residents may be required to attend a certain number of meetings outside the group home each week. In the United States, there tends to be a strong association between such homes and 12-step organizations, AA and NA in particular (Sussman, 2010b; Sussman & Ames, 2008). These types of group homes are alcohol- and drug-free environments where residents generally are expected to pay their own rent and buy their own food but live communally. Sober-living homes provide peer group support for those in recovery. Residents are expected to work or attend school or attend treatment sessions outside of the home. Generally, there are different treatment levels and staff supervision for different clients. For example, some clients may be under house arrest and need to be monitored more closely. Individuals are generally required to undergo random drug testing and there is zero tolerance for alcohol and other drug use or violence. Often, therapeutic community model features are included (e.g., those with more sober time take on more responsibility and have more privileges; peers helping each other recover). As sober living home networks accrue more sober alumni, assistance from within the social network increases (Mueller & Jason, 2014). Suggestion has been made that such homes are successful for a variety of addictions (e.g., alcohol, drugs, eating disorders, gambling; Mueller & Jason, 2014).

Empirical Support for AA

Among the 12-step groups, there has been much anecdotal support of AA, in particular, but relatively little controlled research (e.g., Ferri, Amato, & Davoli, 2006). Often empirical support for the efficacy of AA is based solely on the number of individuals who participate in AA or on the testimony of individual members. However, little empirical outcome research exists. For example, some correlational studies have shown a favorable relationship between AA participation, enhancing one's social network through AA, and sobriety (Kelly et al., 2011). Also, a meta-analysis that investigated the relationship between long-term sobriety among adults and AA attendance and involvement found positive outcomes (Tonigan, Toscova, & Miller, 1996). Alternatively, studies of attrition in AA and experimental studies generally fail to support AA's efficacy over other treatments (see Galaif & Sussman, 1995; Sussman & Ames, 2008). Some work suggests that AA, cognitive-behavioral treatment, and motivational interviewing approaches are about equal in effectiveness for the treatment of alcoholism (Project MATCH; Connors, 1998). Likewise, for substance abuse treatment of teens, AA or NA programs appear to work as well as any other approach but perhaps not better (see Sussman, 2010b for a review). About 10 percent of people who go to AA meetings will remain active in AA for several years and, of them, 50 percent will stay sober particularly if they are involved in helping other alcoholics (Galaif & Sussman, 1995; Pagano, Friend, Tonigan, & Stout, 2004).

One major criticism of 12-step programs is that some researchers and practitioners may think of the organization as having *cult-like* characteristics (Bufe, 1991). Some critics believe that 12-step programs encourage dependence on the program itself, openly discourage skepticism, and may lead to a lack of involvement in other social organizations and resentment toward those not involved in the programs. Also, 12-step programs have been criticized as becoming a substitute of one addiction for another (Sussman & Black, 2008). Furthermore, some members actively promote the idea that 12-step programs are the only "road" to recovery. Those who do not readily embrace 12-step concepts may be made to feel unwelcome at meetings (Bufe, 1991). In addition, those who do not remain in 12-step programs may be accused of having "character defects" or lacking the desire to stop drinking or using instead of being sympathized with or being viewed as individuals pursuing other avenues of gaining sobriety (Trimpey, 1989, 1996).

However, there is no named permanent leader and no hierarchical, authoritarian structure within the organization, and all groups are autonomous. 12-step programs do not exploit members financially, nor do they become actively involved in the political arena, exemplary of cults. They go to no lengths to retain members, nor are they supposed to actively recruit newcomers or provide closed, all-encompassing environments exclusively for members; rather, 12-step programs provide an open environment for anyone who wants to stop drinking, using, or engaging in other addictions. Thus, 12-step programs are not cults, although they appear to have some cult-like qualities, as do many fellowships. 12-step programs provide a *sense of belonging* to a group for many individuals who essentially have become outsiders from mainstream communities. This sense of belonging to a group that has insight into the addicts' experiences, and is willing to provide social support without judgment, is an important aspect that some other treatment protocols may not provide.

12-Step Programs for Addictions Other than Substance Abuse

Overeaters Anonymous (OA) is similar to the AA 12-step program on which it is based, and abstinence emphasizes limiting "trigger foods" such as chocolate, cheese, or fried foods. Yau et al. (2014) could not locate any evaluations of the efficacy of OA. Westphal and Smith (1996) provided a survey to regular attenders of OA who were primarily white females who had been in OA over five years (n = 34 completed questionnaires; n = 27 completed interviews). Only 9 percent were diagnosed as having a current compulsive overeating disorder. Placing importance on abstinence and spirituality were related to retrospective reports of losing a great deal of weight and maintaining the weight loss. Similar results were found in a qualitative focus group study (n = 20; 19 females; mean = 54 years old) by Russell-Mayhew, von Ranson, and Masson (2010). McAleavey (2010) examined six-month effectiveness of a 12-step inpatient program (total n = 42), comparing females suffering from anorexia, bulimia, or eating disorders not otherwise specified, but failed to find differential impact with about a third reporting not exhibiting an eating disorder. It is not clear if an effect was achieved since there was no control condition in any of these very small-scale studies. Controlled trials are needed.

Gamblers Anonymous (GA) is similar to the AA 12-step program on which it is modeled. GA strongly advocates complete abstinence from gambling (Rash & Petry, 2014). Like its sister programs, GA has adopted the disease model and views disordered gambling as a lifelong affliction that can be controlled via gambling abstinence, but not cured. Dropout rates are greater than 50 percent and one-year abstinence rates are approximately 10 percent, though active participants are about a third more likely to achieve abstinence than non-attenders, similar to AA. It is interesting that GA appears to show a dropout/abstinence pattern similar to AA. It is likely that continued participation, which suggests an enhanced social network, is a key reason that GA may work. As discussed in the previous chapter, GA sometimes has been used as an alternative condition to CBT and, in general, did not seem to do as well in the short run. At follow-up there appears little difference across different types of programming, including 12-step. In a review by Cowlishaw et al. (2012), one small study (n = 11 in the GA condition; 54 percent female, mean age = 48 years) compared Twelve-Step Facilitated Group Therapy (a "controlled" version of GA; two sessions per week for eight weeks), with cognitive-behavioral group therapy (n = 18), and a wait-list control condition (n = 9), and suggested beneficial effects in terms of most outcomes (e.g., symptom severity, financial loss from gambling, frequency of gambling), which did not differ from the cognitive-behavioral condition, but differed greatly from the control condition (e.g., frequency of gambling went down to almost zero in the treatment conditions, whereas it went up slightly in the control condition), at 0 to 6 months post-treatment (see original study by Marceaux & Melville, 2011).

As mentioned by Rosenberg et al. (2014), there are five self-help programs modeled after AA that pertain to *sex or love addiction* (i.e., Sex Anonymous, Sexaholics Anonymous, Sex Addicts Anonymous, Sex and Love Addicts Anonymous, and Sexual Compulsives Anonymous), a few of which were mentioned in Chapter 1. While 12-step organizations may be helpful for sex or love addicts, they could serve to be overly inclusive of persons who might not demonstrate extreme love or sexual behaviors in some cases (e.g., Speziale, 1994), or may label as sick some behavior which may be a function of political-social conditions (e.g., racism; Salnier, 1996). There appears to be little in the way of evaluation of these programs.

There does not appear to be a highly organized 12-step program on recovery from *television addiction*, one prevalent type of electronic addiction, though there are some blogs (in particular, see TVAA; http://tvaa.blogspot.com/). These organizations have not been contrasted with each other or other treatments in careful RCTs to assess their relative efficacy.

Workaholism is yet another addiction where 12-step programming might be applied (Sussman, 2012a). In 1983, one of the first formal efforts to create a fellowship around workaholism recovery began in New York when a corporate financial planner and a schoolteacher met. They formed Workaholics Anonymous (WA), using the AA model, including perceiving workaholism as a disease. In their first meetings, spouses joined them and in retrospect this was the first Work-Anon group, analogous to Al-Anon; in which family members of workaholics could seek recovery. On March 31, 1990, after a countrywide exchange of letters among several of the first WA groups, four WA members and two of their "Work-Anon" spouses converged to meet for the first time in St. John's Presbyterian Church in West Los Angeles. Having come from fellowships in New York, Los Angeles, and San Diego, they titled their meeting the "Workaholics Anonymous First World Service Conference." The *Workaholics Anonymous Book of Recovery* (Workaholics Anonymous World Service Organization, 2005), modeled after the AA 12-step framework, was published in 2005. There are no controlled trials on 12-step treatment of workaholism. In fact, as presented in this section, no controlled trials on the efficacy of 12-step groups have been completed for most of the 11 focal addictions and are sorely needed.

Family Therapy

Family therapy tends to view the addictions as a family (systems) problem. In other words, focusing on changing part of the system (e.g., the addict's behavior) may effectively change other parts of the system (e.g., other family members' behavior toward the addict, or toward each other; Horigian et al., 2015). Among addicts, family relationships are viewed as potentially problematic (e.g., given too much expressed emotion, conflict, inappropriate roles) and boundaries within the family are viewed as possibly distorted (e.g., enmeshed or disengaged [lack of boundaries, or too distant]). Family therapy is (and should be) conducted with professional (highly trained) staff (Blum, 1995). In family therapy for an addiction, the family's strengths and resources are utilized to assist in developing means for family members and the addict to live effectively without the problematic addiction and to minimize the negative impact or consequences of the addict's behavior on the family system. That is, the goal is to help the system integrate and heal. Family therapy provides neutral turf for family members to express their feelings and concerns and a means of working toward improved communication among each other.

In the addictions, a vast majority of family therapy research has been conducted pertaining to *alcohol or other drug abuse* (e.g., Horigian et al., 2015; Rowe, 2012; Stanton & Shadish, 1997), with rather promising results (Rowe, 2012), if families can be enrolled in treatment. For example, in a large RCT among families that received Brief Strategic Family Therapy (BSFT; 12 to 16 sessions; parenting and relationship skills, conflict resolution; n = 480 adolescents and their families), adolescents reduced their substance use in families where parents were using drugs at baseline, parents reduced their alcohol use, and BSFT apparently decreased alcohol use among parents by improving family functioning (Horigian et al., 2015).

Family therapy may work for other addictions as well. Family therapy is widely used with *eating disorders* (e.g., 91 percent of eating disorders programs for youth in

Canada involve family therapy; Norris et al., 2013); however, I was not able to locate controlled studies pertaining to food addiction. While there is a fair amount of research on family therapy and eating disorders (i.e., anorexia nervosa, bulimia nervosa, binge eating disorder, or "eating disorders not otherwise specified") showing evidence of efficacy at 6- to 12-month follow-up (e.g., Couturier, Kimber, & Szatmari, 2013; Hay, 2013), more research on family therapy (as well as CBT and self-help approaches) with eating disorders is currently being promoted (e.g., Treasure, 2014), and no research exists on family treatment of food addiction.

Family treatment for *pathological gambling* includes GAM-ANON (GA for families), a self-help workbook of the Community Reinforcement and Family Therapy (CRAFT) model for gambling, and a coping skills training program for families of gamblers. These programs have been evaluated in controlled trials (four studies, with small sample sizes, except for one trial with 168 subjects), indicating no or equivocal effects (Hodgins, Toneatto, Makarchuk, Skinner, & Vincent, 2007). Hodgins et al. (2007) did find some advantage of a workbook ("Helping the Problem Gambler. Helping Yourself: A Self-Help Approach for Family Members") or workbook plus telephone support, compared in a randomized controlled trial to mere provision of treatment resource information, up to a six-month follow-up on days gambling (perhaps a 35 percent reduction in days gambled in last 30 days), satisfaction with the program, and number who had their needs met, though larger trials and much more research is needed.

Liu et al. (2015) examined the effectiveness and underlying mechanism of multi-family group therapy(MFGT) to reduce *Internet addiction* among adolescents. A total of 92 participants consisting of 46 families (adolescents with Internet addiction, aged 12 to 18 years and their parents) were assigned to the experimental group (six-session MFGT intervention; a CBT variant involving instruction in parent–child communication skills and relationship building exercises), or a wait-list control in a quasi-experimental design. Structured questionnaires were administered at pre-intervention (T1), post-intervention (T2), and a three-month follow-up (T3). There was a significant difference in the decline both in the average score and proportion of adolescents with Internet addiction (according to the Adolescent Pathological Internet Use Scale cut-off score) in the MFGT group at post-intervention maintained for three months. Importantly, only 11.1 percent versus 87 percent were still addicted at the three-month follow-up comparing MFGT versus the control condition. Improvement in adolescent Internet use was partially explained by the satisfaction of their psychological needs and improved parent–adolescent communication and closeness.

One small single-group study with children who are *online game addicts* found that family therapy (involving family cohesion enhancement by engaging in cooperative tasks) was associated with improvements in neurobiological response (caudate nucleus activation) to emotional attachment/affection versus game stimuli following three weeks of treatment (Han, Kim, Lee, & Renshaw, 2012). Regarding *TV addiction*, Kubey and Csikszentmihalyi (2002) suggested that families might promote other activities (e.g., involving live social interactions), enforce time limits, make use of channel blocking features, plan which shows to watch ahead of time (decision-making), limit the number of TVs in the home, limit location of TVs, and otherwise learn mindful television viewing (e.g., through media education). However, again, there is rather little research completed on families with various behavioral addictions, and such clinical suggestions, while utilized, have not been systematically tested.

Group Therapy

Group therapy provides peer support, feedback, and confrontation, guided by a trained leader. In-depth attention to psychological issues that might occur in group therapy is relatively unlikely to occur in use of self-help groups. In early recovery, the therapist serves as a coach and a monitor. As recovery progresses, the therapist helps group members resolve issues of trauma and learn intimacy with others, as well as learn how to express feelings appropriately (Sussman & Ames, 2008). Group therapy provides a means for addicts trying to recover to provide corrective feedback to each other (e.g., regarding appropriateness of social behavior) and is relatively less expensive than individual therapy. However, the potential for **deviancy training** (e.g., risk-takers daring each other or learning more risky behavior from each other) could result from group participation (O'Leary et al., 2002).

Among the addictions, certainly most research on group therapy has been conducted with substance use disorder. For example, Stead and Lancaster (2005) provided an in-depth review of 53 controlled trials of group therapy for *cigarette smoking cessation* and found that it was superior to self-help or less intensive programming, and appeared about as effective as individual treatment. There was no evidence to suggest that CBT-type group therapy approaches were superior to other group therapy approaches. This same pattern of findings exists regarding treatment of other *substance use disorders* (Weiss, Jaffee, Menil, & Cogley, 2004).

Rash and Petry (2014) completed a recent review of the research evidence for treatment of *gambling disorder*. They noted that involvement in peer support programs seems to be optimal when combined with professional treatment (e.g., CBT); however, engagement and retention in peer support group programs is limited. Still, there is some promise that group therapy for gambling addiction may be efficacious. Ladouceur et al. (2003) evaluated the efficacy of a group cognitive treatment for pathological gambling. Pathological gamblers were randomly assigned to group treatment (n = 34) or wait-list control (n = 24) conditions. Cognitive correction techniques were used first to target gamblers' erroneous perceptions about randomness, and then to address issues of relapse prevention. Post-treatment results indicated that 88 percent of the treated gamblers no longer met DSM-IV criteria for pathological gambling compared to only 20 percent in the control group. Analysis of data from 6-, 12-, and 24-month follow-ups revealed maintenance of therapeutic gains.

Likewise, Carlbring, Jonsson, Josephson, and Forsberg (2010) tested the effectiveness of motivational interviewing, cognitive-behavioral group therapy, and a no-treatment control (wait-list) in the treatment of pathological gambling. This was completed as a randomized controlled trial at an outpatient addiction dependence clinic. A total of 150 primarily self-recruited patients with current gambling problems or pathological gambling were randomized to four individual sessions of motivational interviewing (MI), eight sessions of cognitive-behavioral group therapy (CBGT), or a no-treatment wait-list control. Gambling-related measures derived from timeline follow-back were administered at baseline, termination, and 6 and 12 months post-treatment. Treatment showed superiority over the no-treatment control in the short run. No differences were found between MI and CBGT at any point in time, both showing significant within-group decreases on most outcome measures up to the 12-month follow-up. Neither treatment, however, showed significant differences from the control group at 6- or 12-month follow-up.

Benson, Eisenach, Abrams, and van Stolk-Cooke (2014) investigated the efficacy of a group treatment model for *compulsive buying disorder*, the "Stopping Overshopping" model, which includes aspects of cognitive-behavioral and dialectical behavior therapy, psychodynamic psychotherapy, psychoeducation, motivational interviewing, acceptance and commitment therapy, and mindfulness. A small pilot randomized controlled trial with 11 participants compared the efficacy of this model (n = 6) with a wait-list control group (n = 5), which received the treatment after a 12-week waiting period. Results showed significant improvement on (a) all compulsive buying measures, (b) amount of money and time spent shopping, and (c) number of compulsive shopping episodes, all of which were maintained at 6-month follow-up.

One may learn through group interaction how to better participate in healthy love relationships, which may be less immediately engrossing but more rewarding in the long run (Sussman & Moran, 2013). One pilot study of eight *love addicts* (defined here as an obsessive need to achieve attraction of one's partner) demonstrated greatly reduced self-reports of love addiction-related feelings over 18 group therapy sessions (Lorena, Sophia, Mello, Tavares, & Ziberman, 2008). Though some data were collected and reported on these subjects other than clinical impressions, no comparison group was identified in that study. One may conjecture that group therapy techniques (e.g., use of psychodrama) may help one decrease illusions toward romantic partners, and help one understand one's feelings toward significant others such as one's nuclear family. One may also learn through group interaction how to better participate in healthy romantic relationships, which may be less exciting but more rewarding in the long run (Sussman, 2010a). No group therapy literature for the other focal addictions was identified.

Social Skills Training

An integral component of cognitive-behavioral programs, or as an adjunct to MI, or as a stand-alone treatment, is social skills training (Grenard, Ames, Pentz, & Sussman, 2006; Sussman & Ames, 2008). Social skills training may include the teaching or reinforcing of **self-control skills** (showing restraint under simulated high-risk conditions in social interactions; urge control), shaping of good listening or conversational skills (e.g., through direction instruction, role play instruction, or by example), instruction of anger or other affect management in social situations (e.g., learning how to cope with feelings in an appropriate manner in interpersonal situations through role playing; conflict resolution skill), and learning stimulus–response control approaches (learning how to remove oneself gracefully from addiction-related cues such as escape from drug using or other addiction-related group participation).

Because a lack of social skills may influence drug use or other addictions (e.g., inability to refuse drug offers and involvement in drug-related activities), social skills training often involves assertiveness training. Methods of ***assertiveness training*** vary, but in general, assertiveness training focuses on (a) enhancing appropriate expression of feelings or personal rights, and (b) skills training in refusal of unreasonable requests of others. ***Role playing*** is a primary vehicle for social skills training. Often modeling of assertive behavior, behavioral rehearsal, practice through role playing, performance, and immediate feedback, and reinforcement components are included in the use of role playing as a treatment strategy (Sussman & Ames, 2008). The utility of contents of social skills training are contingent on whether poor behavioral performance is a learning, practice, or motivation deficit (Turner et al., 1993). If poor performance is a learning deficit, instruction and modeling socially skilled behavior is imperative. If it is a practice deficit, then practice and feedback are important. If it is a motivation deficit, then reinforcement may be most important.

Role playing is a technique used to provide opportunities to practice refusal methods in a non-threatening, simulation environment in which mistakes do not lead to relapse (e.g., see Foy, Miller, Eisler, & O'Toole, 1976). There is little research evidence on the efficacy of social skills training in the addictions arena outside of substance use work. However, even within the substance abuse prevention arena it is not clear whether or not social skills training is a key to effects obtained (see Sussman, 2015). Recall that some aspects of social skill might even enable the addict to procure objects or services of his or her addiction (e.g., Wills et al., 1989 regarding conversation initiation skills). Certainly, more research is needed.

Behavioral Contracting

Behavioral contracting is a method of formalizing or reinforcing an individual's commitment to change and is helpful when individuals express ambivalence about change or have been unable to maintain abstinence or control their behaviors. Contracting usually involves a written agreement, signed and agreed on by involved parties (e.g., the contractee and someone who enforces the contract), that includes behavioral constraints on observable behaviors through the use of reinforcers. Contracting can include contingencies describing penalties for violation of the contract (such as paying a fine in the event of a lapse or relapse) and positive reinforcers (i.e., tangible goods such as food or money) for conforming to the contract (i.e., contingency management). This approach may work while the contract is in operation.

Contracting is not a method shown to be consistently effective in the cigarette smoking cessation literature (Fiore et al., 2008). Conversely, contracting between members of a couple in which one member is alcoholic has shown some promise (e.g., Behavioral Couples Therapy; O'Farrell & Fals-Stewart, 2000). Contracts with chemically dependent patients are the core of primary treatment and continuing care, according to Talbott and Crosby (2001), who described a study of 100 addicts in which a contract for chemical dependence treatment and healthy lifestyles may decrease relapse by 20 percent. Likewise, behavioral contracting between youth and their parents may involve the use of reinforcements contingent on activities that are incompatible with drug use behavior (or other addictive behavior) and adherence to appropriate family roles (Sussman & Ames, 2008). Possibly, the fit needs to be good between the behavioral contract and the relationship involved among the two parties. That is, the person to enforce the contract may need to have an accepted dominant role within the relationship (e.g., dominant role as spouse, parent, or treatment agent).

The use of external restraints or penalties can backfire. For example, when a relapse contract expires or the contingencies lose their incentive appeal, an individual may drink or use other drugs again, or perhaps again engage in another addictive behavior (Sussman & Ames, 2008). The timing of the contract needs to be calculated well, there needs to be a means to monitor the contract closely, and the contract needs to be set up as an enforced understanding rather than as some type of legally binding document. Matching contingencies to reflect the natural social environment is a key to successful use of contracting, but it is not an easy task to accomplish. That is, there must be naturally occurring contingencies to maintain the positive behavior that are long-lasting.

While used with substance use disorders (particularly abuse of opiates), there is little discussion of the use of behavioral contracting (contingency management) with the behavioral addictions. This is a topic for future research.

Mass Media-Related Cessation

One form of cessation programming that has extensive reach is use of mass media *public service announcements* (PSAs; brief messages in the public interest disseminated by the media without charge, with the objective of raising awareness and changing public attitudes and behavior toward a social issue), or more extensive multi-media campaigns. Public health media cessation messages may be defined to include any media announcement, for which there is no charge, which educates and increases awareness about the consequences of an addiction and encourages quitting. A mass media campaign tends to involve multiple PSAs and other media channels (e.g., Internet, flyers, radio, TV). There is also cessation programming on new public media (e.g., YouTube), though it is not clear to what extent such programming is evidence-based.

Richardson et al. (Richardson, Vettese, Sussman, Small, & Selby, 2011) examined *cigarette smoking cessation* content posted on YouTube. The search terms "quit smoking" and "stop smoking" yielded 2,250 videos in October 2007. The researchers examined the top 100 as well as 20 randomly selected videos. Of these, 82 were directly relevant to smoking cessation. Fifty-one were commercial productions that included anti-smoking messages and advertisements for hypnosis and NicoBloc fluid. Thirty-one were personally produced videos that described personal experiences with quitting, negative health effects, and advice on how to quit. Although smoking cessation content is being shared on YouTube, very little is based on strategies that have been shown to be evidence-based.

In addition, Sussman et al. (1994) found that a televised tobacco cessation program could reach a range of diverse individuals but that those who intended to quit smoking in the next three months and who had a tendency to use self-help materials were also those who tended to view programming and read cessation campaign messages. Perhaps, for those who are ready to stop using drugs or engaging in another addiction, and who tend to search their environment for assistance of their own accord, media campaigns may attract their attention and reinforce their intentions to quit using drugs or engaging in another addiction.

Although the effectiveness of PSAs is yet to be fully determined, some *anti-drug misuse* public health messages have been found to be effective. For example, as also mentioned regarding prevention, Palmgreen et al. (2001) found that when targeting sensation-seekers with fast-paced, novel, and stimulating televised campaigns, adolescent marijuana use was reduced in high sensation-seekers; that is, that the campaign reversed upward developmental trends in 30-day marijuana use among high sensation-seeking individuals (i.e., about a 10 percent decrease in use was observed the year following the campaign).

Snyder et al. (2004) conducted a meta-analysis of the effect of mediated health communication campaigns on behavior change, all of which had involved use of at least one form of community-wide mass media. They examined average correlations between exposure to a campaign and behavior change across different arenas (a total of 48 campaigns, most targeting youth). Effect sizes varied from 0.15 for seat belt use, 0.13 for oral health, 0.09 for *alcohol use reduction* (access or education programs, targeted prevention; 0.07 for youth targeted programs), 0.05 for heart disease prevention (diet and exercise), 0.05 for *smoking cessation* (four of 17 campaigns involved youth), 0.04 for mammography and cervical cancer screening, and 0.04 for *sexual behaviors*. Apparently, effects for cessation are weak when programming is conducted only through a mass media modality.

If designed for and targeted to appeal to specific individuals (e.g., sensation-seekers), it appears that some PSAs may be effective, and certainly have the ability to reach large groups of individuals. One caveat, however, is that many public service campaigns assume that individuals behave rationally and want to change drug use or other addictive behaviors and that information regarding consequences can effect behavioral change. As the evidence accumulates implicating implicit and dual processes in guiding addictive behavior, it is becoming increasingly clear that engagement in addictive behaviors is not simply a rational choice behavior. Mass media campaigns may reinforce individuals who are already motivated to change but may have little or no effect on those who appear unwilling to change (labeled in the communications literature as **canalization**; e.g., see Flay, 1981). A new generation of targeted addiction-related public health campaigns developers may want to consider the impact of more automatic influences on behavior and means of tapping into these influences, through new modalities (e.g., smartphones), in addition to the use of more rational-deliberate cognition approaches. Such modalities might even be useful to help prevent relapse (e.g., Just-in-Time smoking cessation support; Naughton, 2016).

There is almost no information on cessation of other addictions through use of the mass media. McKinley and Wright (2012) addressed the presence and nature of *problem gambling* messages on university counseling center websites (CCWs). A total of 203 CCWs were randomly selected to assess how frequently they provided any information about problem gambling, as well as the specific types of communications CCWs offered on this topic. They found that CCWs rarely included any messages about problem gambling. Specifically, only 15 percent of all CCWs contained information about problem gambling. Furthermore, messages about problem gambling were presented significantly less frequently than messages involving *alcohol abuse*, *substance abuse*, depression, anxiety/stress, and psychological struggles with *food*. Certainly, controlled trials of mass media-based cessation programming with a variety of addictions are needed. Implementation of such programming will, of course, be contingent in part on the mores of culture within which it is being considered (e.g., some countries may not permit mass-media messages regarding sex addiction).

Environmental and Policy Changes

The same environmental and policy suggestions, and resources acquisition strategies, discussed in Chapter 12 as being prevention-oriented, also apply as cessation strategies, and are quite relevant. The FCTC (regarding tobacco control), various *prohibitory and regulatory policies* (regarding tobacco, alcohol, other drugs, gambling [e.g., number of casinos in a location], food labeling or alternatives, Internet site prohibitions, sex outlets zoning or prohibition), *disrupting the addiction market* (e.g., through opium field eradication), *taxation* (e.g., of cigarettes, alcohol, marijuana in some locations, sweets), and *law enforcement* are relevant to cessation. If people are restricted from using through lack of opportunity or high price, many will quit possibly without formal treatment. So as not to be redundant I refer the reader back to Chapter 12 for a discussion of these strategies. Applications to cessation are obvious.

One area not covered in Chapter 12 includes types of *diversion programming* for individuals caught engaging in illegal addiction-related behavior. For example, use of *drug courts* in the United States has been attempted. Drug courts arrange for substance abuse treatment (mostly outpatient treatment) and other services and monitor progress in treatment among persons accused of a non-violent drug-related crime in lieu of going to prison. Individuals may receive up to a year of drug abuse treatment and six months of aftercare, and may receive services such as mental health treatment, trauma and family therapy, and job skills training (Huddleston, Marlowe, & Casebolt, 2008). While thought to be promising (Huddleston et al., 2008; Sussman & Ames, 2008), recidivism rates are quite high (e.g., 60 percent at five-years follow-up) and, while most research in this arena is not very good, outcome differences of court diversion graduates and dropouts, or those mandated to treatment versus probation, tend to disappear after a couple of years (DeVall, Gregory, & Hartmann, 2015; Drug Policy Alliance, 2011). A series of controlled trials with at least five-year follow-ups might help improve the interpretability of the utility of drug courts.

Other environmental treatment strategies not discussed in Chapter 12 are discussed in the remainder of this section. That is, modification of the larger physical environment through civil engineering modifications (i.e., introducing changes to the built environment), and person-level decisions relevant to the physical environment, are discussed here.

Geographic Applications

Geographic applications may effectively enhance cessation efforts and decrease relapse rates by providing supportive physical structures (e.g., AA and NA club houses, 24-hour drop-in centers, meditation rooms in public buildings) in addition to removing addiction-related locations (e.g., buildings with lack of defensible space and *alcohol* outlets), or making them more difficult to access, within a given geographical radius (Mason, Cheung, & Walker, 2004).

Increase in locations that provide healthy foods (e.g., fruits and vegetables) might help with *food addiction*. Research is needed, of course, and would need cooperation from the private sector, which may be difficult.

Responsible Gambling Information Centers (RGICs) are located within *gambling* venues. The primary purpose of the RGIC is to provide, on customer request, information and education about the risks of gambling (e.g. odds of winning and losing; demonstrations/tutorials about slot machine workings/random number generation). A second purpose is to identify, support, and refer RGIC visitors who are experiencing problems with gambling. Immediate crisis intervention and counseling may be provided by on-site staff. RGICs are sometimes staffed by casino employees and sometimes by employees of addiction agencies. Utilization rates for RGICs appear to be fairly low by patron utilization standards. No data exist on efficacy of RGICs (Williams et al., 2012). Environmental or large-scale policy modifications have not been envisioned to pertain to most of the addictions, though *workplace or school-based assistance programs* might be considered geographic-based treatment (primarily as locations to assess and refer *tobacco, alcohol, and other drug* abusers; Sussman & Ames, 2008). One may envision such a model to apply to *workaholics*. Again, this is a venue for future research and practice, even by keeping records on number of persons approached and assisted, if not through use of controlled trials.

There is little such environmental-level research regarding the remaining focal addictions, and I am not sure such strategies are applicable. That is, it would seem that love, Internet, shopping, exercise, and probably sex addictions would have no or little relevance to the built environment.

There are some person-level environmental strategies that might be primarily suitable as a means of cessation. These strategies may involve (a) avoiding the location of the object of addiction and (b) approaching healthy alternatives. For example, regarding any addiction it may be important, at least initially, to avoid stimuli associated with the addiction if possible (e.g., having *cigarettes* in the house, ashtrays, *liquor* stores, gambling casinos, massage parlors, match-making websites, perhaps the Internet outside of certain hours). Interestingly, Fisher (2006) suggested that it may be most prudent to avoid all contact with the objects of a *love addiction*, particularly rejecting partners, and for one to become exposed to novel environments to facilitate new, more healthy experiences. Also, the love addict might establish short-term goals that could include signing up for community courses (e.g., photography), participation in meditation or exercise, and learning how to make non-sexual, non-romantic friends (Weiss & Schneider, 2006; Wolfe, 2000). If addiction-related stimuli can't be avoided, one may need to utilize self-talk (e.g., to look the other way, not react, or to restrict what one says) or social support strategies (e.g., strength in numbers) to "walk past" or "work past" the addictive objects, as well as learn to identify and approach non-addiction-related stimuli (e.g., meditation rooms).

Summary

This chapter discussed the motivational intervention, 12-step programs, family therapy, group therapy, social skills instruction, behavioral contracting (contingency management), mass media-aided cessation, and environmental and policy considerations. Along with intrapersonal strategies, these extrapersonal strategies may assist in restoration of life balance – critical in healing any of the 11 focal addictions. A comprehensive approach is important, which includes a healthy diet, monitored exercise, sleep, relaxation techniques, stress management, assertiveness training, and inclusion of identification with some spiritual or existential ideals (e.g., through religious group involvement, or meditation), perhaps, as well as involvement in both intrapersonal and extrapersonal level therapies. It is important to embed the individual in a healthy environment, and make a healthy adjustment to an ongoing environment. Intrapersonal and extrapersonal levels of adjustment likely interact to produce the best outcomes.

Bulleted Summary

- The motivational intervention involves (1) inquiry, (2) assessment, (3) preparation, (4) intervention, and (5) follow-up/case management phases, and is successful in getting people into treatment if families will agree to be a part of this activity (which is very hard to do). 12-step programs exist for the 11 focal addictions but research on their efficacy is sparse and exists primarily for alcohol and other drug use. In general, studies that exist suggest that 12-step programs do no better or worse than other modalities.
- Family and group therapies for the 11 focal addictions have shown equivocal effects. Family therapy might work relatively well when the target addict is the child. Group therapies often show an effect on addictions when combined with other modalities such as individual therapy. Empirical work exists mostly for tobacco, alcohol, and other drug abuse cessation.

- Social skills training is a key extrapersonal strategy that may be used with families or groups. While having a long history in the drug abuse prevention and cessation arena, the usefulness or needed contents of this approach is contingent on whether the "lack" of social skill reflects a learning, practice, or motivation deficit. Behavioral contracting may be a valuable strategy for shaping appropriate behavior; however, it only works as long as it is in place and fading to the natural environment is imperative or behavior will tend to return to the problematic baseline.
- Mass media cessation, given that it has good "reach," likely helps those who are motivated to make use of such material. Physical environmental manipulations (e.g., outlawing cigarette vending machines and cigarette billboard advertisements) may have resulted in lowering the prevalence of tobacco addiction (Sussman & Ames, 2008). RGICs are an example of a physical environment modality that might assist with gambling addiction cessation or moderation. RGICs are located within gambling venues, and might intervene with problem gamblers. Research is needed. Almost no research is available pertaining to physical environmental manipulations and behavioral addictions. Certainly, in zones where gambling casinos are not allowed, prevalence of gambling problems may be lower. More such work is needed regarding all of the 11 focal addictions.

Suggestions for Further Reading

Cowlishaw, S., Merkouris, S., Dowling, N., Anderson, C., Jackson, A., & Thomas, S. (2012). Psychological therapies for pathological and problem gambling. *Cochrane Database of Systematic Reviews*, 11: Article CD008937.

Kelly, J. F., Hoeppner, B., Stout, R. L., & Pagano, M. (2011). Determining the relative importance of the mechanisms of behavior change within Alcoholics Anonymous: A multiple mediator analysis. *Addiction*, 107: 289–299.

Liu, C., Liao, M., & Smith, D. C. (2012). An empirical review of internet addiction outcome studies in China. *Research on Social Work Practice*, 22: 282–292.

Snyder, L. B., Hamilton, M. A., Mitchell, E. W., Kiwanuka-Tondo, J., Fleming-Milici, F., & Proctor, D. (2004). A meta-analysis of the effect of mediated health communication campaigns on behavior change in the United States. *Journal of Health Communication*, 9: 71–96.

Sussman, S. & Ames, S. L. (2008). *Drug Abuse: Concepts, Prevention and Cessation*. Cambridge University Press.

Williams, R. J., West, B. L., & Simpson, R. I. (2012). *Prevention of Problem Gambling: A Comprehensive Review of the Evidence and Identified Best Practices*. Guelph, ON: Report prepared for the Ontario Problem Gambling Research Centre and the Ontario Ministry of Health and Long Term Care, December 1, 2007. http://hdl.handle.net/10133/414; accessed November 25, 2014.

16 Future Considerations for Substance and Behavioral Addictions

Learning Objectives

- To consider more the relations between appetitive needs and addictive effects, and potential implications for future research and practice
- To consider measurement issues such as inclusion and exclusion criteria for the diagnosis of a problematic addiction, and clustering of addictions within and across time
- To revisit consideration of moderation versus abstinence outcomes among the addictions, and breadth of prevention and treatment programming
- To examine the relevance of the "translation-transdisciplinary research matrix" to furthering understanding of the addictions

Introduction

Where is Johnny now? Where is he going? Johnny still works hard, still has a family, as he ages. He has had several repeated alcohol, "love," and work binges followed by periods of attempted balanced living or "going on the wagon" type behavior. His exercise and drug addictions seemed to have resolved naturally. Johnny still got drunk because when he was drunk he really felt self-contained, stronger, insulated from the judgments of others. When his anxiety just seemed too, too much, he could go drink and achieve a real subjective sense of relief and satisfaction. His engagement in other addictions likewise made him feel more self-contained temporarily. He was "willing" to endure any number of negative consequences, including physical pain after a binge period, just to feel better quickly. I don't know where he is headed. I hope he is becoming more balanced as a person and that he will learn happiness and wisdom, and that he is able to remove himself as a "slave" to any number of addictions as he grows older. One thing that Johnny began to assert is that for him to obtain real and lasting "sobriety," he has had to get under control all of his addictions – that is, the underlying functions that they share needed to be arrested. Also, he claimed that he has to change his behavior for himself and only for himself because no one can follow him around 24 hours a day. Conversely, perhaps, he also acknowledged great benefit to his motivation to be "sober" of being exposed to encouraging displays of the "human spirit"; that is, exposure to writings or acts of human kindness. For example, he was moved by the writings of Anne Frank (Frank, 1993) such as the quote: "It's really a wonder that I haven't dropped all my ideals, because they seem so absurd and impossible to carry out. Yet I keep them, because in spite of everything, I still believe that people are really good at heart." He believed that, eventually, he will experience peace due to achieving balance in living. He also knew that the "magic ingredient" to life balance would be acting life in balance no matter how he was feeling, or what thoughts popped to mind. Eventually, it would happen, guided by ideals.

In this final chapter, I investigate future needs in research and practice pertaining to the 11 focal addictions to help people like Johnny. Issues related to research concepts, etiology, and prevalence are discussed first. Next, measurement issues are discussed, followed by issues in practice. Finally, hope for a better understanding of the addictions through a transdisciplinary-translation matrix is discussed. Key concepts discussed in this chapter are depicted in Table 16.1.

Research Concepts, Etiology, Prevalence

The appetitive effects notion is the guiding underlying concept of this text (i.e., associational memory-appetitive system relations-based [AMASR]). The idea is that one's neurobiology is equipped with adaptation-motivation mechanisms (e.g., for survival, contentment, support). These mechanisms can become misdirected, overcharged, or otherwise dysregulated (unreliable) due to the operation of relatively automatic scripts created in associational memory, or due to a misdirected chain of explicit cognitive thought, or to a dual process of implicit and explicit cognition (e.g., Thush et al., 2008), after repeating an addictive behavior–satiation sequence many times, which tie appetitive effects to the addictive behavior rather than to more adaptive behavior (e.g., actual survival enhancement, sustained contentment, or ongoing support). I really like the appetitive effects concept, and believe that it is a binding thread across many research and practice camps that explore addictions (e.g., incentive-sensitization, dysregulation, social learning, or recovery movement).

However, I admit that there is no organized, clear-cut system of "drives" that lead to differential subjective reports of feeling happier, less sad, more sedated or aroused, or more engrossed or quieted cognitively, during an addictive behavioral bout. Investigation into such an organized network of *instincts* (e.g., natural, inherent tendencies such as seeking pleasant events–avoiding harm, fight–flight, dominance–nurturance, or exploration–hibernation) has not yielded a consensus within the scientific community after over 100 years of thought. One may speculate any number of research directions that could convince researchers, and facilitate consensus. For example, possibly, use of Big Behavioral Data (BBD), that can interface and integrate perspectives of psychology, ethology, and neuroscience, will be able to establish a convincing structure of motivation and addiction (see Gomez-Marin, Paton, Kampff, Costa, & Mainen, 2014). Theory is needed as a guide, however. One potential perspective is the assertion that all human motivation is a search for change, and that the locus of change (self, material world, social world) and type of change (potential/expectations

Research Concepts, Etiology, Prevalence

Table 16.1 Future directions

Guiding definition of addiction: the associational memory-appetitive system relations (AMASR) model	One's neurobiology is equipped with adaptation-motivation mechanisms (e.g., for survival, contentment, support). These mechanisms can become misdirected, overcharged, or otherwise dysregulated (unreliable) due to the operation of relatively automatic scripts created in associational memory after repeated exposure to an addictive behavior, which tie appetitive effects to the addictive behavior rather than to more adaptive behavior (e.g., actual survival enhancement, sustained contentment, or ongoing support).
PACE (pragmatics, attraction, communication, expectations) model	Future theoretical development might consider the AMASR model within the context of the PACE model. Pragmatics leads to trying out an addictive behavior. Attraction to appetitive effects achieved leads to experimentation and regular involvement in the addiction. Communication regarding the addiction reflects the depth and breadth of the AM-AS structure. Expectations that the behavior is continuing to fulfill appetitive needs helps maintain the addiction.
Measurement of "inherent" qualities of an addiction experience	It is not clear whether or not behaviors vary in their inherent qualities to become additive. Possibly, slow, contemplative behavior (e.g., with gardening) may indicate a non-addictive quality to some behavior (see discussion in Chapter 2). Work on measuring immediate experience (rush effects, change in phenomenological experience such as feeling more normal) might be attempted.
The paradox of the directions prevention or cessation can take	In the simplest sense, programming needs to either (a) steer involvement in the direction of less harmful expressions (safer substitutes) that serve similar functions or (b) facilitate non-addictive behavioral involvement (slow, deliberate behavioral activities) that may serve rather dissimilar functions. Future program development should consider both directions of work.
Targets of prevention or cessation programming	Addictive behavior prevention or cessation could involve addressing a single addiction or a related set of addictions (e.g., several drugs of abuse). Arguments that favor focusing on a single addiction include being able to provide a sufficient amount of focused information, the possibility that different addictions might be

(cont.)

Table 16.1 *(cont.)*

	engaged in for different reasons, and the need to keep programming to a reasonable length. One main argument that favors the concurrent prevention or treatment of multiple addictions is that information may be efficiently provided that counteracts involvement in any one of several behaviors by focusing on common underlying functions (i.e., counteracting maladaptive AMASR, and related preoccupation and loss of control).
Need for translation-transdisciplinary work	Interestingly, although treated as two different topics, transdisciplinary work and translation work are part of a matrix that may represent a new "revolution" in addictions prevention and cessation research. We are asked to bridge across disciplines and consider solutions that might have an enduring behavioral impact from the onset of our work (Sussman et al., 2006). This text provides one example of an effort to accomplish just that purpose, to represent a bridge to a new transdisciplinary research culture that pertains at the same time to translation work.

for life, process/experience of living, outcomes/evaluations of life activities) delineate a structure of taxonomy of motivation that can guide investigations into situational dynamics in human behavior (Forbes, 2011), including the addictions.

Undoubtedly there will be many years of debate on phenomena such as those described in this text. The various theories presented in the early chapters may suggest to the reader both overlapping and unique aspects to addiction phenomena (Sussman & Sussman, 2011). One may question whether or not behaviors examined are part of the same entity, or whether there are several different disorders that are merely being treated the same way. Thus, there is the current struggle between addictions as examples of OCD or as motivated behavior, for example; of course, there may be some difficulty sometimes distinguishing the difference between OCDs and addictions – depending on how broadly or narrowly they are defined (recall the discussion of this debate in Chapter 1).

When is Excessive Behavior in Pursuit of Appetitive Effects an "Addiction"?

It does seem to be the case that up to 50 percent of adults in a one-year period struggle with one or more of the 11 focal addictions addressed in this text (which may reflect

90 percent of all addictions we experience; e.g., Sussman et al., 2014). Of course, one may debate when to label an excessive behavior as being an addiction as opposed to merely an excessive instance of a behavior that may or may not become addictive. Such a judgment call (outside of extremes of behavior) depends on the "judge" (and the criteria used), the context in which the judgment is made (being drunk or engaging in online gambling in a library would seem different than being drunk or gambling in a bar or casino), and the frequency, severity, and type of negative consequences uncovered. Agreement regarding repeated instances of a negative role consequence (i.e., ability to serve one's home or work functions, and self-care) across judges and contexts likely will be a guiding protocol in this arena. Hopefully an intensionally defined, etiological model will result eventually from such consensus – which I believe the AMASR model could represent. Such a model might contribute more to etiology than would only a taxonomic, extensionally defined expression.

Possibly, it is part of being human that addictive behavior exists (Marks, 1990), as a quantitatively varying phenomenon, and a side-effect of AMASR. Probably everyone has experienced some type of addiction-like phenomenon which merely exists as a temporary fluke within AMASR. On Thanksgiving in the United States, people tend to overeat a great deal. They may be preoccupied about the food they are about to eat, lose control over intake, achieve a self-nurturance appetitive "rush" effect and satiation, and then maybe later on get a stomach ache and be unable to continue their role as host for that evening (a negative consequence). However, the food addictive behavior may be ritualized and constrained within that one holiday week. It is when there exist severe or repeated occurrences of that behavior, such that one even attempts to hide that behavior (on a number of occasions) from others, and one's roles in day-to-day life suffer, continually, that such behavior becomes identified as a "true" addiction (i.e., repeated dysfunction with repeated negative consequences).

Unfortunately, taken across so many behaviors on which AMASR can operate in one's daily life, it may be easy to understand how it is that an addiction to one or more such behaviors can occur among many people – falling under "the radar" in several instances (e.g., particularly regarding food, Internet, sex, love, work, exercise, or shopping addictions). Arguably, the most "visible" addictions – tobacco, alcohol, or illicit drug use, and gambling – are also the ones now officially recognized as addictions by the American Psychiatric Association (APA, 2013). As an addiction's visibility increases consistently above some public awareness threshold, perhaps, it may achieve some type of "official" status (Sinclair et al., 2016).

An alternative way to consider an appetitive needs perspective might be to compare addictive "drives" with survival drives. When a person fails to breathe in enough oxygen or eat enough food, for example, after a while the person will become extremely hungry for air or food, possibly feeling like one will die. Over time, though, the person may no longer experience these cravings. Then later on the person will die. When a person fails to partake in an addictive behavior in which one is entrenched, after a while the person will become extremely hungry for the object of the addiction – possibly feeling like one will die. Over time, the person may no longer experience these cravings. However, later on the person will feel better. That is, the topography of cravings may be identical across (addictive and non-addictive) drives in the earlier phases of withdrawal, but diverge later on. This would make sense in that the same neurobiological systems are activated by different appetitive objects.

There has been a suggestion that such high prevalence of addictive behaviors (i.e., almost 50 percent of the population in the last year) is in part due to modern lifestyle factors that tend to promote trial of and continued engagement in these behaviors, or necessitate coping attempts that are manifested by continued engagement (e.g., Alexander, 2012; Brown, 2014). This problem of lifestyle may interface with neurobiological systems associated with obtaining appetitive effects (e.g., affect, arousal, and thought regulation). One may assert that prevalence of addictions has increased as the pace of life has sped up. Though plausible, there is insufficient information to make such an assertion with confidence. If social contextual factors can be toxic, however, recent clinical thinking includes means to nurture prosociality (cooperative social behavior, conscientiousness), minimize toxic socio-developmental events, and foster psychological flexibility, all of which might result in more protective large social environments (see Biglan & Embry, 2013).

The PACE Model and Appetitive Effects

Assuming that widespread lifestyle factors "set the stage" for addiction to occur, however, such factors do not demarcate which addictions will occur (i.e., besides ones that might be due to changes in technology, and are relatively novel or noticeable). Rather, specificity of forms of addiction likely is due to the PACE variables of Pragmatics (awareness of and access to different avenues of addiction), Attraction (positive affective response, differential subjective effects of the addictive objects and contexts), Communication (learning the language associated with specific addictions [e.g., "chasing losses" in gambling]), and Expectations (meeting one's immediate desires or goals when participating in that behavior). Research that can explore a PACE-type model is needed and may entail the need for a combination of quantitative and phenomenological/qualitative work.

The operation of the PACE variables may vary across different addictive behaviors. For example, *pragmatics* may be a relatively important determinant of addiction pertaining to relatively hard-to-locate addictive behaviors (e.g., injection drug use, perhaps regular alcohol use among preteens), but may not be as important a determinant of easy-to-locate behaviors (e.g., eating, alcohol use among adults). Some addictions may be *attractive* to a relatively small percentage of the population (e.g., exercise), whereas other behaviors may have wide appeal (e.g., food). It is highly likely that each addiction is associated with specialized words or slang (*communication*). It is also possible that relatively socially acceptable addictive behaviors (eating, working, exercise) have fewer words associated with them to disguise their intent from non-participants (i.e., "code words"; not needed). Finally, it is possible that different addictive behaviors are associated with different outcome *expectancies* (e.g., hedonism versus nurturance; recall the discussion in Chapter 5). Examination of the relative importance of different PACE variables with different patterns of addiction specificity will require much work.

It also is important to note that there may be different patterns of addiction specificity within individuals over time, a topic discussed primarily in only one chapter of this text (i.e., Chapter 8). That is, when an addiction or finite set of addictions is terminated, a second addiction or set of addictions may or may not emerge. Longitudinal studies that assess the chronicity and/or fluidity of addictions within individuals will provide valuable information regarding how effectively a PACE model delineates specificity versus co-occurrence; and within-person variability in cross-addiction tendencies. This is an important issue that should be addressed in future work.

The specific causal mechanisms for individual differences in addictive behavior need investigation. It is not clear to what extent one addiction is exchangeable with another in terms of causal mechanisms involved. While the AMASR framework would seem to appear to be a general binding thread, the variable avenues of addiction suggested by the PACE model may indicate operation of different specific causal pathways. The pathways taken may vary as a function of such background variables as geographical location, socioeconomic status, age, gender, and ethnicity, among other demographic, large-scale social variables; these variables need study.

Indeed, this text did not delve much into issues of diversity, ethnicity, or culture. Such topics are becoming well researched in ATOD research (e.g., Sussman & Ames, 2008). Disenfranchised, culturally displaced ethnic minorities do tend to show worse problems with the addictions (e.g., American Indians and alcoholism, gambling addiction, and smoking; Landen, Roeber, Naimi, Nielsen, & Sewell, 2014; Raylu & Oei, 2004; Secades-Villa et al., 2013). Examination of the 11 focal addictions as a function of ethnicity is ongoing. However, tentative findings are indicating almost no publications examining differences in prevalence and co-occurrence of the addictions other than ATOD use as a function of ethnicity (Luczak et al., in press), and almost no studies on all of the 11 addictions examining large-scale nationally representative studies. A few studies, with some equivocal results, have suggested greater BED among whites (compared to African American and Asian groups), but current food addiction results do not appear to favor one ethnicity over another considering the available pool of studies (Luczak et al., in press). One study of the association of gambling addiction with alcohol abuse among Chinese, Korean, and white American college students suggested greater gambling problems among male Chinese students, also being more strongly associated with alcohol use disorders (Luczak & Wall, in press). Unfortunately, there are too few studies to make any statements regarding ethnic variation in prevalence for Internet, love, sex, work, exercise, or shopping addictions. Again, these variables need study.

Some Fundamental Limitations in Multiple Addictions Research

There are limitations with the current field of addictions research and the idea of multiple addictions. At least three limitations need to be mentioned in this chapter on future directions. First, there is a paucity of data on the prevalence and co-occurrence of some of the addictive behaviors (i.e., love, sex, exercise, workaholism, and shopping). More studies on these behaviors with large samples are needed. Second, very few studies examine multiple addictions in the same sample. Further work of this type might be enlightening. Additional research that examines patterns of covariation of multiple addictive behaviors in the same sample over multiple points in time might enable various stakeholder communities (including researchers and practitioners in the addictive behaviors field) to learn more about the underlying etiology and co-occurrence of addictive behaviors and, consequently, how to best treat these behaviors. Finally, very few data on lifetime addiction across the 11 focal addictions exist. I conjecture that if one examines lifetime addiction a majority of the population will indicate having an addiction problem at some point in their lives.

Measurement

There are numerous measurement issues that need to be explored in future research. Five of these issues are discussed as follows. First, inclusion and exclusion criteria for various addictions need better precision. Criteria do vary. Some criteria likely are measures of the same underlying construct (e.g., the DSM includes several criteria that all seem to be tapping preoccupation; which might end up weighting more heavily one underlying dimension). Also, the relative emphasis on negative consequences may vary in the measurement of some addictions (e.g., is enthusiastic workaholism as much an addiction as compulsive workaholism?). I believe that there needs to be an integration of an intensional approach with a criteria-based approach to avoid redundancy in criteria used to establish an addiction.

Second, there is a need to advance a consensus-based set of measurements needed to establish a behavior as being an addiction. Gambling addiction was added to the DSM-V, with the declaration that sufficient research had been completed to "clear it" as an addiction, like tobacco, alcohol, and other drug abuse. The DSM stated that other classes of behaviors were likely to be addictions but that research is needed to validate and formalize their status as an addiction (e.g., national prevalence studies, validated criteria, neurobiological support). Importantly, validation of measures of various behavioral addictions is needed. This may be difficult to do; corroborative reports, use of daily diaries or ecological momentary assessment techniques, and other types of data (e.g., financial records) may assist. Neurobiological assessments may become more realistic as costs go down (current costs of an fMRI may vary between $1100 and $2700 depending on location and the protocol used; e.g., http://geraldguild.com/blog/2011/02/18/brain-waves-and-other-brain-measures/; http://fmri.research.umich.edu/users/billing.php; http://mrrc.yale.edu/users/charges.aspx) and as phenotypic measures become more precise. For example, increased use of brain scanning techniques to identify addictive disorders, or to predict relapse, and associated areas of research may become a reality in the near future (e.g., see Rosenberg & Feder, 2014a).

A very recent example of the prediction of drug abuse relapse through use of neurobiological assessment is instructive in understanding addiction. Gowin et al. (Gowin, Ball, Wittmann, Tapert, & Paulus, 2015) studied 68 methamphetamine-dependent adults (15 female), recruited from 28-day inpatient treatment programs. During treatment, participants completed an fMRI scan that examined brain activation during reward processing. Patients were followed one year later to assess abstinence. Gowin and colleagues examined brain activation during reward processing between relapsing and abstaining individuals. They employed three ***random forest***

prediction models (i.e., clinical and personality measures, neuroimaging measures, or a combined model, using a machine-learning tool which averages many decision-trees according to an algorithm) to generate predictions for each participant regarding their relapse likelihood. Eighteen individuals relapsed. There were significant group by reward-size interactions for neural activation in the left insula and right striatum for rewards. Abstaining individuals showed increased activation for large, risky relative to small, safe rewards, whereas relapsing individuals failed to show differential activation between reward types. Thus, neuroimaging may assist in the prediction of relapse, advancing the tools providers can use to make decisions about individualized treatment of substance use disorders (Gowin et al., 2015). Possibly, a similar approach may be utilized with food or behavioral addictions (e.g., see Balodis et al., 2012, regarding gambling addiction and reduced activity in the ventromedial prefrontal cortex, insula, and ventral striatum during several phases [varying time of presentation and abstractness of a monetary cue] of a monetary incentive gain–loss delay task).

Third, measurement of "inherent" qualities of an addiction experience across different behaviors needs work. It is not clear whether or not behaviors vary in their inherent qualities to become additive. Possibly, slow, contemplative behavior (e.g., with gardening) may indicate a non-addictive quality to some behavior (see discussion in Chapter 2). Work on measuring immediate experience (rush effects, change in phenomenological experience such as feeling more normal) might be attempted. Possibly, qualitative studies are needed to better understand the differences between addictive and non-addictive experience (e.g., through use of ecological momentary assessment approaches).

Fourth, there is much empirical work that needs to be done to understand the clustering of addictions. As examples, it is important to understand which addictive behaviors tend to be more likely to co-occur, or serve as substitutes for each other. Convergent and discriminant validity across different addictions is needed to be able to better understand clustering effects.

Longitudinal Studies

Fifth, there are few longitudinal studies on the trajectories of and the relations among different addictions. Data comparing the age of onset, duration, recurrence, or natural recovery from different constellations of addictions would be beneficial for understanding different patterns of addiction co-occurrence as well as assisting in clinical intervention development. It is plausible that the developmental trajectories for different addictions vary. For example, it is possible that addiction to exercise develops quite slowly because it can take years for one to get in good enough shape to be able to exercise excessively. On the other hand, addiction to cigarette smoking may occur relatively quickly. Different steepness in trajectories may provide one reason why more people may become addicted to one behavior (e.g., cigarette smoking) versus another (e.g., exercise). In addition, possibly, people who become addicted to a lower trajectory addiction (e.g., exercise) may become addicted to other lower trajectory addictions (e.g., workaholism), at least more so than persons who tend to become addicted to higher trajectory addictions.

Regarding longitudinal relations among addictions, a few studies have been completed. Sun et al. (2012) found compulsive Internet use (CIU) was not related to substance use at baseline in a replication samples study among youth from Chinese and US alternative high schools. In addition, though, baseline CIU predicted change in substance use among females, but not males. Baseline substance use failed to predict change in CIU. Understanding why this pattern of effects occurred in both samples is not yet well understood.

Sussman et al. (2015b) found one-year stability among the 11 focal addictions in 538 at-risk emerging adults. They uncovered two classes that were highly stable, through use of latent class analysis (LCA) and latent transitions analysis (LTA). Over 85% of those not addicted to one of the 11 addictive behaviors at the first time point tended not to be addicted to a specific behavior at the second time point. Thus, there was a stable non-addicted class (approximately 65% of the sample). They also examined the percentages of those reporting addiction to a specific behavior at baseline who also reported addiction to that same behavior one year later. While LCA indicated a very stable addicted class over time (90%), there was some apparent switching around within the class. The "stability" for specific addictions was fairly high for cigarettes (73%) and hard drugs (56%); more moderate for sex (47%), work (47%), exercise (46%), Internet (43%), love (42%), eating (41%), and shopping (35%); and relatively low for alcohol (28%) and gambling (18%). Those data suggested that, while some notable specific-addiction stability existed, more work is needed to understand addiction switching over time (e.g., see Carnes et al., 2005).

One other study uncovered a converse set of findings. Konkolÿ Thege et al. (Konkolÿ Thege, Woodin, Hodgins, & Williams, 2015) investigated the five-year trajectories of exercise, sex, shopping, SNS, video gaming, and eating addictions among a cohort of 4,121 adults from Ontario, Canada. Their results revealed that most participants reported having problematic over-involvement for just one of these behaviors and just in a single time period. That study differed from Sussman et al. (2015b) in that they studied a general population of older adults (mean age at baseline = 46.1 years), used only a one-sentence descriptor to identify addictions ("Are there activities that you engage in where your over-involvement has caused significant problems for you in the past 12 months?"), examined fewer addictions, and studied involvement in specific addictions as opposed to membership in latent addiction classes. More work is needed to try to understand when and for whom an addictive behavior is or is not stable over time (e.g., type of population [emerging adult, older adult, at-risk youth]), which addictions are relatively stable (considering a wide breadth of addictions measured), and which measures of addiction are best to use in longitudinal work (addiction matrix items, assessment of severity of behavior).

Practice

In prevention and cessation practice, there needs to be continual monitoring of the potential interplay among different addictions, either (a) steering involvement in the direction of less harmful expressions (safer substitutes) that serve similar functions or (b) facilitating non-addictive behavioral involvement (slow, deliberate behavioral activities) that may serve rather dissimilar functions, perhaps, in the short run but possibly similar functions in the long run (e.g., use of financial planning resources rather than gambling to make money). However, it is not clear whether substitute versus non-compatible alternatives programming should be applied to single addictive behaviors or sets of addictive behaviors.

Breadth of Programming

One area that has not received much research attention in drug abuse or other addictions prevention or cessation, or health behavior research programming in general, is ***breadth of programming***. It is not clear if one prevention program or cessation treatment can be used for all addictions, perhaps even encompassing healthy lifestyles, or whether programming needs to focus on each addictive behavior separately. That is, different addictions may serve similar underlying functions (e.g., mesolimbic dopamine activity, associative learning processes [such as AMASR], problem proneness, peer group solidarity), in which case the underlying mechanism might be targeted for prevention or cessation efforts.

One may consider whether or not there exist ***primary versus secondary addictions*** (e.g., the primary addiction being of most importance, more immediately life-threatening, or earlier in the chain of addictive behaviors; Schneider, 2005). One may want to treat the primary addiction first. Alternatively, one may attempt to treat multiple addictions at one time, as a combined general addiction treatment strategy, regardless of primacy of addiction. After all, if one addiction terminated, the other may gain force unless it too is treated.

Understanding individual trajectories associated with addiction specificity could be useful for treatment planning and tailoring. For example, PACE information could be used to identify those individuals who would benefit from interventions that target a single addictive behavior (e.g., nicotine replacement for tobacco) versus interventions which would be more useful for individuals who experience co-occurring addictions (e.g., impulse-control interventions or learning new ways to manage anhedonia could benefit many different addictions).

Thus, addictive behavior prevention or cessation could involve addressing a single addiction or a related set of addictions (e.g., several drugs of abuse). Arguments that favor focusing on a single addiction include being able to provide a sufficient amount of focused information, the possibility that different addictions might be engaged in for different reasons, and the need to keep programming to a reasonable length. One main argument that favors the concurrent prevention or treatment of multiple addictions is that information may be efficiently provided that counteracts involvement in any one of several behaviors by focusing on common underlying functions (i.e., perhaps counteracting maladaptive AMASR, and related preoccupation and loss of control).

Even more broadly, programming could address healthy lifestyles as well. One may argue that unhealthy lifestyles in general reflect common underlying functions. Sedentary living or exercise addiction, fatty diets or food addiction, drug use, and any of the other behavioral addictions might best be counteracted together as a joint expression of a lack of a sense of wellness, or as problem proneness (Sussman & Ames, 2001). One older review study suggests that prevention programs with a wide breadth of health and risk behaviors are nearly as effective as narrowly focused programs (Johnson, MacKinnon, & Pentz, 1996). Although only a handful of studies were included in that review, the results suggest common underlying mechanisms. Conscientiousness (industriousness and thinking of others, and having a positive attitude), for example, appears to be one such underlying remedial factor in human living (see Sussman et al., 2013b).

Satiation Period and Clinical Solutions

Work is needed to understand the parameters of the satiation period pertaining to an addiction. To feel satiated means that, for at least a brief period, addictive wanting is not operative. As mentioned in Chapter 2, just because a feeling of being satiated is elicited does not necessarily mean that the addict will then discontinue the behavior at that moment. Satiation may dissipate quickly upon termination of the behavior. Still, one may speculate that the experience of satiation may somehow indicate a solution to addictive behavior problems. Perhaps it is possible to tailor safe or "better directed" alternatives to addiction-related satiation of subjective appetitive needs (e.g., Alcoholics Anonymous, 1976), or possibly learn to accept the inevitability of feeling a sense of "wanting" as a side effect of modern living. Acceptance of feeling this wanting ("Sit still and hurt") may, itself, dissipate over time.

Practical Financial Implications of Addressing Multiple Addictions

There are financial implications of multiple addictions work in the practice arena. Given that clients can afford to pay for their own treatment, therapists who specialize in the treatment of multiple addictions provide for themselves a larger client base and potentially more business. However, to label many behaviors as addictions, which might be considered DSM-like diseases, could end up increasing the scope of insurance coverage. This could increase insurance rates for everyone. Deciding which behaviors can be covered by insurance and which ones cannot be covered may prove difficult.

The Future of Work on Multiple Addictions: The Transdisciplinary-Translation Matrix

It has become a truism that addiction is a multifaceted, complex public health problem that requires the efforts of multiple disciplines to address the biological, psychological, and social environmental aspects that contribute to the prevention of the onset and progression of the disorder(s) (APA, 2013). However, merely acknowledging the need for involvement of multiple disciplines is not sufficient. In fact, increasingly it is becoming the case that merely including measures of convenience from multiple disciplines to capture different perspectives, to explain more variance in behavior, or to present a comprehensive prevention or treatment program package, is both theoretically and practically inadequate.

Theories and findings from discrete disciplinary and research foci can be used in integrative ways to build new prevention or treatment science. The transdisciplinary approach creates a synergy through combining diverse theories and findings with the potential for evolving into new entities important in their own right. A transdisciplinary focus may help to "open up the box" to explain for whom specific prevention or cessation approaches work best and under what conditions. A transdisciplinary approach to understanding or controlling for cohort and contextual differences, and statistically controlling for varying influences at different levels of analysis, would help set expectations for future prevention and cessation research.

Rosenfield (1992) provided one of the early reviews of transdisciplinary research, proposing that such an approach could yield qualitatively different results than those discovered by multidisciplinary or interdisciplinary teams. She defined **transdisciplinarity** as a problem-focused approach that blurs the boundaries between disciplines with the assumption that investigators using the approach must have sufficient knowledge of each other's disciplines to enable effective communication. The result is a new assimilation of ideas and methods. Rosenfield provided an informative history of effective but relatively rare transdisciplinary integrations across social and medical sciences beginning in the 1940s. In her view, transdisciplinary research can be differentiated from both multidisciplinary research and interdisciplinary research (which involves investigators from different arenas working on similar research problems, separately or together), with transdisciplinary research having the greatest potential for innovation. In transdisciplinary research, a new integrative vocabulary is forged across disciplines and creates new syntheses (e.g., neurobehavioral science). Of course, one may argue that different types of team approaches may be used to answer different questions and that the transdisciplinary approach may not be needed or desirable to address all research questions. Still, at the very minimum, the transdisciplinary perspective has not been used often and is an exciting perspective to pursue (see Fuqua, Stokols, Gress, Phillips, & Harvey, 2004).

Translation research refers to an extended process that links basic research work to application and application to dissemination. As an example, in the drug abuse prevention arena, examination of associations of D4 dopamine receptor genes with mesolimbic dopamine pathway operations and the trait of sensation-seeking has led to an active model of information exposure that develops fast-paced dramatic portrayals in televised PSAs designed to reduce marijuana use among high sensation-seeking adolescents. Campaigns so developed have been found to reverse upward trends in 30-day marijuana use among high sensation-seeking youth (Palmgreen et al., 2001; Pentz, Jasuja, Rohrbach, Sussman, & Bardo, 2006; Slater et al., 2006).

Of course, a reciprocal and iterative process of using basic science discoveries to develop innovative prevention and treatment strategies is one keystone of translation. Using basic science to inform prevention and treatment research and using discoveries from prevention and treatment research to develop new questions for basic science are important feedback loops of translation. Translation research requires not only different phases (e.g., from basic research to application and back) but also different programmatic and scientific roles within and across phases (Sussman, Valente, Rohrbach, Skara, & Pentz, 2006). These roles may involve persons from rather different academic backgrounds that develop a consensual model of inquiry (i.e., transdisciplinary research) to be able to engage in effective translation. First, there are basic etiologic researchers (e.g., cognitive science, neuroscience, and social inequities) who engage in research that may or may not include suggestion of an application. Second, there are applied etiologic researchers who take basic research in a general area and apply it to a topic (e.g., drug abuse or another addiction etiology). Third, there are strategist-type researchers who take applied etiology and develop strategies that have an ultimate aim to affect behavior (prevention or cessation). Fourth, there are context adapters who take strategies and place them in a context (e.g., schools and homes). Finally, there are "institutionalizers" who "hard-wire" a program into a context (e.g., policy-makers). This list of roles does not exhaust the types of roles that exist or are possible but summarizes some typical roles. Also, although a researcher might focus primarily on one role, he or she might take on additional roles in any category. For example, a basic researcher might suggest an intervention that no other researcher in the chain of translation has considered. Nevertheless, the characterization of roles from basic researcher to institutionalizer seems to map well onto what many researchers do. Consideration of the full breadth of research, from basic research to global institutionalization, may be considered in future work (see Fishbein, Ridenour, Herman-Stahl, & Sussman, 2016).

Interestingly, although treated as two different topics, transdisciplinary work and translation work are part of a matrix that may represent a new "revolution" in addictions etiology, prevention, and cessation research. We are asked to bridge across disciplines and consider solutions that might have an enduring behavioral impact from the onset of our work (Sussman et al., 2006). This text provides one example of an effort to accomplish just that purpose, to represent a bridge to a new transdisciplinary research culture that pertains at the same time to translation work.

Summary

The future of addictions research is bright in that we are now starting to understand the "big picture" of addictions – what an addiction really is, how underlying definitional elements might apply across behaviors, and how we might best assess, prevent, and treat addictive behaviors. I think an AMASR concept explains the commonality of the many behaviors to which one might become addicted, and also how one might minimize the consequences of addiction. One central conclusion from this text is that prevention of some type of addiction-like behavior may not be tenable (or even desirable) across the lifetime; however, prevention of problematic levels of AMASR behavior is feasible. Understanding human neurobiology and its interaction with environmental contexts better will advance our understanding of the addictions, and how to contain them into a manageable "form." I believe that such a perspective is neurobiologically plausible and something that falls beyond social constructivism; that it is a sort of "natural kind." I believe we finally really are getting a sense of what we are talking about.

Bulleted Summary

- Up to 50 percent of adults in a one-year period struggle with one or more of the 11 focal addictions addressed in this text (which may reflect 90 percent of all addictions we experience; e.g., Sussman et al., 2014), and it is argued in this text that the addictions reflect a dysfunctional appetitive motivation system in part due to reactions to lifestyle factors. Possibly, it is part of humankind that addictive behavior exists (Marks, 1990), as a quantitative phenomenon, and a side-effect of AMASR.
- More work is needed on inclusion and exclusion criteria for the addictions, clustering of addictions (e.g., concurrent addictions), and longitudinal course and relations among the addictions.
- In practice, such work as consideration of instruction in healthier substitution behaviors versus incompatible, non-addictive behaviors, or moderation versus abstinence among the addictions, needs to be more comprehensively addressed. Breadth of programming on specific addictive behaviors or healthy lifestyles needs to be considered. Also, implications of the experience of "satiation" on prevention or cessation of the addictions might be contemplated.
- Translation research requires not only different phases (e.g., from basic research to application and back) but also different programmatic and scientific roles within and across phases (Sussman et al., 2006). These roles may involve persons from rather different academic backgrounds that develop a consensual model of inquiry (i.e., transdisciplinary research) to be able to engage in effective translation.

Suggestions for Further Reading

Biglan, A. & Embry, D. D. (2013). A framework for intentional cultural change. *Journal of Contextual Behavioral Science*, 2: 95–104.

Forbes, D. L. (2011). Toward a unified model of human motivation. *Review of General Psychology*, 15: 85–98.

Konkolÿ Thege, B., Woodin, E. M., Hodgins, D. C., & Williams, R. J. (2015). Natural course of behavioral addictions: A 5-year longitudinal study. *BMC Psychiatry*, 15. doi: 10.1186/s12888-015-0383-3.

Marks, I. (1990). Behaviour (non-chemical) addictions. *British Journal of Addiction*, 85: 1389–1394.

Sussman, S., Valente, T. W., Rohrbach, L. A., Skara, S., & Pentz, M. A. (2006). Translation in the health professions: Converting science into action. *Evaluation & the Health Professions*, 29: 7–32.

GLOSSARY

Preface

Addiction of choice	– a most preferred or immediately troublesome addictive behavior
Addiction-related communication	– learning and using the language associated with specific addictions; for example, "chasing losses" in gambling
Appetitive effects	– affect, arousal, and information regulation, inherently associated with biological fitness
Attraction	– finding an appeal of differential subjective effects and contexts
Expectations	– what one expects subjectively from the addictive behavior
Pragmatics	– access to different avenues of addiction

Chapter 1

Addiction	– historical definition is one of giving over or being highly devoted to a person or activity which could have positive or negative implications
Allostasis	– an adaptive response of one's neurophysiology, or the ability to achieve stability through change processes (e.g., often opposing or counteradaptation processes) which can lead to dysregulation such as addictions-related dysfunction
Behavioral addiction	– pertains to engaging in types of behaviors repetitively; objects are not directly taken into the body, are not contain exogenous ligands, such as gambling or sex
Behavioral approach system (BAS)	– general motivational brain system that tends to be relatively automatic, and involves approach behaviors in response to novel cues for reward
Behavioral economics-type models	– a model that sees addiction-related behavior as being a choice (a self-destructive operant behavior), in part derived from multiple competing schedules of reinforcement
Behavioral inhibition system (BIS)	– general motivational brain system that tends to be relatively deliberate, and involves avoidance behaviors in response to novel cues for danger or competing goals

Glossary

Blood–brain barrier	– a filtering mechanism of the capillaries that carries blood to the brain and spinal cord tissue, blocking the passage of certain substances
Catecholamine storm	– flooding of the central nervous system with norepinephrine and epinephrine neurotransmitters upon abrupt withdrawal, resulting typically in high temperature, tachycardia, and tremor
Compulsion	– a simple but intense urge to do something
Craving	– an intense desire to engage in a specific act
Diseases of the spirit	– manias; historically, could have referred to addictive behaviors
Dopamine	– a neurotransmitter, a chemical associated with novelty and reward
Dopamine opponent-process counteradaptation	– e.g., dopamine transduction mechanisms: reduced dopamine output and activation of brain stress systems
Egodystonic	– separate from self
Endogenous ligands	– naturally occurring neurotransmitters
Etiology	– a causal story
Excessive appetite	– an over-attachment to a drug, object, or activity
Exogenous ligands	– neurochemically active substances, which mimic, block, or facilitate the action of naturally occurring neurotransmitters
Extensional definition of addiction	– listing or classification of addiction features
Family resemblances	– things which could be thought to be connected by one essential common feature may in fact be connected by a series of overlapping similarities, where no one feature is common to all
Five-component definition	– a model based on an attempt at synthesis of previous conceptualizations, keeping the number of criteria to a minimum, and considering tolerance and withdrawal as examples of preoccupation. These components are: (a) appetitive effects, (b) satiation, (c) preoccupation, (d) loss of control, and (e) negative consequences
Flue-curing	– four- to eight-week air-cured tobacco, which is low in sugar, and which gives the tobacco smoke a light, sweet flavor, and a high nicotine content
Hallucinosis	– alcohol-related hallucinations or psychosis
Homeostasis	– the tendency toward a relatively stable equilibrium between interdependent elements, especially as maintained by physiological processes
Incentive salience	– neurobiological motivational "wanting" attribute pertaining to reward-predicting stimuli

Glossary

Incentive-sensitization theory	– focuses on the influence of neural adaptation (i.e., sensitization) to addictive behaviors and addictive behavior-conditioned stimuli as the underlying mechanism perpetuating the addictive behaviors
Intensional definition of addiction	– pertains to *causal or process model* type statements of addictions
Liking	– neural substrates of pleasurable effects
Multiaxis diagnosis	– considers multiple life dimensions such as occupational impairment, and medical impairment
Negative reinforcement variant	– when anticipation of negative affect, or experience of negative affect due to stress, which possibly originally stemmed from withdrawal-like reactions, may lead to engagement of addictive behaviors as a negatively reinforcing safety signal
Obsessive-compulsive disorder	– involves repetitive simple behaviors to remove anxiety
Physiological/psychological dependence	– a definition of addiction that pertains to prolonged engagement in a behavior that results in its continued performance being necessary for physiologic and psychological equilibrium
Physiological withdrawal symptoms	– the appearance of both physical and psychological symptoms which are caused by physiological adaptions in the central nervous system and the brain due to chronic exposure to a substance
Polysubstance	– three groups of substances of equal preference, not including caffeine or nicotine; this category of substance abuse appears in the DSM-IV but not the DSM-V
Positive reinforcement variant	– building up of tension or craving for pleasure again (an impulsion, positive reinforcement mostly)
Salience	– refers to the tendency for the addiction to dominate one's thoughts, feelings, and behavior
Self-medication perspective	– pertains to relief from disordered emotions and sense of self-preservation through engaging in the addictive behavior
Self-regulation model	– the "present state" of being cues attempts to reach a "standard" at which point satiation is achieved
Septo-hippocampal system	– detects competing goals and leads to approach or avoidance behavior
Six-component definition	– an extensional model that has been influential among researchers of multiple addictive behaviors involving: (a) salience, (b) mood modification, (c) tolerance, (d) withdrawal symptoms, (e) conflict, and (f) relapse
Sociopathic personality disturbance	– a mental condition in which a person has a long-term pattern of manipulating, exploiting, or violating the rights of others

Glossary

Substance abuse	– according to the DSM-IV, the active American Psychiatric Association definition up until May 2013, a maladaptive recurrent pattern of drug use that is demonstrated by recurrent use over a 12-month period despite persistent (a) social, (b) occupational, (c) legal, or (d) use in physically hazardous situations-related consequences
Substance addiction	– pertains to repetitive intake of a drug (such as alcohol) or of food
Substance dependence provided by the DSM-IV	– a more severe maladaptive pattern of drug misuse than substance abuse disorder involving at least three dependence symptoms over a 12-month period including: tolerance, withdrawal, larger amounts than intended, unable to control, lots of time involved, other activities given up, and continued use despite negative consequences
Substance use disorder	– DSM-V definition, in force since May 2013 to the present, which combines the DSM-IV substance abuse and dependence disorders criteria, but deletes legal consequences and adds craving instead; two or more of 11 criteria are used to diagnose substance use disorder
Tolerance	– the need to engage in the behavior at a relatively greater level than in the past to achieve previous levels of appetitive effects (or achieving diminished effects at previous levels of behavior)
Trauma	– a life threatening or disturbing experience or experiences
Vicariance	– the extent to which one action monopolizes one's working memory, when there is opportunity to consider alternative behaviors
Vice	– behaviors which are pleasurable, popular, possibly voluntary, and wicked
Wanting	– incentive salience to addictive behavior cues
Withdrawal	– an abstinence syndrome, upon abrupt termination of the addictive behavior

Chapter 2

Addictive effects	– immediate impacts of an addictive behavior
Akrasia	– difficulty in refraining from an addictive behavior despite attempting to do so
Appetitive need	– refers to drives, urges, or cravings, often instinctual, that serves to help regulate human function

Glossary

Associational memory-appetitive system relations (AMASR) model	– refers to an appetitive-needs notion of addiction, that one's "instincts/drives," which otherwise would serve important survival and growth functions, through associational memory become excessive, atypically evoked, or misdirected
Automaticity / euphoric recall	– incomplete memory access, or biased memory for initially pleasant effects of engaging in the addictive behavior
Differential socialization	– an aspect of addiction entrenchment, one's values, expectations, and experiences are shaped and directed in potentially counter-normative ways through the avenues in which one learns social behavior
Executive cognitive functions	– controlled brain functions including regulation of one's focus of attention, ability to encode and retrieve and deliberately process different sources of information, ability to discriminate between relevant and irrelevant types of information, ability to evaluate immediate and delayed impacts of engaging in different behaviors, self-reflection, and ability to make self-fulfilling decisions
Hangovers	– negative physical sensations at the end of an addictive behavior sequence
Innate and secondarily acquired instincts	– inborn and tied to associational memory, types of appetitive needs or drives for biological fitness
Meditation practices	– a variety of means of disciplining one's stream of consciousness, including focusing on one's breathing and letting thoughts pass by
Positive addiction	– an addiction which does not cause obvious negative financial, legal, social, role, or mental wellbeing-related consequences, or causes minor consequences
Progression	– a notion within a disease model of addiction, which asserts that continued involvement in an addictive behavior leads to movement to a more advanced state of the disease, eventually leading to institutions or death in the case of alcohol or other drug misuse
Satiation	– at least for a brief period of time, the individual feels as if the appetitive needs are met by the addictive behavior
Subjective adaptation-directed effect	– achieving a sense of being fulfilled or fit
Thought–do loop	– a repetitive thought sequence

Chapter 3

Acquisition skills	– one needs to know how to obtain the addiction object or service from the source
Addiction specificity	– a concept that pertains to why some addictions may not co-occur in individuals; specific addiction developmental pathways
Addictive exploration	– repetitive, out-of control attempts to resolve a generalized sense of personal insecurity though engagement in behavior that "simulates" mastery of the unknown
Aldehyde dehydrogenase (ALDH2)	– an enzyme involved in alcohol metabolism that inadequately breaks down; many Asians have an inactive variant of the liver enzyme, ALDH2, which means that aldehyde takes a long time to clear from the blood, leading to a flushing response
Anhedonia	– inability to experience pleasure
Attention deficit hyperactivity disorders (ADHD)	– a chronic condition marked by persistent inattention, hyperactivity, and sometimes impulsivity
Belief–behavior congruence	– to utilize cognitive processes that serve to distance the perceiver from incongruence between beliefs and behavior, perhaps to keep incongruent information from consciousness
"Cognition-information" errors	– cognitive misperceptions due to the way information is processed that may make an addictive behavior relatively more prevalent, safe, or normatively acceptable than it actually is, and includes such phenomena as illusory correlation, prevalence overestimates, false consensus effect, or unrealistic optimism, as examples
Cognitive level of analysis	– both explicit, deliberate, controlled thinking as well as implicit, well-learned, automatic, or possibly "impulsive" cognitive processes may facilitate engagement in addictive behaviors; these may operate together in "dual process" models
Cognitive processing limits	– of executive functions, related to task demand or time pressure
Compulsive buying disorder (CBD)	– obsession/craving with, addiction to, shopping and buying

Glossary

Deviant subculture	– a group that is reliably deviant from a mainstream, same-age peer group regarding means of achieving appetitive effects
Differential socialization	– introduced in Chapter 2, refers to the group-specific channeling of the development of beliefs, intentions, expectations, norms, perceptions, and modeling of social behaviors
Emerging adulthood	– the developmental period between adolescence and young adulthood, generally 18 to 25 years of age
Etiologic level of analysis	– molar to molecular lens of causation of addictions, including the large physical and social environment, microsocial context, cognitive level, and neurobiological level
Expectancies	– subjective probabilities regarding the likelihood of achieving various outcomes by engaging in some behavior
Explicit and implicit cognitive processes	– deliberate, conscious, and automatic processes
False consensus effect	– tendency to overestimate the extent to which one's opinions, beliefs, preferences, values, and habits are normal and typical of those of others
Flushing response	– red flushing or blotches on the body such as the head, neck, or shoulders
Gender roles	– normative behaviors as a function of one's gender; traditional male roles may tend to be instrumental-based, whereas traditional female roles may tend to be more nurturant or expressive oriented
Geographic/physical environmental and large social climate-level variables	– variables which traverse physical environments and facilitate the development of addictions such as drug distribution channels and effects of the mass media
Gradient of reinforcement value	– different addictive behaviors may vary in steepness, leading to selection of one addiction with a steeper gradient (more reinforcement value per unit time) over another
Group socialization	– a form of learning appropriate behaviors of certain groups and differing across different groups of people
Half and half	– refers to engagement in a combination of oral and vaginal sex

Glossary

Hand release	– refers to a sex worker bringing a client to orgasm by using a hand
Illusory correlation	– tendency to overestimate the co-occurrence of two infrequent events, such as drug use and peak experience
Insider speech	– serves as a symbol of commonality and group identification pertaining to specific addictions within specific contexts
Life Course Theory	– a theory that people tend to select social and physical environments that are similar to earlier experienced environments, which may shape life experiences in part by repetition of learned patterns of communication
Low defensible space	– low monitoring and visibility in one's physical environment; can lead to illicit activity such as distribution or engagement in certain addictive behaviors such as drug misuse
Materialism	– a tendency to consider material possessions and physical comfort as more important than spiritual values
Mere exposure	– a psychological phenomenon by which people tend to develop a preference for things merely because they are familiar with them, sometimes only at the bare-limen realm of awareness
Microsocial (small group) level	– includes the impacts of different groups on one's behavioral options; these groups may include one's family, peers (friends, colleagues), or contact with community agents (e.g., teachers, elected officials, community groups)
Neurobiological level variables	– variables that consider individual differences in neurobiology which may make a person relatively more or less prone to experience different appetitive effects after engaging in various behaviors, including impacts of genetics and differential brain function
Neurodegenerative disorders	– hereditary and sporadic conditions which are characterized by progressive nervous system dysfunction
Neutralization theory	– suggests that those who exhibit risky behaviors, including addictions, actually do internalize dominant social norms; deviant behavior is perhaps viewed as rationalized exceptions to these rules (e.g., victims had it coming to them)

Glossary

Peer prevalence or acceptability overestimates	– tendency to overestimate involvement in an addictive behavior, or acceptability of such involvement, among one's peers
Pragmatics	– availability, access to, and ability to acquire a particular addictive object or service, and engage in the addictive behavior regularly
Prosocial bonding or constraint	– refers to ties to conventional society that might prevent deviant behavior through positive connections, barriers to alternative negative activities, or fear of negative consequences
Representativeness heuristic	– involves making judgments about the probability of an event based on an individual's experiential schema of how representative an event appears to be and the ease with which mental content comes to mind (i.e., cognitive accessibility) rather than relying on further evidence
Reward deficiency syndrome	– some individuals, because of their neurochemistry, have difficulty deriving feelings of reward or pleasure from ordinary activities and this predisposes them to seek alternative behaviors to compensate for the lower level of activation of the brain reward circuitry
Situational/contextual distortions	– one may distort the context of one's lifestyle to normalize one's behavior
Social cognitive/learning theory	– involvement in an addictive behavior or behaviors can develop through vicarious learning and reinforcement, modeling, and/or initially reinforcing consequences
Social images	– general perceived or fanaticized lifestyle characteristics (e.g., appearing sophisticated, sexy, or older, or of appearing happy, by engaging in some behavior or using some product)
Toxicant-induced loss of tolerance (TILT)	– people exposed to pollutants may become more susceptible to the effects of lower quantities of drugs and face greater difficulties with withdrawal; pollution may make one more susceptible to addiction
Unrealistic optimism	– tendency to believe that one is less at risk of experiencing a negative event compared to others

Glossary

Chapter 4

Blood alcohol content (BAC)	– grams of alcohol per deciliter of blood
Compartment syndrome	– excessive pressure build-up in localized area of body, often due to injury
Context	– the circumstances that provide the setting for an event
Natural kind	– "natural grouping" that reflects the underlying order of nature, as opposed to groupings established through consensus or arbitrarily
Nucleus accumbens	– consists of the caudate and putamen and is a region in the basal forebrain rostral to the preoptic area of the hypothalamus; it is an initial "station" for mesolimbic dopamine that runs up the medial forebrain bundle from where it is manufactured in the ventral tegmental area
Positive addictions	– being addicted to an activity that is intrinsically healthy or self-fulfilling
Reintegrative shaming	– a means of recovery or restorative justice by shaming the behavior (e.g., addiction, or other "deviant" act), but not the "offender" him- or herself
Rhabdomyolysis	– death of muscle tissue, myoglobin released into the bloodstream, which can cause kidney damage (related to exercise addiction)
Sobriety	– a balanced life

Chapter 5

11 focal addictions	– cigarettes, alcohol, hard drugs, food/eating, gambling, Internet, shopping, love, sex, exercise, and work
Adrenalin junkies	– people who engage in all sorts of activities for a rush, which may be engaged in repetitively
Body dysmorphic disorder	– self-perceived defects in physical appearance not readily obvious to others
Dominance and submissive-related factors	– appetitive need-addictive dimensions that pertain to a focus on leading a social group or being part of the herd
Hedonist-type addictions	– addictions that focus on immediate pleasure
Hoarding	– a persistent difficulty discarding objects, an experience of distress with discarding them, leading to accumulation of possessions that congest living space, and leads to social, safety, or other impairments
Kleptomania	– characterized by an urge and preoccupation with stealing objects (often the same object which is not needed, and may not even be used) to achieve reduction in tension and pleasure during or following the action

Glossary

Latent class analysis	– a subset of structural equation modeling, used to find groups or subtypes of cases in multivariate categorical data, called "latent classes"
Love addiction	– a constricted pattern of repetitive behavior directed toward a love object that leads to negative role, social, safety, or legal consequences
Nurturant-type addictions	– addictions that focus on personal fulfillment
Pica	– eating of non-nutritive, non-food substances; in the DSM-V, considered a feeding and eating disorder rather than an addiction
Primary exercise dependence	– defined as meeting criteria for exercise dependence and continually exercising solely for the psychological gratification resulting from the exercise behavior itself
Secondary exercise dependence	– defined as meeting criteria for exercise dependence, but using excessive exercise to accomplish some other end (e.g., weight loss or body composition changes) that is related to another disorder such as the development of an eating disorder
Street addiction	– addiction to the action of the streets
Trichotillomania	– hair pulling

Chapter 6

Anorexia nervosa	– an emotional disorder characterized by an obsessive desire to lose weight by refusing to eat is associated with (extreme) over-control, whereas addictions are associated with loss of control; it probably is not reflective of an addictive process
Bulimia nervosa	– an emotional disorder involving distortion of body image and an obsessive desire to lose weight or not gain weight, in which bouts of extreme overeating are followed by depression and self-induced vomiting, purging, or fasting
Eating addiction	– food addiction involves appetitive effect, preoccupation, loss of control, and negative consequences pertaining to food substances; if the focus is more on the behavior of eating, it might be termed "eating" addiction
E-cigarettes	– battery-powered vaporizers that simulate the feeling of smoking, but without tobacco
Harmful dysfunction analysis	– both harm (negative consequences) and dysfunction (dependence; inability to function normally without the addiction) are needed to diagnose an alcohol use disorder using large-scale survey data
Obesity	– grossly fat or overweight (e.g., BMI of 30 or higher)
Prescription drugs	– a more general label that subsumes several categories of medically prescribed drugs misused non-medically (e.g., amphetamines, other narcotics, sedatives, and tranquillizers)

Glossary

Vagus nerve	– each of the tenth pair of cranial nerves, supplying the heart, lungs, upper digestive tract, and other organs of the chest and abdomen; indicates food satiation; vagus nerve stimulation (VNS) has been used for treatment-resistant depression and addiction

Chapter 8

"13th Stepping"	– reflects the tendency to replace one's drug of choice with a sexual compulsion
Addiction of choice	– the primary, most preferred, or most troublesome addiction
Addiction co-occurrence	– two or more addictions that occur at the same time
Addiction spectrum	– the number of co-occurring addictions
Alternating addiction cycles	– pertains to replacement addictions that cycle back and forth, in a systematic way, over stretches of time
Binger	– someone who experiences periods of abstinence followed only by periods of being out of control; there is no controlled engagement in the addictive behavior
Chloriazepoxide	– a benzodiazepine which increases sleepiness and muscle relaxation, and reduces anxiety; may be a substitute addiction for narcotic abuse
Combining	– involves any number of addictions to maintain a certain high; for example, one may combine heroin with cocaine (a "speed ball") in order to obtain the right "edge" to the "high"
Controlled drinker	– someone with consistent, sustained regaining of control over alcohol drinking behavior
Cross-tolerance	– when tolerance from one addiction transfers to another
Disinhibiting	– gathering up courage to be involved in one addiction due to inhibitions that had been lowered while participating in another addiction
"Fused" addictions	– addiction involvement that involves multiple behaviors that are combined (e.g., conjoined smoking and drinking, eating and drinking, love and sex, gambling and drinking); at least four types of fused addictions include cross-tolerance, combining, intensification, and numbing
Implicit contracts	– implicit deals with the world to not engage in an addiction as long as certain events do not occur; in a couple, at a dyadic level, agreeing to tolerate each other's addiction
Intensification	– involves combining addictions for a total experience; for example, some people have suggested that they use cocaine just prior to having sex to intensify the sexual experience
Masking	– hiding of a more normatively unacceptable addiction by first participating in a less shameful one

Glossary

Numbing	– involves following a stimulating addictive behavior with one that is calming or medicating; for example one may follow a sex addiction experience with getting drunk to distance oneself from the first experience
"Periodic" addictive behavior	– when a person whom a researcher, treatment agent, or lay person might label an "addict" demonstrates apparently controlled involvement in the behavior, and then demonstrates periods of being clearly out of control
Replacement	– occurs when one addiction replaces another with a passing of some duration of time; substitute addiction
Ritualizing	– involves a chain of behavior that includes a series of preparation steps and pattern of engaging in a chain of addictive behaviors, all of which invest one into an altered state
Single addiction	– a person is addicted to one substance or behavior
Substitute addictions	– experiencing multiple addictions serially, when a person quits (terminates) one addiction but then begins another addiction
Withdrawal mediation	– occurs when one addiction permits one to avoid withdrawal from another

Chapter 9

Blackouts	– loss or gaps of memory of certain events that occurred while drinking or using
Chromatography	– the separation of a mixture by passing it in solution or suspension or as a vapor, as in gas chromatography, through a medium in which the components move at different rates; a relatively accurate test for the presence of drug metabolites
Corroborative reports	– reports from significant others or professionals about one's status that may serve to corroborate own's self-reports
Cut-off scores	– minimum scores to indicate "true" presence of the addiction
Delirium tremens	– agitation, general confusion, visual and auditory hallucinations; usually resulting from abrupt withdrawal from alcohol; affecting perhaps 2 percent of people who withdrawal from alcohol
Entrenchment	– continued engagement in the behavior despite neglecting other life tasks
False positive rates	– false alarm rates, incorrectly detecting presence of drug use for example
Formication	– a sensation like insects crawling on or under the skin; a perceptual withdrawal symptom

Glossary

Immunoassays	– a procedure for detecting or measuring specific proteins or other substances through their properties as antigens or antibodies; used to detect drug use that should be backed up with confirmatory tests
Mental status examination	– the assessment of appearance, attitude and behavior, speech, affect, thought and language, and perceptions and cognitive functioning, such as insight and judgment
Preoccupation	– perhaps an aspect of or the same thing as entrenchment; generally noticed when the person is engaged in other incompatible behavior; e.g., being on vacation but thinking about working if workaholic
Presenteeism	– going to work despite feeling sick
Proactive assessment	– an assessment used prior to an official referral (e.g., to treatment), to check for the presence, or consequences, of addictions, which may be used to screen out candidates for jobs involving public safety, for example
Pull tabs	– lotto, tickets that may have winning combinations
Reactive assessment	– an assessment used after an official referral to check for medical or social-psychological problem, or due to signs of an addictive behavior
Self-report assessment instruments	– assessments completed by the potential addict, that permit treatment agents and perhaps the suffering person to gage the degree of difficulty with a particular addiction
Structured interview	– an interview that contains a lot of forced-choice or multiple-choice questions and is relatively restricted on number of assessment domains
Unstructured interview	– an interview that contains a lot of open-ended questions and could lead to any number of assessment pathways

Chapter 10

Affective or values-based model	– addresses more global attitudinal changes directed at such factors as enhanced self-esteem, improved decision-making and goal setting, and clarification of one's life values, all of which might prevent drug misuse
Antecedents	– events, contexts, and behaviors that precede and facilitate or deter engagement in the addiction
Cessation programs	– help one quit engagement in an addictive behavior, arrest consequences, recover functioning, live with negative consequences; instruct one how to cope with psychological dependence (emotional reliance) on an addictive behavior, and with withdrawal-like symptoms

Glossary

Cognitive-behavioral techniques	– focuses on uncovering the topography of one's at-risk situations or escalating addictive behavior through stimulus control, organism control (e.g., self-monitoring), response control, and reinforcement control; and learning how to cope effectively with stressful situations to help not relapse
Content-control software	– software that restricts contents that a person (e.g., youth) would be able to access
Extrapersonal	– beyond the individual
Fear-based model	– a model that assumed that if youth were frightened about the potential negative effects of drugs, then they would not want to experiment with drugs
Forbidden fruit contingency	– youth envied what adults are allowed to do (e.g., drink and smoke), and want to engage in such behaviors to demonstrate adult-like behavior
Indicated	– designed to affect high-risk subgroups already identified as having some detectable signs or symptoms of a developing problem
Information-based model	– a model that assumed that providing adolescents with factual information about drug use (or another addiction) would prevent them from engaging in the behavior
Interactive techniques	– e.g., role play, interactive peer discussions, where participants generate the appropriate behavior and are relatively likely to "own" the behavior
Intrapersonal	– within the person
Modalities	– settings, means of delivery (e.g., mass media, policy, schools, churches)
Motivation enhancement	– focuses on techniques to clarify and increase desire for change and reduce ambivalence toward change
Normative beliefs	– the perceptions about the prevalence or acceptability of (an addictive) behavior among close friends and same-age peers
Parent power movement	– a movement that uses testimonials by former drug addicts, drug-free school weeks, removal of drug paraphernalia shops ("head shops"), and a simplified version of social influence programming (e.g., "Just Say No" campaign)
Primary prevention	– before the problem behavior starts
Prohibition	– a US nationwide constitutional ban on the sale, production, importation, and transportation of alcoholic beverages that remained in place from 1920 to 1933
Resistance skills	– the (perceived) ability to identify and resist social pressure to use tobacco, alcohol, and other drugs, intake food, engage in behavioral addictions or try other behavior one does want to do

Response-contingent reinforcement approach	– focuses on reducing occurrence of problem addictive behaviors with extrinsic rewards such as money, prizes, or vouchers; yoking extrinsic rewards to facets of the addictive behavior (e.g., vouchers for demonstrating clean urine tests)
Responsible behavior programs	– emphasize no use of restricted drugs but responsible use of alcohol and waiting until one is grown up (18 years of age) so that one can make a responsible, mature choice
Secondary prevention	– before the disease starts
Selective	– designed to affect subgroups at elevated risk for developing a problem, based on social, psychological, or other factors; e.g., the child of someone suffering from an addiction
Social influence-based programs	– programs that assumed "inoculation" to resist social pressures that serve as precipitants of alcohol, tobacco, and other drug use would prevent initial trial and experimentation
Social influence-oriented approach	– focuses on counteracting social influences that serve to promote or maintain an addiction
Supply reduction approach	– focuses on arranging the social environment so that objects of addiction are more difficult to obtain (e.g., access restriction)
Temperance instruction	– education in self-restraint or abstinence in drinking
Tertiary prevention	– before death is likely
Universal	– designed to affect the general population

Chapter 11

Attitudinal Perspective Theory	– posits that there are two different aspects of one's attitudes about behaviors or events; first, an individual has a general attitudinal perspective and second, the individual has specific attitudes about specific behaviors or events (e.g., being a traditional, moderate, or radical person versus attitudes regarding engagement in specific behaviors, which may depart from one's general perspective of self)
Executive functions	– higher-order cognitive functions, deliberate processing; attentional, memory retrieval, inhibitory processes; e.g., working memory capacity, planning
High-risk situations	– situations in which objects of addiction are readily available or in which addictive behaviors are otherwise promoted

Hot hand fallacy	– the idea that one can elicit winning numbers or determine how one chance event will turn out based on a previous chance event
Implementation intentions programming	– linking specific intentions to perform a behavior with situational cues such that a behavior becomes relatively spontaneously initiated; implementation intentions specify a plan of action
Meditation	– there are many forms of meditation; focusing on thoughts as they "pass by" without acting on them immediately in order to improve cognitive function and mood
Mood management	– self-regulation of negative mood states, use of positive techniques to enhance mood such as meditation
Personalized feedback	– involves understanding where one is situated relative to past behavior and peer norms pertaining to a developing entrenchment in an addiction
Reinterpretation	– normalization of deviant responses or situations
Vigilance programs	– programs developed to target youth at high genetic risk for an addiction; strategies that could be used include (1) screening, (2) assigning youth to receive tailored prevention programming, and (3) use of prophylactic medications to attempt gene function manipulation

Chapter 12

Activism	– the policy or action of using vigorous campaigning to bring about political or social change; in prevention programming learning how to correct social pressures through letter writing or other activities to attempt change in institutions or companies that promote addictions
Alternative resource programming	– in general, attempts to provide community resources to teens (e.g., for education, employment, prosocial recreation), enhance their perception of the availability of these resources, or enhance their self-efficacy to find and utilize these resources
Automated electronic gambling machines	– electronic machines used for gambling (e.g., slot machines or VLTs)
Comprehensive social influences / life skills prevention programming	– generally implemented in schools and occasionally in other community units, generally divided into 11 substantive

Glossary

	components; involves counteracting normative (to be liked) and informational (covert social image) social influences, and also includes physical consequences information
Containment	– reducing engagement in a potentially addictive behavior to a safe level
Conversation initiation skill	– the ability to begin a conversation with another person, possibly a stranger (e.g., a youth being able to walk to a random adult and convincingly request that the adult buy alcohol or another addiction object for the youth)
Decision-making	– involves learning how to rationally combine information to make self-fulfilling decisions in different problem areas; often includes weighing up the pros and cons of different decisions and selecting the one with the most pros and the fewest cons (controlling for valence of the pros and cons)
Diversion programs	– a form of sentencing; such programs are often run by a police department, court, a district attorney's office, or outside agency designed to enable offenders of criminal law to avoid criminal charges and a criminal record (e.g., for non-violent drug crimes)
Employee assistance programs	– employer-sponsored services designed for personal or family problems, including mental health, substance abuse, various addictions, marital problems, parenting problems, emotional problems, or financial or legal concerns; often involves screening, provision of brief materials or counseling, and referral to outside help
Environment enrichment	– providing a more saturated reinforcing environment may decrease negative affect-situation reasons for initiating or continuing to engage in an addictive behavior; appetitive needs being satisfied in productive ways
House edge	– gambling odds favor the gambling establishment and not the customer
Iatrogenic effects	– undesired worsening of an addictive behavior that may occur as the result of some prevention or cessation effort (e.g., increase in drug use)

Glossary

Individual–environment matching	– the idea is to minimize harm of or engagement in addictive behaviors by considering specifically an approach intended to match individual appetitive function to environmental contexts
Interdiction	– delaying or disrupting an addictive behavior (e.g., drug use or distribution); forbid the addiction by actions of authorities (e.g., arrests for prostitution)
Lifestyle matching	– finding a better lifestyle fit to reduce likelihood of addictive behavior initiation or escalation
Media literacy	– engaging in a deliberate analysis of media programming to be made aware of advertising influences
Multisystemic Therapy	– targets individual, family, peer, school, and community influences to prevent future deviant behavior of youth offenders with serious problems that may include violence, substance abuse, and severe emotional problems
Normative restructuring activity	– an activity that confronts persons' perceptions of social norms with actual social norms resulting in a conservative shift in social perception (e.g., youth are instructed to stand under, or hold up if at their desks, approve/disapprove signs regarding acceptability of drug use and realize that most youth disapprove of drug use, contrary to their perceptions)
Open-ended questions	– questions that require more than a one-word answer
Outcome and self-efficacy expectations	– expectancies that completing an action will result in desired outcomes and that one is able to take that action, respectively
Parental monitoring	– being around the youth, showing interest, observing youth behavior
Pre-commitment	– one way to modify the parameters of electronic gambling machines (EGMs), limiting time or amount of money that will be played; perhaps involving electronic smartcards
Prohibitory scheme	– prohibiting supply or engagement in an addictive behavior (e.g., zoning, age restrictions)

Glossary

Refusal assertion skill	– a social skill that involves how one might best refuse an offer or request of someone else
Regulatory scheme	– setting conditions of participation in an addictive behavior (e.g., taxation, legal limits)
Resilience	– ability or skills to buffer oneself from stressful conditions facilitative of addictions
Secure attachment style	– feel connected to and nurtured by significant others
Snus	– moist powder tobacco product originating from a variant of dry snuff in early eighteenth-century Sweden, that may show reduced risks
Social normative perceptions	– beliefs regarding social norms (e.g., prevalence or approval of an addictive behavior)
Social skills training	– instruction in different skills to improve social communication (e.g., listening and communication skills, assertiveness skill), using a well-researched sequential process, including (1) demonstration of appropriate behavior, (2) modeling of appropriate behavior, (3) behavioral rehearsal, and (4) feedback
Sting event	– a carefully planned protocol, typically involving deception, to catch policy violators (e.g., having someone pose as a minor and try to purchase alcohol while law enforcement is watching)
Supply reduction programming	– generally prohibitory policy mechanisms and regulatory policy mechanisms used to limit supply of an addiction service or product
Talk show format	– an activity highly preferred by older teens; psychodramas in the format of "talk shows" can assist in eliciting empathy, responsibility and consequences information, and achieving healthy changes
Tobacco regulatory science	– a relatively new research and policy arena; the emphasis is on minimizing harm of tobacco products and use, as opposed to tobacco prevention or cessation (more directly related to eradication)
Transactional processes	– mutual social interaction and impact (e.g., how a parent and child may impact each other)
Video lottery terminal (VLT)	– gambling on the outcome of a video game (similar to a slot machine)

Glossary

Chapter 13

Abstinence violation effect	– when a person has a single "slip"/"lapse" by engaging in an addiction they had stopped; he or she may experience conflict or guilt, and completely relapse (e.g., drinkers in recovery may think that if they ever drink alcohol, they may feel that they "lost the game" and that they might as well give up and drink regularly again)
Euphoric recall	– a strongly encoded and automatic recall to pleasurable experiences associated with involvement in the addiction
Harm reduction	– attempts to (a) sever connections of the addictive behavior from its consequences to self or others, (b) slowly or in small steps change the form of the addictive behavior to a less dangerous one, and (c) eventually lead to cessation or minimal harm
Intrinsic–Extrinsic Motivation Model	– proposes that goals are more likely to be obtained if the individual identifies with the desirability of obtaining that goal, as opposed to reaching the goal for some other, extrinsic reward; extrinsic motivation can be useful if carefully yoked to desired behavior
Moral treatment	– historically, was an approach to mental disorder based on humane psychosocial care or moral discipline that emerged in the eighteenth century and came to the fore for much of the nineteenth century, deriving partly from psychiatry or psychology and partly from religious or moral concerns; this was also an approach involving community support to help direct the individual away from alcohol or other drug use (e.g., use of inebriate homes)
One drink	– in the United States, one "standard" drink contains roughly 14 grams of pure alcohol, which is found in: 12 ounces of regular beer, which is usually about 5 percent alcohol; 5 ounces of wine, which is typically about 12 percent alcohol; or 1.5 ounces of distilled spirits, which is about 40 percent alcohol
Remission	– cessation, a diminution of the seriousness or intensity of disease
Resistance	– an individual's unwillingness to change or participate in his or her treatment and can be problematic
Stepped-care approach	– involves gradually structuring treatment based on severity and length of time the person has suffered from the addiction (e.g., self-help, outpatient, and residential care if quite severe disruption in function)

Glossary

Stigma	– a mark of disgrace associated with a particular circumstance, quality, or person (e.g., someone suffering from an addiction viewed as weak or immoral by others)
Therapeutic community	– in which the treatment agents include a community of staff and other patients; the approach is usually residential, with the clients and therapists living together, but increasingly residential units have been superseded by day units
Total abstinence	– stopping any involvement with an addictive behavior (e.g., no use of tobacco, alcohol, or any other mood-altering drugs)
Transtheoretical Model	– consists of a series of five stages of change with early stages involving establishing a commitment to a goal and later stages providing the energy to complete the goal (pre-contemplation, contemplation, preparation, action, and maintenance)

Chapter 14

Abstinence violation effect (AVE)	– after having a "slip," the feeling of loss of control over one's addictive behavior and the perceived inability to engage in healthy behaviors
Agonists	– in pharmacological treatment, drugs that provide similar effects as the drug of choice but are relatively safe or produce fewer psychotropic (disabling) effects, used to help a person cease a drug addiction
Antagonists	– in pharmacological treatment, drugs that block the effect of the drug of choice, so that the person using them will not experience pleasant effects when using the drug of choice, used to help a person cease a drug addiction
Attentional retraining	– training one's automatic focus of attention away from an attentional bias for addiction-related cues (e.g., to sodas instead of alcohol, through half-second presentations of alternative cue material); this might decrease cue approach behavior, addiction craving, and addiction-seeking behavior
Behavior modification interventions	– address observable antecedents and consequences of a behavior without acknowledging cognitive mediation of behavior (e.g., stimulus control, shaping behavior, reinforcement control)
Behavioral contracting	– a simple positive-reinforcement intervention to change behavior; it spells out in detail the expectations of the participant in carrying out the intervention plan, with costs and benefits of non-compliance and compliance, time duration, and "out" clauses (e.g; can take a drug if administered by a doctor, when ill)

Glossary

Cognitive interventions	– include strategies to directly modify "thinking" to enhance executive control or other cognitive processes (e.g., classically conditioned, implicit processes, self-instructional training, cognitive restructuring) to facilitate addictive behavior cessation
Cognitive restructuring	– involves recognizing and examining self-defeating cognitions and replacing them with self-fulfilling thoughts that may lead to a better, more rational direction of thought and behavior
Cue exposure treatment protocols	– involves extinguishing conditioned responses through unreinforced exposure to conditioned stimuli (e.g., presentation of drug stimuli repeatedly without using)
Detoxification	– managed withdrawal from drugs involves removing the toxic materials from an individual's body
Dot probe paradigm	– a visual probe task, in which a target replaces an addictive behavior-related picture in a number of cases
Elaborative processing (EP)	– connecting in memory addictive behavior cessation materials with contexts associated with the related addiction
Environmental advocacy	– how to get one's needs met within systems
MI spirit	– client sense of autonomy and collaboration with counselor
Motivational interviewing	– involves a series of procedures for therapists to help clients clarify goals and follow through with their efforts to change behavior (e.g., roll with resistance, MI spirit, personalized feedback)
Organism control	– behavioral techniques to change how a person interprets stimuli, behavior, or reinforcers; changing thinking to change behavior (e.g., self-instructional training, cognitive restructuring)
Personalized feedback intervention	– involves feedback about the participant's behavior in comparison to peers, and tips to change
Post-acute withdrawal (PAW)	– a biopsychosocial syndrome involving the occurrence of a variety of symptoms indicating dysfunction occurring during abstinence, perhaps involving neurobiological readjustment and related to the psychosocial stresses of coping with life addiction-free; includes the period of up to approximately 18 months following acute withdrawal
Problem-solving	– involves a series of steps in cessation programming, including generating as many behavioral options as possible to avoid engaging in the addictive behavior in different life circumstances, examining the benefits and costs of each behavioral option, and then trying to make the best decision or set of decisions based on the available options with the most benefits and least costs

Glossary

Reinforcement control	– behavioral techniques involving introducing new contingencies of reinforcement (e.g., through contingency management or behavioral contracting)
Relapse	– the engagement in an addictive behavior after a period of abstinence; a "lapse" generally is a single instance of engagement whereas a relapse is a return to pre-cessation involvement
Response control	– behavioral techniques to change the responses a person emits after receiving stimuli (e.g., tapering down the number of cigarettes smoked before quitting)
Self-efficacy	– the expectation that one is able to effectively cope with high-risk situations without reverting to prior addictive coping responses is central to relapse-prevention therapy
Self-instructional training	– involves examining and recognizing missing cognitions and adding cognitions through practice so that one is led to a better direction of thought and behavior
Spontaneous recovery	– reintroduction of an addiction object may facilitate reoccurrence of conditioned responses, particularly in varying natural settings
Stimulus control	– altering effects of stimuli confronting the person (e.g., removing objects of addiction from one's home, avoiding going near places where an addictive behavior has occurred)

Chapter 15

Assertiveness training	– focuses on (a) enhancing appropriate expression of feelings or personal rights (general assertiveness), and (b) skills training in refusal of unreasonable requests of others (refusal assertion)
Canalization	– reinforcing individuals, strengthening resolve, who are already motivated to change but may have little or no effect on those who appear unwilling to change
Cult-like	– resembling a cult; belonging to an organization that openly discourages skepticism, and may lead to a lack of involvement in other social organizations and resentment toward those not involved in the organization
Deviancy training	– risk-takers daring each other or learning more risky behavior from each other
Disease model of addiction	– addictions are thought to be "allergies" that are manifested by a baseline subjective sense of restlessness, irritability, and discontent, in conjunction with (implicit) processes that perpetuate uncontrolled participation in the addiction in high-risk situations

Glossary

Family therapy	– in the context of treating the addictions, views the addictions as a family (systems) problem; focusing on changing part of the system (e.g., the addict's behavior) may effectively change other parts of the system (e.g., other family members' behavior toward the addict, or toward each other) depending on the functions the addiction serves within the family and adaptations made to the addiction; it may be important to treat the family unit to successfully treat the addiction and prevent relapse
Group therapy	– treating people at the group level, provides peer support, feedback, and confrontation among participants, guided by a trained leader
Motivational intervention	– confronting the addict with his or her detrimental effects on others, particularly family and close friends, to try to get the addict into treatment
Public service announcements (PSAs)	– brief messages in the public interest disseminated by the media without charge, with the objective of raising awareness, changing public attitudes and behavior toward a social issue
Responsible Gambling Information Centers (RGICs)	– centers located within gambling venues; they provide, on customer request, information and education about the risks of gambling and identify, support, and refer RGIC visitors who are experiencing problems with gambling
Role playing	– a technique used to provide opportunities to practice social skills (e.g., refusal assertion) in a non-threatening, simulation environment in which mistakes do not lead to relapse
Self-control skills	– learning restraint under simulated high-risk conditions in social interactions and other life contexts; urge control; which can then be utilized in real-life situations
Sober-living homes	– safe environments for those who have completed residential treatment or inpatient care or for those who need a structured living situation to maintain sobriety
Therapeutic alliance	– development of a trusting and mutually respectful relationship between the treater and treatee

Glossary

Chapter 16

Breadth of programming	– scope of health behavior being addressed, from a narrow breadth (e.g., one addiction) to a wide breadth (e.g., healthy lifestyles in general)
Instincts	– natural, inherent tendencies such as seeking pleasant events–avoiding harm, fight–flight, dominance–nurturance, or exploration–hibernation
Primary versus secondary addictions	– the primary addiction being of most importance, more immediately life-threatening, or earlier in the chain of addictive behaviors
Random forest prediction models	– clinical and personality measures, neuroimaging measures, or a combined model, using a machine-learning tool which averages many decision-trees according to an algorithm; can be used to generate predictions for each participant regarding their relapse likelihood
Transdisciplinarity	– a problem-focused approach that blurs the boundaries between disciplines with the assumption that investigators using the approach must have sufficient knowledge of each other's disciplines to enable effective communication
Translation research	– an extended process that links basic research work to application and application to dissemination

BIBLIOGRAPHY

Aboujaoude, E., Koran, L. M., Gamel, N., Large, M. D., & Serpe, R. T. (2006). Potential markers for problematic Internet use: A telephone survey of 2,513 adults. *CNS Spectrums*, 11: 750–755.

Ackard, D. M., Brehm, B. J., & Steffen, J. J. (2002). Exercise and eating disorders in college-aged women: Profiling excessive exercisers. *Eating Disorders*, 10: 31–47.

Adams, J. (2009). Understanding exercise dependence. *Journal of Contemporary Psychotherapy*, 39: 231–240.

Adkins, B. J., Rugle, L. J., & Taber, J. I. (1985). A note on sexual addiction among compulsive gamblers. Paper presented at the First National Conference on Gambling Behavior of the National Council on Compulsive Gambling, New York (November).

Adriaanse, M. A., Vinkers, C. D. W., DeRidder, D. T. D., Hox, J. J., & DeWit, J. B. F. (2011). Do implementation intentions help to eat a healthy diet? A systematic review and meta-analysis of the empirical evidence. *Appetite*, 56: 183–193.

Advokat, C. D., Comaty, J. E., & Julien, R. M. (2014). *Julien's Primer of Drug Action: A Comprehensive Guide to the Actions, Uses, and Side Effects of Psychoactive Drugs*. New York: Worth.

Agnew, R. & Peters, A. A. R. (1986). The techniques of neutralization: An analysis of predisposing and situational factors. *Criminal Justice and Behavior*, 13: 81–97.

Agrawal, A., Neale, M. C., Prescott, C. A., & Kendler, K. S. (2004). Cannabis and other illicit drugs: Comorbid use and abuse/dependence in males and females. *Behavior Genetics*, 34: 217–228.

Agrawal, A., Verweij, K. J. H., Gillespie, N. A., Heath, A. C., Lessov-Schlaggar, C. N., Martin, N. G., ... & Lynskey, M. T. (2012). The genetics of addiction: A translational perspective. *Translational Psychiatry*, 2: e140–e154.

Akers, R. L., Krohn, M. D., Lanza-Kaduce, L., & Radosevich, M. (1979). Social learning and deviant behavior: A specific test of a general theory. *American Sociological Review*, 44: 636–655.

Albrecht, U.., Kirschner, N. E., & Grusser, S. M. (2007). Diagnostic instruments for behavioral addiction: An overview. *Psychosocial Medicine*, 4: 1–11.

Alcoholics Anonymous (1976). *Alcoholics Anonymous*. New York: Alcoholics Anonymous World Services.

Alexander, B. K. (2012). Addiction: The urgent need for a paradigm shift. *Substance Use & Misuse*, 47: 1475–1482.

Alexander, B. K. & Hadaway, P. F. (1982). Opiate addiction: The case for an adaptive orientation. *Psychological Bulletin*, 92: 367–381.

Alexander, B. K. & Schweighofer, A. F. (1988). Defining "addiction." *Canadian Psychology*, 29: 151–162.

Alexander, B. K., & Schweighofer, A. R. F. (1989). The prevalence of addiction among university students. *Psychology of Addictive Behaviors*, 2: 116–123.

Alexander, J. F., Barton, C., Schiaro, R. S., & Parsons, B. V. (1976). Systems-behavioral intervention with families of delinquents: Therapist characteristics, family behavior, and outcome. *Journal of Consulting and Clinical Psychology*, 44: 656–664.

Bibliography

Alexander, J. F. & Parsons, B. V. (1973). Short-term behavioral intervention with delinquent families: Impact on family process and recidivism. *Journal of Abnormal Psychology*, 3: 219–225.

Allegre, B., Souville, M., Therme, P., & Griffiths, M. D. (2006). Definitions and measures of exercise dependence. *Addiction Research & Theory*, 14: 631–646.

Allison, K. C., Grilo, C. M., Masheb, R. M., & Stunkard, A. J. (2005). Binge eating disorder and night eating syndrome: A comparative study of disordered eating. *Journal of Consulting and Clinical Psychology*, 73: 1107–1115.

American Psychiatric Association (APA) (2000). *Diagnostic and Statistical Manual of Mental Disorders (DSM-IV-TR)*. Washington, DC: APA.

  (2013). *Diagnostic and Statistical Manual of Mental Disorders* (5th edn.). Washington, DC: APA.

Ames, S. L. & McBride, C. (2006). Translating genetics, cognitive science and other basic science research findings into applications for prevention of substance use. *Evaluation and the Health Professions*, 29: 277–301.

Anderson, K. J. (2001). Internet use among college students: An exploratory study. *Journal of American College Health*, 80: 21–26.

Andreassen, C. S., Hetland, J., Molde, H., & Pallesen, S. (2011) "Workaholism" and potential outcomes in well-being and health in a cross-occupational sample. *Stress and Health*, 27: e209–e214.

Andreassen, C. S., Torsheim, T., Brunborg, G. S., & Pallesen, S. (2012). Development of a Facebook addiction scale. *Psychological Reports*, 110: 501–517.

Angell, J. R. (1906). The important human instincts. In Angell, *Psychology: An Introductory Study of the Structure and Function of Human Consciousness* (3rd edn.). New York: Henry Holt and Company, pp. 294–309.

Anonymous (1929). The nightmare of cocaine by a former "Snow-Bird." *North American Review*, 227: 418–422.

Arnett, J. J. (2000). Emerging adulthood: A theory of development from the late teens through the early twenties. *American Psychologist*, 55: 469–480.

  (2005). The developmental context of substance use in emerging adulthood. *Journal of Drug Issues*, 35: 235–253.

Ashley, D. L., Backinger, C. L., van Bemmel, D. M., & Neveleff, D. J. (2014). Tobacco regulatory science: Research to inform regulatory action at the Food and Drug Administration's Center for Tobacco Products. *Nicotine & Tobacco Research*, 16: 1045–1049.

Atroszko, P. A., Andreassen, C. S., Griffiths, M. D., & Pallesen, S. (2015). Study addiction – a new area of psychological study: Conceptualization, assessment, and preliminary findings. *Journal of Behavioral Addictions*, 4: 75–84.

Auer, M. & Griffiths, M. D. (2015). Theoretical loss and gambling intensity (revisited): A response to Braverman et al. (2013). *Journal of Gambling Studies*, 31: 921–931.

Auerbach, J. D., Hayes, R. J., & Kandathil, S. M. (2006). Overview of effective and promising interventions to prevent HIV infection. *World Health Organization Technical Report Services*, 938: 43–78.

Bagby, R. M., Vachon, D. D., Bulmash, E., & Quilty, L. C. (2008). Personality disorders and pathological gambling: A review and re-examination of prevalence rates. *Journal of Personality Disorders*, 22: 191–207.

Baker, T. B., Piper, M. E., McCarthy, D. E., Majeskie, M. R., & Fiore, M. C. (2004). Addiction motivation reformulated: An affective processing model of negative reinforcement. *Psychological Review*, 111: 33–51.

Bibliography

Bakken, I. J., Wenzel, H. G., Gotestam, K. G., Johansson, A., & Oren, A. (2009). Internet addiction among Norwegian adults: A stratified probability sample study. *Scandinavian Journal of Psychology*, 50: 121–127.

Balodis, I. M., Kober, H., Worhunsky, P. D., Stevens, M. C., Pearlson, G. D., & Potenza, M. N. (2012). Diminished frontostriatal activity during processing of monetary rewards and losses in pathological gambling. *Biological Psychiatry*, 71: 749–757.

Bamber, D., Cockerill, I. M., & Carroll, D. (2000). The pathological status of exercise dependence. *British Journal of Sports Medicine*, 34: 125–132.

Bamber, D. J., Cockerill, I. M., Rodgers, S., & Carroll, D. (2003). Diagnostic criteria for exercise dependence in women. *British Journal of Sports Medicine*, 37: 393–400.

Bancroft, J., Janssen, E., Strong, D., Carnes, L., Vukadinovic, Z., & Long, J. S. (2003). The relation between mood and sexuality in heterosexual men. *Archives of Sexual Behavior*, 32: 217–230.

Bandura, A. (1986). *Social Foundations of Thought and Action: A Social Cognitive Theory*. Englewood Cliffs, NJ: Prentice-Hall.

Barnes, G. M., Welte, J. W., Hoffman, J. H., & Tidwell, M.-C. Q. (2009). Gambling, alcohol, and other substance use among youth in the United States. *Journal of Studies on Alcohol and Drugs*, 70: 134–142.

Barnett, E., Spruijt-Metz, D., Moyers, T. B., Smith, C., Rohrbach, L. A., Sun, P., & Sussman, S. (2014). Bi-directional relationships between client and counselor speech: The importance of reframing. *Psychology of Addictive Behaviors*, 28: 1212–1219.

Barnett, E., Sussman, S., Smith, C., Rohrbach, L. A., & Spruijt-Metz, D. (2012). Motivational interviewing for adolescent substance use: A review of the literature. *Addictive Behaviors*, 37: 1325–1334.

Bauman, K. E., Ennett, S. T., Foshee, V. A., Pemberton, M., King, T. S., & Koch, G. G. (2002). Influence of a family program on adolescent smoking and drinking prevalence. *Prevention Science*, 3: 35–42.

Bauman, K. E., Ennett, S. T., Foshee, V. A., Pemberton, M. K., Tonya, S., & Koch, G. G. (2000). Influence of a family-directed program on adolescent cigarette and alcohol cessation. *Prevention Science*, 1: 227–237.

Bauman, K. E., Foshee, V. A., Ennett, S. T., Pemberton, M., Hicks, K. A., King, T. S., . . . & Koch, G. G. (2001). The influence of a family program on adolescent tobacco and alcohol use. *American Journal of Public Health*, 91: 604–610.

Beard, K. W. & Wolf, E. M. (2001). Modification in the proposed diagnostic criteria for Internet addiction. *Cyberpsychology & Behavior*, 4: 377–383.

Bechara, A. (2005). Decision making, impulse control and loss of willpower to resist drugs: A neurocognitive perspective. *Nature Neuroscience*, 8: 1458–1463.

Beck, J. E. (1998). 100 Years of "Just Say No" versus "Just Say Know": Reevaluating drug education goals for the coming century. *Evaluation Review*, 22: 15–45.

Becker, M. H. (ed.) (1974). *The Health Belief Model and Personal Health Behavior*. Thorofare, NJ: Charles B. Slack.

Becona, E. (1993). The prevalence of pathological gambling in Galicia (Spain). *Journal of Gambling Studies*, 9: 353–369.

Bejerot, N. (1972). A theory of addiction as an artificially induced drive. *American Journal of Psychiatry*, 128: 842–846.

Benson, A. L., Eisenach, D., Abrams, L., & van Stolk-Cooke, K. (2014). Stopping overshopping: A preliminary randomized controlled trial of group therapy for compulsive buying disorder. *Journal of Groups in Addiction & Recovery*, 9: 97–125.

Berczik, K., Griffiths, M. D., Szabo, A., Kurimay, T., Urban, R., & Demetrovics, Z. (2014). Exercise addiction. In K. P. Rosenberg & L. C. Feder (eds.), *Behavioral Addictions: Criteria, Evidence, and Treatment*. London: Academic Press/Elsevier, pp. 317–342.

Bergen-Cico, D. K., Haygood-El, A., Jennings-Bey, T. N., & Lane, S. D. (2013). Street addiction: A proposed theoretical model for understanding the draw of street life and gang activity. *Addiction Research & Theory*, 22: 15–26.

Bernardi, S. & Pallanti, S. (2009). Internet addiction: A descriptive clinical study focusing on comorbidities and dissociative symptoms. *Comprehensive Psychiatry*, 50: 510–516.

Bernhard, B. J. (2007). The voices of vices: Sociological perspectives on the pathological gambling entry in the Diagnostic and Statistical Manual of Mental Disorders. *American Behavioral Scientist*, 51: 8–32.

Berridge, K. C. & Robinson, T. E. (1995). The mind of an addicted brain: Neural sensitization of wanting versus liking. *Current Directions in Psychological Science*, 4: 71–76.

(2003). Parsing reward. *Trends in Neurosciences*, 26: 507–513.

Bickel, W. K., Jarmolowicz, D. P., Mueller, E. T., & Gatchalian, K. M. (2011). The behavioral economics and neuroeconomics of reinforcer pathologies: Implications for etiology and treatment of addiction. *Current Psychiatry Reports*, 13: 406–415.

Bickel, W. K., Mellis, A. M., Snider, S. E., Moody, L., Stein, J. S., & Quisenberry, A. (2016). Novel therapeutics for addiction: Behavioral economic and neuroeconomic approaches. *Current Treatment Options in Psychiatry*, 3: 277–292.

Bickel, W. K., Mueller, E. T., & Jarmolowicz, D. P. (2013). What is addiction? In B. S. McCrady & E. E. Epstein (eds.), *Addictions: A Comprehensive Guidebook* (2nd edn.). Oxford University Press, pp. 3–16.

Biglan, A. & Embry, D. D. (2013). A framework for intentional cultural change. *Journal of Contextual Behavioral Science*, 2: 95–104.

Bindra, D. & Stewart, J. (eds.) (1966). *Introduction to Motivation*. Harmondsworth: Penguin Books.

Bischof, G., Rumpf, H.-J., & Ulrich, J. (2012). Natural recovery from addiction. In H. Shaffer (ed.), *APA Addiction Syndrome Handbook, Volume 2: Recovery, Prevention and Other Issues. 1. Recovering from the Addiction Syndrome*. Washington, DC: American Psychological Association, pp. 133–155.

Bishai, D. M., Mercer, D., & Tapales, A. (2005). Can government policies help adolescents avoid risky behavior? *Preventive Medicine*, 40: 197–202.

Black, D. S., Milam, J., & Sussman, S. (2009). Sitting-meditation interventions among youth: A review of treatment efficacy. *Pediatrics*, 124: e532–e541.

Black, D. W. (2007). A review of compulsive buying disorder. *World Psychiatry*, 6: 14–18.

Black, D. W., Gabel, J., Hansen, J., & Schlosser, S. (2000). A double-blind comparison of fluvoxamine versus placebo in the treatment of compulsive buying disorder. *Annals of Clinical Psychiatry*, 12: 205–211.

Black, D. W., Kehrberg, L. D., Flumerfelt, D. L., & Schlosser, S. S. (1997). Characteristics of 36 subjects reporting compulsive sexual behavior. *American Journal of Psychiatry*, 154: 243–249.

Black, D. W. & Moyer, T. (1998). Clinical features and psychiatric comorbidity of subjects with pathological gambling behavior. *Psychiatric Services*, 49: 1434–1439.

Black, D. W., Shaw, M., McCormick, B., Bayless, J. D., & Allen, J. (2012). Neuropsychological performance, impulsivity, ADHD symptoms, and novelty seeking in compulsive buying disorder. *Psychiatry Research*, 200: 581–587.

Bibliography

Blair, W. (1842). An opium-eater in America. www.druglibrary.org/schaffer/heroin/history/blair.htm; accessed January 8, 2015.

Blanco, C., Garcia-Anaya, M., Wall, M., de los Cobos, J. C. P., Swierad, E., Wang, S., & Petry, N. M. (2015). Should pathological gambling and obesity be considered addictive disorders? A factor analytic study in a nationally representative sample. *Drug and Alcohol Dependence*, 150: 129–134.

Blanco, C., Okuda, M., Wang, S., Liu, S.-M., & Olfson, M. (2014). Testing the drug substitution switching-addictions hypothesis: A prospective study in a nationally representative sample. *JAMA Psychiatry*, 7: 1246–1253.

Blum, K., Bailey, J., Gonzalez, A. M., Oscar-Berman, M., Liu, Y., Giordano, J., ... & Gold, M. (2011a). Neuro-genetics of reward deficiency syndrome (RDS) as the root cause of "addiction transfer": A new phenomenon common after bariatric surgery. *Journal of Genetic Syndromes & Gene Therapy*, 2. doi: 10.4172/2157-7412.S2-001.

Blum, K., Chen, A. L., Giordano, J., Borsten, J., Chen, T. J. H., Hauser, M., ... & Barh, D. (2012). The addictive brain: All roads lead to dopamine. *Journal of Psychoactive Drugs*, 44: 134–143.

Blum, K., Chen, A. L., Oscar-Berman, M., Chen, T. J. H., Lubar, J., White, N., ... & Bailey, J. A. (2011b). Generational association studies of dopaminergic genes in reward deficiency syndrome (RDS) subjects: Selecting appropriate phenotypes for reward dependence behaviors. *International Journal of Environmental Research and Public Health*, 8: 4425–4459.

Blum, K., Febo, M., Badgaiyan, R. D., Braverman, E. R., Dushaj, K., Li, M., & Demetrovics, Z. (2016). Neuronutrient amino-acid therapy protects against reward deficiency syndrome: Dopaminergic key to homeostasis and neuroplasticity. *Current Pharmaceutical Design*, 22.

Blum, K., Noble, E. P., Sheridan, P. J., Montgomery, A., Ritchie, T., Jagadeeswaran, P., ... & Cohn, J. B. (1990). Allelic association of human dopamine D2 receptor gene in alcoholism. *Journal of the American Medical Association*, 263: 2055–2060.

Blum, R. W. (1995). Transition to adult health care: Setting the stage. *Journal of Adolescent Health*, 17: 3–5.

Bluthenthal, R. N., Cohen, D. A., Farley, T. A., Scribner, R., Beighley, C., Schonlau, M., & Robinson, P. L. (2008). Alcohol availability and neighborhood characteristics in Los Angeles, California and southern Louisiana. *Journal of Urban Health: Bulletin of the New York Academy of Medicine*, 85: 191–205.

Bondolfi, G., Osiek, C., & Ferrero, F. (2000). Prevalence estimates of pathological gambling in Switzerland. *Acta Psychiatrica Scandinavica*, 101: 473–475.

Bordua, D. J. (1962). Some comments on theories of group delinquency. *Sociological Inquiry*, 32: 245–260.

Botvin, G. J., Baker, E., Dusenbury, L., Botvin, E. M., & Diaz, T. (1995). Long-term follow-up results of a randomized drug abuse prevention trial in a white middle-class population. *Journal of the American Medical Association*, 273: 1106–1112.

Bouton, M. E. (2014). Why behavior change is difficult to sustain. *Preventive Medicine*, 68: 29–36

Brahm, N. C., Yeager, L. L., Fox, M. D., Farmer, K. C., & Palmer, T. A. (2010). Commonly prescribed medications and potential false-positive urine drug screens. *American Journal of Health-System Pharmacy*, 67: 1344–1350.

Brandon, T. H., Vidrine, J. I., & Litvin, E. B. (2007). Relapse and relapse prevention. *Annual Review of Clinical Psychology*, 3: 257–284.

Brewer, J. A. & Potenza, M. N. (2008). The neurobiology and genetics of impulse control disorders: Relationships to drug addictions. *Biochemical Pharmacology*, 75: 63–75.

Brisman, J. & Seigel, M. C. (1984). Bulimia and alcoholism: Two sides of the same coin. *Journal of Substance Abuse Treatment*, 1: 113–118.

Broning, S., Kumpfer, K., Kruse, K., Sack, P.-M., Schaunig-Busch, I., Ruths, S., . . . & Thomasius, R. (2012). Selective prevention programs for children from substance-affected families: A comprehensive systematic review. *Substance Abuse Treatment, Prevention, and Policy*, 7. doi: 10.1186/1747-597X-7-23.

Brown, R. I. F. (1993). Some contributions of the study of gambling to the study of other addictions. In W. R. Eadington & J. Cornelius (eds.), *Gambling Behavior and Problem Gambling*. Reno, NV: University of Nevada Press, pp. 341–372.

Brown, S. (2014). *Speed: Facing Our Addiction to Fast and Faster – and Overcoming Our Fear of Slowing Down*. New York: Berkley Books.

Brownley, K. A., Berkman, N. D., Sedway, J. A., Lohr, K. N., & Bulik, C. M. (2007). Binge eating disorder treatment: A systematic review of randomized controlled trials. *International Journal of Eating Disorders*, 40: 337–348.

Buddy, L. (2003). Twelve step programs: An update. *Addictive Disorders and Their Treatment*, 2: 19–24.

Bufe, C. (1991). *Alcoholics Anonymous: Cult or Cure?* San Francisco, CA: See Sharp Press.

Buller, D. B., Borland, R., Woodall, W. G., Hall, J. R., Hines, J. M., Burris-Woodall, P., & Saba, L. (2008). Randomized trials on Consider This, a tailored, Internet-delivered smoking prevention program for adolescents. *Health Education & Behavior*, 35: 260–281.

Burgess, V., Dziegielewski, S. F., & Green, C. E. (2005). Improving comfort about sex communication between parents and their adolescents: Practice-based research within a teen sexuality group. *Brief Treatment and Crisis Intervention*, 5: 379–390.

Burke, B. L., Arkowitz, H., & Dunn, C. (2002). The efficacy of motivational interviewing and its adaptations: What we know so far. In W. R. Miller & S. Rollnick (eds.), *Motivational Interviewing: Preparing People for Change*. New York: Guilford Press, pp. 217–250.

Burke, B. L., Arkowitz, H., & Menchola, M. (2003). The efficacy of motivational interviewing: A meta-analysis of controlled clinical trials. *Journal of Consulting and Clinical Psychology*, 71: 843–861.

Burke, R. J. (1999). Workaholism in organizations: Gender differences. *Sex Roles*, 41: 333–345.

(2000). Workaholism in organizations: Concepts, results and future directions. *International Journal of Management Reviews*, 2: 1–16.

Cam, E. & Isbulan, O. (2012). A new addiction for teacher candidates: Social networks. *Turkish Online Journal of Educational Technology*, 11: 14–19.

Campbell, W. G. (2003). Addiction: A disease of volition caused by a cognitive impairment. *Canadian Journal of Psychiatry*, 48: 669–674.

Cao, F. & Su, L. (2006). Internet addiction among Chinese adolescents: Prevalence and psychological features. *Child: Care, Health and Development*, 33: 275–281.

Carlbring, P., Jonsson, J., Josephson, H., & Forsberg, L. (2010). Motivational interviewing versus cognitive behavioral group therapy in the treatment of problem and pathological gambling: A randomized controlled trial. *Cognitive Behaviour Therapy*, 39: 92–103.

Carnes, P. (1991). *Don't Call It Love: Recovery from Sexual Addiction*. New York: Bantam.

Carnes, P. J., Murray, R. E., & Charpentier, L. (2004). Addiction interaction disorder. In R. H. Coombs (ed.), *Handbook of Addictive Disorders: A Practical Guide to Diagnosis and Treatment*. New York: John Wiley, pp. 31–62.

(2005). Bargains with chaos: Sex addicts and addiction interaction disorder. *Sexual Addiction & Compulsivity*, 12: 79–120.

Bibliography

Carroll, J., Padilla-Walker, L., Nelson, L., Olson, C., McNamara Barry, C., & Madsen, S. (2008). Generation XXX: Pornography acceptance and use among emerging adults. *Journal of Adolescent Research*, 23: 6–30.

Carroll, K. M., Connors, G. J., Cooney, N. L., DiClemente, C. C., Donovan, D. M., Kadden, R. R., ... & Zweben, A. (1998). Internal validity of Project MATCH treatments: Discriminability and integrity. *Journal of Consulting and Clinical Psychology*, 66: 290–303.

Carter, B. L. & Tiffany, S. T. (1999). Meta-analysis of cue-reactivity in addiction research. *Addiction*, 94: 327–340.

Carter-Jessop, L., Franklin, L. N., Heath, J. W., Jimenez-Irizarry, G., & Peace, M. D. (2000). Abstinence education for urban youth. *Journal of Community Health*, 25: 293–304.

Casey, B. J., Tottenham, N., Liston, C., & Durston, S. (2005). Imaging the developing brain: What have we learned about cognitive development? *Trends in Cognitive Science*, 9: 104–110.

Castelnuovo, G., Manzoni, G. M., Villa, V., Cesa, G. L., & Molinari, E. (2011). Brief strategic therapy vs cognitive behavioral therapy for the inpatient and telephone-based outpatient treatment of binge eating disorder: The STRATOB randomized controlled clinical trial. *Clinical Practice and Epidemiology in Mental Health*, 7: 29–37.

Castro-Fornieles, J., Diaz, R., Goti, J., Calvo, R., Gonzalez, L., Serrano, L., & Gual, A. (2010). Prevalence and factors related to substance use among adolescents with eating disorders. *European Addiction Research*, 16: 61–68.

Caulkins, J. P. (2006). *Cost-Benefit Analyses of Investments to Control Illicit Substance Abuse and Addiction*. Pittsburgh, PA: Carnegie Mellon University Qatar Campus and Heinz School. Working Paper. http://repository.cmu.edu/cgi/viewcontent.cgi?article=1008& con text=heinzworks; accessed August 25, 2015.

Cavallo, D. A., Smith, A. E., Schepis, T. S., Desai, R., Potenza, M. N., & Krishnan-Sarin, S. (2010). Smoking expectancies, weight concerns, and dietary behaviors in adolescence. *Pediatrics*, 126: e66–e72.

Cerda, M., Wall, M., Keyes, K. M., Galea, S., & Hasin, D. (2012). Medical marijuana laws in 50 states: Investigating the relationship between state legalization of medical marijuana and marijuana use, abuse, and dependence. *Drug and Alcohol Dependence*, 120: 22–27.

Chamberlain, P. & Reid, J. B. (1998). Comparison of two community alternatives to incarceration for chronic juvenile offenders. *Journal of Consulting and Clinical Psychology*, 66: 624–633.

Chamberlain, S. R., Odlaug, B. L., Boulougouris, V., Fineberg, N. A., & Grant, J. E. (2009). Trichotillomania: Neurobiology and treatment. *Neuroscience and Biobehavior Reviews*, 33: 831–842.

Chang, M. K. & Law, S. P. M. (2008). Factor structure for Young's Internet Addiction Test: A confirmatory study. *Computers in Human Behavior*, 24: 2597–2619.

Chapman, C. L. & de Castro, J. M. (1990). Running addiction: Measurement and associated psychological characteristics. *Journal of Sports Medicine and Physical Fitness*, 30: 283–290.

Chapman, R. (2015). *State Health Officer's Report on E-Cigarettes: A Community Health Threat*. Sacramento, CA: California Department of Public Health, California Tobacco Control Program.

Chappel, J. N. (1992). Effective use of Alcoholics Anonymous and Narcotics Anonymous in treating patients. *Psychiatric Annals*, 22: 409–418.

Chatzisarantis, N. L. D. & Hagger, M. S. (2010). Effects of implementation intentions linking suppression of alcohol consumption to socializing goals on alcohol-related decisions. *Journal of Applied Social Psychology*, 40: 1618–1634.

Bibliography

Chen, K., Sheth, A. J., Elliott, D. K., & Yeager, A. (2004). Prevalence and correlates of past-year substance use, abuse, and dependence in a suburban community sample of high-school students. *Addictive Behaviors*, 29: 413–423.

Chiauzzi, E. J. & Liljegren, S. (1993). Taboo topics in addiction treatment: An empirical review of clinical folklore. *Journal of Substance Abuse Treatment*, 10: 303–316.

Chou, C. & Hsiao, M.-M. (2000). Internet addiction, usage, gratification, and pleasure experience: The Taiwan college students' case. *Computers & Education*, 35: 65–80.

Christenson, G. A., Faber, R. J., de Zwaan, M., Raymond, N. C., Specker, S. M., Ekern, M. D., . . . & Mitchell, J. E. (1994). Compulsive buying: Descriptive characteristics and psychiatric comorbidity. *Journal of Clinical Psychiatry*, 55: 5–11.

Christo, G., Jones, S. L., Haylett, S., Stephenson, G. M., Lefever, R. M. H., & Lefever, R. (2003). The Shorter PROMIS Questionnaire: Further validation of a tool for simultaneous assessment of multiple addictive behaviours. *Addictive Behaviors*, 28: 225–248.

Churchland, P. M. (1981). Eliminative materialism and the propositional attitudes. *Journal of Philosophy*, 78: 67–90.

Coffey, C., Carlin, J. B., Degenhardt, L., Lynsky, M., Sanci, L., & Patton, G. C. (2002). Cannabis dependence in young adults: A population study. *Addiction*, 97: 187–194.

Cohen, A. K. (1955). *Delinquent Boys: The Culture of the Gang*. New York: Free Press.

Cohen, P., Cohen, J., Kasen, S., Velez, C. N., Hartmark, C., Johnson, J., . . . & Streuning, E. L. (1993). An epidemiological study of disorders in late childhood and adolescence – I: Age- and gender-specific prevalence. *Journal of Child Psychology and Psychiatry*, 34: 851–867.

Collins, L. M., Graham, J. W., Rousculp, S. S., & Hansen, W. B. (1997). Heavy caffeine use and the beginning of the substance use onset process. In K. Bryant, M. Windle, & S. West (eds.), *The Science of Prevention: Methodological Advances from Alcohol and Substance Abuse Research*. Washington, DC: APA, pp. 79–99.

Compton, W. M., Grant, B. F., Colliver, J. D., Glantz, M. D., & Stinson, F. S. (2004). Prevalence of marijuana use disorders in the United States 1991–1992 and 2001–2002. *Journal of the American Medical Association*, 291: 2114–2121.

Conklin, C. A. & Tiffany, S. T. (2001). The impact of imagining personalized versus standardized urge scenarios on cigarette craving and autonomic reactivity. *Experimental and Clinical Psychopharmacology*, 9: 399–408.

Connors, G. J. (1998). Overview of Project MATCH. *The Addictions Newsletter*, 5: 4–5.

Cook, B. & Hausenblas, H. (2014). Exercise dependence, eating disorders and body dysmorphia. In A. Clow & S. Edmunds (eds.), *Physical Activity and Mental Health*. Champaign, IL: Human Kinetics, pp. 255–280.

Cook, B., Hausenblas, H., & Freimuth, M. (2014). Exercise addiction and compulsive exercising: Relationship to eating disorders, substance use disorders, and addictive disorders. In T. D. Brewerton & A. B. Dennis (eds.), *Eating Disorders, Addictions, and Substance Use Disorders: Research, Clinical and Treatment Perspectives*. Berlin: Springer-Verlag, pp. 127–144.

Cook, B., Karr, T. M., Zunker, C., Mitchell, J. E., Thompson, R., Sherman, R., . . . & Wonderlich, S. A. (2013). Primary and secondary exercise dependence in a community-based sample of road race runners. *Journal of Sport & Exercise Psychology*, 35: 464–469.

Cook, D. R. (1987). Self-identified addictions and emotional disturbances in a sample of college students. *Psychology of Addictive Behaviors*, 1: 55–61.

Cooper, A., Morahan-Martin, J., Mathy, R. M., & Maheu, M. (2002). Toward an increased understanding of user demographics in online sexual activities. *Journal of Sex & Marital Therapy*, 28: 105–129.

Cope, L. M., Vincent, G. M., Jobelius, J. L., Nyalakanti, P. K., Calhoun, V. D., & Kiehl, K. A. (2014). Psychopathic traits modulate brain responses to drug cues in incarcerated offenders. *Frontiers in Human Neuroscience*, 8: Article 87.

Copeland, L., McNamara, R., Kelson, M., & Simpson, S. (2015). Mechanisms of change with motivational interviewing in relation to health behavior outcomes: A systematic review. *Patient Education and Counseling*, 98: 401–411.

Corey, C., Want, B., Johnson, S. E., Apelberg, B., Husten, C., King, B. A., . . . & King, B. A. (2013). Electronic cigarette use among middle and high school students: United States, 2011-2012. *Morbidity and Mortality Weekly Report*, 62: 729–730.

Cornish, J. W. & O'Brien, C. P. (1996). Crack cocaine abuse: An epidemic with many public health consequences. *Annual Review of Public Health*, 17: 259–273.

Corwin, R. L. & Hajnal, A. (2005). Too much of a good thing: Neurobiology of non-homeostatic eating and drug abuse. *Physiology & Behavior*, 86: 5–8.

Council of Philosophical Studies (1981). *Psychology and the Philosophy of Mind in the Philosophy Curriculum*. San Francisco State University.

Courtney, K. E., Schacht, J. P., Hutchison, K., Roche, D. J. O., & Ray, L. A. (2016). Neural substrates of cue reactivity: association with treatment outcomes and relapse. *Addiction Biology*, 21: 3–22.

Courvoisier, D. S. & Etter, J.-E. (2010). Comparing the predictive validity of five cigarette dependence questionnaires. *Drug and Alcohol Dependence*, 107: 128–133.

Couturier, J., Kimber, M., & Szatmari, P. (2013). Efficacy of family-based treatment for adolescents with eating disorders: A systematic review and meta-analysis. *International Journal of Eating Disorders*, 46: 3–11.

Cowlishaw, S., Merkouris, S., Dowling, N., Anderson, C., Jackson, A., & Thomas, S. (2012). Psychological therapies for pathological and problem gambling. *Cochrane Database of Systematic Reviews*, 11: Article CD008937.

Cox, W. M., Fadardi, J. S., Intriligator, J. M., & Klinger, E. (2014). Attentional bias modification for addictive behaviors: Clinical implications. *CNS Spectrums*, 19: 215–224.

Coyle, K. K., Kirby, D. B., Robin, L. E., Banspach, S. W., & Glassman, B. E. (2006). All4You! A randomized trial of an HIV, other STDs, and pregnancy prevention intervention for alternative school students. *AIDS Education and Prevention*, 18: 187–203.

Csikszentmihalyi, M. & Larson, R. (1984). *Being Adolescent: Conflict and Growth in the Teenage Years*. New York: Basic Books.

Cunningham, J. A. (1999). Resolving alcohol-related problems with and without treatment: The effects of different problem criteria. *Journal of Studies on Alcohol*, 60: 463–466.

Cunningham, J. A. & Breslin, F. C. (2004). Only one in three people with alcohol abuse or dependence ever seek treatment. *Addictive Behaviors*, 29: 221–223.

Cunningham-Williams, R. M., Cottler, L. D., Compton, W. M., Spitznagel, E. L., & Ben-Abdallah, A. (2000). Problem gambling and comorbid psychiatric and substance use disorders among drug users recruited from drug treatment and community settings. *Journal of Gambling Studies*, 16: 347–376.

Cuper, P. F. & Lynch, T. R. (2009). When is fantasy proneness associated with distress? An examination of two models. *Imagination, Cognition and Personality*, 28: 251–268.

Curry, S., Wagner, E. H., & Grothaus, L. C. (1990). Intrinsic and extrinsic motivation for smoking cessation. *Journal of Consulting and Clinical Psychology*, 58: 310–316.

Cutler, K. A. (2014). Prescription stimulants are "A Okay": Applying neutralization theory to college students' nonmedical prescription stimulant use. *Journal of American College Health*, 62: 478–486.

Bibliography

Cuzen, N. L. & Stein, D. J. (2014). Behavioral addiction: The nexus of impulsivity and compulsivity. In K. P. Rosenberg & L. C. Feder (eds.), *Behavioral Addictions: Criteria, Evidence, and Treatment*. London: Academic Press/Elsevier, pp. 19–34.

Dalzell, T. & Victor, T. (2008). *Vice Slang*. New York: Routledge.

Davis, A. A., Edge, P. J., & Gold, M. S. (2014). New directions in the pharmacological treatment of food addiction, overeating, and obesity. In K. P. Rosenberg & L. C. Feder (eds.), *Behavioral Addictions: Criteria, Evidence, and Treatment*. London: Academic Press/Elsevier, pp. 185–213.

Davis, C. & Carter, J. C. (2009). Compulsive overeating as an addiction disorder: A review of theory and evidence. *Appetite*, 53: 1–8.

Davis, C., Curtis, C., Levitan, R. D., Carter, J. C., Kaplan, A. S., & Kennedy, J. L. (2011). Evidence that "food addiction" is a valid phenotype of obesity. *Appetite*, 57: 711–717.

Davis, E., Harrell, T. H., & Honaker, L. M. (1989). Content domains of dysfunction in alcohol and polydrug abusers: The Chemical Dependency Assessment Profile. Paper presented at the meeting of the Association for the Advancement of Behavior Therapy, Washington, DC.

Davis, M. M., Gance-Cleveland, B., Hassink, S., Johnson, R., Paradis, G., & Resnicow, K. (2007). Recommendations for prevention of childhood obesity. *Pediatrics*, 120: S229–S254.

Davis, R. A., Flett, G. L., & Besser, A. (2002). Validation of a new scale for measuring problematic Internet use: Implications for pre-employment screening. *Cyberpsychology & Behavior*, 5: 331–345.

Davis, W. A. (2005). Reasons and psychological causes. *Philosophical Studies*, 122: 51–101.

De Bellis, M. D., Clark, D. B., Beers, S. R., Soloff, P. H., Boring, A. M., Hall, J., ... & Keshavan, M. S. (2000). Hippocampal volume in adolescent-onset alcohol use disorders. *American Journal of Psychiatry*, 157: 737–744.

De Quincey, T. (1822). *Confessions of an English Opium Eater*. www.druglibrary.org/schaffer/History/dequinc1.htm; accessed April 20, 2005.

de Wit, H. (1998). Individual differences in acute effects of drugs in humans: Their relevance to risk for abuse. *NIDA Research Monograph*, 169: 176–187.

DeJong, W. (2002). The role of mass media campaigns in reducing high-risk drinking among college students. *Journal of Studies on Alcohol, Supplement*, 14: 182–192.

DeJong, W. & Wallack, L. (1999). A critical perspective on the drug czar's antidrug media campaign. *Journal of Health Communication*, 4: 155–160.

Demetrovics, Z. & Griffiths, M. D. (2012). Behavioral addictions: Past, present and future. *Journal of Behavioral Addictions*, 1: 1–2.

Demetrovics, Z., Szeredi, B., & Rozsa, S. (2008). The three-factor model of Internet addiction: The development of the Problematic Internet Use Questionnaire. *Behavior Research Methods*, 40: 563–574.

Desai, R. A., Desai, M. M., & Potenza, M. N. (2007). Gambling, health, and age: Data from the National Epidemiologic Survey on Alcohol and Related Conditions. *Psychology of Addictive Behaviors*, 21: 431–440.

DeVall, K. E., Gregory, P. D., & Hartmann, D. J. (2015). Extending recidivism monitoring for drug courts: Methods, issues and policy implications. *International Journal of Offender Therapy and Comparative Criminology*, 10. doi: 10.1177/0306624X15590205.

Dickson, L. M., Derevensky, J. L., & Gupta, R. (2002). The prevention of gambling problems in youth: A conceptual framework. *Journal of Gambling Studies*, 18: 97–159.

DiClemente, C. C., Prochaska, J. O., Fairhurst, S. K., Velicer, W. F., Velasquez, M. M., & Rossi, J. S. (1991). The process of smoking cessation: An analysis of precontemplation, contemplation, and preparation stages of change. *Journal of Consulting and Clinical Psychology*, 59: 295–304.

Dierker, L. C., Donny, E., Tiffany, S., Colby, S. M., Perrine, N., & Clayton, R. R. (2007). The association between cigarette smoking and DSM-IV nicotine dependence among first year college students. *Drug and Alcohol Dependence*, 86: 106–114.

DiFranza, J. R., Savageau, J. A., Rigotti, N. A., Fletcher, K., Ockene, J. K., McNeill, A. D., . . . & Wood, C. (2002). Development of symptoms of tobacco dependence in youths: 30 month follow up data from the DANDY study. *Tobacco Control*, 11: 228–235.

DiIorio, C., McCarty, F., & Denzmore, P. (2006). An exploration of social cognitive theory mediators of father–son communication about sex. *Journal of Pediatric Psychology*, 31: 917–927.

Dittmar, H. (2005). Compulsive buying: A growing concern? An examination of gender, age, and endorsement of materialistic values as predictors. *British Journal of Psychology*, 96: 467–491.

Dodder, R. A. & Hughes, S. P. (1993). Neutralization of drinking behavior. *Deviant Behavior: An Interdisciplinary Journal*, 14: 65–79.

Dodes, L. M. (1990). Addiction, helplessness, and narcissistic rage. *Psychoanalytic Quarterly*, 59: 398–410.

Doerfler, M. C. & Kammer, P. P. (1986). Workaholism, sex, and sex role stereotyping among female professionals. *Sex Roles*, 14: 551–560.

Doiron, J. P. & Nicki, R. M. (2007). Prevention of pathological gambling: A randomized controlled trial. *Cognitive Behaviour Therapy*, 36: 74–84.

Donaldson, S. I., Sussman, S., MacKinnon, D. P., Severson, H. H., Glynn, T., Murray, D. M., & Stone, E. J. (1996). Drug abuse prevention programming: Do we know what content works? *American Behavioral Scientist*, 39: 868–883.

Downs, D. S., Hausenblas, H. A., & Nigg, C. R. (2004). Factorial validity and psychometric examination of the exercise dependence scale–revised. *Measurement in Physical Education and Exercise Science*, 8: 183–201.

Drug Policy Alliance (2011). *Drug Courts Are Not the Answer: Toward a Health-Centered Approach to Drug Use*. New York: Drug Policy Alliance. www.drugpolicy.org; accessed October 18, 2015.

Drummond, D. C. (2000). What does cue-reactivity have to offer clinical research? *Addiction*, 95: S129–S144.

Drummond, D. C. & Glautier, S. (1994). A controlled trial of cue exposure treatment in alcohol dependents. *Journal of Consulting and Clinical Psychology*, 62: 809–817.

Duncan, D. F., Nicholson, T., Clifford, P., Hawkins, W., & Petosa, R. (1994). Harm reduction: An emerging new paradigm for drug education. *Journal of Drug Education*, 24: 281–290.

Dunn, C., Deroo, L., & Rivara, F. P. (2001). The use of brief interventions adapted from motivational interviewing across behavioral domains: A systematic review. *Addiction*, 96: 1725–1742.

Durell, J. & Bukoski, W. (1984). Preventing substance abuse: The state of the art. *Public Health Reports*, 99: 23–31.

Dvorak, R. D. & Day, A. M. (2014). Marijuana and self-regulation: Examining likelihood and intensity of use and problems. *Addictive Behaviors*, 39: 709–712.

Edmundson, E., McAlister, A., Murray, D., Perry, C., & Lichtenstein, E. (1991). Approaches directed to the individual. In D. R. Shopland, D. M. Burns, J. M. Samet, & E. R. Gritz (eds.), *Strategies to Control Tobacco Use in the United States: A Blueprint for Public Health in the 1990s*. Washington, DC: US Government Printing Office, pp. 147–199.

Bibliography

Eggleston, A. M., Woolaway-Bickel, K., & Schmidt, N. B. (2004). Social anxiety and alcohol use: Evaluation of the moderating and mediating effects of alcohol expectancies. *Journal of Anxiety Disorders*, 18: 33–49.

Eke, A. N., Mezoff, J. S., Duncan, T., & Sogolow, E. D. (2006). Reputationally strong HIV prevention programs: Lessons from the front line. *AIDS Education and Prevention*, 18: 163–175.

Elder, G. (1998). Life course and human development. In R. M. Lerner (ed.), *Handbook of Child Psychology, Volume 1: Theoretical Models of Human Development*. New York: John Wiley, pp. 939–991.

Elias, M. J. (2006). The connection between academic and social-emotional learning. In M. J. Elias & H. Arnold (eds.), *The Educator's Guide to Emotional Intelligence: An Academic Achievement*. Thousand Oaks, CA: Corwin, pp. 1–14.

Emery, S., Wakefield, M. A., Terry-McElrath, Y., Saffer, H., Szczypka, G., O'Malley, P. M., & Flay, B. (2005). Televised state-sponsored antitobacco advertising and youth smoking beliefs and behavior in the United States, 1999–2000. *Archives of Pediatrics & Adolescent Medicine*, 159: 639–689.

Emmons, K., Glasgow, R. E., Marcus, B., Rakowski, W., & Curry, S. J. (1995). Motivation for change across behavioral risk factors: Conceptual and clinical advances. Paper presented at the Sixteenth Annual Scientific Sessions of the Society of Behavioral Medicine, San Diego, CA.

Engle, B., Macgowan, M. J., Wagner, E. F., & Amrhein, P. C. (2010). Markers of marijuana use outcomes within adolescent substance abuse group treatment. *Research on Social Work Practice*, 20: 271–282.

Epstein, L. H. (1992). Role of behavior theory in behavioral medicine. *Journal of Consulting and Clinical Psychology*, 4: 493–498.

Erickson, P. G. (1995). Harm reduction: What it is and is not. *Drug and Alcohol Review*, 14: 283–285.

Essau, C. A. (2008). Comorbidity of addictive problems: Assessment and treatment implications. In C. A. Essau (ed.), *Adolescent Addiction: Epidemiology, Assessment and Treatment*. New York: Academic Press, pp. 297–313.

Essau, C. A. & Hutchinson, D. (2008). Alcohol use, abuse and dependence. In C. A. Essau (ed.), *Adolescent Addiction: Epidemiology, Assessment and Treatment*. New York: Academic Press, pp. 61–115.

Estok, P. J. & Rudy, E. B. (1996). The relationship between eating disorders and running in women. *Research in Nursing & Health*, 19: 377–387.

Ettorre, E. (2015). Embodied deviance, gender, and epistemologies of ignorance: Re-visioning drugs use in a neurochemical, unjust world. *Substance Use & Misuse*, 50: 794–805.

Evans, R. I. (1998). A historical perspective on effective prevention. In W. J. Bukoski & R. I. Evans (eds.), *Cost–Benefit/Cost-Effectiveness Research of Drug Abuse Prevention: Implications for Programming and Policy*. NIDA Research Monograph 176. Rockville, MD: National Institute on Drug Abuse, National Institutes of Health, pp. 37–58.

Faber, R. J., Christenson, G. A., De Zwaan, M., & Mitchell, J. (1995). Two forms of compulsive consumption: Comorbidity of compulsive buying and binge eating. *Journal of Consumer Research*, 22: 296–304.

Faber, R. J. & O'Guinn, T. C. (1992). A clinical screener for compulsive buying. *Journal of Consumer Research*, 19: 459–469.

Falk, D. E., Yi, H. Y., & Hiller-Sturmhöfel, S. (2006). An epidemiologic analysis of co-occurring alcohol and tobacco use and disorders: Findings from the National Epidemiologic Survey on Alcohol and Related Conditions. *Alcohol Research and Health*, 29: 162–171.

Farabee, D., Prendergast, M., & Anglin, M. (1998). The effectiveness of coerced treatment for drug-abusing offenders. *Federal Probation*, 62: 3–10.

Farrell, M., Howes, S., Bebbington, P., Brugha, T., Jenkins, R., Lewis, G., ... & Meltzer, H. (2003). Nicotine, alcohol and drug dependence, and psychiatric comorbidity: Results of a national household survey. *International Review of Psychiatry*, 15: 50–56.

Fave, A. D., Massimini, F., & Bassi, M. (2011). *Psychological Selection and Optimal Experience across Cultures: Social Empowerment through Personal Growth*. Cross-Cultural Advancements in Positive Psychology 2. New York: Springer.

Feeney, J. A. & Noller, P. (1990). Attachment style as a predictor of adult romantic relationships. *Journal of Personality and Social Psychology*, 58: 281–291.

Feigelman, W., Wallisch, L. S., & Lesieur, H. R. (1998). Problem gamblers, problem substance users, and dual-problem individuals: An epidemiological study. *American Journal of Public Health*, 88: 467–470.

Ferentzy, P., Skinner, W. J. W., & Matheson, F. I. (2013). Illicit drug use and problem gambling. *ISRN Addiction*. doi: 10.1155/2013/342392.

Ferland, F., Ladouceur, R., & Vitaro, F. (2002). Prevention of program gambling: Modifying misconceptions and increasing knowledge. *Journal of Gambling Studies*, 18: 19–29.

Ferri, M., Amato, L., & Davoli, M. (2006). Alcoholics Anonymous and other 12-step programmes for alcohol dependence. *Cochrane Database of Systematic Reviews*, 3. Article CD005032.

Field, M. & Eastwood, B. (2005). Experimental manipulation of attentional bias increases the motivation to drink alcohol. *Psychopharmacology*, 183: 350–357.

Field, M., Munafo, M. R., & Franken, I. H. A. (2009). A meta-analytic investigation of the relationship between attentional bias and subjective craving in substance abuse. *Psychological Bulletin*, 135: 589–607.

Finn, P. R. & Hall, J. (2004). Cognitive ability and risk for alcoholism: Short-term memory capacity and intelligence moderate personality risk for alcohol problems. *Journal of Abnormal Psychology*, 113: 569–581.

Fiori, M. C., Jaen, C. R., Baker, T. B., Bailey, W. C., Benowitz, N. L., Curry, S. J., ... & Wewers, M. E. (2008). *Treating Tobacco Use and Dependence: 2008 Update*. Rockville, MD: US Department of Health and Human Services.

Fishbein, D. H. (2000). The importance of neurobiological research to the prevention of psychopathology. *Prevention Science*, 1: 89–106.

Fishbein, D. H., Ridenour, T., Herman-Stahl, M., & Sussman, S. (2016). The full translational spectrum of prevention science: Facilitating the transfer of knowledge to practices and policies that prevent behavioral health problems. *Translational Behavioral Medicine*, 6: 5–16.

Fishbein, M., & Ajzen, I. (1975). *Belief, Attitude, Intention, and Behaviour: An Introduction to Theory and Research*. Reading, MA: Addison-Wesley.

Fisher, H. (2006). Broken hearts: The nature and risks of romantic rejections. In A. C. Crouter & A. Booth (eds.): *Romance and Sex in Adolescence and Emerging Adulthood: Risks and Opportunities*. Mahwah, NJ: Lawrence Erlbaum Associates, pp. 3–28.

(2014). The tyranny of love: Love addiction – an anthropologist's view. In K. P. Rosenberg & L. C. Feder (eds.), *Behavioral Addictions: Criteria, Evidence, and Treatment*. London: Academic Press/Elsevier, pp. 237–266.

Fisher, J. D., Fisher, W. A., Bryan, A. D., & Misovich, S. J. (2002). Information–motivation–behavioral skills model-based HIV risk behavior change intervention for inner-city high school youth. *Health Psychology*, 21: 177–186.

Bibliography

Flay, B. R. (1981). On improving the chances of mass media health promotion programs causing meaningful changes in behavior. In M. Meyer (ed.), *Health Education by Television and Radio*. Munich: Saur, pp. 56–89.

  (1985). Psychosocial approaches to smoking prevention: A review of findings. *Health Psychology*, 4: 449–488.

Fletcher, B. W., Tims, F. M., & Brown, B. S. (1997). Drug Abuse Treatment Outcome Study (DATOS): Treatment evaluation research in the United States. *Psychology of Addictive Behaviors*, 11: 216–229.

Flynn, B. S., Worden, J. K., Secker-Walker, R. H., Badger, G. J., Geller, B. M., & Costanza, M. C. (1992). Prevention of cigarette smoking through mass media intervention and school programs. *American Journal of Public Health*, 82: 827–834.

Flynn, B. S., Worden, J. K., Secker-Walker, R. H., Pirie, P. L., Badger, G. J., & Carpenter, J. H. (1997). Long-term responses of higher and lower risk youths to smoking prevention interventions. *Preventive Medicine*, 26, 389–394.

Flynn, B. S., Worden, J. K., Secker-Walker, R. H., Pirie, P. L., Badger, G. J., Carpenter, J. H., & Geller, B. M. (1994). Mass media and school interventions for cigarette smoking prevention: Effects 2 years after completion. *American Journal of Public Health*, 84: 1148–1150.

Foddy, B. & Savulescu, J. (2010a). A liberal account of addiction. *Philosophy, Psychiatry, & Psychology*, 17: 1–22.

  (2010b). Relating addiction to disease, disability, autonomy, and the good life. *Philosophy, Psychiatry, & Psychology*, 17: 35–42.

Fong, T. W., Reid, R. C., & Parhami, I. (2012). Behavioral addictions: Where to draw the line? *Psychiatric Clinics of North America*, 35: 279–296.

Forbes, D. L. (2011). Toward a unified model of human motivation. *Review of General Psychology*, 15: 85–98.

Ford, J. D., Gelernter, J., DeVoe, J. S., Zhang, W., Weiss, R. D., Brady, K., . . . & Kranzler, H. R. (2009). Association of psychiatric and substance use disorder comorbidity with cocaine dependence severity and treatment utilization in cocaine-dependent individuals. *Drug and Alcohol Dependence*, 99: 193–203.

Fortson, B. L., Scotti, J. R., Chen, Y.-C., Malone, J., & Del Ben, K. S. (2007). Internet use, abuse, and dependence among students at a southeastern regional university. *Journal of American College Health*, 56: 137–144.

Foster, A. C., Shorter, G. W., & Griffiths, M. D. (2015). Muscle dysmorphia: Could it be classified as an addiction to body image? *Journal of Behavioral Addictions*, 4: 1–5.

Foulds, J., Veldheer, S., Yingst, J., Hrabovsky, S., Wilson, S. J., Nichols, T. T., & Eissenberg, T. (2015). Development of a questionnaire for assessing dependence on electronic cigarettes among a large sample of ex-smoking e-cigarette users. *Nicotine & Tobacco Dependence*, 17: 186–192.

Foy, D. W., Miller, P. M., Eisler, R. M., & O'Toole, D. H. (1976). Social-skills training to teach alcoholics to refuse drinking effectively. *Journal of Studies on Alcohol*, 37: 1340–1345.

Frank, A. (1993). *Anne Frank: The Diary of a Young Girl*, trans. B. M. Mooyaart. New York: Bantam.

Franken, I. H. A. (2003). Drug craving and addiction: Integrating psychological and neuropsychopharmacological approaches. *Progress in Neuro-Psychopharmacology & Biological Psychiatry*, 27: 563–579.

Freedman, A. M., Kaplan, H. I., & Sadock, B. J. (1976). *Modern Synopsis of Psychiatry, Volume 2*. Baltimore, MD: Williams & Wilkins.

Freimuth, M. (2008). *Addicted? Recognizing Destructive Behavior Before It's Too Late*. Lanham, MD: Rowman & Littlefield.

Freimuth, M., Moniz, S., & Kim, S. R. (2011). Clarifying exercise addiction: Differential diagnosis, co-occurring disorders, and phases of addiction. *International Journal of Environmental Research and Public Health*, 8: 4069–4081.

Freimuth, M., Waddell, M., Stannard, J., Kelley, S., Kipper, A., Richardson, A., & Szuromi, I. (2008). Expanding the scope of dual diagnosis and co-addictions: Behavioral addictions. *Journal of Groups in Addiction & Recovery*, 3: 137–160.

French, M. T., Maclean, J. C., & Ettner, S. L. (2008). Drinkers and bettors: Investigating the complementarity of alcohol consumption and problem gambling. *Drug and Alcohol Dependence*, 96: 155–164.

Friend, K. B. & Pagano, M. E. (2004). Smoking initiation among nonsmokers during and following treatment for alcohol use disorders. *Journal of Substance Abuse Treatment*, 26: 219–224.

Fuqua, J., Stokols, D., Gress, J., Phillips, K., & Harvey, R. (2004). Transdisciplinary collaboration as a basis for enhancing the science and prevention of substance use and abuse. *Substance Use and Misuse*, 39: 1457–1514.

Gable, R. S. (2006). The toxicity of recreational drugs. *Scientific American*, 94: 206–208.

Gaboury, A. & Ladouceur, R. (1993). Evaluation of a prevention program for pathological gambling among adolescents. *Journal of Primary Prevention*, 14: 21–28.

Gadalla, T. & Piran, N. (2007). Eating disorders and substance abuse in Canadian men and women: A national study. *Eating Disorders*, 15: 189–203.

Galaif, E. R. & Sussman, S. (1995). For whom does Alcoholics Anonymous work? *International Journal of the Addictions*, 30: 161–184.

Garman, J. F., Hayduk, D. M., Crider, D. A., & Hodel, M. M. (2004). Occurrence of exercise dependence in a college-aged population. *Journal of American College Health*, 52: 221–228.

Gearhardt, A. N., Corbin, W. R., & Brownell, K. D. (2009). Preliminary validation of the Yale Food Addiction Scale. *Appetite*, 52: 430–436.

  (2016). Development of the Yale Food Addiction Scale Version 2.0. *Psychology of Addictive Behaviors*, 30: 113–121.

Gearhardt, A. N., White, M. A., Masheb, R. M., Morgan, P. T., Crosby, R. D., & Grillo, C. M. (2012). An examination of the food addiction construct in obese patients with binge eating disorder. *International Journal of Eating Disorders*, 45: 657–663.

Gearhardt, A. N., Yokum, S., Orr, P. T., Stice, E., Corbin, W. R., & Brownell, K. D. (2011). Neural correlates of food addiction. *Archives of General Psychiatry*, 68: 808–816.

Gibbs, L. E. (1983). Validity and reliability of the Michigan Alcoholism Screening Test: A review. *Drug and Alcohol Dependence*, 12: 279–285.

Giedd, J. N. (2008). The teen brain: Insights from neuroimaging. *Journal of Adolescent Health*, 42: 335–343.

Gillan, C. M. & Robbins, T. W. (2014). Goal-directed learning and obsessive-compulsive disorder. *Philosophical Transactions of the Royal Society, B: Biological Sciences*, 369. doi: 10.1098/rstb.2013.0475.

Glasser, W. (1976). *Positive Addictions*. New York: Harper & Row.

Gleaves, D. H. & Carter, J. D. (2008). Eating addiction. In C. A. Essau (ed.), *Adolescent Addiction: Epidemiology, Assessment and Treatment*. New York: Academic Press, pp. 179–206.

Glynn, K., Levanthal, H., & Hirschman, R. (1985). A cognitive developmental approach to smoking prevention. In C. S. Bell & R. Battjes (eds.), *Prevention Research: Deterring Drug Abuse among Children and Adolescents*. Rockville, MD: National Institute on Drug Abuse, National Institutes of Health, pp. 130–152.

Bibliography

Goeders, N. E. (2004). Stress, motivation, and drug addiction. *Current Directions in Psychological Science*, 13: 33–35.

Goldfried, M. R. & Davison, G. C. (1994). *Clinical Behavior Therapy* (expanded edn.). New York: John Wiley.

Goldman, M. S. (2002). Expectancy and risk for alcoholism: The unfortunate exploitation of a fundamental characteristic of neurobehavioral adaptation. *Alcoholism: Clinical and Experimental Research*, 26: 737–746.

Goldman, M. S. & Darkes, J. (2004). Alcohol expectancy multiaxial assessment: A memory network-based approach. *Psychological Assessment*, 16: 4–15.

Gollwitzer, P. M. (1999). Implementation intentions: Strong effects of simple plans. *American Psychologist*, 54: 493–503.

Gomez-Marin, A., Paton, J. J., Kampff, A. R., Costa, R. M., & Mainen, Z. F. (2014). Big behavioral data: psychology, ethology and the foundations of neuroscience. *Nature Neuroscience*, 17: 1455–1462.

Goodman, A. (1990). Addiction: Definition and implications. *British Journal of Addictions*, 85: 1403–1408.

(2008). Neurobiology of addiction: An integrative review. *Biochemical Pharmacology*, 75: 266–322.

(2009). The neurobiological development of addiction: An overview. *Psychiatric Times*, 26: 1–14.

Goodstadt, M. S. (1978). Alcohol and drug education: Model and outcomes. *Health Education Monogrographs*, 6: 263–279.

Goodwin, R. D., Keyes, K. M., & Hasin, D. S. (2009). Changes in cigarette use and nicotine dependence in the United States: Evidence from the 2001–2002 wave of the National Epidemiologic Survey of Alcoholism and Related Conditions. *American Journal of Public Health*, 99: 1471–1477.

Goossens, L., Soenens, B., & Braet, C. (2009). Prevalence and characteristics of binge eating in an adolescent community sample. *Journal of Clinical Child & Adolescent Psychology*, 38: 342–353.

Gordon, R. (1987). An operational classification of disease prevention. In A. Steinberg & M. M. Silverman (eds.), *Preventing Mental Disorders*. Rockville, MD: Department of Health and Human Services, National Institutes of Health, pp. 20–26.

Gorski, T. T. & Miller, M. (1984). *The Phases and Warning Signs of Relapse*. Independence, MO: Independence Press.

(1986). *Staying Sober: A Guide for Relapse Prevention*. Independence, MO: Independence Press.

Gotestam, K. G. & Johansson, A. (2003). Characteristics of gambling and problematic gambling in the Norwegian context: A DSM-IV based telephone interview study. *Addictive Behaviors*, 28: 189–197.

Gottman, J. M. & Leiblum, S. R. (1974). *How to Do Psychotherapy and How to Evaluate It: A Manual for Beginners*. New York: Holt, Rinehart & Winston.

Gowin, J. L., Ball, T. M., Wittmann, M., Tapert, S. F., & Paulus, M. P. (2015). Individualized relapse prediction: Personality measures and striatal and insular activity during reward-processing robustly predict relapse. *Drug and Alcohol Dependence*, 152: 93–101.

Grall-Bronnec, M., Bulteau, S., Victorri-Vigneau, C., Bouju, G., & Sauvaget, A. (2015). Fortune telling addiction: Unfortunately a serious topic – about a case report. *Journal of Behavioral Addiction*, 4: 27–31.

Grana, R., Benowitz, N., & Glantz, S. A. (2014). E-cigarettes: A scientific review. *Circulation*, 129: 1972–1986.

Bibliography

Grant, B. F., Hasin, D. S., Chou, P., Stinson, F. S., & Dawson, D. A. (2004a). Nicotine dependence and psychiatric disorders in the United States. *Archives of General Psychiatry*, 61: 1107–1115.

Grant, B. F., Stinson, F. S., Dawson, D. A., Chou, P., Dufour, M. C., Compton, W., ... & Kaplan, K. (2004b). Prevalence and co-occurrence of substance use disorders and independent mood and anxiety disorders. *Archives of General Psychiatry*, 61: 807–816.

Grant, J. E., Donahue, C. B., Odlaug, B. L., Kim, S. W., Miller, M. J., & Petry, N. M. (2009). Imaginal desensitization plus motivational interviewing for pathological gambling: Randomized controlled trial. *British Journal of Psychiatry*, 195: 266–267.

Grant, J. E. & Odlaug, B. L. (2014). Diagnosis and treatment of gambling disorder. In K. P. Rosenberg & L. C. Feder (eds.), *Behavioral Addictions: Criteria, Evidence, and Treatment*. London: Academic Press/Elsevier, pp. 35–60.

Grant, J. E., Potenza, M. N., Weinstein, A., & Gorelick, D. A. (2010). Introduction to behavioral addictions. *American Journal of Drug and Alcohol Abuse*, 36: 233–241.

Grant, J. E. & Steinberg, M. A. (2005). Compulsive sexual behavior and pathological gambling. *Sexual Addiction & Compulsivity*, 12: 235–244.

Grant, J. E., Steinberg, M. A., Kim, S. W., Rounsaville, B. J., & Potenza, M. N. (2004). Preliminary validity and reliability testing of a structured clinical interview for pathological gambling. *Psychiatry Research*, 128: 79–88.

Gray, J. A. (1982). Precis of the neuropsychology of anxiety: An enquiry into the functions of the septo-hippocampal system. *Behavioral and Brain Sciences*, 5: 469–484.

Greenberg, J. L., Lewis, S. E., & Dodd, D. K. (1999). Overlapping addictions and self-esteem among college men and women. *Addictive Behaviors*, 24: 565–571.

Greenfield, D. N. (1999). Psychological characteristics of compulsive Internet use: A preliminary analysis. *Cyberpsychology & Behavior*, 2: 403–412.

Grenard, J. L., Ames, S. L., Pentz, M. A., & Sussman, S. (2006). Motivational interviewing with adolescents and young adults for drug-related problems. *International Journal of Adolescent Medical Health*, 18: 53–67.

Griffin, K. W., Botvin, G. J., & Nichols, T. R. (2006). Effects of a school-based drug abuse prevention program for adolescents on HIV risk behavior in young adulthood. *Prevention Science*, 7: 103–112.

Griffin-Shelley, E. (1995). Adolescent sex and relationship addictions. *Sexual Addiction & Compulsivity*, 2: 112–127.

Griffiths, M. A., Harmon, T. R., & Gilly, M. C. (2011). Hubble bubble trouble: The need for education and regulation of hookah smoking. *Journal of Public Policy & Marketing*, 30: 119–132.

Griffiths, M. D. (1996). Behavioral addictions: An issue for everybody? *Journal of Workplace Learning*, 8: 19–25.

(1997). Exercise addiction. *Addiction Research*, 5: 161–168.

(1998). Internet addiction: Does it really exist? In J. Gackenbach (ed.), *Psychology and the Internet: Intrapersonal, Interpersonal, and Transpersonal Implications*. San Diego, CA: Academic Press, pp. 61–75.

(2000a) Internet addiction: Time to be taken seriously? *Addiction Research*, 8: 413–418.

(2000b). Does Internet and computer "addiction" exist? Some case study evidence. *Cyberpsychology & Behavior*, 3: 211–218.

(2005a). A "components" model of addiction within a biopsychosocial framework. *Journal of Substance Use*, 10: 191–197.

(2005b). Workaholism is still a useful construct. *Addiction Research & Theory*, 13: 97–100.

(2008). Internet and video-game addiction. In C. A. Essaru (ed.), *Adolescent Addiction: Epidemiology, Assessment, and Treatment*. London: Academic Press, pp. 231–268.

(2009a). The psychology of addictive behaviour. In M. Cardwell, L. Clark, C. Meldrum, & A. Waddely (eds.), *Psychology for AS Level*. London: HarperCollins, pp. 436–471.

(2009b). *Problem Gambling in Europe: An Overview*. Nottingham Trent University: International Gaming Research Unit and Apex Communications.

Griffiths, M. A., Harmon, T. R., & Gilly, M. C. (2011). Hubble bubble trouble: The need for education and regulation of hookah smoking. *Journal of Public Policy & Marketing*, 30: 119–359.

Griffiths, M. D., Kuss, D. J., & Demetrovics, Z. (2014). Social networking addiction: An overview of preliminary findings. In K. P. Rosenberg & L. C. Feder (eds.), *Behavioral Addictions: Criteria, Evidence, and Treatment*. London: Academic Press/Elsevier, pp. 119–142.

Griffiths, M. D. & Larkin, M. (2004). Conceptualizing addiction: The case for a "complex systems" account. *Addiction Research & Theory*, 12: 99–102.

Griffiths, M. D., Szabo, A., & Terry, A. (2005). The exercise addiction inventory: A quick and easy screening tool for health practitioners. *British Journal of Sports Medicine*, 39: e30.

Griffiths, M. D., Wardle, H., Orford, J., Sproston, K., & Erens, B. (2010). Gambling, alcohol consumption, cigarette smoking and health: Findings from the 2007 British Gambling Prevalence Survey. *Addiction Research & Theory*, 18: 208–223.

Grigsby, T., Forster, M., & Sussman, S. (2015a). A perspective on cigarette smoking during alcohol and substance use treatment. *Substance Use & Misuse*, 50: 1199–1204.

(2015b). Smoking cessation interventions during substance use treatment and recovery: Where do we go from here? *The Addictions Newsletter APA Division 50*, 22: 15–17.

Grigsby, T., Sussman, S., Chou, C.-P., & Ames, S. L. (in press). Assessment of substance misuse. In J. Van Geest, T. Johnson, & S. Alemagno (eds.), *Handbook of Research Methods in the Study of Substance Abuse*. New York: Springer.

Grusser, S. M., Thalemann, R., & Griffiths, M. S. (2007). Excessive computer game playing: Evidence for addiction and aggression? *Cyberpsychology & Behavior*, 10: 290–292.

Guilamo-Ramos, V., Litardo, H. A., & Jaccard, J. (2005). Prevention programs for reducing adolescent problem behaviors: Implications of the co-occurrence of problem behaviors in adolescence. *Journal of Adolescent Health*, 36: 82–86.

Gunduz-Cinar, O., MacPherson, K. P., Cinar, R., Gamble-George, J., Sugden, K., Williams, B., . . . & Holmes, A. (2013). Convergent translational evidence of a role for anandamide in amygdala-mediated fear extinction, threat processing and stress-reactivity. *Molecular Psychiatry*, 18: 813–823.

Gupta, R. & Derevensky, J. L. (2008). Gambling practices among youth: Etiology, prevention and treatment. In C. A. Essau (ed.), *Adolescent Addiction: Epidemiology, Assessment, and Treatment*. New York: Academic Press, pp. 207–229.

Guxens, M. & Sunyer, J. (2012). A review of epidemiological studies on neuropsychological effects of air pollution. *Swiss Medical Weekly*, 141: smw13322. doi: 10.4414/smw.2011.13322.

Guydish, J., Passalacqua, E., Tajima, B., Chan, M., Chun, J., & Bostrom, A. (2011). Smoking prevalence in addiction treatment: A review. *Nicotine & Tobacco Research*, 13: 401–411.

Haertzen, C. A., Kocher, T. R., & Miyasato, K. (1983). Reinforcements from the first drug experience can predict later drug habits and/or addiction: Results with coffee, cigarettes, alcohol, barbiturates, minor and major tranquilizers, stimulants, marijuana, hallucinogens, heroin, opiates and cocaine. *Drug and Alcohol Dependence*, 11: 147–165.

Hafstad, A., Aarø, L. E., Engeland, A., Andersen, A., Langmark, F., & Stray-Pedersen, B. (1997). Provocative appeals in anti-smoking mass campaigns targeting adolescents: The accumulated effect of multiple exposures. *Health Education Research*, 12: 227–236.

Bibliography

Hagger, M. S., Lonsdale, A., Koka, A., Hein, V., Pasi, H., Lintunen, T., & Chatzisarantis, N. L. D. (2012). An intervention to reduce alcohol consumption in undergraduate students using implementation intentions and mental simulations: A cross-national study. *International Journal of Behavioral Medicine*, 19: 82–96.

Hall, W., Degenhardt, L., & Patton, G. (2008). Cannabis abuse and dependence. In C. A. Essau (ed.), *Adolescent Addiction: Epidemiology, Assessment, and Treatment*. New York: Academic Press, pp. 117–148.

Hammond, C. J., Pilver, C. E., Rugle, L., Steinberg, M. A., Mayes, L. C., Malison, R. T., . . . & Potenza, M. N. (2014). An exploratory examination of marijuana use, problem-gambling severity, and health correlates among adolescents. *Journal of Behavioral Addictions*, 3: 90–101.

Han, D. H., Bolo, N., Daniels, M. A., Arenella, L. S., Lyoo, K. I., & Renshaw, P. F. (2011). Brain activity and desire for Internet video game play. *Comprehensive Psychiatry*, 52: 88–95.

Han, D. H., Kim, S. M., Lee, Y. S., & Renshaw, P. F. (2012). The effect of family therapy on the changes in the severity of on-line game play and brain activity in adolescents with on-line game addiction. *Psychiatry Research: Neuroimaging*, 202: 126–131.

Han, D. H., Lee, Y. S., Na, C., & Renshaw, P. (2009). The effect of methylphenidate on Internet video game play in children with attention-deficit/hyperactivity disorder. *Comprehensive Psychiatry*, 50: 252–256.

Hancox, R. J., Milne, B. J., & Poulton, R. (2004). Association between child and adolescent television viewing and adult health: A longitudinal birth cohort study. *Lancet*, 364: 257–262.

Hanh, T. N. (2011). *The Long Road Turns to Joy: A Guide to Walking Meditation*. Berkeley, CA: Parallax Press.

Hanley, A. & Wilhelm, M. S. (1992). Compulsive buying: An exploration into self-esteem and money attitudes. *Journal of Economic Psychology*, 13: 5–18.

Hansen, W. B. (1992). School-based substance abuse prevention: A review of the state of the art in curriculum, 1980–1990. *Health Education Research: Theory and Practice*, 7: 403–430.

(1994). Prevention of alcohol use and abuse. *Preventive Medicine*, 23: 683–687.

(1996). Pilot test results comparing the All Stars program with seventh grade D.A.R.E.: Pilot test integrity and mediating variable analysis. *Substance Use & Misuse*, 31: 1359–1377.

Hansen, W. B., Johnson, C. A., Flay, B. R., Graham, J. W., & Sobel, J. (1988). Affective and social influences approaches to the prevention of multiple substance abuse among seventh grade students: Results from Project SMART. *Preventive Medicine*, 17: 135–154.

Hansen, W. B. & McNeal, R. B. (1997). How D.A.R.E. works: An examination of program effects on mediating variables. *Health Education Quarterly*, 24: 165–176.

Harford, T. C., Grant, B. F., Yi, H.-Y., & Chen, C. M. (2005). Patterns of DSM-IV alcohol abuse and dependence criteria among adolescents and adults: Results from the 2001 National Household Survey on Drug Abuse. *Alcoholism: Clinical and Experimental Research*, 29: 810–828.

Harpaz, I. & Snir, R. (2003). Workaholism: Its definition and nature. *Human Relations*, 56: 291–319.

Harrell, T. H., Honaker, L. M., & Davis, E. (1991). Cognitive and behavioral dimensions of dysfunction in alcohol and polydrug abusers. *Journal of Substance Abuse*, 3: 415–426.

Hartney, E. (2010). The difference between an addiction and a compulsion. About.com Guide. http://addictions.about.com/od/howaddictionhappens/a/addcompulsion.htm?rd=1; accessed July 30, 2010.

Hasin, D. S., Stinson, F. S., Ogburn, E., & Grant, B. F. (2007). Prevalence, correlates, disability, and comorbidity of DSM-IV alcohol abuse and dependence in the United States. *Archives of General Psychiatry*, 64: 830–842.

Bibliography

Hatfield, E. & Sprecher, S. (1986). Measuring passionate love in intimate relationships. *Journal of Adolescence*, 9: 383–410.

Hatterer, L. J. (1982). The addictive process. *Psychiatric Quarterly*, 54: 149–156.

Hausenblas, H. A. & Downs, D. S. (2002). How much is too much? The development and validation of the Exercise Addiction scale. *Psychology and Health*, 17: 387–404.

Hawkins, J. D., Catalano, R. F., & Miller, J. Y. (1992). Risk and protective factors for alcohol and other drug problems in adolescence and early adulthood: Implications for substance abuse prevention. *Psychological Bulletin*, 112: 64–105.

Hay, P. (1998). The epidemiology of eating disorder behaviors: An Australian community-based survey. *International Journal of Eating Disorders*, 23: 371–382.

(2013). A systematic review of evidence for psychological treatments in eating disorders: 2005–2012. *International Journal of Eating Disorders*, 46: 462–469.

Haylett, S. A., Stephenson, G. M., & Lefever, R. M. H. (2004). Covariation in addictive behaviors: A study of addictive orientations using the shorter PROMIS Questionnaire. *Addictive Behaviors*, 29: 61–71.

Heather, N. (1998). A conceptual framework for explaining drug addiction. *Journal of Psychopharmacology*, 12: 3–7.

Heatherton, T. F., Kozlowski, L. T., Frecker, R. C., & Fagerstrom, K.-O. (1991). The Fagerstrom Test for Nicotine Dependence: A revision of the Fagerstrom Tolerance Questionnaire. *British Journal of Addiction*, 86: 1119–1127.

Hebebrand, J., Albayrak, O., Adan, R., Antel, J., Dieguez, C., de Jong, J., ... & Dickson, S. L. (2014). "Eating addiction," rather than "food addiction," better captures addictive-like eating behavior. *Neuroscience and Biobehavioral Reviews*, 47: 295–308.

Henderson, C. S., Witkiewitz, K., George, W. H., & Marlatt, G. A. (2011). Relapse prevention for addictive behaviors. *Substance Abuse Treatment, Prevention, and Policy*, 6. doi: 10.1186/1747-597X-6-17.

Henderson, M. D., Gollwitzer, P. M., & Oettingen, G. (2007). Implementation intentions and disengagement from a failing course of action. *Journal of Behavioral Decision Making*, 20: 81–102.

Henggeler, S. W., Pickrel, S. G., & Brondino, M. J. (1999). Multisystemic treatment of substance-abusing and dependent delinquents: Outcomes, treatment fidelity, and transportability. *Mental Health Services Residual*, 1: 171–184.

Herrnstein, R. J. & Prelec, D. (1991). Melioration: A theory of distributed choice. *Journal of Economic Perspectives*, 5: 137–156.

Heslin, K. C., Singzon, T., Aimiuwu, O., Sheridan, D., & Hamilton, A. (2012). From personal tragedy to personal challenge: Responses to stigma among sober living home residents and operators. *Sociology of Health & Illness*, 34: 379–395.

Hettema, J., Steele, J., & Miller, W. R. (2005). Motivational interviewing. *Annual Review of Clinical Psychology*, 1: 91–111.

Heyman, G. M. (2013a). Addiction and choice: Theory and new data. *Frontiers in Psychiatry*, 4: Article 31.

(2013b). Quitting drugs: Quantitative and qualitative features. *Annual Review of Clinical Psychology*, 9: 29–59.

Heywood, I. (2006). Climbing monsters: Excess and restraint in contemporary rock climbing. *Leisure Studies*, 25: 455–467.

Hill, A., Rumpf, H.-J., Hapke, U., Driessen, M., & John, U. (1998). Prevalence of alcohol dependence and abuse in general practice. *Alcoholism: Clinical and Experimental Research*, 22: 935–940.

Bibliography

Hirsch, E. D., Kett, J. F., & Trefil, J. (eds.) (2002). *The New Dictionary of Cultural Literacy* (3rd edn.). Boston, MA: Houghton Mifflin.

Hirschi, T. (1969). *Causes of Delinquency*. Berkeley, CA: University of California Press.

Hirschman, E. C. (1992). The consciousness of addiction: Toward a general theory of compulsive consumption. *Journal of Consumer Research*, 19: 155–179.

Hodgins, D. C. & el-Guebaly, N. (2004). Retrospective and prospective reports of precipitants to relapse in pathological gambling. *Journal of Consulting and Clinical Psychology*, 72: 72–80.

Hodgins, D. C., Toneatto, T., Makarchuk, K., Skinner, W., & Vincent, S. (2007). Minimal treatment approaches for concerned significant others of problem gamblers: A randomized controlled trial. *Journal of Gambling Studies*, 23: 215–230.

Hodgson, R. J., Budd, R., & Griffiths, M. (2001). Compulsive behaviours. In H. Helmchen, F. A. Henn, H. Lauter, & N. Sartorious (eds.), *Contemporary Psychiatry, Volume 3: Specific Psychiatric Disorders*. London: Springer, pp. 240–250.

Hoek, H. W. & Hoeken, D. V. (2003). Review of the prevalence and incidence of eating disorders. *International Journal of Eating Disorders*, 34: 383–396.

Holden, C. (2001). "Behavioral" addictions: Do they exist? *Science*, 294: 980–982.

Holderness, C. C., Brooks-Gunn, J., & Warren, M. P. (1994). Co-morbidity of eating disorders and substance abuse; Review of the literature. *International Journal of Eating Disorders*, 16: 1–34.

Holland, D. W. (2008). Work addiction: Costs and solutions for individuals, relationships and organizations. *Journal of Workplace Behavioral Health*, 22: 1–15.

Holm, S., Sandberg, S., Kolind, T., & Hesse, M. (2014). The importance of cannabis culture in young adult cannabis use. *Journal of Substance Use*, 19: 251–256.

Horigian, V. E., Feaster, D. J., Brincks, A., Robbins, M. S., Perez, M. A., & Szapocznik, J. (2015). The effects of Brief Strategic Family Therapy (BSFT) on parent substance use and the association between parent and adolescent substance use. *Addictive Behaviors*, 42: 44–50.

Horn, J. L., Wanberg, H. W., & Foster, F. M. (1986). *The Alcohol Use Inventory (AUI)*. Minneapolis, MN: National Computer Systems.

Horvath, A. T. (1999). *Sex, Drugs, Gambling and Chocolate: A Workbook for Overcoming Addictions*. San Luis Obispo, CA: Impact Publishers.

——— (2006). Substitute addictions (President's letter). *Smart Recovery News & Views*, 12: 1–12.

Horvath, C. W. (2004). Measuring television addiction. *Journal of Broadcasting & Electronic Media*, 48, 378–398.

Huang, J.-C., Hu, C., & Wu, T.-C. (2010). Psychometric properties of the Chinese version of the workaholism battery. *Journal of Psychology*, 144: 163–183.

Huddleston, III, C. W., Marlowe, D. B., & Casebolt, R. (2008). *Painting the Current Picture: A National Report Card on Drug Courts and other Problem-Solving Court Programs in the United States*. Washington, DC: National Drug Court Institute.

Hughes, J. R., Helzer, J. E., & Lindberg, S. A. (2006). Prevalence of DSM/ICD-defined nicotine dependence. *Drug and Alcohol Dependence*, 85: 91–102.

Hunter, M. S., Nitschke, C., & Hogan, L. (1981). A scale to measure love addiction. *Psychological Reports*, 48: 582.

Hyde, J. P. (1982). The language game: "Rat" talk – the special vocabulary of some teenagers. *The English Journal*, 71: 98–101.

Iacono, W. G., Malone, S. M., & McGue, M. (2008). Behavioral disinhibition and the development of early-onset addiction: Common and specific influences. *Annual Review of Clinical Psychology*, 4: 325–348.

Bibliography

Ialongo, N., Poduska, J., Werthamer, L., & Kellam, S. (2001). The distal impact of two first-grade preventive interventions on conduct problems and disorder in early adolescence. *Journal of Emotional and Behavioral Disorders*, 9: 146–160.

Irvin, J. E., Bowers, C. A., Dunn, M. E., & Wang, M. C. (1999). Efficacy of relapse prevention: A meta-analytic review. *Journal of Consulting and Clinical Psychology*, 67: 563–570.

Isbister, G. K. (2010). How do we use drug concentration data to improve the treatment of overdose patients? *Therapeutic Drug Monitoring*, 32: 300–304.

Jacobs, D. F. (1986). A general theory of addictions: A new theoretical model. *Journal of Gambling Behavior*, 2: 15–31.

Jacobsen, M. (1993). Time to take a stand against junk food. *PTA Today*, 18: 9–11.

James, A. G., Guo, W., & Liu, Y. (2001). Imaging in vivo brain–hormone interaction in the control of eating and obesity. *Diabetes Technology & Therapeutics*, 3: 617–622.

Jiggens, J. (2008). Australian heroin seizures and the causes of the 2001 heroin shortage. *International Journal of Drug Policy*, 19: 273–278.

Johansson, A., Grant, J. E., Kim, S. W., Odlaug, B. L., & Gotestam, K. G. (2009). Risk factors for problematic gambling: A critical literature review. *Journal of Gambling Studies*, 25: 67–92.

Johnson, C. A., MacKinnon, D. P., & Pentz, M. A. (1996). Integrating supply and demand reduction strategies for drug abuse prevention. *American Behavioral Scientist*, 39: 897–910.

Johnson, E. E., Hammer, R., Nora, R. M., Tan, B., Eistenstein, N., & Englehart, C. (1988). The lie/bet questionnaire for screening pathological gamblers. *Psychological Reports*, 80: 83–88.

Johnson, V. E. (1980). *I'll Quit Tomorrow: A Practical Guide to Alcoholism Treatment*. San Francisco, CA: Harper & Row.

Johnston, L. D., O'Malley, P. M., Bachman, J. G., Schulenberg, J. E.& Miech, R. A. (2014a). *Monitoring the Future: National Survey Results on Drug Use, 1975–2013, Volume 2: College Students and Adults Ages 19–55*. Ann Arbor, MI: Institute for Social Research, University of Michigan.

Johnston, L. D., O'Malley, P. M., Miech, R. A., Bachman, J. G., & Schulenberg, J. E. (2014b). *Monitoring the Future: National Survey Results on Drug Use, 1975–2013: Overview, Key Findings on Adolescent Drug Use*. Ann Arbor, MI: Institute for Social Research, University of Michigan.

Jones, K. D. (2010). The unstructured clinical interview. *Journal of Counseling & Development*, 88: 220–226.

Jonnes, J. (1996). *Hep-Cats, Narcs, and Pipe Dreams: A History of America's Romance with Illegal Drugs*. New York: Scribner.

Julien, R. M. (2005). *A Primer of Drug Action* (9th edn.). New York: W. H. Freeman (13th edn. C. D. Advokat, J. E. Comaty, & R. M. Julien, eds., 2014).

Jusoff, K. & Sahimi, N. N. (2009). Television and media literacy in young children: Issues and effects in early childhood. *International Education Studies*, 2: 151–157.

Kafka, M. P. & Prentky, R. (1992). A comparative study of nonparaphilic sexual addictions and paraphilias in men. *Journal of Clinical Psychiatry*, 53: 345–350.

Kahneman, D. (2003). A perspective on judgment and choice: Mapping bounded rationality. *American Psychologist*, 58: 697–720.

Kalichman, S. C., Johnson, J. R., Adair, V., Rompa, D., Multhauf, K., & Kelly, J. A. (1994). Sexual sensation seeking: Scale development and predicting AIDS-risk behavior among homosexually active men. *Journal of Personality Assessment*, 62: 385–397.

Kalichman, S. C. & Rompa, D. (2001). The Sexual Compulsivity Scale: Further development and use with HIV-positive persons. *Journal of Personality Assessment*, 76: 379–395.

Kaltiala-Heino, R., Lintonen, T., & Rimpela, A. (2004). Internet addiction? Potentially problematic use of the Internet in a population of 12-18-year-old adolescents. *Addiction Research & Theory*, 12: 89–96.

Kaminer, Y., Burleson, J. A., & Jadamec, A. (2002). Gambling behavior in adolescent substance abuse. *Substance Abuse*, 23: 191–198.

Kandel, D. (1990). Parenting styles, drug use, and children's adjustment in families of young adults. *Journal of Marriage and the Family*, 52: 183–196.

Kandel, D., Chen, K., Warner, L. A., Kessler, R. C., & Grant, B. (1997). Prevalence and demographic correlates of symptoms of last year dependence on alcohol, nicotine, marijuana, and cocaine in the US population. *Drug and Alcohol Dependence*, 44: 11–29.

Kaplan, M. S., & Krueger, R. B. (2010). Diagnosis, assessment, and treatment of hypersexuality. *Journal of Sex Research*, 47: 181–198.

Karnell, A. P., Cupp, P. K., Zimmerman, R. S., Feist-Price, S., & Bennie, T. (2006). Efficacy of an American alcohol and HIV prevention curriculum adapted for use in South Africa: Results of a pilot study in five township schools. *AIDS Education and Prevention*, 18: 295–310.

Kaufman, E. (1982). The relationship of alcoholism and alcohol abuse to the abuse of other drugs. *American Journal of Drug and Alcohol Abuse*, 9: 1–17.

Kausch, O. (2003). Patterns of substance abuse among treatment-seeking pathological gamblers. *Journal of Substance Abuse Treatment*, 25: 263–270.

Kaye, W. H., Wierenga, C. E., Bailer, U. F., Simmons, A. N., Wagner, A., & Bischoff-Grethe, A. (2013). Does a shared neurobiology for foods and drugs of abuse contribute to extremes of food ingestion in Anorexia and Bulimia Nervosa? *Biological Psychiatry*, 73: 836–842.

Kedia, S. & Perry, S. W. (2005). Factors associated with client-collateral agreement in substance abuse post-treatment self-reports. *Addictive Behaviors*, 30: 1086–1099.

Kellam, S. G., Wang, W., Mackenzie, A. C. L., Brown, C. H., Ompad, D. C., Or, F., . . . & Windham, A. (2014). The impact of the Good Behavior Game, a universal classroom-based preventive intervention in first and second grades, on high-risk sexual behaviors and drug abuse and dependence disorders into young adulthood. *Prevention Science*, 15: 6–18.

Kelly, J. F., Hoeppner, B., Stout, R. L., & Pagano, M. (2011). Determining the relative importance of the mechanisms of behavior change within Alcoholics Anonymous: A multiple mediator analysis. *Addiction*, 107: 289–299.

Kemps, E., Tiggemann, M., Orr, J., & Grear, J. (2014). Attentional retraining can reduce chocolate consumption. *Journal of Experimental Psychology: Applied*, 20: 94–102.

Khantzian, E. J. (1985). The self-medication hypothesis of addictive disorders: Focus on heroin and cocaine dependence. *American Journal of Psychiatry*, 142: 1259–1264.

(1997). The self-medication hypothesis of substance use disorders: A reconsideration and recent applications. *Harvard Review of Psychiatry*, 4: 287–289.

Kiene, S. M. & Barta, W. D. (2006). A brief individualized computer-delivered sexual risk reduction intervention increases HIV/AIDS preventive behavior. *Journal of Adolescent Health*, 39: 404–410.

Kilpatrick, D. G., Acierno, R., Saunders, B., Resnick, H. S., & Best, C. L. (2000). Risk factors for adolescent substance abuse and dependence: Data from a national sample. *Journal of Consulting and Clinical Psychology*, 68: 19–30.

Kim, K., Ryu, E., Chon, M.-Y., Yeun, E.-J., Choi, S.-Y., Seo, J.-S., & Nam, B.-W. (2006). Internet addiction in Korean adolescents and its relation to depression and suicidal ideation: A questionnaire survey. *International Journal of Nursing Studies*, 43: 185–192.

Kiraly, O., Nagygyorgy, K., Griffiths, M. D., & Demetrovics, Z. (2014). Problematic online gambling. In K. P. Rosenberg & L. C. Feder (eds.), *Behavioral Addictions: Criteria, Evidence, and Treatment*. London: Academic Press/Elsevier, pp. 61–98.

Bibliography

Kirby, D., Obasi, A., & Laris, B. A. (2006). The effectiveness of sex education and HIV education interventions in schools in developing countries. *World Health Organization Technical Report Services*, 938: 103–150.

Kirisci, L., Mezzich, A., & Tarter, R. (1995). Norms and sensitivity of the adolescent version of the Drug Use Screening Inventory. *Addictive Behaviors*, 20: 149–157.

Kleiner, K. D., Gold, M. S., Frost-Pineda, K., Lenz-Brunsman, B., Perri, M. G., & Jacobs, W. S. (2004). Body mass index and alcohol use. *Journal of Addictive Diseases*, 23: 105–118.

Knight, J. R., Sherritt, L., Shrier, L. A., Harris, S. K., & Chang, G. (2002). Validity of the CRAFFT substance abuse screening test among adolescent clinic patients. *Archives of Pediatrics & Adolescent Medicine*, 156: 607–614.

Koc, M. & Gulyagci, S. (2013). Facebook addiction among Turkish college students: The role of psychological health, demographic, and usage characteristics. *Cyperpsychology, Behavior, and Social Networking*, 16: 279–284.

Komro, K., Stigler, M., & Perry, C. (2005). Comprehensive approaches to prevent adolescent drinking and related problems. *Recent Developments in Alcoholism*, 17: 207–224.

Komro, K. A. & Toomey, T. L. (2002). Strategies to prevent underage drinking. *Alcohol Research & Health*, 26: 5–14.

Konkolÿ Thege, B., Woodin, E. M., Hodgins, D. C., & Williams, R. J. (2015). Natural course of behavioral addictions: A 5-year longitudinal study. *BMC Psychiatry*, 15. doi: 10.1186/s12888-015-0383-3.

Koob, G. F. & Le Moal, M. (2001). Drug addiction, dysregulation of reward, and allostasis. *Neuropsychopharmacology*, 24: 97–129.

— (2006). *Neurobiology of Addiction*. London: Academic Press.

Kor, A., Fogel, Y. A., Reid, R. C., & Potenza, M. N. (2013). Should hypersexual disorder be classified as an addiction? *Sexual Addiction & Compulsivity*, 20: 27–47.

Koran, L. M., Faber, R. J., Aboujaoude, E., Large, M. D., & Serpe, R. T. (2006). Estimated prevalence of compulsive buying behavior in the United States. *American Journal of Psychiatry*, 163: 1806–1812.

Kourosh, A. S., Harrington, C. R., & Adinoff, B. (2010). Tanning as a behavioral addiction. *American Journal of Drug and Alcohol Abuse*, 36: 284–290.

Kramer, D. A. & Goldman, M. S. (2003). Using a modified Stroop task to implicitly discern the cognitive organization of alcohol expectancies. *Journal of Abnormal Psychology*, 112: 171–175.

Krueger, R. B. & Kaplan, M. S. (2001). The paraphilic and hypersexual disorders: An overview. *Journal of Psychiatric Practice*, 7: 391–403.

Kubey, R. (1990). Television and the quality of family life. *Communication Quarterly*, 38: 312–324.

Kubey, R. & Csikszentmihalyi, M. (2002). Television addiction is no mere metaphor. *Scientific American*, 286, 74–80.

Kubey, R., Lavin, M. J., & Barrows, J. R. (2001). Internet use and collegiate academic performance decrements: Early findings. *Journal of Communication*, 51: 366–382.

Kumpfer, K. L. (1999). Factors and processes contributing to resilience: The resilience framework. In M. D. Glantz & J. L. Johnson (eds.), *Resilience and Development: Positive Life Adaptations*. New York: Kluwer Academic/Plenum Publishers, pp. 179–224.

Kumpfer, K. L., Alvarado, R., & Whiteside, H. O. (2003). Family-based interventions for substance use and misuse prevention. *Substance Use & Misuse*, 38: 1759–1787.

Kumpfer, K. L. & Bluth, B. (2004). Parent/child transactional processes predictive of resilience or vulnerability to "substance abuse disorders." *Substance Use & Misuse*, 39: 671–698.

Kumpfer, K. L. & DeMarsh, J. P. (1985). Prevention of chemical dependency in children of alcohol and drug abusers. *NIDA Notes*, 5.

Kumpfer, K. L., Molgaard, V., & Spoth, R. (1996). The Strengthening Families Program for the prevention of delinquency and drug use. In R. D. Peters & R. J. McMahon (eds.), *Preventing Childhood Disorders, Substance Abuse, and Delinquency*. Thousand Oaks, CA: Sage, pp. 214–267.

Kumpfer, K. L., Williams, M. K., & Baxley, G. B. (1997). *Drug Abuse Prevention for At-Risk Groups*. Rockville, MD: National Institute on Drug Abuse.

Kunst-Wilson, W. R. & Zajonc, R. B. (1980). Affective discrimination of stimuli that cannot be recognized. *Science*, 207: 557–558.

Kurti, A. N. & Dallery, J. (2012). Review of Heyman's *Addiction: A disorder of choice*. *Journal of Applied Behavioral Analysis*, 45: 229–240.

Kuzma, J. M. & Black, D. W. (2008). Epidemiology, prevalence, and natural history of compulsive sexual behavior. *Psychiatric Clinics of North America*, 31: 601–611.

Kwon, M., Lee, J.-Y., Won, W.-Y., Park, J.-W., Min, J.-A., Hahn, C., ... & Kim, D.-J. (2013). Development and validation of a Smartphone Addiction Scale (SAS). *PLoS One*, 8: e56936.

LaBrie, R. A., Nelson, S. E., LaPlante, D. A., Peller, A. J., Caro, G., & Shaffer, H. J. (2007). Missouri casino self-excluders: Distributions across time and space. *Journal of Gambling Studies*, 23: 231–243.

Lacy, J. H. & Evans, C. D. H. (1986). The impulsivist: A multi-impulsive personality disorder. *British Journal of Addiction*, 81: 641–649.

Ladouceur, R., Boudreault, N., Jacques, C., & Vitaro, F. (1999a). Pathological gambling and related problems among adolescents. *Journal of Child & Adolescent Substance Abuse*, 8: 55–68.

Ladouceur, R., Goulet, A., & Vitaro, F. (2013). Prevention programmes for youth gambling: A review of the empirical evidence. *International Gambling Studies*, 13: 141–159.

Ladouceur, R., Jacques, C., Ferland, F., & Giroux, I. (1999b). Prevalence of problem gambling: A replication study 7 years later. *Canadian Journal of Psychiatry*, 44: 802–804.

Ladouceur, R., Sylvain, C., Boutin, C., Lachance, S., Doucet, C., & Leblond, J. (2003). Group therapy for pathological gamblers: A cognitive approach. *Behaviour Research and Therapy*, 41: 587–596.

Landau, M. E., Kenney, K., Deuster, P., & Campbell, M. (2012). Exertional Rhabdomyolysis: A clinical review with a focus on genetic influences. *Journal of Clinical Neuromuscular Disease*, 13: 122–136.

Landen, M., Roeber, J., Naimi, T., Nielsen, L., & Sewell, M. (2014). Alcohol-attributable mortality among American Indians and Alaska Natives in the United States, 1999–2009. *American Journal of Public Health*, 104: S343–S349.

Larimer, M. E., Neighbors, C., Lostutter, T. W., Whiteside, U., Cronce, J. M., Kaysen, D., & Walker, D. D. (2012). Brief motivational feedback and cognitive behavioral interventions for prevention of disordered gambling: A randomized clinical trial. *Addiction*, 107: 1148–1158.

Larimer, M. E., Palmer, R. S., & Marlatt, G. A. (1999). Relapse prevention: An overview of Marlatt's cognitive behavioral model. *Alcohol Research & Health*, 23: 151–160.

Larkin, M., Wood, R. T. A., & Griffiths, M. D. (2006). Toward addiction as relationship. *Addiction Research & Theory*, 14: 207–215.

Lauderdale, K. L., Roberson, J. L, & Bonilla, C. A. (1999). *Addictive and Compulsive Disorders: A View from the Trenches*. Stockton, CA: ICA.

Lawrence, L. M., Ciorciari, J., & Kyrios, M. (2014). Relationships that compulsive buying has with addiction, obsessive-compulsiveness, hoarding, and depression. *Comprehensive Psychiatry*, 55: 1137–1145.

Bibliography

Lease, H. J. & Bond, M. J. (2013). Correspondence between alternate measures of maladaptive exercise, and their associations with disordered eating symptomatology. *Journal of Behavioral Addictions*, 2: 153–159.

Lee, B., Lee, H., & Kim, J. S. (2015). Prediction model of smartphone addiction in South Korea. *Journal of Behavioral Addictions*, 4: 55.

Lee, B. K. (2014). Where codependency takes us: A commentary. *Journal of Gambling Issues*, 29: 1–5.

Lee, G. P., Stuart, E. A., Ialongo, N. S., & Martins, S. S. (2013). Parental monitoring trajectories and gambling among a longitudinal cohort of youth. *Addiction*, 109: 977–985.

Lejoyeux, M., Avril, M., Richoux, C., Embouazza, H., & Nivoli, F. (2008). Prevalence of exercise dependence and other behavioral addictions among clients of a Parisian fitness room. *Comprehensive Psychiatry*, 49: 353–358.

Lennard, H. L., Epstein, L. J., Bernstein, A., & Ransom, D. C. (1971). *Mystification and Drug Misuse*. New York: Jossey-Bass.

Lent, M. R., Eichen, D. M., Goldbacher, E., Wadden, T. A., & Foster, G. D. (2014). Relationship of food addiction to weight loss and attrition during obesity treatment. *Obesity*, 22: 52–55.

Leonhard, C., Mulvey, K., Gastfriend, D. R., & Schwartz, M. (2000). The Addiction Severity Index: A field study of internal consistency and validity. *Journal of Substance Abuse Treatment*, 18: 129–135.

Leshner, A. I. (1997). Addiction is a brain disease, and it matters. *Science*, 278: 45–47.

Lesieur, H. R. & Blume, S. B. (1987). The South Oaks Gambling Screen (SOGS): A new instrument for the identification of pathological gamblers. *American Journal of Psychiatry*, 144: 1184–1188.

 (1993) Pathological gambling, eating disorders and the psychoactive substance use disorders. *Journal of Addictive Behaviors*, 12: 89–102.

Lesieur, H. R., Blume, S. B., & Zoppa, R. M. (1986). Alcoholism, drug abuse, & gambling. *Alcoholism: Clinical & Experimental Research*, 10: 33–38.

Lesieur, H. R., Cross, J., Frank, M., Welch, M., White, C. M., Rubenstein, G., ... & Mark, M. (1991). Gambling and pathological gambling among university students. *Addictive Behaviors*, 16: 517–527.

Lesieur, H. R. & Rosenthal, R. J. (1991). Pathological gambling: A review of the literature (Prepared for the American Psychiatric Association Task Force on DSM-IV Committee on Disorders of Impulse Control Not Elsewhere Classified). *Journal of Gambling Studies*, 7: 5–39.

Leung, L. (2004). Net-generation attributes and seductive properties of the Internet as predictors of online activities and Internet addiction. *Cyberpsychology & Behavior*, 7: 333–348.

Leventhal, A. M., Chasson, G. S., Tapia, E., Miller, E. K., & Pettit, J. W. (2006). Measuring hedonic capacity in depression: A psychometric analysis of three anhedonia scales. *Journal of Clinical Psychology*, 62: 1545–1558.

Leventhal, A. M., Waters, A. J., Boyd, S., Moolchan, E. T., Heishman, S. J., Lerman, C., & Pickworth, W. B. (2007). Associations between Cloninger's temperament dimensions and acute tobacco withdrawal. *Addictive Behaviors*, 32: 2976–2989.

Leventhal, H., Diefenbach, M., & Leventhal, E. A. (1992). Illness cognition: Using common sense to understand treatment adherence and affect cognition interactions. *Cognitive Therapy and Research*, 16: 143–163.

Levin, E. D., Rezvani, A. H., Montoya, D., Rose, J. E., & Swartzwelder, S. (2003). Adolescent-onset nicotine self-administration modeled in female rats. *Psychopharmacology*, 169: 141–149.

Levine, H. G. (1978). The discovery of addiction: Changing conceptions of habitual drunkenness in America. *Journal of Studies on Alcohol*, 39: 143–174.

Bibliography

Levinthal, C. F. (2005). *Drugs, Behavior, and Modern Society* (4th edn.). Boston, MA: Allyn & Bacon.

Levy, N. (2013). Addiction is not a brain disease (and it matters). *Frontiers in Psychiatry*, 4: Article 24.

Lewinsohn, P. M., Seeley, J. R., Moerk, K. C., & Striegel-Moore, R. H. (2002). Gender differences in eating disorder symptoms in young adults. *International Journal of Eating Disorders*, 32: 426–440.

Lewis, M. D. (2011). Dopamine and the neural "now": Essay and review of addiction – a disorder of choice. *Perspectives on Psychological Science*, 6: 150–155.

Ley, D., Brovko, J. M., & Reid, R. C. (in press). The use of the term "sex addiction" in US legal proceedings. *Current Sexual Health Reports*.

Lindesmith, A. R. (1940). The drug addict as a psychopath. *American Sociological Review*, 5: 914–920.

Lisha, N. E. & Sussman, S. (2010). Relationship of high school and college sports participation with alcohol, tobacco, and illicit drug use: A review. *Addictive Behaviors*, 35: 399–407.

Lisha, N. E., Sussman, S., & Leventhal, A. M. (2013). Physical activity and alcohol use disorders. *American Journal of Drug and Alcohol Abuse*, 39: 115–120.

Littrell, J. (1991). *Understanding and Treating Alcoholism, Volume 2: Biological, Psychological, and Social Aspects of Alcohol Consumption and Abuse*. Hillsdale, NJ: Lawrence Erlbaum Associates.

Liu, C., Liao, M., & Smith, D. C. (2012). An empirical review of Internet addiction outcome studies in China. *Research on Social Work Practice*, 22: 282–292.

Liu, Q.-X., Fang, X.-Y., Yan, N., Shou, Z.-K., Yuan, X.-J., Lan, J., & Liu, C.-Y. (2015). Multi-family group therapy for adolescent Internet addiction: Exploring the underlying mechanisms. *Addictive Behaviors*, 42: 1–8.

Loonis, E. (2002). De la gestion hédonique, prolégomènes à une hédonologie. *Psychologie française*, 47: 83–93.

Loonis, E., Apter, M. J., & Sztulman, H. (2000). Addiction as a function of action system properties. *Addictive Behaviors*, 25: 477–481.

Lorena, A., Sophia, E. C., Mello, C., Tavares, H., & Ziberman, M. L. (2008). Group therapy for pathological love. *Review of Brasilian Psychiatry (Revista Brasileira de Psiquiatria)*, 30: 292–293.

Luczak, S. E., Khoddam, R., Yu, S., Wall, T. L., Schwartz, A., & Sussman, S. (in press). Prevalence and comorbidity of addictions among ethnic groups. *American Journal on Addictions*.

Luczak, S. E. & Wall, T. L. (in press). Gambling behaviors and associations with alcohol use disorders in Chinese, Korean, and White American college students. *American Journal on Addictions*.

Ludlow, F. H. (1857). *The Hashish Eater*. http://users.lycaeum.org/~sputnik/Ludlow/THE/index.html; accessed July 5, 2005.

Machlowitz, M. (1980). *Workaholics: Living With Them, Working With Them*. Reading, MA: Addison-Wesley.

MacKinnon, D. P., Johnson, C. A., Pentz, M. A., Dwyer, D. P., & Hansen, W. B. (1991). Mediating mechanisms in a school-based drug prevention program: First year effects of the Midwestern Prevention Project. *Health Psychology*, 10: 164–172.

MacLaren, V. V. & Best, L. A. (2010). Multiple addictive behaviors in young adults: Student norms for the shorter PROMIS scale. *Addictive Behaviors*, 35: 252–255.

Magill, M. & Ray, L. A. (2009). Cognitive-behavioral treatment with adult alcohol and illicit drug users: A meta-analysis of randomized controlled trials. *Journal of Studies on Alcohol and Drugs*, 70: 516–527.

Bibliography

Mäkelä, K. (2004). Studies of the reliability and validity of the Addiction Severity Index. *Addiction*, 99: 398–410.

Malow, R. M., Rosenberg, R., & Devieux, J. (2006). Human immunodeficiency virus and adolescent substance abuse. In H. A. Liddle & C. L. Rowe (eds.), *Adolescent Substance Abuse: Research and Clinical Advances*. Cambridge University Press, pp. 284–309.

Manderlink, G. & Harackiewicz, J. M. (1984). Proximal versus distal goal setting and intrinsic motivation. *Journal of Personality and Social Psychology*, 47: 918–928.

Mansky, P. A. (1999). Issues in the recovery of physicians from addictive illness. *Psychiatric Quarterly*, 70: 107–122.

Maraz, A., Griffiths, M. D., & Demetrovics, Z. (2016). The prevalence of compulsive buying: A meta-analysis. *Addiction*, 111: 408–419.

Maraz, A., Urban, R., & Demetrovics, Z. (2015). The psychological factors behind dance addiction. *Journal of Behavioral Addiction*, 4: 28.

Marceaux, J. C. & Melville, C. L. (2011). Twelve-step facilitated versus mapping-enhanced cognitive-behavioral therapy for pathological gambling: A controlled study. *Journal of Gambling Studies*, 27: 171–190.

Mariani, J. J., Khantzian, E. J., & Levin, F. R. (2014). The self-medication hypothesis and psychostimulant treatment of cocaine dependence: An update. *American Journal on Addictions*, 23: 189–193.

Marijuana Anonymous World Services (1995). *Life with Hope: A Return to Living through the Twelve Steps and Twelve Traditions of Marijuana Anonymous*. Van Nuys, CA: Marijuana Anonymous World Services.

Markert, L. F. & Nikakhtar, M. (2000). *Addiction or Self Medication? The Truth*. Los Angeles, CA: Ketab Press.

Marks, I. (1990). Behaviour (non-chemical) addictions. *British Journal of Addiction*, 85: 1389–1394.

Marlatt, G. A. (1985). Relapse prevention: Theoretical rationale and overview of the model. In G. A. Marlatt & J. R. Gordon (eds.), *Relapse Prevention*. New York: Guilford Press, pp. 3–70.

Marlatt, G. A., Baer, J. S., Donovan, D. M., & Kivlahan, D. R. (1988). Addictive behaviors: Etiology and treatment. *Annual Review of Psychology*, 39: 223–252.

Marlatt, G. A., Larimer, M. E., & Witkiewitz, K. (eds.) (2012). *Harm Reduction: Pragmatic Strategies for Managing High-Risk Behaviors* (2nd edn.). New York: Guilford Press.

Marlatt, G. A., Somers, J. M., & Tapert, S. F. (1993). Harm reduction: Application to alcohol abuse problems. In L. S. Onken, J. D. Blaine, & J. J. Boren (eds.), *Behavioral Treatments for Drug Abuse and Dependence*. Bethesda, MD: National Institute on Drug Abuse, pp. 147–166.

Mason, M., Cheung, I., & Walker, L. (2004). Substance use, social networks, and the geography of urban adolescents. *Substance Use & Misuse*, 39: 1751–1777.

Mate, G. (2012). Addiction: Childhood trauma, stress and the biology of addiction. *Journal of Rehabilitation Medicine*, 1: 56–63.

Matthey, A. (1816). *Nouvelles recherches sur les maladies de l'esprit*. Paris: Paschoud.

Mattick, R. P., Breen, C., Kimber, J., & Davoli, M. (2014). Buprenorphine maintenance versus placebo or methadone maintenance for opioid dependence. *Cochrane Database of Systematic Reviews*. doi: 10.1002/14651858.CD002207.pub4.

Maze, I. & Nestler, E. J. (2011). The epigenetic landscape of addiction. *Annals of the New York Academy of Sciences*, 1216: 99–113.

McAleavey, K. (2010). Short-term outcomes of a 12-step program among women with anorexia, bulimia, and eating disorders. *Journal of Child and Family Studies*, 19: 728–737.

McCann, U. D., Wong, D. F., Yokoi, F., Villemagne, V., Dannals, R. F., & Ricaurte, G. A. (1998). Reduced striatal dopamine transporter density in abstinent methamphetamine and methcathinone users: Evidence from positron emission tomography studies with [11C] WIN-35,428. *Journal of Neuroscience*, 18: 8417–8422.

McCarthy, D. M., Brown, S. A., Carr, L. G., & Wall, T. L. (2001). ALDH2 status, alcohol expectancies, and alcohol response: preliminary evidence for a mediation model. *Alcohol: Clinical and Experimental Research*, 25: 1558–1563.

McCarthy, K. (1984). Early alcoholism treatment: The Emmanuel Movement and Richard Peabody. *Journal of Studies on Alcohol*, 45: 59–74.

McCuller, W. J., Sussman, S., Wapner, M., Dent, C. W., & Weiss, D. J. (2006). Motivation to quit as a mediator of tobacco cessation among at-risk youth. *Addictive Behaviors*, 31: 880–888.

McEwen, B. S. (2002). Sex, stress and the hippocampus: Allostasis, allostatic load and the aging process. *Neurobiology of Aging*, 23: 921–939.

McGeary, J. E., Meadows, S. P., Amir, N., & Gibb, B. E. (2014). Computer-delivered, home-based, attentional retraining reduces drinking behavior in heavy drinkers. *Psychology of Addictive Behaviors*, 28: 559–562.

McIlwraith, R. (1998). "I'm addicted to television": The personality, imagination, and TV watching patterns of self-identified TV addicts. *Journal of Broadcasting & Electronic Media*, 42: 371–386.

McIlwraith, R., Jacobvitz, R. S., Kubey, R., & Alexander, A. (1991). Television addiction: Theories and data behind the ubiquitous metaphor. *American Behavioral Scientist*, 35: 104–121.

McKinley, C. J. & Wright, P. J. (2012). Examining the presence of problem gambling awareness messages on college counseling center websites. *Health Communication*, 27: 98–106.

McLellan, A. T., Luborsky, L., Cacciola, J., Griffith, J., Evans, F., Barr, H. L., & O'Brien, C. P. (1985). New data from the Addiction Severity Index: Reliability and validity in three centers. *Journal of Nervous and Mental Disease*, 173: 412–423.

McLellan, A. T., Luborsky, L., Woody, G. E., & O'Brien, C. P. (1980). An improved diagnostic evaluation instrument for substance abuse patients: The Addiction Severity Index. *Journal of Nervous and Mental Disease*, 168: 26–33.

McMillan, L. H. W., Brady, E. C., O'Driscoll, M. P., & Marsh, M. V. (2002). A multifaceted validation study of Spence and Robbins' (1992) workaholism battery. *Journal of Occupational and Organizational Psychology*, 75: 357–368.

McMillen, R. C., Gottlieb, M. A., Shaefer, R. M. W., Winickoff, J. P., & Klein, J. D. (2015). Trends in electronic cigarette use among US adults: Use is increasing in both smokers and nonsmokers. *Nicotine & Tobacco Research*, 17: 1195–1202.

Meichenbaum, D. (1977). *Cognitive Behavior Modification: An Integrative Approach*. New York: Plenum.

Meyer, R. E. (1996). The disease called addiction: Emerging evidence in a 200-year debate. *Lancet*, 347: 162–166.

Miele, G. M., Carpenter, K. M., Smith Cockerham, M., Trautman, K. D., Blaine, J., & Hasin, D. S. (2000a). Substance Dependence Severity Scale (SDSS): Reliability and validity of a clinician-administered interview for DSM-IV substance use disorders. *Drug and Alcohol Dependence*, 59: 63–75.

—— (2000b). Concurrent and predictive validity of the Substance Dependence Severity Scale (SDSS). *Drug and Alcohol Dependence*, 59: 77–88.

Miller, C. S. (1999). Are we on the threshold of a new theory of disease? Toxicant-induced loss of tolerance and its relationship to addiction and abdiction. *Toxicology and Industrial Health*, 15: 284–294.

(2000). Toxicant-induced loss of tolerance. *Addiction*, 96: 115–139.

Miller, N. S., Gold, M. S., & Klahr, A. L. (1990). The diagnosis of alcohol and cannabis dependence (addiction) in cocaine dependence (addiction). *International Journal of the Addictions*, 25: 735–744.

Miller, W. R. & Del Boca, F. K. (1994). Measurement of drinking behavior using the Form 90 family of instruments. *Journal of Studies on Alcohol and Drugs*, 12: 112–118.

Miller, W. R., Leckman, A. L., Delaney, H. D., & Tinkcom, M. (1992). Long-term follow-up of behavioral self-control training. *Journal of Studies on Alcohol and Drugs*, 53: 249–261.

Miller, W. R. & Marlatt, G. A. (1984). *Brief Drinker Profile*. Odessa, FL: Psychological Assessment Resources.

(1987). *Manual Supplement for the Brief Drinker Profile, Follow-up Drinker Profile, Collateral Interview Form*. Odessa, FL: Psychological Assessment Resources.

Miller, W. R., Meyers, R. J., & Tonigan, J. S. (1999). Engaging the unmotivated in treatment for alcohol problems: A comparison of three strategies for intervention through family members. *Journal of Consulting and Clinical Psychology*, 67: 688–697.

Miller, W. R. & Rollnick, S. (2013). *Motivational Interviewing: Helping People Change* (3rd edn.). New York: Guilford Press.

Miller, W. R., Walters, S. T., & Bennett, M. E. (2001). How effective is alcoholism treatment in the United States? *Journal of Studies on Alcohol*, 62: 211–220.

Miner, M. H., Coleman, E., Center, B. A., Ross, M., & Rosser, B. R. S. (2007). The Compulsive Sexual Behavior Inventory: Psychometric properties. *Archives of Sexual Behavior*, 36: 579–587.

Mitchell, J. E., Burgard, M., Faber, R., Crosby, R. D., & de Zwaan, M. (2006). Cognitive behavioral therapy for compulsive buying disorder. *Behavior Research and Therapy*, 44: 1859–1865.

Mitchell, J. E., Redlin, J., Wonderlich, S., Crosby, R., Faber, R., Miltenberger, R., . . . & Lancaster, K. (2002). The relationship between compulsive buying and eating disorders. *International Journal of Eating Disorders*, 32: 107–111.

Moeller, K. E., Lee, K. C., & Kissack, J. C. (2008). Urine drug screening: Practical guide for clinicians. *Mayo Clinic Proceedings*, 83: 66–76.

Molnar, B. E., Buka, S. L., & Kessler, R. C. (2001). Child sexual abuse and subsequent psychopathology: Results from the National Comorbidity Survey. *American Journal of Public Health*, 91: 753–760.

Monti, P. M., Abrams, D. B., Kadden, R. M., & Cooney, N. L. (1989). *Treating Alcohol Dependence*. New York: Guilford Press.

Monti, P. M., Rohsenow, D. J., & Hutchison, K. E. (2000). Toward bridging the gap between biological, psychobiological and psychosocial models of alcohol craving. *Addiction*, 95: S229–S236.

Morahan-Martin, J. & Schumacher, P. (2000). Incidence and correlates of pathological Internet use among college students. *Computers in Human Behavior*, 16: 13–29.

Moreno, J. A. (2006). Strategies for challenging police jargon testimony. *Criminal Justice Magazine*, 20: 28–37.

Mudrack, P. E. & Naughton, T. J. (2001). The assessment of workaholism as behavioral tendencies: Scale development and preliminary empirical testing. *International Journal of Stress Management*, 8: 93–111.

Mueller, D. G. & Jason, L. A. (2014). Sober-living houses and changes in the personal networks of individuals in recovery. *Health Psychology Research*, 2: 988. doi: 10.4081/hpr.2014.988.

Mueller, L. A. & Ketcham, K. (1987). *Recovering: How to Get and Stay Sober*. New York: Bantam.

Bibliography

Muller, A., Cook, B., Zander, H., Herberg, A., Muller, V., & de Zwaan, M. (2014). Does the German version of the Exercise Dependence Scale measure exercise dependence? *Psychology of Sport and Exercise*, 15: 288–292.

Murphy, S. A. & Hoffman, A. L. (1993). An empirical description of phases of maintenance following treatment for alcohol dependence. *Journal of Substance Abuse*, 5: 131–143.

Nace, E. P. (1984). Epidemiology of alcoholism and prospects for treatment. *Annual Review of Medicine*, 35: 293–309.

Najavits, L., Lung, J., Froias, A., Paull, N., & Bailey, G. (2014). A study of multiple behavioral addictions in a substance abuse sample. *Substance Use & Misuse*, 49: 479–484.

Narcotics Anonymous (1988). *Narcotics Anonymous* (5th edn.). Van Nuys, CA: Narcotics Anonymous World Services.

National Opinion Research Center (1999). *Gambling Impact and Behavior Study: Report to the National Gambling Impact Study Commission*. University of Chicago Press.

Naughton, F. (2016). Delivering "just-in-time" smoking cessation support via mobile phones: Current knowledge and future directions. *Nicotine & Tobacco Research*, 143, published online, May 28, 14 pp.

Nelson, C. B. & Wittchen, H.-U. (1998). DSM-IV alcohol disorders in a general population sample of adolescents and young adults. *Addiction*, 93: 1065–1077.

Nestler, E. J. & Landsman, D. (2001). Learning about addiction from the genome. *Nature*, 409: 834–835.

Netemeyer, R. G., Burton, S., Cole, L. K., Williamson, D. A., Zucker, N., Bertman, L., & Diefenbach, G. (1998). Characteristics and beliefs associated with probable pathological gambling: A pilot study. *Journal of Public Policy & Marketing*, 17: 147–160.

Neuner, M., Raab, G., & Reisch, L. A. (2005). Compulsive buying in maturing consumer societies: An empirical re-inquiry. *Journal of Economic Psychology*, 26: 509–522.

Newlin, D. B. (2002). The self-perceived survival ability and reproductive fitness (SPFit) theory of substance use disorders. *Addiction*, 97: 427–445.

Nezami, E., Sussman, S., & Pentz, M. A. (2003). Motivation in tobacco use cessation research. *Substance Use & Misuse*, 38: 25–50.

Niaura, R. S., Rohsenow, D. J., Binkoff, J. A., Monti, P. M., Pedraza, M., & Abrams, D. B. (1988). Relevance of cue reactivity to understanding alcohol and smoking relapse. *Journal of Abnormal Psychology*, 97: 133–152.

Niemz, K., Griffiths, M., & Banyard, P. (2005). Prevalence of pathological Internet use among university students and correlations with self-esteem, the General Health Questionnaire (GHQ), and disinhibition. *Cyberpsychology & Behavior*, 8: 562–570.

Noar, S. M., Zimmerman, R. S., Palmgreen, P., Lustria, M., & Horosewski, M. L. (2006). Integrating personality and psychosocial theoretical approaches to understanding safer sexual behavior: Implications for message design. *Health Communication*, 19: 165–174.

Noble, E. P. K., Blum, K., Ritchie, T., Montgomery, A., & Sheridan, P. J. (1991). Allelic association of the D2 dopamine receptor gene with receptor binding characteristics in alcoholism. *Archives of General Psychiatry*, 48: 648–654.

Noonan, W. C. & Moyers, T. (1997). Motivational interviewing: A review. *Journal of Substance Misuse*, 2: 8–16.

Norris, M., Strike, M., Pinhas, L., Gomez, R., Elliott, A., Ferguson, P., & Gusella, J. (2013). The Canadian Eating Disorder Program Survey: Exploring intensive treatment programs for youth with eating disorders. *Journal of the Canadian Academy of Child and Adolescent Psychiatry*, 22: 310–316.

Bibliography

Nurses Research Publication (1999). *Substance Abuse: What You Should Know*. Hayward, CA: Nurses Research Publication. www.nurseslearning.com/courses/nrp/NRP-1600/Nrp1600.pdf; accessed January 22, 2015.

Oates, W. E. (1971). *Confessions of a Workaholic: The Facts about Work Addiction*. New York: World Publishing.

O'Brien, C. P. (2008). Evidence-based treatments of addiction. *Philosophical Transactions of the Royal Society, B: Biological Sciences*, 363: 3277–3286.

O'Brien, C. P. & McLellan, A. T. (1996). Myths about the treatment of addiction. *Lancet*, 347: 237–240.

O'Brien, C. P., Volkow, N., & Li, T.-K. (2006). What's in a word? Addiction versus dependence in DSM-V. *American Journal of Psychiatry*, 163: 764–765.

Ockene, J. K., Nutall, R., Benfari, R. C., Hurwitz, I., & Ockene, I. S. (1981). A psychosocial model of smoking cessation and maintenance of cessation. *Preventive Medicine*, 10: 623–638.

O'Connor, K. P. (1989). Individual differences and motor systems in smoker motivations. In T. Ney & A. Gale (eds.), *Smoking and Human Behavior*. Chichester: John Wiley, pp. 141–170.

O'Farrell, T. J. & Fals-Stewart, W. (2000). Behavioral couples therapy for alcoholism and drug abuse. *The Behavior Therapist*, 23: 49–54.

Ogden, J., Veale, D. M., & Summers, Z. (1997). The development and validation of the Exercise Dependence Questionnaire. *Addiction Research*, 5: 343–355.

O'Leary, T. A., Brown, S. A., Colby, S. M., Cronce, J. M., D'Amico, E. J., Fader, J. S., . . . & Monti, P. M. (2002). Treating adolescents together or individually? Issues in adolescent substance abuse interventions. *Alcoholism: Clinical and Experimental Research*, 26: 890–899.

Olesen, P. J., Westerberg, H., & Klingberg, T. (2004). Increased prefrontal and parietal activity after training of working memory. *Nature Neuroscience*, 7: 75–79.

Orbell, S. & Sheeran, P. (2002). Changing health behaviours: The role of implementation intentions. In D. Rutter & L. Quine (eds.), *Changing Health Behaviour: Intervention and Research with Social Cognition Models*. New York: Open University Press, pp. 123–137.

Orford, J. (1990). Addiction as excessive appetite. *Addiction*, 96: 15–31.

(2001). *Excessive Appetites: A Psychological View of Addictions* (2nd edn.). Chichester: John Wiley.

Pagano, M. E., Friend, K. B., Tonigan, J. S., & Stout, R. L. (2004). Helping other alcoholics in Alcoholics Anonymous and drinking outcomes: Findings from Project MATCH. *Journal of Studies on Alcohol*, 65: 766–773.

Pakpour, A. H., Gellert, P., Dombrowski, S. U., & Fridlund, B. (2015). Motivational interviewing with parents for obesity: An RCT. *Pediatrics*, 135: e644–e652.

Palmer, R. H. C., Young, S. E., Hopfer, C. J., Corley, R. P., Stallings, M. C., Crowley, T. J., & Hewitt, J. K. (2009). Developmental epidemiology of drug use and abuse in adolescence and young adulthood: Evidence of generalized risk. *Drug and Alcohol Dependence*, 102: 78–87.

Palmgreen, P., Donohew, L., Lorch, E. P., Hoyle, R. H., & Stephenson, M. T. (2001). Television campaigns and adolescent marijuana use: Tests of sensation seeking targeting. *American Journal of Public Health*, 91: 292–296.

Panksepp, J., Knutson, B., & Burgdorf, J. (2002). The role of brain emotional systems in addictions: A neuro-evolutionary perspective and new "self-report" animal model. *Addiction*, 97: 459–469.

Pardridge, W. M. (2012). Drug transport across the blood–brain barrier. *Journal of Cerebral Blood Flow & Metabolism*, 32: 1959–1972.

Bibliography

Park, S. K., Kim, J. Y., & Cho, C. B. (2008). Prevalence of Internet addiction and correlations with family factors among South Korean adolescents. *Adolescence*, 43: 895–909.

Payne, B. K. (2005). Conceptualizing control in social cognition: How executive functioning modulates the expression of automatic stereotyping. *Journal of Personality and Social Psychology*, 89: 488–503.

Pearson, M. M. & Little, R. B. (1969). The addictive process in unusual addictions: A further elaboration of etiology. *American Journal of Psychiatry*, 125: 1166–1171.

Pedrelli, P., Bitran, S., Shyu, I., Baer, L., Guidi, J., Tucker, D. D., . . . & Farabaugh, A. H. (2010). Compulsive alcohol use and other high-risk behaviors among college students. *American Journal on Addictions*, 20: 14–20.

Peele, S. (1998). Ten radical things NIAAA Research shows about alcoholism. *The Addictions Newsletter*, 5: 2020-2022.

Peele, S. & Brodsky, A. (1992). *The Truth about Addiction and Recovery*. New York: Fireside.

Pelchat, M. L. (2002). Of human bondage: Food craving, obsession, compulsion, and addiction. *Physiology & Behavior*, 76: 347–352.

Penning, R., Veldstra, J. L., Daamen, A. P., Olivier, B., & Verster, J. C. (2010). Drugs of abuse, driving and traffic safety. *Current Drug Abuse Reviews*, 3: 23–32.

Pentz, M. A., Bonnie, R. J., & Shopland, D. R. (1996). Integrating supply and demand reduction strategies for drug abuse prevention. *American Behavioral Scientist*, 39: 897–910.

Pentz, M. A., Jasuja, G. K., Rohrbach, L. A., Sussman, S., & Bardo, M. T. (2006). Translation in tobacco and drug abuse prevention research. *Evaluation & the Health Professions*, 29: 246–271.

Pentz, M. A., Sussman, S., & Newman, T. (1997). The conflict between least harm and no-use tobacco policy for youth: Ethical ad policy implications. *Addiction*, 92: 1165–1173.

Pepino, M. Y. & Mennella, J. A. (2005). Factors contributing to individual differences in sucrose preference. *Chemical Senses*, 30: i319–i320.

Petraitis, J., Flay, B. R., & Miller, T. Q. (1995). Reviewing theories of adolescent substance use: Organizing the pieces in the puzzle. *Psychological Bulletin*, 117: 67–86.

Petry, N. M. (2005). *Pathological Gambling: Etiology, Comorbidity and Treatment*. Washington, DC: American Psychological Association.

——— (2007). Gambling and substance use disorders: Current status and future directions. *American Journal on Addictions*, 16: 1–9.

Petry, N. M., Ammerman, Y., Bohl, J., Doersch, A., Gay, H., Kadden, R., . . . & Steinberg, K. (2006). Cognitive-behavioral therapy for pathological gamblers. *Journal of Consulting and Clinical Psychology*, 74: 555–567.

Petry, N. M. & Kiluk, B. D. (2002). Suicidal ideation and suicide attempts in treatment-seeking pathological gamblers. *Journal of Nervous and Mental Disease*, 190: 462–469.

Philippe, F. & Vallerand, R. J. (2007). Prevalence rates of gambling problems in Montreal, Canada: A look at old adults and the role of passion. *Journal of Gambling Studies*, 23: 275–283.

Pirkola, S. P., Poikolainen, K., & Lonnqvist, J. K. (2006). Currently active and remitted alcohol dependence in a nationwide adult general population: Results from the Finnish Health 2000 Study. *Alcohol & Alcoholism*, 41: 315–320.

Poelen, E. A. P., Scholte, R. H. J., Engels, R. C. M. E., Boomsma, D. I., & Willemsen, G. (2005). Prevalence and trends of alcohol use and misuse among adolescents and young adults in the Netherlands from 1993 to 2000. *Drug and Alcohol Dependence*, 79: 413–421.

Pope, H. G., Kanayama, G., Athey, A., Ryan, E., Hudson, J. I., & Baggish, A. (2014). The lifetime prevalence of anabolic-androgenic steroid use and dependence in Americans: Current best estimates. *American Journal on Addictions*, 23: 371–377.

Bibliography

Potenza, M. N. (2010). What integrated interdisciplinary and translational research may tell us about addiction. *Addiction*, 105: 790–796.

Potenza, M. N., Fiellin, D. A., Heninger, G. R., Rounsaville, B. J., & Mazure, C. M. (2002). Gambling: An addictive behavior with health and primary care implications. *Journal of General Internal Medicine*, 17: 721–732.

Potenza, M. N., Steinberg, M. A., Wu, R., Rounsaville, B. J., & O'Malley, S. S. (2006). Characteristics of older adult problem gamblers calling a gambling helpline. *Journal of Gambling Studies*, 22: 241–254.

Prestwich, A., Conner, M., & Lawton, R. (2006). Implementation intentions: Can they be used to prevent and treat addiction? In R. W. Wiers & A. W. Stacy (eds.), *Handbook on Implicit Cognition and Addiction*. Thousand Oaks, CA: Sage, pp. 455–469.

Prochaska, J. O. (2008). Decision making in the transtheoretical model of behavior change. *Medical Decision Making*, 28: 845–849.

Prochaska, J. O. & DiClemente, C. C. (1982). Transtheoretical therapy: Toward a more integrative model of change. *Psychotherapy: Theory, Research, Practice*, 19: 275–288.

Prochaska, J. O., DiClemente, C. C., Velicer, W. F., Ginpil, S., & Norcross, J. C. (1985). Prediction change in smoking status for self-changers. *Addictive Behaviors*, 10: 395–406.

Prochaska, J. O., Velicer, S., DiClemente, C. C., Guadagnoli, E., & Rossi, J. S. (1990). Patterns of change: Dynamic typology applied to smoking cessation. *Multivariate Behavioral Research*, 25: 587–611.

Prokhorov, A. V., Kelder, S. H., Shegog, R., Murray, N., Peters, R., Agurcia-Parker, C., ... & Marani, S. (2008). Impact of A Smoking Prevention Interactive Experience (ASPIRE), an interactive, multimedia smoking prevention and cessation curriculum for culturally diverse high school students. *Nicotine and Tobacco Research*, 10: 1477–1485.

Punzi, E. H. & Fahlke, C. (2015). Problems in a substance use disorder treatment population: Treatment perspective. *Alcohol Treatment Quarterly*, 31: 105–117.

Quintero, G. & Nichter, M. (1996). The semantics of addiction: Moving beyond expert models to lay understandings. *Journal of Psychoactive Drugs*, 28: 219–228.

Racine, E., Kahn, T., & Hollander, E. (2014). Compulsive buying disorder. In K. P. Rosenberg & L. C. Feder (eds.), *Behavioral Addictions: Criteria, Evidence, and Treatment*. London: Academic Press/Elsevier, pp. 285–316.

Raines, A. M., Unruh, A. S., Zvolensky, M. J., & Schmidt, N. B. (2014). An initial investigation of the relationships between hoarding and smoking. *Psychiatry Research*, 215: 668–674.

Rash, C. J. & Petry, N. M. (2014). Psychological treatments for gambling disorder. *Psychology Research and Behavior Management*, 7: 285–295.

Ravert, R. D. (2013). Do we want emerging adults to take risks, or not? Paper presented at the 6th Conference on Emerging Adulthood, Chicago, IL, October.

Rawson, R. A. & Condon, T. P. (2007). Why do we need an *Addiction* supplement focused on methamphetamine? *Addiction*, 102: 1–4.

Ray, A. E., Kim, S.-Y., White, H. R., Larimer, M. E., Mun, E.-Y., Clarke, N., ... & Huh, D. (2014). When less is more and more is less in brief motivational interventions: Characteristics of intervention content and their associations with drinking outcomes. *Psychology of Addictive Behaviors*, 28: 1026–1040.

Raylu, N. & Oei, T. P. (2004). Role of culture in gambling and problem gambling. *Clinical Psychology Review*, 23: 1087–1114.

Raymond, N. C., Coleman, E., & Miner, M. H. (2003). Psychiatric comorbidity and compulsive/impulsive traits in compulsive sexual behavior. *Comprehensive Psychiatry*, 44: 370–380.

Bibliography

Rebellon, C. J., Wiesen-Martin, D., Piquero, N. L., Piquero, A. R., & Tibbetts, S. G. (2015). Gender differences in criminal intent: Examining the mediating influence of anticipated shaming. *Deviant Behavior*, 36: 17–41.

Regier, D. A., Farmer, M. E., Rae, D. S., Locke, B. Z., Keith, S. J., Judd, L. L., & Goodwin, F. K. (1990). Comorbidity of mental disorders with alcohol and other drug abuse. *Journal of the American Medical Association*, 264: 2511–2518.

Rehm, J., Marmet, S., Anderson, P., Gual, A., Kraus, L., Nutt, D. J., ... & Gmel, G. (2013). Defining substance use disorders: Do we really need more than heavy use? *Alcohol and Alcoholism*, 48: 633–640.

Reid, R. C. (2013). Personal perspectives on hypersexual disorder. *Sexual Addiction & Compulsivity*, 20: 204–218.

Reid, R. C., Carpenter, B. N., Hook, J. N., Garos, S., Manning, J. C., Gilliland, R., ... & Fong, T. (2012). Report of findings in a DSM-5 field trial for Hypersexual Disorder. *Journal of Sexual Medicine*, 9: 2868–2877.

Reid, R. C., Garos, S., & Carpenter, B. N. (2011). Reliability, validity, and psychometric development of the Hypersexual Behavior Inventory in an outpatient sample of men. *Sexual Addiction & Compulsivity*, 18: 30–51.

Reinert, D. F. & Allen, J. P. (2007). The Alcohol Use Disorders Identification Test: an update of research findings. *Alcoholism: Clinical and Experimental Research*, 31: 185–199.

Rhoades, K. A., Leve, L. D., Harold, G. T., Kim, H. K., & Chamberlain, P. (2014). Drug use trajectories after a randomized controlled trial of MTFC: Associations with partner drug use. *Journal of Research on Adolescence*, 24: 40–54.

Richardson, C. G., Vettese, L., Sussman, S., Small, S. P., & Selby, P. (2011). An investigation of smoking cessation video content on YouTube. *Substance Use & Misuse*, 46: 893–897.

Robinson, B. E. (1998). The workaholic family: A clinical perspective. *American Journal of Family Therapy*, 26: 65–75.

Robinson, T. E. & Berridge, K. C. (1993). The neural basis of drug craving: An incentive-sensitization theory of addiction. *Brain Research Reviews*, 18: 247–291.

  (2000). The psychology and neurobiology of addiction: An incentive-sensitization view. *Addiction*, 95: 91–117.

  (2008). The incentive sensitization theory of addiction: Some current issues. *Philosophical Transactions of the Royal Society, B: Biological Sciences*, 363: 3137–3146.

Robison, A. J. & Nestler, E. J. (2011). Transcriptional and epigenetic mechanisms of addiction. *Nature Reviews Neuroscience*, 12: 623–637.

Rogers, R. W. (1975). A protection motivation theory of fear appeals and attitude change. *Journal of Psychology*, 91: 93–114.

Rohsenow, D. J., Monti, P. M., Rubonis, A. V., Sirota, A. D., Niaura, R. S., Colby, S. M., ... & Abrams, D. B. (1994). Cue reactivity as a predictor of drinking among male alcoholics. *Journal of Consulting and Clinical Psychology*, 62: 620–626.

Rose, S. (2005). Going too far? Sex, sin and social policy. *Social Forces*, 84: 1207–1233.

Rosen, C. S., Henson, B. R., Finney, J. W., & Moos, R. H. (2000). Consistency of self-administered and interview-based Addiction Severity Index composite scores. *Addiction*, 95: 419–425.

Rosenberg, K. P. & Feder, L. C. (eds.) (2014a). *Behavioral Addictions: Criteria, Evidence, and Treatment*. London: Academic Press/Elsevier.

  (2014b). An introduction to behavioral addictions. In K. P. Rosenberg & L. C. Feder (eds.), *Behavioral Addictions: Criteria, Evidence, and Treatment*. London: Academic Press/Elsevier, pp. 1–18.

Bibliography

Rosenberg, K. P., O'Connor, S., & Carnes, P. (2014). Sex addiction: An overview. In K. P. Rosenberg & L. C. Feder (eds.), *Behavioral Addictions: Criteria, Evidence, and Treatment*. London: Academic Press/Elsevier, pp. 215–236.

Rosenfield, P. L. (1992). The potential of transdisciplinary research for sustaining and extending linkages between the health and social sciences. *Social Science and Medicine*, 35: 1343–1357.

Rotgers, F. & Davis, B. A. (2006). *Treating Alcohol Problems*. Hoboken, NJ: John Wiley.

Rotter, J. B. (1954) *Social Learning and Clinical Psychology*. Englewood Cliffs, NJ: Prentice-Hall.

Roumane, N. M. & Conwell, R. H. (1897). *Social Abominations or the Follies of Modern Society*. Whitefish, MT: Kessinger Publishing.

Rounsaville, B. J., Kosten, T. R., Weissman, M. M., & Kleber, H. D. (1986). Prognostic significance of psychopathology in treated opiate addicts: a 2.5-year follow-up study. *Archives of General Psychiatry*, 43: 739–745.

Rowe, C. L. (2012). Family therapy for drug abuse: Review and updates 2003–2010. *Journal of Marital and Family Therapy*, 38: 59–81.

Rozin, P. & Stoess, C. (1993). Is there a general tendency to become addicted? *Addictive Behaviors*, 18: 81–87.

Russell-Mayhew, S., von Ranson, K. M., & Masson, P. C. (2010). How does Overeaters Anonymous help its members? A qualitative analysis. *European Eating Disorders Review*, 18: 33–42.

Rychtarik, R. G., Koutsky, J. R., & Miller, W. R. (1998). Profiles of the Alcohol Use Inventory: A large sample cluster analysis conducted with split-sample replication rules. *Psychological Assessment*, 10: 107–119.

(1999). Profiles of the Alcohol Use Inventory: Correction to Rychtarik, Koutsky, and Miller (1998). *Psychological Assessment*, 11: 396–402.

Sabia, J. J. (2006). Does sex education affect adolescent sexual behaviors and health? *Journal of Policy Analysis and Management*, 25: 783–802.

Sachs, M. L. & Pargman, D. (1979). Running addiction: A depth interview examination. *Journal of Sport Behavior*, 2: 143–155.

Salguero, R. A. T. & Moran, R. M. B. (2002). Measuring problem video game playing in adolescents. *Addiction*, 97: 1601–1606.

Salimi, A., Safari, F., Mohajerani, S. A., Hashemian, M., Kolahi, A.-A., & Mottaghi, K. (2014). Long-term relapse of ultra-rapid opioid detoxification. *Journal of Addictive Diseases*, 33: 33–40.

Salnier, C. F. (1996). Addiction in an alcohol intervention group for black women. *Journal of Drug Issues*, 26: 95–123.

Samet, S., Waxman, R., Hatzenbuehler, M., & Hasin, D. S. (2007). Assessing addiction: Concepts and instruments. *Addiction Science & Clinical Practice*, 4: 19–31.

Sanguanprasit, B., Pacheun, O., & Termsirikulchai, L. (2006). *Health Knowledge and Gender Attitudes Related to Women and Tobacco among Women in Thailand*. Bangkok: Southeast Asia Tobacco Control Alliance (SEATCA) under the Collaborative Funding Program for Tobacco Control Research.

Saunders, J. B., Aasland, O. G., Babor, T. F., de la Fuente, J. R., & Grant, M. (1993). Development of the Alcohol Use Disorders Identification Test (AUDIT): WHO collaborative project on early detection of persons with harmful alcohol consumption – II. *Addiction*, 88: 791–804.

Sawyer, A. M. & Borduin, C. M. (2011). Effects of multisystemic therapy through midlife: A 21.9-year follow-up to a randomized clinical trial with serious violent juvenile offenders. *Journal of Consulting and Clinical Psychology*, 79: 643–652.

Bibliography

Sbraga, T. P. & O'Donohue, W. T. (2003). *The Sex Addiction Workbook: Proven Strategies to Help You Regain Control of Your Life*. Oakland, CA: New Harbinger Publications.

Schaef, A. W. (1987). *When Society Becomes an Addict*. New York: HarperCollins.

Scharkow, M., Festl, R., & Quandt, T. (2014). Longitudinal patterns of problematic computer game use among adolescents and adults: A 2-year panel study. *Addiction*, 109: 1910–1917.

Schaufeli, W. B., Bakker, A. B., van der Heijden, F. M. M. A., & Prins, J. T. (2009). Workaholism among medical residents: It is the combination of working excessively and compulsively that counts. *International Journal of Stress Management*, 16: 249–272.

Schaufeli, W. B., Shimazu, A., & Taris, T. W. (2009). Driven to work excessively hard: The evaluation of a two-factor measure of workaholism in the Netherlands and Japan. *Cross-Cultural Research*, 43: 320–348.

Schneider, J. P. (2005). Coexisting disorders. In R. H. Coombs (ed.), *Addiction Counseling Review*. Mahwah, NJ: Lawrence Erlbaum Associates, pp. 293–316.

Schneider, J. P. & Irons, R. R. (2001). Assessment and treatment of addictive sexual disorders: Relevance for chemical dependency relapse. *Substance Use & Misuse*, 36: 1795–1820.

Schofield, G., Mummery, K., Wang, W., & Dickson, G. (2004). Epidemiological study of gambling in the non-metropolitan region of central Queensland. *Australian Journal of Rural Health*, 12: 6–10.

Schottenfeld, R. S. & Pantalon, M. V. (1994). Assessment of the patient. In M. Galanter & H. D. Kleber (eds.), *The American Psychiatric Press Textbook of Substance Abuse Treatment*. Washington, DC: American Psychiatric Press, pp. 25–33.

Schutz, A. & Luckmann, T. (1973). *The Structure of the Life World*. Evanston, IL: Northwestern University Press.

Secades-Villa, R., Olfson, M., Okuda, M., Velasquez, N., Perez-Fuentes, F., Liu, S.-M., & Blanco, C. (2013). Trends in the prevalence of tobacco use in the United States, 1991–1992 to 2004–2005. *Psychiatric Services*, 64: 458–465.

Seegers, J. A. (2003). The prevalence of sexual addiction symptoms on the college campus. *Sexual Addiction & Compulsivity*, 10: 247–258.

Selzer, M. L. (1971). The Michigan Alcoholism Screening Test: The quest for a new diagnostic instrument. *American Journal of Psychiatry*, 127: 1653–1658.

Selzer, M. L., Vinokur, A., & Rooijen, L. V. (1975). A self-administered Short Michigan Alcoholism Screening Test (SMAST). *Journal of Studies on Alcohol and Drugs*, 36: 117–128.

Shaffer, H. J. & Hall, M. N. (2001) Updating and refining prevalence estimates of disordered gambling behavior in the United States and Canada. *Canadian Journal of Public Health*, 92: 168–172.

Shaffer, H. J., Hall, M. N., & Vander Bilt, J. (1999). Estimating the prevalence of disordered gambling behavior in the United States and Canada: A research synthesis. *American Journal of Public Health*, 89: 1369–1376.

Shaffer, H. J. & Jones, S. B. (1989). *Quitting Cocaine: The Struggle against Impulse*. Lanham, MD: Lexington Books.

Shaffer, H. J., LaBrie, R., Scanlan, K. M., & Cummings, T. N. (1994). Pathological gambling among adolescents: Massachusetts Gambling Screen (MAGS). *Journal of Gambling Studies*, 10: 339–362.

Shapira, N. A., Lessig, M. C., Goldsmith, T. D., Szabo, S. T., Lazoritz, M., Gold, M. S., & Stein, D. J. (2003). Problematic Internet use: Proposed classification and diagnostic criteria. *Depression and Anxiety*, 17: 207–216.

Bibliography

Shi, Y. (2016). Impacts of medical marijuana policies on initiation of marijuana use: Evidence from national longitudinal surveys of youth 1997. Podium presentation at the 2016 Conference of the American Academy of Health Behavior, Ponte Vedra Beach, Florida, February.

Shields, I. W. & Whitehall, G. C. (1994). Neutralization and delinquency among teenagers. *Criminal Justice and Behavior*, 21: 223–235.

Shimazu, A. & Schaufeli, W. B. (2009) Is workaholism good or bad for employee well-being? The distinctiveness of workaholism and work engagement among Japanese employees. *Industrial Health*, 47: 495–502.

Shimazu, A., Schaufeli, W. B., & Taris, W. (2010) How does workaholism affect worker health and performance? The mediating role of coping. *International Journal of Behavioral Medicine*, 17: 154–160.

Silberg, J., Rutter, M., D'Onofrio, B., & Eaves, L. (2003). Genetic and environmental risk factors in adolescent substance use. *Journal of Child Psychology and Psychiatry*, 44: 664–676.

Simons, J. S., Dvorak, R. D., & Lau-Barraco, C. (2009). Behavioral inhibition and activation systems: Differences in substance use expectancy organization and activation in memory. *Psychology of Addictive Behaviors*, 23: 315–328.

Sinclair, H., Lochner, C., & Stein, D. J. (2016). Behavioral addiction: A useful construct? *Current Behavioral Neuroscience Reports*, 3: 43–48.

Singer, D. G. & Singer, J. L. (1998). Developing critical viewing skills and media literacy in children. *Annals of the American Academy of Political and Social Science*, 557: 164–179.

Single, E. (1995). Defining harm reduction. *Drug and Alcohol Review*, 14: 287–290.

Skara, S. & Sussman, S. (2003). A review of 25 long-term adolescent tobacco and other drug use prevention program evaluations. *Preventive Medicine*, 37: 451–474.

Skolnick, J. H. (1988). The social transformation of vice. *Law and Contemporary Problems*, 51: 9–29.

Slater, M. D., Kelly, K. J., Edwards, R. W., Thurman, P. J., Plested, B. A., Keefe, T. J., … & Henry, K. L. (2006). Combining in-school and community-based media efforts: Reducing marijuana and alcohol uptake among younger adolescents. *Health Education Research*, 21: 157–167.

Slutske, W. S. (2006). Natural recovery and treatment-seeking in pathological gambling: Results of two US national surveys. *American Journal of Psychiatry*, 163: 297–302.

Smith, D. E., Marcus, M. D., Lewis, C. E., Fitzgibbon, M., & Schreiner, P. (1998). Prevalence of binge eating disorder, obesity, and depression in a biracial cohort of young adults. *Annals of Behavioral Medicine*, 20: 227–232.

Smith, G. T. (1994). Psychological expectancy as mediator of vulnerability to alcoholism. *Annals of the New York Academy of Sciences*, 708: 165–171.

Snir, R. & Zohar, D. (2008). Workaholism as discretionary time investment at work: An experience-sampling study. *Applied Psychology: An International Review*, 57: 109–127.

Snyder, J., Schrepferman, L., Oeser, J., Patterson, G., Stoolmiller, M., Johnson, K., & Snyder, A. (2005). Deviancy training and association with deviant peers in young children: Occurrence and contribution to early-onset conduct problems. *Development and Psychopathology*, 17: 397–413.

Snyder, L. B., Hamilton, M. A., Mitchell, E. W., Kiwanuka-Tondo, J., Fleming-Milici, F., & Proctor, D. (2004). A meta-analysis of the effect of mediated health communication campaigns on behavior change in the United States. *Journal of Health Communication*, 9: 71–96.

Solomon, J., Card, J. J., & Malow, R. M. (2006). Adapting efficacious interventions: Advancing translational research in HIV prevention. *Evaluation & the Health Professions*, 29: 162–194.

Bibliography

Sommers, I. (1988). Pathological gambling: Estimating prevalence and group characterstics. *International Journal of the Addictions*, 23: 477–490.

Sommers, P. V. (1972). *The Biology of Behavior*. Sydney: John Wiley.

Speigel, E. & Mudler, E. A. (1986). The anonymous program and ego functioning. *Issues in Ego Psychology*, 19: 34–42.

Spence, J. T. & Robbins, A. S. (1992). Workaholism: Definition, measurement, and preliminary results. *Journal of Personality Assessment*, 58: 160–178.

Speziale, B. A. (1994). Marital conflict versus sex and love addiction. *Families in Society*, 75: 509–512.

Spitzer, R. L., Devlin, M., Walsh, B. T., Hasin, D., Wing, R., Marcus, M., . . . & Nonas, C. (1992). Binge eating disorder: A multisite field trial of the diagnostic criteria. *International Journal of Eating Disorders*, 11: 191–203.

Spoth, R., Reyes, M. L., Redmond, C., & Shin, C. (1999). Assessing a public health approach to delay onset and progression of adolescent substance use: Latent transition and log-linear analyses of longitudinal family preventive intervention outcomes. *Journal of Consulting and Clinical Psychology*, 67: 619–630.

Spunt, B., Dupont, I., Lesieur, H., Liberty, H. J., & Hunt, D. (1998). Pathological gambling and substance misuse: A review of the literature. *Substance Use & Misuse*, 33: 2535–2560.

Stacy, A. W. & Ames, S. L. (2001). Implicit cognition theory in drug use and driving under the influence interventions. In S. Sussman (ed.), *Handbook of Program Development in Health Behavior Research and Practice*. Thousand Oaks, CA: Sage, pp. 107–130.

Stacy, A. W., Ames, S. L., & Knowlton, B. (2004). Neurologically plausible distinctions in cognition relevant to drug abuse etiology and prevention. *Substance Use & Misuse*, 39: 1571–1623.

Stanton, M. D. & Shadish, W. R. (1997). Outcome, attrition, and family-couples treatment for drug abuse: A meta-analysis and review of the controlled, comparative studies. *Psychological Bulletin*, 122: 170–191.

Stead, L. F. & Lancaster, T. (2005). Group behaviour therapy programmes for smoking cessation. *Cochrane Database of Systematic Reviews*, 2. Article CD001007.

Steinberg, M. A., Kosten, T. A., & Rounsaville, B. J. (1992). Cocaine abuse and pathological gambling. *American Journal on Addictions*, 1: 121–132.

Stewart, D. G. & Brown, S. A. (1995). Withdrawal and dependency symptoms among adolescent alcohol and drug abusers. *Addiction*, 90: 627–635.

Stice, E., Rohde, P., Shaw, H., & Marti, C. N. (2013). Efficacy trial of a selective prevention program targeting both eating disorders and obesity among female college students: 1- and 2-year follow-up effects. *Journal of Consulting and Clinical Psychology*, 81: 183–189.

Stinson, F. S., Ruan, W. J., Pickering, R., & Grant, B. (2006). Cannabis use disorders in the USA: Prevalence, correlates and co-morbidity. *Psychological Medicine*, 36: 1447–1460.

Stone, A. L., Becker, L. G., Huber, A. M., & Catalano, R. F. (2012). Review of risk and protective factors of substance use and problem use in emerging adulthood. *Addictive Behaviors*, 37: 747–775.

Storti, E. (2001). Motivational intervention: The only failure is the failure to act. In R. H. Coombs (ed.), *Addiction Recovery Tools: A Practical Handbook*. Thousand Oaks, CA: Sage, pp. 3–16.

Strang, J., Babor, T., Caulkins, J., Fischer, B., Foxcroft, D., & Humphreys, K. (2012). Drug policy and the public good: Evidence for effective interventions. *Lancet*, 379: 71–83.

Stucki, S. & Rihs-Middel, M. (2007). Prevalence of adult problem and pathological gambling between 2000 and 2005: An update. *Journal of Gambling Studies*, 23: 245–257.

Bibliography

Sullivan, S. (1999). Development of the "EIGHT" problem gambling screen. Unpublished doctoral dissertation, Auckland University, New Zealand.

  (2007). Don't let an opportunity go by: Validation of the EIGHT gambling screen. *International Journal of Mental Health Addiction*, 5: 381–389.

Sun, D. L., Chen, Z. J., Ma, N., Zhang, X. C., Fu, X. M., & Zhang, D. R. (2009). Decision-making and prepotent response inhibition functions in excessive Internet users. *CNS Spectrum*, 14: 75–81.

Sun, P., Johnson, C. A., Palmer, P., Xie, B., Arpawong, T. E., Unger, J., . . . & Sussman, S. (2012). Concurrent and predictive relationships between compulsive Internet use and substance use: Findings from vocational high school students in China and the USA. *International Journal of Environmental Research and Public Health*, 9: 660–673.

Sun, P., Unger, J. B., Palmer, P. H., Gallaher, P., Chou, C.-P., Baezconde-Garbanati, L., . . . & Johnson, C. A. (2005). Internet accessibility and usage among urban adolescents in southern California: Implications for web-based health research. *Cyberpsychology & Behavior*, 8: 441–453.

Sunderwirth, S. G. & Milkman, H. (1991). Behavioral and neurochemical commonalities in addiction. *Contemporary Family Therapy*, 13: 421–433.

Sussman, S. (1996). Development of a school-based drug abuse prevention curriculum for high-risk youths. *Journal of Psychoactive Drugs*, 28: 169–182.

  (ed.) (2001). *Handbook of Program Development in Health Behavior Research and Practice*. Thousand Oaks, CA: Sage.

  (2002a). Effects of sixty-six adolescent tobacco use cessation trials and seventeen prospective studies of self-initiated quitting. *Tobacco Induced Diseases*, 1: 35–81.

  (2002b). Smoking cessation among persons in recovery. *Substance Use & Misuse*, 37: 1275–1298.

  (2002c). Tobacco industry youth tobacco prevention programming: A review. *Prevention Science*, 3: 57–67.

  (2005). Cognitive misperception as determinants of drug misuse. *Salud y drogas*, 5: 9–31.

  (2007). Sexual addiction among teens: A review. *Sexual Addiction & Compulsivity*, 14: 257–278.

  (2010a). Love addiction: Definition, etiology, treatment. *Sexual Addiction & Compulsivity*, 17: 31–45.

  (2010b). A review of Alcoholics Anonymous/Narcotics Anonymous programs for teens. *Evaluation & the Health Professions*, 33: 26–55.

  (2012a). Workaholism: A review. *Journal of Addiction Research & Therapy*, S6. doi: 10.4172/2155-6105.S6-001.

  (2012b). Steve Sussman on Matilda Hellman's "Mind the Gap!" Failure in understanding key dimensions of an addicted drug user's life – addictive effects. *Substance Use & Misuse*, 47: 1661–1665.

  (2013). A lifespan developmental-stage approach to tobacco and other drug abuse prevention. *ISRN-Addiction*. doi: 10.1155/2013/745783.

  (2015). Evaluating the efficacy of Project TND: Evidence from seven research trials. In L. M. Scheier (ed.), *Handbook of Adolescent Drug Use Prevention: Research, Intervention Strategies, and Practice*. Washington, DC: American Psychological Association.

Sussman, S. & Ames, S. L. (2001). *The Social Psychology of Drug Abuse*. Buckingham: Open University Press.

  (2008). *Drug Abuse: Concepts, Prevention and Cessation*. Cambridge University Press.

Sussman, S., Ames, S. L., & Avol, E. (2015a). Could environmental exposures facilitate the incidence of addictive behaviors? *Evaluation & the Health Professions*, 38: 53–58.

Sussman, S. & Arnett, J. (2014). Emerging adulthood: Developmental period facilitative of the addictions. *Evaluation & the Health Professions*, 37: 147–155.

Sussman, S., Arpawong, T. E., Sun, P., Tsai, J., Rohrbach, L. A., & Spruijt-Metz, D. (2014). Prevalence and co-occurrence of addictive behaviors among former alternative high school youth. *Journal of Behavioral Addictions*, 3: 33–40.

Sussman, S. & Black, D. S. (2008). Substitute addiction: A concern for researchers and practitioners. *Journal of Drug Education*, 38: 167–180.

Sussman, S., Craig, S., & Moss, M. A. (2002). *Project TND: Towards No Drug Abuse*. Los Angeles, CA: University of Southern California.

Sussman, S., Dent, C. W., Mestel-Rauch, J. S., Johnson, C. A., Hansen, W. B., & Flay, B. R. (1988). Adolescent nonsmokers, triers, and regular smokers' estimates of cigarette smoking prevalence: When do overestimates occur and by whom? *Journal of Applied Social Psychology*, 18: 537–551.

Sussman, S., Dent, C. W., Stacy, A. W., Burton, D., & Flay, B. R. (1995). *Developing School-Based Tobacco Use Prevention and Cessation Programs*. Thousand Oaks, CA: Sage.

Sussman, S., Dent, C. W., Wang, E., Cruz, N. T. B., Sanford, D., & Johnson, C. A. (1994). Participants and nonparticipants of a mass media self-help smoking cessation program. *Addictive Behaviors*, 19: 643–654.

Sussman, S., Earleywine, M., Wills, T., Cody, C., Biglan, T., Dent, C. W., & Newcomb, M. D. (2004). The motivation, skills, and decision-making model of drug abuse prevention. *Substance Use & Misuse*, 39: 1971–2016.

Sussman, S., Grana, R., Pokhrel, P., Rohrbach, L. A., & Sun, P. (2010). Forbidden fruit and the prediction of cigarette smoking. *Substance Use & Misuse*, 45: 1683–1693.

Sussman, S., Horn, J. L., & Gilewski, M. (1990). Alcohol relapse prevention: Need for a memory modification component. *International Journal of the Addictions*, 25: 921–929.

Sussman, S., Leventhal, A., Bluthenthal, R. N., Freimuth, M., Forster, M., & Ames, S. L. (2011a). A framework for the specificity of addictions. *International Journal of Environmental Research and Public Health*, 8: 3399–3415.

Sussman, S., Levy, D., Hassmiller, K., Cena, D. W., Kim, M., Rohrbach, L. A., & Chaloupka, F. (2013a). A speculation on modalities of tobacco use prevention. *Tobacco Induced Diseases*, 11.

Sussman, S. & Lisha, N. (2014). Reasons for co-occurrence of team sports participation and alcohol misuse. In J. Raines (ed.), *Substance Abuse: Prevalence, Genetic and Environmental Risk Factors and Prevention*. Hauppauge, NY: Nova Science Publishers, pp. 1–18.

Sussman, S., Lisha, N., & Griffiths, M. (2011b). Prevalence of the addictions: A problem of the majority or the minority? *Evaluation & the Health Professions*, 34: 3–56.

Sussman, S., Milam, J., Arpawong, T. E., Tsai, J., Black, D. S., & Wills, T. A. (2013b). Spirituality in addictions treatment: Wisdom to know ... what it is. *Substance Use & Misuse*, 48: 1203–1217.

Sussman, S. & Moran, M. B. (2013). Hidden addiction: Television. *Journal of Behavioral Addictions*, 2: 125–132.

Sussman, S., Patten, C. A., & Order-Connors, B. (2005). Tobacco use. In R. H. Coombs (ed.), *Addiction Counseling Review: Preparing for Comprehensive, Certification and Licensing Examinations*. Mahwah, NJ: Lawrence Erlbaum Associates, pp. 203–224.

Sussman, S., Pokhrel, P., Sun, P., Rohrbach, L. A., & Spruijt-Metz, D. (2015b). Prevalence and co-occurrence of addictive behaviors among former alternative high school youth: A longitudinal follow-up study. *Journal of Behavioral Addictions*, 4: 189–194.

Sussman, S., Reynaud, M., Aubin, H.-J., & Leventhal, A. M. (2011c). Drug addiction, love, and the Higher Power. *Evaluation & the Health Professions*, 34: 362–370.

Sussman, S., Rohrbach, L., Patel, R., & Holiday, K. (2003). A look at an interactive classroom-based drug abuse prevention program: Interactive contents and suggestions for research. *Journal of Drug Education*, 33: 355–368.

Sussman, S., Skara, S., & Pumpuang, P. (2008). Project Towards No Drug Abuse (TND): A needs assessment of a social service referral telephone program for high risk youth. *Substance Use & Misuse*, 43: 2066–2073.

Sussman, S., Stacy, A. W., Dent, C. W., Simon, T. R., & Johnson, C. A. (1996). Marijuana use: Current issues and new research directions. *Journal of Drug Issues*, 26: 695–733.

Sussman, S., Sun, P., Rohrbach, L., & Spruijt-Metz, D. (2012). One-year outcomes of a drug abuse prevention program for older teens and emerging adults: Evaluating a motivational interviewing booster component. *Health Psychology*, 31: 476–485.

Sussman, S. & Sussman, A. N. (2011). Considering the definition of addiction. *International Journal of Environmental Research and Public Health*, 8: 4025–4038.

Sussman, S. & Unger, J. B. (2004). A "drug abuse" theoretical integration: A transdisciplinary speculation. *Substance Use & Misuse*, 39: 2055–2069.

Sussman, S., Valente, T. W., Rohrbach, L. A., Skara, S., & Pentz, M. A. (2006). Translation in the health professions: Converting science into action. *Evaluation & the Health Professions*, 29: 7–32.

Sutton, S. R. & Eiser, J. R. (1984). The effect of fear-arousing communications on cigarette smoking: An expectancy-value approach. *Journal of Behavioral Medicine*, 7: 13–33.

Swarz, R. (2010). Medical marijuana users in substance abuse treatment. *Harm Reduction Journal*, 7. doi: 10.1186/1477-7517-7-3.

Swisher, J. D. & Hu, T. W. (1983). Alternatives to drug abuse: Some are and some are not. In T. J. Glynn, C. G. Leukefeld, & J. P. Ludford (eds.), *Preventing Adolescent Drug Abuse: Intervention Strategies*. Rockville, MD: National Institute on Drug Abuse, pp. 141–153.

Sykes, G. & Matza, D. (1957). Techniques of neutralization: A theory of delinquency. *American Sociological Review*, 22: 664–670.

Szabo, A., Frenkl, R., & Caputo, A. (1997). Relationships between addiction to running, commitment to running, and deprivation from running: A study on the Internet. *European Yearbook of Sport Psychology*, 1: 130–147.

Talbott, G. D. & Crosby, L. R. (2001). Recovery contracts: Seven key elements. In R. H. Coombs (ed.), *Addiction Recovery Tools: A Practical Handbook*. Thousand Oaks, CA: Sage, pp. 127–144.

Tam, L., Bagozzi, R. P., & Spanjol, J. (2010). When planning is not enough: The self-regulatory effect of implementation intentions of changing snacking habits. *Health Psychology*, 29: 284–292.

Tao, R., Huang, X., Wang, J., Zhang, H., Zhang, Y., & Li, M. (2010). Proposed diagnostic criteria for Internet addiction. *Addiction*, 105: 556–564.

Taris, T. W., Schaufeli, W. B., & Verhoeven, L. C. (2005). Workaholism in the Netherlands: Measurement and implications for job strain and work-nonwork conflict. *Applied Psychology: An International Review*, 54: 37–60.

Tarter, R. E. & Hegedus, A. M. (1991). The Drug Use Screening Inventory: Its applications in the evaluation and treatment of alcohol and other drug abuse. *Alcohol Health & Research World*, 15: 65–75.

Tarter, R. E., Kirisci, L., Mezzich, A., Conelius, J. R., Pajer, K., Vanyukov, M., ... & Clark, D. (2003). Neurobehavioral disinhibition in childhood predicts early age at onset of substance use disorder. *American Journal of Psychiatry*, 160: 1078–1085.

Bibliography

Tarter, R. E., Laird, S. B., Bukstein, O. G., & Kaminer, Y. (1992). Validation of the adolescent drug use screening inventory: preliminary findings. *Psychology of Addictive Behaviors*, 6: 233–236.

Taylor, C. Z. (2002). Religious addiction: Obsession with spirituality. *Pastoral Psychology*, 50: 291–315.

Teesson, M., Baillie, A., Lynskey, M., Manor, B., & Degenhardt, L. (2006). Substance use, dependence and treatment seeking in the United States and Australia: A cross-national comparison. *Drug and Alcohol Dependence*, 81: 149–155.

Terry, A., Szabo, A., & Griffiths, M. (2004). The exercise addiction inventory: A new brief screening tool. *Addiction Research & Theory*, 12: 489–499.

Thaxton, L. (1982). Physiological and psychological effects of short-term exercise addiction on habitual runners. *Journal of Sport & Exercise Psychology*, 4: 73–80.

Thomas, N. D. (1997). Hoarding: Eccentricity or pathology –when to intervene? *Journal of Gerontological Social Work*, 29: 45–55.

Thompson, E. L. (1978). Smoking education programs 1960–1976. *American Journal of Public Health*, 68: 250–257.

Thush, C., Wiers, R. W., Ames, S. L., Grenard, J. L., Sussman, S., & Stacy, A. W. (2008). Interactions between implicit and explicit cognition and working memory capacity in the prediction of alcohol use in at-risk adolescents. *Drug & Alcohol Dependence*, 94: 116–124.

Timmerman, M. G., Wells, L. A., & Chen, S. (1990). Bulimia nervosa and associated alcohol abuse among secondary students. *Journal of the American Academy of Child & Adolescent Psychiatry*, 29: 118–122.

Timmreck, T. C. (1990). Overcoming the loss of love: Preventing love addiction and promoting positive emotional health. *Psychological Reports*, 66: 515–528.

—— (1998). *An Introduction to Epidemiology*. Boston, MA: Jones and Bartlett.

Tobler, N. S. (1986). Meta-analysis of 143 adolescent drug prevention programs: Quantitative outcomes results of program participants compared to a control or comparison group. *Journal of Drug Issues*, 15: 535–567.

Tobler, N. S., Roona, M. R., Ochshorn, P., Marshall, D. G., Streke, A. V., & Stackpole, K. M. (2000). School-based adolescent drug prevention programs: 1998 meta-analysis. *Journal of Primary Prevention*, 20: 275–336.

Toneatto, T. (2008). Reliability and validity of the Gamblers Anonymous Twenty Questions. *Journal of Psychopathology and Behavioral Assessment*, 30: 71–78.

Toneatto, T. & Brennan, J. (2002). Pathological gambling in treatment-seeking substance abusers. *Addictive Behaviors*, 27: 465–469.

Toneatto, T., Sobell, L. C., Rubel, E., & Sobell, M. B. (1999). Natural recovery from cocaine dependence. *Psychology of Addictive Behaviors*, 13: 259–268.

Tong, V., McIntyre, T., & Silmon, H. (1997). What's the flavor? Understanding inmate slang usage in correctional education settings. *Journal of Correctional Eduction*, 48: 192–197.

Tonigan, J. S., Toscova, R., & Miller, W. R. (1996). Meta-analysis of the literature on Alcoholics Anonymous: Sample and study characteristics moderate findings. *Journal of Studies on Alcohol*, 57: 65–72.

Topalli, V. (2005). When being good is bad: An expansion of neutralization theory. *Criminology*, 43: 797–836.

Treasure, J. (2014). The time is right to launch large-scale controlled treatment effectiveness studies of early-onset binge eating disorders and bulimia nervosa in student populations. *Epidemiology and Psychiatric Sciences*, 23: 47–49.

Bibliography

Tremblay, L. K., Naranjo, C. A., Cardenas, L., Herrmann, N., & Busto, U. E. (2002). Probing brain reward system function in major depressive disorder: Altered response to dextroamphetamine. *Archives of General Psychiatry*, 59: 409–417.

Trevisan, L. A., Boutros, N., Petrakis, I. L., & Krystal, J. H. (1998). Complications of alcohol withdrawal: Pathophysiological insights. *Alcohol Health & Research World*, 22: 61–66.

Trimpey, J. (1989). *The Small Book: A Revolutionary Alternative for Overcoming Alcohol and Drug Dependence*. New York: Delacorte Press.

  (1996). *Rational Recovery: The New Cure for Substance Addiction*. New York: Pocket Books.

Tsai, C.-C. & Lin, S. S. J. (2003). Internet addiction of adolescents in Taiwan: An interview study. *Cyberpsychology & Behavior*, 6: 649–652.

Tsai, J., Huh, J., Idrisov, B., Galimov, A., Espada, J. P., Gonzalvez, M. T., & Sussman, S. (under review). Prevalence and co-occurrence of addictive behaviors among Russian and Spanish youth: A replication study. *Journal of Drug Education*.

Tsoh, J. Y., Chi, F. W., Mertens, J. R., & Weisner, C. M. (2011). Stopping smoking during the first year of substance use treatment predicted 9-year alcohol and drug treatment outcomes. *Drug and Alcohol Dependence*, 114: 110–118.

Turner, G. E., Burciaga, C., Sussman, S., Klein-Selski, E., Craig, S., Dent, C. W., ... & Flay, B. R. (1993). Which lesson components mediate refusal assertion skill improvement in school-based adolescent tobacco use prevention? *International Journal of the Addictions*, 28: 749–766.

Ulrich, J., Hill, A., Rumpf, H.-J., Hapke, U., & Meyer, C. (2003). Alcohol high risk drinking, abuse and dependence among tobacco smoking medical care patients and the general population. *Drug and Alcohol Dependence*, 69: 189–195.

Unger, J. B., Hamilton, J. E., & Sussman, S. (2004). A family member's job loss as a risk factor for smoking among adolescents. *Health Psychology*, 23: 308–313.

Upshaw, H. S. & Ostrom, T. M. (1984). Psychological perspective in attitude research. In J. R. Eiser (ed.), *Attitudinal Judgment*. New York: Springer-Verlag, pp. 23–42.

US Department of Health and Human Services (1988). *The Health Consequences of Smoking – Nicotine Addiction: A Report of the Surgeon General*. Rockville, MD: US DHHS, PHS, CDC, NHPE, OSH.

  (2014). *The Health Consequences of Smoking – 50 Years of Progress: A Report of the Surgeon General*. Atlanta, GA: US DHHS, CDC, NCCDPHP, OSH.

Vaillant, G. E. (1966). A twelve-year follow up of New York narcotic addicts: Some characteristics and determinants of abstinence IV. *American Journal of Psychiatry*, 123: 573–585.

  (1983). *The Natural History of Alcoholism: Causes, Patterns, and Paths to Recovery*. Cambridge, MA: Harvard University Press.

  (1988). What can long-term follow-up teach us about relapse and prevention of relapse in addiction? *British Journal of Addiction*, 83: 1147–1157.

Valence, G., d'Astous, A., & Fortier, L. (1988). Compulsive buying: Concept and measurement. *Journal of Consumer Policy*, 11: 419–433.

Varley, R., Webb, T. L., & Sheeran, P. (2011). Making self-help more helpful: A randomized controlled trial of the impact of augmenting self-help materials with implementation intentions on promoting the effective self-management of anxiety symptoms. *Journal of Consulting and Clinical Psychology*, 79: 123–128.

Veerman, J. L., Healy, G. N., Cobiac, L. J., Vos, T., Winkler, E. A. H., Owen, N., & Dunstan, D. W. (2012). Television viewing time and reduced life expectancy: A life table analysis. *British Journal of Sports Medicine*, 46: 927–930.

Bibliography

Victor, S. E., Glenn, C. R., & Klonsky, E. D. (2012). Is non-suicidal self-injury an "addiction"? A comparison of craving in substance use and non-suicidal self-injury. *Psychiatry Research*, 197: 73–77.

Villella, C., Martinotti, G., Di Nicola, M., Cassano, M., La Torre, G., Gliubizzi, M.D., . . . & Conte, G. (2011). Behavioral addictions in adolescents and young adults: Results from a prevalence study. *Journal of Gambling Studies*, 27: 203–214.

Vincent, E. C., Zebelman, A., & Goodwin, C. (2006). What common substances can cause false positives on urine screens for drugs of abuse? *Journal of Family Practice*, 55: 893–897.

Volberg, R. A. (1994). The prevalence and demographics of pathological gamblers: Implications for public health. *American Journal of Public Health*, 84: 237–241.

Volberg, R. A., Gupta, R., Griffiths, M. D., Olason, D., & Delfabbro, P. H. (2010). An international perspective on youth gambling prevalence studies. *International Journal of Adolescent Medicine and Health*, 22: 3–38.

Volberg, R. A. & Steadman, H. J. (1988). Refining prevalence estimates of pathological gambling. *American Journal of Psychiatry*, 145: 502–505.

Volkow, N. D., Chang, L., Wang, G.-J., Fowler, J. S., Ding, Y.-S., Sedler, M., . . . & Pappas, N. (2001). Low level of brain dopamine D2 receptors in methamphetamine abusers: Association with metabolism in the orbitofrontal cortex. *American Journal of Psychiatry*, 158: 2015–2021.

Volkow, N. D., Wang, G.-J., & Baler, R. D. (2011). Reward, dopamine and the control of food intake: Implications for obesity. *Trends in Cognitive Sciences*, 15: 37–46.

Volkow, N. D., Wang, G.-J., Tomasi, D., & Baler, R. D. (2013). The addictive dimensionality of obesity. *Biological Psychiatry*, 73: 811–818.

Volkow, N. D. & Wise, R. A. (2005). How can drug addiction help us understand obesity? *Nature Neuroscience*, 8: 555–560.

Wagenaar, A. (2006). Alcohol and injury: A surfeit of solutions. Presentation at the 2nd Symposium on Addictive and Health Behaviors Research, Jacksonville, Florida, June.

Wagenaar, A., Lenk, K., & Toomey, T. (2005). Policies to reduce underage drinking: A review of the recent literature. *Recent Developments in Alcoholism*, 17: 275–297.

Wagner, H. S., Ahlstrom, B., Redden, J. P., Vickers, Z., & Mann, T. (2014). The myth of comfort food. *Health Psychology*, 33: 1552–1557.

Wakefield, J. C. & Schmitz, M. F. (2014). How many people have alcohol use disorders? Using the harmful dysfunction analysis to reconcile prevalence estimates in two community surveys. *Frontiers in Psychiatry*, 5: Article 10 (Corrigendum: *Frontiers in Psychiatry*, 5: Article 144).

Waldron, H. B., Slesnick, N., Brody, J. L., Turner, C. W., & Peterson, T. R. (2001). Treatment outcomes for adolescent substance abuse at 4- and 7-month assessments. *Journal of Consulting and Clinical Psychology*, 69: 802–813.

Walters, S. T., Wright, J. A., & Shegog, R. (2006). A review of computer and Internet-based interventions for smoking behavior. *Addictive Behaviors*, 31: 264–277.

Walther, B., Hanewinkel, R., & Morgenstern, M. (2013). Short-term effects of a school-based program on gambling prevention in adolescents. *Journal of Adolescent Health*, 52: 599–605.

Wardman, D., el-Guebaly, N., & Hodgins, D. (2001). Problem and pathological gambling in North American Aboriginal populations: A review of the empirical literature. *Journal of Gambling Studies*, 17: 81-100.

Warner, J. (1992). Before there was "alcoholism": Lessons from the medieval experience with alcohol. *Contemporary Drug Problems*, 19: 409–429.

Warner, L. A., Kessler, R. C., Hughes, M., Anthony, J. C., & Nelson, C. B. (1995). Prevalence and correlates of drug use and dependence in the United States. *Archives of General Psychiatry*, 52: 219–229.

Waterman, B. R., Liu, J., Newcomb, R., Schoenfeld, A. J., Orr, J. D., & Belmont, P. J. (2013). Risk factors for chronic exertional compartment syndrome in a physically active military population. *American Journal of Sports Medicine*, 41: 2545–2549.

Waters, E., de Silva Sanigorski, A., Hall, B. J., Brown, T., Campbell, K. J., Gao, Y., ... & Summerbell, C. D. (2011). Interventions for preventing obesity in children. *Cochrane Database of Systematic Reviews*, 3. doi: 10.1002/14651858.CD001871.pub3.

Weinstein, A., Feder, L. C., Rosenberg, K. P., & Dannon, P. (2014). Internet addiction disorder: Overview and controversies. In K. P. Rosenberg & L. C. Feder (eds.), *Behavioral Addictions: Criteria, Evidence, and Treatment*. London: Academic Press/Elsevier, pp. 99–118.

Weinstein, A. & Weinstein, Y. (2014). Exercise addiction: Diagnosis, bio-psychological mechanisms and treatment issues. *Current Pharmaceutical Design*, 20: 4062–4069.

Weiss, R., Jaffee, W. B., Menil, V. P., & Cogley, C. B. (2004). Group therapy for substance use disorders: What do we know? *Harvard Review of Psychiatry*, 12: 339–350.

Weiss, R. & Schneider, J. (2006). *Untangling the Web: Sex, Porn, and Fantasy Obsession in the Internet Age*. New York: Alyson Books.

Welte, J., Barnes, G. M., Tidwell, M.-C. O., & Hoffman, J. H. (2008). The prevalence of problem gambling among US adolescents and young adults: Results from a national survey. *Journal of Gambling Studies*, 24: 119–133.

Welte, J., Barnes, G. M., Wieczorek, W. F., Tidwell, M. C., & Parker, J. (2001). Alcohol and gambling pathology among US adults: Prevalence, demographic patterns and comorbidity. *Journal of Studies on Alcohol*, 62: 706–712.

Werdell, P. R. (2009). *Bariatric Surgery and Food Addiction: Preoperative Considerations*. Aberdeen, SD: EverGreen Publications.

Westphal, J. R., Rush, J. A., Steven, L., & Johnson, L. J. (2000). Gambling behavior of Louisiana students in Grades 6 through 12. *Pediatric Services*, 51: 96–99.

Westphal, V. K. & Smith, J. E. (1996). Overeaters Anonymous: Who goes and who succeeds? *Eating Disorders*, 4: 160–170.

Whang, L. S., Lee, S., & Chang, G. (2003). Internet over-users' psychological profiles: A behavior sampling analysis on Internet addiction. *Cyberpsychology & Behavior*, 6: 143–150.

White, W. (2005). Recovery: Its history and renaissance as an organizing construct. *Alcoholism Treatment Quarterly*, 23: 3–15.

Wiers, R. W., Bartholow, B. D., Wildenberg, E. V. D., Thush, C., Engels, R. C. M. E., Sher, K. J., ... & Stacy, A. W. (2007). Automatic and controlled processes and the development of addictive behaviors in adolescents: A review and a model. *Pharmacology, Biochemistry and Behavior*, 86: 263–283.

Wiers, R. W., de Jong, P. J., Havermans, R., & Jelicic, M. (2004). How to change implicit drug use-related cognitions in prevention: A transdisciplinary integration of findings from experimental psychopathology, social cognition, memory and experimental learning psychology. *Substance Use & Misuse*, 39: 1625–1684.

Wiers, R. W. & Stacy, A. W. (2006). *Handbook of Implicit Cognition and Addiction*. Thousand Oaks, CA: Sage.

Wilkinson, C., Allsop, S., Cail, D., Chikritzhs, T., Daube, M., Kirby, G., & Mattick, R. (2009). *Alcohol Warning Labels: Evidence of Effectiveness on Risky Alcohol Consumption and Short*

Bibliography

Term Outcomes. Shenton Park, Australia: The National Drug Research Institute of Curtin University. www.foodstandards.govt.nz/code/applications/documents/Alcohol-warning-labels-report-1.pdf; accessed August 26, 2015.

Williams, C. L. & Perry, C. L. (1998). Lessons from Project Northland: Preventing alcohol problems during adolescence. *Alcohol Research & Health*, 22: 107–116.

Williams, N. E. (2011). Arthritis and nature's joints. In J. K. Campbell, M. O'Rourke, and M. H. Slater (eds.), *Carving Nature at Its Joints: Natural Kinds in Metaphysics and Science*. Topics in Contemporary Philosophy 8. Cambridge, MA: MIT Press, pp. 199–223.

Williams, R. J., West, B. L., & Simpson, R. I. (2012). *Prevention of Problem Gambling: A Comprehensive Review of the Evidence and Identified Best Practices*. Guelph, ON: Report prepared for the Ontario Problem Gambling Research Centre and the Ontario Ministry of Health and Long Term Care, December 1, 2007. http://hdl.handle.net/10133/414; accessed November 25, 2014.

Williams, R. J., Wood, R. T., & Currie, S. (2010). Stacked deck: An effective school-based program for the prevention of problem gambling. *Journal of Primary Prevention*, 31: 109–125.

Wills, T. A. (1986). Stress and coping in early adolescence: Relationships to substance use in urban school samples. *Health Psychology*, 5: 503–529.

Wills, T. A., Baker, E., & Botvin, E. M. (1989). Dimensions of assertiveness: Differential relationships to substance use in early adolescence. *Journal of Consulting and Clinical Psychology*, 57: 473–478.

Wingood, G. M., DiClemente, R. J., Harrington, K. F., Lang, D. L., Davies, S. L., Hook, E. W., . . . & Hardin, J. W. (2006). Efficacy of an HIV prevention program among female adolescents experiencing gender-based violence. *American Journal of Public Health*, 96: 1085–1090.

Winters, K. C., Specker, S., & Stinchfield, R. (2002). Measuring pathological gambling with the Diagnostic Interview for Gambling Severity (DIGS). In J. J. Marotta, J. A. Cornelius, & W. R. Eadington (eds.), *The Downside: Problem and Pathological Gambling*. Reno, NV: University of Nevada Press, pp. 143–148.

Winters, K. C., Stinchfield, R., & Fulkerson, J. (1993). Patterns and characteristics of adolescent gambling. *Journal of Gambling Studies*, 9: 371–386.

Wise, R. A. & Koob, G. F. (2014). Circumspective: The development and maintenance of drug addiction. *Neuropsychopharmacology*, 39: 254–262.

Wittgenstein, L. (1953). *Philosophical Investigations*. Oxford: Basil Blackwell.

Wolfe, J. L. (2000). Assessment and treatment of compulsive sex/love behavior. *Journal of Rational-Emotive & Cognitive-Behavior Therapy*, 18: 235–246.

Wong, I. L. & So, E. M. (2003). Prevalence estimates of problem and pathological gambling in Hong Kong. *American Journal of Psychiatry*, 160: 1353–1354.

Wong, U. & Hodgins, D. C. (2013). Development of the Game Addiction Inventory for Adults (GAIA). *Addiction Research & Theory*, 22. doi: 10.3109/16066359.2013.824565.

Wood, E., Stolz, J.-A., Li, K., Montaner, J. S. G., & Kerr, T. (2006). Changes in Canadian heroin supply coinciding with the Australian heroin shortage. *Addiction*, 101: 689–695.

Woodward, V. H., Misis, M. L., & Griffin, O. H. (2014). Examining the effects of social bonds and shame on drug recovery within an on-line support community. *Deviant Behavior*, 35: 938–958.

Workaholics Anonymous World Service Organization (2005). *The Workaholics Anonymous Book of Recovery*. Menlo Park, CA: Workaholics Anonymous World Service Organization. (See also www.workaholics- anonymous.org/book_of_recovery.html and www.workaholics- anonymous.org/page.php?page=history; accessed October 1, 2011.)

Bibliography

Wyer, R. S., Chiu, C.-Y., & Hong, Y-Y. (eds.) (2013). *Understanding Culture: Theory, Research, and Application*. New York: Psychology Press.

Yau, Y. H. C., Gottlieb, C. D., Krasna, L. C., & Potenza, M. N. (2014). Food addiction: Evidence, evaluation, and treatment. In K. P. Rosenberg & L. C. Feder (eds.), *Behavioral Addictions: Criteria, Evidence, and Treatment*. London: Academic Press/Elsevier, pp. 143–184.

Yehuda, R. (ed.) (2002). *Treating Trauma Survivors with PTSD*. Washington, DC: American Psychiatric Publishing.

Yin, H. H. & Knowlton, B. J. (2006). Addiction and learning in the brain. In R. W. Wiers & A. W. Stacy (eds.), *Handbook on Implicit Cognition and Addiction*. Thousand Oaks, CA: Sage, pp. 167–173.

Yoder, B. (1990). *The Recovery Resource Book*. New York: Simon & Schuster.

Young, K. (1996). Psychology of computer use: XL. Addictive use of the Internet – a case that breaks the stereotype. *Psychological Reports*, 79: 899–902.

  (1998). *Caught in the Net*. New York: John Wiley.

  (1999). Internet addiction: Symptoms, evaluation, and treatment. In L. Van de Creek & T. Jackson (eds.), *Innovations in Clinical Practice, Volume 17: A Source Book*. Sarasota, FL: Professional Resource Press, pp. 19–31.

Young, P. T. (1936). *Motivation of Behavior*. New York: John Wiley.

Young, S. E., Corley, R. P., Stallings, M. C., Rhee, S. H., Crowley, T. J., & Hewitt, J. K. (2002). Substance use, abuse and dependence in adolescence: Prevalence, symptom profiles and correlates. *Drug and Alcohol Dependence*, 68: 309–322.

Yung, K., Eickhoff, E., Davis, D. L., Klam, W. P., & Doan, A. P. (2015). Internet addiction disorder and problematic use of Google Glass^{TM} in patients treated at a residential substance abuse treatment program. *Addictive Behaviors*, 41: 58–60.

Zhang, S., Qi, J., Li, X., Wang, H.-L., Britt, J. P., Hoffman, A. F., ... & Morales, M. (2015). Dopaminergic and glutamatergic microdomains in a subset of rodent mesoaccumbens axons. *Nature Neuroscience*, 18: 386–392.

Zimmerman, M., Chelminski, I., & Young, D. (2006). Prevalence and diagnostic correlates of DSM-IV pathological gambling in psychiatric outpatients. *Journal of Gambling Studies*, 22: 255–262.

Zuckerman, M. (1994). *Behavioral Expressions and Biosocial Bases of Sensation Seeking*. Cambridge University Press.

Zweben, J. E. (1987). Eating disorders and substance abuse. *Journal of Psychoactive Drugs*, 19: 181–192.

  (1993). Recovery oriented psychotherapy: A model for addiction treatment. *Psychotherapy*, 30: 259–268.

INDEX

Underline refers to definitions (both text and glossary)

Italic refers to figures/diagrams

Bold refers to tables

12-step programs **6–7**, *6*
   behavioral addictions 6
   case study 4
   extrapersonal-level approaches, cessation **283–284**, 285–290
   historical perspectives 12
   replacement/substitute addictions 141
13th Stepping 141, 327

AA. *see* Alcoholics Anonymous
ABM (attentional bias modification) 273–275, 337–338
abstinence goals, cessation 246–249
abstinence violation effect (AVE) 277, 336, 337
acceptance phase, treatment process model 254
acetaldehyde dehydrogenase (ALDH2) 64, 321
ACORN Assessment tool 162, **176–177**
acquisition skills, PACE model 63, 321
ACTH (adrenocorticotropic hormone) 20–21
action, motivation to change 256
activism 211, 215, **216–217**, 332–335
adaptation-motivation mechanisms, dysregulation 302
addiction co-occurrences. *see* co-occurrence
addiction, definitions 304–306, 317–318. *see also* associational memory-appetitive system relations (AMASR) model
addiction entrenchment. *see* entrenchment
addiction of choice 136, 316, 327
addiction patterns 134–136, *137*, 146–147
   fusion addictions 138–139
   lifestyle demands 143–145
   longitudinal and developmental perspectives **138**, 138
   multiple, concurrent addictions 139–140, **143–144**
   replacement/substitute addictions 140–143, **143–144**
   single addiction 135–137
addiction-related communication 316
Addiction Severity Index (ASI) 153, **176–177**
addiction-specific consequences 74 75, 78–81
addiction specificity 61, 311, 321
addiction spectrum 138, 327
addiction to body image (ABI) 93. *see also* physical attractiveness
addiction transfer 138
addiction types 89–90. *see also specific addictions*
   11 focal addictions 100–102, 325

appetitive motives **96**, 96–98
catalogue of types **90–91**, 90–95
matrix self-report measure 98–101, *99–101*
addictive effects 32–33
addictive exploration 61, 321
additive effects 69, 319–320
ADHD. *see* attention deficit hyperactivity disorder
admission phase, treatment process model 254
adolescents. *see also* emerging adulthood
   critical points for addiction 65
   drug education models 193–195
   gambling studies 120
   patterns of addiction **138**, 138
   prevention strategies 196–197, **224–225**, 291
adrenalin junkies 95, 325–326. *see also* thrill seeking
adrenocorticotropic hormone (ACTH) 20–21
adult role models, social skills training 215, **216–217**
adulthood, emerging. *see* emerging adulthood
adventure seeking **90–91**, 95, 231. *see also* adrenaline junkies
affect enhancement, assessment
   exercise addiction 169–170
   food addiction 161–162
   gambling disorder 163
   sex addiction 168–169
   shopping/spending 166
   social network addiction 165–166
affective/values-based model 193, **194–195**, 329
ages targeted, prevention strategies 196–197
agitated withdrawal, gaming assessment 165
agonists 261
air pollution facilitators/predictors of addiction 47, **48–49**, 51–52
akrasia 41, 319
alcohol addiction 106. *see also* substance addictions
   appetitive needs and addictive effects 35–36
   assessment 152–153, 158–160, **176–177**
   case study 3–5
   cessation 269–270
   cognitive-behavior therapy 265
   co-occurrence with other addictions 112–114, **130**, 134–136
   detoxification and pharmacotherapy 262
   family therapy 290
   flushing response 65
   goals of abstinence vs. moderation 246–247
   historical perspectives 9–10

Index

implicit cognition oriented approaches 273–274
lethal to effective dose ratio **82**
negative effects **80**
prevalence 104–105, **104–105**, 108–110, **109**, **130**
prevention 187, 212–216, **216–217**, 224–232, **230**, 234–235
replacement/substitute addictions 142–143
and team sports 127
withdrawal symptoms **15–16**
alcohol, tobacco, and other drug abuse (ATOD). *see individual addictions*
Alcohol Use Disorders Identification Test (AUDIT) 159, **176–177**
Alcohol Use Inventory (AUI) 159–160, **176–177**
Alcoholics Anonymous (AA) **6–7**, 134
    12-step programs 285–288
    case study 4
    historical perspectives 250
    replacement/substitute addictions 141–142
    self-report assessment instruments 157, **176**, 329
    treatment process model 254
ALDH2 (acetaldehyde dehydrogenase) 64, 321
allostasis theory **13–14**, 20–21
alternating addiction cycles 141, 327
alternative behaviors available 35, 195–196
alternative programs 238–239
AMASR. *see* associational memory-appetitive system relations model
American Psychological Association 89, 92
amphetamines, withdrawal symptoms **15–16**
amygdala 19–21
An Opium-Eater in America (Blair) 10
anandamide, neural system 33
anhedonia 321. *see also* reward deficiency syndrome
anonymity of membership, 12-step programs 286
anorexia nervosa 114, 326. *see also* eating disorders
antagonists 261
antecedents of behavior 185, 329–330
antihistamines, case study 4
anti-social behavior, compulsive **90–91**, 92
anxiety, negative consequences of addiction 77
anxious-ambivalent attachment style 93
appetite, excessive 21. *see also* entrenchment
appetitive effects 316
appetitive effects model of addiction 6–7, 22, 32–33, 44–45, 319–320
    addictive effects 32–33
    contrast with alternative models *36–37*, 36–38, **37**
    diagnostic criteria 148–149
    exercise addiction assessment 169–170
    five-component definition **13–14**, 23–24, 38–41, **38–39**
    historical perspectives 9
    motivation to change 257
    non-addictive behaviors 42–44
    relationship between appetitive needs and addictive effects 35–36
    sedentary habits in modern society 34–35
    types of addiction **96**, 96–98
appetitive needs 33–34, 319
arrests/court orders for treatment, and cessation 243
ASI. *see* Addiction Severity Index
ASPIRE (A Smoking Prevention Interactive Experience) 231

assertiveness training 283, 294, 339
assessment 148–149, **176–177**, 180–182, 329–330
    behavioral addictions 154–157, 162–173, **176–177**
    clinical interview overview 149–151, **176–177**
    comparison of different measures 177–180, **180**
    matrix self-report measures *99–101*, 173, **176–177**
    motivational interventions 283
    other methods 174–175
    self-report assessment instruments overview 157
    substance addictions 152–154, 157–162, **176–177**
assistance-seeking skills, mediators of change 195–196
associational memory-appetitive system relations (AMASR) model *36–37*, 36–38, 44, 320. *see also* appetitive effects model of addiction
    and cessation 242
    facilitators and predictors of addiction 47, 70
    future research directions 302–306, **303–304**, 314–315
associative learning 20, 64
ATOD (alcohol, tobacco and other drug abuse). *see individual addictions*
attention deficit hyperactivity disorder (ADHD) 51, 60–61, 321
attentional bias modification (ABM) 273–275, 337
attitudinal perspective theory 204–205, 331
attraction 62, 63–65, 306–307, 316. *see also* PACE model
attractiveness, physical **90–91**, 93. *see also* tanning addiction
AUDIT (Alcohol Use Disorders Identification Test) 159, **176–177**
AUI (Alcohol Use Inventory) 159–160, **176–177**
automated electronic gambling machines (EGMs) 236, 332–335
automatic processing 59
automaticity 320. *see also* euphoric recall
AVE (abstinence violation effect) 277, 336, 337
avoidance, behavioral coping strategies 205–206

BAC (blood alcohol content) 81, 325–326
bartering, social contexts of addiction 140
BED. *see* binge eating disorder
behavior modification 264. *see also* cognitive-behavior therapy
behavioral addictions 6–8. *see also* exercise; gambling; Internet; love; sex addictions; workaholism
    assessment **176–177**
    case study 3–5, 118
    cessation 245–247, 270–271
    cognitive-behavior therapy 266–268
    definitions **3**, **5–6**, **8**, **29–31**, 316
    historical perspectives 11–12
    incentive-sensitization theory 20
    prevalence/co-occurrence 118–119, **119–120**, **130**, 131–133, **132**
    self-report assessment instruments 162–173
    structured interviews 154–157
    withdrawal symptoms 15
behavioral approach system (BAS) **13–14**, 19–20, 316
behavioral contracting 267–268, **283–284**, 294–295, 337–338
behavioral coping strategies, intrapersonal-level approaches 205–206
behavioral economics-type models 21–22

Index

behavioral inhibition system (BIS) **13–14**, 19–20, <u>316</u>
belief–behavior congruence 47, **48–49**, 59, **200–201**, 204–205, <u>321</u>
beliefs, negative consequences of addiction 195–196
benzodiazepines, replacement/substitute addictions 142
Bergen Facebook Addiction Scale (BFAS) 166, **176–177**
big behavioral data (BBD) 302
binge eating disorder (BED) 90–92, 115, 153–154, 265–266. *see also* food addiction
bingers 136, **137**, <u>327</u>
biochemical methods of assessment 174–175, **176–177**
BIS-BAS addiction self-regulation model **13–14**, 19–20, <u>316</u>
blackouts 179, <u>328</u>
blood alcohol content (BAC) 81, <u>325</u>
blood–brain barrier 6, <u>317</u>
body dysmorphic disorder 93, <u>325</u>
brain disease, addictions as. *see* disease model of addiction
brain regions implicated, reward deficiency syndrome 60
breadth of programming 311–312, <u>341</u>
breathalyzers 175
Brief Drinker Profile (structured interview) 152, **176–177**
bulimia nervosa 114, <u>326</u>. *see also* eating disorders
buying. *see* compulsive buying disorder; shopping/spending addiction

caffeine, withdrawal symptoms **15–16**
canalization 296, <u>339</u>
cannabinoids. *see* marijuana
case study (Johnny) 3–5
   appetitive needs and addictive effects 32
   assessment 148
   cessation programs 242, 259, 282–283
   facilitators and predictors of addiction 46
   future directions 301–302
   negative consequences 71
   patterns of addiction 134
   prevalence and co-occurrence of addictions 103, 118
   prevention strategies 185, 199, 210
   types of addiction 89
catalogue, types of addiction **90–91**, 90–95
catecholamine storms 15, <u>317</u>
caudate nucleus 104
causal mechanisms for specific addictions 307. *see also* etiology
CBD. *see* compulsive buying disorder
CBMS (Compulsive Buying Measurement Scale) 166, **176–177**
CBS (Compulsive Buying Scale) 166, **176–177**
CBT. *see* cognitive-behavior therapy
CDAP (Chemical Dependency Assessment Profile) 160, **176–177**
CDP (Comprehensive Drinker Profile) 152, **176–177**
CDS (Cigarette Dependence Scale) 158, **176–177**
cessation <u>229</u>, 242–243, 257–258. *see also* extrapersonal-level approaches; intrapersonal-level approaches
   due to negative consequences 243–244
   future research directions **303–304**, 310–312
   goals of abstinence vs. moderation 246–249
   historical perspectives 249–252
   motivation to change 255–257, *255*
   natural recovery 244–245
   vs. prevention 188–190
   stages-of-recovery model 252–255, *253*
   stepped-care approach 245–246
Chemical Dependency Assessment Profile (CDAP) 160, **176–177**
childhood obesity, prevention strategies 219
children, patterns of addiction **138**, 138, 143–145
chloriazepoxide 142, <u>327</u>
chocolate, attentional bias modification 274
chromatography 175, <u>328</u>
Church of the Latter Day Saints 66–67
Cigarette Dependence Scale (CDS) 158, **176–177**
cigarette smoking. *see* tobacco addiction
CIU (Compulsive Internet Use) scale 164, **176–177**
clinical interviews 149–151, **176–177**. *see also* structured interviews
clustering effects, future research directions 309
CMA (Crystal Meth Anonymous) **6–7**
cocaine 9.140, 10–11, **15–16**, 82
Cocaine Anonymous (CA) **6–7**
codeine 82, 174–175
codependency, social contexts of addiction 140
coercion into treatment 243–244
cognitive-behavior therapy (CBT) **190–191**, 190, 263–268, **278–280**, <u>330</u>
cognitive behavioral group therapy (CBGT) 293
cognitive coping strategies 206
cognitive distortions/biases **200–201**, 205–207, 264–265, 277
cognitive-information based prevention strategies **200–201**, 203–206, 208–209
cognition-information errors **48–49**, 57, 69, 203, 221, <u>321</u>
cognitive interventions 264. *see also* cognitive-behavior therapy
cognitive level of analysis 47, **48–49**, 57–59, 69, <u>321</u>
cognitive processing limits 47, **48–49**, 58–59, <u>321</u>
cognitive restructuring 206, 264, 266–268, 277, <u>338</u>
cognitive style, coping strategies 206
Collateral Interview Form (structured interview) 152, **176–177**
combining 139, **143–144**, <u>327</u>
commercial interests 187, <u>219</u>
commitment to avoid addiction 195–196, **216–217**, 216
communication 62, 65–67, 306–307. *see also* PACE model
communication skills, life skills approach 212–213, **216–217**
communications related types of addiction **90–91**, 92. *see also* Internet addiction; television addiction
Community Reinforcement and Family Therapy (CRAFT) model 291
comorbidity, facilitators and predictors of addiction **48–49**, 60–61
compartment syndrome 83, <u>325</u>
compliance phase, treatment process model 254
Comprehensive Drinker Profile (CDP) 152, **176–177**
comprehensive social influences approach 212–216, **216–217**, **332–333**

Index

compulsion 18, 146, 317. *see also* obsessive compulsive disorder
compulsive buying disorder (CBD) **48–49**, 53, 95, 263, 267, 321. *see also* shopping/spending addiction
Compulsive Buying Measurement Scale (CBMS) 166, **176–177**
Compulsive Buying Scale (CBS) 166, **176–177**
compulsive Internet use (CIU) 309–310. *see also* Internet addiction disorder
Compulsive Internet Use (CIU) scale 164, **176–177**
concurrent addiction patterns 139–140. *see also* multiple addictions
Confessions of a Workaholic (Oates) 12
Confessions of an English Opium Eater (De Quincey) 10
conflict, six-component definition **13–14**, 23
consequences of addiction. *see* negative consequences of addiction
constraint (prosocial bonding) 47, **48–49**, 57, 324
containment 239
contemplation, motivation to change 256
content-control software 186, 330
context 83, 325. *see also* lifestyle
contextual distortions 47, **48–49**, 59, 324
controlled drinking 136, 246–247, 327
conversation initiation skill 212–213, 333
co-occurrence of addictions 103, 118, **130**, 307–308. *see also specific addictions*
coping, gaming addiction assessment 165
coping, prevention strategies **200–201**, 205–207
corroborative reports 174, 328
corticotropin-releasing factor (CRF) 20–21
court orders, treatment 243
CRAFFT (car, relax, alone, forget, family or friends complain, trouble) assessment instrument 160
CRAFT (Community Reinforcement and Family Therapy) model 291
cravings 16–17, 27, 33, 39, 317. *see also* wanting
CRF (corticotropin-releasing factor) 20–21
critical periods 65, 197
cross-tolerance 138, **143–144**, 327
Crystal Meth Anonymous (CMA) **6–7**
cue exposure treatment protocols 271–273, **278–280**, 338
cultlike characteristics, 12-step programs 288, 339
cultural norms 30, 55–57, 59
cultural perspectives
 ethnicity 307.
 facilitators and predictors of addiction 47, **48–49**, 52–55, 66–67
 negative consequences 83
cut-off scores 157, 328

danger, physical **74–75**, 79, **80**, 179, **180**. *see also* risky behavior
death/serious injury **74–75**, 81–83, **82**, 116–117
Debtors Anonymous (DA) **6–7**
decision-making skills 195–196, 216, **216–217**, 333
deep vein thrombosis, exercise addiction 83
delay, behavioral coping strategy 205–206
delirium tremens 159, 328
depression 77

detoxification 260–263, **278–280**
developmental perspectives
 patterns of addiction **138**, 138
 prevention strategies 196–197
development-related lifestyle factors 143–145
deviancy training 292, 339
deviant subcultures 47, **48–49**, 56–57, 322
diagnostic criteria **13–14**, 16–17, 24–28, 148–149. *see also* DSM (Diagnostic and Statistical Manual of the American Psychiatric Association)
Diagnostic Interview for Gambling Severity (DIGS) 154
differential socialization 37, **37**, 47, **48–49**, 56–57, 322
DIGS (Diagnostic Interview for Gambling Severity) 154
direction-energy model, motivation to change 256
disease model of addiction 8, 339
 12-step programs 285
 alternatives to appetitive needs model **37**, 38
 cessation goals 246
 patterns of addiction 145
diseases of the spirit 12, 317
disinhibiting 140, 327
distorted thinking **200–201**, 205–207, 264–265, 277
distraction, coping strategies 205–206
distribution routes for drugs 47–48, **48–49**, 62
diversion programming 235, 297, 333
diversity, ethnic 307. *see also* cultural perspectives
dominance-related factors **96**, 96–98, 325
dopamine 317
dopamine opponent-process counteradaptation 20–21
dopaminergic system 33
 air pollution effects 51–52
 BIS-BAS addiction self-regulation model 19
 five-component definition 40
 incentive-sensitization theory 20
 multigenic etiology of addiction 201
 negative consequences 82
 patterns of addiction 146
 reward deficiency syndrome 47, **48–49**, 59–60, 324
 spiritual obsession 94
 transdisciplinary-translation matrix 313
dot probe paradigm 273, 338
Dr. Jekyll/Mr. Hyde effect, cessation 247
dramatic consequences of addiction **74–75**, 81–83, **82**, 116–117. *see also* danger, physical
drinking alcohol. *see* alcohol addiction
drug addiction. *see also* alcohol; substance; tobacco addictions
 appetitive needs and addictive effects 35–36
 assessment 152–153, 160, **176–177**
 case study 3–5
 categories 105–106
 cessation 269–270
 cognitive-behavior therapy 265
 co-occurrence with other addictions 112–114, **130**
 detoxification and pharmacotherapy 261–262
 family therapy 290
 goals of abstinence vs. moderation 246–247
 lethal to effective dose ratio **82**
 negative consequences **80**, 81–83
 policy-based prevention programs 235–236
 prescription drugs 111, 326

Index

drug addiction (*cont.*)
    prevalence 104–105, **104–105**, 110–112, **130**, **132**
    prevention strategies 187, 212–216, **216–217**, 224–232, **230**
    tolerance 15
    types of addiction 90, **90–91**
    withdrawal symptoms **15–16**
drug therapies. *see* pharmacotherapy
Drug Use Screening Inventory (DUSI) 160, **176–177**
drunk driving 175
DSM I-IV (Diagnostic and Statistical Manual of the American Psychiatric Association), historical perspectives 24–27
DSM-V (Diagnostic and Statistical Manual of the American Psychiatric Association), current diagnostic criteria **13–14**, 16–17, 27–28, 148–149
    substance addiction categories 105–106
    types of addiction 89, 91–93, 95
Dutch Work Addiction Scale (DUWAS) 172, **176–177**
dyadic-level addiction 140
dysfunctional television viewing. *see* television addiction
dysregulation, adaptation-motivation mechanisms 302

EAA (Exercise Addicts Anonymous) **6–7**
EAI (Exercise Addiction Inventory) 169–170, **176–177**
eating addiction 115–116, 326. *see also* binge eating disorder; food addiction
eating disorders 114, 290–291, 325–327
e-cigarettes 107–108, 326
education in schools 193–194, **194–195**, 211. *see also* comprehensive social influences approach; extrapersonal-level approaches, prevention
EDQ (Exercise Dependence Questionnaire) 169–170, **176–177**
EDS (Exercise Dependence Scale) 156–157, 169–170, **176–177**
egodystonic urges 18, 317
elaborative processing 203, 274, 338
electronic cigarettes. *see* e-cigarettes
electronic devices addiction 12. *see also* Internet addiction disorder
electronic gambling machines (EGMs) 236, 332
eleven focal addictions. *see* addiction types. *see also specific addictions by name*
emerging adulthood 322
    critical points for addiction 65
    facilitators and predictors of addiction 47, **48–49**, 52–55
    patterns of addiction **138**, 138
    prevention strategies 219
emotional competence enhancement **200–201**, 202–203
emotional negative consequences 74–75, 77, **80**
emotional self-regulation, BIS-BAS model 19. *see also* loss of control
Employee Assistance Programs 237
endogenous ligands 6–8, 20, 317

energy to change 255–256
engagement, assessment 165, 178, **180**
entrenchment 328
    diagnostic criteria 148–149
    exercise addiction assessment 169–170
    food addiction assessment 161–162
    gambling disorder assessment 163
    intensional models/definitions of addiction **13–14**, 21–22
    PACE model 66
    sex addiction assessment 168–169
    shopping/spending assessment 166
environment enrichment 239, 333
environmental advocacy 267, 338
environmental changes, approaches to cessation **283–284**, 297–299
environmental level of etiology 47, **48–49**, 48–55, 62, 69. *see also* lifestyle
ethnicity, and addictions 307. *see also* cultural perspectives
etiology 13, 46–48, **48–49**, 69–70, 302, 317. *see also* macro-level; microsocial level of etiology
    addiction specificity 61
    AMASR model 47, 70
    cognitive level 47, **48–50**, 57–59, 69, 322
    environmental level 47, **48–49**, 48–55, 62, 69, 322
    future research directions 305, 314
    neurobiological level 47, **48–49**, 59–61, 322
    PACE model **48–52**, 61–70
euphoric recall 245, 320, 336
excessive appetite 21. *see also* entrenchment
exclusion criteria, various addictions 308–309
executive cognitive functions 42, **200–201**, 203–204, 274, 320, 331
exercise addiction. *see also* behavioral addictions
    appetitive needs and addictive effects 35–36
    assessment 156–157, 169–170, **176–177**
    case study 3–5
    cessation 251
    cognitive-behavior therapy 267–268
    co-occurrence with other addictions 113–114, 116, 126–127, **130**
    longitudinal perspectives 309
    negative consequences 72, **80**, 83
    opioid system 60
    prevalence **119–120**, 125–126, **130**, **132**
    prevention strategies 211, 218–219, 229
    replacement/substitute addictions 142–143
    terminology 194
    tolerance 15
    types of addiction **90–91**, 93–94
    unusual thinking 74–77
    withdrawal symptoms 15
Exercise Addiction Inventory (EAI) 169–170, **176–177**
Exercise Addicts Anonymous (EAA) **6–7**
Exercise Dependence Questionnaire (EDQ) 169–170, **176–177**
Exercise Dependence Scale (EDS) 156–157, 169–170, **176–177**
exogenous ligands 6, 317
expectations/expectancies 206, 316
    outcome expectancies 229, 279, 334
    PACE model **52**, 62, 67–68, 306–307

Index

explicit cognitive processes 58, 302, 322
extensional definition of addiction 13–14, 13–14, 13, 22–29, 317. *see also* five-component definition; six-component definition
external addiction-related cues 185
extrapersonal-level approaches, cessation 299–300, 330
   12-step programs 283–284, 285–290
   behavioral contracting 283–284, 294–295
   case study 282–283
   family therapy 283–284, 290–292
   group therapy 283–284, 292–293
   mass media related 282–283, 283–284, 295–297
   motivational intervention 283
   policy-based cessation programs 283–284, 297–299
   social skills training 283–284, 293–294
extrapersonal-level approaches, prevention 186, 210–212, 239–240
   alcohol, tobacco, and other drugs 212–216, 216–217, 224–236, 230
   family-based programs 224–229, 224–225
   media-based programs 229–233, 230
   other addictions 216–223, 228–229, 232–233, 236–237
   policy-based programs 233–237
   resources acquisition instruction/alternatives programming 238–239

FA (Food Addicts in Recovery Anonymous) 6–7
FAA (Food Addicts Anonymous) 6–7, 162
Facebook (FB) Addiction Scale (FAS) 165–166, 176–177
factors leading to addiction. *see* etiology
Fagerstrom Scale for Nicotine Dependence (FTND) 157, 176–177
false consensus effect 58, 322–324, 322
false positive rates 175, 328
family-based prevention programs 224–229, 224–225
Family Matters prevention program 224–225, 226
family resemblances conceptualization 29, 317
family therapy 283–284, 290–292, 340
fantasizing types of addiction 90–91, 93
fear-based model 193, 194–195, 330
FFT (Functional Family Therapy) program 224–225, 226–227
fight/flight responses 96, 96–98, 341
financial consequences of addiction 74–75, 78, 80
financial implications, assessment 179, 180
five-component definition of addiction 13–14, 23–24, 38–41, 38–39, 317
flue-curing 9, 317
flushing response 65, 322
follow-up, motivational interventions 283
Follow-Up Drinker Profile (structured interview) 152, 176–177
food addiction 90–92, 104, 114–116. *see also* binge eating disorder; eating addiction; substance addictions
   appetitive needs and addictive effects 35–36
   assessment 153–154, 160–162, 176–177
   attentional bias modification 274
   biochemical assessment 175
   cessation 247, 270

   cognitive-behavior therapy 265–266
   co-occurrence with other addictions 112, 116, 130
   diagnostic criteria 27–28
   historical perspectives 11–12
   negative consequences 80
   pharmacotherapy 262–263
   prevalence 104–105, 104–105, 130, 132
   prevention strategies 187, 219–220, 228, 236
   tolerance 15
   types of addiction 90–91
   unusual thinking 74–77
   withdrawal symptoms 15
Food Addicts Anonymous (FAA) 6–7, 162
Food Addicts in Recovery Anonymous (FA) 6–7
food labeling 186
forbidden fruit contingency 192–193, 202, 330
formication 159, 328
foster care. *see* multidimensional treatment foster care
FTND (Fagerstrom Scale for Nicotine Dependence) 157, 176–177
Functional Family Therapy (FFT) program 224–225, 226–227
fusion addictions 138–139, 143–144, 327
future research directions 301–302, 303–304, 314–315
   AMASR model 302–306, 303–304
   cessation and prevention strategies 303–304, 310–312
   measurement issues 303–304, 308–310
   PACE model 303–304, 306–307
   transdisciplinary-translation matrix 303–304, 312–314

GAIA (Gaming Addiction Inventory for Adults) 165, 176–177
Gamblers Anonymous (GA) 6, 6–7, 254, 289
gambling disorder 5. *see also* behavioral addictions
   appetitive needs and addictive effects 35–36
   assessment 154–155, 162–163, 176–177
   cessation 251
   cognitive-behavior therapy 266
   co-occurrence with other addictions 112–113, 121–122, 130
   diagnostic criteria 28
   extensional models 28
   family therapy 291
   group therapy 292–293
   historical perspectives 11–12
   media-based prevention programming 232
   negative consequences 80
   personalized feedback intervention 270–271
   pharmacotherapy 263
   prevalence 119–120, 120–121, 130, 132
   prevention strategies 187, 206–209, 220–221, 236–237
   types of addiction 90–91, 92
   unusual thinking 74–77
   withdrawal symptoms 15
Gambling Impact and Behavior Study 244–245
Game Addiction Scale for primary school age children 165, 176–177
gaming, online. *see* online gaming
Gaming Addiction Inventory for Adults (GAIA) 165, 176–177

Index

gardening (non-addictive activity) 42, 146, 309
gender roles 47, **48–49**, 52–55, 322
genetics
    multigenic etiology of addiction 201
    reward deficiency syndrome 60
geographic applications, policy-based cessation programs 298
geographic-level variables. *see* environmental level of etiology
GHB (gamma-hydroxybutyrate), lethal to effective dose ratio **82**
Glasse, William 194
glucocorticoids, allostasis theory 20–21
glutamatergic system, five-component definition 40
goal-setting skills, mediators of change 195–196
goals, motivation to change 255–256
Gorski and Miller treatment process model 254–255
gradient of reinforcement value 68, 322
Gray's BIS-BAS addiction self-regulation model 19–20
group level. *see* micro-social (small group) level of etiology
group polls, peer group acceptability of addictions 214
group socialization 56–57, 322. *see also* differential socialization
group therapy **283–284**, 292–293, 340

HA (Heroin Anonymous) **6–7**
hair pulling (trichotillomania) 94, 326
half and half 66
hallucinogens, withdrawal symptoms **15–16**
hallucinosis 24, 317
hand release 66, 323
hangovers 40, 320
harm reduction strategies 248–249, 336
harmful dysfunction analysis 108, 326
HBI (Hypersexual Behavior Inventory) 168, **176–177**
HD-DCI. *see* Hypersexual Disorder-Diagnostic Criteria Interview
hedonism 199
hedonist-type addictions **96**, 96–98, 325
heroin 10, 48, **82**, 174–175
Heroin Anonymous (HA) **6–7**
high-risk situations 277, 331
historical perspectives 9–13
    cessation 249–252
    diagnostic criteria 24–27
    prevention 191–194, **194–195**
HIV/sexually transmitted diseases 207–208, 222
hoarding **90–91**, 95, 325
homeostasis 21, 257. *see also* allostasis theory
honesty, open-mindedness, and willingness (HOW) 12-step programs 286
Hooked on Nicotine Checklist (HONC) 158, **176–177**
hot hand fallacy 206, 332
house edge 220, 333
Houston, University of 194
Hypersexual Behavior Inventory (HBI) 168, 176–177
Hypersexual Disorder-Diagnostic Criteria Interview (HD-DCI) 156, **176–177**
hypothalamic–pituitary–adrenal axis (HPA) 20–21, 33

I Can Problem Solve (ICPS) program 202
IAD. *see* Internet addiction disorder

IAT (Internet Addiction Test) 164, **176–177**
iatrogenic effects of treatment 239, 292
IGD (Internet gaming disorder) 89, 155. *see also* online gaming
illness model. *see* disease model of addiction
illusory correlation 58, 323
imaginal desensitization 264–265
immediate danger. *see* danger
immoral personality 37, **37**
immunoassays 174, 329
implementation intentions **200–201**, 204, 274–275, 332
implicit cognitive processes 58, 302, 322
    five-component definition 39, 41
    incentive-sensitization theory 20
    intrapersonal-level approaches to cessation 273–275, **278–280**
    Internet addiction disorder 59
implicit contracts 140, 327
implicit memory, euphoric recall 245
impulse control disorder 95
impulsive-obsessive/compulsive behavior **13–14**, 17–18
incentive salience 20
incentive-sensitization theory **13–14**, 20, 318
inclusion criteria, addictions 308–309
indicated prevention strategies 188, **189**, 330
individual difference factors 63–65, 67. *see also* personality
individual–environment matching 239
information-based model **190–191**, 193, 330
inherent qualities of addiction experience, measurement issues 309
injury **74–75**, 81–83, **82**, 116–117. *see also* danger
innate instincts 33, 320
inoculation 194
inquiry, motivational intervention 283
insider speech 66, 323
instinctive drives 302, 341
insurance coverage, multiple addictions 312
intensification 139, **143–144**, 327
intensional models of addiction 13–22, **13–14**, 318
    addiction entrenchment 21–22
    impulsive-obsessive/compulsive behavior 17–18
    physiological and psychological dependence **13–16**, 15–17
    self-medication 19
    self-regulation 19–21
interactive techniques 196, 330
interdiction 233, 334
internal addiction-related cues 185
International Conferences on Behavioral Addictions 7, 23
Internet addiction disorder (IAD). *see also* behavioral addictions; media addiction; online gaming
    appetitive needs and addictive effects 35–36
    assessment 155, 164, **176–177**
    automatic processing 59
    cessation 248, 251
    cognitive-behavior therapy 266–267
    co-occurrence with other addictions 113–114, 123–124, **130**
    family-based prevention programs 229, 291
    historical perspectives 12

Index

negative consequences **80**
pharmacotherapy 263
prevalence **119–120**, 122–123, **130**, **132**
prevention strategies 187
tolerance 15
withdrawal symptoms 15
Internet Addiction Test (IAT) 164, **176–177**
Internet and Tech Addiction Anonymous (ITAA) **6–7**
Internet gaming disorder (IGD) 89, 155. *see also* online gaming
interviews, structured 151–157, **176–177**, 329
intrapersonal-level approaches, cessation 259–260, **278–280**, 280
    cognitive-behavior therapy 263–268, **278–280**
    cue exposure/reactivity approaches 271–273, **278–280**
    detoxification and pharmacotherapy 260–263, **278–280**
    implicit cognition oriented approaches 273–275, **278–280**
    motivational interviewing 268–271, **278–280**
    relapse/relapse prevention 275–279, **278–280**
intrapersonal-level approaches, prevention 186, 199, **200–201**, 208–209, 330
    application to other addictions 207–208
    belief–behavior discrepancies reduction **200–201**, 204–205
    cognitive-information strategies **200–201**, 203–206, 208–209
    coping skills to reduce cognitive distortions **200–201**, 205–207
    executive functioning capacity enhancement **200–201**, 203–204
    gambling disorder 206–209
    implementation intentions programming **200–201**, 204
    neurobiological-related strategies 199–203, **200–201**, 208–209
    social and emotional competence enhancement **200–201**, 202–203
intrinsic–extrinsic motivation model 256–257, 336
irrational perceptions, assessment 179, **180**
ITAA (Internet and Tech Addiction Anonymous) **6–7**

Jacobsen, Michael 193
Johnny. *see* case study (Johnny)
Johnson Institute-style motivational intervention 283
Johnson treatment process model 254
junk food 193

kernels of truth 203, 221
kleptomania 12, 92, 325

LAA (Love Addicts Anonymous) **6–7**, **176–177**
labeling, addicts 84, 145. *see also* disease model of addiction; stigma
labeling, food 186
language of addiction, PACE model 65–67. *see also* communication
latent class analysis 100, 326
Latter Day Saints, Church of the 66–67
law enforcement-based cessation programs 297
legal negative consequences **74–75**, 79, **80**

assessment 180, **180**
cessation and 243
Lie/Bet Questionnaire 163, **176–177**
Life Course Theory 65, 323
life skills approach 212–216, **216–217**, 332. *see also* social skills training
Life Skills Training Program 222
lifestyle 34–35, 44
    and addictions 306
    behavioral coping strategies 205–206
    cessation and prevention strategies 311–312
    mediators of change 195–196
    patterns of addiction 143–145
    sedentary habits 34–35, 79–81, 83
lifestyle matching 239
ligands, endogenous/exogenous 6–8, 20, 317
liking 20, 318
listening skills, life skills approach 212–213, **216–217**
loneliness, negative consequences of addiction 77
long-term consequences 213–214, **216–217**. *see also* negative consequences
longitudinal perspectives
    future research directions 309–310
    patterns of addiction **138**, 138
loss of control 6–7, 22
    appetitive needs 33
    case study 5
    diagnostic criteria 148–149
    exercise addiction assessment 169–170
    five-component definition **13–14**, 23–24, **38–39**, **40–41**
    food addiction assessment 161–162
    gambling disorder assessment 163
    gaming assessment 165
    historical perspectives 9, 12–13
    love addiction assessment 167
    negative consequences 73–74, **74–75**, **80**
    non-addictive behaviors 43
    relapse/relapse prevention 276
    sex addiction assessment 168–169
    shopping/spending assessment 166
    social network addiction assessment 165–166
love addiction 326. *see also* behavioral addictions
    12-step programs 289
    appetitive needs and addictive effects 35–36
    assessment 156, 167, **176–177**
    cessation 251, 271, 299
    cognitive-behavior therapy 267
    co-occurrence with other addictions 113, 125, **130**
    group therapy 293
    negative consequences **80**
    prevalence **119–120**, 124–125, **130**, **132**
    prevention strategies 207, 211, 221, 228, 237
    reward deficiency syndrome 60
    types of addiction **90–91**, 93
Love Addicts Anonymous (LAA) **6–7**, **176–177**
Love Scale 167, **176–177**
low defensible space, 48, 323
LSD, lethal to effective dose ratio **82**

MA (Marijuana Anonymous) **6–7**
macro level of etiology 47
    facilitators and predictors of addiction 47, **48–49**
    PACE model 62
    patterns of addiction 145

Index

maintenance of behavior
  motivation to change 256
  PACE model 68
  treatment process model 254–255
marijuana
  case study 4
  cessation goals 246
  historical perspectives 11
  incidence and prevalence 110–112
  lethal to effective dose ratio 82
  prevalence **104–105**
  retention time 174–175
  withdrawal symptoms **15–16**
Marijuana Anonymous (MA) **6–7**
masking 140, **143–144**, 327
mass media. *see* media
MAST (Michigan Alcohol Screening Test) 158, **176–177**
materialism 61, 95, 323. *see also* shopping/spending
matrix self-report measures 98–101, *99–101*, 173, **176–177**
measurement issues, future research directions 303–304, 308–310
media addiction. *see also* online gaming; television addiction
  facilitators and predictors of addiction 47, **48–49**, 54–55
  policy-based prevention programs 237
  social network addiction 165–166
  social skills training 215, **216–217**
media literacy 333–334
media-related cessation/prevention campaigns 229–233, **230**, **283–284**, 295–297. *see also* public service announcements
medical consequences **74–75**, 79, **80**
  assessment 179, **180**
  dramatic consequences 81–83. *see also* danger; death/serious injury
medical model. *see* disease model of addiction
meditation practices 320, 332
  as non-addictive behavior 43
  cessation 264, 299
  prevention strategies 207
  relapse/relapse prevention 279
memory
  cognitive processing limits 58–59
  euphoric recall 245
  implicit 39, 41, 274
Mental Status Examination 150, **176–177**, 329
mere exposure effect 55, 323
mescaline, lethal to effective dose ratio 82
mesolimbic dopaminergic system. *see* dopaminergic system
methadone, retention time 174–175
MFGT (multi-family group therapy) 291
MI (motivational interviewing) 264–265, 268–271, **278–280**, 338
MI spirit 270, 338
Michigan Alcohol Screening Test (MAST) 158, **176–177**
microsocial (small group) level of etiology 47, 323
  extrapersonal-level approaches to prevention 211

facilitators and predictors of addiction 47, **48–49**, 55–57, 69
  PACE model 62
  patterns of addiction 145
Minnesota Impulsive Disorder Interview (MIDI) 155–156, **176–177**
mirror-checking, for attractiveness **90–91**, 93. *see also* tanning addiction
modalities 330
moderation goals 141, 246–249
modern alcoholism movement 250
modern society 34–35, 306. *see also* lifestyle
molar. *see* macro level of etiology
mood management 207, 332
mood modification **13–14**, 23
moral treatment approach 250, 336
morality, and negative consequences 84
motivation enhancement **190–191**, 191, 255–257, *255*, 330
motivational drives, and addictions 302–306
motivational interventions 283, 340
motivational interviewing (MI) 264–265, 268–271, **278–280**, 338
mournful withdrawal, gaming assessment 165
MST (multisystemic therapy) **224–225**, 227, 334
mu opioid neural system 33
Mueller and Ketcham treatment process model 252–254
multiaxis diagnosis 25, 318
multidimensional treatment foster care (MTFC) **224–225**, 227–228
multidisciplinary approach to cessation 251. *see also* transdisciplinary-translation matrix
multi-family group therapy (MFGT) 291
multigenic etiology of addiction 201
multiple addictions 6–8
  case study 3–5
  cessation, historical perspectives 251
  future research directions 311
  insurance coverage 312
  patterns of addiction 139–140
multi-response self-report matrix 98–101, *99–101*, 173, **176–177**
multisystemic therapy (MST) **224–225**, 227, 334
myth formation 203, 221

Narcotics Anonymous (NA) **6–7**, 254, 285–288
National Epidemiological Survey on Alcohol and Related Conditions (NESARC) 163, 245
natural kind 83, 325
natural recovery 244–245, 272
necessary and sufficient conditions for addiction 28–29
need–behavior–satiation cycles 39–40
negative consequences of addiction 6–7, 22, 71–72, 85–86
  addiction-specific consequences **74–75**, 78–81
  and cessation 243–245
  and morality 84
  appetitive needs 33
  contextual factors 83
  diagnostic criteria 148–149
  dramatic consequences 81–83, **82**
  five-component definition **13–14**, 23–24, **38–39**, 40–41

Index

food addiction assessment 161–162
gambling disorder assessment 163
gaming assessment 165
historical perspectives 9, 13
long- and short-term, social skills training 213–214, **216–217**
loss of control 73–74
love addiction assessment 167
non-addictive behaviors 44
preoccupation 72–73
sex addiction assessment 168–169
social network addiction assessment 165–166
table of consequences by type of addiction **80**
television 79–81, 83
universal consequences 74–77, **74–75**
negative reinforcement variant model 17, 30, 39, 318
nested model, facilitators and predictors of addiction 69
neurobiological assessments 174, 308–309
neurobiological-level variables 47, **48–49**, 59–61, 323
neurobiological-related prevention strategies 199–203, **200–201**, 208–209
neurocircuitry, reward deficiency syndrome 60. *see also* dopaminergic system
neurodegenerative disorders 51, 323
neurotransmission-hormonal system **13–14**, 20–21, 33, 59–60, 70
neutralization theory **48–49**, 56–57, 323
nicotine 9, **15–16**, 82. *see also* e-cigarettes; tobacco addiction
Nicotine Anonymous (NicA) **6–7**
nitrous oxide, lethal to effective dose ratio **82**
non-addictive behaviors 42–44. *see also* gardening
non-conscious processes. *see* implicit cognitive processes
non-suicidal self-injury (NSSI) 94. *see also* pain seeking
norepinephrine 33
normative beliefs 195–196, 213, 218, 233, 330. *see also* cultural norms
normative restructuring activity 214, 334
NSSI. *see* non-suicidal self-injury
nucleus accumbens 20–21, 82, 325
numbing 139, **143–144**, 328
nurturant-type addictions **96**, 96–98, 326

OA (Overeaters Anonymous) 4, **6–7**, 161–162, 288–289
Oates, Wayne 12, 193
obesity 90–92, 114, 326. *see also* food addiction
Obligatory Exercise Questionnaire (OEQ) 169–170, **176–177**
obsessive compulsive disorder (OCD) 93–95, 318
 addiction differentiation 304
 impulsive-obsessive disorders differentiation 18, 30
 facilitators and predictors of addiction 60–61
 prevention strategies 187
one drink 247, 336
Online Gamers Anonymous (OLGA) **6–7**
online gaming 155. *see also* Internet addiction
 assessment 165
 diagnostic criteria 89
 family therapy 291
 prevalence **132**

open-ended questions 212, 334
opioid system 60
opium
 detoxification and pharmacotherapy 262
 distribution routes for drugs 48
 historical perspectives 10–11
 retention time 174–175
 withdrawal symptoms **15–16**
organism control 339
organizational interventions 202
outcome expectancies 229, 279, 334
over-attachment to drug, object, or activity. *see* entrenchment
Overeaters Anonymous (OA) 4, **6–7**, 161–162, 288–289
oxytocin 60

PA (Pills Anonymous) **6–7**
PACE model (pragmatics, attraction, communication, expectations)
 etiology of addiction **48–52**, 62–70
 future directions **303–304**, 306–307
pain seeking, types of addiction **90–91**, 94–95
parent power movement 193, 330
parental monitoring 228, 334
Passionate Love Scale (PLS) 167, **176–177**
patterns of addiction. *see* addiction patterns
PAW (post-acute withdrawal) 275–276, 338
PCP (phencyclidine) **15–16**, 105, 174–175
peer pressure, extrapersonal-level approaches to prevention 211
peer prevalence/acceptability overestimates 58, 214, **216–217**, 324
pejorative labeling 84. *see also* stigma
Penn State Electronic Cigarette Dependence Index (PSECI) 158, **176–177**
period of engagement, diagnostic criteria 148–149
periodic addictive behavior 136, **137**, 328
personality
 and attraction 63–65
 facilitators and predictors of addiction 47, **48–49**, 60–61
 immoral 37, **37**
 individual difference factors 63–65, 67
 sociopathic 24, 318
personalized feedback 206–207, 270–271, 332, 337
pharmacotherapy 261–263, **278–280**. *see also* prescription drugs
phencyclidine (PCP) **15–16**, 105, 174–175
physical attractiveness **90–91**, 93. *see also* tanning addiction
physical consequences. *see* negative consequences
physical danger. *see* danger
physiological dependence **13–16**, 15–17, 179, **180**, 318
physiological withdrawal symptoms 3, 317–318
pica (eating of non-nutritive, non-food substances) 90–92, 326
Pills Anonymous (PA) **6–7**
pituitary–adrenal axis 20–21, 33
PLS (Passionate Love Scale) 167, **176–177**
policy-based cessation programs **283–284**, 297–299
policy-based prevention programs 233–237
pollution, air 47, **48–49**, 51–52, 324

Index

polysubstance abuse 25, 318
pornography, family-based prevention programs 229. *see also* sex addiction
positive addictions 72, 320, 325
positive reinforcement variant 17–18, 30, 39, 318
post-acute withdrawal (PAW) 275–276, 338
pragmatics 62–63, 306–307, 316, 324. *see also* PACE model
pre-commitment 237
pre-contemplation, motivation to change 256
predictors of addiction. *see* etiology
preoccupation 6–7, 22, 329
    appetitive needs 33
    diagnostic criteria 148–149
    exercise addiction assessment 169–170
    five-component definition **13–14**, 23–24, **38–39**, 40–41
    food addiction assessment 161–162
    gambling disorder assessment 163
    historical perspectives 9, 12–13
    love addiction assessment 167
    negative consequences 72–73, **74–75**, 80
    non-addictive behaviors 43
    PACE model 66
    sex addiction assessment 168–169
    shopping/spending assessment 166
    social network addiction assessment 165–166
preparation, motivation to change 256, 283
prescription drugs 111, 326. *see also* pharmacotherapy
presenteeism 172, 329
prevalence 112–114, 245–246
    alcohol addiction 104–105, **104–105**, 108–110, **109**, **130**
    behavioral addictions 118–119, **119–120**, **130**, 131–133, **132**
    binge eating disorder 115
    drug addiction 110–112
    future directions 307–308
    patterns of addiction 146
    spontaneous recovery 244
    substance addictions 6, 63, 104–105, **104–105**
    tobacco addiction 106–108
    TV addiction 79–81
prevalence of addiction overestimates, social skills training 214–215, **216–217**
prevention 185–187, **189**, 197–198. *see also* extrapersonal-level; intrapersonal-level approaches
    ages targeted 196–197
    cessation vs. 188–190
    classifications **189**
    drug education models 193–194, **194–195**
    future research directions **303–304**, 310–312
    historical perspectives 191–194, **194–195**
    levels 188
    main strategies/themes **190–191**
    mediators of change 195–196
    modalities 188
primary addictions 311, 341
primary drug use disorder 136. *see also* drug addiction
primary exercise dependence 93–94, 326. *see also* exercise addiction
primary gambling disorder 136. *see also* gambling disorder

primary prevention 188, **189**, 330
proactive assessment 149, 329
problem-solving 206, 264, 338
Problem Video Game Playing Scale (PVP) 165, **176–177**
process addictions 12. *see also* Internet addiction disorder
programs for quitting. *see* 12-step programs
progression 320
prohibition 192, 330
prohibitory schemes 233, 297–299, 334
Project Towards No Tobacco Use 212–216
prosocial bonding/constraint 47, **48–49**, 57, 324
prosociality, future directions 306
protective environments 306
PSECI. *see* Penn State Electronic Cigarette Dependence Index
psychological dependence **13–16**, 15–17, 179, **180**, 318
public commitment, social skills training 216. *see also* commitment
public service announcements (PSAs) 233, 295–297, 313, 340. *see also* media-related cessation/prevention campaigns
pull tabs 163, 329
PVP (Problem Video Game Playing Scale) 165, **176–177**

questions, open-ended 212, 334

random forest prediction models 308–309, 341
reactive assessment 149, 329
recovery period, treatment process model 252–255
refusal assertion skill 213, **216–217**, 335
regular addicts **137**, 137
regulatory schemes 233, 297–299, 335
reinforcement control 339
reintegrative shaming 84, 325
reinterpretation 205–206, 332
relapse 338–340
    cessation programs 189, 275–279, **278–280**
    food addiction 161
    negative consequences **74–75**, 77, **80**
    six-component definition **13–14**, 23
relationship addictions. *see* love addiction; sex addiction
religion. *see* spiritual obsessions
remission 244, 336
repetitive simple behaviors 18. *see also* obsessive compulsive disorder
repetitive thought–do loops 43, 320. *see also* preoccupation
replacement addictions 135, 140–143, **143–144**, 328
representativeness heuristic 58, 324
research roles 314. *see also* future research directions
residential cognitive-behavior therapy programs 268
resilience 224, 334–335
resistance, to social pressure 195–196, 330
resources acquisition instruction 238
response-contingent reinforcement approaches **190–191**, 191, 331
response control 339

Index

responsible behavior programs, historical perspectives 192, 331
Responsible Gambling Information Centers (RGICs) 298, 340
restructuring, cognitive 206, 264, 266–268, 277, 338
retention time, biochemical assessment 174
reward circuitry. *see* dopaminergic system
reward deficiency syndrome 47, **48–49**, 59–60, 324
rhabdomyolysis 83, 325
risk reduction, intrapersonal-level approaches to prevention 206–207
risky behavior. *see also* danger, physical
  emerging adulthood 53–54
  gender roles 52
  sex addiction 207–208, 221–222
ritualizing 140, 328
rohypnol, lethal to effective dose ratio **82**
role consequences, negative **74–75**, 78–79, **80**
role models, social skills training 215, **216–217**
role play 196, 294, 340
roles, research 314. *see also* future research directions
rule-based definitions of addiction. *see* intensional models
rush effects 32, 34–35, 42. *see also* mood modification

SA (Sexaholics Anonymous) **6–7**
SAA (Sex Addicts Anonymous) **6–7**, 169
salience **13–14**, 23, 35
SAST (Sex Addiction Screening Test) 168, **176–177**
satiation 33
  five-component definition **13–14**, 23–24, **38–39**, 39–40
  future research directions 312
  non-addictive behaviors 42–43
SCA (Sexual Compulsives Anonymous) **6–7**
scare tactics, as prevention strategies 193
school-based assistance programs 298. *see also* education in schools
SCID. *see* Structured Clinical Interview for the Diagnostic Statistical Manual
SCI-PG. *see* Structured Clinical Interview for Pathological Gambling
screening interviews 149–151, **176–177**. *see also* structured interviews
SDSS (Substance Dependence Severity Scale) 152–153, **176–177**
secondarily acquired instincts 33, 320
secondary addictions 311, 341
secondary exercise dependence 93–94, 326. *see also* exercise addiction
secondary prevention 188, **189**, 331
secure attachment styles 228, 335
sedentary habits 34–35, 79–81, 83. *see also* lifestyle
selective prevention strategies 188, **189**, 331
self-confidence building 215–216, **216–217**
self-control skills 293, 340
self-efficacy expectations 334, 339
self-esteem 77, 195–196
self-initiated cessation 244. *see also* natural recovery
self-instructional training 206, 264, 339
self-medication **13–14**, 19, 65, 318
self-regulation model **13–14**, 19–21, 257, 318
self-report assessment instruments 157–173, **176–177**, 329

self-talk 267, 299
sensation-seeking **90–91**, 95, 231. *see also* adrenalin junkies
septo-hippocampal system 19, 318
serious injury 74–75, 81–83, **82**, 116–117. *see also* danger
serotonin neural system 33
seven deadly sins, historical perspectives 12
sex addiction. *see also* behavioral addictions
  12-step programs 289
  appetitive needs and addictive effects 35–36
  assessment 156, 168–169, **176–177**
  biochemical assessment 175
  cognitive-behavior therapy 267
  co-occurrence with other addictions 113, 125, **130**
  historical perspectives 11–12
  negative consequences **80**
  obsessive compulsive disorders 18
  pharmacotherapy 263
  prevalence **119–120**, 124–125, **130**, **132**
  prevention strategies 207–208, 211, 221–222, 228–229, 233, 237
  tolerance 15
  types of addiction **90–91**
  withdrawal symptoms 15
Sex Addiction Screening Test (SAST) 168, **176–177**
Sex Addicts Anonymous (SAA) **6–7**, 169
Sex and Love Addicts Anonymous (SLAA) **6–7**, 167
Sexaholics Anonymous (SA) **6–7**
Sexual Compulsives Anonymous (SCA) **6–7**
Sexual Recovery Anonymous (SRA) **6–7**
sexually transmitted diseases, prevention strategies 207–208, 222
shame, gaming 165
shopping/spending addiction. *see also* behavioral addictions
  appetitive needs and addictive effects 35–36
  assessment 155–156, 166
  cessation 251
  cognitive-behavior therapy 267
  co-occurrence with other addictions 129
  group therapy 293
  historical perspectives 12
  negative consequences **80**
  prevalence 129, **132**
  prevention strategies 211, 218, 229
  types of addiction **90–91**, 95
  unusual thinking 74–77
short-term consequences. *see* negative consequences
single addiction 135–137, 328
situational/contextual distortions 47, **48–49**, 59, 324
six-component definition **13–14**, 23
SLAA (Sex and Love Addicts Anonymous) **6–7**, 167
sleeping, non-addictive behaviors 42
slippery slope, implicit cognition oriented approaches 275
Smith, Robert 134, 285
smoking. *see* tobacco addiction
snus 234, 335
sober-living homes 287, 340
sobriety 71, 137, 325
social cognitive learning theory 47, **48–49**, 55, 324
social competence enhancement **200–201**, 202–203
social consequences of addiction 74, **74–75**, **80**

Index

social contexts of addiction 140. *see also* lifestyle
social group-related types of addiction **90–91**, 93. *see also* love addiction; sex addiction
social images 68, <u>324</u>
social influence-based programs 190, **190–191**, 194, <u>331</u>. *see also* social skills training
social influences 212–216, **216–217**, <u>331</u>, <u>332–333</u>
social level. *see* micro-social level of etiology
social media addiction 165–166. *see also* media addiction
social normative perceptions 195–196, 213, 218, 233, <u>335</u>. *see also* cultural norms
social skills training **216–217**, <u>335</u>. *see also* social influences
   activism 215
   adult role models 215
   cessation 283, **283–284**, 293–294
   commitment to avoid addiction 216
   decision-making skills 216
   listening and communication skills 212–213
   media/advertising influences 215
   mediators of change 195–196
   peer group unacceptability of addictions 214
   prevalence of addiction overestimates 214–215
   refusal assertion skill 213
   self-confidence building 215–216
   short- and long-term physical consequences information 213–214
   talk show format 216, **216–217**
social support 205–206, 286
socialization models 37, *37*
society, Western 34–35, 306. *see also* lifestyle
sociopathic personality disturbance 24, <u>318</u>
SORR. *see* stimulus-organism-response-reinforcement techniques
South Oaks Gambling Screen (SOGS) 163
spending addiction. *see* shopping/spending addiction
spiritual consequences, food addiction assessment 162
spiritual obsessions **90–91**, 94
sponsors, 12-step programs 286–287
spontaneous recovery 244–245, 272, <u>339</u>
SRA (Sexual Recovery Anonymous) **6–7**
stabilization period, treatment process model 252–255
Stacked Deck program 220
stages-of-recovery model, cessation 252–255, *253*
state of readiness to change 255–256
stepped-care approach 245–246, 258. *see also* 12-step programs
stigma 63–65, 84, 244, <u>337</u>
stimulus control 339
stimulus-organism-response-reinforcement techniques (SORR) 264. *see also* cognitive-behavior therapy
sting events 235, <u>335</u>
stopping over-shopping model, group therapy 293
STRATOB (Systemic and STRATegic psychotherapy for OBesity) study 265
street addiction 92, <u>326</u>. *see also* anti-social behavior
Strengthening Families Program **224–225**, 224–226, 228

stress management skills, mediators of change 195–196
Structured Clinical Interview for Pathological Gambling (SCI-PG) 154, **176–177**
Structured Clinical Interview for the Diagnostic Statistical Manual (SCID) 153–154, **176–177**
structured interviews 151–157, **176–177**, <u>329</u>
structuring interventions 202
study addiction 92. *see also* workaholism
style, cognitive coping strategies 206
subjective adaptation-directed
   addictive effects 32–33
   additive effects 319–320
submissive-related factors **96**, 96–98, <u>325</u>
substance abuse, DSM diagnostic criteria 25, <u>319</u>
substance addictions **6–7**. *see also* alcohol; drugs; food; tobacco addictions
   assessment 152–154, 157–162, **176–177**
   case study 103
   cessation 245–246
   cognitive-behavior therapy 265
   definitions **5–6**, 8, 29–31, 103, <u>319</u>
   group therapy 292
   historical perspectives 9–11
   incentive-sensitization theory 20
   prevalence and co-occurrence 103–105, **104–105**, 112–114, 116–117
substance dependence, DSM diagnostic criteria 26, <u>319</u>
Substance Dependence Severity Scale (SDSS) 152–153, **176–177**
substance use disorder, DSM diagnostic criteria 27, <u>319</u>
substitute addictions 135, 140–143, **143–144**, <u>328</u>
substitution behavior, behavioral coping strategies 205–206
suicidal ideation 77
supply reduction approaches/programming **190–191**, 191, 234, <u>331</u>, <u>335</u>
support networks 205–206, 286
surrender phase, treatment process model 254

talk show format 216, **216–217**, <u>335</u>
tanning addiction 36
taxation 186, 236, 297, 332–335
team sports, and alcohol misuse 127
technology related types of addiction **90–91**, 92. *see also* Internet addiction; television addiction
television addiction 29, 39, 116–117. *see also* media addiction
   case study 3
   cessation 289, 291–292
   negative consequences 79–81, 83
   prevention strategies 223, 233
temperance movement 9, 192, <u>331</u>
termination of addictions 135
tertiary prevention 188, **189**, <u>331</u>
Thanksgiving, United States 305
theory-based definitions. *see* intensional models
therapeutic alliance 283, <u>340</u>
therapeutic community model 287, <u>337</u>

Index

thinking, unusual 74–77, **74–75**, **80**. *see also* cognitive distortions
thought–do loops 43, 320. *see also* preoccupation
thrill seeking **90–91**, 95, 231. *see also* adrenalin junkies
TILT (toxicant-induced loss of tolerance) **48–49**, 51, 324
TNT (Towards No Tobacco Use) project 212–216
tobacco addiction 9, **15–16**, **82**, 106. *see also* e-cigarettes; substance addiction
   appetitive needs and addictive effects 35–36
   assessment **176–177**
   cessation 269–270
   cognitive-behavior therapy 265
   co-occurrence with other addictions 112–114, **130**, 134–136
   detoxification and pharmacotherapy 262
   financial consequences 78
   goals of abstinence vs. moderation 246–247
   group therapy 292
   historical perspectives 9
   lethal to effective dose ratio **82**
   longitudinal perspectives 309
   media-based prevention programming 229–232, **230**
   prevalence 104–108, **104–105**, **130**, **132**
   prevention strategies 187, 212–216, **216–217**, 224–228, 233–234
   replacement/substitute addictions 142–143
   self-report assessment instruments 157–158
   structured interview 152–153
   table of consequences **80**
   withdrawal symptoms **15–16**
tobacco regulatory science 234, 335
tolerance 23–24, 319. *see also* preoccupation
   diagnostic criteria 26, 148–149
   negative consequences **74–75**, 77, **80**
   physiological and psychological dependence 15
   sex addiction assessment 168–169
   six-component definition **13–14**, 23
total abstinence 246–247, 337
Towards No Tobacco Use (TNT) project 212–216
toxicant-induced loss of tolerance (TILT) **48–49**, 51, 324
transactional framework of resilience 224
transactional processes 334–335
transdisciplinarity 313, 341
transdisciplinary-translation matrix **303–304**, 312–314
transition period, treatment process model 254–255
translation research 313, 341. *see also* transdisciplinary-translation matrix
transtheoretical model 256, 337
trauma 19, 319
treatment process model, cessation 252–255, *253*. *see also* 12-step programs
trichotillomania (hair pulling) 94, 326
TV addiction. *see* television
types of addiction. *see* addiction types

unconscious processes. *see* implicit cognitive processes
universal consequences of addiction **74–75**, 74–77
universal prevention strategies 188, **189**, 331
University of Houston 194
unrealistic optimism 58, 324
unstructured interviews 150–151, **176–177**, 329
unusual thinking **74–75**, 74–77, **80**. *see also* cognitive distortions
urge management, relapse prevention 277

vagus nerve 104, 327
validation of addiction criteria, future research directions 308–309
values-based model 193, **194–195**, 329
variables and predictors of addiction. *see* etiology
vasopressin 60
ventral tegmental area (VTA) 20–21, 82
vicariance, addiction 21, 35, 55
vices, historical perspectives 12
video lottery terminal (VLT) gamblers 232, 335
vigilance programs 201, 332
voluntary cessation 243–244
voyeurism **90–91**, 95

WA (Workaholics Anonymous) **6–7**
wanting 20, 33, 40, 319. *see also* cravings
WAQ (Work Attitude Questionnaire) 171, **176–177**
WART (Work Addiction Risk Test) 171, **176–177**
Washington Temperance Society (Washingtonians) 9
Western society 34–35, 306. *see also* lifestyle
willpower 44
Wilson, Bill 134, 285
withdrawal mediation 139, **143–144**, 328
withdrawal symptoms 23–24, 318. *see also* preoccupation
   behavioral addictions 6
   detoxification and pharmacotherapy 260
   diagnostic criteria 26, 148–149
   drugs **15–16**
   exercise addiction assessment 169–170
   food addiction assessment 161
   individual differences 65
   negative consequences **74–75**, 77, **80**
   shopping/spending assessment 166
   six-component definition **13–14**, 23
   social network addiction assessment 165–166
Work Addiction Risk Test (WART) 171, **176–177**
Work Attitude Questionnaire (WAQ) 171, **176–177**
Workaholics Anonymous (WA) **6–7**
workaholism. *see also* behavioral addictions
   12-step programs 289–290
   appetitive needs and addictive effects 35–36
   assessment 157, 170–173, **176–177**
   biochemical assessment 175
   case study 5
   cessation 251, 271
   cognitive-behavior therapy 267
   co-occurrence with other addictions 128, **130**
   cultural norms 30
   historical perspectives 12
   negative consequences 72, **80**
   prevalence **119–120**, 127–128, **130**, **132**

Index

workaholism (*cont.*)
   prevention strategies 187, 208, 211, 223, 229, 237,

   terminology 193
   types of addiction **90–91**, 92
Workaholism Battery (WorkBAT) 171, **176–177**
workplace assistance programs 298

Yale-Brown Obsessive Compulsive Scale-Shopping Version 166, **176–177**
Yale Food Addiction Scale (YFAS) 161, **176–177**
'you only live once' (YOLO) 53–54
Young's Internet Addiction Test 164, **176–177**
YouTube, extrapersonal-level approaches to cessation 295